纳提什瓦

孟加拉国毗诃罗普尔古城
2013—2017年发掘报告

Nateshwar: An Interim Excavation Report (2013-2017) of the Vikrampura Ancient City in People's Republic of Bangladesh

（中国）湖南省文物考古研究所
（孟加拉国）阿哥拉萨－毗诃罗普尔基金会   编著

柴焕波 S.M.诺曼   主编

Edited by
Agrashar Vikrampur Foundation in Bangladesh
Hunan Provincial Institute of Cultural Relics
and Archaeology in China

Chief Editor
Sufi Mostafizur Rahman   Chai Huanbo

科学出版社
北京

内 容 简 介

孟加拉国考古学家于2010年发现毗诃罗普尔（Vikrampura）古城，并于2013年首次发掘古城的纳提什瓦（Nateshwar）遗址。2014—2018年，中国湖南省文物考古研究所和阿哥拉萨-毗诃罗普尔（Agrashar Vikrampur）基金会聘请的欧提亚·欧耐斯恩考古研究中心（Oitihya Onneswan Archaeological Research Center）组成联合考古队，先后三次对纳提什瓦遗址进行了大规模的考古发掘，取得了重大成果。通过地层学和一系列测年数据，纳提什瓦遗址可分为两个时期，年代为8—13世纪。考古发现遗址早晚的规模庞大、具有不同功能的大型佛教遗址，证实了这座都城的存在。作为南亚次大陆最后一个佛教中心的珍贵遗产，这个遗址将载入世界考古学的史册。

本书可供从事考古、历史、佛教研究的专家、学者、教师、学生参考、阅读。

图书在版编目(CIP)数据

纳提什瓦：孟加拉国毗诃罗普尔古城2013—2017年发掘报告 / 柴焕波，（孟加拉）S.M.诺曼主编；湖南省文物考古研究所，（孟加拉）阿哥拉萨-毗诃罗普尔基金会编著.—北京：科学出版社，2019.3

ISBN 978-7-03-060913-7

Ⅰ.①纳… Ⅱ.①柴… ②S… ③湖… ④孟… Ⅲ.①佛教-宗教建筑-文化遗址-发掘报告-孟加拉国 Ⅳ.①K883.548.6

中国版本图书馆CIP数据核字(2019)第051329号

责任编辑：张亚娜　郑佐一／责任校对：彭　涛
责任印制：肖　兴／书籍设计：北京美光设计制版有限公司

科学出版社 出版
北京东黄城根北街16号
邮政编码：100717
http://www.sciencep.com

北京华联印刷有限公司 印刷
科学出版社发行　各地新华书店经销

*

2019年3月第　一　版　　开本：889×1194　1/16
2019年3月第一次印刷　　印张：29
字数：750 000

定价：480.00元
（如有印装质量问题，我社负责调换）

序一

毗诃罗普尔是孟加拉国历史上的一个重要名字，曾是文伽和三摩达吒地区统治者的胜利之营（Jayskandhavara）。今天，当地人在耕种、掘池或其他家庭动土过程中，经常发现有建筑遗迹、金属造像、铜板、陶塑、陶器、金属以及木制品。在毗诃罗普尔发现的造像、柱子和碑铭如今正在达卡的孟加拉国国家博物馆、拉贾希的瓦伦德拉研究博物馆、加尔各答的印度博物馆和世界不同国家的其他博物馆里展出。此外，许多偶然发现的文物也在国内外的个人收藏中。

尽管有一些历史记载和大量考古证据，但该地区一直没有进行过考古研究，特别是发掘工作。达卡博物馆当时的馆长、毗诃罗普尔地区的儿子纳利尼坎塔·巴塔萨利曾试图在1913年进行发掘，但未能启动。在将近一个世纪之后，我于2010年邀请苏菲·马斯塔费珠·诺曼教授领导的欧提亚·欧耐斯恩考古研究中心在毗诃罗普尔地区开展了发掘工作。在大范围的调查过程中，在许多地点都发现有古代聚落。在9个地点的试掘探沟内揭露出了文化遗存。2010年，在蒙希甘杰县沙德乡朗帕尔村的拉库罗普尔遗址开始了大面积发掘，并一直持续到2013年。到目前为止，此处已经发现了一个大型佛教寺院的一部分，值得一提的是，这是这一地区第一个发现的该类型寺院。^{14}C测定其年代为公元990年至1050年，正处于毗诃罗普尔伟大儿子阿底峡尊者的生活时期。2013年，考古学家开始在纳提什瓦遗址进行工作，发现了密集的古砖和部分古代建筑遗迹。由于期望在毗诃罗普尔地区进行大量的考古研究工作，2013年，阿哥拉萨－毗诃罗普尔基金会通过孟加拉国谢赫·哈西娜总理的国际事务顾问利慈维教授向中国驻孟加拉国大使馆提出了寻求资金和技术援助、开展中孟联合考古发掘的想法。2013年4月17日至22日，在中国驻孟加拉国大使馆的安排下，湖南省文物局代表团访问了孟加拉国，他们考察了拉库罗普尔和纳提什瓦两个遗址，并决定与孟加拉国团队进行联合考古研究。

自2014年以来，在苏菲·马斯塔费珠·诺曼教授和柴焕波教授的领导下，年度的联合考古发掘工作一直在继续，并且有了重大发现。我必须感谢考古学家们如此迅速地出版了这份中期报告；我也感谢阿哥拉萨－毗诃罗普尔基金会所有成员在研究项目中的友好支持；我要感谢尊敬的文化部和财政部的各位部长和所有政府官员，以及蒙希甘杰地方政府在研究项目中的慷慨帮助；感谢孟加拉国文化部和中国湖南省文物考古研究所的经费资助。希望这份中期报告能够满足国内外学者和读者长期以来的需求，这是我们第一次能够通过它了解到毗诃罗普尔地区丰富的文化遗产。

努·奥·阿拉姆·列林　博士
孟加拉国阿哥拉萨－毗诃罗普尔基金会主席

Preface 1

Vikrampura is an important name in Bangladesh history, once being a *Jayskandhavara* (camp of victory) of the rulers of Vanga and Samatata region. Present-day locals have been discovering architectural remains, metal statues, copper plates, terracotta objects, potteries, metal and wooden objects during cultivation, digging ponds or conducting other activities for a long time. Sculptures, pillars and inscriptions found in Vikrampura are displayed in Bangladesh National Museum, Dhaka; Varendra Research Museum, Rajshahi; Indian Museum, Kolkata and other museums worldwide. Besides, many accidentally discovered artifacts are also in personal collections at home and abroad.

Despite several historical accounts and numerous archaeological evidences, no archaeological research, especially excavation, was conducted in this area for a long time. Nalinikanta Bhattasali, the then Curator of Dhaka Museum and a son of Vikrampura, attempted to excavate in 1913, yet failed to continue the initiative. After almost a century, I took the initiative in 2010 for excavation in Vikrampura involving 'Oitihya Onneswan' (archaeological research centre) under the leadership of Prof. Sufi Mostafizur Rahman. From extensive exploration, human settlements are revealed in test trenches at nine places. Large scale excavation commenced at Raghurampur, under Rampal union of Munshiganj Sadar upazila in 2010 to 2013. Part of a large Buddhist Vihara has been discovered so far. It is worth mentioning that this Vihara is the first of its kind in Vikrampura. ^{14}C dating of this Vikrampura Vihara is c. 990 – 1050 AD. During this time Atisha Dipankara Srijnana, the great son of Vikrampura was alive. In 2013, our archaeologists started excavation at Nateshwar, revealing dense old bricks and parts of ancient architectures. Expecting massive archaeological research in Vikrampura region, the Agrashar Vikrampur Foundation proposed the China-Bangladesh joint excavation plan for financial and technical assistance to the Chinese Embassy in Bangladesh through Prof. Gowher Rizvi, International Affairs Advisor to the Honorable Prime Minister of Bangladesh Sheikh Hasina in 2013. Under the arrangement of the Chinese Embassy in Bangladesh, the delegation of Hunan Provincial Institute of Cultural Relics and Archaeology visited Bangladesh from 17th to 22nd April, 2013. They investigated the Raghurampur and Nateshwar sites and decided to cooperate with Bangladesh team for joint archaeological research.

Since 2014 the joint annual excavation has been continuing under the leadership of Prof. Sufi Mostafizur Rahman and Prof. Chai Huanbo. Significant discoveries have been made. I must thank the archaeologists stitude for taking such a quick attempt to publish an interim report. I also thank all the members of Agrasor Vikrampur Foundation for their kind support. I would like to thank honorable ministers and all government officials of the Ministry of Cultural Affairs and Ministry of Finance, local administrations of Munshiganj for their generous help. I acknowledge the financial support of the Ministry of Cultural Affairs, People's Republic of Bangladesh and Hunan Provincial Institute of Cultural Relics and Archaeology, China. I wish the interim report will fulfill the long awaiting demand of scholars and readers at home and abroad. For the first time, we will be able to learn about the rich heritage of Vikrampura through the Interim Report.

Dr.Nooh-Ul- Alam Lenin
President of Agrasor Vikrampur Foundation, Bangladesh

序二

通过中孟考古工作者五年多的艰辛努力，毗诃罗普尔古城考古取得了骄人的成绩，《纳提什瓦——孟加拉国毗诃罗普尔古城2013—2017年发掘报告》是这个项目的阶段性成果，也是我们在"一带一路"倡议下交出的一份沉甸甸的答卷。

孟加拉国地处海上和陆上丝绸之路的要道，是我国在南亚的友好邻邦。在中国古籍中，孟加拉被称作朋加剌、榜葛剌等，自秦汉以来，就有友好交往的记录。毗诃罗普尔古城是孟加拉国历史上旃陀罗、跋摩、犀那三个王朝的都城，纳提什瓦遗址是古城内的一处重要的佛教遗址，年代在公元8—12世纪。考古发掘表明，纳提什瓦遗址无论在规模还是建筑特性上，在孟加拉都是前所未有的，具有重要的学术价值。同时，毗诃罗普尔古城作为阿底峡尊者的故乡，在藏传佛教中具有重要的影响。作为经济与文化、宗教的重要地带，纳提什瓦一直是中孟交流的重要纽带。

毗诃罗普尔古城的考古工作才刚刚开始，任重而道远，我们愿意与孟加拉国同行一道，在考古发掘、学术研究和考古遗址公园建设方面进行全方位的合作，共赏孟加拉国古代灿烂的文明，共享中国在考古发掘和考古遗址公园建设方面的成功经验，增进中孟文化交流和孟加拉国民生福祉，使这一项目成为中孟友谊新的里程碑。

郭伟民　博士
湖南省文物考古研究所所长

Preface 2

The archaeological work in the Vikrampura ancient city has made remarkable achievements through the arduous efforts of Chinese and Bangladesh archaeologists over five years. *Nateshwar: An Interim Excavation Report (2013 – 2017) of the Vikrampura Ancient City in People's Republic of Bangladesh* is the fruit of this project and an impressive answer paper under the initiatives of "One Belt and One Road". Bangladesh is a friendly neighbor of China, which is located in the junction of the maritime and land silk roads. In Chinese ancient literature, Bangladesh was called Peng-jia-la, Bang-ge-la, etc. Since Qin and Han dynasties, friendly exchanges between Bangladesh and China has been recorded. Vikrampura ancient city was the capital of three dynasties. From archaeological work, Nateshwar is an important religious site from 8th to 12th centuries AD, unprecedented in scale and architectural characteristics in Bangladesh, holding great academic value. Also, Vikrampura has an remarkable influence in Tibet as the hometown of venerable Atisha Dipankara Srijnana. Since 1950s, it has been a key link in China-Bangladesh relations. Archaeological work in Vikrampura ancient city has just begun, with a long way to go. We are willing to promote a full cooperation with our Bangladesh counterparts in archaeological excavation, academic research and archaeological park construction, to share the splendid ancient civilization of Bangladesh and China's successful experience in archaeological work. This project will also enhance cultural exchanges between China and Bangladesh, improving local livelihood, making it a new milestone of friendship between China and Bangladesh.

Dr.Guo Weimin
Director of Hunan Provincial
Institute of Cultural Relics and Archaeology, China

目录

第一章　绪论
　　第一节　地理位置　　2
　　第二节　自然环境　　6
　　第三节　历史沿革　　9
　　第四节　考古历程　　15

第二章　地层
　　第一节　地层综述　　44
　　第二节　地层举例　　49
　　第三节　地层年代的 ^{14}C 数据分析　　64

第三章　遗迹
　　第一节　第一期遗迹　　76
　　　一　早段遗迹　　76
　　　二　中段遗迹　　80
　　　三　晚段遗迹　　90
　　第二节　第二期遗迹（上）——十字形中心神殿建筑　　101
　　　一　发掘经过　　101
　　　二　层位关系　　101
　　　三　遗迹描述　　102
　　　四　年代推断　　118
　　　五　对于建筑复原的设想　　119
　　第三节　第二期遗迹（下）——其他遗迹　　134
　　　一　八边形佛塔1　　134
　　　二　八边形佛塔2　　134
　　　三　八边形佛塔3　　139
　　　四　曲折形围墙1　　139
　　　五　路面1　　139
　　　六　路面3　　141
　　第四节　第三期遗迹　　148

v

第四章　遗物
第一节　陶器 224
第二节　其他出土遗物 308

第五章　结语
第一节　纳提什瓦遗址的年代分期和遗址兴废过程的历时性描述 326
第二节　纳提什瓦遗址的核心价值 335
第三节　纳提什瓦遗址进一步发掘、保护的设想 337

附录
附录一　美国贝塔（Beta）实验室 ^{14}C 测定数据 342
附录二　孟加拉国纳提什瓦遗址出土动物遗存 347
附录三　孟加拉国纳提什瓦遗址炭化米分析 359

专文
8—12 世纪东印度佛教建筑、造像对于西藏的传播 / 柴焕波 361

Contents

Chapter I   Preface

    Section 1   Geographical Background   2
    Section 2   Natural Environment   6
    Section 3   Brief History   9
    Section 4   Archaeological Process   15

Chapter II   Stratigraphy

    Section 1   Comprehensive Introduction   44
    Section 2   Section Description   49
    Section 3   Analysis of Stratigraphy Radiocarbon Dates   64

Chapter III   Cultural Remains

    Section 1   The First Period Cultural Remains   76
        1. Early Stage   76
        2. Middle Stage   80
        3. Late Stage   90

    Section 2   The Second Period Cultural Remains (Part I): Cruciform Central Temple   101
        1. Excavation Process   101
        2. Stratigrapical Context   101
        3. Remains Description   102
        4. Age of the Construction   118
        5. Conception on the Architectural Reconstruction   119

    Section 3   The Second Period (II): Other Features   134
        1. Octagonal Stupa 1   134
        2. Octagonal Stupa 2   134
        3. Octagonal Stupa 3   139
        4. Zigzag Boundary Wall 1   139
        5. Floor 1   139

	6. Floor 3	141
Section 4	The Third Period	148

Chapter IV Unearthed Artifacts

Section 1	Pottery	224
Section 2	Other Unearthed Objects	308

Chapter V Conclusion

Section 1	The Chronological Periods and the Rise and Decline of the Site	326
Section 2	The Main Value of the Nateshwar Site	335
Section 3	The Further Excavation and Conservation at Nateshwar Site	337

Appendix

Appendix 1: Radiocarbon Dates from US Beta Laboratory	342
Appendix 2: Identification Report of Fauna Specimens at Nateshwar Site	347
Appendix 3: Study of Carbonized Rice in Nateshwar site, Bangladesh	359

Special Paper

Research on the Buddhist Remains of Bangladesh During the 8th to 12th Centuries and Their Influences on Tibet (by Chai Huanbo) — 361

插图目录

图1-1	毗诃罗普尔古城地理位置图	3
图1-2	纳提什瓦遗址平面位置图	4
图1-3	拉库罗普尔（Raghurampur）遗址、纳提什瓦遗址、阿底峡故乡金刚瑜伽（Vairajogini）村平面位置图	7
图1-4	纳提什瓦遗址历年发掘探方分布图	17
图2-1	纳提什瓦遗址地层剖面位置图	49
图2-2	UnitJ10GridA10、B10、C10、D10、E10、E9剖面图	50
图2-3	UnitJ11GridE1、D1、C1、B1、A1剖面图	51
图2-4	UnitJ11GridE6、E5、E4、E3、E2、E1剖面图	51
图2-5	UnitI11GridH6、I6、J6，UnitJ11GridA6、B6、C6、D6、F.6剖面图	52
图2-6	UnitI10GridG8、G9、G10，UnitI11GridG1、G2、G3、G4、G5剖面图	53
图2-7	UnitK9GridA8、B8、C8、D8、E8、F8、G8、H8剖面图	54
图2-8	UnitL9GridA9、B9、C9、D9、E9、F9剖面图	55
图2-9	UnitL8GridF2、F3、F4剖面图	56
图2-10	UnitK7GridI10，UnitK8GridI1-I10，UnitK9GridI1-I7剖面图	57
图2-11	UnitH10GridJ5-J1，UnitI9GridA10-A3剖面图	59
图2-12	UnitI9GridJ1，UnitJ9GridA1、B1、C1、D1、E1、F1、G1、H1剖面图	59
图2-13	UnitJ9GridH5、G5、F5、E5、D5、C5、B5、A5，UnitI9GridJ5、I5、H5剖面图	60
图2-14	UnitJ10GridD8、D7、D6、D5、D4、D3、D2、D1，UnitJ9GridD10、D9、D8、D7、D6、D5剖面图	62
图3-1	纳提什瓦遗址第一期遗迹总平面图	76
图3-2	神殿1前期建筑平剖面图	78
图3-3	神殿1后期建筑平剖面图	78
图3-4	神殿1西壁立面图	79
图3-5	道路3北段、道路4、墙1平剖面图	81
图3-6	道路3中段平剖面图	81
图3-7	浴室及排水沟平剖面图	82
图3-8	神殿2平剖面图	84
图3-9	房屋1平剖面图	86
图3-10	房屋5平剖面图	88
图3-11	墙3平剖面图	89

图3-12	十字形中心神殿建筑平面图	103
图3-13	十字形中心神殿建筑柱厅1平剖面图	104
图3-14	十字形中心神殿建筑柱厅1柱基平剖面图	105
图3-15	十字形中心神殿建筑柱厅2平剖面图	109
图3-16	十字形中心神殿建筑柱厅2柱基平剖面图	110
图3-17	十字形中心神殿建筑柱厅3平剖面图	112
图3-18	十字形中心神殿建筑柱厅4平剖面图	115
图3-19	十字形中心神殿建筑北门遗迹平剖面图	119
图3-20	纳提什瓦遗址第二期遗迹总平面图	135
图3-21	八边形佛塔1平剖面图	136
图3-22	八边形佛塔2平剖面图	138
图3-23	曲折形围墙1平剖面图	140
图4-1	UnitL10GridI5-J6，UnitJ11GridC1-D2①层出土陶器	225
图4-2	UnitL10GridE6②层出土陶器	226
图4-3	UnitI10GridI3，UnitL10，UnitJ11，UnitK9GridF10，UnitI11②层出土陶器	227
图4-4	H1出土陶器	228
图4-5	H1出土陶器	229
图4-6	H1出土陶器	230
图4-7	UnitI10-I11④层出土陶器	231
图4-8	UnitI10-I11，UnitL10GridE6，UnitL10GridE5-F6④层出土陶器	232
图4-9	UnitI10GridI11，UnitJ10-I6，UnitK10GridI3④层出土陶器	233
图4-10	UnitK10-I4，UnitL10GridD6，UnitL10GridE5-F6④层出土陶器	234
图4-11	UnitI10-I11，UnitL10GridE6④层出土陶器	234
图4-12	UnitL10GridE5-F6，UnitI10-I11，UnitL10GridF6④层出土陶器	235
图4-13	UnitI10-I11，UnitL10GridA6、B6、C6、D6、E6，UnitL10GridE5、F6④层出土陶器	236
图4-14	UnitK10GridI2-I6、J2-J6⑤层出土陶器	238
图4-15	UnitK10GridI2-I6、J2-J6，UnitL10GridE5-F6⑤层出土陶器	239
图4-16	UnitL8GridG5-F5⑤层下部出土陶器	240
图4-17	UnitL8GridG5-F5⑤层下部出土陶器	241
图4-18	UnitL8GridG5-F5⑤层下部出土陶器	242
图4-19	UnitL8GridG5-F5⑤层下部出土陶器	243
图4-20	UnitL8GridG5-F5⑤层下部出土陶器	244
图4-21	UnitL8GridG5-F5⑤层下部出土陶器	245
图4-22	UnitL10GridA2-A3⑤—⑥层之间出土陶器	246
图4-23	瓮（W1∶19）	247

图4-24	瓮1内出土陶器	248
图4-25	瓮1内出土陶器	248
图4-26	瓮1内出土陶器	249
图4-27	瓮1内出土陶器	249
图4-28	瓮1内出土陶器	251
图4-29	瓮2内出土A型壶	252
图4-30	瓮2内出土B型罐	252
图4-31	瓮2内出土陶器	253
图4-32	UnitI11GridG2-G3⑥层表层出土陶器	255
图4-33	UnitI11GridG3，UnitI11GridG2-G3⑥层表层出土陶器	256
图4-34	UnitI10GridG9-I11、G2、G3、G4、G5，UnitL10 GridE5-F6，UnitL8GridF5-G5⑥层出土陶器	257
图4-35	UnitI10GridG9-I11、G2、G3、G4、G5，UnitL8 GridF5-G5⑥层出土陶器	258
图4-36	UnitL11GridE5-F6，UnitI10GridG9-I11、G2、G3、G4、G5⑥层出土陶器	259
图4-37	UnitL8GridF5-G5⑥层B型罐	259
图4-38	UnitL10GridE5-F6，UnitI10GridG9-I11、G2、G3、G4、G5⑥层出土陶器	260
图4-39	UnitL8GridF5-G5，UnitL10GridE6⑥层出土陶器	262
图4-40	UnitL10GridE5-F6，UnitI10GridG9-I11、G2、G3、G4、G5⑥层出土陶器	263
图4-41	UnitL10GridE5-F6，UnitI10GridG9-I11、G2、G3、G4、G5，UnitL8GridF5-G5⑥层出土陶器	264
图4-42	UnitL10GridE5-F6，UnitI10GridG9-I11、G2、G3、G4、G5⑥层出土陶器	265
图4-43	UnitL10GridE6，UnitL8GridF5-G5⑥层出土陶器	266
图4-44	UnitI10GridG9-I11、G2、G3、G4、G5，UnitL10GridE5-F6，UnitL8GridF5-G5⑥层出土陶器	267
图4-46	UnitI10GridG9-I11、G2、G3、G4、G5⑦层出土陶器	269
图4-45	UnitI10GridG9-I11、G2、G3、G4、G5，UnitI11Grid G3⑦层出土陶器	269
图4-47	UnitI10GridG9-I11、G2、G3、G4、G5⑦层出土陶器	270
图4-48	UnitI10GridG9-I11、G2、G3、G4、G5⑦层出土陶器	271
图4-49	UnitI10GridG9-I11、G2、G3、G4、G5⑦层出土陶器	272
图4-50	UnitI10GridG9-I11、G2、G3、G4、G5⑦层出土陶器	273
图4-51	UnitI10GridG9-I11、G2、G3、G4、G5⑦层出土陶器	273
图4-52	UnitI10GridG9-I11、G2、G3、G4、G5⑦层出土陶器	274
图4-53	UnitI10GridG9-I11、G2、G3、G4、G5⑦层出土陶器	275
图4-54	铁钉	308
图5-1	纳提什瓦遗址遗迹总平面图	327

Figures

Fig. 1-1	Geographical map of Vikrampura site	3
Fig. 1-2	The location plan of Nateshwar area	4
Fig. 1-3	The location plan of Raghurampur site, Nateshwar site and Vairajogini Village of the hometown of Atisha Dipankara Srijnana	7
Fig. 1-4	The distribution of test grids over the years at Nateshwar site	17
Fig. 2-1	The location map of the stratigraphic sections at Nateshwar site	49
Fig. 2-2	The section of UnitJ10GridA10, B10, C10, D10, E10, E9	50
Fig. 2-3	The section of UnitJ11GridE1, D1, C1, B1, A1	51
Fig. 2-4	The section of UnitJ11GridE6, E5, E4, E3, E2, E1	51
Fig. 2-5	The section of UnitI11GridH6, I6, J6, UnitJ11GridA6, B6, C6, D6, E6	52
Fig. 2-6	The section of UnitI10GridG8, G9, G10, UnitI11GridG1, G2, G3, G4, G5	53
Fig. 2-7	The section of UnitK9GridA8, B8, C8, D8, E8, F8, G8, H8	54
Fig. 2-8	The section of UnitL9GridA9, B9, C9, D9, E9, F9	55
Fig. 2-9	The section of UnitL8GridF2, F3, F4	56
Fig. 2-10	The section of UnitK7GridI10, UnitK8GridI1-I10, UnitK9GridI1-I7	57
Fig. 2-11	The section of UnitH10GridJ5-J1, UnitI9GridA10-A3	59
Fig. 2-12	The section of UnitI9GridJ1, UnitJ9GridA1, B1, C1, D1, E1, F1, G1, H1	59
Fig. 2-13	The section of UnitJ9GridH5, G5, F5, E5, D5, C5, B5, A5, UnitI9GridJ5, I5, H5	60
Fig. 2-14	The section of UnitJ10GridD8, D7, D6, D5, D4, D3, D2, D1, UnitJ9GridD10, D9, D8, D7, D6, D5	62
Fig. 3-1	The master plan of the cultural remains of the first Period at Nateshwar site	76
Fig. 3-2	The plan and section of the early phase of Temple 1	78
Fig. 3-3	The plan and section of the late phase of Temple 1	78
Fig. 3-4	The elevation of the western wall of Temple 1	79
Fig. 3-5	The plan and section of the northern part of Road 3, Road 4 and Wall 1	81
Fig. 3-6	The plan and section of the middle part of Road 3	81
Fig. 3-7	The plan and section of bathroom and drainage	82
Fig. 3-8	The plan and section of Temple 2 (pyramid-shaped stupa)	84
Fig. 3-9	The plan and section of House 1	86
Fig. 3-10	The plan and section of House 5	88
Fig. 3-11	The plan and section of Wall 3	89
Fig. 3-12	The plan of Cruciform Central Temple	103
Fig. 3-13	The plan and section of Pillared-hall 1, Cruciform Central Temple	104
Fig. 3-14	The plan and section of Pillar-plinth of Pillared-hall 1, Cruciform Central Temple	105

Fig. 3-15	The plan and section of Pillared-hall 2, Cruciform Central Temple	109
Fig. 3-16	The plan and section of pillar-plinth of the Pillared-hall 2, Cruciform Central Temple	110
Fig. 3-17	The plan and section of Pillared-hall 3, Cruciform Central Temple	112
Fig. 3-18	The plan and section of Pillared-hall 4, Cruciform Central Temple	115
Fig. 3-19	The plan and section of the north entrance of the Cruciform Central Temple	119
Fig. 3-20	The master plan of the second period cultural remains at Nateshwar site	135
Fig. 3-21	The plan and section of Octagonal Stupa 1	136
Fig. 3-22	The plan and section of Octagonal Stupa 2	138
Fig. 3-23	The plan and section of Zigzag Boundary Wall 1	140
Fig. 4-1	The unearthed potteries of Layer 1 from UnitL10GridI5-J6, UnitJ11GridC1-D2	225
Fig. 4-2	The unearthed potteries of Layer 2 from UnitL10GridE6	226
Fig. 4-3	The unearthed potteries of Layer 2 from UnitI10GridI3, UnitL10, UnitJ11, UnitK9GridF10 and UnitI11	227
Fig. 4-4	The unearthed potteries from H1	228
Fig. 4-5	The unearthed potteries from H1	229
Fig. 4-6	The unearthed potteries from H1	230
Fig. 4-7	The unearthed potteries of Layer 4 from UnitI10-I11	231
Fig. 4-8	The unearthed potteries of Layer 4 from UnitI10-I11, UnitL10GridE6, UnitL10GridE5-F6	232
Fig. 4-9	The unearthed potteries of Layer 4 from UnitI10GridI11, UnitJ10-I6, UnitK10GridI3	233
Fig. 4-10	The unearthed potteries of Layer 4 from UnitK10-I4, UnitL10GridD6, UnitL10GridE5-F6	234
Fig. 4-11	The unearthed potteries of Layer 4 from UnitI10-I11, UnitL10GridE6	234
Fig. 4-12	The unearthed potteries of Layer 4 from UnitL10GridE5-F6, UnitI10-I11, UnitL10GridF6	235
Fig. 4-13	The unearthed potteries of Layer 4 from UnitI10-I11, UnitL10GridA6, B6, C6, D6, E6, UnitL10GridE5, F6	236
Fig. 4-14	The unearthed potteries of Layer 5 from UnitK10GridI2-I6, J2-J6	238
Fig. 4-15	The unearthed potteries of Layer 5 from UnitK10GridI2-I6, J2-J6, UnitL10GridE5-F6	239
Fig. 4-16	The unearthed potteries of lower Layer 5 from UnitL8GridG5-F5	240
Fig. 4-17	The unearthed potteries of lower Layer 5 from UnitL8GridG5-F5	241
Fig. 4-18	The unearthed potteries of lower Layer 5 from UnitL8GridG5-F5	242
Fig. 4-19	The unearthed potteries of lower Layer 5 from UnitL8GridG5-F5	243
Fig. 4-20	The unearthed potteries of lower Layer 5 from UnitL8GridG5-F5	244
Fig. 4-21	The unearthed potteries of lower Layer 5 from UnitL8GridG5-F5	245
Fig. 4-22	The unearthed potteries between Layer 5 and layer 6 from UnitL10GridA2-A3	246
Fig. 4-23	The Urn (W1∶19)	247
Fig. 4-24	The unearthed potteries from Urn 1	248
Fig. 4-25	The unearthed potteries from Urn 1	248
Fig. 4-26	The unearthed potteries from Urn 1	249

Fig. 4-27	The unearthed potteries from Urn 1	249
Fig. 4-28	The unearthed potteries from Urn 1	251
Fig. 4-29	The A-type jug unearthed from Urn 2	252
Fig. 4-30	The B-type pot unearthed from Urn 2	252
Fig. 4-31	The unearthed potteries from Urn 2	253
Fig. 4-32	The unearthed potteries of Layer 6 from UnitI11GridG2-G3	255
Fig. 4-33	The unearthed potteries of top Layer 6 from UnitI11GridG3, UnitI11GridG2-G3	256
Fig. 4-34	The unearthed potteries of Layer 6 from UnitI10GridG9-I11, G2, G3, G4, G5, UnitL10GridE5-F6, UnitL8GridF5-G5	257
Fig. 4-35	The unearthed potteries of Layer 6 from UnitI10GridG9-I11, G2, G3, G4, G5, UnitL8GridF5-G5	258
Fig. 4-36	The unearthed potteries of Layer 6 from UnitL11GridE5-F6, UnitI10GridG9-I11, G2, G3, G4, G5	259
Fig. 4-37	The B-type pot of Layer 6 from UnitL8GridF5-G5	259
Fig. 4-38	The unearthed potteries of Layer 6 from UnitL10GridE5-F6, UnitI10GridG9-I11, G2, G3, G4, G5	260
Fig. 4-39	The unearthed potteries of Layer 6 from UnitL8GridF5-G5, UnitL10GridE6	262
Fig. 4-40	The unearthed potteries of Layer 6 from UnitL10GridE5-F6, UnitI10GridG9-I11, G2, G3, G4, G5	263
Fig. 4-41	The unearthed potteries of Layer 6 from UnitL10GridE5-F6, UnitI10GridG9-I11, G2, G3, G4, G5, UnitL8GridF5-G5	264
Fig. 4-42	The unearthed potteries of Layer 6 from UnitL10GridE5-F6, UnitI10GridG9-I11, G2, G3, G4, G5	265
Fig. 4-43	The unearthed potteries of Layer 6 from UnitL10GridE6, UnitL8GridF5-G5	266
Fig. 4-44	The unearthed potteries of Layer 6 from UnitI10GridG9-I11, G2, G3, G4, G5, UnitL10GridE5-F6, UnitL8GridF5-G5	267
Fig. 4-45	The unearthed potteries of Layer 7 from UnitI10GridG9-I11, G2, G3, G4, G5, UnitI11GridG3	269
Fig. 4-46	The unearthed potteries of Layer 7 from UnitI10GridG9-I11, G2, G3, G4, G5	269
Fig. 4-47	The unearthed potteries of Layer 7 from UnitI10GridG9-I11, G2, G3, G4, G5	270
Fig. 4-48	The unearthed potteries of Layer 7 from UnitI10GridG9-I11, G2, G3, G4, G5	271
Fig. 4-49	The unearthed potteries of Layer 7 from UnitI10GridG9-I11, G2, G3, G4, G5	272
Fig. 4-50	The unearthed potteries of Layer 7 from UnitI10GridG9-I11, G2, G3, G4, G5	273
Fig. 4-51	The unearthed potteries of Layer 7 from UnitI10GridG9-I11, G2, G3, G4, G5	273
Fig. 4-52	The unearthed potteries of Layer 7 from UnitI10GridG9-I11, G2, G3, G4, G5	274
Fig. 4-53	The unearthed potteries of Layer 7 from UnitI10GridG9-I11, G2, G3, G4, G5	275
Fig. 4-54	Iron nail	308
Fig. 5-1	The master plan of cultural remains at Nateshwar excavation site	327

附表目录

表1	房屋1柱洞登记表	85
表2	UnitI10、I11、J10、J11 ①层陶器统计表	224
表3	UnitI10、I11、J10、J11 ②层陶器统计表	226
表4	UnitI10、I11、J10、J11 ④层陶器统计表	229
表5	UnitK10GridI2-I6、J2-J6 ⑤层陶器统计表	237
表6	UnitL8GridG5-F5 ⑤层下部陶器统计表	237
表7	UniL10GridA2-A3 ⑤—⑥层之间陶器统计表	238
表8	UnitI10GridG9，UnitI11GridG2、G3、G4、G5 ⑥层陶器统计表	254
表9	UnitL10GridE5-F6（神殿1北部探坑）⑥层陶器统计表	254
表10	UnitI10GridG9，UnitI11GridG2、G3、G4、G5 ⑦层陶器统计表	268
表11	纳提什瓦遗址地层和遗迹单位的分期表	326

Table Catalogue

Table 1	Statistic table of postholes in House 1	85
Table 2	Statistic table of the potteries of Layer 1 in Unit I10, I11, J10 and J11	277
Table 3	Statistic table of the potteries of Layer 2 in Unit I10, I11, J10 and J11	278
Table 4	Statistic table of the potteries of Layer 3 in Unit I10, I11, J10 and J11	279
Table 5	Statistic table of the potteries of Layer 5 in UnitK10GridI2-I6-J2-J6	280
Table 6	Statistic table of the potteries of lower Layer 5 in UnitL8GridG5-F5	280
Table 7	Statistic table of the potteries of between Layer 5 and Layer 6 in UnitL10GridA2-A3	281
Table 8	Statistic table of the potteries of Layer 6 in UnitI10GridG9, UnitI11GridG2、G3、G4、G5	282
Table 9	Statistic table of the potteries of Layer 6 in UnitL10GridE5-F6	282
Table 10	Statistic table of the potteries of Layer 7 in UnitUnitI10GridG9, UnitI11GridG2、G3、G4、G5	283
Table 11	The periodization of layers and cultural remains at Nateshwar site	331

彩版目录

彩版 1-1	纳提什瓦遗址环境	23
彩版 1-2	纳提什瓦村环境	24
彩版 1-3	蒙希甘杰县内名胜	25
彩版 1-4	达卡法王寺阿底峡相关文物和纪念堂	26
彩版 1-5	拉库罗普尔遗址	27
彩版 1-6	纳提什瓦遗址的原貌	28
彩版 1-7	2014—2015 年中孟第一次联合发掘	29
彩版 1-8	2015—2016 年中孟第二次联合发掘	30
彩版 1-9	2017—2018 年中孟第三次联合发掘	30
彩版 1-10	部分考古队员合影	31
彩版 1-11	队员风采	32
彩版 1-12	工地掠影	33
彩版 1-13	工地掠影	34
彩版 1-14	生活花絮	35
彩版 1-15	工作、生活花絮	36
彩版 1-16	领导的关注	37
彩版 1-17	领导的关注	38
彩版 1-18	领导的关注	39
彩版 1-19	来自各国的来访者	40
彩版 1-20	公共考古宣传	41
彩版 1-21	"毗诃罗普尔遗址考古发掘和文物保护国际研讨会"在达卡贾汉吉纳格尔大学举行	42
彩版 2-1	地层及灰坑 H2	67
彩版 2-2	地层及出土陶器	68
彩版 2-3	地层剖面	69
彩版 2-4	UnitI10GridG8、G9、G10，UnitI11GridG1、G2、G3、G4、G5 剖面	70
彩版 2-5	UnitK9GridA8、B8、C8、D8、E8、F8、G8、H8 剖面	71
彩版 2-6	地层剖面	72
彩版 2-7	UnitK7GridI10，UnitK8GridI1-I10，UnitK9GridI1-I7 剖面	73
彩版 2-8	地层剖面	74
彩版 3-1	第一期遗迹全景	150
彩版 3-2	神殿 1 外墙	151
彩版 3-3	神殿 1 全景	152

彩版 3-4	神殿 1 门厅	153
彩版 3-5	神殿 1 相关遗迹	154
彩版 3-6	神殿 1 墙角瓮 1、瓮 2	155
彩版 3-7	房屋 6、房屋 7 和道路 1	156
彩版 3-8	道路 3 北部	157
彩版 3-9	道路 3 中南部	158
彩版 3-10	浴室和排水沟	159
彩版 3-11	神殿 2	160
彩版 3-12	神殿 2 东墙基	161
彩版 3-13	神殿 2 东墙外遗迹	162
彩版 3-14	神殿 2 东墙外陶器和河光石	163
彩版 3-15	神殿 2 北墙	164
彩版 3-16	隔墙	165
彩版 3-17	隔墙根下出土陶器	166
彩版 3-18	隔墙根下出土陶器	167
彩版 3-19	房屋 1	168
彩版 3-20	房屋 2	169
彩版 3-21	房屋 3、4	170
彩版 3-22	房屋 5 全景	171
彩版 3-23	房屋 5 局部	172
彩版 3-24	墙 1、2、3	173
彩版 3-25	路面 4、道路 4	174
彩版 3-26	十字形中心神殿全景	175
彩版 3-27	中心塔基地层和柱厅 1 发掘前地表	176
彩版 3-28	柱厅 1 全景	177
彩版 3-29	柱厅 1 全景	178
彩版 3-30	柱厅 1 东墙基	179
彩版 3-31	柱厅 1 北墙基	180
彩版 3-32	柱厅 1 南墙基、西墙基	181
彩版 3-33	柱厅 1 柱基 1	182
彩版 3-34	柱厅 1 柱基 2	183
彩版 3-35	柱厅 1 柱基 3、4	184
彩版 3-36	柱厅 2 全景	185
彩版 3-37	柱厅 2 全景（2014—2015 年发掘后）	186
彩版 3-38	柱厅 2 全景（2015—2016 年发掘后）	187
彩版 3-39	柱厅 2 东墙基、南墙基	188

彩版 3-40	墙柱厅 2 西墙基	189
彩版 3-41	柱厅 2 北墙基	190
彩版 3-42	柱厅 2 柱基 1	191
彩版 3-43	柱厅 2 柱基 2、3、4	192
彩版 3-44	柱厅 3 全景	193
彩版 3-45	柱厅 3 墙基	194
彩版 3-46	柱厅 3 柱基	195
彩版 3-47	柱厅 4 全景	196
彩版 3-48	柱厅 4 全景	197
彩版 3-49	柱厅 4 东墙基、南墙基	198
彩版 3-50	柱厅 4 西墙基、北墙基	199
彩版 3-51	柱厅 4 柱基 1、2	200
彩版 3-52	柱厅 4 柱基 1、2	201
彩版 3-53	柱厅 4 柱基 3、4	202
彩版 3-54	连接墙基 1	203
彩版 3-55	连接墙基 2	204
彩版 3-56	连接墙基 3、4	205
彩版 3-57	中心塔基和柱厅 4 全景	206
彩版 3-58	中心塔基局部遗迹	207
彩版 3-59	中心塔基东、北、西端	208
彩版 3-60	北门道全景	209
彩版 3-61	北门道局部	210
彩版 3-62	护墙基和巴哈布尔遗址复原图	211
彩版 3-63	出土装饰砖	212
彩版 3-64	八边形佛塔 1 全景	213
彩版 3-65	八边形佛塔 1 内部	214
彩版 3-66	八边形佛塔 1 局部	215
彩版 3-67	八边形佛塔 2 全景	216
彩版 3-68	八边形佛塔 2 塔身部分	217
彩版 3-69	八边形佛塔 2 前厅部分	218
彩版 3-70	八边形佛塔 3、曲折形围墙 1	219
彩版 3-71	路面 1 平面位置	220
彩版 3-72	路面 1 遗迹	221
彩版 3-73	路面 3、H2	222
彩版 4-1	①、②层陶器	285
彩版 4-2	②、④层陶器	286

彩版 4-3	H1 陶器	287
彩版 4-4	④层陶器	288
彩版 4-5	④层陶器	289
彩版 4-6	⑤层陶器	290
彩版 4-7	⑤层陶器	291
彩版 4-8	瓮 1 陶器	292
彩版 4-9	瓮 1 陶器	293
彩版 4-10	瓮 1 陶器	294
彩版 4-11	瓮 1、瓮 2 陶器	295
彩版 4-12	瓮 2 陶器	296
彩版 4-13	⑥层表面陶器	297
彩版 4-14	⑥层陶器	298
彩版 4-15	⑥层陶器	299
彩版 4-16	⑥层陶器	300
彩版 4-17	⑥层陶器	301
彩版 4-18	⑦层陶器	302
彩版 4-19	⑦层陶器	303
彩版 4-20	⑦层陶器	304
彩版 4-21	陶片纹饰	305
彩版 4-22	陶片纹饰	306
彩版 4-23	陶片纹饰	307
彩版 4-24	毗诃罗普尔地区出土文物	314
彩版 4-25	出土瓷片	315
彩版 4-26	出土文物	316
彩版 4-27	毗诃罗普尔地区出土砖雕	317
彩版 4-28	毗诃罗普尔地区出土砖雕	318
彩版 4-29	毗诃罗普尔地区出土石雕造像	319
彩版 4-30	毗诃罗普尔地区出土石雕造像	320
彩版 4-31	毗诃罗普尔地区出土石雕造像	321
彩版 4-32	毗诃罗普尔地区出土石雕造像	322
彩版 4-33	毗诃罗普尔地区出土石雕造像	323
彩版 4-34	毗诃罗普尔地区出土石雕造像	324

Color Plates

Color Plate 1-1	The environment at Nateshwar site	23
Color Plate 1-2	The environment of the Nateshwar Village	24
Color Plate 1-3	The places of interest in Munshiganj district	25
Color Plate 1-4	The related relics of Atisha Dipankar at Dharmarajika Buddhist temple in Dhaka and the memorial hall under construction	26
Color Plate 1-5	The cultural remains at Raghurampur site, Vikrampura	27
Color Plate 1-6	The original landscape of Nateshwar site	28
Color Plate 1-7	The China-Bangladesh first joint excavation during 2014-2015	29
Color Plate 1-8	The China-Bangladesh second joint excavation during 2015-2016	30
Color Plate 1-9	The China-Bangladesh third joint excavation during 2017-2018	30
Color Plate 1-10	The group photo of some archaeological team members	31
Color Plate 1-11	Team members	32
Color Plate 1-12	A glance at excavation site	33
Color Plate 1-13	A glance at excavation site	34
Color Plate 1-14	Life trivia	35
Color Plate 1-15	Trivia of work and life	36
Color Plate 1-16	The care from the leaders	37
Color Plate 1-17	The care from the leaders	38
Color Plate 1-18	The care from the leaders	39
Color Plate 1-19	The visitors from all over the world	40
Color Plate 1-20	Public archaeology	41
Color Plate 1-21	The "Seminar on Archaeological excavation and Conservation of Nateshwar Site, Vikrampura" was held at Jahangirnar University	42
Color Plate 2-1	The layers and ash pit (H2)	67
Color Plate 2-2	The layers and unearthed potteries	68
Color Plate 2-3	Stratigraphic section	69
Color Plate 2-4	The section of UnitI10GridG8, G9, G10, UnitI11GridG1, G2, G3, G4, G5	70
Color Plate 2-5	The section of UnitK9GridA8, B8, C8, D8, E8, F8, G8, H8	71
Color Plate 2-6	Stratigraphic section	72
Color Plate 2-7	The section of UnitK7GridI10, UnitK8GridI1-I10 and UnitK9GridI1-I7	73
Color Plate 2-8	Stratigraphic section	74
Color Plate 3-1	The panorama of the first period's cultural remains	150
Color Plate 3-2	The outer wall of Temple 1	151

xxi

Color Plate 3-3	The panorama of Temple 1	152
Color Plate 3-4	The entrance hall of Temple 1	153
Color Plate 3-5	The related relics of Temple 1	154
Color Plate 3-6	The Urn 1 and Urn 2 at the corners of Temple 1	155
Color Plate 3-7	House 6, House 7 and Road 1	156
Color Plate 3-8	The north of Road 3	157
Color Plate 3-9	Southern and central part of Road 3	158
Color Plate 3-10	Bathroom and drainage	159
Color Plate 3-11	Temple 2 (pyramid-shaped stupa)	160
Color Plate 3-12	The eastern wall foundation of Temple 2 (pyramid-shaped stupa)	161
Color Plate 3-13	The remains outside of the eastern wall of Temple 2 (pyramid-shaped stupa)	162
Color Plate 3-14	The unearthed potteries and processed cobbles outside the eastern wall of Temple 2 (pyramid-shaped stupa)	163
Color Plate 3-15	The northern wall of Temple 2 (pyramid-shaped stupa)	164
Color Plate 3-16	Partition wall	165
Color Plate 3-17	The potteries unearthed at the foot of partition wall	166
Color Plate 3-18	The potteries unearthed at the foot of partition wall	167
Color Plate 3-19	House 1	168
Color Plate 3-20	House 2	169
Color Plate 3-21	House 3, House 4	170
Color Plate 3-22	The panorama of House 5	171
Color Plate 3-23	Some parts of House 5	172
Color Plate 3-24	Wall 1, Wall 2, and Wall 3	173
Color Plate 3-25	Floor 4, Road 4	174
Color Plate 3-26	The panorama of the Cruciform Central Temple	175
Color Plate 3-27	The stratigraphy of central temple foundation and the surface of Pillared-hall 1 before excavation	176
Color Plate 3-28	The panorama of Pillared-hall 1	177
Color Plate 3-29	The panorama of Pillared-hall 1	178
Color Plate 3-30	The eastern wall foundation of Pillared-hall 1	179
Color Plate 3-31	The northern wall foundation of Pillared-hall 1	180
Color Plate 3-32	The southern and western wall foundations of Pillared-hall 1	181
Color Plate 3-33	The Pillar-plinth 1 of Pillared-hall 1	182
Color Plate 3-34	The Pillar-plinth 2 of Pillared-hall 1	183
Color Plate 3-35	The Pillar-plinth 3, 4 of Pillared-hall 1	184
Color Plate 3-36	The panorama of Pillared-hall 2	185
Color Plate 3-37	The panorama of Pillared-hall 2 (after excavation during 2014-2015)	186
Color Plate 3-38	The panorama of Pillared-hall 2 (after excavation during 2015-2016)	187
Color Plate 3-39	The eastern and southern wall foundations of Pillared-hall 2	188
Color Plate 3-40	The western wall foundation of Pillared-hall 2	189

Color Plate 3-41	The northern wall foundation of Pillared-hall 2	190
Color Plate 3-42	The Pillar-plinth 1 of Pillared-hall 2	191
Color Plate 3-43	The Pillar-plinth 2, 3 and 4 of Pillared-hall 2	192
Color Plate 3-44	The panorama of Pillared-hall 3	193
Color Plate 3-45	The wall foundation of Pillared-hall 3	194
Color Plate 3-46	The Pillar-plinth of Pillared-hall 3	195
Color Plate 3-47	The panorama of Pillared-hall 4	196
Color Plate 3-48	The panorama of Pillared-hall 4	197
Color Plate 3-49	The eastern and southern wall foundations of Pillared-hall 4	198
Color Plate 3-50	The western and northern wall foundations of Pillared-hall 4	199
Color Plate 3-51	The Pillar-plinth 1,2 of Pillared-hall 4	200
Color Plate 3-52	The Pillar-plinth 1, 2 of Pillared-hall 4	201
Color Plate 3-53	The Pillar-plinth 3, 4 of Pillared-hall 4	202
Color Plate 3-54	The Connective Wall Foundation 1	203
Color Plate 3-55	The Connective Wall Foundation 2	204
Color Plate 3-56	The Connective Wall Foundation 3 and 4	205
Color Plate 3-57	The panorama of central temple foundation and Pillared-hall 4	206
Color Plate 3-58	The partial remains of central temple foundation	207
Color Plate 3-59	The east, north and west ends of central temple foundation	208
Color Plate 3-60	The panorama of north entrance	209
Color Plate 3-61	Some local parts of north entrance	210
Color Plate 3-62	The parapet wall and the imagination reconstruction of central temple at Paharpur monastery	211
Color Plate 3-63	The unearthed decorative bricks	212
Color Plate 3-64	The panorama of Octagonal Stupa 1	213
Color Plate 3-65	The interior of Octagon Stupa 1	214
Color Plate 3-66	The exterior of Octagon Stupa 1	215
Color Plate 3-67	The panorama of Octagonal Stupa 2	216
Color Plate 3-68	The body of Octagonal Stupa 2	217
Color Plate 3-69	The mandapa of Octagonal Stupa 2	218
Color Plate 3-70	The Octagonal Stupa 3, Zigzag Boundary Wall 1	219
Color Plate 3-71	The location plan of Floor 1	220
Color Plate 3-72	Floor 1	221
Color Plate 3-73	Floor 3, ash pit H2	222
Color Plate 4-1	The potteries of Layer 1 and Layer 2	285
Color Plate 4-2	The potteries of Layer 2 and Layer 4	286
Color Plate 4-3	The potteries from H1	287
Color Plate 4-4	The potteries of Layer 4	288
Color Plate 4-5	The potteries of Layer 4	289
Color Plate 4-6	The potteries of Layer 5	290

Color Plate 4-7	The potteries of Layer 5	291
Color Plate 4-8	The potteries from Urn 1	292
Color Plate 4-9	The potteries from Urn 1	293
Color Plate 4-10	The potteries of Urn 1	294
Color Plate 4-11	The potteries of Urn 1 and Urn 2	295
Color Plate 4-12	The potteries from Urn 2	296
Color Plate 4-13	The potteries on the surface of Layer 6	297
Color Plate 4-14	The potteries of Layer 6	298
Color Plate 4-15	The potteries of Layer 6	299
Color Plate 4-16	The potteries of Layer 6	300
Color Plate 4-17	The potteries of Layer 6	301
Color Plate 4-18	The potteries of Layer 7	302
Color Plate 4-19	The potteries of Layer 7	303
Color Plate 4-20	The potteries of Layer 7	304
Color Plate 4-21	Pottery decoration	305
Color Plate 4-22	Pottery decoration	306
Color Plate 4-23	Pottery decoration	307
Color Plate 4-24	The artifacts unearthed in Vikrampura area	314
Color Plate 4-25	The unearthed porcelain fragments	315
Color Plate 4-26	The unearthed artifacts	316
Color Plate 4-27	The brick scuptures unearthed in Vikrampura area	317
Color Plate 4-28	The brick scuptures unearthed in Vikrampura area	318
Color Plate 4-29	The stone statues unearthed in Vikrampura area	319
Color Plate 4-30	The stone statues unearthed in Vikrampura area	320
Color Plate 4-31	The stone statues unearthed in Vikrampura area	321
Color Plate 4-32	The stone statues unearthed in Vikrampura area	322
Color Plate 4-33	The stone statues unearthed in Vikrampura area	323
Color Plate 4-34	The stone statues unearthed in Vikrampura area	324

提要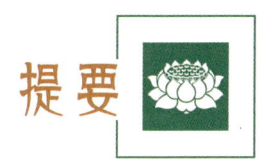

毗诃罗普尔（Vikrampura）古城是2010年由孟加拉国考古学家发现的，2013年，孟加拉国考古学家首次在纳提什瓦（Nateshwar）遗址进行了考古发掘。2014年12月—2018年1月，中国湖南省文物考古研究所和阿哥拉萨－毗诃罗普尔（Agrashar Vikrampur）基金会聘请的欧提亚·欧耐斯恩考古研究中心（Oitihya Onneswan Archaeological Research Center）组成联合考古队，先后三次对纳提什瓦遗址进行了大规模的考古发掘，发掘面积达5236平方米，取得了重大成果。

通过地层学和一系列测年数据，纳提什瓦遗址可分为两个时期。第一期年代约在公元780—950年，即修建于德瓦（Devas）王朝（750—800年）时期，沿续至旃陀罗（Chandra）王朝（900—1050年）的前期。第二期年代约在公元950—1223年，这段时期为旃陀罗王朝后期、跋摩（Varman）王朝（1080—1150年）和犀那（Sena）王朝（1100—1223年）时期。据考证，这三个王朝都曾建都于毗诃罗普尔。作为阿底峡尊者的故乡，毗诃罗普尔在藏文典藏中，也是一个神圣的名字。这个规模庞大、具有不同功能的大型佛教遗址的发现，证实了这座都城的存在。纳提什瓦遗址的早期遗迹，是一组塔院（stupa court）和僧院（vihara）的综合体，遗址规模、整体布局及单体建筑的特点，在孟加拉国都是前所未有。晚期遗迹主要为十字形中心神殿建筑及多边形塔等附属建筑，这是孟加拉国10—13世纪金刚乘建筑的典型范例。作为南亚次大陆最后一个佛教中心的珍贵遗产，这个遗址将载入世界考古学的史册。

Abstract

The Vikrampura ancient city site was discovered by Bangladeshi archaeologists in 2010. In 2013, Bangladesh archaeologists carried out the archaeological excavation at Nateshwar site for the first time. From December 2014 to January 2018, the joint archaeological team composed of Agrashar Vikrampur Foundation in Bangladesh and Hunan Provincial Institute of Cultural Relics and Archaeology in China successively conducted three large-scale excavations at Nateshwar site. More than five thousand square meters were exposed and a series of significant results were achieved by the time.

According to the site's stratigraphy and carbon fourteen dating, two periods were confirmed in Nateshwar Buddhist settlement. The first period is around between 780 – 950 AD, which was the Deva dynasty (750 – 800AD) and lasted to early Chandra dynasty (900 – 1050AD). The second period is circa between 950 – 1223AD, when late Chandra, Varman dynasty (1080 – 1150AD) and Sena dynasty (1100 – 1223AD) successively ruled this region. Their capitals were all located in Vikrampura according to the research on several copper plate inscription data. The name of Vikrampura, the hometown of venerable Atisha Dipamkara Srijnana, appeared also in Tibetan historical texts. The discovery of this large-scale Buddhist site with different functional zones proves the existence of the capital in the text. The earlier features at Nateshwar site are a complex of stupa court and vihara. The scale of the site, the overall layout and the characteristic of the single structure are unique in Bangladesh. The main later features are the cruciform central temple and octagonal stupas dating from 10th to 13th century, which are the typical structure of Vajrayana Buddhism in Bangladesh. This site will be written into the history of world archaeology as the last precious heritage of Buddhist center in South Asia subcontinent.

Chapter

I

第一章

Preface

绪 论

第一节
Section 1
Geographical Background

地理位置

孟加拉国位于南亚次大陆的东北部，地处恒河与布拉马普特拉河下游的三角洲上，西面、北面分别与印度的西孟加拉邦接壤，东北部与印度的阿萨姆（Assam）邦和梅加拉亚（Meghalaya）邦相邻，东部与印度的特里普拉（Tripura）邦和米左拉姆（Mizoram）邦毗连，东南与缅甸交界，南部濒临浩瀚的孟加拉湾。

毗诃罗普尔（Vikrampura）古城位于孟加拉国中东部地区，行政区划属达卡专区的蒙希甘杰（Munshiganj）县，西北距首府达卡市区约34千米（图1-1），北面为纳拉扬甘杰（Narayangj）县，东北为库米拉（Comilla）县，东面为坚德布尔（Chandpur）县，南面为沙里亚德布尔（Shakhipur）县和马达里布尔县（Madaripur）县，西面为达卡县和福里德布尔（Faridpur）县。

毗诃罗普尔古城目前包括东、西两个遗址，分别为拉库罗普尔（Raghurampur）遗址和纳提什瓦（Nateshwar）遗址，两者核心区相距约2千米。拉库罗普尔（Raghurampur）遗址2010年试掘面积约300平方米，未进行大面积的勘探，初步推测遗址面积可达数万平方米。

中孟联合发掘的纳提什瓦（Nateshwar）遗址，位于蒙希甘杰县峒吉巴日（Tongibari）乡的纳提什瓦村所在地，遗址因此而命名。中心基点坐标为北纬23°31′53.11″，东经90°28′10.67″。纳提什瓦遗址的微地貌为平原中的一个馒头形土丘，高出周围地面2—3米，地势较为开阔，中心部位最高，向四周渐低。土台中心部位为村民的公共用地，被杂草覆盖，有着大量香蕉树和零星蔬菜，围绕台子中心的四周长有大量高大树木，现代民居、村小学、水塘以及菜地散布于台子的边缘，再往外围则主要为较为密集的民居和低地农田，一条大致呈南北走向的莫喀第（Mirkadim）人工运河从遗址的西侧流经（图1-2；彩版1-1、1-2）。

孟加拉盆地处于喜马拉雅山和孟加拉群山碰撞形成的褶皱带上，连接印度板块与亚欧板块地质构造不稳定，其东部边缘吉大港和锡尔赫特分布有陡峭的山地，蒙希甘杰县的地貌单元属古老的梅格纳河口冲积平原，平稳宽阔的近水平状海脊被厚厚的泥沙堆积覆盖。分析显示，这些古老沉积主要来源自布拉马普特拉河。县境内土壤类型主要为古恒河、梅格纳河所带来的非钙质棕色冲积平原土壤。

图 1-1 毗诃罗普尔古城地理位置图
Fig. 1-1 Geographical map of Vikrampura site

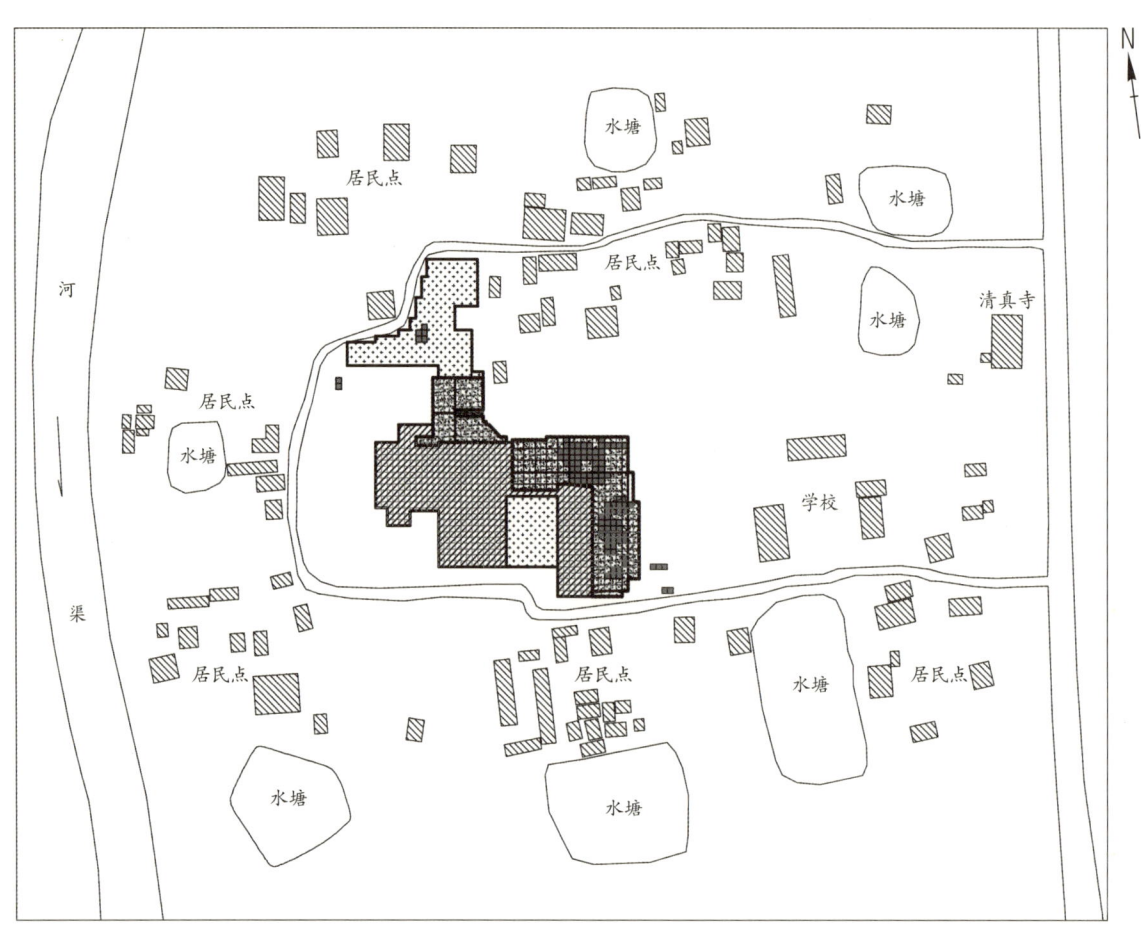

图 1-2 纳提什瓦遗址平面位置图
Fig. 1-2　The location plan of Nateshwar site

Bangladesh is situated in the northeastern part of the South Asian subcontinent, lying on the delta of the lower reaches of the Ganges and the Brahmaputra River. It is bordered on the west and north by the West Bengal of Indian state. On the east, it is adjacent to the Tripura and Mizoram of Indian state and on the southeast, it is bordered by a part of Myanmar. To the south lies the Bay of Bengal.

Vikrampura ancient city is located in the central-eastern region of Bangladesh, belonging to Munshiganj district. It is about 34 kilometers northwest of the capital city of Dhaka (Figure 1-1). The neighboring districts include Narayangaj on the north, Comilla on the northeast, Chandpur on the east, Shakhipur and Madaripur on the south, as well as Dhaka and Faridpur districts on the west. Present exploration and survey shows that Raghurampur area and Nateshwar area are the two sites of the Vikrampura ancient city, and the distance between their core regions is about 2 km. In 2010, Raghurampur was tentatively excavated about 300 m^2, but its area was speculated to be thousands of square meters according to the exposed monuments.

The Nateshwar site, which was jointly excavated by Bangladesh and China, is located in the village of Nateshwar of Tongibari upazila in Munshiganj District. The site is named after the village name of Nateshwar. Its central point coordinates are 23°31'53.11" North latitude and 90°28'10.67" East longitude. The current geomorphology of the site area is a bread-shaped mound in the plain, which is about 3 m above the ground. Before the excavation, the central part of the mound used to be the public land, covered with various weeds, a large amount of banana trees and sporadic planted vegetables. Besides, there are a large number of tall trees surrounding the mound while modern farmers' houses, a primary school, ponds and vegetable fields are scattered in the periphery area. A roughly north to south direction active Mirkadim channel flows past on the west side of the site (Figure 1-2, Color Plate 1-1, 1-2).

第二节 自然环境
Section 2 Natural Environment

孟加拉国也被认为是"喜马拉山脉水流冲击形成的三角洲",是水脉和淤泥之地。蒙希甘杰县处于三河交汇处,除西部与邻县接壤为陆地外,其余三面均被河流所包围,除了旧冲积层有小块地区地势较高外,整个平原都是坦荡如砥的新冲积层,坡度舒缓,海拔不超过10米。县境北部流淌着拖莱索里河(Dhaleshwari),与拉克什亚(Lakhya)河在弗郎纳杰巴札尔(Firingi Bazar)附近相汇,东部流经梅格纳(Meghna)河,帕德玛(Padma)河从南部蜿蜒而过。这三条河流均是孟加拉国内的大河,其中恒河发源于喜马拉雅山南麓冈戈里冰川,向东流经印度斯坦平原,在孟加拉西北部拉吉沙希(Rajshahi)县西面一隅流入孟加拉国,然后向东南,在孟加拉国中心地带和首都达卡西北的戈阿隆多(Goelundo)附近的贾木纳(Jamuna)河汇流,再继续向东南方向奔流,与梅格纳河汇合,恒河在孟境内的河段被称为博多河(或帕德玛河)。贾木纳河发源于中国西藏境内的喜马拉雅山北麓,上游是雅鲁藏布江,在印度境内称为布拉马普特拉河,之后流经阿萨姆平原,从正北方向进入孟加拉国,贾木纳河与博多河汇合后,水势浩大。梅格纳河源自印度,从东北部进入孟加拉国,上游水源众多,降雨量极大,下游在昌德布林(Chandpur)与博多河、贾木纳河汇流,雨季时河面宽度可达8千米。在地质时期和历史时期,这些河流改道较为频繁,如仅在2个世纪以前,孟加拉北部马哈斯坦(Mahastan)遗址附近的蒂斯塔(Tista)河曾是当地的主要河流,也是现今一些小型河流的主要水源地,1787年之后则向东改道并与贾木纳河汇合;贾木纳河古河道曾经紧邻达卡蒙希甘杰地区东部,其后由于构造运动大幅度向西改道,并最终形成现今位于达卡以西的贾木纳河;同样,博多河曾经主要为南北向的一条河流,但2个世纪以前也开始向东改道并与贾木纳河汇合形成新的博多河(图1-3)。

蒙希甘杰县以平原为主,大量的溪流和被大河灌溉的低地构成境内水陆兼具的地形特征,雨季时大部分低地处于水位之下,大量的泥沙也由河流上游带来,聚集于河流泛滥的陆地处,不断抬升着陆地的高度,也为农业生产带来了肥沃的土壤,因此,境内也是孟加拉国最大的土豆生产地之一,重要的作物还包括麻、水稻、小麦和其他蔬菜,也生产甘蔗和香蕉。

蒙希甘杰县属热带季风性气候,具有高温、多雨、潮湿和季节性变化明显的特点。一年之中主要有4个季节:夏季(4—6月)、秋季(9—11月)、冬季(12—1月)、春季(2—3月),大部分雨水发生在季风季节(7—8月),冬季的雨水很少。秋季气候宜人,春季色彩斑斓。1月是最冷的月份,最低气温12.7℃,4月是最炎热的月份,最高气温一般在33—36℃。在蒙希甘杰地区,年均降雨量为2376毫升。

图1-3 拉库罗普尔（Raghurampur）遗址、纳提什瓦遗址、阿底峡故乡金刚瑜伽（Vairajogini）村平面位置图

Fig. 1-3 The location plan of Raghurampur site, Nateshwar site and Vairajogini Village of the hometown of Atisha Dipankara

主要参考书目

MD. ABU MUSA. Archaeological survey report: Munshiganj district. Department of Archaeology, Ministry of Cultural Affairs, Bangladesh. 2000. pp1-91.

Md. Shafiqul Alam, Jean-francois Salles (eds). France-Bangladesh Joint venture excavations at Mahastangarh: first interim report 1993-1999. Department of Archaeology, Mission Francaise de Cooperation archaeologique au Bangladesh. 2001, pp1-58.

The Bengal basin is in contact with the Indian and Eurasian plates, lying on a Precambrian platform. The geological structure in Bangladesh is unstable with a series of folds and faults. With steep mountains and hilly areas in the northeast of Sylhet and southeast of Chittagong, the landform of Munshiganj District is the old alluvial floodplain. The springs of the Ganges and the Brahmaputra rivers are located on the ridges of the Himalayas ranges, where most of the sediments mainly originate. The soils around Munshiganj are mainly non-calcareous brown floodplains originated from the ancient Ganges River and Meghna River.

Bangladesh is also considered to be a river delta caused by large rivers flowing down from the Himalayas. Munshiganj district lies in the confluence of three main rivers, the Padma, the Meghna and the Dhalesewari. In addition to bordering land on the west, the other three sides of the District are surrounded by rivers. Most parts of the land are less than 10 m above sea level. These three rivers are the main rivers in Bangladesh, of which the Ganges originates in the south of the Himalayas glaciers, flows eastward through the Indian flat plain, comes into Bangladesh in Rajshahi, and then merges with Jamuna river in Goalanda in the heart of Bangladesh and northwest of the capital of Dhaka. The Ganges in the territory of Bangladesh is called the Padma River. The Brahmaptura-Jamuna River originates in the northern ridge of the Himalayas in the territory of Tibet of China, its upper reaches is called the Tsangpo River, known as the Brahmaputra River in India and Bangladesh, and then flows through the Assam plain, and finally enters into Bangladesh from the north. The river Meghna originates from India, and enters Bangladesh from the northeast. The upper reaches of the river posseses a large amount of rainfall and lots of water sources. After converging with Padma and Jumana Rivers in Chandpur, the river width of the downstream is up to 8 km in the rainy season. This river system was quite altered as the rivers changed their courses frequently during the geological and historical time. For example, about two centuries ago, the Karatoya River near the Mahasthangarh site in northern Bangladesh was once the main river in the area flowing southward to join the Ganges and also the main source for many of the smaller rivers; however, because of the uplift of the Barind tract, it diverted eastward and became a tributary of the Jamuna. In a similar situation, the ancient Jamuna river course used to be immediately adjacent to the eastern part of the Dhaka-Munshiganj area, but it was diverted to the west of the present Dhaka, following by a significant tectonic movement. Similarly, the Padama River was once a river in the north-south direction, but it began to divert eastward two centuries ago and merged with the Brahmaputra River (Figure 1-3).

Munshiganj district is dominated by plains. A large number of streams and lowlands irrigated by rivers constitute the terrain characteristics of both land and water here. In the rainy season, most of the lowlands are inundated by raining water, and a lot of sand sediments, which are brought from the upper reaches of the river, and are deposited in the low-lying territory, providing rich fertile soils for local agricultural production. It is one of the largest potato production areas in Bangladesh; other important crops include rice, wheat and various vegetables, sugar cane and banana .

Munshiganj has a tropical monsoon climate, typical of the Southeast Asian region, with a hot, humid summer, a warm, rainy monsoon season and a dry, mild winter. There are 4 seasons in a year, roughly including summer (April – June), autumn (September – November), winter (December – January) and Spring (February – March). Most rains occur during the monsoon and there is a little rain in winter. Fall is pleasant and spring is very colorful. January is the coolest month, with the minimum temperature of 12.7 °C, and April is the warmest, with temperature ranging from 33 °C to 36 °C. The total annual rainfall in Munshiganj area is 2376 ml.

第三节 历史沿革
Section 3 Brief History

"孟加拉"一词源于太阳神的南方语词"邦加"（Bonga），后又演变为"文伽"（Vanga），在孟加拉语中，V 的发音与 B 同一。成书于前 4 世纪到公元 4 世纪之间的印度古代梵语史诗《摩诃婆罗多》以及《往世书》、《诃利世系》记载，文伽是文伽王国创立者瓦利的一个养子，古国在孟加拉国东部，贾木纳河与博多河之间。德干高原 805 年一处铭文提到"文伽拉"（Vangala）。

孟加拉地区历史悠久，西孟加拉邦发现过一万年前的石器；孟加拉地区出土的公元前 3000 年左右的有肩石斧，在东南亚、长江流域、日本都有分布；公元前 1000 年更早，孟加拉地区出现了一定程度的文明，其中有分布在河畔的从事贸易的小镇废墟；源自西亚和印度河流域的琉璃珠、蚀花肉红石髓珠，通过孟加拉国北部的贸易小镇和滇缅古道，传入中国的云南、四川和南方地区；早期的佛教造像也由此道传入中国。

根据出土碑刻铭文、钱币和文献资料，南亚次大陆 16 个古代地理疆域（王国）名称中，有 4 个与现代的孟加拉国领土密切相关，它们分别是般达拉（Pundra 或 Pundravarddhana）、文伽（Vanga）、三摩达吒（Samatata）和诃利科罗（Harikela）。在孔雀王朝、笈多王朝时期，般达拉疆域范围主要在北部孟加拉，而波罗-犀那王朝时期，般达拉疆域已覆盖到了毗诃罗普尔所在的地区。12 世纪时期的文伽疆域的核心地区主要在毗诃罗普尔和孟加拉中南部的巴里萨尔（Barisal）县。三摩达吒则是一个流传更广的名字，公元 4 世纪就已出现在铭文中，7 世纪玄奘的记述中也有记载，一般认为它的核心在库米拉-诺阿卡利（Comilla-Noakhali）地区，都城德瓦帕哇吒（Devaparvata），位于现今迈纳马蒂（Mainamati）的南部，也有资料显示，旃陀罗（Chandra）王朝时期，三摩达吒王国的都城迁移至毗诃罗普尔地区。大约在公元 9 世纪时期，诃利科罗主要疆域从最初的吉大港地区，随后囊括了锡尔赫特山区。

毗诃罗普尔古城所在的蒙希甘杰地区的早期历史资料较为缺乏，信史大约追溯至公元前 4 世纪。大约在公元前 321 年建国的北印度帝国的孔雀王朝（Mauyan dynasty）也统治着孟加拉北部地区，后来势力范围向东扩展至布拉马普特拉河和梅格纳河交汇区域，这个时期的佛教开始日益繁盛。其后，巽伽（Shungas）王朝和贵霜（Kushana）王朝分别在公元前 187—前 75 年、公元前 30—147 年间，将政权影响波及这里，但是它们的政治核心主要在北部和中部印度。笈多（Gupta）王朝（320—500 年）是孔雀王朝之后最重要的几个王朝之一，也是印度历史上一个最兴盛的时期，这个时期孟加拉国从北部直至中部的库米拉地区均在笈多王朝的势力范围内，为北印度政治中心的繁荣发挥了重要的作用。笈多王朝瓦解之后的二百多年间，尤其是公元 7 世纪中期至 8 世纪中期的历史面貌相对比较模糊，这阶段的主要特点之一是政权不稳定、地区混战和分裂割据不断，另外一个特点则是在后期阶段与北印度、尼泊尔等地区的多个外部政治势力之间有着错综复杂的关系。北部孟加拉地区在笈多王朝失去其在印度的统治之后，直至 6 世纪末仍有较长一段时间维系着脆弱的统治。这一时期孟加拉主要分裂成两个重要的独立政权，在东部和南部地区的文伽王国，核心区在现今福里德布尔（Faridpur）县的高达利帕尔（Kotalipara）地区；西部和北部在设赏迦（Sasanka）王（606—637 年）的领导下，在公元 7 世纪初于高达（Gauda）建立王国，势力范围主要在现今的西孟加拉邦地区，也曾一度控制了北、西、东部孟加拉和印度的奥里萨（Orissa）邦和马格达（Magadha）邦，但设赏迦王朝很快衰败，其后经历了多个独立的小王国和短暂的吞并统一过程。650—700年间，克哈德（Khadaga）王朝打败了之前在三摩达吒地区的一些小势力，统一了孟加拉地区的整个东部和南部，国都可能位于现在库米拉县的卡尔曼塔（Karmantavasaka）。

从笈多王朝及之前的早期历史时期，再经过较长时间的"黑暗"阶段，孟加拉终于又重新组建了强大的政权，直到穆斯林建立政权之前的这一段时间，在孟加拉国历史上称为"前中世纪（pre-medieval）"时期。从公元8世纪中期至12世纪的孟加拉以帕德玛河和布拉马普特拉－贾木纳河交汇处为界，大致分为北部孟加拉和东部、南部孟加拉两个相对独立的地区，并各自经历王朝的兴衰更替。蒙希甘杰地区一直受控于孟加拉东、南部的几个王朝政权。

波罗（Pala）王朝（750—1174年）由高波罗（Gopala）建立，主要势力范围在孟加拉北部的高达（Gauda）境内，统治长达400余年，并将领土一直西扩至印度中部疆域内。

波罗王朝在达玛波罗（Dharmapala，781—821年）和德瓦波罗（Devapala，821—861年）两任国王时进入兴盛时期，建立了帝国；玛亥波罗一世（Mahipala Ⅰ，995—1043年）时期经过中间短期衰退后又得以中兴，重新恢复帝国的势力，处于王朝的稳定时期；在雷玛波罗（Ramapala，1082—1124年）及之后的继任者的虚弱统治下，波罗王朝走向衰落和瓦解。在波罗王朝统治时期，北部孟加拉营建了大量佛教僧院、佛塔、寺庙等建筑，其中苏摩普里寺（Somapuri）佛教遗迹是世界上第二大单体佛教僧院。

与波罗王朝同时期存在的孟加拉东、南部地区，先后经历了德瓦（Deva）王朝、旃陀罗（Chandra）王朝和跋摩（Varman）王朝时期。德瓦王朝（750—800年）历经四任统治者：Sri Santideva、Sri Viradeva、Sri Anandadeva 和 Sri Bhavadeva，它的势力范围主要在三摩达吒疆域，统治中心在库米拉地区，国都位于德瓦帕瓦吒（Devaparvata），即现今的拉尔迈－迈纳马蒂（Laimai-mainamati）区域。德瓦王朝时期佛教兴盛，迈纳马蒂是佛教发展的中心地区，分布在那里的两座佛教僧院阿难陀寺（Ananda Vihara）和萨尔班寺（Salban Vihara）均以国王的名字命名。800—900年间的历史记载较少，噶里德瓦（Kanideva）于公元9世纪在诃利科罗（Harikela）建立王国，统治了孟加拉东南部，包括吉大港地区、库米拉地区，东北部的锡尔赫特可能也在其政治范围之内，都城位于布德旺普尔（Burdwanpur）。同时，在迈纳马蒂地区可能也曾在公元8—9世纪时期出现过阿伽尔（Akara）王朝，短暂存在于德瓦王朝之后。旃陀罗王朝（900—1050年）是一个非常强大的时期，是孟加拉东部和南部一个长久繁荣的黄金时代，完全能够与孟加拉西部和北部的波罗王朝相抗衡，都城位于蒙希甘杰地区的毗诃罗普尔。此后，跋摩王朝（1080—1150年）、犀那（Sena）王朝（1100—1223年）也建都于毗诃罗普尔地区。

公元1204年，巴克蒂亚克洛杰（Ikhtiaruddin Mohammad Bakhtiar Khalji）打败了犀那王朝，于1205年在高达（Gauda）建立了穆斯林政权，至英国殖民统治之前，孟加拉历史进入了中世纪（Medieval）和后中世纪（Late-Medieval）时期。在13—14世纪中叶，孟加拉名义上属德里苏丹国（Delhi Sultans），但派驻各地的将领往往拥兵自重，因而多个地区有独立的政治势力。公元1338年，孟加拉苏丹建立，都城在Sonargaon，至公元1538年，孟加拉一直处于独立的王国政权控制下。1539年至1576年，孟加拉先后处于Pathans和多个地方封建首领（Bara Bhuiyans）的统治下。1576年，莫卧尔（Mughal）王朝阿克巴（Akabar）征服孟加拉，使其成为帝国的一部分，首都先是在高达（Gauda），稍后迁至Tanda、Rajmahal，至1610年实际控制了孟加拉后又将达卡作为其国都。1707年后，莫卧尔帝国急剧衰落，1717年莫卧尔王朝派驻孟加拉的总督穆尔希德·库利·汗（Murshid Quli Khan）宣布独立，将首府从达卡迁往穆尔希达（Murshidabad），孟加拉地区此后进入一个由独立总督治理时期，在这期间佛教和印度教先后式微，伊斯兰教成为主要宗教。1757年，英国殖民者通过普拉西战役征服孟加拉，其通过东印度公司推行殖民统治，加尔各答作为早期首府（1771—1911年），其后英属印度政府迁都至德里。1947年，印度和巴基斯坦分治，孟加拉地区进入巴基斯坦时期。1971年，孟加拉国独立，成立孟加拉人民共和国。

蒙希甘杰县地属达卡专区，政府驻地在达里布尔，北纬23°27′36″，东经90°32′24″。全县包括6个乡69个村950个组，总人口150.5万。县境呈东西狭长形，面积约1000平方千米。人口密度为每平方千米1400人。可耕种面积为560平方千米，另有23平方千米为休耕面积。单季作物占23%，双季作物占44%，三季作物占33%。纳提什瓦（Nateshwar）遗址所在的峒吉巴日（Tongibari）乡面积约为150平方千米，共有家庭31346户，176881人（1991年），男女比例分别为52.46%和47.54%，平均识字率为35.7%。

县境内居民宗教信仰以伊斯兰教为主，占88%，另外印度教占9.7%，佛教占1.3%，基督教占1%。境内的各类历史遗迹数量众多，包括14处以上的古代池塘（ponds），Idrakpur城堡（fort）（1660年，位于蒙希甘杰镇），Baba Adam清真寺（1483年），Kharia Jame清真寺（18世纪），Radha Govinda印度教寺庙（16世纪），Dhipur寺庙（犀那王朝），Sonarang寺庙（1843—1886年），Mir Kadim古桥（17世纪莫卧尔王朝），Chowdhury Bazar、Outshahi、Tangibari、Fegunasar等莫卧尔王朝及其后的方形尖塔，以及著名的阿底峡（Atisha Dipankar Srijnan）出生地金刚瑜伽（Vairajogini）村（彩版1-3）。

The word of "Bengal" originated from the word "Bonga", and later evolved into "Vanga". In the ancient Vedic epics, the *Ramayana* and the *Mahabharata*, Vanga was mentioned that he was an adopted son of the founder of the Kingdom, which situated in the eastern part of Bangladesh, and between the Jamuna River and the Padma River. An 805 AD inscription, which was discovered in Deccan Plateau, was also referred to Vangala. The history of Bangladesh dates back millennia. Stone Age tools have been found in a few places. The Lalmai-Tripura prehistoric fossil wood industry was attributed to late upper Pleistocene age. The discovered ground stones bear close resemblance to the finds in Southeast Asia, the Yangtze River of China and Japan. The stone and glass beads as well as the etched carnelian beads, which originated from the Indian subcontinent, were diffused into Yunnan, Sichuan and other southern China regions through the ancient commercial centers in Bangladesh or the Yunnan-Burma trading route. It is also speculated that the early Buddhism spread into China in the same way.

According to the inscriptions, coins and literatures, four of the sixteen ancient historical territorial units (*Janapadas*), Pundra or Pundravarddhana, Vanga, Samatata and Harikela are closely connected with the territory of modern Bangladesh (Chakrabarti, 1992). Recently, a *janapada* of sixth century BC named Louhitya has been discovered in the northeast part of Bangladesh centering Wari-Bateshwar (Sufi and Ahmed, 2015). However, In the period of Mauryan and Gupta dynasties, the territory of Pundra was mainly limited in the north of Bangladesh, while during the Pala-Sena dynasties it had covered the area of Vikrampura. The main territory of Vanga would comprise Vikrampura and Bakla / Bakerganj. Around in the 12th century AD, Vanga generally corresponded to the eastern and southern Bangal, comprising mainly of modern Chittagong and Dhaka divisions. Samatata has been widely used since the 4th century AD and appeared in the records of the Chinese pilgrim Hiuen Tsang in the seventh century. It is generally believed that the Comilla-Nokphali area is its core region, where Devaparvata is known as its capital. The data shows that since the Chandra dynasty began, the capital of Samatata kingdom was transferred to Vikrampura. At about the 9th century AD, the main territory of Harikela had covered Sylhet mountain tract from the original Chittagong area.

The Mauryan Empire, which was founded in northern India around 321 BC, ruled the northern part of Bangladesh, and later expanded to the east of the Brahmaputra and Meghna rivers. At that time, Buddhism became increasingly prominent, spreading to Bangladesh. The following Shungas dynasty and the Kushana dynasty influenced this area during 187 – 75 BC, 30 BC – 147AD respectively, but their political powers remained in the north and the middle India. The Gupta dynasty (320 – 500 AD) is one of the most important dynasties after the Mauryan dynasty, and it is also an important phase in the history of India. During this period, Bangladesh became fully integrated into the great north Indian Gupta Empire, which performed considerably as the part of the so-called Gupta golden age. The post-Gupta political history of Bengal including Bangladesh is not clear, especially in the mid-7th to mid-8th century. A number of foci of power existed and very much within the tide of political events in north India. There existed a complicated relationship with the political forces of North India, Nepal and other regions in that later period. The northern Bengal region remained loosely under the rule of Gupta dynasty until the end of the 6th century after the Empire of Gupta went into decline in India. In this period, Bangladesh splintered into the kingdoms of Vanga, Samatata and Harikela. In the west the Gauda kingdom aroused. Shashanka proclaimed independence and unified the smaller principalities of Bengal, but after his death Bengal descended once more into a period of disunity and foreign invasion. During 650 – 700 AD, the Khadaga dynasty defeated some of the small forces in the previous Samatata area, unifying the entire east and south of Bangladesh, and built its capital in Karmantavasaka, where is current Comilla district. From about the middle of the eighth century AD, Bangladesh was more or less separated into northern Bangladesh between the Padma and the Brahamaputra-Jamuna and eastern and southern Bangladesh, and each experienced several successive dynasties.

The Pala dynasty (750 – 1174 AD), which was the first independent Buddhist dynasty of Bengal, was established by Gopala, dominating the territory of Gauda in northern Bangladesh for more than 400 years and extended the territory to the territory of present India.

The subsequent rulers of Dharmapala (781 – 821 AD) and Devapala (821 – 861 AD) expanded the boundaries and made the empire the dominate power in northern and eastern India, much of South Asia, and beyond. After some time of weak rule, Mahipala I recovered control of Bengal and expanded the empire further. After him the Pala dynasty again went into decline until Ramapala, the last great Pala ruler, managed to retrieve its fortunes to some extent. In the period, the Buddhist arts flourished, a large number of stupas, temples and monasteries were built. Among them, Somapura (Paharpur) Buddhist monastery is the world's largest single Buddhist monastery.

The dynastic successions of Devas, Chandras and Varmans constitute the political history of eastern and southern Bangladesh till the 12th century AD. The Deva dynasty (750 – 800 AD) genealogy as given in the copper-plate is the following: Sri Santideva, Sri Viradeva, Sri Anandadeva and Sri Bhavadeva, ruling in Samatata or the Tripora-Nooakhali plain. It had their headquarters in the Lalmai-mainamati region, and Devaparvata was the capital. During the Deva dynasty, Buddhism was flourishing; Mainamati became the center of Buddhism, where the two Buddhist monasteries of Ananda Vihara and Salban Vihara were named by their kings' names Anandadeva and Bhavadeva respectively. Little is known about the period between 800 AD and 900 AD. Kanideva established the kingdom in Harikela in the 9th century, and ruled the southeastern part of Bangladesh including Chittagong, Comilla areas, whose capital was located in Burdwanpur. Chandra dynasty (900 – 1050 AD) was a very powerful period, and was also the golden age in the east and south of Bangladesh, which could compete with the northern contemporary Pala dynasty. The capital of this dynasty was located in Vikrampura, present-day Munshiganj area. Since then, the Varman dynasty (1080 – 1150 AD), and the Sena dynasty (1100 – 1223 AD) also built their capitals there.

In 1204, a military commander from the Delhi Sultanate, Mohammad Bakhtiar Khalji, defeated the Sena dynasty and established Muslim rule in Gauda including Bihar and Bengal as far east as Rangpur, Bogra and the region of Brahmaputra river. During 13 – 14th century, Bangladesh was ruled intermittently under the Sultanate of Delhi. In 1338, Fakhruddin Mubarak Shah declared independence and proclaimed Sultan of Bengal in Sonargaon. The Sultanate started to disintegrate into many Pathans and a number of local feudal leaders after the fall of the Hussain Shahi dynasty in the 16th century, and was finally absorbed into the Mughal Empire. In 1576, the great Mughal emperor Akabar conquered Bengal and once more brought it under the control of Delhi. Dhaka became the capital of the province of Bengal. After 1707, the Mughal Empire declined dramatically, and in 1717. Murshid Quli Khan, the Governor of the Mughal dynasty in Bangladesh, declared independence, moving the capital from Dhaka to Murshidabad. Bangladesh later entered a period of governorship by an independent governor, during which time Buddhism and Hinduism had already declined, and Islam occupied Bengal. In 1757, the East India Company, under the leadership of Robert Clive, returned to Bengal as a political power, effectively governing it on behalf of the British Crown. Kolkata was built as the early capital (1771 – 1911 AD), and then the capital moved to Delhi. In 1947, Britain announced the decision to end its rule in India. Bengal was then split into the state of West Bengal, India and the Muslim region of East Bengal under Pakistan, to be renamed East Pakistan. In 1971, Bangladesh was independent; the People's Republic of Bangladesh was established. Munshiganj district, part of the Dhaka division, lies in 23°27′36″ of north latitude and 90°32′24″ of east longitude. There are six upzilas, 69 unions and 650 mauzas in the district. The total area of the zila is about 1000 sq. km, of which 93 sq km is riverine. According to the Population Census 2001, the total number of households in Munshiganj zila was 251,000, which was 0.98% of total households in the District. Estimated population of the zila in 2008 was 1505,000, which was 1.04% of the total population of the country. The population density is about 1400/km^2. The area of cultivated land is 560 km^2, and another 23 square kilometers is fallow area. Single season crops accounted for 23%, double season crops accounted for 44%, and three seasons of crops accounted for 33%. The Tongibari upazilla, where Nateshwar site is located, is about 150 km^2, with a total of 31,346 households and 176,881 persons (in 1991). The proportions of male and female are 52.46% and 47.54%, and the average literacy rate was 35.7%.

Most people of the District are Muslim, accounting for 88%, while Hindus accounted for 9.7%, Buddhists accounted for 1.3%, and Christians accounted for 1%. There are a large number of historical sites, including more than 14 ancient ponds, Idrakpur Fort (1660 AD), Baba Adam Mosque (1483 AD), Kharia Jame Mosque (18th Century), Radha Govinda Hindu temple (16th century), Sonarang temple (1843 – 1886 AD), Mir Kadim ancient bridge (17th century, Mughal dynasty), Chowdhury Bazar, Outshahi, Tangibari, Fegunasar, and the subsequent square towers, as well as the famous Atisha Dipankar Srijnan a birthplace in Vajrajogini village (Color Plate 1-3).

第四节 考古历程
Section 4 Archaeological Process

孟加拉国地处海上和陆上丝绸之路的必经之地。在中国古籍中，孟加拉地区被称作朋加剌、榜葛剌等。中国伟大的僧人法显（335—422年）、玄奘（600—664年）都曾访问过孟加拉地区。明代以后，孟加拉成为中外交往史籍上出现最频繁的名字，明朝政府还在孟加拉的吉大港设立官厂，作为郑和船队的基地。孟加拉国成立以来，历届政府都奉行对华友好政策，是中国在南亚地区的友好邻邦。

在中孟关系史上，毗诃罗普尔是一个光辉的名字，这里是佛教大师阿底峡尊者（982—1054年）的出生地。1038年，阿底峡应藏王的邀请来到西藏，从事传教、著述、译经活动，奠定了藏传佛教后弘期显密双修以及严格的修习次第，阿底峡在西藏创立的噶丹派，影响深远，是现行达赖、班禅系统格鲁派（黄教）的源头。作为西藏佛教后宏期的开山祖师，阿底峡尊者在西藏享有崇高的地位，据大多数藏文史料记载，他诞生于古印度东部邦伽罗国萨诃罗（萨霍尔）王室。那措·崔臣杰瓦（1011—1064年）在对阿底峡的颂词中，这样描写他的出生地："东方萨霍尔（Zahor）殊胜地，坐落一座大城镇，名叫毗扎玛普热（Vikramapar，威德城），城中便是大王殿，宫殿辉煌宽又广，人称金色胜幢宫。"（宗喀巴：《菩提道广论》，藏文铅印版，青海民族出版社，1985年，第4页。）

法尊法师译《阿底峡尊者传》说："中天竺金刚座之东方，有国曰伽邦罗。国内大都，曰萨诃啰，有二十七亿户。城中王宫，平洁高广，有无量金幢宜饰，故名金幢宫，受用圆满可见一斑耳。"

《白史》的作者更敦群培曾游历次大陆，在《印度诸圣地旅游纪实》中说，"从那里（超戒寺的旧址）动身可到旁遮普，那里是古代旁嘎拉国即静命大师和觉沃杰阿底峡的诞生地。藏巴地区亦指此处。据传萨霍尔或撒霍尔也在其附近，那里亦有古代王宫的遗址。"（《更敦群培文集精要》，中国藏学出版社，1996年）

阿底峡尊者在西藏生活了十余年，圆寂后，安葬于拉萨附近的聂塘寺。1963年，孟加拉佛教复兴会会长维苏塔难陀长老在一次会议上，向周恩来总理提出，拟将阿底峡尊者部分灵骨奉迎回国供奉，周总理欣然应允。阿底峡尊者的部分灵骨于1978年6月被迎请至孟加拉国达卡法王寺供奉。1982年2月，在孟加拉国首都达卡举行了纪念阿底峡尊者诞生一千周年国际讨论会。来自12个国家的130多位佛教界人士出席了讨论会。会后在阿底峡出生地，达卡郊区的金刚瑜伽村，举行了阿底峡大师纪念柱奠基典礼（彩版1-4）。

毗诃罗普尔古城发现于2010年。包括东、西两个遗址，分别为拉库罗普尔（Raghurampur）和纳提什瓦（Nateshwar）。在拉库罗普尔遗址，孟加拉国考古学家先后于2011年、2012年、2013年进行了三次考古工作，共发掘了约300平方米的面积，揭露出六个3.5平方米的小型僧侣房间以及五个佛塔的联合体，^{14}C测定年代约990—1050年，与阿底峡的生活年代同时（彩版1-5）。2013年，考古学家在纳提什瓦遗址进行了首次考古发掘，发掘面积344平方米，揭露出密集的古砖（彩版1-6）。这项发掘工作，是由努·奥·阿拉姆·列林（Nooh-UI-Alam Lenin）博士领导的孟加拉国地方文化组织阿哥拉萨－毗诃罗普尔（Agrashar Vikrampur）基金会主持的。具体的业务工作由苏菲·马斯塔费珠·诺曼（Sufi Mostafizur Rahman）博士领导的欧提亚·欧耐斯恩（Oitihya Onneswan）考古研究中心承担。

2013年，主持这个项目的阿哥拉萨－毗诃罗普尔基金会通过孟加拉国外交部，向中国驻孟大使馆提出了中孟联合发掘的意向，希望得到资金和技术方面的援助。在中国驻孟大使馆的精心安排下，2014年4月17—22日，湖南省文物局组织由何强、瞿伟建、高成林、柴焕波组成的代表团访问了孟加拉国，实地考察了毗诃罗普尔遗址，并确定了中孟联合发掘的意向。

2014年12月—2015年2月，湖南省文物考古研究所派出柴焕波、莫林恒、李意愿、贾英杰四人赴孟，和孟加拉国阿哥拉萨-毗诃罗普尔基金会聘请的欧提亚·欧耐斯恩考古研究中心组成联合考古队，对纳提什瓦遗址进行了第一次大规模的联合考古发掘，历时七十余天，发掘面积1746平方米。

2015年6—7月，湖南省文物考古研究所派出柴焕波、莫林恒、李意愿、贾英杰、朱元妹、汪华英、付林英七人赴孟，对该遗址出土的全部文物进行整理和陶器的修复。

2015年11月—2016年1月，湖南省文物考古研究所派出柴焕波、莫林恒、李意愿、袁伟、贾英杰、谭何易、胡重等七人赴孟，和欧提亚·欧耐斯恩考古研究中心组成联合考古队，对纳提什瓦遗址进行了第二次联合考古发掘，发掘面积2122平方米。

2017年1—3月，欧提亚·欧耐斯恩考古研究中心发掘了十字形神殿建筑北门道遗迹，发掘面积约400平方米。

2017年11月—2018年1月，湖南省文物考古研究所派出柴焕波、莫林恒、李意愿、贾英杰等四人赴孟，和欧提亚·欧耐斯恩考古研究中心组成联合考古队，对纳提什瓦遗址进行了第三次联合考古发掘，发掘面积约800平方米。至此，遗址发掘总面积达5236平方米（彩版1-7—1-9）。

纳提什瓦遗址的探方系统是2013年首次发掘时设定的，2014—2015年度的布方区域位于遗址的东部和北部，用全站仪对原来的布方系统进行信息化记录，方向为350°（北偏西10°）。以2米×2米作为记录和发掘的探方（Grid）规格，每100个2米×2米规格的探方形成的正方形区域构成一个更大的发掘单元（Unit），由基点向北和向东发掘单元分别用数字（1、2、3……）和英文字母（A、B、C……）表示，在每个发掘单元（Unit）中，也采用同样的数字和字母结合的方式，以记录每个探方（Grid）的名称（如UnitK11GridJ1……）。在发掘过程中，遗迹和出土物的位置，都按这个系统记录。准确地说，它更像是一套发掘记录系统，实际发掘探方的大小，并不限于2米×2米，而是按发掘的实际需要，采用4米×4米甚至更大的面积（图1-4）。

在田野发掘方法上，孟加拉国采用欧洲国家普遍的发掘方法，强调按深度和平面位置对发掘品作详细的记录，从理想的角度，如果与地层划分并重，资料将更具有科学性。但在实际操作过程中，特别是在大面积发掘过程中，许多遗迹和遗物，虽然有空间位置，却很难落实到具体的统一地层上，遇到复杂的遗迹现象，往往难以作出及时的判断。在这次联合发掘中，经过中孟双方广泛深入的交流，在发掘方法上达成了共识，即在地层划分和解释方面，更多采用中国比较成熟的地层学方法，按照文化层和堆积单元，由晚及早，逐层向下发掘，除了探方隔梁的地层剖面外，根据堆积的具体状况，有针对性地设计剖面，以把握遗迹的堆积状况和形成过程。重要的人工遗物收集，除记录层位外，还记录其空间位置的坐标。发掘结束后，对收集土样进行了及时浮选，对各种动植物标本进行详细鉴定，对^{14}C标本进行了测试。

这个项目的中方队长为湖南省文物考古研究所郭伟民所长，孟方队长为阿哥拉萨-毗诃罗普尔基金会努·奥·阿拉姆·列林主席。主持发掘的中方领队为湖南省文物考古研究所柴焕波研究员，孟方领队为贾汉吉纳格尔大学苏菲·马斯塔费珠·诺曼（Sufi Mostafizur Rahman）教授。中方发掘成员有莫林恒、李意愿、袁伟、贾英杰以及技术工人朱元妹、汪华英、付林英、谭何易、胡重等。孟方主要发掘队员有：Md. Mamum Dewan，Muhammad Mahbubul Alam Himel，Muhammad Shohrab Uddin Shourav，Md. Sadequzzaman Tanu，Md. Awlad Hossain。此外有

20多名其他工作人员参加了发掘（彩版1-10—1-15）。

中孟联合发掘得到了中国湖南省人民政府、中国驻孟大使馆和孟加拉国阿哥拉萨－毗诃罗普尔基金会的资金支持。在考古发掘期间，孟加拉国总理外交事务顾问Gauhar Rizvi先生、财政部长Abul Mal Abdul Muhit先生、孟加拉国文化部长Asaduzzaman Noor先生、建设部长Obaidul Quader先生、考古局局长Altaf Hossain先生，孟加拉国议会文化委员会主席Simin Hossam Rimi女士，中国全国政协常委及中国佛教协会副主席珠康·土登克珠活佛、前任中国驻孟大使李军先生、中国驻孟大使马明强先生、临时代办陈伟先生先后视察了考古工地。孟加拉国总理哈西娜、到访的中国国务院副总理刘延东，也在不同场合盛赞毗诃罗普尔古城的考古发掘。五个国家副总理级别的高官，也实地考察了遗址，包括中国新华社在内的二十多家媒体报道了这次联合发掘，孟加拉国所有报纸都以显著的篇幅予以报道（彩版1-16—1-20）。

经过连续几年的发掘，考古工作取得了很多重要的成果，为了充分论证成果的遗产价值并开展后续的保护工作，在湖南省文物考古研究所和孟加拉国阿哥拉萨－毗诃罗普尔基金会的筹备下，2018年1月4日，"毗诃罗普尔遗址考古发掘和文物保护国际研讨会"在达卡古老的贾汉吉纳格尔大学举行。湖南省文物局代表团出席了会议，孟方也会组织相关的官员、专家学者和媒体记者参会（彩版1-21）。

在考古发掘期间中，双方已经开始谋划报告编写工作，2016年发掘工作结束后，进入了报告的正式编写阶段，2017年12月，报告最后编写

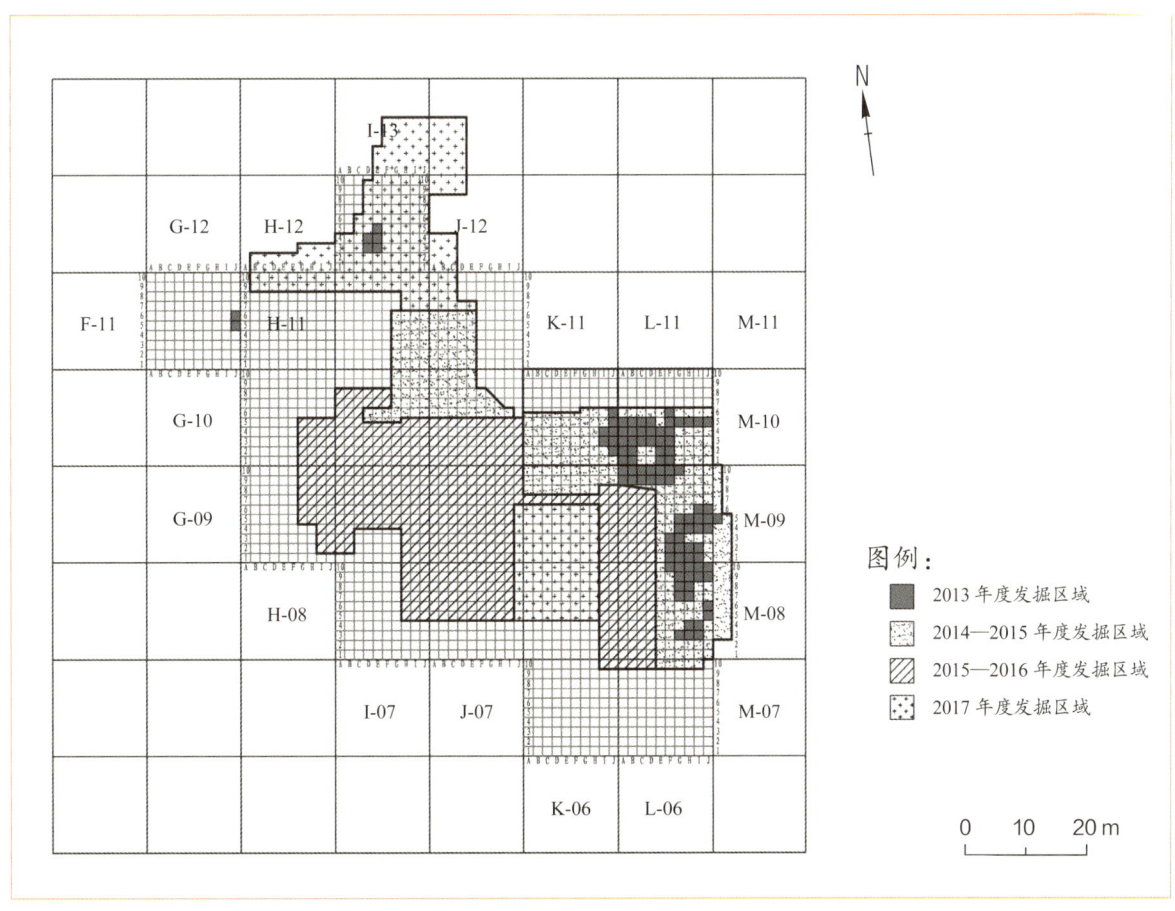

图1-4　纳提什瓦遗址历年发掘探方分布图

Fig. 1-4　The distribution of test grids over the years at Nateshwar site

完成。本报告的主编为柴焕波研究员和苏菲·马斯塔费珠·诺曼（Sufi Mostafizur Rahman）教授；编写者为柴焕波、李意愿、莫林恒、穆罕默德·海穆尔（Muhammad Mahbubul Alam Himel）、穆罕默德·玛门（Muhammad Mamum Dewan）、穆罕默德·肖热沃（Muhammad Shohrab Uddin Shourav）等；绘图为贾英杰、谭何易、胡重；摄影为柴焕波、贾英杰；航拍：贾英杰；中英文翻译为李意愿；校对苏菲·马斯塔费珠·诺曼（Sufi Mostafizur Rahman）、莫莉莎（Moneesha Rahman Kalamder）。

这本报告囊括了2013年至2017年的主要发掘成果，因为报告编写截止日期与考古发掘同时完成，2017年的某些发掘成果，尤其是出土陶器，未能体现在报告中，有待下一部报告进行公布。

Bangladesh was an important hub of the ancient maritime silk road and the land silk road. It was recorded in ancient Chinese texts by the name of Peng-jia-la or Bang-ge-la. Chinese great monk Fa Xian (335 – 422 AD) and Hiuen Tsang (600 – 664 AD) had ever visited here. The name of Bangladesh has become the most frequent used word since the Ming Dynasty (1368 – 1664 AD) in ancient Chinese history. It is said that the Ming government set up official factories in Chittagong as the base for the Chinese great Admiral Zheng He's fleet. Since the independence of Bangladesh, every government has pursued a friendly policy towards China and become a friendly neighbor of China in South Asia.

In the history of China-Bangladesh relations, Vikrampura is a glorious name, the birthplace of the Buddhist master Venerable Atisha Dipankara Srijnana (982 – 1054 AD). In 1038, Atisha was invited to Tibet by the king to teach, write and translate the Buddhist texts, which laid the foundation for the Tibetan Buddhism in the post-propagation period, characterized by emphasizing rigorous ethics, a gradual path to enlightenment, and systematic doctrines in both exoteric and esoteric Buddhism. The Genden, which was founded by Atisha in Tibet, was deeply influential, becoming the source of Gelu-pa of the current Dalai Lama and Panchen Lama system. As the pioneer of Buddhism, Venerable Atisha enjoys a very high status in Tibet.

According to most of the Tibetan historical records, Atisha was born in a royal family of zahor in the eastern ancient India. In the eulogy about Atisha, Nacuo Cuichengjiewa (1011–1064 AD) described his birthplace "The east of Zahor is located in a large town, named Vikrampur (pronunciation in Chinese is pi-zha-ma-pu-re). In the city, there is a palace, which is brilliant and spacious, known as the Golden Palace." (Zong Kaba, 1985)

It was written in *the Biography of Venerable Atisha* that "on the east of India, there is a country named Jia Bang Luo. There are billions of households in the city. The palace of the city is decorated with golden ornaments". (Ven Fazun,1995)

Venerable Atisha Dipankara lived in Tibet for more than ten years, and was buried in Nie Tang Temple near Lhasa city after his death. In 1963, the president of Bangladesh Bouddha Kristi Prachar Sangha proposed to Premier Zhou Enlai at a meeting, that China should return some parts of his remains to Bangladesh. Premier Zhou was pleased to promise, and the remains finally reached to the monastery of Dhaka in June 1978 due to the joint efforts of the two countries. In February 1982, an international symposium was held in the capital of Bangladesh, to commemorate the Thousandth Anniversary of the Birth of the Atisha. More than 130 Buddhists from 12 countries attended the seminar. After the meeting, the breaking ground ceremony of Atisha Dipankara Memorial Hall was held in the Vajrajogini village of Vikrampura (Color Plate 1-4).

Vikrampura is an important name in the early history of Bangladesh as well. Vikrampura was a Jayskandhavara (camp of victory) of the rulers of Vanga and Samatata region, as revealed from many copper plate inscriptions of the Chandra (c. 900 – 1050 AD), Varman (c. 1080 – 1150 AD) and Sena (c. 1095 – 1230 AD) dynasties of early medieval Bangladesh. It is significant that for a long period of time, people had been discovering architectural remains, sculptures of stone, wood and metal, copper plates, terracotta objects, potteries, metal and wooden objects during cultivation, digging ponds or other domestic digging activities in Vikrampura (Ghosh 1275BS; Gupta, 1316BS). Sculptures, pillars and inscriptions found in Vikrampura are being displayed in Bangladesh National Museum, Dhaka; Varendra Research Museum, Rajshahi; Indian Museum, Kolkata and other museums in different countries of the world. Besides museums, many accidentally discovered artefacts are in personal collections at home and abroad. It is worthwhile to mention that more than 50% sculptures of Bangladesh National Museum are from Vikrampura alone.

Despite several historical accounts and numerous archaeological evidences, unfortunately there was no serious archaeological investigation in this area for a long time. Nalinikanta Bhattasali, the then Curator of Dhaka Museum and a son of Vikrampura, took initiative in 1913 for excavation, but no specific archaeological site or discovery is mentioned in his short report (Bhattasali, 1929). Almost after one hundred years, another son of Vikrampura, Nooh-Ul-Alam Lenin, President of 'Agrashar Vikrampur Foundation', took the initiative in 2010 for excavation in Vikrampura involving 'Oitihya Onneswan' (archaeological research centre) under the leadership of Sufi Mostafizur Rahman. During extensive exploration, ancient human settlements have been discovered in many places in Munshiganj Sadar and Tangibari upazila. Test trenches at 9 places have revealed ancient human settlements in Vikrampura area. In the ancient city of Vikrampura, Raghurampur site is in the east and Nateshwar site is in the west. In Raghurampur site, excavation was carried out for three seasons from 2011 to 2013. An area of about 300 square meters was exposed and 6 monastic cells were uncovered, each measuring 3.5 m^2 (Color Plate 1-5). The date of Raghurampur is about 990 – 1050 AD according to Carbon 14 dating, which is contemporary with the living time of Atisha Dipankara. According to a Chinese source, this Buddhist Vihara was known as Vikramapuri Vihara (Barua, 1969). It is worth mentioning that this Buddhist Vihara is the first of its kind among the discovered ancient monuments in 2013. Archaeologists from Oitihya Onneswan, Bangladesh excavated about 344 m^2 for the first time in the Nateshwar site, revealing dense old bricks and part of ancient architectures (Color Plate 1-6).

Expecting massive archaeological research in Vikrampura region, the Agrashar Vikrampur Foundation proposed the idea of China-Bangladesh joint excavation for financial and technical assistance to the Chinese Embassy in Bangladesh through the Ministry of Foreign Affairs of Bangladesh in 2013. Under the arrangement of the Chinese Embassy in Bangladesh, the delegation of Hunan Provincial Bureau of Cultural Relics consisted by Mr. He Qiang, Mr. Qu Weijian, Prof. Gao Chenglin and Porf. Chai Huanbo visiting Bangladesh from 17th to 22th in April, 2013. They investigated the Raghurampur and Nateshwar site and determined to cooperate with Bangladesh team for joint excavation.

During December 2014 – February 2015, the field team of Hunan Provincial Institute of Cultural Relics and Archaeology, composed of Prof. Chai Huanbo, Associate Prof. Mo Linheng, Dr. Li Yiyuan and Jia Yingjie came to Bangladesh, and formed a joint archaeological team with Oitihya Onneswan (Archaeological Research Center) of Agrashar Vikrampur Foundation. A large scale of joint excavation was conducted at Nateshwar, with an area of 1746 m^2, lasting more than 70 days.

From June to July in 2015, another three members, Zhu Yuanmei, Wang Huaying and Fu Linying, from Hunan Provincial Institute of Cultural Relics and Archaeology, came to Bangladesh for repairing the unearthed potteries. All the artifacts were studied during this period.

From November 2015 to January 2016, the Bangladesh-China joint team carried out the second collaborative excavation at Vikrampura, exposing an area of 2122 m^2.

From November 2017 to January 2018, the Bangladesh-China joint team carried out the third collaborative excavation at Vikrampura, exposing an area of 800 m^2 (Color Plate 1-7 – 1-9).

The grids mapping system of the site was set up by Oitihya Onneswan (Archaeological Research Center) when it conducted the first excavation in 2013. The mapping grids in 2014–2015 were located in the eastern and northern parts of the excavation area. Before the formal excavation, the recording system was digitalized with the total station. Under this system, the whole site was divided into different 400 m^2 size square units, of which each was composed of 100 grids of 2 × 2 m^2 size. Consequently, the grid provides a basic excavation and recording context. Starting from the base point, the grids and units are represented by numbers to the north, and represented by alphabet letters to the east respectively. During the excavation, all the cultural features and artifacts were recorded in this way (such as UnitK11GridJ1) (Figure 1-4).

During the excavation process, the joint team adopted the method of stratigraphy and typology, which are well-developed methodology in China. The important special finds are collected not only by cultural layers, but the coordinates of their spatial positions are also recorded. The flotation for the collected soil samples was also conducted in time, and identified the samples of various animals and plants were identified. The carbon samples were tested after the complete of excavation.

The project leader of Bangladesh is Dr. Nooh-Ul-Alam Lenin, the president of the Agrashar Vikrampur Foundation, and the Chinese project leader is Dr. Guo Weimin, the director of the Hunan Provincial Institute of Cultural Relics and Archaeology. The excavation was carried out under the supervision of two field-directors: Prof. Sufi Mostafizur Rahman and Prof. Chai Huanbo. The members of Bangladeshi team are Md. Mamum Dewan, Muhammad Mahbubul Alam himel, Muhammad Shohrab Uddin Shourav, Md. Sadequzzaman Tanu, Md. Awlad Hossain. The members of Chinese team are Mo Linheng, Li Yiyuan, Yuan Wei, Jia Yingjie, Zhu Yuanmei, Wang Huaying, Fu Linying, Tan He Yi, Hu Zhong (Color Plate 1-10 – 1-15). Moreover, over 20 research assistants of Bangladesh side took part in the excavation.

The Joint project was supported by Ministry of Cultural Affairs, Government of the People's Republic of Bangladesh, Hunan Provincial Government of China, the embassy of China in Bangladesh, and the Agrashar Vikrampur Foundation. During the archaeological excavation, many special guests had visited the archaeological site: Mr. Gauhar Rizvi, advisor (Foreign Affairs) to the Honorable Prime Minister of Bangladesh, Mr. Asaduzzaman Noor, Minister of Cultural Affairs of Bangladesh, Mr. Obaidul Quader, Minister of Road Construction and Bridge, Mr. Altaf Hossain, the Director General of the Department of Archaeology, Ms. Simin Hossam Rimi, the Chairman of the Parliamentary Standing Committee of ministry of cultural affair of the Bangladesh, living Buddha Tudeng Kezhu of the Standing Committee of the Chinese People's Political Consultative Conference (CPPCC) and Vice-Chairman of the Chinese Buddhist Association, Mr. Ma Mingqiang of the Chinese ambassador to Bangladesh. The Bangladesh Prime Minister Sheikh Hasina and Chinese vice Premier Liu Yandong also praised the archaeological excavations of the Vikrampura site on different occasions. More than 20 media outlets, including China's Xinhua News Agency, reported the joint excavation, and all newspapers and TV channels in Bangladesh highlighted their reports (Color Plate 1-16 – 1-20).

After several years of excavation, many important achievements have been accomplished in the archaeological work. In order to fully demonstrate the heritage value and carry out the protection work, a seminar on the excavation and conservation of Nateshwar Buddhist site was held in Jahangir Nagar University in Dhaka from 2nd January to 3rd January 2018. The delegation consisted of scholars, experts on heritage protection and media reporters from Hunan Province, China took part in the seminar. Officials, experts, scholars and media reporters in Bangladesh also attended the conference. The meeting has achieved fruitful results (Color Plate 1-21).

The excavation report was planned during the starting of joint archaeological excavation. After the excavation work in 2016, the mission was implemented. In December 2017, this report was finally completed and proofread by both the team members. The co-editors of the report are Prof. Sufi Mostafizur Rahman (Bangladesh) and

Prof. Chai Huanbo (China). The compliers include Bangladeshi members of Sufi Mostafizur Rahman, Muhammad Mahbubul Alam Himel, Muhammad Mamum Dewan, Muhammad Shohrab Uddin Shourav and Chinese members of Chai Huanbo, Li Yiyuan, Mo Linheng. All the drawings were finished by Jia Yingjie, Tan Heyi, Hu Zhong, and photos were provided by Chai Huanbo and Jia Yingjie. Aerial photography was taken by Jia Yingjie. Translation was finished by Li Yiyuan and was revised by Sufi Mostafizur Rahman. The language of the text was edited by Moneesha Rahman Kalamder and Sufi Mostafizur Rahman.

This report includes the main excavation achievements from 2013 to 2017. However, as the deadline for preparing the report was completed along with archaeological excavation, some of the discoveries in 2017, especially the unearthed potteries, failed to be reflected in this report. They will be published in the next report.

彩版 1-1
纳提什瓦遗址环境
Color Plate 1-1
The environment at Nateshwar site

1. 遗址台地（西—东）

2. 遗址周边环境

彩版 1-2
纳提什瓦村环境
Color Plate 1-2
The environment of the Nateshwar Village

1. 莫喀第（Mirkadim）人工运河从遗址的西侧流过

2. 纳提什瓦村西的印度教神庙

3. 村民用遗址旧砖辅地

4. 村民

彩版 1-3
蒙希甘杰县内名胜
Color Plate 1-3
The places of interest in Munshiganj district

1. 莫卧尔时代Mir Kadim石桥，17世纪

2. 莫卧尔时代Idrakpur城堡，17世纪

彩版 1-4
达卡法王寺阿底峡相关文物和纪念堂
Color Plate 1-4
The related relics of Atisha Dipankar at Dharmarajika Buddhist temple in Dhaka and the memorial hall under construction

1. 达卡法王寺函有阿底峡尊者灵骨的灵塔

2. 达卡法王寺珍贵的藏文经书

3. 正在建筑的阿底峡纪念堂

彩版 1-5
拉库罗普尔（Raghurampur）遗址
Color Plate 1-5
The cultural remains at Raghurampur site, Vikrampura

1. 寺庙建筑

2. 僧舍

彩版 1-6

纳提什瓦（Nateshwar）遗址的原貌
Color Plate 1-6
The original landscape of Nateshwar site

1. 出露的砖墙

2. 建筑遗迹

3. 遗址地表

彩版 1-7
2014—2015 年中孟第一次联合发掘
Color Plate 1-7
The China-Bangladesh first joint excavation during 2014 – 2015

彩版 1-8
2015—2016 年
中孟第二次联合发掘

Color Plate 1-8
The China-Bangladesh second joint excavation during 2015 – 2016

彩版 1-9
2017—2018 年
中孟第三次联合发掘

Color Plate 1-9
The China-Bangladesh third joint excavation during 2017 – 2018

彩版 1-10
部分考古队员合影
Color Plate 1-10
The group photo of some archaeological team members

左起：
Aditi，Nusrat Jahan Kanan，莫林恒，袁伟，Sufi Mostafizur Rahman，
Md. Mamum Dewan，李意愿，柴焕波，谭何易，Azmal Hossain Selim，Md.Tahmidun Nabi，Md. Sadequzzaman Tanu，胡重，Murad，贾英杰
From left:
Farzana Aditi, Nusrat Jahan Kanan, Mo linheng, Yuan Wei,
Sufi Mostafizur Rahman, Md. Mamum Dewan, Li Yiyuan, Chai Huanbo, Tan Heyi, Azmal Hossain Selim,
Md. Tahmidun Nabi, Md. Sadequzzaman Tanu, Hu Zhong, Murad, Jia Yingjie

彩版 1-11
队员风采
Color Plate 1-11
Team members

Sufi Mostafizur Rahman

Muhammad Shohrab Uddin Shourav

Muhammad Mahbubul Alam Himel、Md. Mamum Dewan、Md. Awlad Hossain、李意愿

袁伟

莫林恒

柴焕波

Nusrat Jahan Kanan

贾英杰和Md. Mamum Dewan

彩版 1-12
工地掠影
Color Plate 1-12
A glance at excavation site

交流

分析

勘探

测绘

航拍

记录

彩版 1-13
工地掠影
Color Plate 1-13
A glance at excavation site

1. 修复陶器

2. 陶器拼接

3. 器物绘图

4. 考古调查

5. 陶片拼接

6. 文物登记

彩版 1-14
生活花絮
Color Plate 1-14
Life trivia

1. 遗址所在的 Tongibari 地方长官宴请中方考古队员

2. 在工地过生日

3. 在孟加拉国同事家作客

4. 工地烧烤

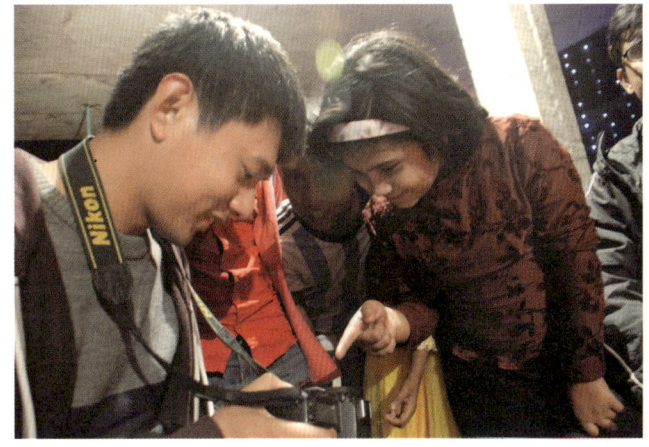

5. 异域采风

6. 参观旅行

彩版 1-15
工作、生活花絮
Color Plate 1-15
Trivia of work and life

1. 发掘现场

2. 工地用餐

3. 日常的祈祷

4. 工作人员与民工合影

彩版 1-16
领导的关注
Color Plate 1-16
The care from the leaders

1. 湖南省文物局代表团首访孟加拉国

2. 马明强大使会见柴焕波领队

3. 陈伟代办、孙延参赞与湖南代表团一行考察工地

4. 全国政协常委珠康活佛和考古队员合影

彩版 1-17
领导的关注
Color Plate 1-17
The care from the leaders

1. 孟加拉国总理外交顾问Rizvi先生、Lenin先生和马明强大使出席新闻发布会

2. 前任中国驻孟大使李军先生视察考古工地

3. 孟加拉国财政部长Muhith先生视察工地

4. 孟加拉国建设部长Quader先生视察工地

彩版 1-18
领导的关注
Color Plate 1-16
The care from the leaders

1. 孟加拉国财政部长Muhit先生会见湖南代表团

2. 孟加拉国议会文化委员会主席Rimi女士视察工地

3. 孟加拉国文化部长Noor先生会见郭伟民所长

4. 阿哥拉萨-毗诃罗普尔基金会主席Lenin博士感谢中国考古人为孟加拉国文化遗产事业所作的贡献

彩版 1-19
来自各国的来访者
Color Plate 1-19
The visitors from all over the world

1. 联合国教科文组织考古学家David先生（左三）、孟加拉国资深考古学家Hossain先生（左四）访问考古工地

2. 亚洲佛教代表团访问工地

3. 不丹议会代表团访问工地

4. 印度考古调查局前局长拉克西－坦瓦利（DR.Rakesh Tewari）先生访问工地

5. 日本参观团访问工地

彩版 1-20
公共考古宣传
Color Plate 1-20
Public archaeology

1. 新闻发布会现场

2. 公众宣传

3. 媒体采访考古工地

4. 考古体验

5. 参加考古活动的当地青少年

彩版 1-21

"毗诃罗普尔遗址考古发掘和文物保护国际研讨会"在达卡贾汉吉纳格尔大学举行

Color Plate 1-21
The "Seminar on Archaeological excavation and Conservation of Nateshwar Site, Vikrampura" was held at Jahangirnar University

1. 毗诃罗普尔遗址考古发掘和文物保护国际研讨会在达卡隆重召开

2. 湖南文物局代表团访问古老的贾汉吉纳格尔大学考古系

Chapter

II

第二章

Cultural Layers

地层

纳提什瓦
Nateshwar

第一节
地层综述
Section 1 Comprehensive Introduction

纳提什瓦遗址的地层堆积，有的呈水平，有的呈坑状，有的呈坡状，这些都与地层的具体成因有关。现将各个地层的概况和成因逐一叙述如下，并将不同时期的遗迹单位，归属于相应的地层中。

①层：地表层，浅灰色沙性土，大致呈水平堆积，一般厚度0.1米左右。该层包含有砖块、瓦砾、玻璃、现代钱币等，分布在整个遗址范围内，为现代居民的活动地面（彩版2-1，1）。

②层：为黄褐色沙性土，一般厚约1米，最深处厚约3米。土质越接近地表越疏松。该层的堆积形态为长坑状或圆坑状，这是当地居民大规模的挖土取砖后留下的凹坑，此后又将土回填，平整为公共活动的地面，由此形成了②层，实际上就是取砖坑和取砖沟。该层普遍分布于整个遗址区，一些深坑大多位于建筑的四角拐角处，这些地方往往是砖材集中的地方，且连接成片，在发掘过程中将其作为坑状地层进行处理，各个坑内的堆积大体一致，内部可细分许多小层，剖面上呈"夹心饼干"状的层理，体现了具体的回填过程。由于各个坑内堆积难以彼此对应，因此各自编分层号。回填是一种随机的行为，不同来源的土会有不同程度的混杂，从实际观察到的情况看，这种取砖行为并不是同时的，很可能是多次形成的。②层普遍打破④层，并在取砖坑的邻近部位对④层产生了扰动。②层包含物有碎砖块、砖颗粒、石灰、陶片、玻璃等。开口于②层下的遗迹单位有灰坑H1—H5（彩版2-1，2、3）。

③层：灰青绿色淤泥层，集中分布在Unit I9、J9、I10、J10内，平面为一直径为30米左右的圆形堆积，深度达到2米。该层土质土色明显区别于遗址的其他地层，内部又可分为许多细密的自然层次，土质纯净，不见出土遗物。对于这个地层的成因，目前尚不能确定。第一种可能，是后期居民取某处淤积土、人工填筑而成，由于土方量大，可能与某次特定的建筑行为有关。第二种可能，由于这一区域处在中心神殿废墟的边缘，地势较低，长期从高到低的积水可能会形成了这样的自然层。鉴于③层尚需进一步的发掘，这个问题有待进一步的观察和讨论（彩版2-1，4）。③层下为第二期众多的遗迹，包括：十字形中心神殿建筑、八边形佛塔、路面1、曲折形围墙1等。

④层：以带黏性浅灰色沙性土为主。一般厚2—3米，最厚处4米左右，在整个遗址有大面积分布。从发掘情况看，④层呈环状分布于遗址的中心部分，而在遗址的外围，并没有④层分布。一般来说，上部土质沙性较重，底部黏性较重，由上到下黏性逐渐增强，沙性逐渐减弱。中央部位的沙性较重，边缘部位的黏性较重，这可能是由于工程的技术原因造成的，下部的土在承受上部建筑重量后更容易走形，向四周扩散。纯沙土和纯黏土都是不适合做垫基土的，需要将两者按一定比例掺合起来，这也解释了为什么④层上部的棕灰色沙土中掺入混杂的灰青色黏土，而在下部的灰青色黏土中也有棕灰色沙土成分，也就是说，④层是沙土、黏土按一定比例掺和混杂的，越靠近底部，黏土比例越大，越靠近上部，沙土比例越大。总体而言，④层是一种较为纯净的带黏性灰沙土，在遗址不同区域、不同深度，含沙量、黏性、含砖块、砖颗粒的比例不完全相同，以柱厅4的东、西、南三个剖面为例，这三个剖面的④层填土都为沙性土，但颜色、含沙量、黏性都不一致。

④层是建造第二期寺院而进行的大规模、有序的填土活动所致，其作用是将整个地面抬高，从现有的迹象看，地面被普遍提高了2—3米，有些地方可能填高了4米以上。④层地层由多层

呈倾斜状的填土堆积而成，但在底部，可见到水平堆积层次，因为底部有原先的早期建筑，因地面不平整，一方面拆除早期建筑，一方面需要平整地面。因此，在局部区域的底部有一、二层含砖块、砖颗粒较多的填土层，相对上部的沙土层而言，较为杂乱，这与利用废墟作为填土有关。如在神殿1南侧墙体外的堆积，呈西北向东南倾倒，北高南低，厚度逐渐减少，直至消失，明显是拆早期建筑直接倾倒而形成的倾斜地层，再在其上方倾斜填筑2米多厚的沙土层。这类地层，有的相对较水平，有的则倾斜混杂不齐，不论形态如何不同，都属于铺垫层的底部，并不是为了形成一个生活地面而铺垫的。

④层上部的沙土层是从附近取来的，这些灰沙土并不是河边或河流中的纯沙土，而是带黏性的，因此，推测其可能来源于附近的冲积平原，这种沙土经过长时间的沉淀而略带黏性，遗址附近一系列现存的水塘，很可能是取土留下的遗迹。有迹象显示，④层的填筑次序是从遗址的中心区域开始，中心部位填土较高，然后向四周边缘扩散，这在东部边缘的UnitL9、L10的相关剖面上最为明显。倾倒填筑方向不完全一致，属于随机行为。④层底部有一层碎砖渣层，在柱厅4中心的碎砖渣层比东部边缘的碎砖渣层高出约1米，这也反映出先填中心区域，然后向四周扩展的填筑过程。此外，在遗址东部碎砖渣层之下，有局部的白色沙土层，连续至南部边缘逐渐只有一线痕迹，很可能是由于雨水沉积后形成的。④层上部堆积中的包含物较少，主要为少量砖块、砖颗粒、陶片。由于是搬动所致，其中的包含物要早于地层形成的年代。有些局部可能经过夯筑，这表现在各个小层之间倾斜角度大致相近，厚薄大致相近，但很难从平面上找到夯窝的痕迹（彩版2-2，1）。开口于④层下的遗迹有道路4等。据初步分析，第一期遗存废弃后，与④层形成之前，局部地段有过小规模的平整、修建、并继续使用的迹象，此即为第一期晚段的遗存。

⑤层：分布于遗址东部，主要在Unit K11、L11、L10、L9内，在很多区域缺失。主体为黄褐色沙性土，较疏松，厚约1米，最厚处1.3米。该层含较多的砖颗粒、炭末及一定数量的陶片。⑤层由多个小的水平层堆积而成，其间包含有密集的砖砾层，每小层的厚度在10—30厘米不等，这些分层与遗迹糅合在一起，情况比较复杂。该层局部有因聚水形成的浅坑沉积，表明其形成过程经历较长的时间，并非一次性填筑行为。⑤层的性质为第一期寺院早、中段建筑毁弃以后形成的废弃堆积层（彩版2-2，2）。开口于⑤层下的遗迹有：神殿1后期遗迹、神殿2、道路3（延用早段）、隔墙、房屋1、房屋2、房屋3、房屋4、房屋5、墙1、墙2、墙3、路面2、路面4等。属于第一期寺院早、中段建筑遗存。

⑥层：灰黄色沙性土，一般厚度0.4米，最厚处1.1米。目前仅在Unit I11、I10、L10、L8、J11有局部分布，呈水平堆积。⑥层含较多陶片，地层中含有较多的碳末、烧土颗粒。在Unit I11的⑥层表面，局部分布有二十余件较完整的陶器，呈水平分布，由此推测，⑥层可能是第一期的生活堆积（彩版2-2，3）。目前在Unit I11、L10、L8各处发掘的⑥层，并没有直接的地层连接，且土质土色并不完全一致，因此不同区域的⑥层可能有早晚，这有待以后进一步观察。此外，在Unit I11的G2、G3、G4、G5以及J11的A4⑥层之上，有一层厚的10厘米的纯沙层，可以判断是由积水造成的。由于发掘面积有限，⑥层堆积的性质以及相对应的遗迹关系，有待进一步的确定。开口于⑥层下的遗迹包括：神殿1前期遗迹、道路1、道路2、道路3、道路5、浴室和排水沟等。

⑦层，为青灰色膏泥土，基本呈水平堆积。从土质土色分析，接近当地原生土，在遗址附近有广泛的分布。⑦层目前只在Unit I11、I10、L10、L8有局部发掘，发掘厚度约0.8米，未发掘到最底部。⑦层表面出土几件可修复的完整陶器，在地层中也含有较多陶片，以及少量小石块、铁器、玻璃器、网坠、炭末等。

⑦层是遗址最早的人类活动堆积，因发掘面积所限，对该层的认识还不够充分，它是早期建筑的填土层，还是相应的生活堆积，尚不能确定。⑦层下的原生自然层为青色膏泥土，在附近地区有广泛的分布。目前未发现开口于⑦层下的遗迹（彩版2-2，4）。

Due to the different specific formation processes of the deposits, the cultural layers of the Nateshwar site present various accumulation patterns, such as the horizontal, pit-shaped, and slope-like. The general information, the possible causes and the corresponding cultural features are described as follows.

Layer 1: Surface humus, loose light gray clayey powder sand is roughly horizontally distributed in the whole site. The common thickness is about 0.1 m. This layer contains potsherds, brick bats, glass, modern coins, etc (Color Plate 2-1, 1).

Layer 2: Brown clayey powder sand is about 1 m thick in general, but the deepest thickness is about 3 m. It is much looser on the top because of being closer to the ground. This layer is distributed in the shape of long ditches and round pits, which were caused by taking away the bricks and filling with soils again by the later residents. It is generally distributed throughout the site; some of the deeper pit-like deposits are mostly located in the four corners of constructions. These kinds of pits, whose nature and inclusions are roughly the same, and were recorded as the pit-shaped layer during the excavation. However, it can be subdivided into many different sub-layers. Because the backfilling with mixed soils of different sources is a random behavior, the color and texture of the accumulation in each pit are difficult to be compared and coordinated. According to the observation, the behaviors of brick hunting probably happened several times on this site.

The pit-like Layer 2, which contains broken brick pieces, brick dusts, limes, potteries, and glass etc., cut the Layer 4 and disturbed the vicinity of the brick walls. The pits of H1 – H5 are under this layer (Color Plate 2-1, 2, 3).

Layer 3: Grey green silt, concentrating in the Unit I9, J9, I10 and J10, is roughly distributed in a circular area of 30 m in diameter and 2 m in depth. The color of the deposit is obviously different from that of other layers of the site, and it can be divided into several natural sub-layers without artifacts. The cause of this layer is still not fully understood. The first possibility is that the later residents carried the silty soils from elsewhere to dump here, which probably reflects some habitation behavior. The second possibility is that it is the long-term accumulation of the sediments due to the natural process of raining water. Since the excavation is continuing, the above question about this layer should await further observation and discussion. There are many cultural features of the second period under Layer 3, including the cruciform central temple, octagonal stupa, Floor 1, zigzag boundary wall (Color Plate 2-1, 4).

Layer 4: Yellowish clayey sand, is distributed in the whole excavation area, 2 – 3 m thick in general, and the thickest position is about 4 m. The deposit of Layer 4 looks like a bread-like mound, thicker in the center and gradually becomes thinner in the periphery. Generally speaking, the soil of the upper layer contains more sand, and the soil of the lower layer is more clayey. The proportion of the inclusions of sand, clay, brickbats, and brick dusts in the Layer is various in different location and depth. Taking the Pillared-hall 4 for example, all the Layer 4 soils in the eastern, western and southern sections are clayey sand, but they are inconsistent in terms of soil color, viscosity and sand proportion containing.

The cause of the Layer 4 is mainly the large-scale and well-planned activities of soil piling for raising the basement elevation during the second period. According to the present archaeological data, the ground surface significantly raises 2 – 4 m. Layer 4 is divided into many sloping sub-layers, with the exception of the horizontal sub-layer at the bottom. Because the constructions of the second period are partially built above the earlier architectures of the first period, the previous uneven surface should be covered with soils. That is the reason why we can observe one or two sub-layers of the bottom Layer 4 includes more brick bats and brick particles. It also reflects the reuse of the previous architectural ruins. For instance, the deposit outside the southern wall of the Temple 1 is higher on the north and lower on the south; sloping distribution from northwest to southeast with the thickness also gradually reduces. This phenomenon is clearly caused by the demolition and immediate dumping of the earlier constructions. These sub-layers, regardless of the variety of existing situation, are all used as the basement to build the new structures.

Unlike the pure sand in the river or on the riverbed, the soil in the upper part of the Layer 4 is the clayey sand with stickiness, which could be collected from nearby alluvial plain and, has experienced a long period of precipitation to become compact. Partial soils may be rammed, although it is difficult to find the trace of ramming at present. The existing ponds and channels near the site likely contain the traces as a result of the soil digging. The slopping direction of the layer indicates that the soils were firstly dumped in the center and then expanded to the periphery, which clearly showed from the related sections of the Unit L9, L10 in the eastern excavation area. The soil dumping is a random behavior, without any strict and consistent way. At the bottom of Layer 4 in the Pillared-hall 4, the depth of the brickbats in sub-layer is 2 m higher in the center than the eastern edge, which reflects that the central region was dumped earlier than other areas. Since the soils of this layer were carried from outside, the age of the inclusions should be earlier than that of the layer itself. There are few inclusions in the upper Layer 4, which mainly are a small amount of bricks, brick particles and pottery shreds (Color Plate 2-2, 1).

The cultural features under this layer include Road 4. According to our preliminary analysis, there are probably a small group of people living here for a short time before the formation of the Layer 4 and after the abandonment of the first period, belonging to the last remains of the first period.

Layer 5: It is distributed in the eastern excavation area, mainly in Units K11, L11, L10 and L9, and it is absent in many excavation grids. The soil of the layer is yellowish brown clayey sand, loose texture, about 1 – 1.3 m thick. A certain number of brick particles, pottery shreds and charcoals were found inside. It can be divided into several small horizontal sub-layers; the thickness ranges from 10 to 30 cm. The shallow water deposition can also be observed in some locations, indicating that the formation of the layer took a relative long time, rather than forming at a single occasion. The nature of the Layer 5 is so far interpreted to the abandonment deposit of the early and middle phase of the first period monuments. The cultural features under Layer 5 include late phase of Temple 1, Temple 2 (pyramid-shaped stupa), Road 3, partition wall, House 1, House 2, House 3, House 4, House 5, Wall 1, Wall 2, Wall 3, Floor 2 and Floor 4 (Color Plate 2-2, 2).

Layer 6: Grayish yellow clayey sand, its common thickness is 0.4 m and 1.1 m at the thickest position. It is limited in Unit I11, I10, L10, L8, J11, and was horizontally deposited. Many potteries were found in this layer; some charcoals and burnt soil were also discovered. Over 20 complete potteries were horizontally unearthed on the surface of Layer 6 in Unit I11, which leads to the speculation that the Layer 6 is formed by the everyday living debris of the first period (Color Plate 2-2, 3). The Layer 6 distributed separately in Unit I11, L10, and L8 is not uniform, and the color and texture of this soil in these different units are not exactly the same. Therefore, whether these layers in the units are actually the same thing will be awaiting for the further analysis. Due to the limited exposure of layer 6, the understanding about the nature and corresponding cultural remains are still obscure and incomplete. The early phase of the Temple 1, Road 1, Road 2, Road 3, Road 5, Wall 13, bathroom and the drainage were found under this layer.

Layer 7: It is green gray sandy clay, mainly horizontally distributed in the site. The color and texture are close to the natural soil, widely distributed around the site. It is currently exposed in Unit I11, I10, L10, L8, only excavated 0.8 m deep, and its total depth remains unknown. There are several repairable potteries unearthed on the surface of Layer 7. A small amount of small stones, iron nails, glass pieces, fishing net sinkers, charcoals were discovered in the layer.

The Layer 7 is the earliest cultural deposit in the excavation area. However, the understanding about the layer is not enough owing to limited excavation. It is uncertain that this layer is the foundation of earlier constructions or the habitants' everyday living deposits. The deposit beneath this layer is the blue virgin soil, which can be widely found in the vicinity (Color Plate 2-2, 4).

第二节
Section 2
Section Description
地层举例

现选择若干地层剖面加以具体介绍，由此说明整个遗址的地层堆积情况，选用地层照片上的地层号，有些有改动，皆以线图为准（图2-1）。

一、UnitJ10GridA10、B10、C10、D10、E10、E9 剖面

（图2-2；彩版2-3，1）

①层：表土层。

②层：为取砖后的回填坑，可分为13个小层。

②A层：红褐色土，厚0—0.95米，土质略疏松，含较多碎砖块，由东向西逐渐倾斜加厚。

②B层：灰色沙土，厚0—0.35米，土质较疏松，含较多砖颗粒，由东向西倾斜。

②C层：红褐色土，厚0—0.9米，土质略疏松，含较多砖块，砖块直径在10厘米以下。

②D层：深灰色沙土，厚0—0.75米，土质较疏松，含少量砖颗粒，呈坑状堆积。

②E层：浅灰色沙土，厚0—0.7米，呈坑状堆积，土质较疏松，含少量砖块。

②F层：深灰色沙土，厚0—0.7米，土质略紧，含部分砖块，呈坑状堆积。

②G层：浅红色沙土，厚0—0.3米，土质略紧，含较多细小砖颗粒，呈坡状堆积。

②H层：浅红色沙土，厚0—1.3米，土质略紧，含部分砖块，呈坡状堆积。

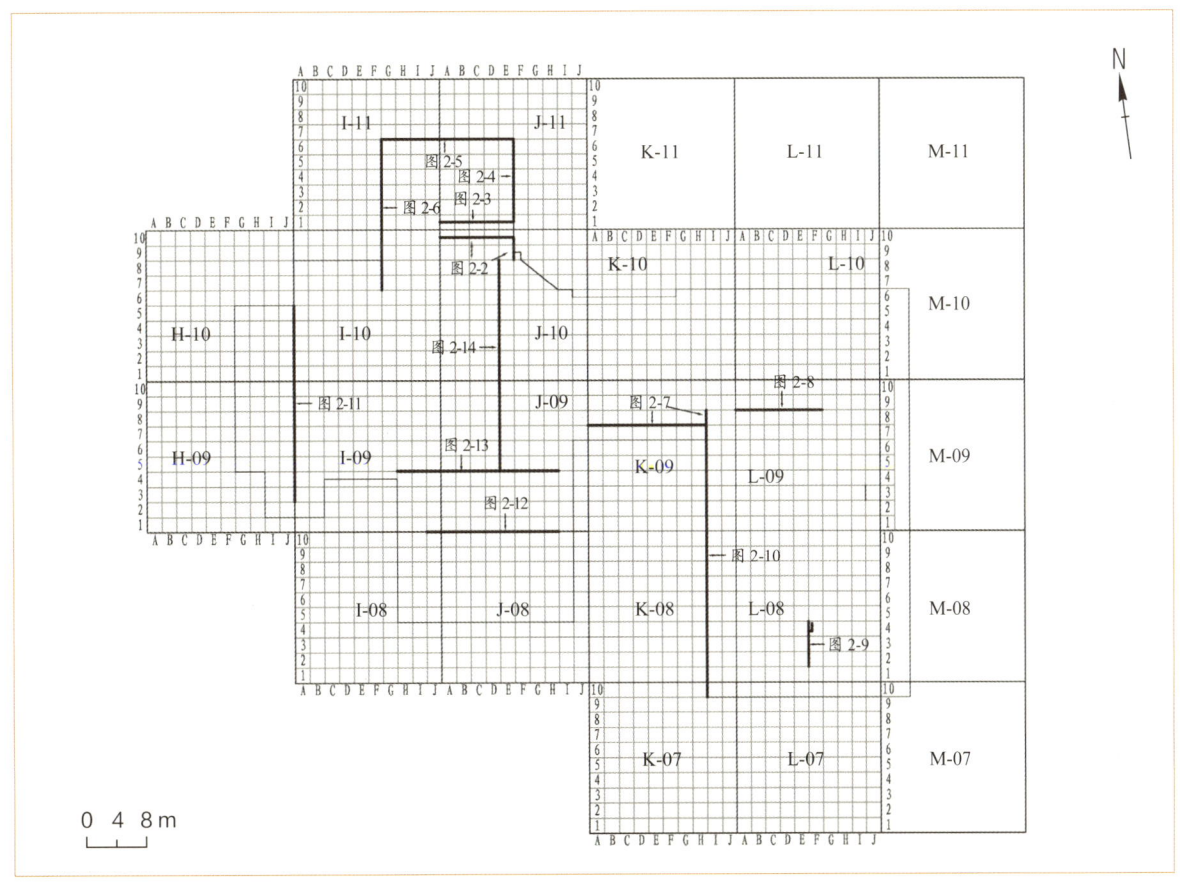

图2-1 纳提什瓦遗址地层剖面位置图
Fig. 2-1 The location map of the stratigraphic sections at Nateshwar site

②I层：深灰色沙土，厚0—0.65米，土质略紧，含少量砖颗粒，呈坡状堆积，由东向西倾斜。

②J层：红褐色土，厚0—0.3米，土质略紧，含部分砖块，呈坡状堆积。

②K层：浅灰色沙土，厚0—0.25米。土质略紧，含少量砖块，东高西低，呈坡状堆积。

②L层：浅红褐色沙土，厚0—0.6米，含少量砖颗粒。

②M层：深红褐色沙土，厚0—0.8米，含较多砖颗粒。

二、UnitJ11GridE1、D1、C1、B1、A1剖面

（图2-3；彩版2-3，2）

①层：表土层。

②层：为取砖后的回填坑，可分为8个小层。

②A层：红褐色沙性土，厚0—1.3米，土质略疏松，含较多碎小砖块，呈坑状堆积。H1开口于②A下。

②B层：灰色沙土，厚0—0.8米，土质略疏松，含部分碎砖块。

②C层：浅灰褐色沙性土，厚0—0.3米，土质略疏松，含部分碎砖块，由东向西呈坡状堆积。

②D层：深灰色，厚0—0.8米，含少量砖块，水平堆积。

②E层：浅红褐色沙性土，厚0—0.8米，含较多砖块，水平堆积。

②F层：深灰色沙性土，厚0—0.35米，含部分砖块，水平堆积。

②G层：浅红色带黏性沙土，厚0.1—0.78米，含较多小砖块和陶片。

②H层：浅灰褐色带黏性沙土，厚0.25—0.9米，含部分小碎砖和陶片。

④层：深灰色沙性土，厚0—1.4米，含部分砖块、陶片，未发掘到底。

三、UnitJ11GridE6、E5、E4、E3、E2、E1剖面

（图2-4；彩版2-3，3）

①层：表土层，厚0—1.1米，浅灰色沙土，土质疏松。

②层：为取砖后的回填坑，可分为8个小层。

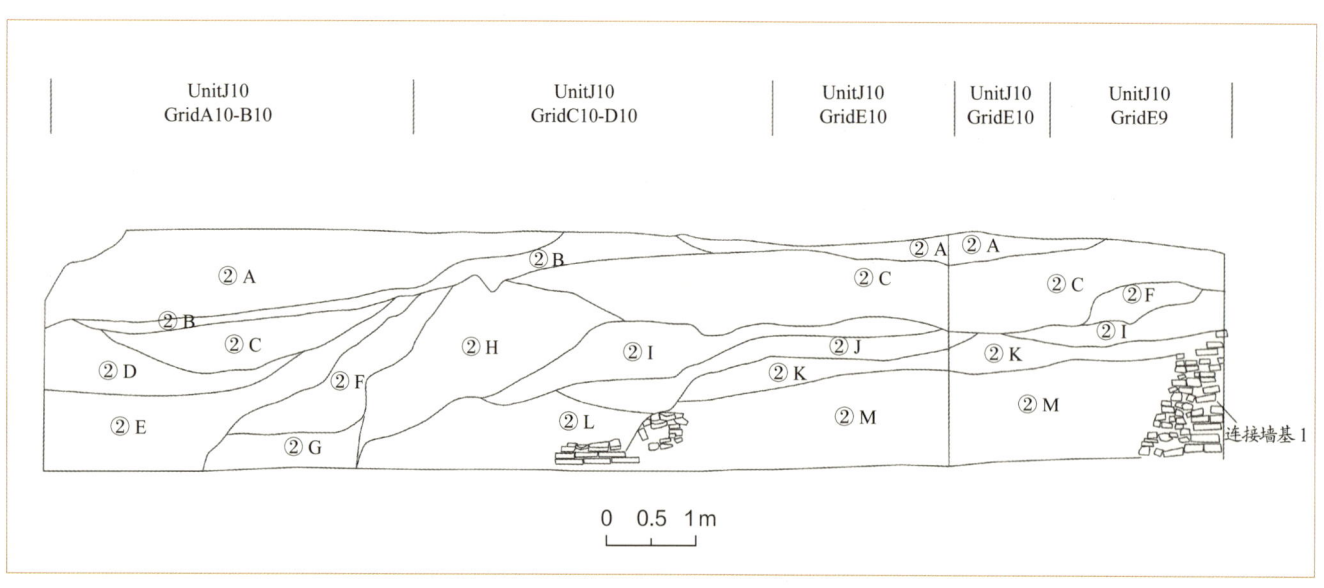

图2-2　UnitJ10GridA10、B10、C10、D10、E10、E9剖面图
Fig. 2-2　The section of UnitJ10GridA10, B10, C10, D10, E10, E9

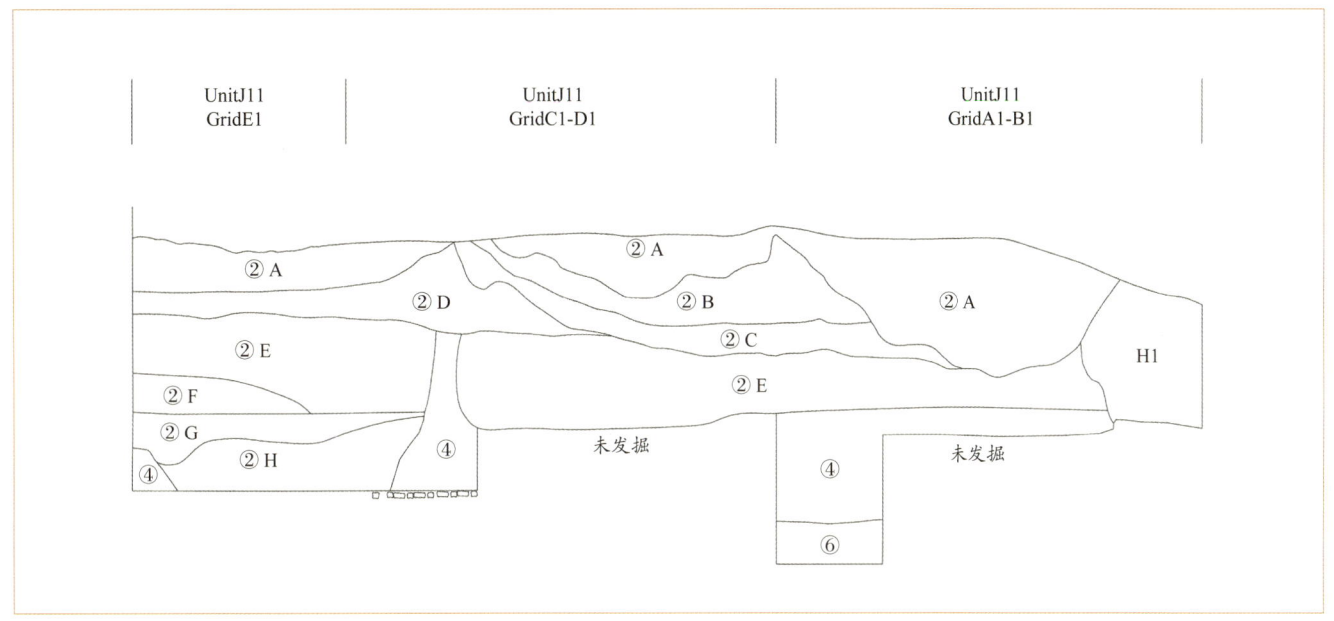

图 2-3　UnitJ11GridE1、D1、C1、B1、A1 剖面图
Fig. 2-3　The section of UnitJ11GridE1, D1, C1, B1, A1

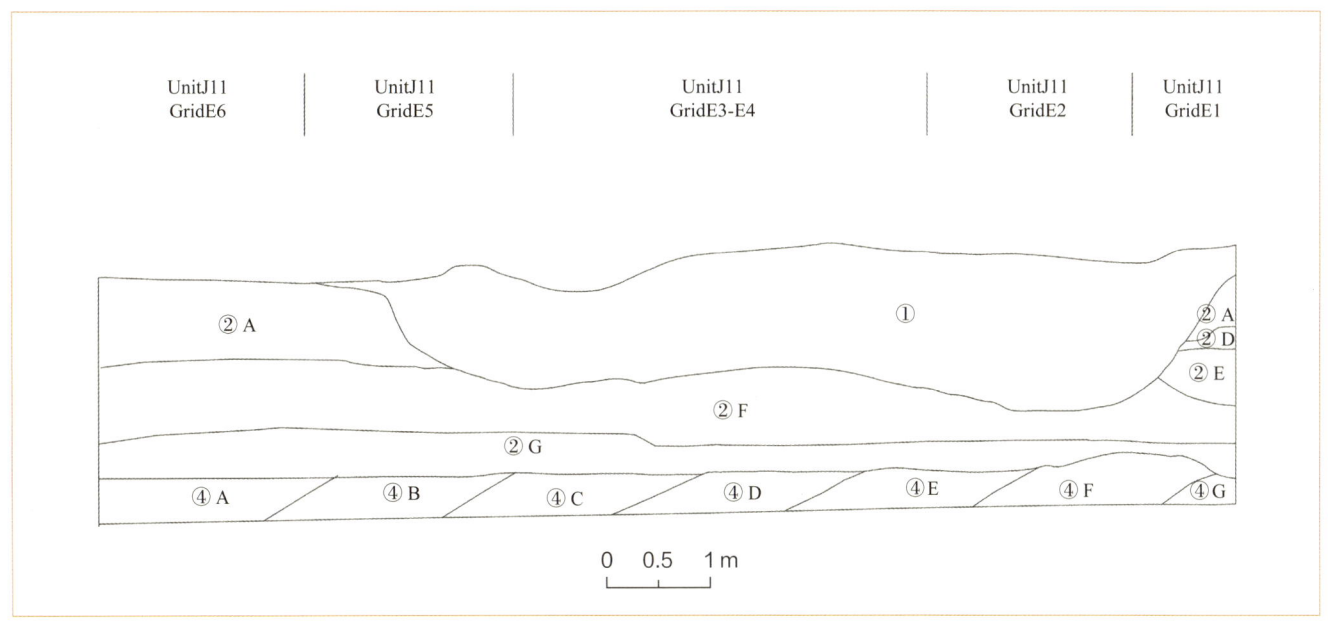

图 2-4　UnitJ11GridE6、E5、E4、E3、E2、E1 剖面图
Fig. 2-4　The section of UnitJ11GridE6, E5, E4, E3, E2, E1

②A 层：厚 0—0.7 米，红褐色沙性土，土质疏松，含较多砖块。

②D 层：厚 0.12—0.2 米，深灰色沙土，土质疏松。

②E 层：厚 0.25—0.55 米，浅红褐色沙性土，土质略紧，含较多砖块。

②F 层：厚 0.35—0.85 米，深灰色沙性土，土质略紧。水平状堆积，剖面上可见多个小夹层。含碎砖块、少量陶片等。

②G 层：浅红色黏性沙土，厚 0.25—0.55 米。水平状堆积，局部可见小的坑状纹理。含部分砖块、陶片。

④层：呈水平堆积，但可见明显的倾斜小层层理，每个小层在厚度、宽度、倾斜度上都较为接近。可分为 7 个小层。

④ A 层：厚 0.5—0.6 米，浅灰色沙土，含少量砖颗粒、陶片。

④ B 层：厚 0.4—0.5 米，浅黄色沙土，含少量砖颗粒。

④ C 层：厚 0.4—0.5 米，深灰色沙土，含少量砖颗粒、陶片。

④ D 层：厚 0.4—0.5 米，浅灰色沙土，含少量砖颗粒。

④ E 层：厚 0.4—0.5 米，浅灰白色沙土，含少量砖颗粒、陶片。

④ F 层：厚 0.4—0.5 米，浅灰褐色带黏性沙土。

④ G 层：灰白色沙土。

在④层底部含大量倾斜砖块，为柱厅 2 东墙基底部砖。

四、UnitI11GridH6、I6、J6，UnitJ11GridA6、B6、C6、D6、E6 剖面

（图 2-5）

①层：表土层，厚约 0.2 米，呈水平状堆积。

②层：呈坑状堆积，为取砖后的回填坑，分 3 个小层。

② A 层：厚 0.85—1.2 米，红褐色沙性土，含较多碎砖块、石灰颗粒及部分陶片。

② B 层：红色黏性沙土，厚 0.2—1.1 米，含较多碎砖块。

② C 层：浅红色黏性沙土，厚 0.4—1.05 米，含较多碎砖块、麻石块和少量陶片。

④层：呈水平状堆积，分 3 个小层。

④ A 层：深灰色沙土，厚 0.5—0.75 米，含少量碎砖块、石块、陶片。

④ B 层：浅红褐色沙土，厚 0.3—0.5 米，含较多碎砖块、小石块。

④ C 层：深灰色沙土，厚 0.1—1.2 米，含少量小砖块、陶片。

④层下为柱厅 2 北墙基底部砖。

五、UnitI10GridG8、G9、G10，UnitI11GridG1、G2、G3、G4、G5 剖面

（图 2-6；彩版 2-4）

①层：地表层，浅灰色沙性土层，厚 0.1—1 米。①层下有近现代的土坑 H5。

②层：为取砖后的回填坑，坑底为建筑遗迹墙 12 的红砖，坑内堆积为取砖后的回填土，可分 3 个小层。

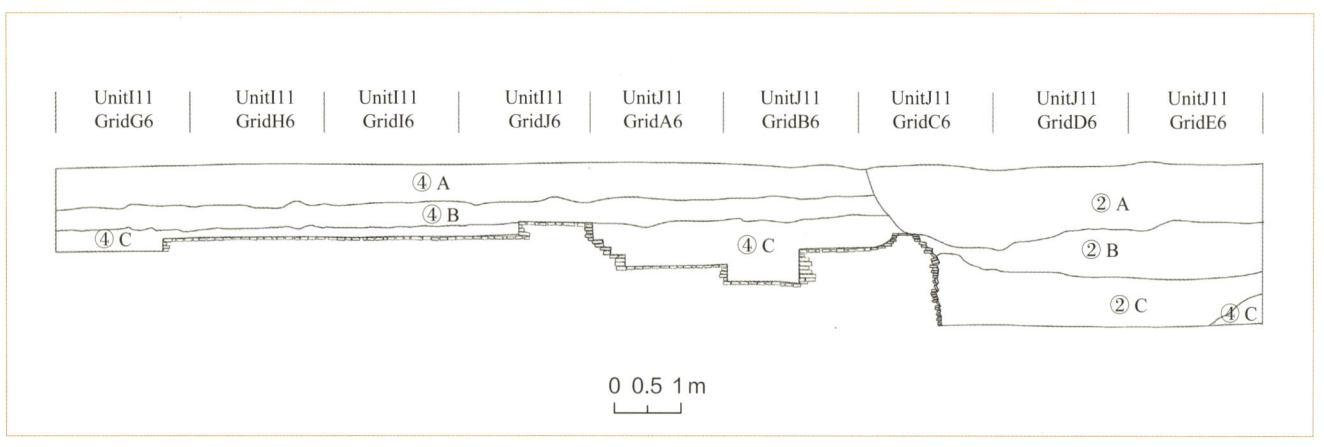

图 2-5　UnitI11GridH6、I6、J6，UnitJ11GridA6、B6、C6、D6、E6 剖面图
Fig. 2-5　The section of UnitI11GridH6, I6, J6, UnitJ11GridA6, B6, C6, D6, E6

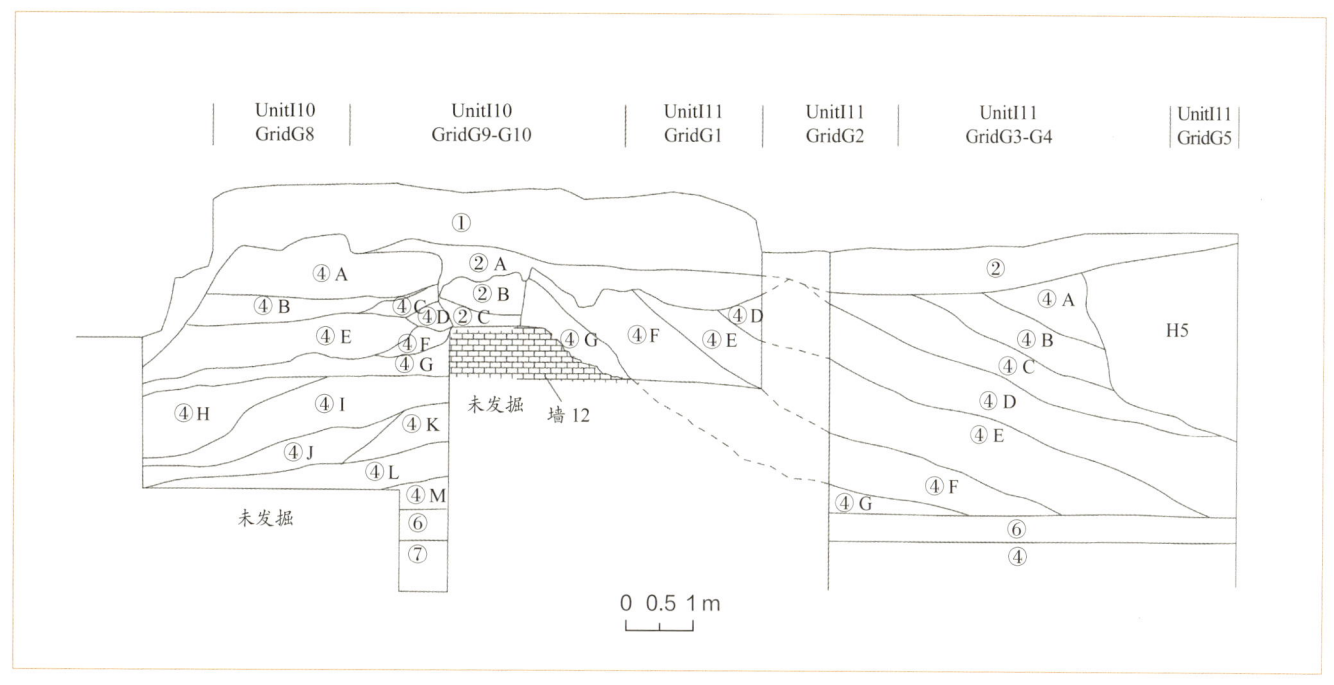

图 2-6 UnitI10GridG8、G9、G10，UnitI11GridG1、G2、G3、G4、G5 剖面图
Fig. 2-6 The section of UnitI10GridG8, G9, G10, UnitI11GridG1, G2, G3, G4, G5

②A 层：红褐色沙土，厚 0—0.65 米，含较密集的残碎砖块，少量石灰颗粒。

②B 层：浅灰色沙土，厚 0—0.6 米，含少量砖块。

②C 层：浅黄色沙土，厚 0.15—0.35 米，含少量砖颗粒。

④层：南部④层（大致为 UnitI10GridG8、G9 区域）整体为深灰色沙土，总厚度为 3.95 米。各个小层由北向南倾斜，厚度、倾斜度不等，可分 13 小层。

④A 层：深灰色，厚 0.4—0.95 米，含少量砖块。

④B 层：浅黄色，厚 0—0.45 米，含少量砖颗粒。

④C 层：浅灰黑色，厚 0—0.35 米，含少量炭末。

④D 层：灰黄色，厚 0—0.45 米，土质较纯净。

④E 层：深灰色，厚 0—0.65 米，含少量陶片。

④F 层：灰黄色，厚 0—0.35 米，含少量砖块。

④G 层：浅灰色，厚 0.3—0.75 米，含少量陶片、炭末。

④H 层：浅灰色，厚 0—0.95 米，含少量陶片、炭末。

④I 层：深灰色，厚 0.2—0.7 米，含少量砖颗粒。

④J 层：浅灰黑色，厚 0—0.75 米，土质较纯净。

④K 层：浅黄色，厚 0—0.65 米，含少量陶片。

④L 层：浅灰色，厚 0.5—0.65 米，含少量砖颗粒。

④M 层：深灰色，厚 0.2—0.45 米，土质较纯净。

北部④层（大致为 UnitI10GridG10，UnitI11GridG1、G2、G3、G4、G5 区域）：总厚度 3.45 米，由南向北倾斜，各小层的厚度、倾斜度大致相等，可分为 7 小层。

④A 层：深灰色土，厚 0—1.05 米，含少量砖颗粒。

④B 层：深灰色沙土，厚 0—0.3 米，含少量砖块。

④C层：浅灰黄色沙土，厚0—0.4米，较纯净。

④D层：浅灰色沙土，厚0—1.15米，含少量砖颗粒和陶片。

④E层：深灰色沙土，厚0—1米，含较多砖块。

④F层：深灰色沙土，厚0—0.8米，含部分砖颗粒。

④G层：灰白色沙土，厚0—0.4米，含大量砖块，为最底层的铺垫层。

④层下有墙12遗迹。

⑥层：灰褐色土，厚0.3—0.35米，水平堆积，在该层表面出土较多可修复的完整陶器，主要器形为碗、器盖，还含有较多炭末和烧土颗粒。

⑦层：灰黑色膏泥土，已发掘厚度为1.05米，水平堆积，可分为20厘米左右的小层，出土较多陶片及少量网坠、玻璃器等。

六、UnitK9GridA8、B8、C8、D8、E8、F8、G8、H8剖面

（图2-7；彩版2-5）

①层：表土层，分为2个小层。

①A层：褐灰色沙性土，厚0.2—0.48米，土质疏松，夹杂砖块碎末、纸屑、陶片等。

①B层：棕黄色黏土质粉沙，厚0.15—0.97米，夹杂较多砖块、陶片、少量石灰颗粒。

②层：为取砖后的回填坑，有东、西两坑。东部坑在GridF8、G8、H8内，距离地表最浅0.63米，最深0.96米，厚1.94—2.35米。坑内土质土色斑驳，整体呈褐黄色，堆积可以分10个小层。

②A层：褐色黏土质粉沙土，土质较紧密。

②B层：浅褐黄色粉沙土，土质较紧密，由西向东倾斜。

②C层：深褐黄色粉沙土，含大量红色碎砖块，由西向东倾。

②D层：褐色粉沙土，由西向东坡状分布，土质较疏松。

②E层：黄褐色粉沙土，含少量碎砖块。

②F层：青灰色粉沙土，少量碎砖块，由东向西坡状分布。

②G层：褐色粉沙土，土质较紧密。

②H层：深褐黄色，含大量碎砖块。

②I层：褐色粉沙土。

②J层：棕黄色粉沙土，土质较紧密，有少

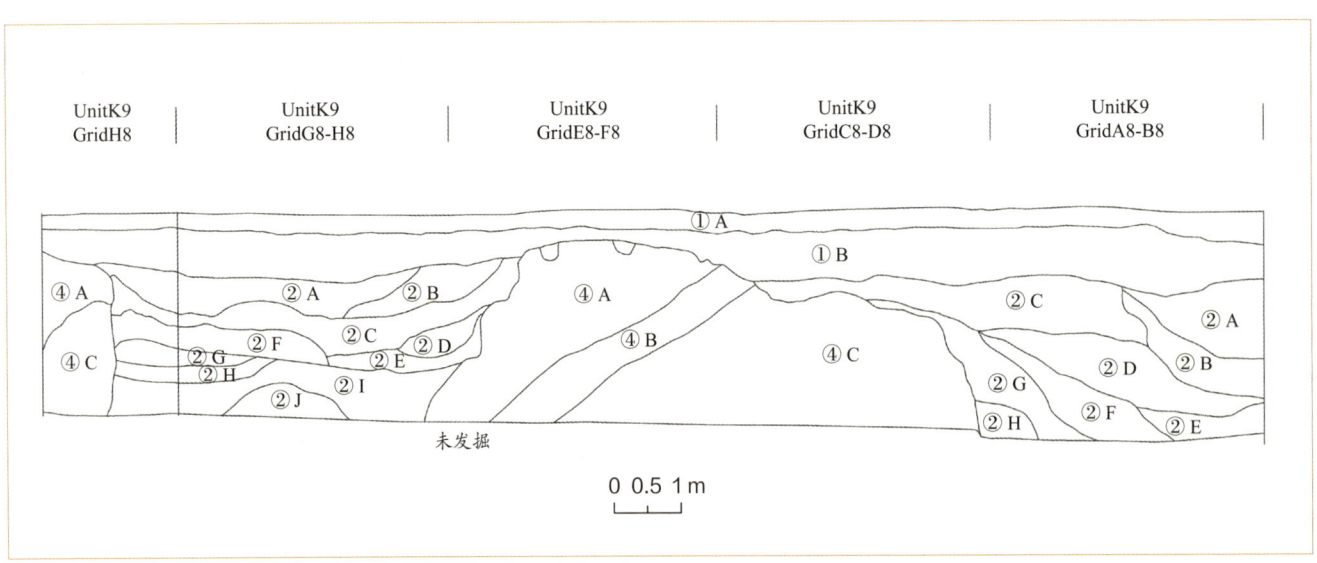

图2-7 UnitK9GridA8、B8、C8、D8、E8、F8、G8、H8剖面图
Fig. 2-7 The section of UnitK9GridA8, B8, C8, D8, E8, F8, G8, H8

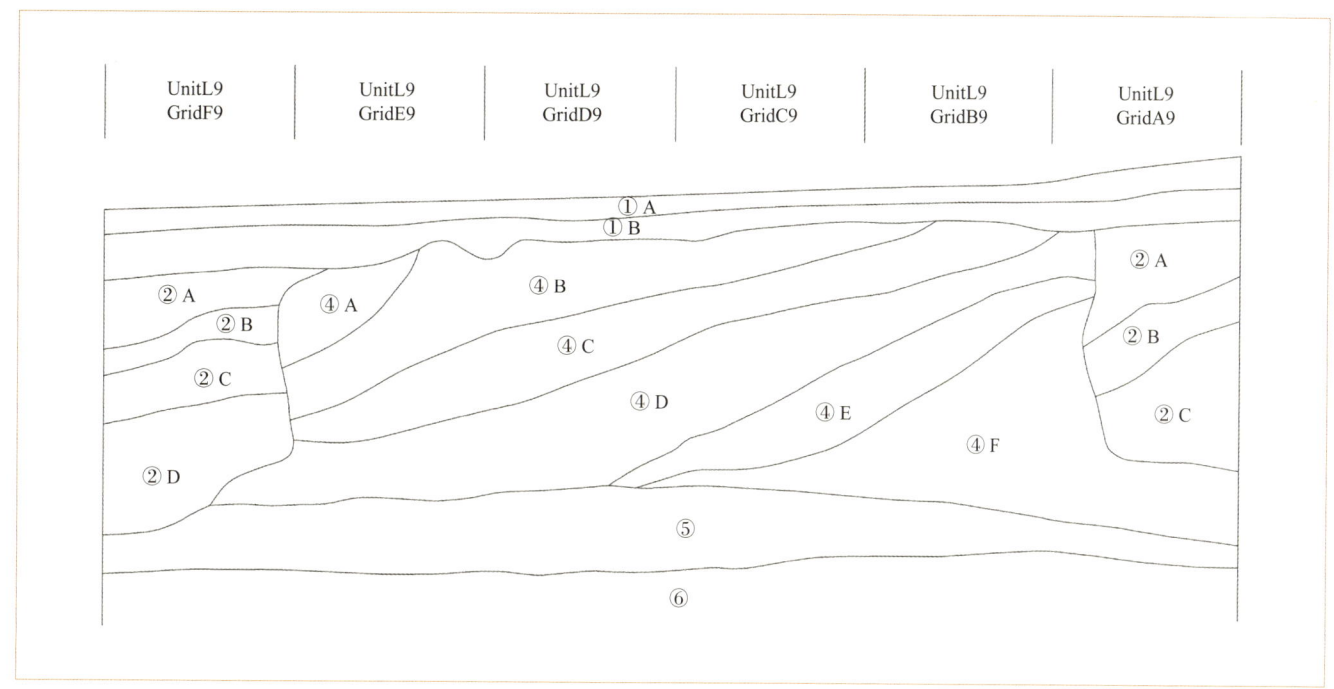

图 2-8　UnitL9GridA9、B9、C9、D9、E9、F9 剖面图
Fig. 2-8　The section of UnitL9GridA9, B9, C9, D9, E9, F9

量碎石块和大量陶片。

西部坑在 GridA8、B8、C8、D8 内，距离地表最浅 0.96 米，最深 1.22 米，厚 2—2.3 米。坑内堆积可分为 8 个小层，由东向西呈斜坡状分布。

②A 层：棕黄色粉沙土，土质较紧密，含大量碎砖块。

②B 层：浅黄褐色粉沙土，土质较紧密。

②C 层：棕黄色粉沙土，土质较紧密，含大量碎砖块和少量石灰颗粒。

②D 层：褐灰色粉沙土，土质较疏松，含零星碎砖块。

②E 层：深褐色粉沙土，土质较紧密。

②F 层：棕黄色粉沙土，土质较紧密，含较多碎砖块和少量石灰颗粒。

②G 层：浅灰黄色粉沙土，土质较紧密，含少量石灰颗粒。

②H 层：浅黄色粉沙土，土质较疏松，含少量碎砖块、陶片。

④层：浅黄色泥沙土，较为纯净，土质较紧密，距离地表最浅 0.47 米，最深 1.22 米，厚 1.57—2.59 米。堆积由西向东倾斜，可分为 3 个小层。

④A 层：浅黄色泥沙土，土质较紧密，厚 0—1.65 米，有少量陶片。

④B 层：深黄色泥沙土，土质较紧密，呈条带状倾斜分布，厚 0—0.64 米。

④C 层：浅黄色泥沙土夹杂有灰褐色土块，土质较紧密，厚 0—1.9 米，有少量陶片。

该层下遗迹有砖墙 11。

七、UnitL9GridA9、B9、C9、D9、E9、F9 剖面

（图 2-8；彩版 2-6，1）

①层：表土层，分为 2 个小层。

①A 层：褐灰色沙性土，土质疏松，厚 0.16—0.32 米，包含少量碎砖块和现代垃圾。

①B 层：褐黄色黏土质粉沙土，夹杂有较多碎砖块，厚 0.17—0.46 米，包含较多陶片。

②层：为取砖后的回填坑，有东、西两坑。东部坑在 GridF9 内，可分为 4 个小层。

②A层：棕黄色粉沙土，带黏性，土质较紧密，由东向西略呈斜坡状分布。厚0.4—0.7米，夹杂大量碎砖块和较多陶片。

②B层：浅褐黄色黏土质粉沙，土质较紧密，由西向东呈缓坡状分布，厚0.24—0.4米，含零星碎砖块。

②C层：浅黄色黏土质粉沙，土质较紧密，略呈坡状分布，厚0.5—0.67米，夹杂零星砖碎块。

②D层：棕黄色黏土质粉沙，土质较紧密，由西向东呈坡状分布，厚0.71—1.21米，夹杂大量碎砖块、石灰颗粒和较多陶片。

西部坑在GridA9内，堆积可分为3个小层。

②A层：棕黄色黏土质粉沙，由西向东呈坡状分布，厚0.8—1.1米。出土大量陶片、碎砖块和零星石灰颗粒。

②B层：灰黄色黏土质粉沙，由西向东呈坡状分布，厚0.4—0.67米，夹杂零星碎砖块。

②C层：深褐黄色黏土质粉沙，由西向东呈坡状堆积，厚0.62—1.52米，出土有较多陶片、碎砖块和少量石灰颗粒。

④层：浅黄色黏土质粉沙土，较为纯净，土质较紧密。距地表最浅0.34米，最深0.67米，厚2.41—3.02米。堆积由西向东呈斜坡状分布，可分为5个小层。

④A层：青褐色粉沙土，土质较紧密，厚0—1.02米，无包含物。

④B层：青黄色粉沙土，含有青褐色土块，土质较紧密，厚0—1.16米，出土少量碎陶片。

④C层：青褐色粉沙土，含有少量黄色土块，土质较紧密，厚0—0.8米，无包含物。

④D层：深褐黄色粉沙土，含有少量红色砖灰，土质较紧密，厚0.31—1.18米，出土较多陶片。

④E层：碎砖块夹粉沙土条带层，结构较紧密，厚0.18—0.83米。

④F层：褐黄色黏土质粉沙土，土质较紧密，厚0—2.34米，无出土物。

⑤层：褐色黏土质粉沙，含大量砖灰、碎砖块等建筑废弃，基本呈水平状分布于整个探方。距地表最浅2.96米，最深3.99米，厚0.23—0.86米。出土有较多陶片、炭末及少量玻璃、石质遗物。分布于神殿1西北、西南部位的大型陶瓮开口于此层下。

⑥层：灰褐色黏土质粉沙土，土质较疏松，基本呈水平状分布于整个探方。距地表最浅3.74米，最深3.86米，已发掘厚度约0.7米，出土少量陶片。⑥层未发掘至底，但从附近的解剖坑显示，⑥层下为一种纯净的黄色泥沙土堆积，可见厚度可达2米，仍未至底，不见任何遗物，这层堆积的性质不明。

八、UnitL8GridF2、F3、F4 剖面

（图2-9；彩版2-6，2）

这是发掘过程中开挖的一个探坑，现将其剖面介绍如下：

④层：深灰色沙土，厚1.7—1.75米。略呈水平状堆积，内部层理未细分，含少量陶片。

⑤层：浅灰褐色沙土，厚1—1.2米。呈水平状堆积，局部含较多砖块。该层下有L1，另有一

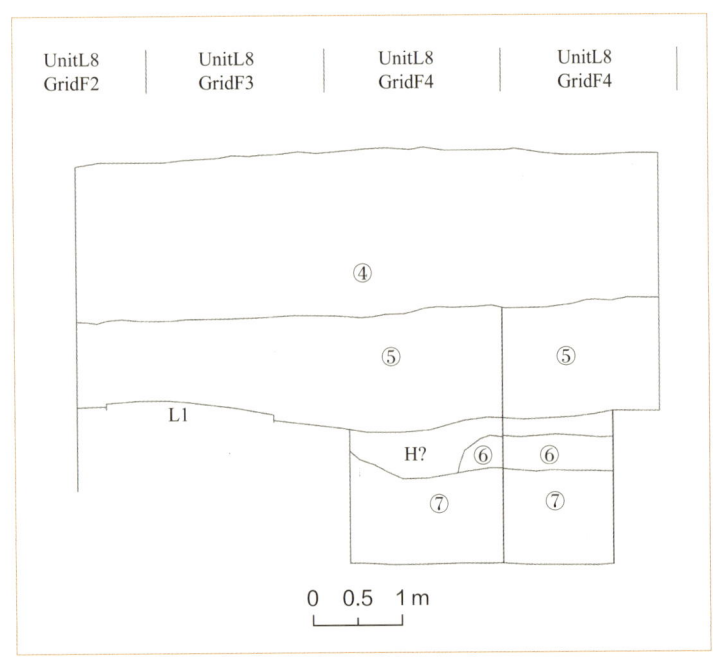

图2-9　UnitL8GridF2、F3、F4剖面图
Fig. 2-9　The section of UnitL8GridF2, F3, F4

个灰坑，未编号，出土大量陶片。

⑥层：深灰色土，厚0—0.4米。呈水平状堆积，含部分陶片。

⑦层：青灰色膏泥土，厚1—1.2米。呈水平状堆积，含部分陶片，未发掘到底。

九、UnitK7GridI10，UnitK8GridI1–I10，UnitK9GridI1–I7 剖面

（图2-10；彩版2-7）

现将剖面分为北段、中段、南段，分别予以记录。

1. 北段

位于UnitK9GridI1、I2、I3、I4、I5、I6、I7内。

①层：浅红褐色沙土，厚0.2—0.4米，含较多红砖颗粒，水平状分布。

②层：深红褐色沙土，厚0.41—2.88米，含较多砖块、砖颗粒及少量石灰、陶片。②层有南北两处坑状堆积。北部坑较规整，上部长3.2米，底部长3.41，底部与建筑遗迹相连。南部坑上部长4.31米，边缘不规整，坑深2.42米。

④层：灰色沙土层，土质较纯净，包含物少，可见由南向北倾斜层，可分为4个小层。

④A层：浅棕黄色，沙性较强，厚0.79—3.12米，斜坡状堆积。

④B层：深棕黄色，沙性略强，厚0—1.2米，斜坡状堆积，含零星砖块及少量砖末。

④C层：浅灰青绿色，厚0—1.3米，黏性略强，斜坡状堆积，含少量砖颗粒。

④D层：灰青绿色，黏性较重，可见块状的泥与沙混杂，厚0.21—0.46米，近水平状堆积，底部有一层散落的红砖。

⑤层：浅红褐色沙土，黏性较大，厚0—0.2米，呈水平状堆积，夹有较多碎砖块、砖颗粒、陶片、炭末及动物骨骼。该层覆盖在道路L3之上，应为L3时期的生活堆积。

2. 中段

位于UnitK8GridI5、I6、I7、I8、I9内。其中GridI5、I6、I7部分只发掘到②层，因地面有遗迹现象，未做进一步的发掘。

①层：浅红褐色沙土，厚0.3—1米，水平堆积，含较多小砖块和砖颗粒。

②层：深红褐色沙土，厚0.92—2.08米，含砖块、砖颗粒。②层底部有砖结构。

④层：由上至下土色由浅渐深，沙性由强至弱，黏性不断加强，含砖的颗粒逐渐变大。堆积西高东低，结合这一区域④层的分布，这里应为④层堆积的东部边缘。可分为7个小层。

④A层：浅灰棕黄色沙土，沙性较强，厚0.5米，含少量砖颗粒。

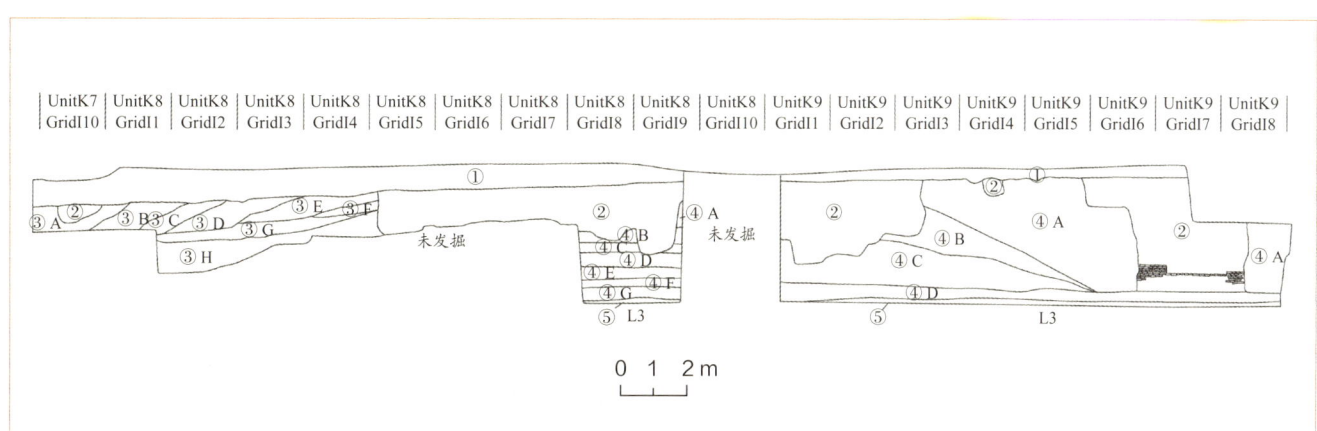

图2-10 UnitK7GridI10，UnitK8GridI1-I10，UnitK9GridI1-I7 剖面图
Fig. 2-10 The section of UnitK7GridI10, UnitK8GridI1-I10, UnitK9GridI1-I7

④B层：浅灰黄色沙土，厚0.4米，含少量砖颗粒。

④C层：灰黄色沙土，厚0.4米，含少量砖颗粒。

④D层：浅灰青绿色沙土，带黏性，厚0.3米，含少量砖颗粒。

④E层：灰青绿色沙土，黏性较强，厚0.4米，含少量砖颗粒。

④F层：灰青绿色沙土，黏性较强，厚0.5米，含少量砖块及砖颗粒。

④G层：浅灰绿色土，黏性重，厚0.5米，含有少量砖颗粒。

④层底部有较密集砖层，砖多为1层，少量为2层，以平铺为主，也有少量砖略有倾斜。其中保存最完整一块砖长29厘米、宽18厘米、厚5厘米。

⑤层：浅灰黑色沙土，厚0.2米，含较多陶片、砖颗粒及黑色炭末，并出土一块中国唐宋瓷片。该层覆盖在道路L3之上，应为L3时期的生活堆积。

3. 南段

位于UnitK7GridI10，UnitK8GridI1、I2、I3、I4、I5内。

①层：浅红褐色沙土层，厚0.7—1米，含较多碎砖块、砖颗粒。

②层：局部坑状堆积，厚0.7米，含碎小砖块。

③层：整体为灰青绿色，表现为较有层次的由北向南的倾斜堆积，局部可见板结块状纹理。上部含沙的板结纹理较多，较密集，下部黏性土的纹理较多，较密集。土质纯净，不见包含物。从堆积的倾斜形态，显示出从遗址中心部位向边缘逐渐形成的过程。根据地层的自然肌理，可分为8个小层。

③A层：灰棕色沙土及少部分灰青绿色黏性沙土，厚0—0.75米。

③B层：灰棕色沙土，局部可见灰青绿色黏性沙土，厚0—0.75米。

③C层：灰青黏性沙土，厚0—0.95米。

③D层：青绿色黏土，厚0—0.76米。

③E层：灰青绿色沙土，厚0—0.6米。

③F层：浅灰黄色沙土，厚0—0.3米。

③G层：灰棕色沙土及灰青色黏土，厚0.18—0.85。

③H层：灰青绿色沙土，黏性较大，厚0—0.9米。在该小层下，有局部倾斜的红砖颗粒层分布，与路面1相接，显示为新的活动界面。

十、UnitH10GridJ1J5，UnitI9GridA3-A10剖面

（图2-11；彩版2-8，1）

①层：表土层，可分3小层。

①A层：灰白色土，土质较松，厚0.17—0.72米，夹杂有红色砖粒。

①B层：红褐色土，土质较紧，厚0.19—0.74米，夹杂有少量红色砖粒。

①C层：红褐色土，土色略深，夹杂有较多红色砖粒。

②层：为取砖后的回填坑，可分2个小层。

②A层：红褐色土，土质紧密，含有密集的碎砖块。

②B层：灰褐色土，土质略软，内含较多的砖颗粒。

④层：上部土色较浅、较杂，下部土色变灰褐。堆积近水平分布，厚度约3.00米，包含物较少，可分4个小层。

④A层：灰黄色土，土色较杂，略呈倾斜状分布，厚0—1.15米。

④B层：灰黄色土，略偏白，厚0.50—1.44米。

④C层：灰色土，略偏黄，厚0.60—1.02米。

④D层：灰褐色土，色较深，厚0.44—0.71米。

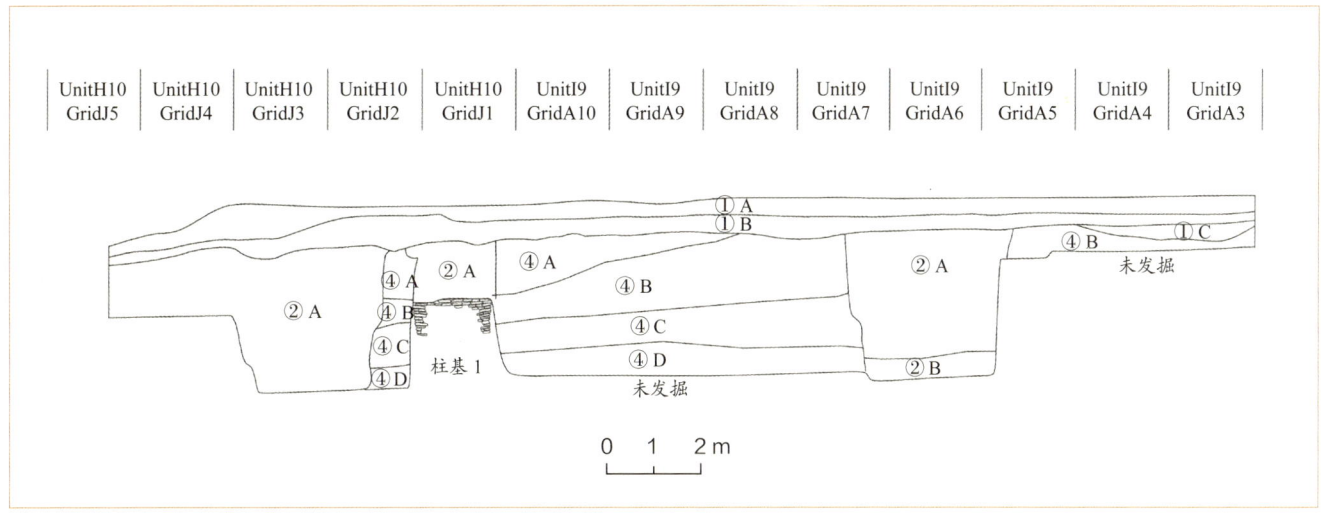

图 2-11　UnitH10GridJ5-J1，UnitI9GridA10-A3 剖面图
Fig. 2-11　The section of UnitH10GridJ5-J1, UnitI9GridA10-A3

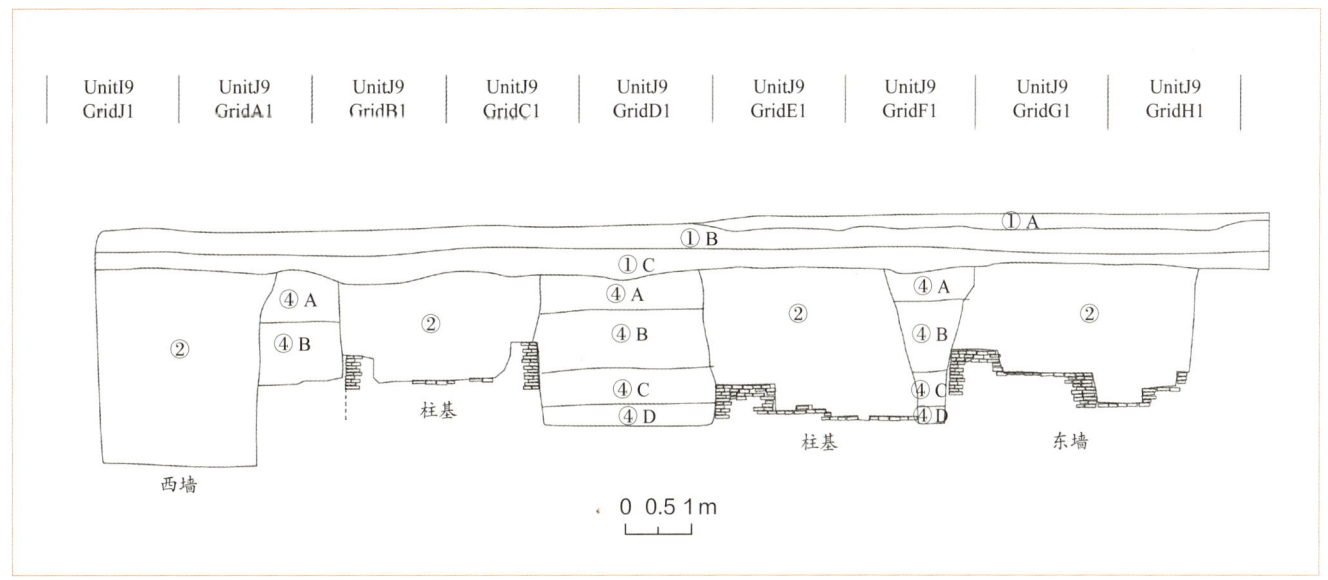

图 2-12　UnitI9GridJ1，UnitJ9GridA1、B1、C1、D1、E1、F1、G1、H1 剖面图
Fig. 2-12　The section of UnitI9GridJ1, UnitJ9GridA1, B1, C1, D1, E1, F1, G1, H1

④层下为⑥层，未作发掘。

十一、UnitI9GridJ1，UnitJ9GridA1、B1、C1、D1、E1、F1、G1、H1 剖面

（图 2-12）

①层：表土层，呈水平堆积，厚 0.65 米，分 3 小层。

①A 层：灰沙土，厚 0—0.23 米。

①B 层：浅灰褐色沙土，厚 0.24—0.46 米，含少量红砖颗粒。

①C 层：深褐色沙土，厚 0.14—0.46 米，含较密集的红砖颗粒。

②层：红褐色沙土，呈坑状分布，为取砖后的回填坑，层理呈多层水平堆积，包含较多的砖块、砖颗粒、陶片、螺壳、石灰等。厚 0.98—2.87 米。

④层：灰色沙土，土质较纯净，厚 2.5 米，

包含有零星砖颗粒及少量陶片，分4小层。

④A层：浅灰黄色土，厚0.45—0.81米，呈水平堆积，内含较多砖块、砖颗粒。

④B层：灰黄色土，沙性较大，厚0.84—0.91米。

④C层：浅灰青色沙土，带黏性，厚0.45—0.53米。

④D层：深灰青色沙土，黏性较强，厚0.27—0.32米。该层表面有一层砖末。

④层被柱厅4的西墙、柱基4、柱基2、东墙打破。

十二、UnitJ9GridH5、G5、F5、E5、D5、C5、B5、A5，UnitI9GridJ5、I5、H5 剖面

（图2-13；彩版2-8，2）

此为中心塔基区东西向剖面。

①层：褐灰色粉沙黏土，土质较疏松，呈水平状分布于整个探方中，夹杂零星红砖碎末。根据土质土色，可分为3个小层：

①A层：深灰褐色，土质较疏松，西部略高，东部略低，厚0.27—0.44米，包含有零星碎砖块、纸屑、陶片等，是现代居民的活动层。

①B层：浅灰褐色，土质较疏松，厚0.74—1.01米，含少量碎砖末和陶片。

①C层：褐红色粉沙黏土，土质较紧密，呈起伏状分布于探方中，厚0—0.86米，夹杂较多红色碎砖块、陶片和少量石灰颗粒。从分布形态看，应是回填取砖坑之后，平整地面所形成的堆积。

②层：取砖后回填土形成的堆积，呈坑状堆积，坑底一般都直达建筑基础，剖面的东、中、西共有3处堆积，现分别进行描述。

东部堆积：应为取连接墙基4的砖块后，回填形成的堆积层，根据土质土色，可分为5个小层。

②A层：灰黄色粉沙黏土，土质较疏松，基本水平分布，厚0.18—0.26米。

②B层：红色粉沙黏土，含大量碎砖，土质较紧密，由西向东略呈坡状分布，厚0.27—0.38米。

②C层：红黄色粉沙黏土，夹少量碎砖块，土质较紧密，由西向东略呈坡状分布，厚0.11—0.18米。

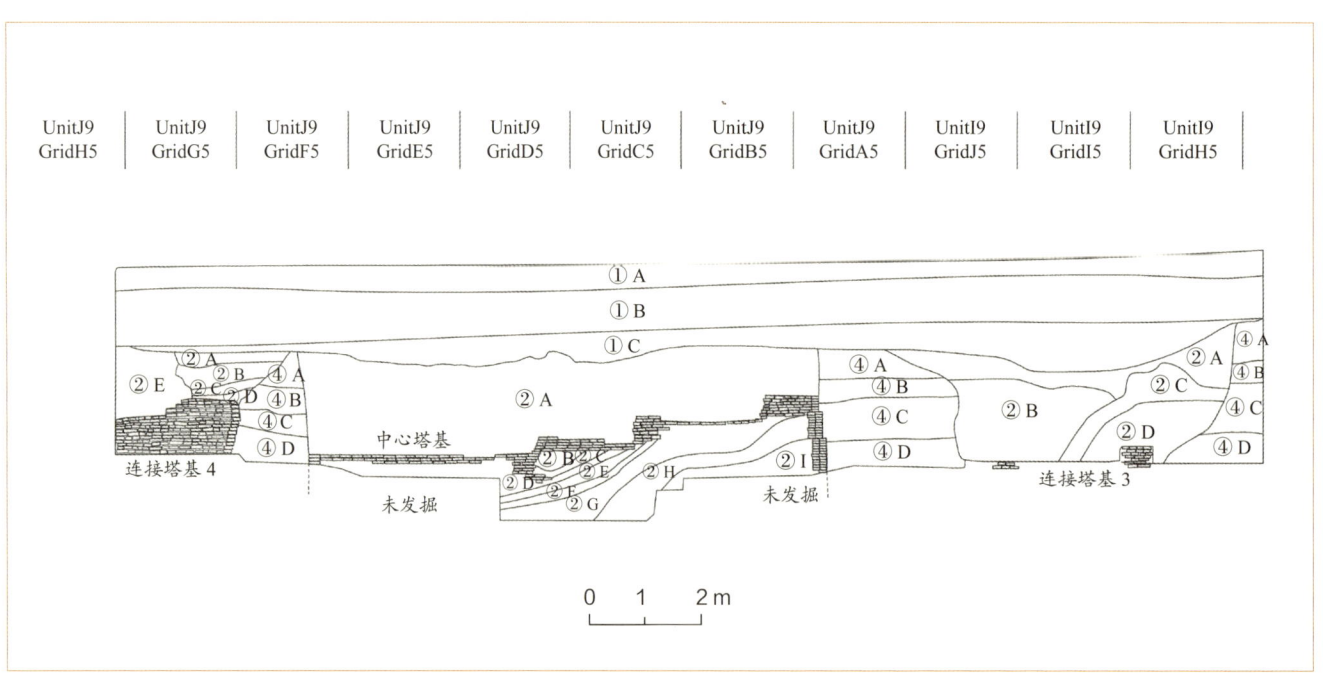

图2-13　UnitJ9GridH5、G5、F5、E5、D5、C5、B5、A5，UnitI9GridJ5、I5、H5 剖面图
Fig. 2-13　The section of UnitJ9GridH5, G5, F5, E5, D5, C5, B5, A5, UnitI9GridJ5, I5, H5

②D层：灰黄色粉沙黏土，含零星碎砖末，土质较疏松，略呈坡状，厚0.04—0.15米。

②E层：褐红色粉沙黏土，土质较紧密，厚0.96—1.26米，含较多陶片、少量碎砖块、石灰颗粒。

中部堆积：应为取中心塔基南部砖墙后，回填形成的堆积层。大部分砖墙已被掏空，上部尚保留部分墙体，厚2.26—2.92米，距地表最浅2.31米，最深3.33米。据土质土色可以分为9个小层。

②A层：褐红色粉沙黏土，土质较紧密，基本呈水平状分布，厚0.75—1.59米，含大量碎砖块、陶片、少量石块，还有多个大型树根，这些树根应是当时生长的，由此推测，在此层与①C层之间，应存在一个自然间隙期，时间为树木生长的时期。

②B层：棕褐色粉沙黏土，含零星砖末，土质较紧密，厚0—0.25米。

②C层：浅青灰色黏土，含少量碎砖末，土质较疏松，由西向东呈坡状堆积，厚0.11—0.21米。

②D层：褐红色粉沙黏土，含较多碎砖块，土质较紧密，由西向东呈坡状堆积，厚0.12—0.15米。

②E层：浅青灰色黏土，含零星碎砖末，土质较疏松，由西向东呈坡状堆积，厚0.11—0.22米。

②F层：深褐红色粉沙黏土，含较多碎砖块，土质较紧密，由西向东呈坡状堆积，厚0.12—0.18米。

②G层：浅灰褐色粉沙黏土，含零星碎砖块，土质较紧密，由西向东呈坡状堆积，厚0.32—0.56米。

②H层：浅褐红色粉沙黏土，含少量碎砖块，土质较紧密，由西向东呈坡状堆积，厚0.22—0.42米。

②I层：浅青褐色粉沙黏土，土质较疏松，由西向东呈坡状堆积，未发掘至底，厚0.18—0.61米。

西部堆积：应为取连接墙基3的墙砖后，回填形成的堆积层。厚1.28—1.85米，距地表最浅1.87米，最深2.38米。据土质土色可分为4个小层。

②A层：浅褐红色粉沙黏土，含较多碎砖块，土质较紧密，厚0.09—1.06米。

②B层：深褐红色粉沙黏土，含较多碎砖块，土质较紧密，厚1.02—1.43米。

②C层：灰黄色粉沙黏土，含极少量碎砖块，由西向东倾斜分布，厚0.22—0.66米。

②D层：浅红褐色粉沙黏土，含较多碎砖块，土质较紧密，基本水平状分布，厚0.35—1.06米。

④层：灰黄色黏土质粉沙，含有较多碎砖块，土质较疏松，基本呈水平状分布。这层土有许多水平层，且含碎砖块较多，较其他探方中大部分区域的④层土有一些区别，可能系修建砖墙后在不同墙体之间填土行为所致。据土质土色，可分为4个小层。

④A层：浅黄色黏土粉沙，含少量较大的碎砖块，土质较疏松，水平状分布，厚0.51米。

④B层：深灰黄色黏土粉沙，含少量较大的碎砖块，土质较疏松，水平状分布，厚0.41米。

④C层：灰黄色黏土质粉沙，含较多大块的碎砖，土质较紧密，东高西低，略呈坡状，厚0.72米。

④D层：灰黄灰青色黏土粉沙，含零星碎砖块，土质较疏松，东高西低，略呈坡状，未见底，厚0.5米。

④层下为⑥层，未作进一步发掘。

十三、UnitJ10GridD8、D7、D6、D5、D4、D3、D2、D1，UnitJ9GridD10、D9、D8、D7、D6、D5剖面

（图2-14；彩版2-8，3）

此为中心塔基南北向剖面。

①层：褐灰色粉沙黏土，土质较疏松，基本呈水平状分布于整个探方中，夹杂零星红砖碎末、陶片、纸屑等。根据土色的深浅可分为2个小层：

①A层：深灰褐色，西部略高，东部略低，厚0.45—0.55米，局部含有碎砖块，是现代居民的活动层。

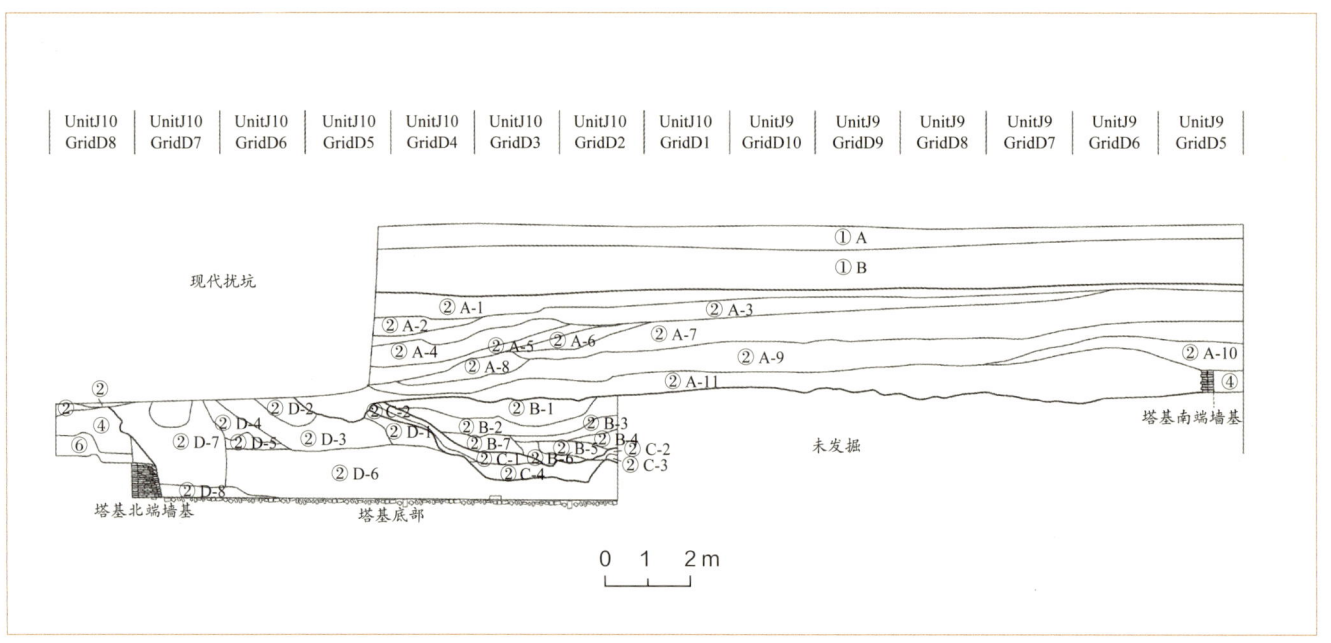

图 2-14　UnitJ10GridD8、D7、D6、D5、D4、D3、D2、D1，UnitJ9GridD10、D9、D8、D7、D6、D5 剖面图
Fig. 2-14　The section of UnitJ10GridD8, D7, D6, D5, D4, D3, D2, D1, UnitJ9GridD10, D9, D8, D7, D6, D5

①B层：浅灰褐色，厚0.92—1.14米，含极少量砖末和陶片。

②层：因位于塔基的中心部位，建筑基础最深，取砖后形成的坑也最深，回填层的堆积也相应更厚，与其他区域的②层相比，因在较长时间内处于一种低洼的状态，所以形成一些淤泥沉积。根据土质土色及形成原因，将其分为②A、②B、②C、②D 4个亚层，每个亚层内又形成了一些更小的层次。

②A层：褐色粉沙黏土，土质较紧密，为最后一次填满中心区域的低洼地带所形成的堆积，整体较为水平，但其中的一些小层可见由南向北呈坡状分布。厚2.28—2.7米，距地表最浅3.68米，最深4.03米。含有大量碎砖块、陶片、少量石制品残件。根据土质土色，可将②A层分为11个小层：

②A-1：深红褐色粉沙黏土，含大量碎砖块，北部较厚，南部较薄，厚0.11—0.7米。

②A-2：褐红色粉沙黏土，含大量碎砖块，由南向北坡状分布，厚0—0.41米。

②A-3：深灰褐色粉沙黏土，含少量碎砖块，由南向北呈坡状分布，厚0—0.41米。

②A-4：深棕褐色粉沙黏土，含大量碎砖块，由南向北呈坡状分布，厚0—0.56米。

②A-5：青灰色粉沙黏土，含极少量碎砖末，由南向北呈坡状分布，厚0—0.42米。

②A-6：浅红褐色坟山黏土，含少量碎砖末，由南向北呈坡状分布，厚0—0.39米。

②A-7：深灰褐色粉沙黏土，含少量碎砖块，南部较厚，略呈坡状，厚0—0.82米。

②A-8：棕褐色密集碎砖块层，由南向北呈坡状分布，厚0—0.49米。

②A-9：红褐色粉沙黏土，含少量碎砖块，略带坡状，厚0—0.72米。

②A-10：深青褐色粉沙黏土，含极少碎砖块，厚0—0.66米。

②A-11：红褐色粉沙黏土，含较多碎砖块，为水平状分布，厚0—1.2米。

②B层：棕褐色粉沙黏土，局部泛青，含有少量碎砖块，土质较疏松，大致由北向南呈坡状分布，与②A在整体上较为接近，但可能由于地处低洼，使该层土色变成近棕褐色。该层出土保

存较好的树根、树干、树叶、种子等植物遗存，也有少量楠竹和螺壳等。这些树根应是当时生长的，由此推测，在此层与②A层之间，存在一个自然间隙期，正是树木生长的时期，这反映了遗址在破坏之后，在较长时间内的形成过程。厚1.17—1.55米，距地表最浅5.21米，最深5.47米。根据土质土色的细微差异，将②B层分为7个小层：

②B-1：棕褐色，局部泛青，含较多碎砖块，厚0.35—0.65米。

②B-2：棕褐色，可见含大量黑色植物遗存和较多碎砖块，厚0.22—0.44米。

②B-3：浅棕褐色，厚0.12—0.37米。

②B-4：浅青褐色，含少量碎砖块，厚0.2—0.4米。

②B-5：深青褐色，含少量碎砖块，厚0.3—0.39米。

②B-6：深灰褐色，含较多碎砖块，厚0.13—0.25米。

②B-7：深黄褐色，含较多碎砖块，厚0.33—0.38米。

②C层：由灰色和黑色淤泥状条带构成的堆积，反映了一种静水环境下的水成沉积。此层较薄，厚0.38—0.61米，距地表最浅4.67米，最深5.85米，由北向南呈坡状分布。该层是取砖之后，较长时期保持低洼状态、因泥水积聚沉淀而成。据土质土色的差异，可将②C层分为4个小层：

②C-1：浅褐灰色淤泥条带，黏性强，由北向南呈坡状，厚0.13—0.27米。

②C-2：黑褐色淤泥条带，黏性强，含有较多植物腐殖物，由北向南呈坡状，厚0.02—0.18米。

②C-3：浅青色淤泥条带，土质松软，厚0.1—0.17米。

②C-4：浅灰色黏土，土质松软，含少量黑色植物腐殖物，与上层淤泥层及下部粉沙黏土层呈过渡状态，锅底状分布，厚0.24—0.5米。

②D层：浅黄褐色粉沙黏土，含有较多的碎砖块，是挖坑取砖后最初回填的堆积，出土少量陶片、树根等，主要可以分为两种性质的堆积，一种在靠近砖墙边缘处挖坑时破坏④层后就地填埋的泥土，土质土色与④层较为接近，但土色偏黄，较为疏松，且含少量砖块，主要分布在边缘；另一种为朝向中心部位倾斜的堆积，混杂有大量的碎砖块和回填土，土色偏浅红，这一部分填土由于中心低凹蓄水成塘的缘故，使得靠近"堤岸"部位浸染成浅青色，其余部分基本保持原来的土色。厚0.36—2.29米，距地表最浅4.15米，最深6.24米。据土质土色分为8个小层。

②D-1：黄褐带青色，黏性较大，含少量碎砖块，北高南低，厚0.21—0.55米。

②D-2：浅褐黄色，含较多碎砖末，土质较疏松，厚0.4—0.64米。

②D-3：浅黄色黏土，靠南部分被浸染成青色，含零星碎砖，土质较疏松，北高南低呈坡状，厚0.58—0.85米。

②D-4：褐红色粉沙黏土，含大量碎砖块，北高南低，土质较疏松，厚0.24—0.69米。

②D-5：浅褐黄色黏土，含零星碎砖块，土质较疏松，分布较水平，厚0.17—0.38米。

②D-6：黄褐带浅红色粉沙黏土，含大量细小砖块，土质较紧密，厚0.46—1.26米。

②D-7：浅褐黄色粉沙黏土，含零星碎砖块，为扰动后的原④层，土质较紧密，厚1.5—1.98米。

②D-8：黄褐带青色粉沙黏土，含较多细小碎砖块，土质较疏松，厚0—0.24米。

④层：青褐色粉沙黏土，局部含有较多碎砖末，土质较紧密，北高南低，北薄南厚，厚0.5—1.1米，距地表最浅4.72米，最深5.24米，根据土色的细微差异，可分出一些亚层。

⑥层：青黑色粉沙黏土，含少量残砖，土质较紧密，局部含红色砖末薄层带，厚0.2—0.7米，距地表最浅5.27米，最深5.35米，出土有较多陶片。该层只作局部发掘，未至底部。

第三节

Section 3
Analysis of Stratigraphy Radiocarbon Dates

地层年代的 ^{14}C 数据分析

我们选取 29 个样本，送交美国贝塔（Beta）实验室，因 3 个样本数量不足，实际测试 26 个（附录 1）。标本的编号为原始地层号（有些有附注），有些层位后来有些调整，以下列最后确定的地层为准。各个数据的树轮校正皆为 ±30 年。

根据最后确定的地层，现将这批样本分为四组。

第 1 组：④层，根据检测的结果，共得 3 个数据。

SAMPLE：12，J11G—D3 ⑤：840AD（原始标本附注：取自④层下部，可能是早期扰乱土，标本并不代表地层形成的年代）

SAMPLE：19，K10E3 ④：800AD

SAMPLE：20，K9J9 ④：890AD

第 2 组：⑤层，共得 8 个数据。

SAMPLE：13，K10I4 ⑤：960AD（原始标本附注：地层性质主要为第一期的生活堆积）

SAMPLE：14，K9J9 ⑤：830AD（原始标本附注：地层性质主要为第一期的生活堆积）

SAMPLE：15，K10J3 ⑤：910AD（原始标本附注：地层性质主要为第一期的生活堆积）

SAMPLE：17，K10I1J2 ⑤：800AD（原始标本附注：地层性质主要为第一期的生活堆积）

SAMPLE：18，K10I3 ⑤：950AD（原始标本附注：地层性质主要为第一期的生活堆积）

SAMPLE：21，L10E5F6 ④：860AD（原始标本附注：地层性质主要为第一期的生活堆积）

SAMPLE：28，L8G3H4 ⑤：950AD（原始标本附注：为⑤层及其下纯黄土层）

SAMPLE：29，L8G3H4 ⑤：890AD（原始标本附注：为⑤层及其下纯黄土层）

第 3 组：⑥层，共得 12 个数据。

SAMPLE：1，I11G3 ④：830AD（原始标本附注：取自⑥层表面）

SAMPLE：2，I11G3 ④：880AD（原始标本附注：取自⑥层表面）

SAMPLE：3，I11G2—G3 ④：870AD（原始标本附注：取自⑥层内部）

SAMPLE：4，I11G2—G3 ⑦：780AD（原始标本附注：取自⑥层内部）

SAMPLE：5，J11G—A4 ⑤：810AD（原始标本附注：取自⑥层表面）

SAMPLE：6，J11G—A4 ⑦（？）：840AD（原始标本附注：取自⑥层表面）

SAMPLE：22，L10G—B5：870AD（原始标本附注：取自密集的烧土层，应与建筑行为有关，地层相当于⑥层）

SAMPLE：23，L10G—B5：820AD（原始标本附注：取自密集的烧土层，应与建筑行为有关，地层相当于⑥层）

SAMPLE：24，L10G—B5：790AD（原始标本附注：取自密集的烧土层，应与建筑行为有关，地层相当于⑥层）

SAMPLE：25，L10G—B5：770AD（原始标本附注：取自密集的烧土层，应与建筑行为有关，地层相当于⑥层）

SAMPLE：26，L10B4：780AD（原始标本附注：取自大瓮内上部，土层可能受到干扰）

SAMPLE：27，L10B4：860AD（原始标本附注：取自大瓮内下部）

第 4 组：⑦层，共得 3 个数据。

SAMPLE：7，I11G2—G3 ⑧：880AD（原始标本附注：相当于⑦层）

SAMPLE：9，I11G2—G3 ⑧：780AD（原始标本附注：相当于⑦层）

SAMPLE：10，I10G9 ⑧：800AD（原始标本附注：相当于⑦层）

分析上述数据，可以看出：⑥、⑦层之间变

化不大；关键性的变化发生在⑤⑥层之间，这是关键的地层叠压证据；从表面上看，④层的数据有点偏早，但分析了它的成因是取早期的堆积筑填新建筑的地基，就可以理解了它的合理性，这也与发掘时所推测的情况一致。需要说明的是，影响 ^{14}C 数据的因素很多，如树龄的大小，数据本身也有一个上下30年的摆动空间，所以，它所提供的只是一个相对准确的框架性年代序列，在分期中使用了具体到年份的绝对年代，显然带有很强的推测性，有些则是依据当地历史背景所做的设定，如第二期的下限公元1223年。这些数据中，年代上限的 ^{14}C 标本较为丰富，年代也比较清晰；下限因为没有采集到理想的标本，尚缺。

About 29 charcoal samples were selected and sent to the Beta laboratory in the United States for radiometric dates, but due to the three samples being too poor in carbon content, only 26 samples were actually submitted for analyses (Appendix 1). The serial numbers of the specimen are the original stratigraphic context (some with the notes), some of which have been corrected according to our later analysis.

The charcoal samples can be divided into the following four groups corresponding to the layers. All the dendrological calibration resolution is ±30 years.

Group 1: The Layer 4, three radiometric results are obtained.

Sample 12: J11G – D3, 840AD (The original note: collected from the lower part of Layer 4; possibly from the earlier disturbed soil; the date of the specimen does not represent the formation age of the layer itself).

Sample 19: K10E3 ④, 800AD.

Sample 20: K9J9 ④, 890AD.

Group 2: Layer 5, eight radiometric data are obtained:

Sample 13: K10I4 ⑤, 960AD (The original note: the nature of the layer is the everyday living remains of the first period).

Sample 14: K9J9 ⑤, 830AD (The original note: the nature of the layer is the everyday living remains of the first period).

Sample 15: K10J3 ⑤, 910AD (The original note: the nature of the layer is the everyday livelihood remains of the first period).

Sample 17: K10I1J2 ⑤, 800AD (The original note: the nature of the layer is the everyday living remains of the first period).

Sample 18: K10I3 ⑤, 950AD (The original note: the nature of the layer is the everyday living remains of the first period).

Sample 21: L10E5F6 ④, 860AD (The original note: the nature of the layer is the everyday living remains of the first period).

Sample 28: L8G3H4 ⑤, 950AD (The original note: the Layer 5 and beneath yellowish layer).

Sample 29: L8G3H4 ⑤, 890AD (The original note: the Layer 5 and the yellowish layer beneath it).

Group 3: Layer 6, twelve radiometric dates are obtained:

Sample 1: I11G3 ④, 830AD (The original note: collected from the surface of Layer 6).

Sample 2: I11G3 ④, 880AD (The original note: collected from the surface of Layer 6).

Sample 3: I11G2 – G3④, 870AD (The original note: collected from the Layer 6).

Sample 4: I11G2–G3⑦, 780AD (The original note: collected from the Layer 6).

Sample 5: J11G–A4 ⑤, 810AD (The original note: collected from the surface of Layer 6).
Sample 6: J11G–A4 ⑦, 840AD (The original note: collected from the surface of Layer 6).
Sample 22: L10G – B5, 870AD (The original note: collected from the densely distributed burnt earthen layer, equal to Layer 6, probably be related to construction behavior).
Sample 23: L10G – B5, 820AD (The original note: collected from the densely distributed burnt earthen layer, equal to Layer 6, probably be related to construction behavior).
Sample 24: L10G – B5, 790AD (The original note: collected from the densely distributed burnt earthen layer, equal to Layer 6, probably be related to construction behavior).
Sample 25: L10G – B5, 770AD (The original note: collected from the densely distributed burnt earthen layer, equal to Layer 6, probably be related to construction behavior).
Sample 26: L10B4: 780AD (The original note: collected from the upper part sediment inside of the urn, but may be disturbed).
Sample 27: L10B4, 860AD (The original note: collected from the lower part sediment inside of the urn).
Group 4: Layer 7, three radiometric dates are obtained:
Sample 7: I11G2 – G3⑧, 880AD (The original note: it is equivalent to Layer 7).
Sample 9: I11G2 – G3⑧, 780AD (The original note: it is equivalent to Layer 7).
Sample 10: I10G9⑧, 800AD (The original note: it is equivalent to Layer 7).

Based on the above dates, some conclusions can be given as follows: there is little difference between Layer 6 and Layer 7, but the crucial changes happen between Layer 5 and Layer 6, showing the key stratigraphic evidence. The age of Layer 4 is a bit younger than that of the under layers, probably because the soils used for the foundation are carried from outside and earlier deposits are mixed during this process. However, the radiocarbon dates are consistent with our speculation about the cause of Layer 4. It should also be noted that there are many factors that affect the accuracy, such as the age of the trees and the errors of the dating itself, so it provides us only a relatively accurate framework of the chronological sequence. It is obviously with a strong speculation and uncertainty that we use the absolute dates for the periodization of the site. For example, we use the year of 1223 as the lower limit age of the second period by referring to the historical background of ancient Bangladesh. In general, the ^{14}C samples for the upper limit are abundant and the dates obtained are relatively clear, while the ideal samples for lower limit are insufficient. In conclusion, the above data, including some cultural features' age and stage attribution, have to be verified by further archaeological excavation.

彩版 2-1
地层及灰坑 H2
Color Plate 2-1
The layers and ash pit (H2)

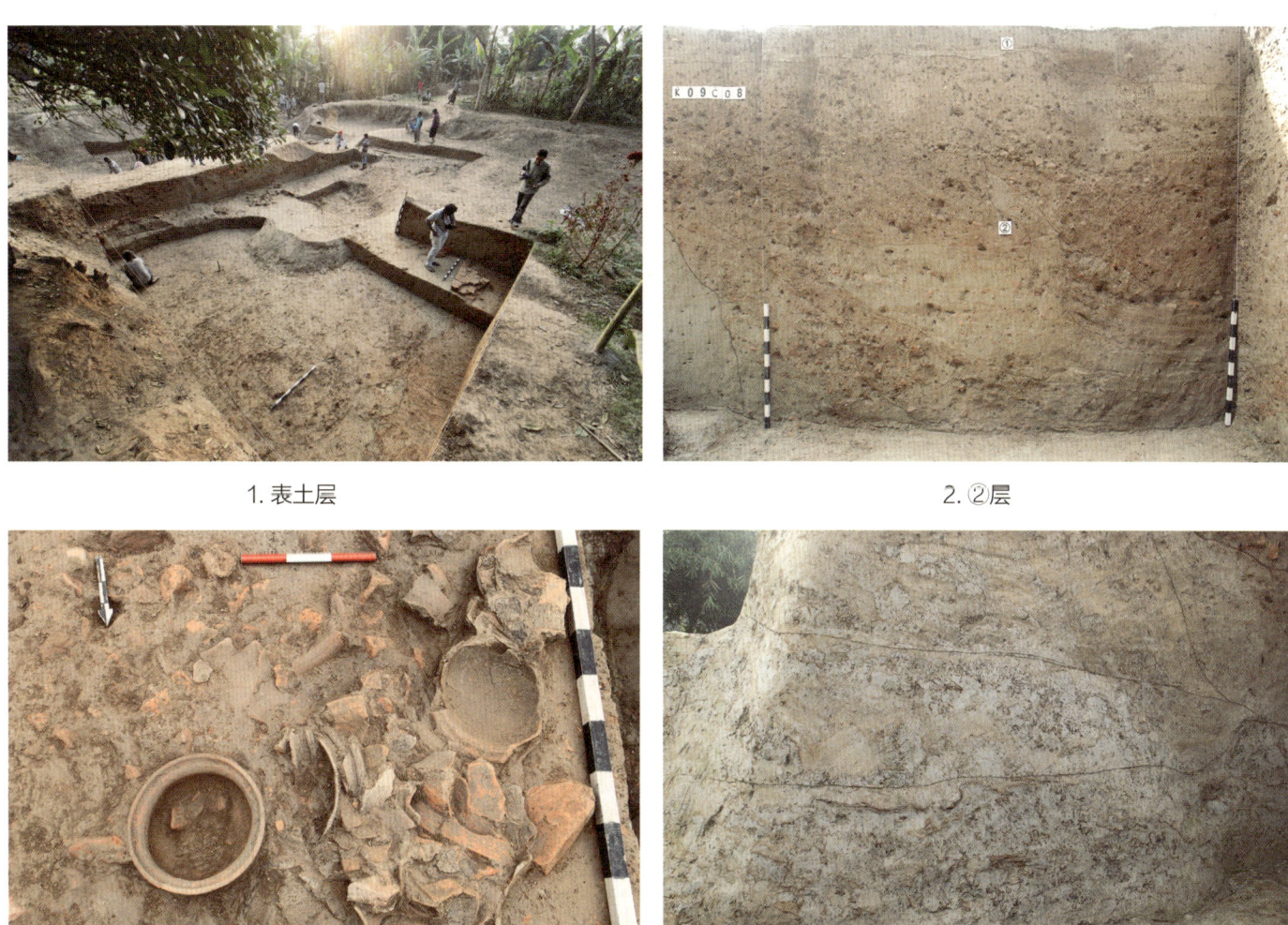

1. 表土层

2. ②层

3. ②层下灰坑H2

4. ③层

彩版2-2
地层及出土陶器
Color Plate 2-2
The layers and unearthed potteries

1. ④层

2. ⑤层

3. ⑥层下陶器

4. ⑥、⑦层

彩版2-3 地层剖面
Color Plate 2-3
Stratigraphic section

1. UnitJ10GridA10、B10、C10、D10、E10、E9剖面
The section of UnitJ10GridA10, B10, C10, D10, E10, E9

2. UnitJ11GridE1、D1、C1、B1、A1剖面
The section of UnitJ11GridE1, D1, C1, B1, A1

3. UnitJ11GridE6、E5、E4、E3、E2、E1剖面
The section of UnitJ11GridE6, E5, E4, E3, E2, E1

彩版2-4
UnitI10GridG8、G9、G10，
UnitI11GridG1、G2、G3、
G4、G5剖面

Color Plate 2-4
The section of UnitI10GridG8, G9, G10, UnitI11GridG1, G2, G3, G4, G5

彩版 2-5
UnitK9GridA8、B8、C8、D8、E8、F8、G8、H8 剖面
Color Plate 2-5
The section of UnitK9GridA8, B8, C8, D8, E8, F8, G8, H8

彩版2-6
地层剖面
Color Plate 2-6
Stratigraphic section

1. UnitL9GridA9、B9、C9、D9、E9、F9剖面
The Section of UnitL9GridA9, B9, C9, D9, E9, F9

2. UnitL8GridF2、F3、F4剖面
The section of UnitL8GridF2, F3, F4

彩版2-7
UnitK7GridI10，UnitK8GridI1-I10，UnitK9GridI1-I7剖面
Color Plate 2-7
The section of UnitK7GridI10, UnitK8GridI1-I10 and UnitK9GridI1-I7

彩版2-8
地层剖面
Color Plate 2-8
Stratigraphic section

1. UnitH10GridJ5-J1，UnitI9GridA10-A3剖面
The section of UnitH10GridJ5-J1, UnitI9GridA10-A3

2. UnitJ9GridH5、G5、F5、E5、D5、C5、B5、A5，UnitI9GridJ5、I5、H5剖面
The section of UnitJ9GridH5, G5, F5, E5, D5, C5, B5, A5, UnitI9GridJ5, I5, H5

3. UnitJ10GridD8、D7、D6、D5、D4、D3、D2、D1，UnitJ9GridD10、D9、D8、D7、D6、D5剖面
The section of UnitJ10GridD8, D7, D6, D5, D4, D3, D2, D1, UnitJ9GridD10, D9, D8, D7, D6, D5

Chapter

第三章

Cultural Features

遗 迹

纳提什瓦
Nateshwar

第一节 Section 1
The First Period Cultural Remains
第一期遗迹

第一期的遗迹包括早段、中段和晚段三个阶段，目前的发现以中段的遗存为主（图 3-1；彩版 3-1）。

一、早段遗迹

早段遗迹包括：神殿 1 前期遗迹、房屋 6、房屋 7、道路 1、道路 2、道路 3、道路 5、浴室和排水沟等。

（一）神殿 1

神殿 1 位于遗址的东北部，方向 5°，分布于 UnitL9GirdA9–F10 和 UnitL10GridA1–F4 等探方内。根据建筑的墙体之间的接触关系，神殿 1 可以分为前、后两个建筑阶段。

前期神殿保留的建筑基础，平面形状大致呈方形，相邻两边夹角呈直角。东西长 9.5、南北宽 9.4、残高 0.5 米。残存的基础砖块外壁砌筑不规整，部分使用火砖。在其北墙中部还残存部分门道遗迹，向外凸出，大体呈长方形，东西长 2.7、南北宽 2、残高约 1 米，但由于后期的破坏及叠压，具体分布及结构还不清楚。

现存建筑主要是后期阶段的神殿。主体仍建造在前期阶段的基础之上，平面形状呈规整的方形，边长均为 9 米。大部分已被破坏，保留部分外墙及基础部分，西南角和东南角墙体保存较好，

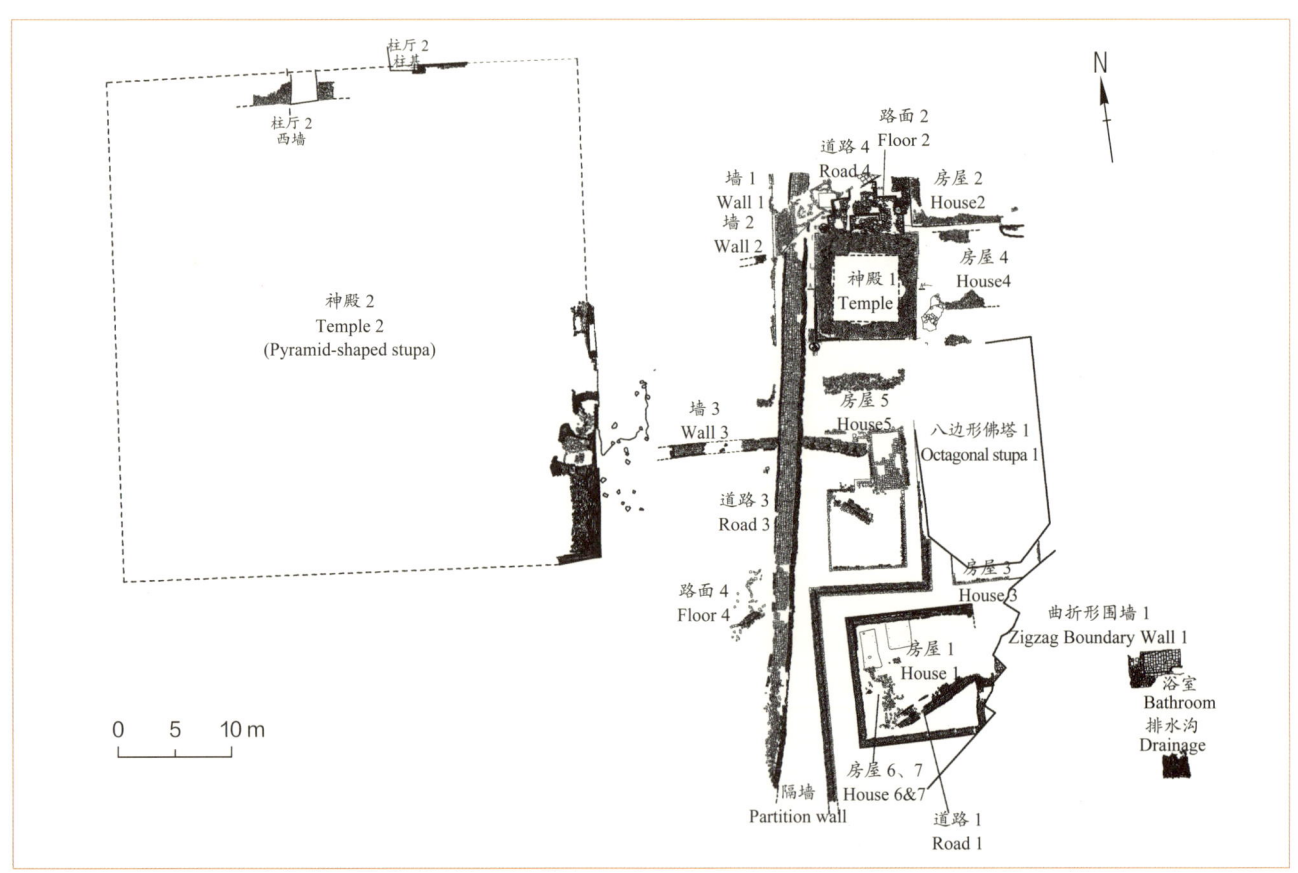

图 3-1　纳提什瓦遗址第一期遗迹总平面图
Fig. 3-1　The master plan of the cultural remains of the first Period at Nateshwar site

北部门道也保存较好，墙体宽 1.5 米，残存最高处 2.8 米。室内东西长 5.8、南北宽 5.6 米。东、南、西三面外壁设计非常精巧，由几排弧状砖叠涩而成，外凸内收，另有两道装饰砖砌成的精致花卉图案，显示出整个建筑在遗址中的重要性。在后期佛殿的北部有明显的门道建筑结构，由北向南，在东、西两侧墙壁以连续三次直角转折，最终与神殿北墙相连，显示门道内部空间由神殿中轴线向外连续扩展二次。在门道东侧的砖面上发现三个半圆形柱洞，直径 35—40 厘米，残深 30—50 厘米，推测门道原属于有屋顶的柱廊结构。

在后期神殿的四角，可能各安放有圜底大瓮，现发现两处，瓮 1 位于 UnitL10GridB4 内，瓮 2 位于 UnitL9GridB9 内，两者皆一半掩埋在地面以下，瓮 1 内放置了数十件陶器。推测它们皆是神殿存在期间放置在屋檐下，作为日常使用的。

神殿 1 开口于⑤层下，打破⑥层，与道路 3 同时，建筑年代属于第一期（图 3-2、3-3、3-4；彩版 3-2、3-3、3-4、3-5、3-6）。

（二）房屋 6

房屋 6 分布于 UnitL8GridC2–C7、D2–D7、E2–E7、F2–F8、G2–G8、H2–H8、I2–I8 等探方内，叠压在房屋 7 之上，部分叠压在房屋 1 之下，未能发掘，其整体的形状结构不甚清楚。根据清理，其南北长 9 米、东西长度不清。

房屋 6 在房屋 7 之上铺垫一层青灰色黏土，厚度 20 厘米，水平分布，在房屋 6 局部可见 3 块经过处理的地面。分别编为 A、B、C 三处。A 处位于房屋 6 北侧中部，平面呈长方形，东西长 2.1、南北宽 1.9、厚 0.1 米，为青灰色黏土夯筑，局部边缘有一单线竖砌砖块围绕。发现小型柱洞 6 个，呈圈状分布在 A 处地面边缘约 20 厘米处，柱洞直径约 5 厘米，大小相近，深度在 10 至 24 厘米之间，根据柱洞大小，推测这是一简易的窝棚式建筑。B 处地面位于房屋 6 西北部，平面呈长方形，南北长 3.4、东西宽 1.6、厚 0.1 米。为青灰色黏土夯筑，局部边缘有一单线竖砌砖块围绕，发现柱洞 12 个，多为小型柱洞，直径约 5 厘米，大小相近，深度在 12 至 42 厘米之间，部分柱洞内保存有木柱外壳。在南侧有一较大柱洞，直径为 30、深 25 厘米，坑内为灰褐色填土。推测也是一简易的窝棚式建筑。C 处地面位于房屋 6 西侧南部，平面呈椭圆形，南北长 2.6、东西宽 1.65、厚 0.06 米。由青灰色黏土拌以粒径在 1.5 厘米左右的砖粒夯筑，表面平整。推测这是一种有意的防潮处理。

在房屋 6 西北部出土了炭化米粒、植物皮壳、指甲以及鱼类、家禽、老鼠等多种动物骨骼，推测房屋 6 应作为食堂的用途。根据房屋 6 发现的柱洞都较小，推测可能是一种临时性的房屋建筑。

根据地层关系，房屋 6 应属于早期早段（见图 3-9；彩版 3-7，1、2）。

（三）房屋 7

房屋 7 分布于 UnitL8GridC2–C7、D2–D7、E2–E7、F2–F8、G2–G8、H2–H8、I2–I8 等探方内，开口于房屋 6 之下，打破道路 1。由于房屋 7 叠压在房屋 1、房屋 6 之下，只能做局部清理，其形状结构不甚清晰。根据显露的室内面，其东西向长度至少为 9 米，南北向清理长度 2 米。

房屋东侧有一道南北向墙体，清理长度 5.6 米、宽度 0.4 米、高度 0.28 米。室内面由一层红砖平铺。在墙体中部西侧，有一疑似柱础痕迹。柱础直径 0.7 米、厚 6 厘米，由一层直径约 10 厘米的小砖块铺筑。沿房屋 7 东墙东侧，有一宽度约 1.5 米的砖层分布，砖块多呈西高东低，推测是将房屋 7 东墙砖体拆除后简易铺垫，作为房屋 6 的铺垫层。

根据房屋 7 所在的位置，推测其有可能作为食堂功能。根据地层关系，房屋 7 应属于早期早段（见图 3-9；彩版 3-7，3）。

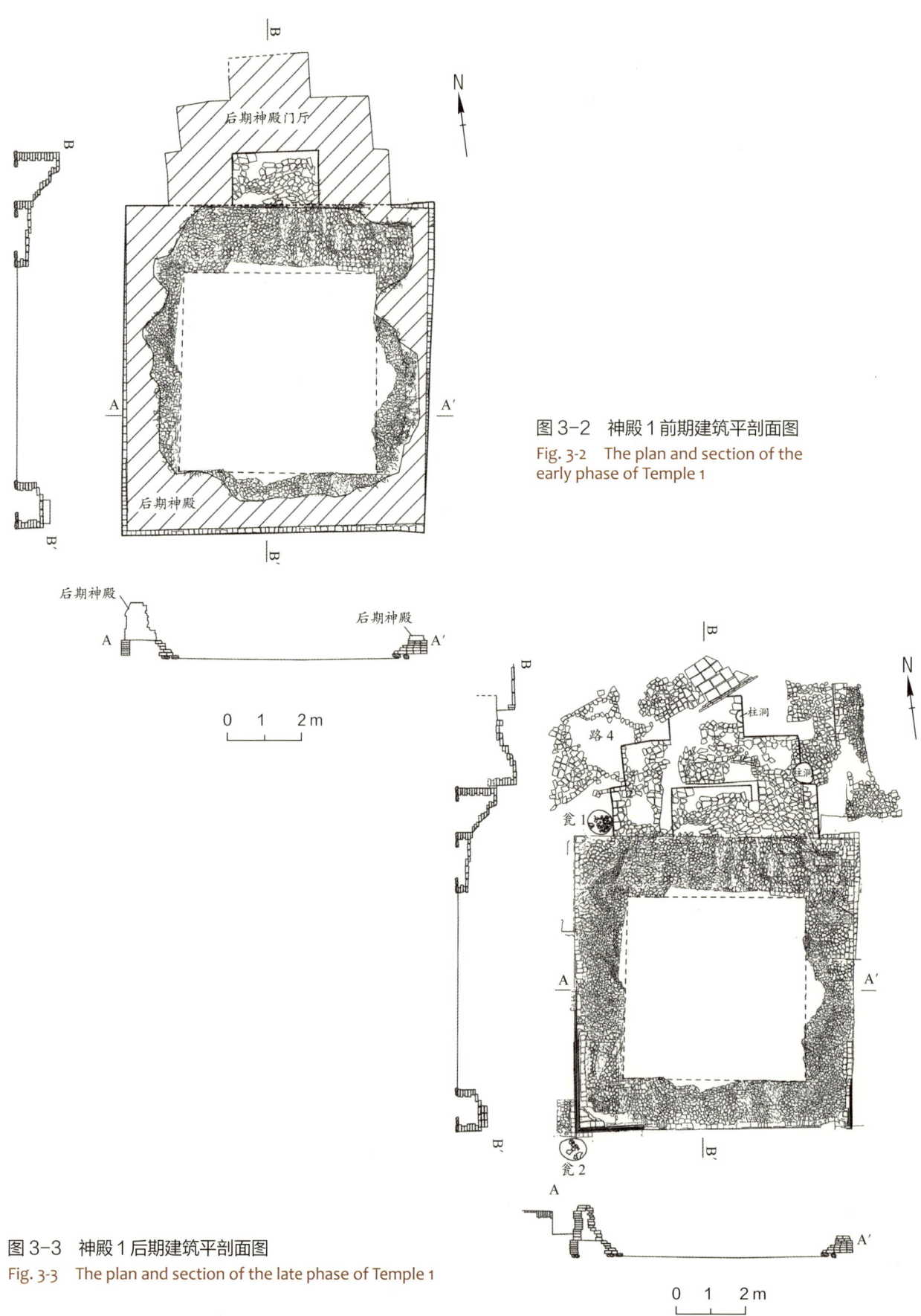

图 3-2　神殿 1 前期建筑平剖面图
Fig. 3-2　The plan and section of the early phase of Temple 1

图 3-3　神殿 1 后期建筑平剖面图
Fig. 3-3　The plan and section of the late phase of Temple 1

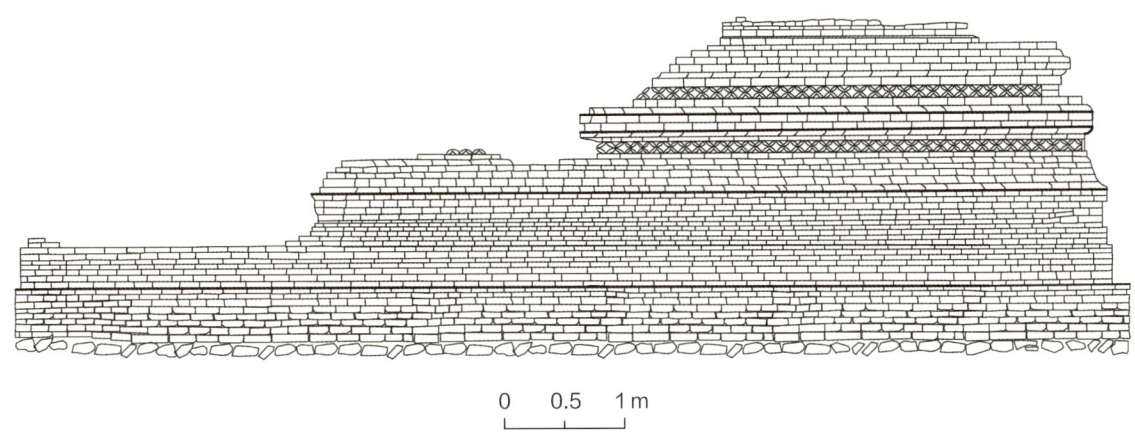

图 3-4　神殿 1 西壁立面图
Fig. 3-4　The elevation of the western wall of Temple 1

（四）道路 1

位于遗址东南角，揭露部分分布于 UnitL8 GridE2、E3、F2、F3、G4、H4、H5 内。2014、2017 两个年度进行了考古发掘。方向 245°。揭露部分长 9.5、宽 1.5、厚 0.2 米，保存基本完整，东北部被后期破坏，情况不明，西南方向继续延伸。两侧三层竖砖，中间两层竖砖将道路平均分成两半，其余部分均为平砖铺砌。在道路西南部（房屋 1 西南角）发现大量砖块叠压在其上，可能系同时期遗迹，在修建房屋 1 时拆毁并作为地基部分。

道路 1 叠压在房屋 1 之下，推测为第一期早段（见图 3-9；彩版 3-7，4）。

（五）道路 2

分布于 UnitL8GridI8 探方内，仅残存小块区域，长约 1 米，宽 0.5 米，方向为 90°。由一层砖平铺砌造而成，但由于保存状况很差，详细情况不明。道路 2 部分也叠压在房屋 1 之下，推测应为第一期早段。

（六）道路 3

位于遗址东部，为早期遗址中一条连接不同建筑间的重要通道，其两侧分布有同时期的建筑和辅道。2014—2015 年度中孟联合发掘时首次发现，2015—2016、2017—2018 经过两个季度的扩方发掘。已发掘部分位于 UnitK8GridJ1、J2、J3、J4、J5、J6、J7、J8、J9、J10，UnitL8GridA8、A9，UnitK9GridJ1、J2、J3、J4、J5、J6、J7、J8、J9、J10，UnitL9GridA1、A2、A3、A4、A5、A6、A7、A8、A9、A10，UnitK10GridJ1、J2、J3、J4、J5、J6，UnitL10GridA1、A2、A3、A4、A5、A6 内，两端分别进入北部和南部未发掘区。

道路 3 保存完整，平面形状呈规则的条带形，东西两侧近平行，方向为 10°。已发掘部分长 53.4 米，宽 2.2 米，厚约 0.25 米。道路由两侧的竖向砌砖和中间的平铺砌砖共同构成。其中，每一行平铺的砖块一般为 8—10 块，西侧砌砖均为 4 层（宽 0.21 米），东侧砌砖一般为 9 层（宽 0.53 米），但在 UnitL9GridA5 以南增加成 12 层（宽 0.65 米）。在 UnitL9GridA5、B5 与道路 6 相交处，外侧砖块由纵向设计改成横向和横斜竖交错铺砌。

路面可见由 2 层铺砖构成，上层铺砖较为整齐，地面较平整，中心部位略高，两侧略低，横剖面略呈凸弧状；下层铺砖因大部分叠压在上层砖下，具体情况不明，从局部观察，较上层粗糙和稀疏，主要用于路面的基础。路面砖块之间形成的砖缝与道路的方向一致，所用砖大小、形状规格并不统一，部分残砖也被使用。完整砖块的最小尺寸为24厘米×12.5厘米，最大尺寸为34厘米×24.6厘米。道路3下部在局部可见叠压着早期道路，建筑方式与上部相似，但由于揭露面积很有限，详细情况不明，该道路可能因延续时间长，历经多次维修。

道路3开口于⑤层下，北部被道路4打破，在中段东侧与道路6呈丁字形相接。道路3与其东侧神殿1的前期墙基基本平行，相距30厘米；与神殿1的后期墙基不甚平行，相距62—97厘米。从设计角度考虑，道路3可能与神殿1前期同时修建，当神殿1后期扩建时，该道路仍在使用，并与神殿周围分布的地面2共同构成神殿1的活动地面（图3-5，3-6；彩版3-8，3-9）。

（七）道路5

位于UnitI11GridH2内。2015年1月，在此挖解剖沟时发现，距地表深度5米。仅揭露出东西方向0.4米，路宽0.6米，厚0.25米，中部有两道砖竖砌，两侧有2层平铺砖，方向180°，开口于⑥层下，打破⑦层。推测这是一条东西向的道路遗迹，路面正是⑦层的表面，年代应为遗址的第一期早段。

（八）浴室和排水沟

浴室位于UnitM8GridE5、F5内。东墙、西墙和南墙大部分被破坏，北墙部分被发现。平面形状呈长方形，东西长7米，南北宽2.8米。北墙仅揭露部分；西墙长2.8米，宽0.8米，残剩21层砖块，高0.99米。在北墙上距离地面以上20厘米处有一个长宽均为30厘米的壁龛。南墙长7米，基本被后期完全破坏，残高0.61米。浴池内建有很好的砖铺地面，东西长3.45米，南北宽1.8米。所用砖块包括完整砖块以及用于填充缝隙的切割砖块，整个地面砖块的构造设计相当讲究。

排水沟位于UnitM8GridG1、H1内。北部基本被破坏，南部仅部分保留，发掘仅揭露这个遗迹的很少一部分。已揭露排水沟包括两侧南北向的砖墙和中间宽0.5米的砖铺水沟，砖墙残存宽1—1.2米，水沟底部砖块以人字形铺造，应用于浴室的排水（图3-7；彩版3-10）。

二、中段遗迹

中段遗迹包括：神殿1后期遗迹（内容在早段提及）、神殿2、道路3（延用早段）、隔墙、房屋1、房屋2、房屋3、房屋4、房屋5、墙1、墙2、墙3、路面2、路面4。

（一）神殿2

神殿2位于遗址的中部，方向5°。2017年揭露部分为建筑的东墙和南墙东段，分布于UnitK8GridA10，B10，UnitK9GridA1–A10、B1–B10，UnitK10GridA1、A2、A3等探方内。北墙原为2015年度发掘揭露的墙体，2017年的发掘证实其应为该神殿的北墙部分，分布于UnitI10GridG9、H9、I9、G10、H10、I10、J10，UnitI11GridI1，以及UnitJ11GridD1、D2等探方内。东墙的南端保存较好，北端仅存基部，全长43米，南墙东段揭露长3.9米，北墙揭露长达19米。建筑的整体被十字形中心神殿破坏，其下或许还有局部残存，但未作勘探。从东壁剖面图中，可以看到神殿2被柱厅4东墙基和连接墙基4的填土破坏的情况。

从残存的东墙的剖面上看，墙体可分为两部分，下部墙体与墙基相连，墙基宽度为1.7米，底砖距地表深度5.1米，下部叠砌比较杂乱，上部有10块砖叠砌整齐，高约0.5米，外侧与外墙壁面齐平。下部墙体内侧不整齐，与内部地面或建筑结构的结合部，目前尚不清晰，宽度约为1.7米，上部墙体向中心倾斜上升，从已揭露的剖面看，墙体的宽度约为4.3米。

从东墙外壁地面以上的墙体观察，自下而

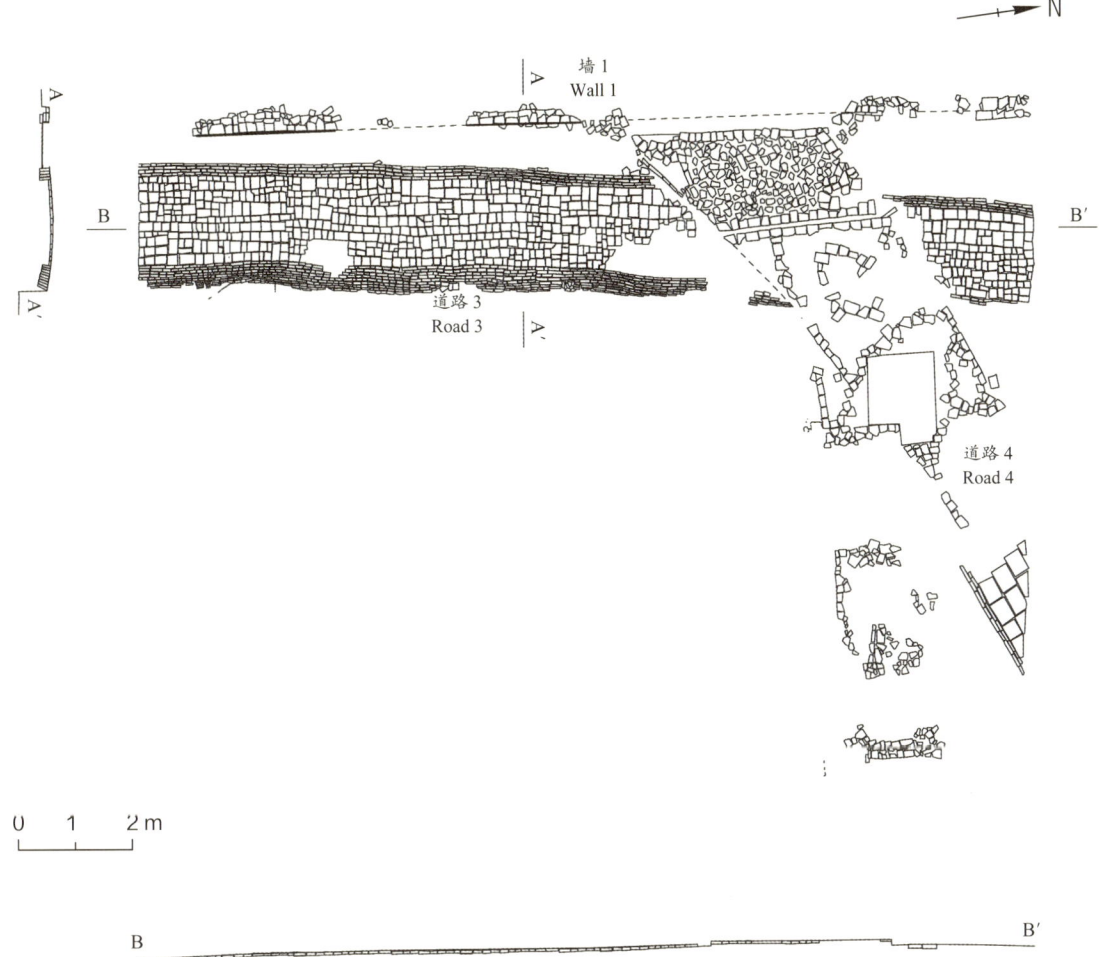

图 3-5　道路 3 北段、道路 4、墙 1 平剖面图
Fig. 3-5　The plan and section of the northern part of Road 3, Road 4 and Wall 1

图 3-6　道路 3 中段平剖面图
Fig. 3-6　The plan and section of the middle part of Road 3

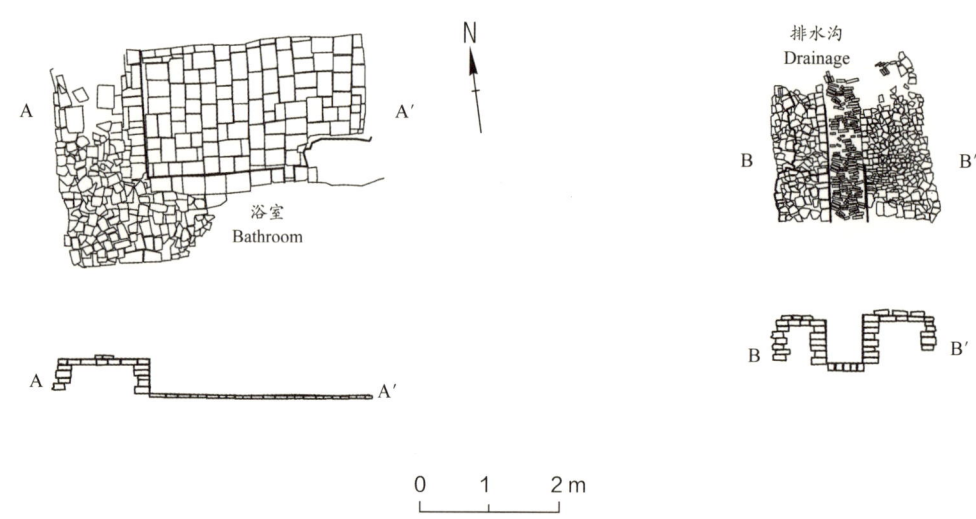

图 3-7　浴室及排水沟平剖面图
Fig. 3-7　The plan and section of bathroom and drainage

上，底部是由14层砖垂直平砌，高0.8米，其上则是用斜侧面砖砌成，保存最高处残存30层砖，残高1.6米，再上部的建筑结构不清，但从残砖中，多见斜侧面砖，从墙体的斜向上升趋势，坡度为53度。东墙中部外壁砌成几道凹凸或斜角，结合东墙的中部外侧墙体上有一些起棱和嵌入式结构，也许与相关的附属设施有关。

北墙残存东、西两段，柱厅2的西墙基和柱基1叠压、打破北墙西段，并将其作为建筑的基础。西段平面呈长方形，西端未发掘到头，发掘部分长7.4米，最宽处1.9米，最窄处0.66米。表面最高点地面以下2.7米，最低点地面以下5.3米，保存高度为2.6米。从南侧墙面观察，剖面分为4个层级，最低部为一层厚约20—30厘米的不规则形火砖斜砌，火砖之上有一层很薄的红色砖末层，厚约3—5厘米；其上为19层砖平铺，高度0.9米；其上又有9层砖平铺，略向外伸出墙体，高度0.3米；最上面31层砖，略向外伸出，高度1.4米。墙体使用砖的形制、大小不一，绝大部分为薄砖，厚度为4厘米，少量厚度为7厘米。值得注意的是，墙体北部有④G层，该层含有大量的倾斜砖体，这些倾斜砖的厚度大部分在3.5—4厘米，与神殿2北墙的用砖尺寸一致，可能是拆除北墙的砖体作为④层最底层的铺垫层。墙体的北侧由于被第二期遗迹所叠压，未能清理，目前清理的部分是北墙的南侧，大部分应是墙基部分，同时期室内地面情况不清。北墙东段与西段相隔7.6米，东段残长2.1米，残高0.7米，局部有15层砖平铺砌筑。北侧面的砖体呈现出一段规整的斜面，显然是出露于地表的墙体部分，墙体往下还有延伸，从目前解剖的迹象分析，外墙露出光洁墙面时，内侧未见光洁封面，从东墙和北墙保存的顶部说明，神殿2是一个带有巨大厚墙的实心建筑，也许在中心部位，存在一个面积不太大的方形空间，作为神殿的神圣中心。

根据这个时期神殿的一般性情况，推测整体为正方形，建筑内部可能是一个方形的空间，也可能是支撑塔顶的复杂的建筑结构，目前尚不能确定。此外，也许还有门厅或台阶一类的附属建筑，但目前发掘面积有限，也不能确定。

建筑砖体的形制、大小不一，最大的完整砖30厘米×18.7厘米，最小的完整砖21厘米×12.5厘米，砖块之间以灰黄色粉沙质黏土勾缝。在清理建筑东侧地面时发现，堆积中的残砖呈从西向东的倾倒状，应是修建第二期十字形中心神殿时，将神殿2的高耸部分平整所致，堆积中还散落着各种块石，主要为个体较大的河流砾石，岩性多为粗砂岩或石英砂岩，大部分可见到自然砾石面，但皆有一侧凿成平整面，可能是放置在建筑上部使用的，也有部分方形，其中一件可能是造像的基座。

神殿2叠压在④层之下，也被十字形中心神殿部分建筑墙基叠压，打破⑥⑦层，结合第一期遗存的整体情况，推测年代为第一期中段，但也可能建于早段（图3-8；彩版3-11，3-12，3-13，3-14，3-15）。

（二）隔墙

目前发掘出来的隔墙位于遗址东部，南端继续向南延伸，北端已被破坏，可能向东延伸，有待进一步发掘。揭露部分分布于UnitL8GridA6–A9、B1–B9、C9–F9、F10，UnitL9GridF1–F9、G9、H9内。墙体大致由西南向东北带状展布，其间可见有两处90°的直角转折，将隔墙分成了分别长18.7、10、13.1米的三段。在北部还残存有长0.5米、1米左右的两段，从墙体走向和砖块特征等判断，隔墙可能在神殿1东南角直角转折后继续向东延伸。

隔墙宽0.9、残高0.7米，砖墙两侧外部用砖较完整，中间填充有碎砖，外壁面平滑、规整，基础深度与房屋1、房屋5基本相同，约0.1米，基本为平地起建。从隔墙与其他建筑的平面布局可以看出，其功能是将第一期寺院的不同功能建筑进行区分，形成以中心神殿为主的神圣空间和以僧舍为中心的生活空间。

隔墙开口于⑤层以下，打破⑥层，推定时代为第一期中段（彩版3-16，3-17，3-18）。

（三）房屋1

位于遗址东南部，分布于UnitL8GridC2–C7、D2–D7、E2–E7、F2–F8、G2–G8、H2–H8、I2–I8等探方内。2014年度发掘时，发现南墙、东墙和部分西墙和北墙。2017年全部发掘。揭露部分全为墙基，除东北角被后期破坏外，其余部分保存相对较好。

房屋1平面形状近方形，方向5°，南北长11.2、东西宽11、残高0.6米。在东墙中部有向外凸出的长方形的门道，南北残长约1米（推测原来长3米），东西宽1米，大部分被叠压在曲折形围墙下。四面墙体残存最高处保留有13层平铺砖块，外墙用砖均较为完整，而内墙由碎砖砌造；墙壁宽度基本相同，约0.62—0.73米；墙壁外部呈阶梯状向上内收，南北两侧保留3个梯级，南侧保留2个梯级，每次内收宽度介于3—7厘米之间。在房屋外的西面与隔墙之间发现有一段砖铺通道，应为当时的生活地面。据此观察，四面墙体的基础部分应该均出露于当时的地面之上，与外墙壁面规整、平滑的特征也相符，这表明房屋的修建大体是平地起建。在房屋四壁的内部填充有混杂部分碎砖渣的黏土质粉沙土，较为紧密，可能经过有意夯实，起到防潮作用。从墙体的基础砌筑深度、砖墙的宽度等方面考虑，推测该房屋基础以上的部分可能以木构建筑材料为主。

F1内现存三排四列柱洞，分布在墙体内侧和室内，柱洞都为较规整圆形，相邻柱洞的间距均为3米。根据房屋朝向东，将柱洞分为前、中、后三排，从左向右逐一记录（表1）。

房屋1开口于⑤层下，打破⑥层，被曲折形围墙叠压，其下叠压道路1及房屋6、7，因此判断遗址年代为第一期中段。据其室内空间可达上百平方米面积考虑，该房屋应非一般性住房，推测可能属食堂性质的建筑（图3-9；彩版3-19）。

（四）房屋2

位于遗址东北部，紧邻神殿1。揭露部分全为墙基，包括完整南墙和部分西墙，分布于UnitL10GridF4、F5、F6、G4、H4、I4等探方内，其余部分在北部未发掘区。房屋方向5°。南墙长

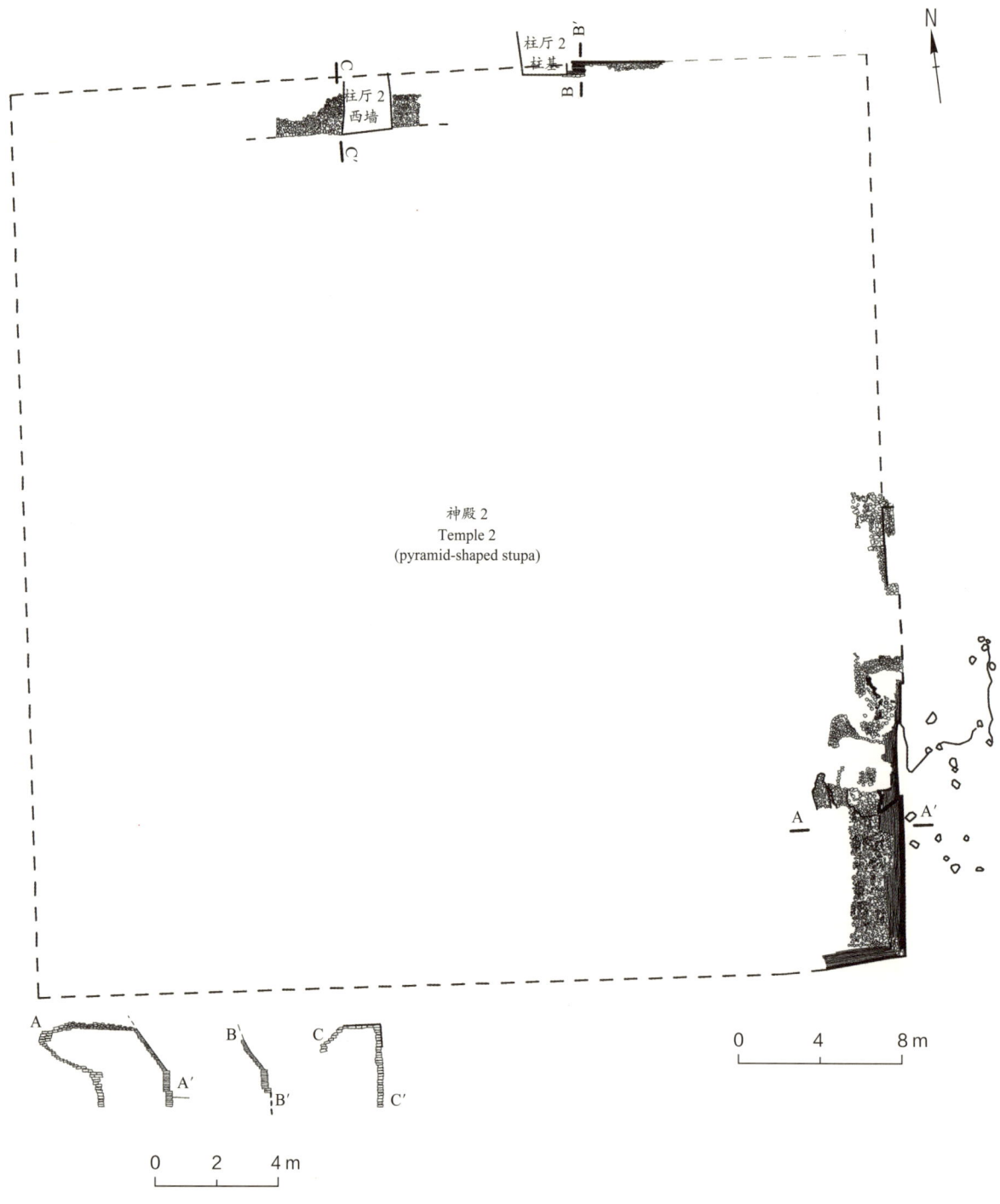

图 3-8 神殿 2 平剖面图
Fig. 3-8 The plan and section of Temple 2 (pyramid-shaped stupa)

7.1、宽 0.8、残高 0.7 米；西墙残长 4.3、宽 0.7、残高 0.6 米。墙体最高处保存有 15 层砖，内墙壁面参差不齐，但外墙壁面除底部 2 层砖外均相当规整、平滑，表明该房屋的基础应大部分出露于当时地面之上，推测修建时可能仅向下开挖很浅的基槽。由于房屋 2 所在区域已被后期取土破坏，开口层位不明，打破⑥层，推测与神殿 1 晚期时代相当，属第一期中段（彩版 3-20）。

（五）房屋 3

位于遗址东部，与房屋 5 分处于隔墙的两侧。大部分被叠压在八边形佛塔 1 之下，仅南墙完整揭露，部分东墙和西墙可见。根据同时期房屋大致呈方形的情况，推测房屋 3 也为方形。揭露部分分布于 UnitL8GridG9、G10、H9、I9、J9 等探方内。房屋方向为 5°。破坏严重，仅存墙基部分。南墙长 5.4、宽 0.4—0.6、残高 0.3 米，在外墙面可见一个宽 5—10 厘米阶梯状内收。西墙出露长 2.3、宽 0.5、残高 0.3 米。

房屋 3 开口于⑤层下，打破⑥层，被八边形佛塔 1 叠压，年代应为第一期中段，其性质推测属僧房。在其西南角外探坑中发现有大量陶片、黑色炭化物，应为第一期早段的废弃堆积（彩版 3-21，1、2）。

（六）房屋 4

位于遗址东北部，神殿 1 的正东面。保存很差，仅有南、北两部分墙体残存，均为房屋的基础部分。平面形状不清。主要分布于 UnitL10 GridG1、H1、I1、G3、G4、H3、H4 等探方内。南墙残长 3.6、宽 1.5、残高 0.5 米；北墙残长 2.7、宽 1、残高 0.6 米。发掘的外墙用砖粗糙、砖壁面不整齐，可见部分火砖，显然应属地面以下部分。但与北部相邻的房屋 2 相比，其埋在地下的基础部分明显高于房屋 2 出露在地面以上的墙体部分，因此推测该房屋 4 的时代要晚于房屋 2，但仍属于第一期中段。

此外，根据房屋残存的墙体明显宽于一般性

表 1　房屋 1 柱洞登记表

编号	尺寸（厘米）	描述
D1	直径 40，深 70	下部有 5 层砖块填充 上部有 20 厘米的青灰色柱洞填土
D2		破坏不见
D3	外圈直径 70，内圈直径 30	外圈打破 L1 路面，内圈由砖块填筑
D4	直径 22，深 42	碎砖填筑
D5	外圈直径 40，深 70； 内圈直径 15，深 38	外圈为青灰色柱洞填土， 内圈为一腐朽木柱痕迹
D6	直径 60，深 6	一层红砖平铺
D7	直径 60，深 6	一层红砖平铺
D8	直径 40，深度未清理	碎砖填筑
D9	直径 40，深 47	碎砖填筑
D10	直径 35，深 50	青灰色柱洞填土
D11	直径 45，深 30	碎砖填筑
D12	直径 35，深 20	红砖平铺砌筑

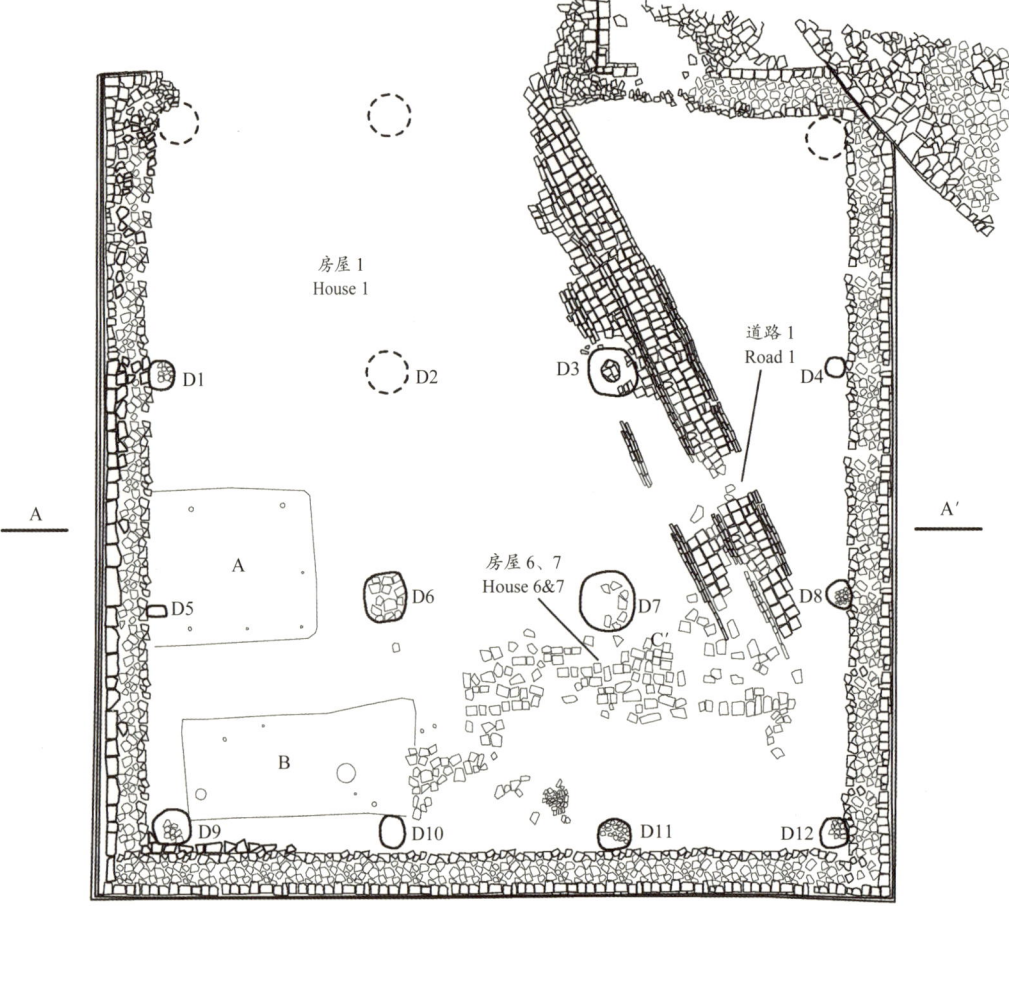

图 3-9 房屋 1 平剖面图
Fig. 3-9 The plan and section of House 1

的僧舍住房墙体（如房屋3、房屋5等），推测房屋4可能为神殿性质的建筑（彩版3-21，3、4）。

（七）房屋5

位于遗址东部，东、南两侧位于隔墙的转角处，与隔墙形成约1.3米的通道。2017年度在清理完其上的路面1之后，发现该建筑遗迹。主要分布于UnitL9GridB1–E1、B2–E2、B3–E3、B4–E4、B5–E5、B6–E6、B7–E7、B8–E8以及UnitL8GridB10–E10等探方内。从墙体之间砌筑的接触关系可以判断，该房屋存在后期的扩建。

早期房屋（房间1）平面大致呈方形，方向为5°，南北长7、东西宽6.7米；在北墙中部有向外凸出的长方形房门，东西长1.42、南北宽0.82米。揭露的砖墙均为房屋的基础部分，外墙壁平滑、规整，内墙参差不齐，根据同时期的建筑地面可知，这些房基均应出露于当时的地面之上，也属平底起建的方式。墙体较窄，厚0.3—0.4米，残高约0.4米，保存7层平铺砖块。在墙体内部填充有灰黄色的黏土质粉沙，共同作为整个建筑的基础。在房间内北部仍残存部分砖铺的地面，与房门连接在一起，推测当时室内地面应由一或两层平砖铺垫而成。房门残存高度与其余墙体相当，外墙壁呈阶梯状向上内收，可见三个梯级，第二个梯级内收宽度达20厘米，其余两个仅4—8厘米；壁面规整平滑。与房间1可能同时存在的还有位于其正北部约3.4米处的另一房间（房间2），但现仅残存部分南墙和门道，以及可能同时存在的一条砖路，具体平面结构不清。南墙残长5.1、宽0.8、残高0.4米。门道与该墙相连，入口处有一规整的凹形结构，长0.73、宽0.22、残高0.2米，其具体功用尚不清楚。砖路建筑方式与道路3相同，两侧为三排竖砖，中间为平铺铺砌，其西端连接道路3，东端则以令人惊讶的弧形转弯直通这间房屋的门道处，表明这两者之间应有密切的联系，也可能是安置梯子处。

晚期阶段的改造主要发生在房屋5的东北角，在东部、北部各新建了一堵墙，南部和西部利用房屋5北部的部分墙体，从而形成了一个长方形的房间（房间3）。该房间长5、宽3.4、残高0.5米，在其北部还存在有房门的痕迹。房内底部为砖铺地面，但其深度低于房间1的室内地面，而与屋外的地面高度相当。在砖铺地面之上发现有大量的石灰、黏土粉沙混杂而成紧实土层，类似于"三合土"，起防潮作用，发掘中虽仅存局部，但推测原应分布于整个房内。内壁较为规整、平滑，推测房间3应作为储藏室修建的。在北部可能同时还有砖铺地面，由碎砖平铺而成，构成屋前的庭院式路面，目前仅保留长约7米、宽约2米的不规整部分。

房屋5开口于⑤层下，打破⑥层，与道路3的晚期同时，推测为第一期中段。房屋5与房屋1、房屋3以隔墙分隔，但与中心神殿形成一个更加紧密的空间关系，表明这座房屋与神殿的日常供奉存在着密切的关系，可能为供奉用品储藏和专职管理人员的居住场所（图3-10；彩版3-22，3-23）。

（八）墙1

主要分布于UnitK9GridJ9、J10，UnitK10GridJ1、J2、J3、J6、I5、I6内。北端位于探方UnitK10GridI7下，南端情况不明。揭露部分位于道路3的西侧80—130厘米距离处，方向为5°。墙10破坏严重，仅保存部分东侧外墙，西侧均被破坏，中部多段也被破坏。墙体残长14.8米，分成三个不相连的残段，北至南分别长3.5米、1.66米和2.55米，残存宽度0.36米左右，残高0.2米。最高处残存4层平铺砖块，以纵向平铺砌筑为主。砖块形制规格不统一，使用较多的残砖，最大砖块主要见于北段，尺寸为30厘米×17厘米×7厘米，较小砖块尺寸为20厘米×13厘米×5厘米。

墙1开口于⑤层下，基础深度与道路3、道路4基本水平或略高，据此推测其时代为遗址的第一期中段。由于发掘有限，对于砖墙结构和功能尚不清楚（见图3-5；彩版3-24，1）。

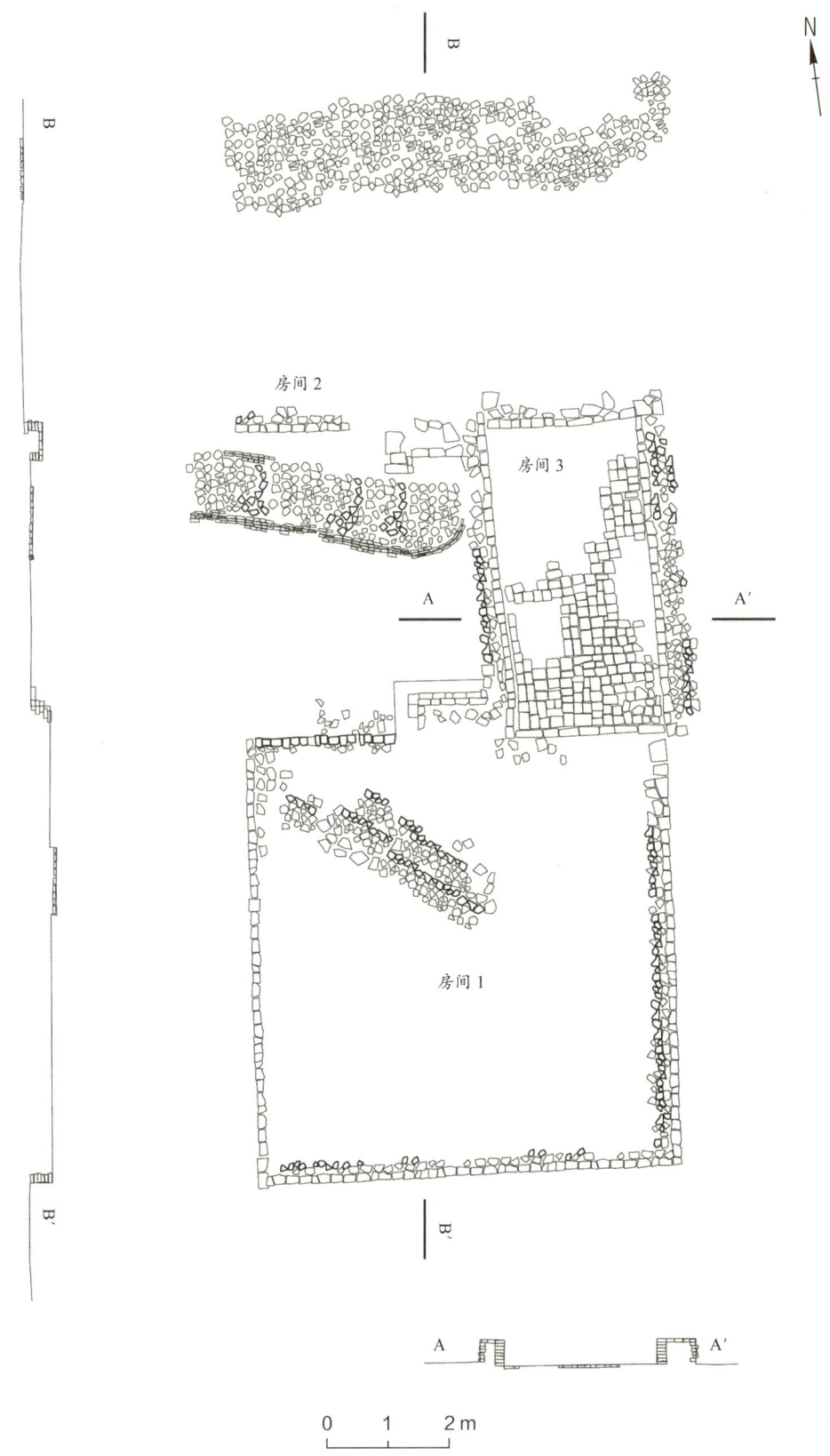

图 3-10　房屋 5 平剖面图

Fig. 3-10　The plan and section of House 5

（九）墙 2

位于 UnitK10GridI2、I3 内。2015 年 1 月发掘十字形中心神殿建筑的柱厅 1 时发现。墙体东侧被后期破坏，西侧向西部继续延伸，因叠压在柱厅 1 之下，未作进一步发掘。

墙 2 仅残存部分墙基，高出道路 3 约 40 厘米。残存墙体由 5 层砖东西向平铺砌筑，北侧砖壁平整，南侧被后期损毁。残长 1.6、残宽 0.7、残存厚度 0.26 米。墙的方向为 100°。墙砖的形制和大小不统一，厚度在 4.5—6 厘米之间。在清理过程中，北侧发现有较多的炭灰、陶片、玻璃残器和动物骨骼。在墙 2 的底部，隔着约 25 厘米的灰黄色泥沙土层，分布有早于墙 2 的面积较大的散乱砖层，推测是神殿 1 同时期建筑的废弃堆积。

墙 2 开口于④层下，被柱厅 1 叠压，打破⑤层。从其深度、用砖大小等观察，推测年代为遗址第一期的中晚段，墙 2 的性质不清楚（彩版 3-24，2、3）。

（十）墙 3

墙 3 位于神殿 2 的东部，分布于 UnitK9GridE4–I4、E5–J5 探方内。方向 275°。长 9.5 米，宽 1 米，残高 0.4 米，保存 8 层砖块。两侧砖块较完整，中间铺砌大量残砖。从南北两侧外墙壁面较为规整和平滑的特征推测，该墙体大部分应出露在当时的地面之上。

其东端连接道路 3，西端终点不明，目前尚未发现与其对应墙体，因此，对它的功能尚不能做出确切的认识，可能与中心神殿 2 存在一定的关联。

墙 3 开口于⑤层下，打破⑥层，推测年代属于第一期中段（图 3-11；彩版 3-24，4）。

（十一）路面 2

零星分布在 UnitL10GridB5、E5、E6 等探方内，由一层碎砖水平铺砌而成，由于保存较差及北部未发掘，详细分布和结构不太清楚。部分叠压在道路 4 之下，与神殿 1 第 2 段的北门外墙相连。根据其与周邻建筑的关系，推测应为神殿 1 使用时期的地面，时代为第一期中段。

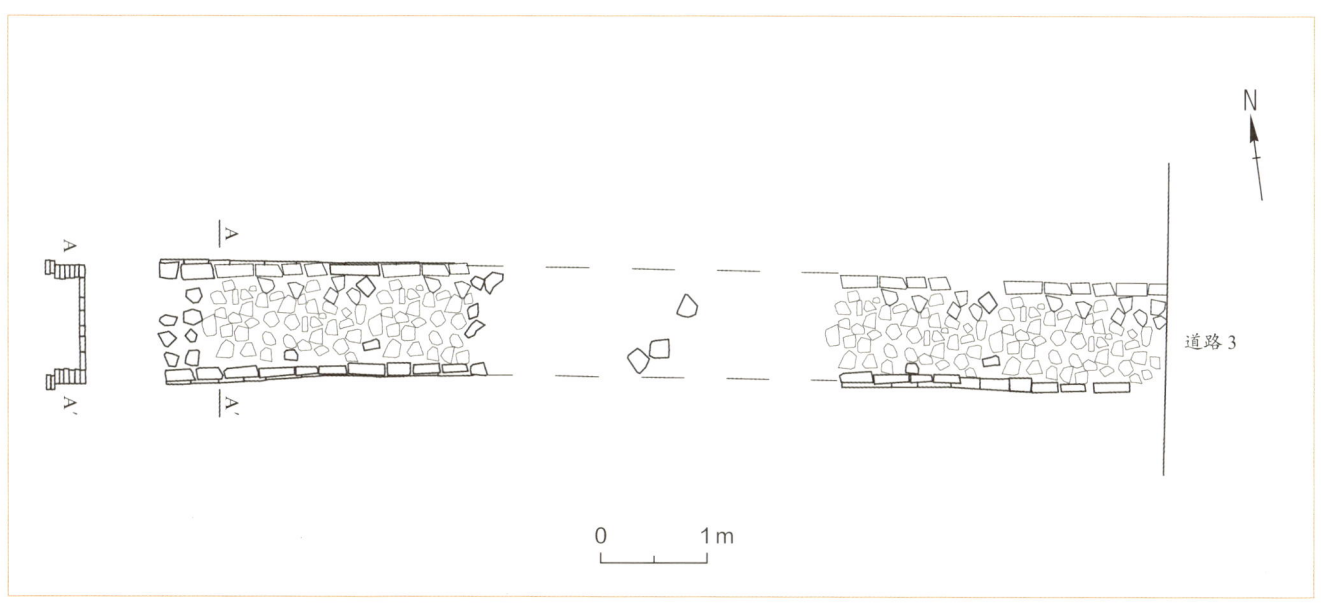

图 3-11　墙 3 平剖面图
Fig. 3-11　The plan and section of Wall 3

（十二）路面 4

路面 4 位于神殿 2 的东部，破坏严重，目前确切的路面遗迹主要发现于 UnitK8GridH7、I7、H8、I8、G9、H9、I9 等探方内。路面较平整，保存较好的部分长、宽均约 5 米，由不完整的砖块平铺而成，保存的完整宽度有 12、24、18 厘米三类，砖块大小、方向不一，砖缝较宽，从局部有二层叠砖的情况推测，原来的路面可能由 2 层砖平砌形成。在路面以下发现铺垫有一层厚约 10 厘米的纯净粉沙层，有明显的水平层理，应是有意置于路面砖块以下的建筑材料，起到过滤雨水的作用。此外，在现存路面的北部 UnitK9Grid G2–G7、H1–H7、I1–I6 探方内，也有大量的不规则砖块，局部区域也可见平铺成路面的砖块，推测应是原始路面被后期破坏以后所致。因此，很可能这部分区域均有砖铺地面，作为神殿 2 东部广场性质的活动地面（彩版 3-25，1）。

二、晚段遗迹

可以明确的晚段遗迹为道路 4。

道路 4 位于遗址的东部，分布于 UnitK10Grid J3、J4、J5，UnitL10GridA4、A5、A6、B5、B6、C6、D6 内。2015 年 1 月，在清理道路 3 的过程中，发现在其北部路面上叠压着另外一层铺砖，揭露后，发现是相互叠压的两期道路遗迹。

道路 4 平面形状不甚规则，方向为东北—西南走向，东北端较窄，西南端较宽。已发掘部分长 12 米，宽 1.7—2.5 米，厚 0.05—0.2 米。南侧近西端处略向南折，形成一个约 165° 的钝角。道路两侧为侧砖竖立砌筑，北侧较完整，南侧保存较差；中间部分为碎砖平铺，彼此交错，无固定方向。在 GridB5、B6 内，路面向下凹陷，以该处为界，以东路面在普通铺砖上面另铺砌一层大而厚的完整砖块，而以西路面仅见一层普通铺砖。完整底砖至少有三种规格，分别为 23 厘米 × 17 厘米 × 5 厘米，21 厘米 × 15 厘米 × 4 厘米和 19 厘米 × 12 厘米 × 4 厘米；在 GridC6 内的上层铺砖则明显较底层砖尺寸偏大，尺寸为 39 厘米 × 27 厘米 × 5 厘米，可能与后期的道路重新修补有关。在道路的西端还发现一条南北向的浅沟，长 292 厘米，宽 8 厘米，深 6.5 厘米，其功能可能与排水有关。道路 4 的用砖大小、形态不统一，在中部大量使用残砖铺砌，仅在两侧和排水沟处的竖砌砖块较为完整。

道路 4 开口于⑤层下，叠压着神殿 1 第 2 阶段的门厅和地面 2，打破道路 3。东北端继续向北部未发掘区域延伸，可能连接着同时期的其他建筑。推断年代为遗址的第一期晚段（见图 3-5；彩版 3-25，2）。

The first period of the remains includes the early stage, the middle stage and the late stage. The current findings are mainly based on the remains of the middle stage (Figure3-1；Color Plate 3-1).

The early stage

The cultural remains of the early stage of the first period include the early phase of the Temple 1, Road 1, Road 2, Road 3, Road 5, bathroom and drainage.

1. Temple 1

The temple 1, which is located in the squares of UnitL9GirdA9 – F10 and UnitL10GridA1 – F4, has two constructive processes of early and late phases. The direction is 5°.

Only part of the foundation is preserved from the early phase of the temple except the northern gateway, which contains a higher part. It is roughly a square in shape, but the angle between two intersected sides is not 90°. It measures 9.45 m from north to south, 9.37 m from east to west and the preserved height is 0.5 m. The exposed outer bricks of the foundation are not regular and some are over-burnt (picket) bricks. In the middle of the northern wall, the doorway is projected and only partially is preserved, but the complete architectural feature is still not clear. The surviving part is oblong in shape, measuring 2.7 m from east to west, 2 m from north to south and 1 m high. The exposed temple belongs to the later phase. It was built above the first constructive phase. Except the northern projection part, the size of the temple is almost the same as that of the early phase. It is a regular square in shape, each side measuring 9 m. Most of the architecture was seriously destroyed; only part of outer walls and foundation were preserved. In general, the walls of southwestern corner and southeastern corner as well as the doorway are in good condition. The exposed wall is 1.5 m wide and is 2.8 m at the highest position. The dimension of the inner space is 5.8m from east to west and 5.6 m from north to south. The outer walls above the ground floor are highly decorated. In the middle, the fascinating decoration is created by a few rows of curved bricks. Two and some decorative bricks form a delicate floral pattern.

The northern doorway clearly survives in the late phase. The entrance is attached with northern wall of temple. It resembles a three-terraced shape. From north to south, both of the eastern and western faces of the entrance structure continuously turn outwards at the angle of 90°, which means that the inner space of the doorway is expanded two times. There are three semi-circular postholes in the bricks of the entrance, measuring 35-40 cm in diameter and 30-50 cm in depth, which indicate that the entrance is possiblely a pillared structure with a roof.

Two big urns are discovered in the corners of the late phase, one is in UnitL10GridB4, and the other one is in UnitL9GridB9. It is probably that each corner of the temple is placed with such an urn. The two uncovered urns are half buried in the ground when firstly discovered, and dozens of potteries in them. It thus served as the daily use during the functional period of the temple. Temple 1 is under the Layer 5, cuts the Layer 6, and contemporary with Road 3.It belongs to the first period (Figure 3-2, 3-3, 3-4; Color Plate 3-2, 3-3, 3-4.3-5, 3-6).

2. House 6

House 6 is distributed in the squares of Unit L8 Grid C2 – C7, D2 – D7, E2 – E7, F2 – F8, G2 – G8, H2 – H8, I2 – I8. As a result of partial overlay of the House 1 and House 7, the overall shape and structure are not clear. The exposed part is 9 m long from north to south.

In this area, a 20 cm thick layer of grayish-brown clay, which is horizontally distributed, is put above the previous House 7. Three special process floors are visible in the houses 6, recorded as A, B and C. A is located in the middle of the northern side of the House 6, rectangular in shape, measuring 2.1 m long form north to south, 1.9 m wide form east to west, and 0.1 m thick. The surface inside is possibly rammed, and it is surrounded by some vertical bricks at its periphery. Six small postholes, which are round shaped and 5 cm in diameter, 10-24 cm in depth, are found at the edge. According to the size of the holes, it is a simple shelter-style structure. B is located in the northwest of House 6, with a rectangular ground plan, 3.4 m long from north to south, 1.6 m wide from east to west and 0.1 m thick. The surface inside is possibly rammed, and some vertical bricks surround its periphery. 12 small postholes, about 5 cm in diameter and 12-42 cm in depth, are found in this area. On the south side there is larger posthole, 30 cm in diameter and 25 cm in depth, filled with gray brown soil. It is presumably also a simple shelter-type building. C is located in the south west of the House 6, and is oval in shape, 2.6 m long form north to south, 1.65 m wide in east-west, and 0.06 m thick. It is a typical smooth earthen floor made of the mixture of charcoals, gray clayey sand and brick particles, which are probably used for damp-proofing function.

Some charred rice grains, plant seeds, nails, and animal bones of fishes, poultry and mice are unearthed in the northwest of the house, suggesting that House 6 should be used as a dining room. According to the small size of exposed postholes in the house, it might be a temporary construction. It belongs to the early stage of the first period judged from the stratigraphic relationship (Color Plate 3-7: 1, 2).

3. House 7

House 7, which is located in UnitL8GridC2 – C7, D2 – D7, E2 – E7, F2 – F8, G2 – G8, H2 – H8, I2 – I8, opens under the House 6 and destroys the Road 1. As the House 7 is under the House 1 and House 6, it is only partially excavated, and the shape and structure are not clear. According to the exposed indoor floor, the east-west length is at least 9 m, and 2 m wide is also exposed from north to south. In the east of the house is a north-south wall with a length of 5.6 m, a width of 0.4 m and a height of 0.28 m. A layer of bricks is paved as the floor inside the house. In the middle of this eastern wall, an uncertain pillar base, measuring 0.7 m in diameter and 6 cm in thickness is discovered. It is made of a layer of broken bricks. Along the eastern side of the east wall of the House 7, there are some bricks with a width of 1.5 m. Most of the bricks are higher in the west and lower in the east. It is presumed that the wall is demolished to directly creat the base of House 6.

According to the location of House 7, it might have served as the dining room. According to the stratigraphic relations, House 7 belongs to the early stage of the first period (Color Plate 3-7, 3).

4. Road 1

It is located in the southeast corner of the excavation area; the exposed part is distributed in UnitL8GridE2, E3, F2, F3, G4, H4, and H5. Archaeological excavations were conducted in 2014 and 2017. The direction is 245°, and the exposed part is 9.5 m long, 1.5 m wide, 0.2 m thick. It is almost well preserved with the exception of the destructive northeast part, but the southwestern end continues to extend westwards. Three vertical bricks on both sides, two vertical bricks in the middle which divide the road into two halves, and the rest are paved by horizontal bricks. On the southwest of the road (inside House 1) a large number of bricks were found to be superimposed on it, which were possibly built contemporarily with the Road 1 and were then demolished to be used as foundation during the construction of House 1.

Road 1 is under the House 1, and it is presumed to be the early stage of the first period (Color Plate 3-7, 4).

5. Road 2

A small area of Road 2 is distributed in Unit L8GridI8, about 1 m long and 0.5 m wide. The direction is 90°. It was made by one layer of horizontal brick. However, the details are not clear due to poor conditions. Part of the Road 2 is also under House 1, and it is presumably to be the early stage of early period.

6. Road 3

It is located in the eastern part of the excavation area, and the exposed part is distributed in the UnitK8GridJ1 – J10, UnitL8GridA8, A9, UnitK9 GridJ1 – J10, UnitL10GridA1 – A10, UnitK10GridJ1, J2, J3, J4, J5, J6, UnitL10GridA1, A2, A3, A4, A5, A6. Both the northern and southern ends of the road extend to the unexcavated squares.

Road 3 is in a regular straight belt shape, with the two roughly parallel outer sides. It is well preserved, 10° in direction. The exposed part measures 58.4 m in length, 2.2 m in width and 0.25 m in thickness. The road is composed of vertically placed bricks of both outer sides and horizontal bricks in between. Among them, each row in the center contains about 8-10 bricks, and 4 vertical bricks (0.21 m wide) in the west and 9 vertical bricks (0.53 m wide) in the east, but the number of the vertical bricks in the east increases to 12 (0.65 m wide) from the UnitL9GridA5 southwards. It is worthwhile to mention that the design of eastern outer side is a little altered at the junction with Road 6 in the UnitL9GridA5 and B5, where the vertical bricks are built in cross design.

Two layers of bricks are observed in the centre of the road, of which the bricks of upper layer are relatively neat and flat with a slightly convex cross-section, and the configuration of lower part is not clear due to the overlay of the upper part. Observed from some small areas, the lower bricks are more rough and sparse, possibly because they are mainly used as the basement of the road. The shape and size of the bricks are not uniform; some broken bricks are also used. The minimum size of the complete bricks is 24 x 12.5 cm and the maximum size is 34 x 24.6 cm.

Road 3 opened under the Layer 5 and above the Layer 6, broken by Road 4 in the north, and linked with the Road 6 in the middle. It is parallel to the east wall of the early phase of Temple 1 with a distance of 0.3 m, but its distance from the west wall of the late phase of the Temple 1 is not the same, ranging from 0.62 m to 0.97 m in distance. Considering the design, Road 3 may be built simultaneously with the first phase of the Temple 1, but it continued to be used when the temple was expanded in the second phase. Together with the Floor 2 around the temple, it functioned as the outside floor at that time (Figure 3-5, 3-6; Color Plate 3-8, 3-9). The length of the Road 3 suggested that it was an important passage connecting different buildings and ancillary roads on both sides in the first period.

7. Road 5

It is located in UnitI11GridH2. In January 2015, it was found at the depth of 5 m when a test ditch was explored. The exposed portion is east-west direction, 0.4 m long, 0.6 m wide and 0.25 m thick. There are two vertical bricks in the middle and two layers of bricks at both sides. It is under the Layer 6, and cuts the Layer 7. The ground surface of the road is presumably on the top of Layer 7, belonging to the early stage of the first period.

8. Bathroom and drainage

The Bath Complex is located in the Squares of UnitM8GridE5 and F5. At the time of digging, we discovered the bath complex which was maximally destroyed. Undamaged part was exposed from north to south. It is composed of two parts: one looks like a bathroom and another is like a drain. Most of the parts of the eastern, western and southern walls are destroyed later. The northern wall was partially found. The ground is rectangular in shape, and its length is 7 m from east to west and width is 2.8 m from north to south. The northern part is not excavated completely. The western wall is 2.8 m long, 0.8 m wide and 0.99 m high. The preserved segment of the wall has 21 layers of bricks. In this wall, there is a 30×30 cm niche which is 20 cm above the floor. The southern wall measuring 7 m long, is almost totally destroyed by later residents, and the preserved height is 0.61 m.

This room has a nice brick-paved floor which is built with fascinating brick combination. The floor is nicely made of both entire and cut bricks form east to west, making a good and sustainable inner look. Inner part of this floor is 3.45 m form east to west and is 1.8 m from south to north.

The drainage part is located in UnitM8GridG1 H1. Northern part of the drain is destroyed. A small area is exposed by excavation. It has two walls from north to south which are separated by a 50 cm wide brick-paved lower channel. This channel is built by Herringbone Technique. (Figure 3-7; Color Plate 3-10)

The middle stage

The cultural remains of the middle stage include the late phase of the Temple 1, Temple 2 (pyramid-shaped stupa), Road 3, partition wall, House 1, House 2, House 3, House 4, House 5, Wall 1, Wall2, Wall 3, Floor 2 and Floor 4.

1. Temple 2 (pyramid-shaped stupa)

The stupa is located in the center of the site, with a direction of 5° from north to south. The complete eastern wall and part of southern wall of the structure, located in UnitK8GridA10, B10, UnitK9GridA1 – A10, B1 – B10, UnitK10GridA1, A2, A3, were exposed in 2017. The northern wall, which is located in UnitI10GridG9, H9, I9, G10, H10, I10, J10, UnitI11GridI1 and UnitJ11GridD1, D2, was excavated in 2015 and confirmed by the excavation in 2017. The eastern wall measures 43.4 m long, the south end is well conserved, but the north end only the foundation part is preserved for the north end foundation part. The exposed southern wall is 3.9 m long and the northern wall is 19 m long. Most of the pyramid structure is destroyed by the later cruciform central temple, other parts may be preserved under it, but can not be excavated. From the section of the eastern wall, the stupa is clearly observed to be destroyed by the eastern wall of the Pillared-hall 4 and the Connective Wall Foundation 4.

For the section of the surviving eastern wall, it can be divided into upper and lower parts. The lower wall is connected with the foundation, the inner side is not regular, and the boundary line between the wall and the inside ground or other structures is not clear. The width of the foundation is 1.7 m, and the depth of the bottom brick is 5.1 m from the ground surface. The foundation appears a little bit irregular at the bottom while the top is neatly arranged with 10 layers of bricks, to a height of about 0.5 m high. The upper wall is constructed upwards towards the center, and the width of the exposed east wall is about 4.3 m.

For the northern wall two separated sections were preserved. The western wall foundation of Pillared-hall 2 and the Pillar-plinth 1 destroys this wall, overlying on it as a new foundation for the second period construction. The preserved western section of the northern wall is rectangular, 7.4 m long, 0.66-1.9 m wide, and 2.6 m high. The highest position of the wall is 2.7 m deep from the ground, while the lowest position is 5.3 m below the ground. If viewed from the southern face of the wall, it can be divided into 4 parts from bottom to top. The lowest part is paved by a layer of irregular over-burnt (picket) bricks, about 20-30 cm thick, with another thin brick dust layer above it. Then 19 layers of bricks are on top of it, measuring 0.9 m high. Again 9 layers of horizontal bricks are 0.3 m high. The top has 31 layers of bricks, slightly outward, measuring 1.4 m high. The shape and size of the used bricks are various. Most bricks are 4 cm thick and a small amount of bricks are 7 cm. It is worth noting that the size of the bricks in the layer ④G on the north of the wall is similar to the bricks of this exposed northern wall, which is probably caused by the demolishment of the earlier structure as the later foundation in the second period. Currently the western part of the northern wall is not completely exposed and several other structures also exist. Complete understanding about this part will be achieved after further excavation. Located on the east of the western part with a distance of 7.6 m, the eastern part of the northern wall is 2.1 m long and the maximum preserved height is 0.7 m, with 15 layers of bricks. The architectural feature of the northern face of this part is similar with that of the eastern wall of the stupa. The lower part is a straight wall and the upper part is a regular and nicely inclined-wall. According to the distribution of the exposed walls and the general situation of the temple in this period, it is presumed that the ground plan of the stupa is a square in shape. The interior of the stupa is not yet certain; it might be a square space, or a complicated building structure supporting the top of the stupa. In addition, there may be ancillary buildings, such as halls or stairs, but so far it is also uncertain due to the limited excavation.

If we observ the outer eastern wall from bottom to top, the bottom is vertically built with 14 layers of horizontal bricks with the height of 0.8 m, on top of which 30 layers of bevel cut bricks are used to build the slanting wall, measuring 1.6 m high. The superstructure of the stupa is not clear because of the destruction. In the middle of the eastern outer wall, several special projections, offsets and bevels are found, which may relate to ancillary facilities.

The shape and size of the bricks are not uniform. The largest complete brick is 30×18.7 cm, and the smallest complete brick is 21×12.5 cm. The mortar is the gray-yellow silty clay. A large number of the bricks are deposited sloping from west to east on the east of the stupa, which is probably formed by demolishing and leveling the earlier structure while building the cruciform central temple in the later period. Some stones, mainly the river cobbles of coarse sandstone or quartz sandstone, are also found in the deposit. Most of the stones keep the natural gravel surface but one side is chiseled to form a flat surface, indicating that they should have been placed in the upper part of the stupa. Among them, one stone is probably used as the pedestal of the sculpture.

This stupa opens under Layer 4, partially destroyed by the foundations of the cruciform central temple, and cuts Layer 6 and Layer 7. According to the above context, it is attributed to the middle stage of the first phase, but might also have been built in early stage (Figure3-8; Color Plate 3-11, 3-12, 3-13, 3-14, 3-15).

2. Partition wall

The excavated wall is located in the eastern excavation area, the south end continues to extend southward and the northern end has been destroyed but is possibly extending eastward. The exposed part is distributed in UnitL8Grid A6 – A9, B1 – B9, C9 – F9, F10, UnitL9GridF1 – F9, G9, H9. The wall roughly spreads from southwest to northeast, and the wall has two right-angled 90° turns. It divides the wall into three continuous parts, measuring 18.7 m, 10m and 13.1 m respectively. On the north, there are two remaining sections with length of 0.5 m and 1 m. Judged from the direction of the wall and the features of the bricks, the partition wall may extend eastward after turning at a right angle in the southeast corner of the temple.

The width of the partition wall is 0.9 m and the height is 0.7 m. The external bricks of the wall are relatively complete whereas the middle is filled with broken bricks. The outer wall surface is smooth and regular. The foundation depth is basically the same as that of the House 1 and the House 5, about 0.1 m. From the spatial arrangement of the partition wall and other constructers, it can be concluded that the function of this wall is to distinguish the different functional zones of the first monastery and form an independent district centering on the main stupa. The Partition wall is under Layer 5 and cuts Layer 6, presumed to be the middle stage of the first period (Color Plate 3-16, 3-17, 3-18).

3. House 1

The House 1 is located in the southeastern excavation area, and is distributed in units L8GridC2 – C7, D2 – D7, E2 – E7, F2 – F8, G2 – G8, H2 – H8, I2 – I8. The southern wall, eastern wall and part of the western and northern walls were excavated in 2014; they all were exposed entirely in 2017. The exposed part of house is the foundation. Except the northeast corner, the else are relatively well preserved.

The ground plan of the House 1 is roughly square in shape, 11.2 m long from north to south, 11 m wide from east to west and preserved with a height of 0.6 m. The direction is 5°. In the middle of the eastern wall there is an outwardly protruding rectangular doorway, which is 1 m long from north to south (the original length is presumable 3 m) and 1m wide from east to west. Most of the doorway was under the zigzag boundary wall. About 13 layers of bricks were maximally preserved in the four walls. The bricks of the outer walls are more complete, while the center of the walls is filled with broken bricks. The width of the walls is basically the same, about 0.62 – 0.73 m.

The terrace-like architectural structure of the outer walls can be observed. The northern wall and southern wall have three inward steps, the western wall has two inward steps, and the width of each step ranges in 3 – 7 cm. There is a brick floor between the western wall and the partition wall, which is clearly the contemporary living ground surface. Based on this observation, the foundation of the four walls should be above the ground at that time, which is consistent with the regular and smooth features of the outer walls. This shows that the construction is directly built from the ground without foundation ditches. The enclosed wall-foundations of the house are filled with soils mixed with some small broken brickbats, which may have also been intentionally ramped to provide a damp-proof effect.

Twelve postholes (D1 – D12) in three rows, with 3 m distance between them, are located on the inner side of the walls and inside of the house. They are almost regular round in shape, 35-70 cm in diameter, 6-70 cm in preserved depth. Some irregular bricks are found at the bottom of the postholes.

Considering the depth of the foundation and width of the brick wall, it is presumed that the superstructure above the foundation of the house is probably built with wood materials in a pillared style.

The House 1 opens under the Layer 5, cuts Layer 6, overlaid by the zigzag boundary wall and covers the Road 1. It is thus attributed to the middle stage of the first period. Considering its interior space of over 100 m^2, the house seems not to be a normal living room, but is probably the dining room (Figure 3-9; Color Plate 3-19).

4. House 2

It is located in the northeast of the excavation area, adjacent to the Temple 1. The exposed part is the wall foundation, including the complete southern wall and part of the western wall, which is located in UnitL10GridF4, F5, F6, G4, H4, and I4. The other part of the house is in the northern unexplored area. Its direction is 5°. The southern wall is 7.1 m in length, 0.8 m in width and 0.7 m in height. The western wall is 4.3 m in length, 0.7 m in width and 0.6 m in height. There are 15 layers of bricks preserved in the highest part of the wall, where the interior walls are uneven, but the external walls are quite regular and smooth except for the two bottom layers of bricks. This indicates that the foundation of the house should be mostly exposed above the ground at that time, and the foundation ditch is shallow during construction. Since the area where House 2 is located is destroyed by later brick-hunters, the opening layer is unknown. But it cuts the Floor 6. It is presumed to be built in the middle stage of the first period

(Color Plate 3-20).

5. House 3

It is located in the eastern excavation area, and on west side of the partition wall. Most of them are under the Octagonal Stupa 1. The southern wall is completely exposed, but only parts of the eastern and western walls are visible. Similar to other exposed houses from the same period, the House 3 is probably also square in shape. The exposed part is distributed in UnitL8GridG9, G10, H9, I9 and J9. The direction of the house is 5°. All the preserved parts are foundation because of serious damage. The southern wall is 5.4 m long, 0.4 – 0.6 m wide, and 0.3 m high. A 5-10 cm wide terraced-like inward projection is visible in the outer wall. The exposed western wall is 2.3 m long, 0.5 m wide and 0.3 m high.

House 3 opens under the Layer 5, cuts the Layer 6, and is overlaid by the Octagonal Pagoda 1. The age is speculated to be the middle stage of the first period, and the nature of the house is probably the living room for monks. A large number of potteries and black charred remains, which were found in the grid of the outside of its southwest corner, should be the debris of the first stage of the first period (Color Plate 3-21:1,2).

6. House 4

It is located in the northeast excavation area, east of Temple 1, and mainly distributed in UnitL10GridG1, H1, I1, G3, G4, H3, and H4. The house is poorly preserved, so the ground plan is unclear. Only the southern and northern parts of the walls remain, which all belong to the foundation. The preserved southern wall measures 3.6 m long, 1.5 m wide, 0.5 m high; preserved northern wall is 2.7 m long , 1 m wide , and 0.6 m high.

The exterior wall is not built with regular bricks but rather rough, and occasionally used overburnt (picket) bricks, indicating that the exposed part should have been underground. However, compared with the adjacent House 2 on the north, the foundation level is significantly higher than the above ground wall of the House 2, so it can be inferred that the House 4 is later than the House 2. But it still belongs to the middle stage of the first period according to the layers and layout of the structures.

In addition, considering the width of the preserved wall is significantly wider than the ordinary wall of the living room (such as House 5), it is speculated that House 4 may be related to the construction of the temple (Color Plate 3-21: 3, 4).

7. House 5

It is located in the eastern excavation area and the east and south sides are surrounded by the partition wall. The passage width between the house 5 and the partition wall is about 1.3 m. It was discovered after we cleared up the deposit of the Floor 1 in 2017. It was mainly distributed in the UnitL9GridB1 – E1, B2 – E2, B3 – E3, B4 – E4, B5 – E5, B6 – E6, B7 – E7, B8 – E8, and UnitL8GridB10 – E10. Judging from the masonary contact relationship between the walls, there was an expansion phase after the house was originally built.

The ground plan of the early house (Room 1) is roughly square, 5° in direction, 7 m long from north to south and 6.7 m width from east to west. There is an outwardly projecting rectangular door in the middle of the northern wall, with an east-west length of 1.42 m and a north-south width of 0.82 m. The exposed brick walls are the foundation of the house. The external walls are smooth and regular whereas the interior walls are uneven and rough. Referring to the ground floor of the same period of the construction, the foundation of the House 5 should also be exposed above the ground at that time, which means the builder constructed the buildings almost on the top of the ground surface. The wall is 0.3 – 0.4 m wide and 0.4 m high, with 7 preserved layers of bricks. The wall is filled with gray-yellow clayey sand inside, serving as the plinth of the entire building. A part of the brick-paved floor, which is connected with the doorway, is found indoors in the northern room. The floor is possibly made of one or two layers of horizontal bricks. The height of the preserved doorway is the same as the walls. Its outer wall has three upward narrow steps, of which the second step width is 20 cm and the remaining two are only 4 – 8 cm. The wall face of the entrance is smooth and neat. Another room (Room 2) is situated on the north of the Room 1, about 3.4 m in distance. However, only part of the southern wall and the doorway, and possibly a brick road are preserved. The specific architectural structure is unclear at present. The remained southern wall is 5.1 m long, 0.8 m wide, and 0.4 m high. The doorway which has an unidentified regular concave structure with 0.73 m in length, 0.22 m in width and 0.2 m in height, is connected with the southern wall. A brick road, which is partially overlaid by the Room 2, is constructed the same way as the Road 3, with three rows of vertical bricks on both sides and horizontal paved-bricks in the middle. This road is linked with the Road 3 at the western end and connected with the doorway of Room 2 with a surprisingly curved turn at the eastern end, strongly indicating that there are close relationship between the road and the Room 2, and perhaps there is a placement of ladders to upstairs.

The expansion work of the later phase is mainly occurred in the northeast corner of the House 5. Two walls are newly added in the east and north of the Room 1, and a wall is also built to connect the northern wall of Room 1 with the southern wall of Room 2. In this way, a rectangular room (Room 3), measuring 5 m long, 3.4 m wide is created. The maximum preserved height is 0.5 m. There is also a trace of doorway in the middle of northern wall. Inside the room, a brick floor is found at the bottom, but its depth is obviously lower than that of the indoor floor of Room 1 whereas equal to the level of the outside ground surface at that time. A lot of lime possibly mixed with sand is put on the paved floor, which is probably used to make it damp-proof. Although only a small part is exposed during the excavation, but it is possibly distributed throughout the room. The inner wall of the Room 3 is also regular and smooth, suggesting that it should be built as a storage room. Meanwhile, a part of brick-paved floor measuring 7 m long and 2 m wide is preserved on the north. It looks like to function as the courtyard in front of the house. House 5 opens under the Layer 5, cuts the Layer 6, and is contemporary with the late phase of the Road 3. It is presumed to be the middle stage of the first period. House 5 is separated from House 1 and House 3 by the partition wall, but in this way it forms a closer spatial relationship with the central temple of the first period, indicating a close relationship between the house and the daily service of the shrine. It is possibly for the storage and also the residence of full-time managers (Figure 3-10; Color Plate 3-22, 3-23).

8. Wall 1

It is mainly distributed in UnitK9GridJ9, J10, UnitK10GridJ1, J2, J3, J6, I5, I6, and the northern end is clearly located in UnitK10GridI7, but the southern end is not clear. The exposed part is situated on the west of the road 3 at a distance of 80 – 130 cm with a direction of 5°. The wall is severely damaged, only part of the eastern outer wall is preserved, and all the western part and partial middle part are destroyed. The remained wall is preserved as three unconnected segments, of which the lengths are 3.5 m, 1.66 m and 2.55 m, respectively. In general, the preserved length is 14.8 m, the width is about 0.36 m and the height is about 0.2 m. The highest position of the east outer wall contains 4 layers of horizontal bricks, whose shape and size are not uniform. The largest brick is 30×17×7 cm, and the smallest brick is 20×13×5 cm. The wall is under the Layer 5, and its foundation depth is basically the same or slightly higher than the Road 3 and the Road 4. According to this and the characteristics of the bricks, the wall is presumably attributed to the middle stage of the first period. However, the function and structure of this wall are not clear because of limited exposure (Figure 3-5; Color Plate 3-24, 1).

9. Wall 2

It is located in UnitK10GridI2, I3, and is discovered during the excavation of the pillared-hall 1 in January 2015. The eastern side of the wall is destroyed, and the western side enters the western unexcavation area, under the Pillared-hall 1.

The Wall 2, which is about 40 cm higher than the surface of the Road 3, is severely damaged and only five layers of the bricks are preserved. The wall is horizontally built, and the preserved length is 1.6 m, width up to 0.7 m, and height up to 0.26 m. The direction of the wall is 100°. The shape and size of the bricks are the non-uniform. During the excavation, many ashes, potteries, glass objects and animal bones are uncovered on the north side. In addition, a number of bricks are found under the Wall 2, which are probably the abandoned structures contemporary with the Temple 1.

The Wall 2 is under the Layer 4, cuts the Layer 5 and overlaid by the Pillared-hall 1. According to the depth of the foundation and the size of the bricks, this wall might belong to the late stage of the first period (Color Plate 3-24, 2, 3).

10. Wall 3

Wall 3 is located on the east of pyramid-shaped, and distributed in Unit K9 Grid E4 – I4, E5 – J5. The direction is 275°. It is 9.5 m long, 1 m wide, and 0.4 m high with 8 layers of bricks. The bricks on both sides are more complete, and a large number of broken bricks are built in the middle. Judged from the features of regularity and smooth of the outer wall on both sides, most of the Wall 3 should be above the ground at that time.

Its east end is connected with the Road 3, and the terminus of the west end is unknown. At present, no corresponding wall has been found. Therefore, understanding of its function is still unclear, and it may be related to the main stupa.

The Wall 3 is under the Layer 5, cuts the Layer 6, and presumably belongs to the middle stage of the first period (Figure 3-11; Color Plate 3-24, 4).

11. Floor 2

Due to poor preservation and partial exploration, it is sporadically distributed in UnitL10GridB5, E5 and E6, and the detailed structure is not clear. Part of the floor is under the Road 4, and connects with the outer wall of the north gate of the early phase Temple 1. The exposed floor is paved with a layer of broken bricks. According to its relationship with the adjoining constructions, it is supposed to be the ground floor of the late phase of Temple 1, which belongs to the middle stage of the first period.

12. Floor 4

Floor 4, located on the east of main stupa, is seriously damaged. Currently the floor is mainly distributed in UnitK8GridH7, I7, H8, I8, G9, H9 and I9. The surface of the floor is relatively flat, and the length and width of the well-preserved part are about 5 m. It was made of incomplete bricks with dimension of 24×18×5 cm. The brick size and the gap between paved bricks are various. It is speculated that the original floor may have been built with two layers of bricks. A layer of pure silt sand, about 10 cm thick, is found beneath the floor, which is probably deliberately placed to filter rainwater. In addition, a large number of irregular bricks are also found in UnitsK9GridG2 – G7, H1 – H7, I1 – I6 in the north of the definite floor area, and a few floor-like paved bricks can be also seen in some areas. It thus led to the consumption that the original floor of this area was disturbed by later residents. It is likely that the brick-paved floor functions as the eastern square of the main stupa (Color Plate 3-25, 1).

The Late stage

The definite cultural remains of the late stage is Road 4.

1. Road 4

It is located in the east of the excavated area and distributed in UnitK10GridJ3, J4, J5, UnitL10GridA4, A5, A6, B5, B6, C6, and D6. It was found in January 2015, when the Road 3 was excavated. At first, some paved bricks were found above the Road 3; finally it was identified and named as Road 4 after carefully being cleaned. The ground plan of the road is irregular; the northeastern end is narrow and the southwestern end is wide. The direction is northeast-southwest in general, but the southern edge slightly turns southwards with the angle of 165° at the western end. The exposed part is 12 m long, 1.7-2.5 m wide, and 0.05-0.2 m thick.

The two outer sides of Road 4 are constructed with erected bricks, whose northern side is relative complete while the southern side is poorly preserved. The central part is paved horizontally with broken bricks without any fixed direction. But the northeastern end of the road is covered by another layer of big size bricks. In Grid B5 and B6, the surface of the road is a little depressed. At least three kinds of bricks are used, which measure 23×17×5 cm, 21×15×4 cm, and 19x12x4 cm, respectively. However, the upper layer of bricks in the GridC6 are larger than others, and the brick size is 39×27×5 cm. Interestingly, a longitudinal small ditch measuring 2.92×0.065×0.08 m was discovered in the western end of the road, which was probably used for drainage.

The Road 4 is under Layer 5, and cuts Road 3, and overlies the top of the northern entrance of early phase of Temple 1. The northeast part extends to the northeast unexcavated area, and the southwest part might continue to the bottom of the Pillared-hall 1. The age of Road 4 is inferred to be in the later stage of the first period(Figure 3-5; Color Plate 3-25, 2).

第二节

Section 2

The Second Period Cultural Remains (Part I): Cruciform Central Temple

第二期遗迹（上）——十字形中心神殿建筑

十字形中心神殿建筑分布在 UnitH9、H10、I8、I9、I10、I11、J8、J9、J10、J11、K9、K10 等单元内。东西长 62.3 米，南北长 62.8 米，遗迹残存最高点距地表 -0.7 米，最低基础砖距地表 -6.2 米，保存部分相对高度 5.5 米，总面积 1980 平方米，方向近正南北（彩版 3-26）。

一、发掘经过

2013 年，孟加拉国欧提亚·欧耐斯恩（Oitihya Onneswan）考古研究中心的考古学家在发掘神殿 1 时，在西部扰坑的自然剖面上露出部分发现墙砖，因面积有限，对其性质判断不清。2014 年 12 月，中孟联合考古队组织首次联合发掘，在清理该处遗迹时，意外发现这是一段规整且长的砖墙，从已显示的部分，初步判断为一处大型的建筑的墙基。因此，在清理神殿 1 西侧的道路 3、墙 2 等遗迹后，于 2015 年 1 月 16 日，将发掘区往西部扩大，试图通过大面积发掘来弄清该建筑的形制和性质。发掘采用探沟方法，迅速找到该大型建筑墙基的四至，再整体布方全部揭露。发掘和记录工作至 2 月 17 日基本结束。与此同时，从 2015 年 1 月 5 日至 2015 年 2 月 7 日，考古队又完成了其西北部另一处建筑遗迹的发掘。此时，意外地发现，这两处遗迹结构相似，且呈犄角状分布，由于未能认识其确切的性质，暂称之为“塔院”（stupa court），对建筑墙基内的方形柱状物，暂称为“塔基”。2016 年 11 月，中孟联合考古队组织第二次联合考古发掘，在此两座“塔院”的正对面，又发现了形制与尺寸完全相同的建筑体，且呈对称的分布，由此构成一个更为庞大的建筑整体，地层上也处在同一时期，这显然是经过精心的设计的建筑整体，故正式命名为十字形中心神殿（Cruciform Central Temple）建筑。并将原来的“塔院”“塔基”分别更名为“柱厅”“柱基”。2016 年 11 月至 12 月，考古队完成了对柱厅 3、柱厅 4 遗迹的发掘，并对柱厅 1、柱厅 2 未完成的局部以及四个柱厅之间的连接墙基进行了补充发掘。与此同时，从 2015 年 12 月 1 日至 2016 年 1 月 5 日，将中心区域所有上部红褐色的②层土发掘完毕，大部分出露的青褐色（黑色）堆积层面，又在中心区域先后发掘了北、东、南、西四条呈十字形相交的 4 米宽探沟，以及南侧一条东西向的探沟，局部发掘至底部基础面，发掘工作遂告结束。2017 年 1 月—3 月，欧提亚·欧耐斯恩考古研究中心考古队员，在遗址的北部发现了北门道遗迹和一座八边形佛塔。在 2017 年 11 月—12 月的联合发掘中，他们又对中部八边形塔基进行清理，并在柱厅外侧发现了局部护墙，使这座十字形中心神殿建筑的内涵更加完整。至此，根据出露的砖墙建筑及底部基础等情况，已经可以复原出这个十字形中心神殿建筑的整体结构。

二、层位关系

整个遗迹被②层叠压，打破④层，遗迹的墙体被后期取砖严重破坏。在发掘过程中，还有一些局部的遗迹叠压关系，如：柱厅 1 东墙基下叠压遗迹墙 2，西墙基下叠压着另外一处早期砖墙（未编号，可能与墙 2 为同一遗迹）。柱厅 2 西墙基南端，打破了神殿 2 北墙，并局部利用此墙作为基础。柱厅 3 柱基部分打破⑤层，该层土质非常紧密，且较平整，似为早期建筑的活动面。图 2-12 是 UnitI9GridJ1、UnitJ9GridA1、B1、

C1、D1、E1、F1、G1、H1 剖面图，反映了柱厅4的西墙、西北柱基、东北柱基、东墙打破④层的地层关系。

在四个柱厅之间，有四条墙基将柱厅连接在一起，目前发现的都是地表以下的墙基部分，故称之为"连接墙基"。四条"连接墙基"均开口于②层下，打破④层。以连接墙基3为例，该墙基在UnitI9GridE7、F7内出露的最底层基础砖块，距地表深3.9米，与柱厅3围墙基础相连且处于同一水平，而且，连接墙基与柱厅墙基之间相互勾连的建筑方式，表明这两个建筑是统一设计、并同时营建的，没有先后关系。由此推断，连接墙基与柱厅属于同一时期。

中心塔基遗迹普遍被②层叠压，②层为取砖后回填土形成的堆积，呈坑状堆积，坑底一般都直达建筑基础，因位于塔基的中心部位，建筑基础最深，回填层的堆积也相应更厚。由于取砖后形成的坑很深，此后曾形成一个低洼的水塘，与其他区域的②层相比，因较长时间处于一种积水状态，所以形成一些淤泥沉积。该层内还出土保存较好的树根、树干、树叶、种子等植物遗存，少量楠竹、小编织物和螺壳等，它们在饱水、厌氧的环境里得到了保存。由此推测，在此层存在一个自然间隙期，这些树根应是当时生长的，这反映了遗址在破坏之后，在较长时间内的形成过程（彩版3-27，1、2）。根据中心塔基区域东西向横剖面（UnitJ9GridH5、G5、F5、E5、D5、C5、B5、A5，UnitI9GridJ5、I5、H5 剖面图，见图2-13）和南北向纵剖面（UnitJ10GridD8、D7、D6、D5、D4、D3、D2、D1，UnitJ9GridD10、D9、D8、D7、D6、D5 剖面图，见图2-14），可以反映中心塔基的地层堆积情况。

三、遗迹描述

这座十字形中心神殿建筑，由四座柱厅、四条连接墙基和一个中心塔基组成（图3-12），现将遗迹的各个部分描述如下。

（一）柱厅

1. 柱厅1

主要位于UnitK10内，部分分布于UnitK9内。其中东墙基外壁分布于UnitK10GridI1、I2、I3、I4、I5、H6，UnitK9GridI9、I10内；南墙基外壁分布于UnitK9GridA8、B8、C8、D8、E8、F8、G8、H9、I9内；西墙基外壁分布至UnitK10GridA1、A2、A3、A4、A5、A6，并少部分进入UnitJ10内；北墙基外壁已揭露部分分布于UnitK10GridA6、B6、C6、D6、E6、F6、G6、H6内。已发掘部分面积约300平方米（彩版3-27，3）。

柱厅1为墙基和柱基的联合体，东、南、西、北四面墙基大致呈回字形，墙基内有4处柱基。外围东西长17.7米，南北长15.6米（根据南墙基壁的宽度，推测北墙基壁约有0.3米宽度叠压在北部未发掘探方下，因此实际长度也在17.7米左右），内围南北长9.7米，东西长9.7米。方向近正南北（图3-13，3-14；彩版3-28，3-29）。

东墙基：保存状况相对较好。墙基南北两端残存较高，中间部分破坏较严重。主要分布在UnitK9GridH9、I9、H10、I10，Unit10GridG1、G2、G3、G4、G5、G6、H1、H2、H3、H4、H5、H6内，部分叠压在UnitK10Grid的探方G7、H7下，未进行发掘。墙基宽3.8米，残存最高处2.3米。

墙基的结构可分为上部和下部两个部分。

下部砖墙共有24层砖块以平铺形式砌筑而成，东、西两壁均从上至下逐渐内收至底，上宽下窄，剖面略呈倒梯形。最底部的铺砖局部可见有高温形成的火砖，根据在UnitI11、J11等探方中发掘的同时期墙基推测，这种火砖在墙基底面均有分布。

据观察，砖墙下部的东侧（外侧）砖壁立面形态从北部至南部并不完全相同，砖块向外凸出的起始位置没有一致性，整个砖壁没有追求严格平齐的概念，不同部分砖块凹进凸出的情况各不

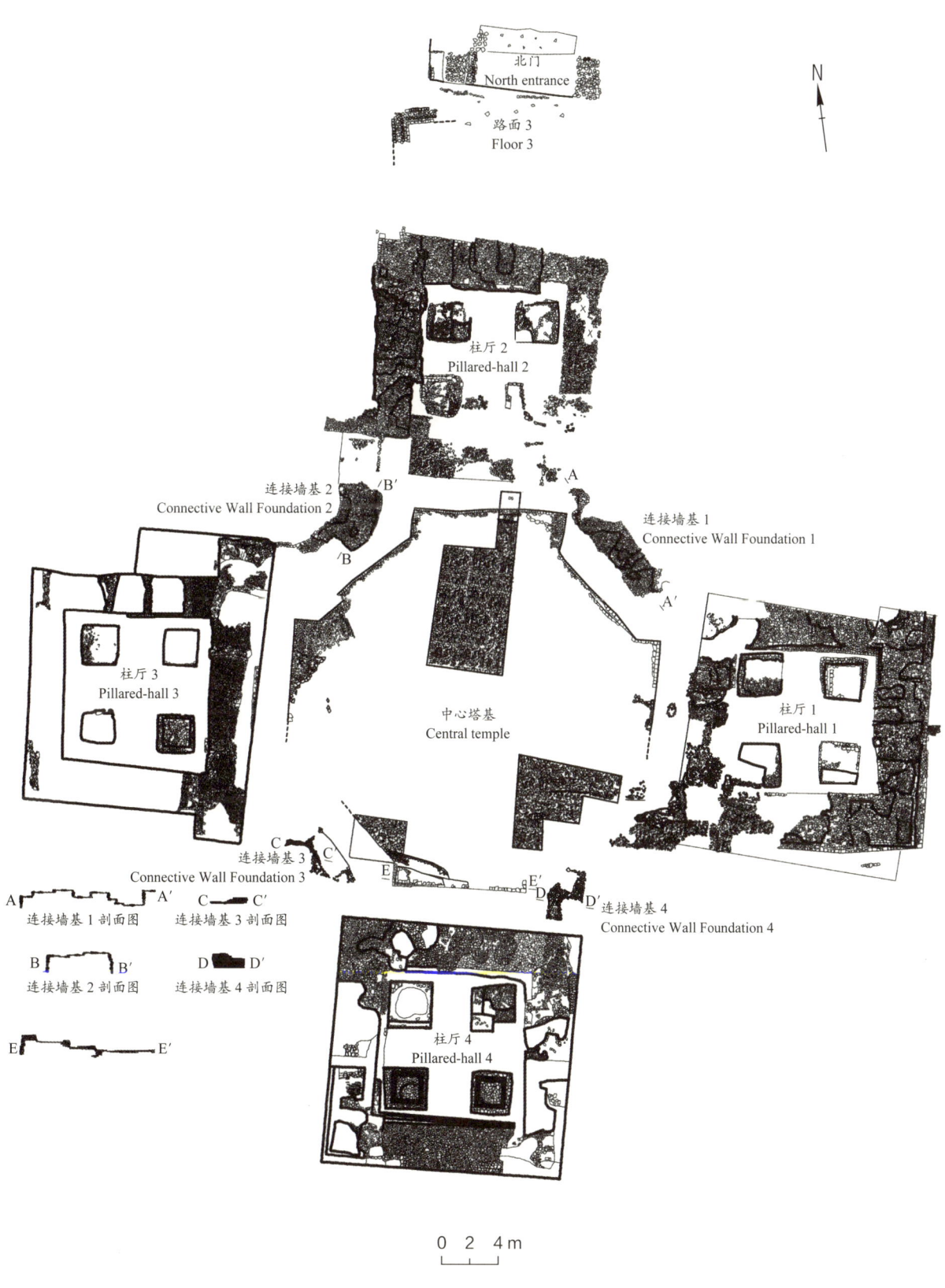

图 3-12 十字形中心神殿建筑平面图
Fig. 3-12 The plan of Cruciform Central Temple

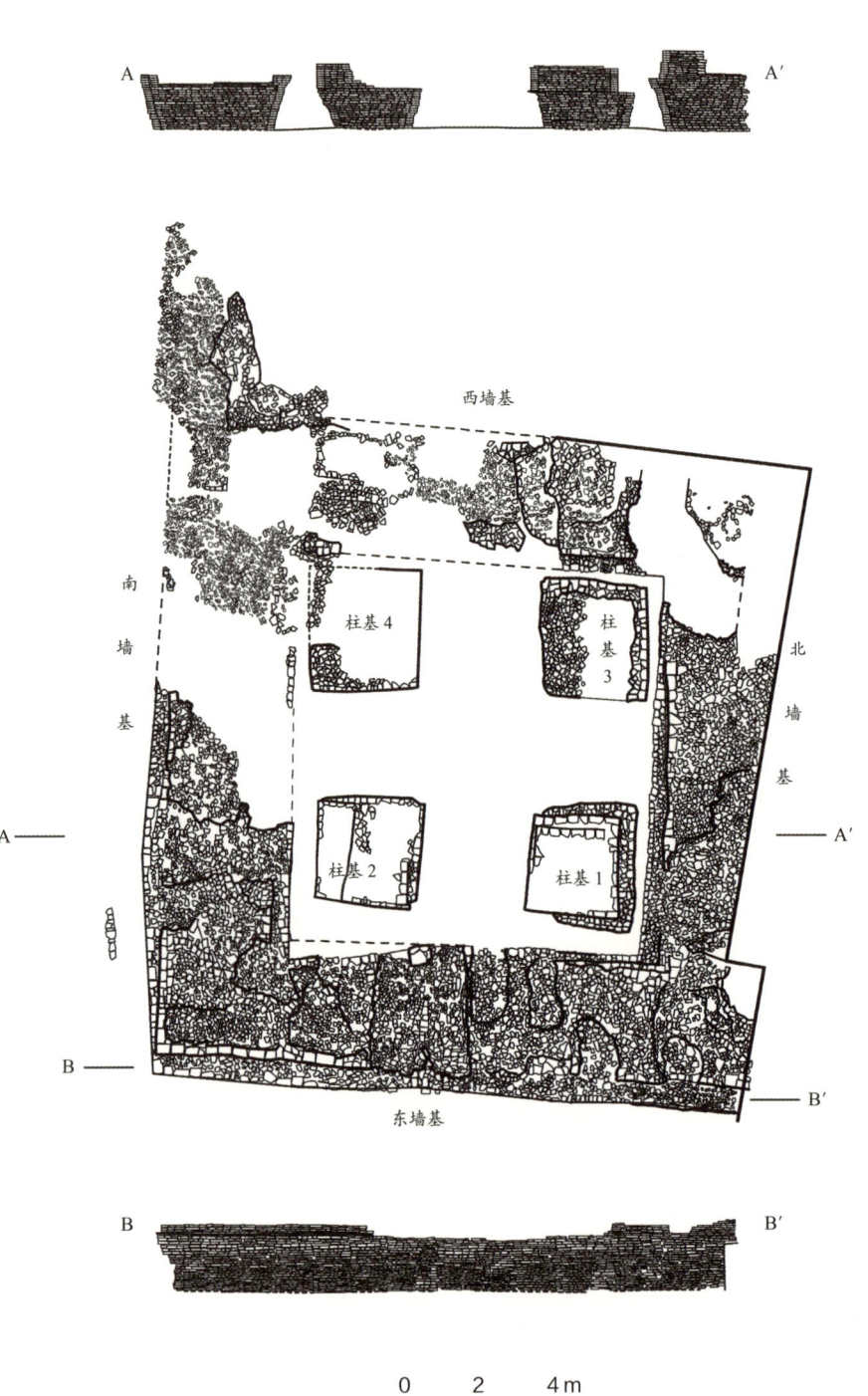

图 3-13 十字形中心神殿建筑柱厅 1 平剖面图
Fig. 3-13　The plan and section of Pillared-hall 1, Cruciform Central Temple

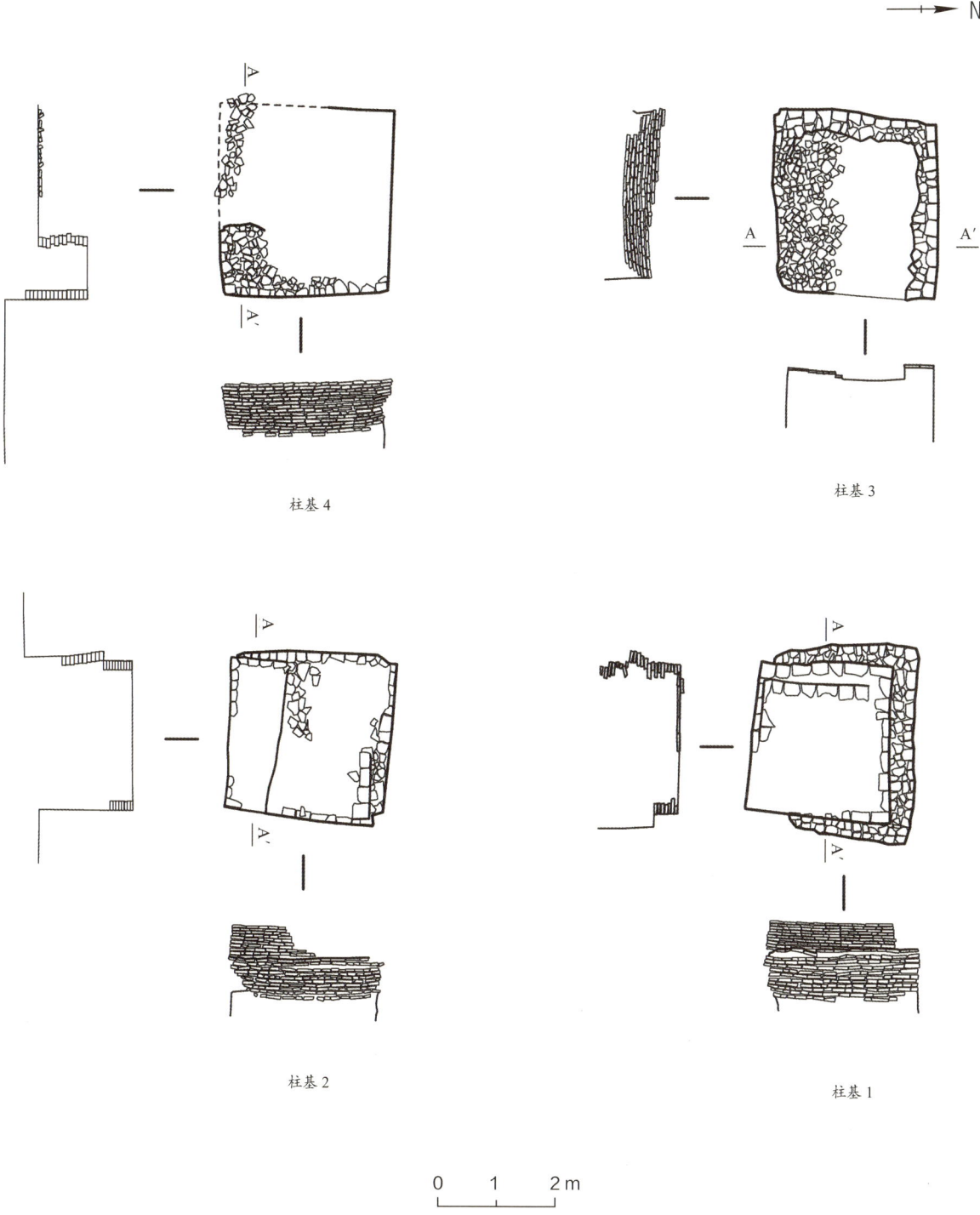

图 3-14　十字形中心神殿建筑柱厅 1 柱基平剖面图

Fig. 3-14　The plan and section of Pillar-plinth of Pillared-hall 1, Cruciform Central Temple

相同。但整体而言，东墙基下半部分在砌筑至最顶部砖时，砖墙东侧边缘仍基本呈水平直线，整个墙基也在表面形成一个相对水平的面，这一点又体现工匠对建筑的结构是有控制的。墙基下部的西侧面（内壁）也与上述东侧面相似，均是由上向下内收至底。据观察，分别从底部向上的第10层砖、第19层砖开始往上逐渐向外伸出，形成三个小的梯级，至第19层砖时不再向外，第20—24层铺砖形成的砖壁较为平齐。

这段砖墙整体高约1.6米，顶面宽约3.8米，为整个墙基的最宽处，底部宽度推测约2.6米，内、外两侧较为粗糙，多不平齐，一些不甚规则的火砖块也掺杂其中，凹进凸出现象十分明显，没有刻意追求外观效果。

下部砖墙砌筑形成一个较宽的水平"台面"之后，上部砖墙宽度开始收缩，整体宽约3米，最高残存0.7米。这部分砖墙在砌筑时，呈三个小梯级向上逐渐缩进。首先，在东侧（外侧）向内收缩0.66米，西侧（内侧）内收0.34米后，铺砌一层厚约7厘米的砖块，在此基础上再分别向内各收缩5—6厘米，向上砌筑5层砖，高约34厘米。从GridG5、H6处保存的墙基观察，保存最高的砖墙西侧（内侧）内收18厘米，东侧（外侧）内收3—6厘米后，又向上砌筑新的砖墙，目前仅残存4层砖的厚度，其上情况不清。在靠近东、西两侧壁处使用的砖块相对较为完整，完整砖的最大规格为38厘米×30厘米×5厘米。用这些砖块形成墙基的四周外框后，再在中间部分砌以各种大小、形状大小不一的破碎砖块，这种现象相当普遍，体现了当时旧物再用的建筑工艺（彩版3-30）。

北墙基：主要分布在UnitK10GridA5、B5、C5、D5、E5、F5、A6、B6、C6、D6、E6、F6内，部分仍叠压在发掘区的北部。GridA5、B5、A6、B6处破坏极为严重，仅残存少量底部的基础。北墙基残存最高处2.4米，据东墙基、南墙基的结构情况，推知该墙的最宽处约3.8米。

该墙基在结构上也分为上、下两个部分，基本情况与东墙基相近。下部墙基呈倒梯形，上面宽下面窄，发掘揭露了18层砖，厚1.43米，未至底。从最宽的顶面开始向下至第5层砖，砖壁较为平齐，再向下，砖墙逐渐内收，至第17层砖时突然内收18厘米。上部砖墙残存最高为0.8米，在砌筑方式上，南侧面（内壁）也是平砌内缩，而西端则保持与原墙基的平齐状态。在砌筑过程中，工匠为保持墙基的总体水平，局部使用灰浆填补，处理因砖块厚度不一而造成的问题。

据观察，南侧（内侧）砖层形成的边缘略呈曲线状，用砖没有统一规格，完整砖最大尺寸为38厘米×28厘米×5厘米，其他砖规格有27厘米×18厘米×6厘米、28厘米×15.5厘米×5厘米等。多种规格砖块混杂使用，砖块间多呈锯齿状凸出，显得粗糙。北侧砖壁（外侧）因未发掘，详细情况不清，推测应与东墙基外壁类似（彩版3-31）。

南墙基：主要分布在UnitK9GridF10、G10、B9、C9、E9、F9、G9、H9、E8、F8、G8内；主体残长10.2米，残存最高处为2.4米。砖墙破坏严重，除A9、B9部分缺失外，其他部分只保存了最底部的基础，由大量火候过高的火砖和普通残砖密集交错铺垫，没有明显的间隙，形成非常坚实的底面。

保存的墙基也由上、下两部分构成。下部砖墙的大部分均未完全发掘，揭露深度约1.35米，结构与东墙基外壁相似，其南、北两侧均上宽下窄，略呈倒梯形，顶部砖面为墙基最宽处，约3.8—4米，值得注意的是，下部砖墙顶层砖面的东南部有一段（位于GridF8、G8中）非常明显的向外突出的弧形，其余部分又基本为直线形，这种现象在其他砖墙中不见，原因不清。

上部砖墙向上内收砌筑，残高0.8米。北侧（内壁）内收43厘米，南侧（外壁）内收30—52厘米，后铺砌一层砖，厚6—7厘米；然后南侧内收5厘米，北侧内收6厘米，再向上平砌4层砖，厚29厘米；南侧继续内收20厘米，北侧则向外伸出8厘米，向上再平铺砌筑砖墙，仅残存7层砖，厚44厘米。完整的砖块不多，最大的砖块尺寸为38厘米×28厘米×5厘米，大部分都是残损砖，形状、大小不一，还有少量火砖，此外，砖缝的尺寸也不一，竖向砖缝约在0.5—2厘米之间，平铺的砖缝在0.5—1厘米之间（彩版3-32，1、2）。

西墙基：主要分布在UnitK10GridA1、A2、A3、A4、A5、B2、B3、B4，UnitK9GridA10、B10内，保存状况较差，残存最高处为1.98米。

在UnitK10GridA1、A2、B2，UnitK9 GridA10、A8、B10内，分布有密集的底层基础火砖和碎砖，部分仅零星分布，但均可见直接叠压在一条南北向长9.05、宽1.75、高0.7米（未见底）的早期砖墙（未编号）之上，可能是利用该墙基作为基础的一部分。

残存墙基的结构与其他三面墙基基本相近，已揭露的东侧壁（内壁）包括下部和上部两部分墙基。下部砖墙应与东墙基基本相同，推测高为1.6米；上部砖墙残高0.38米，先内收40厘米铺建一层砖，厚6厘米；然后内收8—10厘米，向上砌筑3层砖，厚约19厘米；最后又向外伸出约10厘米，向上再次砌筑砖墙，仅残存2层砖。这与南墙基的内侧砖壁砌筑方式相似（彩版3-32，3、4）。

西墙基南端与连接墙基4相接。

柱厅1回字形的围墙内，均匀分布着四个柱基。

柱基1：位于墙内的东北角，主要分布于UnitK10GridE4、F4内，部分进入GridE5、F5、E3、F3内，保存状况较好，距离东墙基0.48—0.7米，距离北墙基约0.4米，残高1.75米。方向近正南北。

该柱基主要由上、中、下三部分呈叠涩状砌筑而成，最底基座部分高约1米，由14层砖平铺砌筑而成，平面呈不规则方形，北壁边缘为不规则曲线状，东、南、西三壁边缘相对较直。四周砖壁由上向下逐渐内收至底，整体形态似方形漏斗状。基座上部长、宽为3.27米×2.7米，下部长、宽为2.54米×2.4米。用砖大小、形状存在很大差异，除边框外，大部分使用残砖铺砌而成，最底层普遍使用火砖，侧壁不平齐，砌筑不很讲究，凹进凸出明显，砖缝也较宽。基座部分与上部柱基有部分错位，柱体北、西、东三侧壁，分别内收46、28、40厘米，南面则向外伸出约10—20厘米。

砌筑在基座之上的中部柱体，平面呈较为规整的正方形，边长均为2.5米，平铺10层砖，残高0.7米。这部分柱体四周的砖壁平直，较下部整齐，砌筑也较为讲究。所用砖多为27厘米×17厘米×5厘米，少量为26厘米×20厘米×5厘米。其东南角和中间部分局部破坏。

砌筑在中部柱体之上的上部柱体，平面也呈正方形，四周边长均为2.1米，其西壁和南壁均分别内收24厘米、10厘米，但破坏严重，仅在西部和南部残存高约5厘米的砖块痕迹。

值得注意的是，包括柱基1在内的其他柱基，破坏最严重的部分均在中心部位，而四周相对较好，这与后期挖坑取砖的行为有关（彩版3-33）。

柱基2：位于墙内的东南角，主要分布于UnitK10GridE1、F1内，部分进入GridE2、F2内，保存较好。距离东墙基1.3—1.5米，距离南墙基0.58米，残高1.46米，方向近正南北。

柱基2由上、下两部分叠涩而成。下部柱基呈不规则方形漏斗状，上宽下窄，由上向下逐渐内收，四角略带弧状，南北长2.85、东西宽2.76、高0.96米，共由12层砖平铺砌筑而成，最底层砌以火砖。北侧砖壁较为整齐，略向外呈弧凸状；东侧最上面一层砖则向外伸出约13厘米；南侧砖壁从底部向上至第11层砖逐渐向外凸出，至12层砖又内收缩约4厘米；西侧砖壁从底部向上第1—10层砖较平直，略向外凸，第11—12层砖向外凸出近12厘米。总体上，南壁和西壁相对较为平直整齐。

上部柱基的柱体略向南偏移，东侧内收约9厘米，北侧内收约31厘米，西侧内收约20厘米，南侧与下部柱基的顶砖平齐。柱体平面形状为方形，四周边长均为2.5米。柱体北部多被后期损毁，仅残存一层砖，南部保存有9层铺砖，厚约50厘米。中间部分的砖块均被后期破坏。砖壁外侧明显较下部分平齐，砖缝也较小，但仍使用少部分火砖（彩版3-34）。

柱基3：位于墙内西北角，主要分布于UnitK10GridB3、C3、B4、C4内。柱基北、西、南三面均完整，东侧和中间部分破坏较为严重，仅保存最下面部分。柱基距离北墙基0.36米，距西墙基0.36米，方向近正南北。

残存柱基为底座部分，共有12层砖，残高约0.84米，平面形状略呈方形漏斗状，上宽下窄，北侧、南侧和西侧壁缘均为不甚规整的直线，东西长3—3.1米，南北宽2.75—2.83米。四周侧壁不平齐，砖缝厚薄不一，较为粗糙，使用的砖块形制和大小不一，大部分均为残损砖块。中间部分由大量形状、大小不一的碎砖块砌筑而成。柱基的底部西侧叠压着大量杂乱的砖块，推测为前期建筑倒塌后的废弃堆积，类似情况在其他探方中也可见到（彩版3-35，1、2）。

柱基4：位于墙内的西南角。主要分布于UnitK10GridC1、D1，UnitK9GridC10、D10内。距离南墙基0.34米，残高0.9米，方向近正南北。柱基破坏严重，西部已全部损毁，南北长2.96米，东西残长1.3米，推测柱基4的尺寸应与其他柱基相近，完整边长3米左右。

柱基残存部分为底座部分，共保存16层砖，由砖块平铺砌筑而成。东侧砖壁由下至上略向外凸出，南侧砖壁较直，北侧砖壁上部5—7层砖明显较下部的砖块向外凸出，西侧壁情况不明。柱基的用砖的规格大小不一，多为残损砖块，砖壁凹进凸出明显，砖缝在0.5—3.5厘米之间（彩版3-35，3、4）。

2. 柱厅2

柱厅2位于UnitI10、J10、I11、J11内，北部有很小部分未发掘。东侧边界分布于UnitI10GridE9、E10，UnitJ11GridE1、E2、E3、E4、E5、E6内；南侧边界分布于UnitI10GridI8、J8，UnitJ10GridA8、B8、C9、D8、E8内；西侧边界分布于UnitI10GridH9、H10，UnitI11GridH1、H2、H3、H4、G4、G5、G6内；北侧边界分布于UnitI11GridG6、H6、I6、J6，UnitJ11Grid A6、B6、C7、D7、E7内。

柱厅结构为内有四个立柱的方形建筑。外侧边长约16米，方向近正方向，面积约256平方米。柱基平面呈方形。大小相近，南北长2.7—2.8米，东西长2.8—2.9米之间，长度的差异与各柱基保留的水平高度有关。在东南、西南各以连接墙基1、连接墙基2与相邻的柱厅1、柱厅3相连（图3-15，3-16；彩版3-36、3-37、3-38）。

东墙基：复原长15.9米，保存长9.4米，宽2.3—2.4米。墙基的砖体基本已被挖掘殆尽，只保留了底部的砖层，多为火砖。最底部有一层厚约5厘米的红褐色黏沙土，掺入较多的砖末和小砖块，其上砌筑一层以火烧砖为主的不规则砖，火砖大多斜砌，少见平铺。火砖长度一般在10—20厘米之间，火砖之间用残砖块塞垫，其上用中小型砖块向上逐层平铺，砖与砖之间用一种灰黄黏土勾缝黏合（彩版3-39，1）。

南墙基：复原长度15.5米，保存长度12.8米，宽度2.3—2.5米。墙基已被完全破坏，只在底部长7.2、宽2.5米范围内保留一段火砖层，火砖之上有局部的平铺砖层。南墙基东端与连接墙基1相连，西端与连接墙基2相连。从整体的结构看，连接墙基与柱厅墙基是连为一体的（彩版3-39，2）。

西墙基：墙基总长度为16.2米，一般宽度为3.2米，最大宽度为3.5米，高度1—1.5米。其中，北部13.7米墙基保存较完整，表面可见多处取砖形成的圆弧形坑状遗迹，靠近南部的一个取砖坑，长3.2、深1.1米，北部有一些小的取砖坑，直径1—1.5米，深0.2—0.3米。南端破坏较严重，只剩下局部的火砖层。

通过清理墙基西侧的④层堆积，显露出墙基的外侧面，经观察发现，在底部火砖之上有6层红砖向上平铺，从7—23层，红砖向外凸出，此

图 3-15　十字形中心神殿建筑柱厅 2 平剖面图
Fig. 3-15　The plan and section of Pillared-hall 2, Cruciform Central Temple

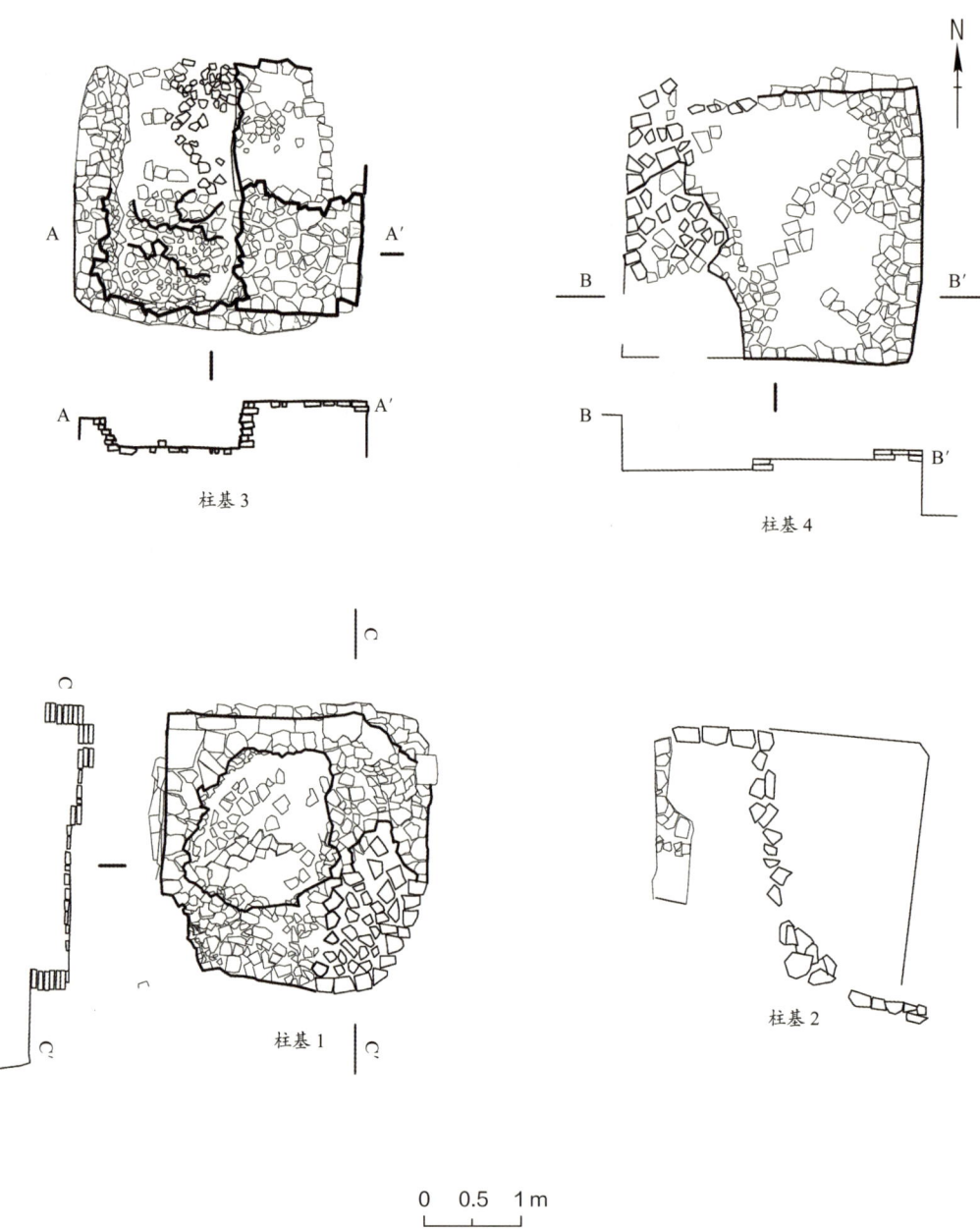

图 3-16 十字形中心神殿建筑柱厅 2 柱基平剖面图
Fig. 3-16 The plan and section of pillar-plinth of the Pillared-hall 2, Cruciform Central Temple

后，又向上逐渐内收。墙基砖体结构的宽度大于底部火烧砖的宽度。墙基两侧边缘砖的尺寸略大，一般长度在15厘米左右，中部的砖料多为残碎，长度多在10厘米左右。这种情况与柱厅1的墙基是一致的。墙基南端打破了早期遗迹神殿2北墙基，并局部利用作为基础（彩版3-40）。

北墙基：复原长度为16米，保存部分长度11.5米，一般宽度为3.2米，最大宽度为3.4米，高度1—1.5米。墙基表面还可以见多个南北向的取砖坑，长度为2—3米，宽度为1—2.8米，深度在0.5—0.8米。

从东端断面观察，墙基最底层为火砖层，其上平铺的19层砖，渐次向外凸出，第20—22层砖为垂直平铺，第23层砖凸出成为最宽处，下部高1.42米。墙基以此分为上、下两部分。向上第24—26层垂直平铺，第27—29层逐渐内收。在北墙基基与西墙基基转角处，有一南北长2.52米，东西残长1.7米的墙基上部，保存有7层砖平铺，残高0.4米。最大一块砖的尺寸为30厘米×20厘米×45厘米（彩版3-41）。

柱厅2回字形的围墙内，均匀分布着四个柱基。

柱基1：呈方形，边长2.8米，最高点水平高程-2.55米，最低点水平高程-3.71米，残存高度1.16米。表面被H1打破，基础压在④层底部的倾斜砖层上。靠近柱基外侧的砖相对较大且完整，里面的砖较残碎。所见最大砖的尺寸为27厘米×20厘米×4.5厘米，柱基西侧尚保存14层砖（彩版3-42）。

柱基2：呈方形，复原边长2.8米，最高点水平高程-2.67米，最低点水平高程-3.6米，残存高度0.93米。柱基2砖体已被后期全部取走，仅保留北侧和西侧的局部砖块（彩版3-43，1、2）。

柱基3：南北长2.7米，东西长2.9米，最高点水平高程-2.89米，最低点水平高程-4.42米，残存高度1.53米。柱基修建在④层最底部一层倾斜砖层上。由东向西观察，下部19层砖向下内收，中部3层砖平铺外凸，上部2层砖垂直平铺（彩版3-43，3、4）。

柱基4：平面形状较完整，西南角略有残破，南北长2.7米，东西长2.8米，最高点水平高程-3.55米，最低点水平高程-4.13米（未发掘到底），残存高度0.58米。柱基修建在④层底部倾斜砖层上。从剖面观察，外缘用砖都是相对较好的砖块，中间砖块相对碎小（彩版3-43，5、6）。

3. 柱厅3

柱厅3位于遗址的西部，主要分布在Unit I9、I10、H9、H10内。其中东墙基外壁分布于UnitI9GridF6、F7、F8、F9、E10，UnitI10Grid E1、E2、E3、E4内，南墙基外壁分布于UnitH9 GridH5、I6、J6，UnitI9GridA6、B6、C6、D6、E6、F6内，西墙基外壁分布于UnitH9GridH5、H6、H7、H8、H9、H10，UnitH10GridH1、G2、G3内，北墙基外壁分布于UnitH10GridG3、H3、I3、J3，UnitI10GridA3、B4、C4、D4、E4内。总面积约300平方米。

柱厅3为柱基和围墙的联合体，包括东、南、西、北四个墙基和墙内的4个柱基。墙基平面呈"回"字形，外围东部长16.1米，南部长15.75米，西部长15.95米，北部长16.25米；内围东部长10.6米，南部长10.2米，西部长10.2米，北部长10.1米。方向近正方向。柱基2、3略有保存，柱基1、4破坏严重，出于对遗迹的保护，未作全面的清理（图3-17；彩版3-44）。

东墙基：主要分布在UnitI9GridD8、D9、D10、E6、E7、E8、E9、E10，UnitI10GridD1、D2、D3、D4、E1、E2、E3、E4，少量进入UnitI9 GridF6、F7、F8、F9、F10。整个墙基除北端略有残存，整体破坏较为严重。墙基上部宽3.2米，底部宽1.90—2.60米，深度约2.98米。据残存的墙基剖面分析，东、西两侧壁均从上至下逐渐内收至底，上宽下窄，剖面形状略呈倒梯形，残存砖墙最高处约1.55米，是由17层砖块以平铺形式砌筑而成。使用砖的形状、大小均不一，大量使用残损砖，少量使用火砖，完全完整的砖块不多。竖向砖缝约在0.5—2厘米，平铺的砖缝介

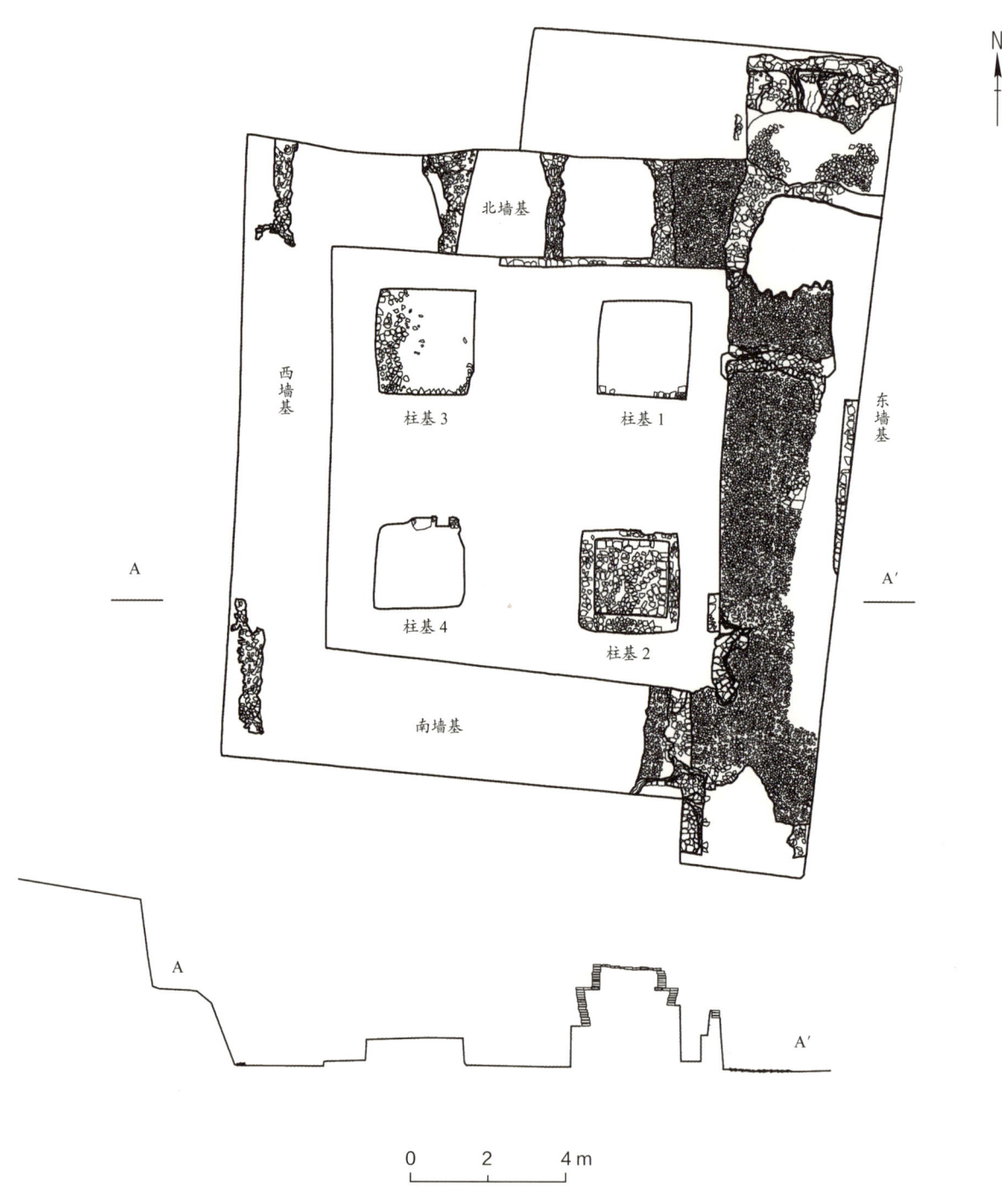

图 3-17 十字形中心神殿建筑柱厅 3 平剖面图

Fig. 3-17 The plan and section of Pillared-hall 3 , Cruciform Central Temple

于0.5—5毫米之间。常见砖的规格为33厘米×24厘米×6厘米，最大的砖块尺寸为40厘米×28厘米×6厘米（彩版3-45，1）。

南墙基：主要分布在UnitH9GridH6、H7、I6、7、J6、J7，UnitI9GridA6、A7、B6、B7、C6、C7、D6、D7、E6、E7，少量进入UnitI09GridF6、F7中。墙基上部宽约3.1米，底部宽约2.20米，深度约3.05米。破坏严重，仅东面残存一部分。该墙基结构与东墙基相近，东面砖墙残高约1.05米，由12层砖块以平铺形式砌筑而成，其底部铺以杂乱的火砖，厚约0.2米（彩版3-45，2）。

西墙基：主要分布在UnitH9GridH6、H7、H8、H9、I6、I7、I8、I9、I10，UnitH10GridH1、H2、H3内。墙基基本上已破坏殆尽，仅存残迹。该墙基保存的建筑结构与东墙基相近，呈倒梯形，上宽下窄。墙基上部宽约3.10，底部宽约2.40米，深度约2.70米。其中UnitH9GridH6、H7中的一段残长约3.50米；UnitI10GridH2、H3中一段残长约3.00米，残高约0.60米，由6层砖块平铺砌筑而成，其底部铺以杂乱的火砖，厚约0.20米（彩版3-45，3）。

北墙基：主要分布在UnitH10GridH2、H3、I2、I3、J2、J3，UnitI10GridA2、A3、B2、B3、C3、C4、D3、D4、E3、E4内。北墙基破坏较严重，仅在东面、中间和西面各残存一小段。墙基上部宽约3.00米，底部宽约2.20米，深度约2.65米。该墙基在结构上基本与东墙基相近。墙基呈倒梯形，上面宽下面窄。砖墙残存最高为0.40米，由3层砖块以平铺砌筑而成，其底部铺以杂乱的火砖，厚约0.20米（彩版3-45，4）。

柱厅3回字形的围墙内，均匀分布着四个柱基。

柱基1：位于墙内东北角，主要分布于UnitI10GridB1、B2、C1、C内。距离东墙基0.95米，距离北墙基约0.80米。柱基平面近正方形，南北长2.55，东西宽2.40，残高2.00米，方向近正方向。柱基南面略为完整，东、西、北和中间被破坏，残存部分由大量形状、大小不一的碎砖块平铺砌筑而成。部分所用砖规格为27×17×5厘米，少量为26厘米×20厘米×5厘米。未作完全清理（彩版3-46，1）。

柱基2：位于墙内东南角，主要分布于UnitI9GridB8、B9、C8、C9、D8、D9内。距离东墙基1.05米，距离南墙基1.10米，保存情况较好。柱基平面近正方形，东西长2.65米，南北宽2.56米，残高2.50米，方向近正方向。保存的柱基由上、中、下三部分叠涩而成，通过对南侧下部砖壁的局部解剖，下部基座上宽下窄，由30层砖平铺砌筑而成，从上向下内收，下部约有0.61米未做解剖。下部侧壁不平齐，砖缝厚薄不一，较为粗糙，大部分使用的砖块大小不一，大部分均为残损砖块。中部柱基略偏东北位置，由6层砖平铺砌成，四周边长均为2米，东侧内收27厘米，北侧内收20厘米，西侧内收38厘米，南侧内收36厘米。墙面砌筑整齐。上部柱基位于中部柱基的中心位置，四侧各内收7—8厘米。平面形状为方形，边长1.85、残高0.18米，墙面砌筑工整，四面整齐，仅存2—3层砖平铺，其上已被破坏（彩版3-46，2）。

柱基3：位于墙内的西北角，主要分布于UnitH10GridJ1内，少量进入UnitH9GridJ10、UnitH10GridI1、J2、UnitI10GridA1、UnitI9GridA10内。距离西墙基1.01米，距离北墙基0.84米。柱基南北长2.70米，东西宽2.55米，残高1.65米，方向近正方向。柱基西面、南面较完整，东北角和中间被破坏，残存部分由碎砖块平铺砌筑而成。柱基3未作完全清理。通过对南部墙面局部解剖，下部柱基为略呈不规则的方形，上宽下窄，从上向下的5层砖四面均规整，第6层开始内收，下部约有0.63米未做解剖。四周侧壁不平齐，砖缝厚薄不一，较为粗糙，使用的砖块形制和大小不一，大部分均为残损砖块（彩版3-46，3）。

柱基4：位于墙内的西南角，主要分布于UnitH9GridJ8、J9，UnitI9GridA8、A9内。距离南墙基1.1米，距离西墙基0.95米。柱基东西长2.6米，南北宽2.35米，残高为0.55米，方向近正方向。柱基上方有一近方形的取砖坑，柱基已经破坏殆尽，仅保存最底部的火砖层，未作清理（彩版3-46，4）。

4. 柱厅4

柱厅4位于遗址的南部，分布于UnitI8、UnitJ8、UnitI9、UnitJ9内。东侧边界分布于UnitJ8GridH6、H7、H8、H9、H10，UnitJ9GridH1、H2、H3、H4内；南侧边界分布于UnitJ8GridA6、B6、C6、D6、E6、F6、G6、H6内；西侧边界分布于UnitI8GridA6、A7、A8、A9、A10，UnitI9GridJ1、J2、J3内；北侧边界分布于UnitI9GridJ3，UnitI9GridA3、B3、C3、D3、E3、F4、G4、H4内。

柱厅4是一个边长约16米的方形建筑，由外围四道墙基和中间的4个柱基组成，方向近正方向。目前发现的四个柱厅的墙基和柱基的结构大体一致，柱厅4保存相对较好。墙基皆上宽下窄，向下内收，边缘砖体砌筑规整，中间部位多随意平铺。方形柱基可分为上、下两个部分。下部呈四方漏斗状，砖体砌筑不甚规整，砖与砖之间缝隙较大，在3—5毫米之间，所用砖体较厚；上部所用砖较薄，砌筑规整，砖与砖之间缝隙较小，在2—3毫米之间（图3-18；彩版3-47、3-48）。

东墙基：分布于UnitJ8GridG6、H6、G7、H7、G8、H8、G9、H9、G10、H10，UnitJ9Grid G1、H1、G2、H2、G3、H3、G4、H4内。其中北部保存一段，残长1.5米，上部宽3.4米，底部宽2.4米，保存高度2.1米。其余部分砖结构都不超过1米（彩版3-49，1）。

南墙基：分布于UnitJ8GridA6、B6、C6、D6、E6、F6、G6、H6、B7、C7、D7、E7、F7、G7、H7内，复原长度15.4米，保存长度14.4米，最宽处3.55米，残高2.55米。在东端南墙基与东墙基连接处，墙基保存不甚完整。在西端与西墙基转角连接处，有一边长1.5米的三角形取砖坑。中间有9米长的墙基保存较好，墙基外侧砌筑规整，内部铺砖较为随意。通过北侧的墙基剖面，呈现由下往上5个层级：先是垂直砌砖13层砖，高1米；再砌筑5层砖，高0.37米，向外伸出0.1米；再向上砌筑4层砖，高0.25米，伸出0.14米；再向上砌筑2层砖，高0.12米，内收0.16米；再向上砌筑7层砖（上部缺失），高0.45米，内收0.16米（彩版3-49，2、3、4）。

西墙基：分布于UnitI8GridA6、A7、A8、A9、A10，UnitI9GridJ1、J2、J3，UnitI8GridA6、A7、A8、A9、A10，UnitI9GridA1、A2、A3内；长度16米，宽度2.6米，保存高度2.1米。大部分已经被破坏，只剩下局部的砖结构和底部砖。在西墙的②层积堆中，发现一块可能用于建筑的石材（彩版3-50，1）。

北墙基：分布于UnitI9GridJ2、J3，UnitI9 GridA2、A3、B2、B3、C2、C3、D2、D3、E2、E3、F2、F3、G2、G3、H3、H4内。北墙基长16.2米，保存最宽处3.05米，高度2.1米，表面有大小、深浅不一的取砖坑，在西、东两端分别可与东北、西北方向连接墙基3、4的砖结构相连接。

北墙基内侧保存较好，观察其剖面结构，由下往上可分为3个层级，底部高度0.76，有11层砖砌筑，外侧边缘不甚规整；向上砌筑12层砖，高0.82米，内收0.4米；再砌筑7层砖，高0.37米，内收0.14米（彩版3-50，2、3、4）。

柱厅4回字形的围墙内，均匀分布着四个柱基。

柱基1：分布于UnitJ8GridB7、B8、C7、C8内，距西墙0.3米，距南墙0.4米。南北长2.8米，东西长2.9米，通高2.7米，保存较好。下部共有砖17层，高度1.25米，底部的12层砖至17层砖逐层凸出，伸出0.25米。上部规整，自下而上分5级逐级内缩：第1级砖4层，高0.23米；第2级砖4层，高0.23米；第3级砖9层，高0.55米；第4级砖4层，高0.23米；第5级砖4层，高0.21米。柱基1北侧面基本垂直的，没有明显的凸出（彩版3-51，1、2）。

柱基2：分布于UnitJ8GridE8、E9、F8、F9内，距东墙0.8米，距南墙0.44米。柱基2南北

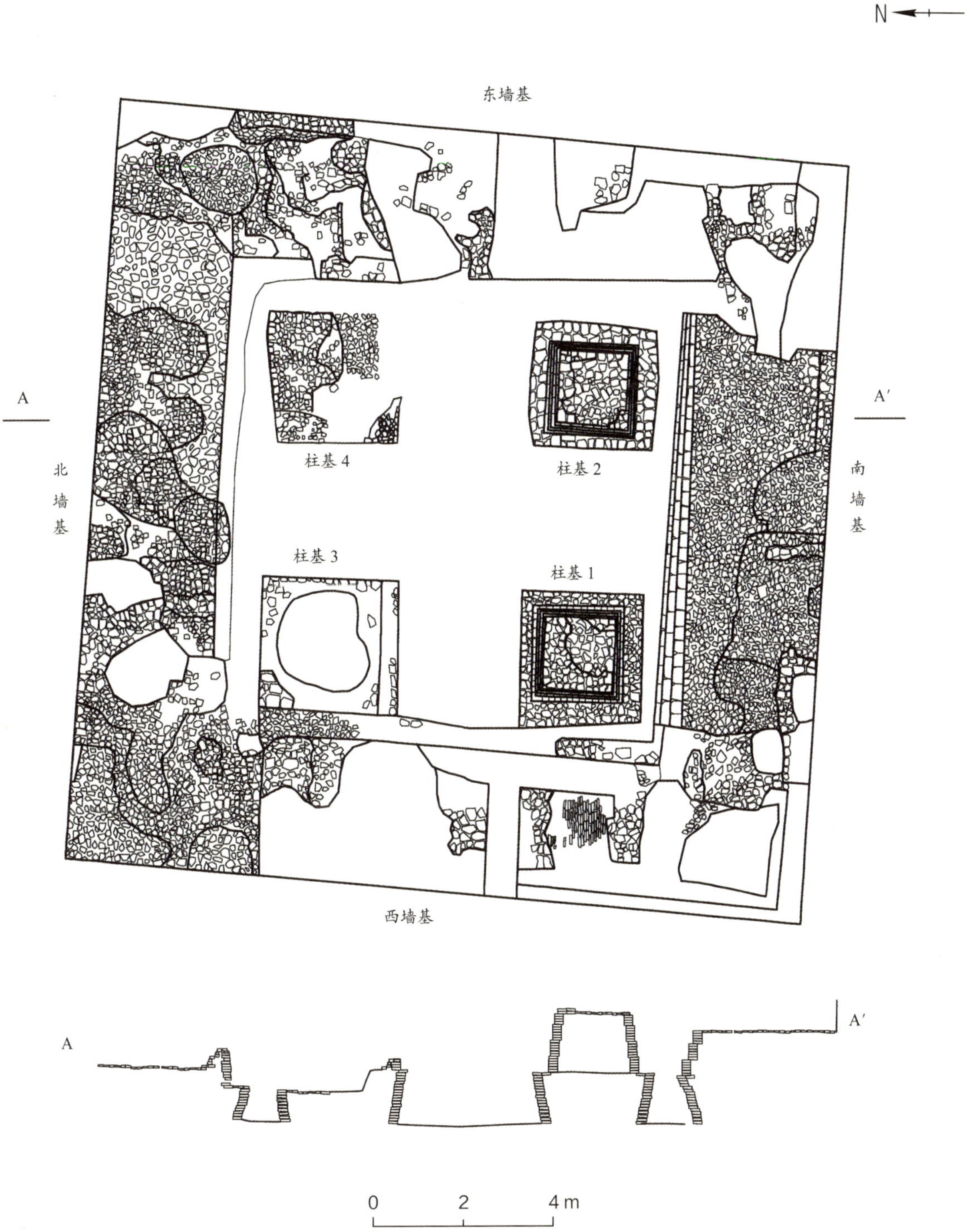

图 3-18 十字形中心神殿建筑柱厅 4 平剖面图
Fig. 3-18 The plan and section of Pillared-hall 4, Cruciform Central Temple

长 2.6 米，东西长 2.7 米，保存较好。上部高 1.4 米，下部高 1.28 米，通高 2.68 米。

柱基 2 下部以西侧剖面为例，自下而上可分为 3 级：第 1 级高 0.7 米，垂直砌砖 11 层，边缘砌筑不整齐；第 2 级高 0.14 米，垂直砌砖 2 层，较第一级边缘伸出 0.1 米；第 3 级高 0.33 米，垂直砌砖 5 层，较第 2 级边缘伸出 0.19 米。柱基 2 东侧面，共有砖 16 层，基本垂直，没有外伸结构。

柱基 2 上部砌筑规整，由下向上分 5 级逐级收缩：第 1 级砌砖 7 层，高 0.41 米；第 2 级砌砖 6 层，高 0.34 米，边缘内收 0.05 米；第 3 级砌砖 6 层，高 0.33 米，边缘内收 0.05 米；第 5 级砌砖 4 层，高 0.21 米，边缘内收 0.05 米；第 5 级砌砖 3 层，高 0.16 米，边缘内收 0.06 米（彩版 3-51，3、4；彩版 3-52）。

柱基 3：分布于 UnitJ8GridB10、C10，7、C8，UnitJ9GridB1、C1 内，距西墙 0.25 米，距北墙 0.66 米。柱基 3 上部已被破坏，下部大致保存外部轮廓，南面保留 12 层砖，高 0.85 米；东面保留 12 层砖，高 0.74 米；北面保留 11 层砖，高 0.8 米。柱基 3 下部有一种四周向中间内陷的现象，其他柱基也有不同程度向中心内陷的情况，可能与承受柱子重量所致（彩版 3-53，1、2）。

柱基 4：分布于 UnitJ8GridE10，UnitJ9GridE1、E2、F1、F2 内，距北墙 0.72 米，距东墙 0.8 米。柱基 4 只残存柱基下部，底部南北长 2.4 米，东西长 2.76 米。东侧保留砖 2—4 层，残高 0.05—0.3 米；西北端保留砖 11 层，残高 0.72 米；西南角保留砖 9 层，残高 0.5 米（彩版 3-53，3、4）。

（二）连接墙基

1. 连接墙基 1

位于中心神殿建筑的东北部，连接柱厅 1 的西北部和柱厅 2 的东南部。位于 UnitJ10Grid G6、H6、I6、F7、G7、H7、E8、F8、G8、E9、F9 内。

连接墙基 1 呈东南—西北走向，北端略呈弧形转弯，中部呈长条形，方向 322 度，南端未发掘。砖体结构已被后期取砖破坏，多处有挖砖留下的坑。墙基残长 9.23 米。北部西侧弧形位置，下部砌出三个三角形凸出砖体，其上为垂直平铺。北部最高处保留 23 层砖体，高 1.2 米（彩版 3-54）。

2. 连接墙基 2

位于中心神殿建筑的西北部，连接柱厅 2 的西南部和柱厅 3 的东北部。位于 UnitI10GridD4、E4、D5、E5、F5、G5、G6、H6、I6、G7、H7、I7、G8、H8、G9、H9 内。

连接墙基 2 可分为 3 个部分，北部与柱厅 2 南墙相连，南部与柱厅 3 的北墙相连。中部弧形部分起转向的作用。目前保存的最高点水平为 -1.96 米，最低点水平为 -3.93 米，保存高度为 1.97 米。北部墙体南北长 4.5 米，东西宽 2.7 米，大部分已被取砖破坏。从剖面上看，墙体可分上下两部分，下部高 1.5 米，上部砖体内收 0.34 米，保留砖 8 层，高 0.5 米。从剖面上还可观察到，修建时首先是在④层中挖槽，然后填筑一种纯净的青灰色沙土，底部用火砖斜砌，其上用红砖平铺，逐层上砌。这种修筑方法与其他 3 处连接墙基一致。中部两侧弧线基本平行，宽度 2.8 米。南部墙体东西长 4.7 米，南北宽 2.5 米，保存高度 2 米，局部露出底部火砖。

连接墙基 1 与连接墙基 2 有所差别，连接墙基 1 是两端呈弧形，中部是呈长条形，而连接墙基 2 是两端为长条形，中部是弧形。由于连接墙基处于柱厅建筑的四角，墙基的形制可能与墙体的具体需要有关（彩版 3-55）。

3. 连接墙基 3

位于中心神殿建筑的西南，连接柱厅 3 东南角和柱厅 4 西北角。未全部发掘，揭露部分分布于 UnitI9GridJ5、I5、I6、H5、H6、F6、F7、E6、E7、D5 内。

连接墙基 3 遭后期取砖破坏甚大，主体部分砖墙已所剩不多。但根据残迹和取砖坑的形状，可推知其平面形状为圆弧形结构，与连接墙基 2 相似。揭露部分长 13.36 米，宽 3.05 米，残高 1.9 米。

墙体东部在 Grid J3 内与柱厅 4 北墙呈直角相接，此处残存 4 层砖，残高 0.2 米，残长 1.5 米。墙基由砖块平铺砌筑而成，边缘砖块尺寸相对较大，中心部位由残缺砖块填充砌筑，青灰色粉沙黏土填缝，砖缝宽近 3 厘米。残存部分保存 5 层砖，残高 0.45 米。在 GridE7、F7 内出露最底层基础砖块，距地表深 3.9 米，与柱厅 3 围墙基础相连且处于同一水平。墙体西部 GridD5、D6 内残存相对较好的墙基，与柱厅 3 的南墙呈直角相连，南北残长 1.7 米，东西残宽 0.75 米，残高 1.9 米，共存 22 层平铺砖，底部为火砖（彩版 3-56，1、2）。

4. 连接墙基 4

位于中心神殿建筑的东南部，北端与柱厅 1 的西墙相连，南端与柱厅建筑 4 的北墙相连，未全部发掘，揭露部分分布于 UnitJ9GridJ8、J7、I8、I7、H6、H5、G6、G5、G4 内。

连接墙基 4 平面形状为两端带圆弧的长条形，结构与连接墙基 1 相似。因后期的取砖破坏，在 UnitJ9GridI6、I7、J6、J7 内，露出最底层基础砖，用密集的红色碎砖块竖立铺垫而成，基础面基本呈水平，连接墙基 4 北端与柱厅 1 的西墙下叠压着早期的一个砖墙建筑（未编号），其基础面较柱厅 1 砖墙的基础面高出 0.6 米，与其他 3 处连接墙基有所不同。墙基长 13.2 米，宽 2.9 米，残高约 1 米，顶砖距地表深 2.3 米。建筑时直接在底层基础砖面上平铺砖块，墙基底窄上宽，呈倒梯形，多用残缺不完整砖，较完整的砖尺寸为 25 厘米×18 厘米×6 厘米、30 厘米×25 厘米×5 厘米（彩版 3-56，3、4）。

（三）中心塔基

中心塔基位于中心神殿建筑的中心部位，处于由东、北、西、南四座柱厅及附属的连接墙基所构成的近八角形的封闭空间内，为十字形中心神殿建筑的核心部分，主要分布于 UnitJ10 和 UnitJ9 的大部分，以及 UnitI10 和 UnitI9 的小部分，总面积约 580 平方米（彩版 3-57）。

中心塔基的发掘采取探方和探沟相结合的方式，目前未全部揭露至底，但根据出露的砖墙及底部基础等情况，已经可以复原出中心塔基的平面结构。

中心塔基的平面形状为八边形，在东、南、西、北四个正方位略有向外凸出的塔基部分，长 9.2 米、宽 1.6 米左右（距地表 2.6 米处的墙宽 1.6 米，因它是逐层向上递减的，因此，向上会略小于 1.6 米，向下会略大于 1.6 米）。中心部位塔心区的砖基被后期完全取走，仅存形状不规则的底砖，塔基的四周边缘残存着部分墙基，以南部保存较好，北部、西部和东部也有局部的残存（见图 3-12）。

目前揭露的南部塔基南端保存相对较好，主要分布于 UnitJ9GridA5、B5、C5、D5、E5、F5、A6 和 B6 等 7 个探方内，墙基东西长 9.2 米，残宽 0.7—2.98 米，已发掘部分残高 2.02 米，顶砖距地表深约 2.6 米。方向大致为 270°。两侧外缘可见墙基的连接转折，西侧外缘保存较完整，从内拐角点（位于 GridA5 探方东北部和 GridF6 的西南部）以 135°的角度分别向两侧延伸，并与中心区域东、西两端相同规格的墙基相接，从而可能复原出整体上的八边形塔基。南侧凸出墙基砌筑方式为错缝平铺，自下而上分 4 个梯级，以 7—9 厘米宽度收缩，呈梯级逐层内收，每一梯级为高约 0.43 米的 7 层砖砌。从外侧墙基观察，砌筑较为规整，壁面基本平整、垂直，没有明显凹进凸出的现象，砖缝较为均匀，较柱厅的墙基建筑更为讲究。其西南角距离连接墙基 3 为 2.57 米，距离柱厅 4 北围墙为 2.35 米，东南角距离连接墙基 4 为 1.52 米，距离柱厅 4 北围墙为 2.61 米。

东部塔基北端墙体形状保存较完整，分布在 UnitJ10GridI1、I2、I3、I4 内，长 3.4 米、宽 1.7 米、清理高度 1.36 米，南端 UnitJ9GridI9 内有些经扰乱散落的砖块，从取砖坑所形成的形状和范围，以及残存砖墙的排列，可知东部塔基与南部塔基结构相似，多数砖块不完整，完整砖尺寸为 30 厘米×19 厘米×4 厘米，东壁距离柱厅 1 西墙基底部 2.46 米。东部至北部外侧直线连接墙体，分布在 Unit J10GridE10、F9、G8、H7 内，长 7.9 米、宽 0.4 米、清理高度 0.98 米，部分墙体略呈倒塌倾斜状态。

北部塔基保存两端外侧边缘轮廓，分布在 UnitI10GridJ6、J7，UnitI11GridA6、A7、B6、B7、C7、D7 内，长 10.4 米、宽 2.64 米、高 1.98 米。西端部分保存较高墙体，南北长 1.75 米、残宽 0.66 米、高 1.98 米，顶砖距离地表深 3.89 米，在转角部位有一段长 0.56 米、宽 0.35 米、高 0.65 米的墙体，该段修筑方式也与南塔基相近，呈梯级状平铺砌筑，结构应与南部塔基相近。

西部塔基中北部轮廓清楚，分布在 Unit I9GridG8、G9、G10、H8、H9、H10 和 UnitI10 GridG1、G2、G3、H1、H2、H3 内，长 6.9 米、宽 1.74 米、残高 1.5 米，完整砖尺寸为 39 厘米×29 厘米×6 厘米。顶砖距地表深 4.15 米，西端外壁缘距离柱厅 3 东墙基约 2.18 米。西部至北部外侧直线连接墙体，分布在 UnitI10GridH2、H3、H4、I3、I4、I5、J5、J6 内，长 8.4 米、宽 3 米、清理高度 1.5 米。

通过对 UnitJ10GridB3、C3、B4、C4、B5、C5、B6、C6 探方的发掘，发现塔基底部分布有一层密集的基础砖，距离地表深约 6.1 米，低于柱厅建筑围墙基础约 2.6 米，由大量棕褐色的火砖和红色的碎砖块铺垫而成，基本呈水平，其上还残存部分砖块，显示是直接从这个基础面向上平铺砌筑的，砖尺寸较大，规格为 45 厘米×30 厘米×5 厘米。通过对 UnitJ9GridE7、F7、E8、F8、G8、E9、F9、G9、H9 的发掘，也全部揭露出底层基础砖，底层基础距离地表深约 5.9 米，局部还残存 2—3 层平铺砖块，规格和铺砌方式也大致与上述探方相近，但在 GridF8、G8 与 F9、G9 交界处，底部基础铺砌略有不同，此处用砖多使用残断砖块，火砖的数量较少，铺砌方式为砖块竖立砌筑，因而两者之间形成较为明显的界限，由于发掘有限，这种情况是否与中心塔基的结构有关，尚待进一步分析（彩版 3-58，3-59）。

（四）北门和护墙遗迹

2017 年 1 月—3 月，欧提亚·欧耐斯恩（Oitihya Onneswan）考古研究中心考古队员，在遗址的北部发掘了北门遗迹。北门西南部毗邻八边形佛塔 2，揭露的墙体分布于 UnitI12GridE10、F10、G10，UnitI13GridF1、G1、H1、F2–J2、F3–J3，UnitJ13GridA2–D2、A3–D3 等探方内，西侧和东侧继续向两端方向延伸。整体保存较差，大部分被后期破坏，多残存基础部分，其中北部和东部破坏尤甚，但幸运的是在西北角保存了部分完整的墙体，残存高度达 1.5 米，使我们能够对门道的基本结构有初步的认识。已揭露的遗迹东西长 23.1、宽 3 米。

北门的结构大体可以分为三部分，中间为长 11.6 米、宽 3 米的门道，两侧为与门道相连的东西两侧墙体。西侧墙体为直角曲折状，呈之字形，由南向北，墙体向北 1 米后，向东转折 4.2 米，然后再往北 1.2 米，而与中间门道相连。东侧墙体破坏较大，但残存的部分基础表明与西侧具有相同的构造，推测两侧应基本对称。在残存最高的墙体外壁使用了部分装饰砖以营造出弧形结构，整个外壁规整而平滑，显示了高超的建筑技艺。

北门建筑开口于②层下，打破④层，推测属于遗址第二期，应为十字形中心神殿的北部门道（图 3-19；彩版 3-60，3-61）。

根据巴哈布尔十字形建筑的复原图，在柱厅外有一层平行分布的护墙，在纳提什瓦十字形神殿的柱厅外侧，也发现类似的护墙建筑迹象，如 UnitK9GridJ8 就是柱厅 1 东南角护墙的基部（彩版 3-62，1）。

四、年代推断

建筑的年代为遗址的第二期。根据④层、⑤层 ^{14}C 年代测定数据，我们认为建筑的建造和使用年代在 10 世纪至 13 世纪，具体的年代定在 950—1223 年。由于②层尚缺乏相关的测年数据和其他可以确定年代的遗物，我们根据本地区的历史沿革，推测②层属于穆斯林统治时期，约公元13世纪上半期。

五、对于建筑复原的设想

中心佛塔和东、南、西、北四个柱厅及相应的连接墙基，是这座十字形中心神殿建筑的主体。柱厅的墙基结构及砌筑方式大体是一致的，四个柱基的形制和结构也基本相同，且在墙基内分布对称，构成较为固定的程式，表明这是经过统一设计和规划的。从④层的奠基到建筑主体及同时期附属建筑的修筑，都是同时的。在其使用的几百年中，总的格局没有大的改动，只是周围建筑有些局部的修缮和扩建，如八边形佛塔就存在一个改扩建的现象。

（一）关于建筑方式

④层堆积作为十字形中心神殿建筑的奠基层，普遍分布于整个遗迹范围内。建筑的修造过程是：先搬运大量泥沙于此，填土以抬升地面，待沉实后，挖建筑的基槽，再砌筑建筑的墙基。理由如下：

1. ④层的分布是有边界的，基本上与十字形

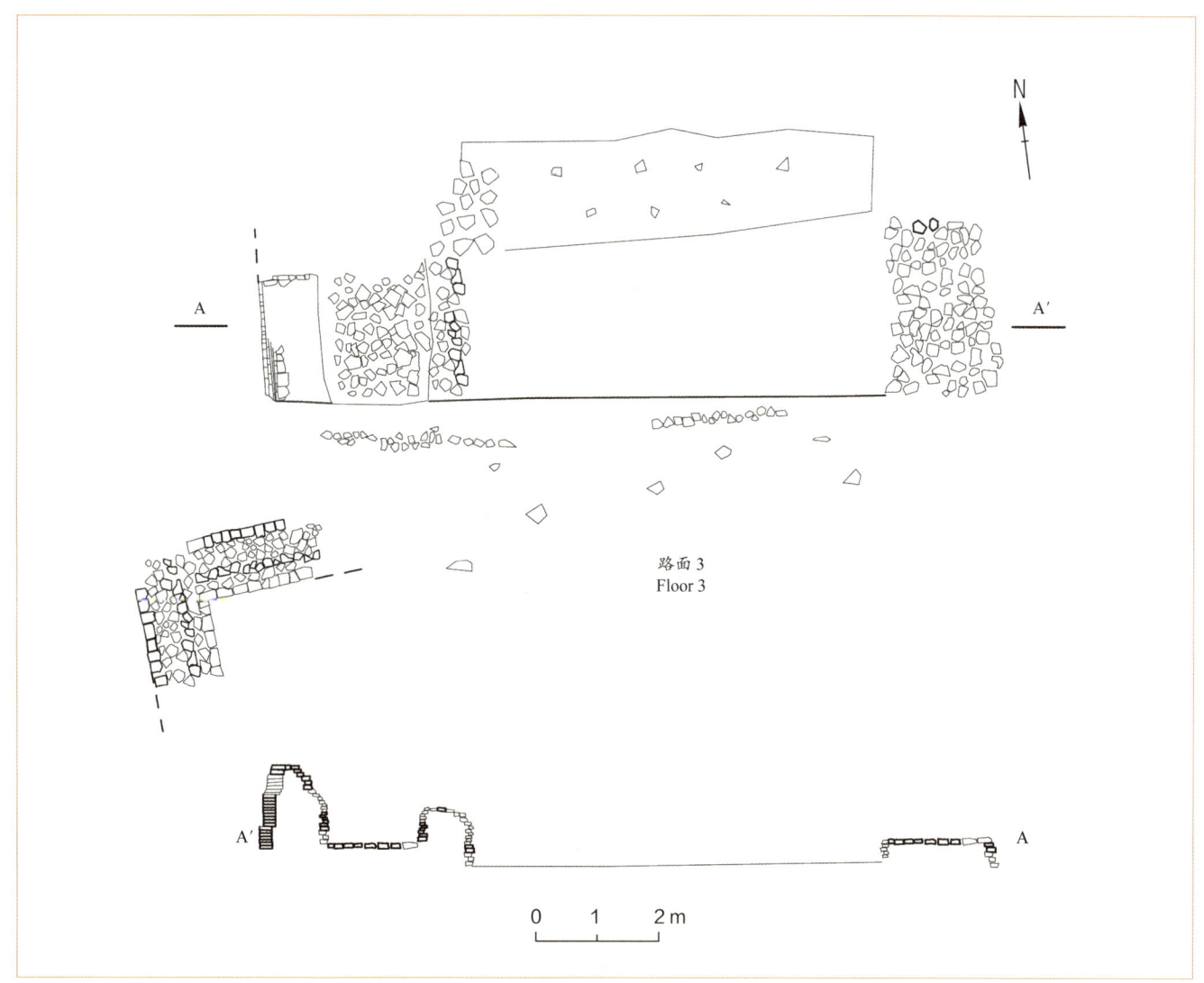

图 3-19　十字形中心神殿建筑北门遗迹平剖面图
Fig. 3-19　The plan and section of the north entrance of the Cruciform Central Temple

中心神殿建筑范围重合，目前明确的东部的边界在 UnitL9GridB8、B9、B10 附近。

2. 以柱厅 1 为例，④层的堆积形态在四围墙基内外均基本相同，都呈坡状的结构；此外，在发掘该建筑的过程中，其中④层的一个亚层（红色"砖灰"层）由西向东倾斜状分布于柱基外部并一直延伸至其底部，很明显，只有先堆填土层再进行砌筑，才能形成这样的现象。

3. 柱厅的下部墙基都呈倒梯形状的结构，从稳定性上考虑，只有在两侧有泥土支撑的情况下才能砌筑，这符合先挖基槽的做法。

4. 从柱基的形态看，从上到下，普遍不对称，甚至有错位现象，这只能解释为在狭窄的土坑中施工时难免发生的现象。此外，通过对柱厅 2 柱基 3 附近的土质观察，距柱基 10 厘米左右的填土与周围填土略有区别，推测当时先在④层填土中挖出柱基的空间，然后修筑砖结构的柱基。此后再填充之间的缝隙，观察多个柱基、墙基周围的填土，都有类似的情况。

5. 中心塔基体量极大，基础较深，可能先直接在⑥层之上砌塔基，然后在四周填筑④层土，这有待进一步的观察。

（二）关于建筑的地面

原始地面是什么样的形貌？可惜地面部分基本上被后期取砖活动破坏了，所以遗址中还没有找到确切的原始地面。不过，从一些迹象中，我们可以加以推测。以柱厅 3 柱基 2 为例，其下部使用的砖块形态不一，工艺粗糙，从中部开始砌筑工整、四面整齐，越向上结构越精致，这不是偶然现象，目前遗址内所见柱基都带有这种特征，可以肯定，下部的塔基埋于地面之下，中部和上部可能出露在地面之上。结合地层剖面中④层顶部的保存情况推测，建筑的原始地面的水平高度，应与目前的地面接近。

此外，在 UnitK8GridI7 处②层下，存在距地表 1.5 米的建筑砖砌面，从结构上看，不像是墙体，似乎是一条道路的北侧边缘。在柱厅 4 的东墙基之外，也有两块平砌的方形砖，似乎有原始地面的可能性。此外，路面 1 也可能是十字形中心神殿建筑的外围地面，路面上有局部平铺的方形砖块，它符合中心神殿的阶梯状廊庑的结构，叠压其上的是③层，从理论上说，③层与④层之间的交界面，可视作建筑地面的分界线，只是由于③层在遗址中只是局部分布，对路面 1 的性质也有待继续探讨。

（三）关于建筑结构的复原

目前发掘的建筑遗迹，基本上是原来建筑的墙基部分，地面上的建筑已不可寻，曾经辉煌的建筑形态，只能停留在复原中了。事实上，作为成熟的佛教建筑风格，总是带有固定程式的，这次发现的十字形中心神殿建筑，在孟加拉地区已多有发现，最典型的是孟加拉国西北部拉杰沙希县恼冈（Naogaon）地区的巴哈尔布尔村巴哈布尔（Pahapur）遗址，这是历史上的苏摩普里寺（Somapuri）遗址，这处遗址已列为世界文化遗产。经过实地比对，其建筑结构与纳什提瓦遗址的这处建筑遗迹十分相似，应该属于同一类建筑模式，因此，它可为我们的建筑复原提供某些依据（彩版 3-62，2、3）。

1. 中心塔基

中心佛塔是整个建筑的核心，所有的单个建筑都是围绕着这个中心对称布局。根据塔基中部的局部发掘、解剖可知，中心塔基是一个边长为 9.2 米的八边形，其上原是一个高高耸立的八边形的巍峨佛塔。由于体量极大，故其基础深度超过了四周柱厅的墙基。整个中心塔基均有火砖和残断砖铺垫，在整体上应以实心为主，塔体内可能存在塔心室，里面供奉的应是"五部佛"中的本尊毗卢遮那佛。《大日经》的密法称之为胎藏界，喻众生自心中含藏有菩提净心之种子，以大悲万行之所含藏养育，以三密方便之巧艺，终至发生圆满无上之菩提佛果。《大日经》组织的胎藏曼陀罗正是由八叶莲花组成中胎，毗卢遮那佛住于花台正中。八边形佛塔的象征意义正与此有关。

八边形塔基与四个方向的柱厅之间，有一条宽 2.36 的环形道，应是围绕佛塔的行经道，每个柱厅与中央佛塔之间，都会设立一门，通过这个门，就可进入行经道，也可以通往其他三处柱厅，所有建筑之间的关系也显得圆融有序了。

在塔基靠近柱厅的边缘，各有一个 1.6 米左右的凸出部分，与柱厅的内门相对，推测其功能应与佛像的座基有关，依照"四方佛"的佛教概念，四个方位会各供奉一位主供佛，佛像位于此处塔身的壁龛上，这与巴哈布尔遗址佛塔四周的墙内佛龛相似，也可能依墙安置佛像。位于库米拉（Comilla）县迈纳马蒂（Mainamati）地区的雷拔坪神庙（Rupban Mura），建于 8 世纪，也具有类似的结构。

2. 柱厅

东南西北四个柱厅，围绕着八边形中心佛塔，各自朝着塔身四面佛龛上的"四方佛"，柱厅，实际上是带有四个柱基的柱厅，除用于僧徒礼拜外，也可能用于集会、讲解教义、诵经等功能。柱厅中间发现的四座砖砌柱基，承担屋顶的重量，或许上面还有石柱础和立柱。从目前的考古资料，可以对柱厅的结构作出以下推测：

A. 柱厅的高度：从地基深度分析，建筑不仅有较大的内部平面空间，也应有相当大的供人们使用的高度空间。中心佛塔墙基深约 6 米，柱厅的墙基深约 3 米，由此也可推测出地面部分的墙体有相当的高度。中心佛塔与柱厅具有附属关系，从而构成中央高、四面低的结构布局。

B. 柱厅的面积：以柱厅 4 的南墙为例，除去东西两端墙基宽度，室内的宽度约为 11 米，从柱厅的结构来看，室内面积约为 100 多平方米。

C. 柱厅的门道：目前没有发现明显的门道结构信息。参照巴哈布尔遗址的建筑结构，柱厅的外门道应是朝东南西北四个正方向的。以柱厅 4 为例，其门道是正南北向的，而且处于遗址南北轴心的位置。由南门进入柱厅，再由北门进入中心佛塔。根据在巴哈布尔遗址调查的情况，结合遗址上已采集的石构件，推测存在门槛之类的石构件。据调查，地面上原来有一些石材，现在，大多被移走了。

D. 柱厅的屋顶：由于柱厅体量大，考虑到这里雨季降水量大，屋顶不应该是平顶，而是四面坡顶或尖顶，这种屋顶有其历史渊源，且与整个建筑形态和谐一致，印度中世纪这类建筑的模式，在孟加拉的许多印度教神庙建筑中，至今仍在延用。

E. 连接墙基：每个柱厅都与弧形的连接墙基相连，砌筑的手法和结构也与柱厅的墙基一致，推测墙的高度也应与柱厅的高度接近。

F. 砖雕装饰：在库米拉、巴哈布尔等地，建筑遗址的外墙上都镶嵌有砖雕，因此，这里也应存在砖雕装饰，但目前尚无发现，仅采集到莲瓣、双股胶索、棋格纹等装饰砖（彩版 3-63）。

（四）关于建筑的宗教象征

十字形中心神殿建筑的宗教本质，即为金刚乘中的曼陀罗，这是金刚乘对于世界结构的想象，具体化为寺院建筑的形式。

所谓曼陀罗，又称坛城，是象征化的小宇宙，是摆脱了任何干扰的、封闭的地盘，这是整个亚洲的一种古老的宇宙模式。从曼陀罗形式出发，十字形建筑又与四阶梯（修行的步骤）、"五部佛"（佛的空间分布）的概念相配置。本尊毗卢遮那佛居于中心，相当于空；阿閦佛位于东方，相当于风；宝生佛位于南方，相当于火；阿弥陀佛位于西方，相当于水；不空成就佛位于北方，相当于地。"五部佛"本身就构成了一个曼陀罗。修行者通过观想，将召到的神祇，分置于各自的空间中，金刚乘认为，人和宇宙之间存在着某种对应性，观想、修习的要旨，在于使两个宇宙重叠。

波罗（Pala）王朝（750—1174 年）统治时期，佛教偏于东印度和孟加拉一隅，经历了近 500 年的发展，这一时期，金刚乘取得了压倒性的优势，成为印度佛教最后一个辉煌时期。以怛特罗为基础的宗教修习是当时最流行的宗风。在波罗、斯那王朝时期，一批按其教法和仪轨而修建的金刚乘中心诞生了。除了大乘中心那烂陀寺（Nalanda）本身也是金刚乘中心之一外，由护法王达摩波罗（Dharmapala，770—810年）创建了三座著名的金刚乘寺庙，超戒寺（Vikramacila）、奥丹塔普里寺（Odantapuri）和苏摩普里寺（Somapuri）。超戒寺在印度的比哈尔邦，经过印度考古部门发掘，寺院中间也有十字形塔；苏摩普里寺在孟加拉国的巴哈布尔（Paharpur），是世界上第二大单体佛教僧院，也有十字形中心塔和多角围墙。位于库米拉（Comilla）县迈纳马蒂（Mainamati）地区的鲁帕班神庙（Rupban Mura），它的中心建筑也是这种结构。这次纳提什瓦遗址出土的十字形中心神殿建筑，结构正好与上述寺庙吻合，是金刚乘曼陀罗的典型模式。

波罗王朝被认为是孟加拉历史上的黄金时代，孟加拉民族的荣耀和对外影响在这一时期达到了前所未有的程度，十字形中心神殿建筑风格也传播到周边的许多地区。加德满都博达佛塔，相传11世纪重修，塔修在三层宽阶之上，四周有108个供有阿弥陀佛的佛龛，外形为曼陀罗坛城，中心为塔顶的伞盖；桑耶寺是西藏历史上的第一座寺庙，创建于8世纪后半期，位于中心的乌策大殿平面呈四方形，每一边的中部四门凸出，形成曼陀罗形状，据《巴协》记载，桑耶寺仿自同时期的奥丹塔普里寺（Odantapuri），本身就是一个"吉祥毗卢遮那救度恶趣曼陀罗"；建于10世纪末的阿里古格的托林寺朗巴朗则拉康，是典型曼陀罗图式的例证。在东南亚，柬埔寨的吴哥窟、爪哇的婆罗浮屠佛塔（Borobudhur），也是这种十字形风格。

据 ^{14}C 测定，纳提什瓦这座十字形中心神殿建筑的年代为10—13世纪，正处在金刚乘最后的鼎盛时期。通过与巴哈布尔的苏摩普里寺（Somapuri）遗址的柱厅比较，其建筑规模要大于后者，因此，很可能是孟加拉国同类建筑中最大的单体建筑。

The cruciform central temple structure is located in the squares of Unit H9, H10, I8, I9, I10, I11, J8, J9, J10, J11, K9 and K10. It is north-south in direction with a total area of 1980 m², which is 62.3 m long from east to west, 62.8 m long from north to south, and the survived height is 5.5 m. The highest position is 0.7 m under the ground floor while the lowest brick is at the depth of 6.2 m (Color Plate 3-26).

Excavation Process

It was firstly discovered by the China-Bangladesh joint archaeological team during the trial excavation is December 2014. On January 16, 2015, the exposure area was extended westward and the layout of this massive structure was first clarified through excavation of trenches. The systematical grid system was then completely excavated on 17th, February, 2015. In the meantime, another monument in the northwestern site, which unexpectedly has a similar structure and is angularly connected with the previous one, was also exposed during January 5 and February 7, 2015. In November 2016, the joint team carried out the second collaborative excavation and uncovered other two structures with the same size and shape, which were symmetrically distributed in four wings. These different architectural components constitute an unexpected massive well-designed monument, which was officially named as the cruciform central temple architecture. According to the exposed brick walls and the foundations, the architectural characteristics of the cruciform central temple can be partially reconstructed.

Stratigraphic Context

This construction opens under Layer 2, cuts Layer 4, and is seriously destroyed by later brick hunters. Figure 2-12 shows the cross-section of the UnitI9GridJ1, UnitJ9GridA1, B1, C1, D1, E1, F1, G1, and H1, reflecting the layers relationship among the western and eastern walls, northwest and northeast foundations of Pillared-hall 4 as well as the Layer 4.

Although only the foundations were discovered, they clearly show that the four pillared-halls were connected with each other by four massive walls, which were named as the "connective wall foundation" in this report. The construction system of interlocked bricks between them obviously indicates that they were built at the same time under a unified plan.

The foundation of central part was universally covered by the pit-like Layer 2, which was formed by the backfilling soils after removing the bricks from the regular walls. Since the foundation is the deepest in the center, the deposit here is also correspondingly the thickest. As a result of a pond in the center formed by later destruction, the soil color of the central deposit was unusually blue or black, and many silty sub-layers were observed. Moreover, many tree roots, wooden sticks, leaves, seeds and other organic remains such as bamboo mats and shells were also preserved in a good condition, indicating that probably there was a time gap before it was completely filled by soils. The layer information of the central stupa can be inferred from the east-west section (UnitJ9GridH5, G5, F5, E5, D5, C5, B5, A5, UnitI9GridJ5, I5 and H5 cross-section, see Figure 2-13) and the north-south section (J10GridD1 – D8, UnitJ9GridD5 – D10, see Figure 2-14).

Remains Description

The cruciform central temple consists of four pillared-halls, four connecting wall foundations and a main temple base (Figure 3-12). The various parts of the monument are described below.

(A) Pillared-hall

1. Pillared-hall 1

It is mainly located in Unit K10 and partly in UnitK9. The outer wall of the eastern foundation is distributed in UnitK10GridI1, I2, I3, I4, I5, H6 and UnitK9GridI9, I10; the outer wall of the southern foundation is distributed in UnitK9GridA8, B8, C8, D8, E8, F8 , G8, H9 and I9. The outer wall of the western foundation is distributed in UnitK10Grid A1 – A6, and part of it extends to Unit J10. The outer wall of the northern foundation has been partially exposed in UnitK10GridA6, B6, C6, D6, E6, F6, G6, and H6. In total, about 300 m² has already been exposed (Color Plate 3-27, 3).

The Pillared-hall 1 is a combination of the wall foundation and the pillar-plinth. The foundations of the east, south, west and north constitute the enclosure structure with four pillar plinths inside. The outer length is 17.7 m from east to west and the exposed width is 15.6 m from north to south (a part of the northern wall is still unexposed, but by inferring from the width of the southern wall foundation, the actual length should also be 17.7 m), the inner lengths of north-south and east-west walls all measure 9.7 m. The direction is nearly north-south (Figure 3-13, 3-14; Color Plate 3-28, 3-29).

Eastern wall foundation: It is in a relatively good condition and measures 3.8 m wide, 2.3 m at the highest preserved position. The northern and southern walls are preserved while the middle wall is seriously destroyed.

It is composed of two parts: The upper part and the lower part. The lower part of the foundation is built with 24 layers of horizontal bricks, which is wider on the top and narrower at the bottom, resembling an inverted trapezoid. Above this platform-like lower part, the width of the upper part is gradually reduced in three stages. It is 3 m wide and 0.7 m high. The size of the complete bricks measures 38×30×5 cm. Using broken bricks at the center of the wall while using complete bricks to build the outer sides of the wall is a common phenomenon that reflects the old building technique (Color Plate 3-30).

Northern wall foundation: It is mainly distributed in UnitK10GridA5, B5, C5, D5, E5, F5, A6, B6, C6, D6, E6, and F6 and partly is still unexcavated. The preserved maximum width is 2.4 m, whose complete width is estimated to be 3.8 m according to the structure of other similar foundations. It is also composed of the upper and lower parts, similar to the east wall foundation (Color Plate 3-31). The upper part is preserved with 0.8 m in height.

Southern wall foundation: It is mainly distributed in UnitK9GridF10, G10, B9, C9, E9, F9, G9, H9, E8, F8 and G8. The preserved part is 10.2 m in length and 2.4 m in height, consisting of the upper and lower parts (Color Plate 3-32: 1, 2).

Western wall foundation: It is mainly distributed in UnitK10GridA1 – A5, B2, B3, B4, UnitK9GridA10, B10, but is poorly preserved with 1.98 m in height at the highest position. The structure and construction technique of this wall are similar with those of the other three exposed foundations. The lower part is preserved 1.6 m high, and the upper part is only 0.38 m in height (Color Plate 3-32: 3, 4). Four pillar-plinths are systematically distributed inside of the well-enclosed area of the Pillared-hall 1.

Pillar-plinth 1: It is located in the northeast corner

of the enclosed area, mainly distributed in UnitK10GridE4, F4, and part of GridE5, F5, E3 and F3. The plinth is relatively well preserved, with a distance of 0.48 – 0.7 m away from the eastern wall and 0.4 m away from the northern wall. The preserved height is 1.75 m, and its orientation is nearly north-south.

Three overlapped parts of upper, middle and lower can be observed from the pillar-plinth. Among them, the lowest part, composed of 14 horizontal brick layers, is irregular square shape and about 1 m in height. The middle part, with 10 layers of horizontal bricks, is regular square shape of 2.5 m long in each side, preserved with a height of 0.7 m. The upper part is also square shaped and 2.1 m long in each side.

It is noteworthy that the worst damaged parts of the pillar-plinths in Pillared-hall 1 are in the center, which clearly reflects the behavior of bricks hunting by the later residents (Color Plate 3-33).

Pillar-plinth 2: It is composed of upper and lower parts. The lower part is irregular square shape, measuring 2.85 m in south-north length, 2.76 m in east-west width and 0.96 m in height. For the upper part, 9 layers of bricks are preserbed, about 0.5 m in height. Some over-burnt (picket) bricks can be seen to be used (Color Plate 3-34).

Pillar-plinth 3: It is located in UnitK10GridB3, C3, B4, C4. About 12 layers of bricks are preserved, 0.84 m high. The ground plan is square shape, measuring 3 – 3.31 m from east to west and 2.75 – 2.83 m from north to south. Most of the used bricks are broken. A large number of irregular bricks are found to below the pillar-plinth, which are possibly the remains of the constructions of the Layer 5 (Color Plate 3-35: 1, 2).

Pillar-plinth 4: It is located in UnitK10GridC1, D1, UnitK9GridC10, D10. It is seriously destroyed, 2.96 m long from north to south, and the preserved is 1.3 m from east to west. About 16 layers of bricks remain (Color Plate 3-35: 3, 4).

2. Pillared-hall 2

It is located in UnitI10, J10, I11, J11 and a small northern part remains unexcavated. The eastern boundary is distributed in UnitI10GridE9, E10, UnitJ11GridE1, E2, E3, E4, E5, and E6. The southern border is distributed in UnitI10GridI8, J8, UnitJ10GridA8, B8, C9, E8; the western boundary is located in UnitI10GridH9, H10, UnitI11GridH1, H2, H3, H4, G4, G5, G6; the northern border is located in UnitI11GridG6, H6, I6, J6, J11 Grid A6, B6, C7, D7, E7.

Pillared-hall 2 is a square building with four upright pillars inside. The outer dimension is about 16 m, covering an area of about 256 m^2, and the direction is nearly north-south. The pillar foundations are square in shape and same in size, which are 2.7 – 2.8 m long from north to south and 2.8 – 2.9 m long from east to west. The variation in length is related to their preserved height. The Connective Wall Foundation 1 and 2 are linked with the adjacent Pillared-hall 1 in the southeast and Pillared-hall 3 in the southwest, respectively (Figure 3-15, 3-16; Color Plate 3-36, 3-37, 3-38).

Eastern wall foundation: The reconstructed length is 15.9 meters, but only 9.4 meters was preserved in length, and 2.3 – 2.4 meters preserved in width. Expect that the over-burnt (picket) bricks at the lowest bottom were left, the upper walls almost have been destroyed (Color Plate 3-39, 1).

Southern wall foundation: the reconstructed length is 15.5 meters, but only 12.8 meters preserved in length, 2.3 – 2.5 meters preserved in width. The over-burnt (picket) bricks with the dimension of 7.2×2.5 m at the bottom; the upper walls have been completely destroyed (Color Plate 3-39, 2).

Western wall foundation: the overall length is 16.2 m, the general width is 3.2 m, but 3.5 m at the widest point, and the preserved height is 1 – 1.5 m. Among them, a 13.7 m long northern part of the foundation is relatively intact, except several pit-shaped features caused by brick hunters on the surface. Another pit in the south is 3.2 m long and 1.1 m deep. The southern part of the wall is seriously destroyed, leaving only some over-burnt (picket) bricks(Color Plate 3-40).

Northern wall foundation: The reconstructed length is 16 m, but only 11.5 m is preserved in length. The most common width is 3.2 m, the maximum width is 3.4 m, and the preserved height is 1 – 1.5 m. Some pits in north-south direction pits distribute on the surface, which are 2 – 3 m in length, 1 – 2.8 m in width and 0.5 – 0.8 m in depth (Color Plate 3-41).

Four pillar-plinths are evenly distributed inside of the wall-enclosed area of Pillared-hall 2.

Pillar-plinth 1: It likes square in shape, 2.8 m in length, and the preserved height is 1.16 m (Color Plate 3-42).

Pillar-plinth 2: It likes square in shape, estimated length is 2.8 m, and the preserved height is 0.93 m. Most of the bricks are completely removed (Color Plate 3-43: 1, 2).

Pillar-plinth 3: It measures 2.7 m long from north to south, 2.9 m long from east to west, and the preserved height is 1.53 m. It was built above a sloping brick sub-layer of the Layer 4. Observed from east to west, the lower 19 brick layers gradually reduce their width downwards, the middle three brick layers are projected, and the upper two brick layers are vertically built (Color Plate 3-43: 3, 4).

Pillar-plinth 4: The ground plan is complete, except the southwest corner which is slightly broken. It is 2.7 m long from north to south, 2.8 m long from east to west, and the preserved height is 0.58 m. It is built above the sloping sub-layer of bricks of the Layer 4.

From the cross-section observation, the outer wall are made of good and complete bricks while the core bricks are broken (Color Plate 3-43: 5, 6).

3. Pillared-hall 3

It is located in the western excavation area, mainly in UnitI9, I10, H9, H10. The outer wall of the eastern foundation is distributed in UnitI9GridF6, F7, F8, F9, E10 and UnitI10GridE1, E2, E3 and E4. The outer southern wall foundation is distributed in UnitH9GridH5, I6, J6, UnitI9GridA6, B6, C6, D6, E6 and F6, the outer western wall foundation is distributed in UnitH9GridH5, H6, H7, H8, H9, H10, UnitH10GridH1, G2 and G3, and the outer northern wall foundation is distributed in UnitH10GridG3, H3, I3, J3, I10 Grid A3, B4, C4, D4, E4. In total, the exposed area is about 300 m^2.

Pillared-hall 3 is a combination complex of the walls and the pillars, including four wall foundations of east, south, west and north directions and four pillar-plinths inside. The ground plan of the structure is square, and the outer dimensions are 16.1 m long on the east, 15.75 m on the south, 15.95 m on the west, 16.25 m on the north; the inner dimension is 10.6 m long on the east, 10.2 m on the south, 10.2 m on the west, and 10.1 m on the north. The direction is nearly north-south. Pillar-plinth 2 and 3 are partially preserved while Pillar-plinth 1 and 4 are severely damaged. They are not fully excavated in order to protect some parts of the structure (Figure 3-17; Color Plate 3-44).

Eastern wall foundation: It is mainly distributed in UnitI9GridD8, D9, D10, E6, E7, E8, E9, E10, UnitI10GridD1, D2, D3, D4, E1, E2, E3, E4, and some is located in UnitI9GridF6, F7, F8, F9, F10. The northern end is partially preserved, while the rest of the wall is almost completely destroyed. The width is 3.2 m on the top and 1.9 – 2.6 m at the bottom, and the depth is 2.98 m. The most common size of the bricks is 0.33×0.24×0.06 m, and the biggest brick is 0.40×0.28×0.06 m. (Color Plate 3-45, 1).

Southern wall foundation: It is mainly distributed in UnitH9GridH6, H7, I6, I7, J6, J7, UnitI9GridA6, A7, B6, B7, C6, C7, D6, D7, E6, E7, and some is located in UnitI9GridF6, F7. The width on the top is 3.1 m, and 2.2 m at the bottom, and the depth is 3.05 m. The wall is seriously destroyed; only eastern face is partially preserved. (Color Plate 3-45, 2).

Western wall foundation: It is mainly located in UnitH9GridH6, H7, H8, H9, I6, I7, I8, I9, I10, UnitH10GridH1, H2, H3. The wall foundation is almost entirely destroyed, only some remained. It is 3.1 m on the top and 2.4 m at the bottom, and 2.7 m in depth. In UnitH10GridH2, H3, some over-burnt (picket) bricks with a length of 3 m and

height of 0.2 m were used (Color Plate 3-45, 3).
Northern wall foundation: It is mainly distributed in UnitH10GridH2, H3, I2, I3, J2, J3, UnitI10GridA2, A3, B2, B3, C3, C4, D3, D4, E3, E4. The foundation is 3 m wide on the top and 2.2 m wide at the bottom, 2.65 m deep. The preserved height of the wall is 0.4 m, and it contains about 3 layers of horizontal bricks (Color Plate 3-45, 4).

Four pillar plinths are evenly distributed inside of the well-enclosed area of the Pillared-hall 2.
Pillar-plinth 1: It is located in the northeast corner of the well enclosed areas, mainly distributed in UnitI10GridB1, B2, C1, and C2, measuring 0.95 m away from eastern wall and 0.80 m away from northern wall. It is roughly square in shape, measuring 2.55 m long from north to south, 2.4 m wide from east to west, and 2 m high. The direction is nearly north-south (Color Plate 3-46, 1).
Pillar-plinth 2: It is relatively well preserved and located in the southeast corner of the enclosure, mainly distributed in UnitI9GridB8, B9, C8, C9, D8, and D9. It measures about 1.05 m away from the east wall, and 1.1 m away from the south wall (Color Plate 3-46, 2).
Pillar-plinth 3: It is located in the northwest corner of the well enclosed areas, mainly distributed in UnitH10GridJ1, and a small part is under the ground in UnitH9GridJ10, UnitH10GridI1, J2, UnitI10GridA1, and UnitI9GridA10. It is about 1.01 m away from the west wall, and 0.84 m away from the north wall. The north-south length is 2.7 m, east-west width is 2.55 m, and the preserved height is 1.65 m (Color Plate 3-46, 3).
Pillar-plinth 4: It is located in the southwest corner of the well enclosed area, mainly distributed in UnitH9GridJ8, J9, UnitI9GridA8, and A9. The east-west length is 2.6 m, north-south width is 2.35 m, and preserved height is 0.55 m (Color Plate 3-46, 4).

4. Pillared-hall 4

It is distributed in the south of the excavation area and mainly distributed in UnitI8, UnitJ8, UnitI9, and UnitJ9. The eastern boundary is located in UnitJ8GridH6, H7, H8, H9, H10, UnitJ9GridH1, H2, H3, H4; the southern boundary is located in UnitJ8GridA6, B6, C6, D6, E6, F6, G6, H6; the western boundary is distributed in UnitI8GridA6, A7, A8, A9, A10, UnitI9GridJ1, J2, J3; the northern border is located in UnitI9GridJ3, UnitJ9GridA3, B3, C3, D3, E4, F4, G4, H4.

It is a square-shaped structure with 16 m long on each side, consisting of four enclosure walls that enclose the area and four pillar-plinths in the center. The orientation is nearly north-south direction. The structures of the current exposed Pillared-halls and pillar-plinths are almost similar. Among them, the Pillared-hall 4 is relatively well preserved. All the foundations of the walls are wider on the top and narrower at the bottom; the outer parts are well built while the central parts are constructed roughly and randomly. The pillar-plinth, which is square in ground plan, can be divided into upper and lower parts: The latter is shaped like a square funnel and the brick masonary is not good, referring from the large gaps among bricks (3 – 5 mm); the former is built with thinner bricks and there are smaller gaps among bricks, including better design (Figure 3-18; Color Plate 3-47, 3-48).

Eastern wall foundation: It is distributed in UnitJ8GridG6, H6, G7, H7, G8, H8, G9, H9, G10, H10, UnitJ9GridG1, H1, G2, H2, G3, H3, G4, H4. One preserved part on the north measures 1.5 m long, 2.1 m high, 3.4 m wide on the top and 2.4 m at the bottom. Other preserved sections measure no more than 1 m in height (Color Plate 3-49, 1).
Southern wall foundation: It is located in UnitJ8GridA6, B6, C6, D6, E6, F6, G6, H6, B7, C7, D7, E7, F7, G7, H7, with an estimated length of 15.4 m, but it is preserved with 14.4 m in length, 2.55 m in height, and 3.55 m at the widest position. The excavation of the junction area between the eastern wall and the southern wall is not completed (Color Plate 3-49: 2, 3, 4).
Western wall foundation: It is distributed in UnitI8GridA6, A7, A8, A9, A10, UnitI9GridJ1, J2, J3, UnitJ8GridA6, A7, A8, A9, A10, UnitJ9GridA1, A2, A3. It is 16 m in length, 2.6 m in width, and 2.1 m in preserved height. Most walls are destroyed, only a

part of the brick structure and some bricks at the bottom remain. An architectural stone, probably used for construction, was found in the Layer 2 near the western wall (Color Plate 3-50, 1).

Northern wall foundation: It is distributed in UnitI9GridJ2, J3, UnitJ9GridA2, A3, B2, B3, C2, C3, D2, D3, E2, E3, F2, F3, G2, G3, H3, H4. It measures 16.2 m in length, and the preserved part is 3.05 m wide and 2.1 m high. Various size and shape pits were discovered on the surface of the foundation. The Connective Wall 3 and 4 were linked with the northeast and northwest walls, respectively (Color Plate 3-50: 2, 3, 4).

Four pillar-plinths were systematically distributed inside of the well-enclosed area the Pillared-hall 4.

Pillar-plinth 1: It is well preserved and distributed in UnitJ8GridB7, B8, C7, and C8, measuring 2.8 m long from north to south, 2.9 m long from east to west, and 2.7 m in preserved height (Color Plate 3-51: 1, 2).

Pillar-plinth 2: It is located in UnitJ8GridE8, E9, F8, F9, and measures 2.6 m long from north to south, 2.7 m long from east to west. The total height is 2.68 m, the upper part being 1.4 m high and the lower part being 1.28 m high (Color Plate 3-26: 3, 4; Color Plate 3-52).

Pillar-plinth 3: It is located in UnitJ8GridB10, C10, 7, C8, UnitJ9GridB1, and C1. The upper part was destroyed, and the lower part was partially preserved (Color Plate 3-53: 1, 2).

Pillar-plinth 4: It is distributed in UnitJ8GridE10, UnitJ9GridE1, E2, F1, and F2; only the lower part was preserved with the dimension of 2.4 m from north to south and 2.76 m from east to west (Color Plate 3-53: 3, 4).

(B) Connective Wall Foundation

1. Connective Wall Foundation 1

It is located in the northeastern area of the cruciform central temple, linking the northwest corner of Pillared-hall 1 and the southeast corner of Pillared-hall 2. It is distributed in UnitJ10Grid G6, H6, I6, F7, G7, H7, E8, F8, G8, E9, and F9.

It is southeast-northwest in direction, and 9.23 m in preserved length. The general ground plan is arc-like, the middle part is running in a long strip-shape, and the northern part turns curvedly. The whole structure was almost destroyed by later brick hunters, and the pits were left on the wall (Color Plate 3-54).

2. Connective Wall Foundation 2

It is located in the northwestern part of the cruciform central temple, connecting the southwestern corner of Pillared-hall 2 and the northeast corner of the Pillared-hall 3. It is mainly distributed in UnitI10GridD4, E4, D5, E5, F5, G5, G6, H6, I6, G7, H7, I7, G8, H8, G9, and H9. Connective Wall Foundation 2, which is a little different from the Connective Wall Foundation 1, is arc-shaped in the middle and stripe-shaped at both ends (Color Plate 3-55).

3. Connective Wall Foundation 3

It is located in the southwest of the cruciform central temple, connecting the southeast corner of Pillared-hall 3 and the northwest corner of Pillared-hall 4. The exposed parts are distributed in UnitI9GridJ5, I5, I6, H5, H6, F6, F7, E6, E7 and D5.

It is seriously damaged by later destruction and only a small part of the brick wall is preserved. However, according to the remnants of the pit's shape, the structure of the arc-shaped ground plan can be inferred, which is similar to Connective Wall Foundation 2. The exposed part is 13.36 m long, 3.05 m wide and 1.9 m high (Color Plate 3-56: 1, 2).

4. Connective Wall Foundation 4

It is located in the southeast of the cruciform central temple, the northern end is connected to the western wall of Pillared-hall 1 and the southern end is connected to the northern wall of Pillared-hall 4. The partially exposed wall is distributed in UnitJ9GridJ8, J7, I8, I7, H6, H5, G6, G5, and G4. Its plan is similar to Connective Wall Foundation 1 (Color Plate 3-56: 3, 4).

(C) The Foundation of Central Temple

The foundation of main temple, in the middle of the cruciform central temple, is located in the enclosed octagonal space formed by the four pillared-halls of the cardinal directions and also the adjoining connective wall foundations. It is the nuclear of the cruciform construction, and is mainly distributed in the UnitJ10, UnitJ9 and part of the UnitI10 and UnitI9, with a total area of about 580 m^2 (Color Plate 3-57).

The exposed foundation of the main temple, which is 9.2 m long and 1.6 m wide, is octagonal in shape with four additional slightly protruding parts in each of the east, south, west and north directions. The bricks of the central structure are completely destroyed; only some part of peripheral walls and the irregular bricks at the bottom are preserved. The southern part is comparatively well preserved, and the outer walls of northern, western and eastern parts also remain (see figure 3-6).

The southern foundation, which is 9.2 m wide from east to west and 0.7 – 2.98 m wide and 2.02 m high, is mainly distributed in the squares of UnitJ9GridA5, B5, C5, D5, E5, F5, A6 and B6. The top brick is about 2.6 m deep from the ground surface and the direction is approximately 270°. The wall turns at an angle of 135° at the east and west ends of the foundation, and extends separately to the eastern and western directions. According to this, it is possible for us to reconstruct the ground plan of the main temple. The northern end of the eastern wall foundation is well preserved whereas some scattered bricks are found at the southern end. It is distributed in UnitJ10GridI1, I2, I3 and I4 and the exposed area measures 3.4 m long and 1.7 m wide, 1.36 m high. Judged from the shape and scope of pits caused by brick-hunters and the arrangement of the preserved brick wall, the architectural structure of the eastern foundation of the central temple is similar to the southern counterpart. Majority of the bricks are incomplete, and the size of a complete brick is 30×19×4 cm. It is 2.46 m distance from the side of the eastern wall to the bottom of western wall foundation of Pillared-hall 1.

The northern foundation of central temple, contains two preserved ends and partial outer walls, and is distributed in UnitI10GridJ6, J7, UnitI11GridA6, A7, B6, B7, C7, and D7. It is 10.4 m long, 2.64 m wide and 1.98 m high. The wall at the western end is preserved at a relatively bigger height, measuring 1.75 m long from north to south, 0.66 m wide, and 1.98 m high. The top brick is 3.89 m deep from the ground surface, and in the corner there is a collapsed wall of 0.56 m long, 0.35 m wide, 0.65 m high. The building structure of this section is also similar to the southern counterpart. The contour of the northern side of western wall is clear and is distributed in UnitI9GridG8, G9, G10, H8, H9, H10 and UnitI10GridG1, G2, G3, H1, H2, H3. It measures 6.9 m long, 1.74 m wide and 1.5 m high. The size of a complete brick is 39×29×6 cm. The top brick is 4.15 m deep from the surface, and the distance between the outer edge of the western end and the eastern wall foundation of the Pillared-hall 3 is about 2.18 m. The northwest wall is located in UnitI10GridH2, H3, H4, I3, I4, I5, J5 and J6, measuring 8.4 m long, 3 m wide and 1.5 m high. During excavations in UnitJ10GridB3, C3, B4, C4, B5, C5, B6 and C6, a layer with densely distributed bricks was found at the bottom. It was paved horizontally with a large number of brown over-burnt (picket) bricks and broken bricks. Some bricks of the size of 45×30×5 cm are also found above it, showing that the central temple is probably built on this platform. The bottom of the foundation is 6.1 m deep from the ground surface, and it is about 2.6 m lower than that of the pillared-halls. The burnt bricks are also found at the bottom in the UnitJ9GridE7, F7, E8, F8, G8, E9, F9, G9 and H9, about 5.9 m deep from the ground surface. Two or three layers of bricks are also partially preserved in some places above the bottom burnt bricks. But on the border of Grids of F8, G8 and Grids of F9, G9, it is vertically built with many broken bricks at the bottom instead of the burnt bricks. The difference in building style is obvious in this area. However, whether it is related to the structure of the central temple awaits for future research (Color Plate 3-58, 3-59).

North Entrance and Parapet Wall

It is located in UnitI12GridE10, F10, G10, UnitI13 GridF1, G1, H1, F2 – J2, F3 – J3, UnitJ13GridA2 – D2, A3 – D3, and is discovered in the north of Octagonal Stupa Complex 2. It has exposed 23.1 m in the direction of east to west and 3 m in width from north to south. The east and west ends of the wall continue to extend into the unexcavated area. Most of the gate wall is destroyed, and the exposed part is mainly the foundation. But fortunately the wall in the northwestern corner is relatively well preserved up to 1.5 m high. It allows to get a general understanding about the architectural structure of the gate.

The gate is roughly composed of three parts. A doorway measuring 11.6 m long and 3 m wide is in the middle, and eastern and western walls are located in two sides connecting with the doorway. The western wall is of zigzag shape, starting from the south and extending 1 m before turning 4.2 m in the east and then 1.2 m to the north. The eastern wall is seriously destructed, but the preserved foundation shows that it is symmetrical with the eastern wall. The outer wall of the maximum preserved part is decorated with slanted plane bricks in order to create a special arc structure. The outer wall is regular and smooth, exhibiting a sophisticated technique.

The north gate is exposed under Layer 2 and cuts the Layer 4. It is speculated to belong to the second period as the gateway of the cruciform central temple (Figure3-19; Color Plate 3-60, 3-61). According to the reconstruction of the main temple in Paharpur, there is a parallel parapet wall outside of the pillared-halls. At Nateshwar site, a similar trace of parapet wall is also discovered. The brick structure found in UnitK9GridJ8 is the base of the parapet wall in the southeast corner of Pillared-hall 1 (Color Plate 3-62, 1).

Age of the Construction

The cruciform central temple belongs to the second period. According to the radiocarbon dates of the Layer 4 and Layer 5, it is speculated that the structure is built and used between 10th and 13th century, specifically around 950 – 1223 AD. However, it is noteworthy that the time of the Layer 2 is inferred from local historical background due to lack of related dating data and other artifacts. Muslims ruled here in the first half of the 13th century AD according to some texts.

Conception on the Architectural Reconstruction

The central temple, the four pillared-halls as well as the corresponding connective walls constitute the entire structure of the cruciform central temple. As mentioned above, the building structure and masonary technique of the foundation of these Pillared-halls are generally the same, so are the shape and structure of the pillar-plinths, which are symmetrically distributed in enclosing walls. This fixed form indicates that it is a well-planned and designed architecture. The overall construction including the cruciform central temple and ancillary buildings should have been built almost simultaneously. During centuries of existence, no major change occurred in the general pattern, except some repairs and extensions for the surrounding buildings. For example, archaeological evidence shows that the octagonal stupa was ever rebuilt.

(A) About the Building Method

The Layer 4, as the foundation base of the cruciform central temple, is widely distributed in the mound. After our analysis on the layers and features, the building process can be concluded as follows: firstly clay sandy soils were carried to significantly raise the ground surface, then they were made compacted and solid, and afterwards the foundation ditches were dig before finally constructing the monuments.

The reasons for the above speculation are as follows:

1. The distribution of Layer 4 coincides with the area of the cruciform central temple architecture in this period. At present, the definite eastern boundary is clearly located in UnitL9GridB8, B9, and B10.

2. Taking the deposit in pillared-hall 1 as an example, the distribution of the Layer 4 deposit is basically the same both inside and outside of the enclosure, directly sloping from the very top to the bottom. In addition, during the excavation, a sub-layer of Layer 4 composed of the red brick dusts was observed at the bottom of the pillar-plinth, clearly indicating that the behavior of carrying and dumping soils here took place earlier than the building of the structures.

3. All the exposed lower parts of the wall foundations were inverted trapezoid in shape. If considering the stability and safety of the building process, the two sides of the walls need the support coming from the surrounding earth.

4. For the plinth's morphology, it is asymmetry from top to bottom, or slightly misplaced, which can only be interpreted as the inevitable mistakes during the construction in a narrow base-ditch. Moreover, by observing the soil near the Pillar-plinth 3 of Pillared-hall 2, there is a slight difference between the filling soil and the surrounding soil. This phenomenon happened in several other pillar-plinths as well, which can be speculated that the base-ditch was created before building the pillar-plinth, and soil was finally used to fill the gap between them.

5. As for the main temple, because of the massive and deep foundation, it is probably built directly above the Layer 6 firstly, and then fills with the soil of Layer 4. However, this needs further observation and analysis.

(B) About the Ground Floor of the Structures

What is the original ground surface of the cruciform central temple? Unfortunately, it is almost destroyed by later brick-hunters and the exact original ground surface has not been found yet. However, some speculation can be made from the indications of a few traces. Taking the Pillar-plinth 2 in the Pillared-hall 3 as an example, the bricks used in the lower part are various in shapes and roughly built, but from the middle to the top, they were built neatly and seemed more delicate. This is not an accidental phenomenon. The same situation can be observed from other pillar-plinths. Judged from this feature, it is safe to say that the lower plinth is buried under the ground, while the upper part may have been exposed above the ground. Combined with the preservation of the Layer 4, it is presumed that the original ground surface level of the construction should have been close to the current ground level.

In addition, there is a brick feature at a depth of 1.5 m from the ground surface under Layer 2 in UnitK8Grid I. The structure is unlike the wall and appears to be an edge of a road. Outside the east wall of Pillared-hall 4, there are also two square-shaped bricks that appear to be the original ground floor. Besides, the Floor 1, which is partially paved with square-shaped bricks, may also be the peripheral ground surface of the cruciform central temple architectures. It conforms to the structure style of the central temple with a high terraced porch.

(C) About the Reconstruction of the Building Structure

The architectural monuments exposed at Nateshwar site are mainly the foundation parts of the original buildings. The superstructures above the ground floor are no longer traceable. The complete understanding about the once brilliant architecture should rely on reconstruction and imagination. Even though, as a mature Buddhist architectural style, it almost has a fixed pattern. Similar architectures such as the cruciform central temple have been found in many sites in Bangladesh. For instance, the Paharpur monastery, which is located in Naogaon, Rajshahi district, is the most distinctive one. It is known as the Somapura Mahavihar in ancient times and now has been named as a UNESCO world heritage site. By on-site comparison, the building structure of Paharpur central temple is very close to the architectural monument found in Nateshwar site, and they probably belong to the same type of building styles (Dikshit 1938). If so, the Paharpur central temple can provide us much information for the reconstruction task (Color Plate 3-62: 2, 3).

1. The Main Temple

The central main temple is the nucleus of the entire building, and all individual buildings are symmetrically distributed around the center. According to the excavation of the central foundation, it is an octagonal shape, measuring 9.2 m long each side. It originally had a towering octagonal super-structure at its central location. Due to the huge size, the depth of the foundation in the centre is deeper than surrounding pillar-halls foundation. Since the entire foundation was built with over-burnt (picket) bricks and broken bricks, the main temple could be a solid structure and possibly with a chamber in the hearth, where the deity Vairochana Buddha (one of the Five Buddhas) was worshiped.

Between the octagonal main temple and the pillared-halls in four directions, there is a 2.36 m wide circular passage, which is the circumambulatory path for worshiping. There should be a gate (doorway) between each pillared-hall and the central main temple, leading to the veranda and other 3 pillared-halls.

2. Pillared-hall

Around the central octagonal shrine, each of the Pillared-halls in the four wings is facing the "Four-direction Buddha" in the chamber respectively. The Pillared-hall is actually a hall with four pillar-plinths, which can be used for worship and may also for assembly, teaching, chanting and other functions. The four brick pillar-plinths were found in the inside of the hall, bearing the weight of the roof, and perhaps some stone pedestals and wood or stone pillars were also set above the plinths. According to current archaeological data, we can make the following assumptions about the structure of the Pillared-halls:

A. The height: Judged from the depth of the foundation, the building not only had substantial horizontal space, but also should have a considerable height for performing activities here. The foundations of the main temple and the pillared-halls are 6 m and 3 m deep respectively from the ground surface, from which it can be inferred that the walls above the ground floor shoule also have a considerable height. Because the pillared-halls were affiliated to the main temple, the center should be higher than the surrounding halls, the roof rising in receding tiers over the vaults spanning the different corridors, forming the dome-like structure.

B. The size: Taking the south wall of Pillared-hall 4 as an example, the width of the inner room is about 11 m, if the foundation width at eastern and western ends is discounted. Consequently, the area of the inner room is around 100 m^2.

C. The doors: No clear and definite trace of door was found at present. However, if we construct a wall above 3 m wide foundation, the wall should be at least 2 m wide. With reference to the architectural structure of Paharpur site, the outer door of the Pillared-hall should be oriented in the four cardinal directions of East, South, West, and North. For instance, the door of the Pillared-hall 4 is set in north-south direction and also located in the north-south axis of the site. One can enter into the Pillared-hall from the south gate, and then into the main temple from the north gate. Based on the survey conducted at the Paharpur site, stone thresholds possibly existed. Indeed some kinds of stone artifacts were previously on the ground of the site, but were removed later.

D. The roof: Due to the large size of the pillared-hall, and taking into account the large rainfall during the rainy season in this place, the roof of the architectures shoule be spire shape or slopping downwards the top around four sides instead of a flat shape. This type of roof has its historical origins in medieval buildings in India, and is still in use in many Brahmanical temples in Bangladesh.

E. The connective walls: The arc-shaped connective wall foundations link with pillared-halls, and the masonary techniques and structures are also consistent with the wall of the pillared-hall, suggesting that the height of the connective walls should be close to the height of the pillared-hall.

F. The terracotta decoration: It is revealed that many terracotta plaques are decorated on the outside of the architectures in Comilla, Paharpur and other Buddhist sites. So, the outer walls of Nateshwar site should also be ornamented with terracotta plaques. However, at present only some bricks with lotus petals and checkerboard design are found (Color Plate 3-63).

(D) About the Religious Symbol of the Architecture

The religious nature of the cruciform central temple is the *mandala*; it is the imagination of *Vajrayana* on the world structure embodied with monastic architecture. The Pala dynasty was considered to be the golden age in the history of ancient Bangladesh. The glory and its radiating influence in Bangladesh reached an unprecedented level during this period. The architectural style of the cruciform central temple also spread out in many surrounding areas. The Sangye temple, which was the first temple in the history of Tibet, was founded in the latter half of the 8th century. The main temple in the center is square in shape with four protruding doors on each side, which form a mandala shape. In Southeast Asia, Angkor Wat in Cambodia, Borobudur Temple in Java, are also built in this cruciform style.

According to radiocarbon dates, the age of the cruciform central temple at Nateshwar is from the 10th to the 13th centuries, when is at the peak of *Vajrayana*. Compared to the pillared-halls of the Somapura Mahavihar at Paharpur, the size of the building at Nateshwar is greater than that of the Paharpur site, so it is likely to be the largest single Buddhist architecture in Bangladesh.

第三节
Section 3
The Second Period (II): Other Features

第二期遗迹（下）
——其他遗迹

第二期的遗迹除了十字形中心神殿建筑，还包括八边形佛塔 1、2、3，曲折形围墙 1，路面 1、3 等（图 3-20）。

一、八边形佛塔 1

八边形佛塔 1 位于 UnitL8、L9、M8、M9 内。正南北方向，南北长 19 米，东西宽 11 米。整体包括八边形佛塔和前厅两个部分。但是根据建筑的砖墙砌筑特征，可以将它分为前、后两个时期。

前期佛塔分布于 UnitL8GridG1、G2、H1、H2、H3、I1、I2、I3、J1、J2 等探方中。由于村民在此取土发现了一些砖块，揭露出基本完整的南墙、东南墙和西南墙，佛塔的每一墙均长 3 米，相邻两墙的夹角为 137°。根据这些特点，可以推测前期佛塔应为八边形。保存最高的地方有 36 层砖，高约 1 米。在前期佛塔的底部，发现一个作为其基础的砖砌平台，由于后期建筑的叠压，它的具体形状和尺寸难以完整获取，从局部的清理可知，它的下部为平砖铺砌，但上部则是由竖砖砌筑而成。同时，佛塔有可能建在这个砖台的南部，而北部可能作为这一时期的外部功能区的建筑基础。重要的是，在佛塔的内部中心发现一个塔心室，长 0.63 米、宽 0.57 米，残高 1.4 米。它大约在砖台以上 0.8 米，有比较精致的设计，自下至上可能可以观察到三个不同形状的组成部分，下部为方形、中部为八边形（每边 22 厘米）、上部位圆形。除了这个内室之外，佛塔的其他区域均有砖块，推测这应是一个实心的建筑。

后期佛塔在前期的基础上向外同时增加了 1.9 米，同时在北部新建了一个前厅。南墙、东南墙、西南墙、东墙、西墙均可以观察到，长度均为 4.6 米，这些墙体之间的转角也均为 137°。南墙位于 UnitL8GridH10、I10、J10；东南墙位于 UnitM8GridA10，UnitM9UnitA1、B2；西南墙位于 UnitL8GridG10，UnitL9gridF2、F3、F4；东墙位于 UnitM9GridB3、B4；西墙位于 UnitL9GridF1、F2、F3；其他三面墙体皆在前厅屋顶的覆盖下。大部分佛塔的墙体均被后期破坏，残存最高约 2.5 米。在后期佛塔外的东北部，有一个面积 1.5 米×1.5 米的区域铺垫有砖块，保留有 5—6 层砖厚，但具体功能不详。

前厅建于后期八边形佛塔的北部，分布于 UnitL9GridF4–J9 和 UnitM9GridA4–A9 内，呈长方形，后期佛塔的北墙也同时被用于前厅的南墙，东西两墙分别与佛塔的东墙和西墙成直线。东墙保存较好，但北墙和西墙破坏严重。前厅内部东西长 5.8 米，南北宽 4.4 米。西墙宽 2.8 米，北墙宽 2.5 米，保存最高为 1.4 米。北墙基础外壁部分，中部砖块平滑，规整，而上部砖块粗糙，且用砖的尺寸变大，底部基础砖凹凸不平，这表明前厅可能经历了多次维修。

八边形佛塔 1 开口于②层下，打破④层，隔墙、房屋 3 叠压在其下，推测其年代为第二期，为十字形中心神殿的附属建筑（图 3-21；彩版 3-64、3-65、3-66）。

二、八边形佛塔 2

八边形佛塔 2 发现于 2016—2017 年度的考古发掘，该遗迹分布于 UnitH12GridG2–J2，G3–J3，I4、J4 以及 UnitI12GridA3–D3，A4–F4，C5–E5，C6–E6，D7、F7，D8、F8 中。它与八边形佛塔 1 有大致相同的结构特征。塔体为东西向，东西长 18 米，南北宽 10 米，保存高度 1.8 米。

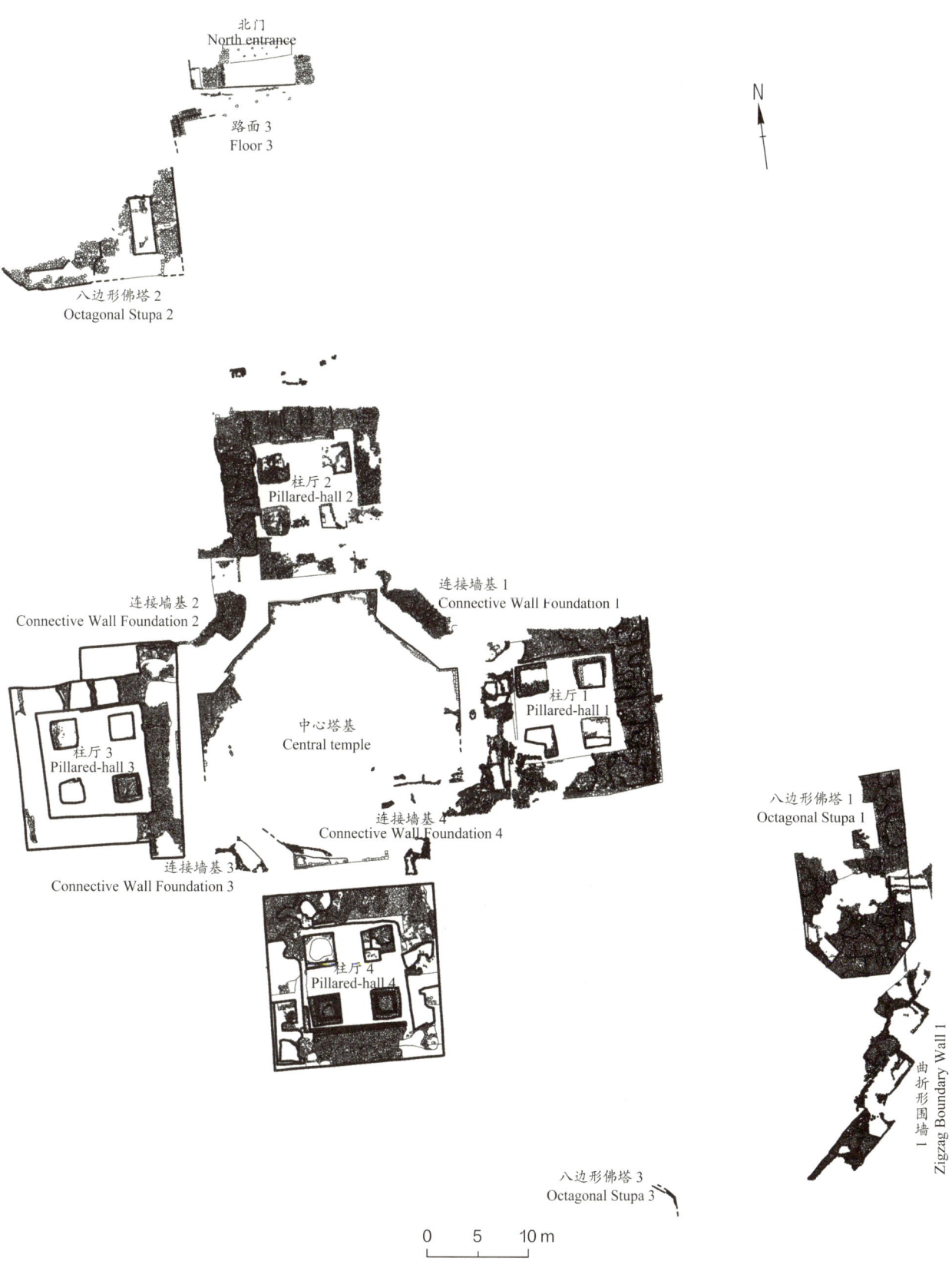

图 3-20 纳提什瓦遗址第二期遗迹总平面图

Fig. 3-20 The master plan of the second period cultural remains at Nateshwar site

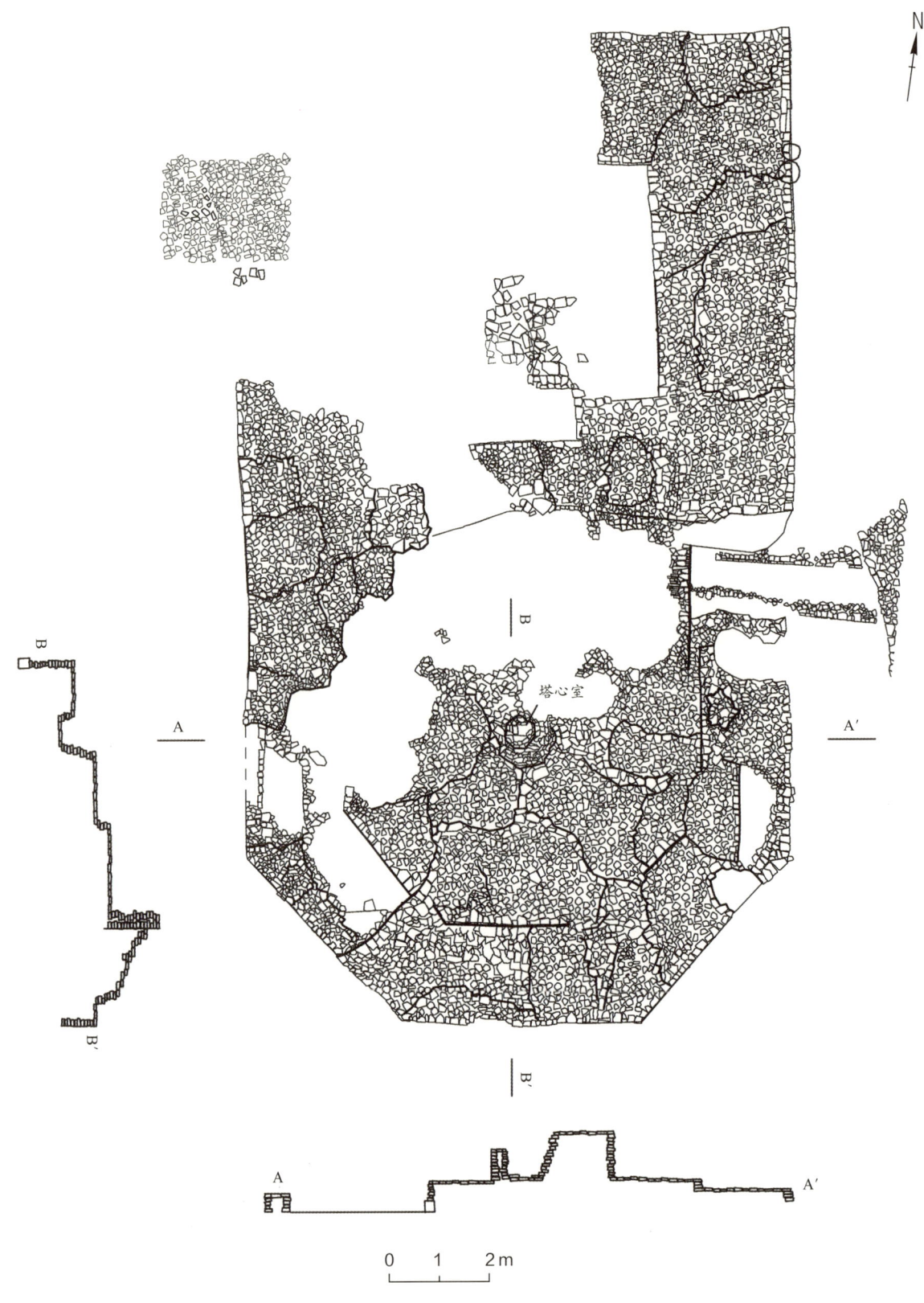

图 3-21 八边形佛塔 1 平剖面图
Fig. 3-21 The plan and section of Octagonal Stupa 1

其前后历经多次维修和扩建，大致能分为前后两个建筑时期。

前期佛塔大部分已被后期破坏，分布于Unit H12GridH3、I3、J3、I4、J4 和 UnitI12GridA3、A4 内，其余部分叠压在村级公路下。残存塔体自下至上发现有两个宽度约2.5厘米的阶梯状内收，第一级在位于墙体顶部以下51厘米处，再往下61厘米则为第二级，往下仅发掘28厘米。由于后期建筑的叠压，塔基部分没有进行发掘，但佛塔的南部和东南部已完全揭露，南墙长2.78米，东南墙长1.92米，东南墙的东端向东凸出0.7米后，再向北延伸形成东墙，这一部分目前仅揭露0.4米，此外西南墙体也仅揭露0.19米。东南墙和西南墙均向北部以137°方向延伸，可以推知佛塔的平面形状应为八边形，且在东部有向外略凸出的部分。据墙体长度和结构，推测八边形各边长度可能存在两种情况：第一，西南墙、西墙、西北墙、北墙和东墙可能和南墙长度相同，而东南墙和东北墙长度相同；第二，南墙、北墙、西墙和东墙长度相同，而东南墙、西南墙、东北墙和西北墙长度相同。但以上的推测，只有待全部揭露后，才能最终确定。

后期的佛塔在前期佛塔的规整壁面外开始扩建，均向外扩建了1.8米，两期之间的砖块没有镶嵌关系。此外，在佛塔东部新建了一个前厅。每一个外墙的平面和立面均可发现墙体的凹凸转折设计，一些纵向和横向的阶梯状构造，增加了这一期建筑的美观性。西南墙长4米，已揭露部分距离地表18—43厘米，向北以137°的角度转折延伸。在该墙体的南端向东85厘米后向外凸出14厘米，然后32—37厘米以后向内凹进14—16厘米，再继续向东约22—28厘米。距离南墙的西端约30厘米、在残存顶砖以下约40厘米处的外墙壁缩进4—6厘米。南墙长3.5米，外墙壁也具有与西南墙相同的砌筑特征。南墙平面向内凹进15厘米后继续向东延伸11.9米，并作为前厅的南墙。

前厅南墙外墙长11.9米，内墙长5.52米，南墙最高处的底部宽度为2.2—2.6米。外墙立面有5级向上内收结构，每级缩进宽度3—8厘米，而内部仅有1级内收。其中，第一级位于保存墙体最高处以下90厘米处，第二至五级阶位于依次向下67、18、10、11厘米处，其下再发掘46厘米。内墙里面保存墙体最高处以下58厘米处，向内缩进宽度为8厘米，其下另发掘深度28厘米。东墙外墙长10米，内墙长5.27米，保存最高部分位于现今地面以下40厘米处，其墙体下部宽2.2—2.6米。东墙的外墙有6级凹进或凸出的建筑结构。在保存墙体最高处向下66厘米为第一梯级，再向下53厘米墙体缩进，其下5厘米处再次向内缩进，再往下29厘米又向外凸出，其下5厘米仍向外凸出，再往下18厘米则重新缩进，在此处往下46厘米后发掘停止。东墙内壁立面有4级向上内收特征，第一级位于保存墙体最高处向下23厘米，第二至四级分别依次向下23、23、12厘米。此外，外墙的第二梯级以上的墙面规整且光滑，而其下部分则相反。北墙从东北角往西揭露长度4.06米，保存最大宽度在底部为2.2—2.6米，最高处距离现今地表35厘米。已发掘部分在外墙立面最高处以下74厘米处可见1个阶梯状内收，而内墙立面有3个阶梯状内收，依次在最高处往下46、48、13厘米。

前厅内部东西长5.52米，南北宽5.27米。在内部西侧有一个类似祭台的砖构建筑，南北长5.27米，东西宽2.89米。其与前厅的西墙相接，北侧和南侧与前厅的墙壁间没有镶嵌关系，可能为后期扩建。在前厅内部东北角和东南角还发现两个更晚阶段的似柱基方形建筑物（功能不详），东北角方形物保存较好，东西长2.2米，南北宽1.5米，残高1米。

八边形佛塔2开口于③层下，打破④层，其时代推测为第二期（图3-22；彩版3-67，3-68，3-69）。

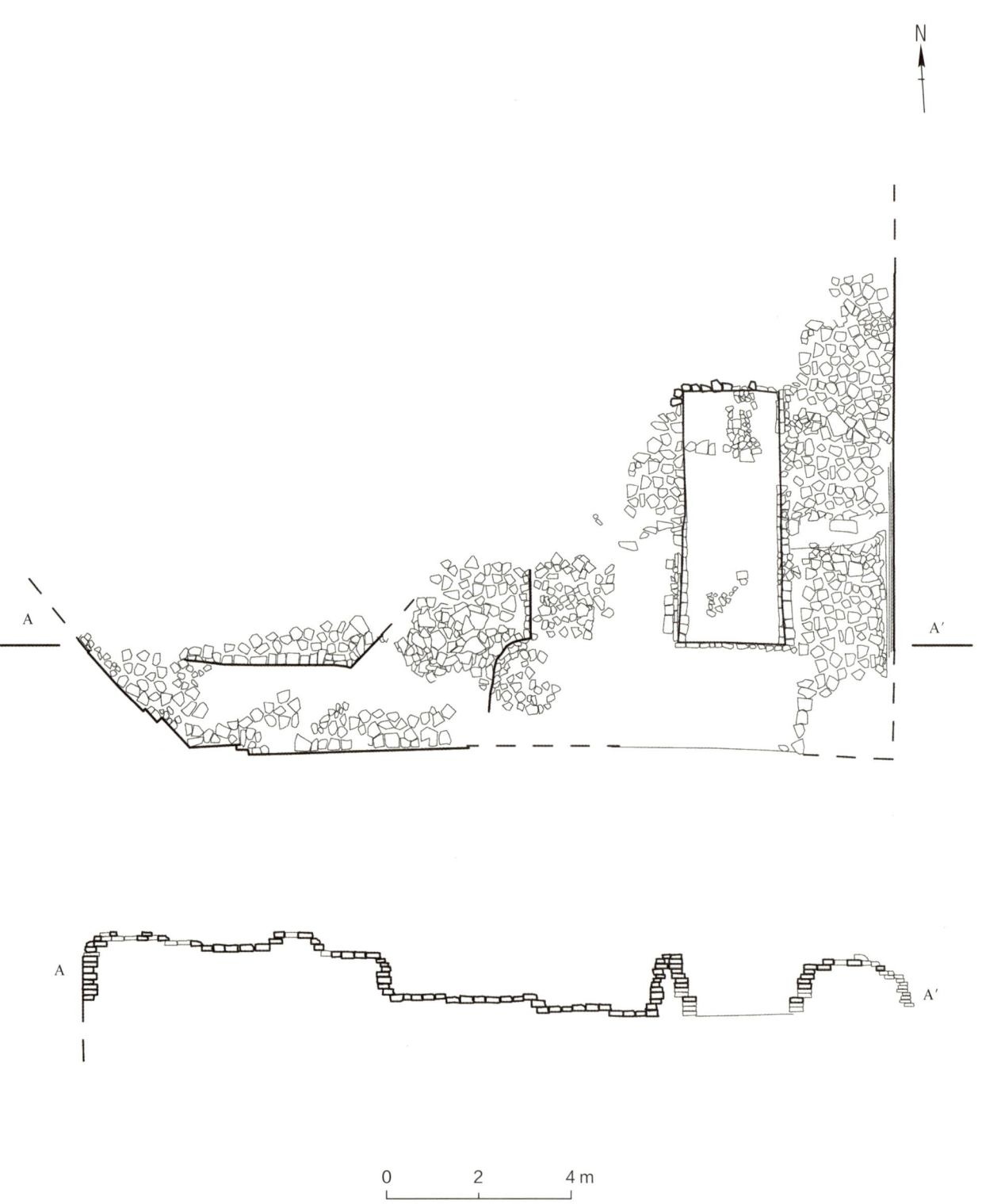

图 3-22 八边形佛塔 2 平剖面图
Fig. 3-22 The plan and section of Octagonal Stupa 2

三、八边形佛塔 3

八边形佛塔 3 位于遗址的东南角，UnitK7 GridI9、I10、J9、J10 内，目前只在探方隔梁中显露，尚未发掘（彩版 3-70，1）。

四、曲折形围墙 1

曲折形围墙 1 主要分布于 UnitL7GridF10、G10，UnitL8GridG1、H1、H2、I1、I2、I3、I4、I5、J2、J3、J4、J5、J6 和 UnitM8GridA3、A4、A5、A6、A7、A8、A9、B5、B6、B7、B8、B9、B10 探方内。此外，在 UnitM9GridC3、C4、C5 可能也有它的构成部分。该墙破坏严重，其曲折形态与遗址中发现的其他墙体明显不同。

此围墙大致呈西南—东北走向，残长 23.2 米、宽 3.1 米、残高 1.9 米。已揭露部分在平面上有 3 个 90° 角度的曲折转弯，内墙体凸出均约 1.5 米，外墙凹进均约 2.15 米。墙体的里、外两面均发现有阶梯状向上的内收结构，从底部向上，墙体宽度逐渐减少。残存墙体内墙仅发现一个阶梯的内收，而外墙有六个阶梯的内收，每次缩进宽度在 5—10 厘米之间。外墙面下部砖块不规整，上部则规整而平滑。

曲折形围墙 1 开口于②层下，打破④层，房屋 1 和路面 1 叠压其下。根据层位关系，推测它属于遗址的第二期。很可能是十字形中心神殿建筑的内围墙。（图 3-23；彩版 3-70，2、3）。

五、路面 1

位于十字形中心神殿建筑的东部，东邻八边形佛塔和曲折形围墙等建筑，北部、东部因后期破坏仅有少量残痕，西南向未发掘区延伸，已发掘部分主要分布于 UnitL8 和 UnitL9 两个单元内，少部分进入到 UnitK8 内，共涉及 95 个 Grid 单位，面积约 350 平方米。目前揭露的路面北界至 UnitL9GridB8、C8、D8、E8 内；西界至 UnitL9GridB1、B2、B3、B4、B5、B6、B7，UnitL8GridB4、C5、B6、B7、B8、B9、B10，UnitK8GridI2、J3 内；南界至 UnitL8GridA1、B1、C1 内，再往南则仅有不足 1 厘米的薄薄的残痕及至消失，可能由于雨水的冲刷所造成；东界分布至 UnitL9GridE8、E7、E6、E5、E4、F3、F2、F1，UnitL8GridF10、F9、F8、G7、G6、F5、E4、D3、C2、C1 内。此外，在 UnitL9、L8 中的八角形佛塔周围有局部分布；在靠近曲折形围墙西侧的 Unit L8 Grid J9 内也有分布；在神殿 1 北部，同样有一层较厚的红色碎砖粉末层和少量较平整砖块，尽管其结构与路面 1 遗迹有些差异，但不排除是路面 1 向北的继续延伸，直至 UnitL10 的北端，这在北部剖面上也有所反映（彩版 3-71）。

2013 年发掘八边形佛塔西南部时，已出露该遗迹，当时判断为与之共存的地面遗迹，但揭露面积有限。2015 年 11—12 月，中孟联合发掘时，对此区域进行了大面积揭露，清理了叠压在其上面的堆积层，并进行了局部解剖。清理了上部灰青、灰黄色黏土堆积，将发掘面停留在出露的红色碎砖块和黏土的层面，未将后期的扰动或废弃层全部剥离掉，具体、准确的红色砖末层的分布情况，还有待下一步的发掘。

已揭露的遗迹大致呈南北向带状分布，北部较直，南部向西部呈弧状延伸，南北最长处 34.3 米，东西最宽处 11.6 米。堆积形态西高东低，呈缓坡状分布，东部则相对较为平整，表面距离地表深度最浅处 2.45—2.85 米，最深处 3.55—3.97 米。路面遗迹并不是水平的，而是呈现出凹凸不平状。

遗迹的堆积包括上、下两部分，上部分为后期扰乱或废弃堆积，下部分则为路面上的原生堆积，这种关系在发掘的剖面上能清楚地观察出来。上部分堆积由碎砖、粉沙黏土交替出现而形成的多个夹层，其分布由北向南或由西向东逐层叠压，呈坡状的形态，砖块绝大部分为大小不一的残砖，北部分布较密集，南部碎砖相对较少；这种多个

图 3-23 曲折形围墙 1 平剖面图
Fig. 3-23 The plan and section of Zigzag Boundary Wall 1

小层斜坡分布的形态特点，表明它是一种倾倒垃圾式的堆积，推测可能是遗址中一些砖墙或台阶建筑破坏后所形成的废弃遗存。

下部则是以红色砖末为特征的堆积，在平剖面上均显示其在这一区域是较为连续且有较大面积的分布，具有人为铺垫和使用的特点，作为"路面"的功用较为清晰。其出露部分距离地表3.55—3.87米之间，上下高差可达30厘米左右，可能由于后期的扰动破坏所形成。该红色砖末层在东北部相当规整，近水平状，厚约5厘米，层内主要由较为细腻的砖末层构成，呈板块结构，同时也掺杂有极少的平铺砖块；南部厚5—12厘米，堆积相对较松散，表面起伏变化较大，层内除细腻的砖末外，也包含颗粒更大的一些碎块，局部可见较多的混杂其中的平铺砖块。在此砖末层之下，另有一层厚约6厘米的白色纯净粉沙呈大面积分布，与此"路面"遗迹相伴生，对它的解释还没有确定，一种可能是人工有意填铺而成，另一种可能是由于雨水在边缘低洼处的一种淤积现象所造成，因为白色粉沙带中可见明显的细部层理结构。在该纯净的砖末层之上的局部区域，如 UnitL8GridD10、D9，还可见有一些完整的砖块呈条状或块状分布，可能是完整路面或庭院性质的设施（彩版3-72）。

④层在路面1西缘渐趋消失，从叠压关系可知，路面1西缘叠压在④层之上，大部分则直接叠压在⑤层之上。根据它与八边形佛塔外墙的接触关系，外墙与地面紧密衔接，表明应是同时形成的，作为分布在室外的路面遗迹或活动面，更确切地说，它很可能就是环绕着十字形中心神殿建筑的道路（行经道）或者围廊建筑的残迹。据目前整个遗址的布局推测，在路面1与神殿建筑的中心区之间，可能存在有一些相应的砖结构廊庑或台阶建筑，从而构成了整个遗址从低处通往高处的通道。

它符合中心神殿的曼陀罗式的阶梯状的形式。从理论上说，叠压其上的③层与其下④层之间的交界面，正是建筑地面的分界线。此外，从④层的分布情况看，显然没有到达八边形佛塔1所在的遗址东部区域。因为，将塔心室置于地下，并不是当地的习俗，而且从塔身的位置看，佛塔的地面不可能与遗址中央④层地面的高度相同。

六、路面3

路面3主要分布于UnitI12GridF6–J6、F7–J7、F8–J8、F9–J9、F10–J10，UnitI13Grid G3–J3、G4–J4等探方内，位于八边形佛塔2东部的北门的南北两侧。揭露部分东西长约16米，南北宽约13米，厚约14厘米。发现时，路面与北门紧密相连，但与佛塔之间存在有约30厘米左右的空缺。路面整体较为平坦，局部因破坏而凹凸不平。

从断面观察，其主要由较细腻的砖末构成，底部掺杂有少量的碎砖末，而上层则为纯净砖末，在路面以下还发现厚约3厘米的浅白色纯净粉沙层。北门北侧的路面东西长3米，南北宽1米，与北门南侧的路面相比，修建得更好，砖末更为细腻且铺垫更平整。从路面的水平高度看，北门北侧要高于南侧约40厘米，这很可能更接近于这一区域的原始路面高度。路面3之上，很可能铺有完整的地面砖，只是已经不存，所以，严格地说，现在所留存的，只是路面下的路基部分。

路面3开口于③层下，位于④层以上，应是与北门及八边形佛塔同时期的活动面（彩版3-73，1、2）。

The cultural remains of the second period also include the Octagonal Stupa 1 – 3, Zigzag Boundary Wall, Floor 1 and Floor 3 (Figure 3-20).

Octagonal Stupa 1

Octagonal Stupa 1 is located in UnitL8, L9, M8, and M9. It is in north-south direction. It is 19 m long from north to south, and 11 m wide from east to west. In general, it comprises of two parts; one is octagonal stupa and the other is pillared-hall. Two different constructive phases, which are described below, were found in Octagonal Stupa 1.

The early phase stupa is located in UnitL8GridG1, G2, H1, H2, H3, I1, I2, I3, J1, and J2. Before excavation, some bricks were discovered because the villagers collected soil from here. With expansion of the excavation, the southern wall, southeastern wall and southwestern wall were almost completely exposed while eastern wall and western wall were partially excavated. Each wall of the stupa measures 3 m long and the angle between the two consecutive walls is 137°. According to the characteristic of the spatial distribution, the first phase stupa is supposed to be an octagonal shape. The highest preserved position is about 1 m height with 36 brick-layers. At the bottom of the stupa, a wide solid brick basement was found. However, because of the overlay by the later structure, the shape and dimension can not be measured. From a small area test trench, it was observed that the basement was built with horizontal bricks firstly and then vertical bricks were constructed above it. The stupa was possibly constructed in the south of the brick basement rather than in the center, and the northern part of the basement was used for other purposes. But this conclusion needs future excavation and analysis.

Importantly, a relic chamber, which measures about 0.63 m long, 0.57 m wide and 1.4 m high, was found in the center of this stupa. It was built 0.8 m above the basement. The chamber is well-designed, and three components can be recognized from bottom to top. The lower part is square shape, the middle part is an octagonal (each side is 22 cm long) and the upper part is round. Except this small chamber inside, the stupa should be a solid structure since inner the stupa was fully built with broken bricks.

The late phase of stupa extended 1.9 m in a pillared-hall called *mandapa* was also added in the second phase. The southern side is in UnitL8GridH10, I10, J10; southeastern side is in UnitM8GridA10, Unit M9 Unit A1, B2; the southwestern side is in UnitL8GridG10 Unit L9 grid F2, F3, F4; the eastern side is in UnitM9GridB3, B4 and the western side is in UnitL9GridF1, F2, F3. The other three sides are covered by the pillared-hall, which is in UnitL9GridF4-J9 and UnitM9GridA4-A9. The outer walls of the northern wall were found and they were also used as the southern wall of the pillared-hall. Each side of the preserved walls is 4.6 m long. Moreover, the second phase stupa was a little shifted in the direction from the first phase. Most of the structure was destroyed by later residents, and the maximum preserved height is about 2.5 m. Some paved bricks, which measure 1.5×1.5×0.3 m, were located in front of second phase stupa on the east. It possibly functioned as the entrance or pillared-hall-like hall. Due to limited distribution and excavation, the final conclusion awaits for further analysis.

A rectangular pillared-hall was created in the northern octagonal stupa of the second structural phase. The constructive time of the pillared-hall is not contemporary with the second phase stupa, and is possibly a little later than the latter. The western wall of the pillared-hall is preserved in a relatively good condition, but the northern wall and western wall are seriously destroyed. The western wall is 2.8 m wide, and the northern wall is 2.5 m wide and preserved up to 1.4 m high. In addition, the western side and eastern side of the pillared-hall are in a line with the edge of western wall and eastern wall respectively. The inner dimension of the hall is about 5.8 m from east to west and 4.4 m from north to south.

If considering the differences of the brick size and degree of the exposed outer walls, it seems that the pillared-hall itself was repaired several times. For example, some bricks in the middle part of the northern wall were smooth and regular whereas the upper part was constructed with larger size but less smooth bricks.

Octagonal Stupa 1 is under Layer 2, cuts the Layer 4 Partition Wall 1 and House 3 are found to under it, which is speculated to belong to the second period, which is contemporary with the cruciform central temple (Figure 3-21; Color Plate 3-64, 3-65, 3-66).

Octagonal Stupa 2

The Octagonal Stupa 2, which was constructed with nearly the same characteristics of Octagonal Stupa Complex 1 in Unit L8 and M8, was discovered in 2016-2017. It is located in Grid G2 – J2, G3 – J3, I4, J4 under H12 unit and A3 – D3, A4 – F4, C5 – E5, C6 – E6, D7, F7, D8, F8 grid under Unit I12. This stupa complex is in the east-west direction measuring 18 m long from east to west and 10 m width from north to south and the preserved height of structure is up to 1.8 m. It has two different constructive phases which were also repaired and extended several times.

The early phase of stupa has been located in Grid I4, I5, J4 and J5 of Unit H12 and grid A4, A5 of Unit I12. The rest of area could not be exposed as it is presently used as a village road. At first, we discovered some bricks lying 44 cm under present surface ground and 80×44 cm² area was exposed. Then more structures were found below it and excavation was expanded. Two projections have been discovered in vertical elevation. The 1st projection is located 51 cm below the top of the discovered wall. About 61 cm under 1st projection, the 2nd projection was discovered. The width of the projection is 2.5cm. Up to 28 cm below the 2nd projection has been discovered. The projections of south, south-east and south-west have been located in same level. The foundation has not been exposed where it started due to later constructive period. But the south face and south-east face have been completely exposed. The south face of stupa is 2.78 m long and southeast face of stupa is 1.92 m long. The east end of south-east face continued 70cm to the east then turned it to the north. 40cm of the east face of structure and 19 cm of the south-west face of structure are also exposed. Presence of the 2nd constructive phase and current village road makes a tough situation for measuring length of the northern and the north-west faces of structure.

South-eastern face and south-western face of this structure have turned in a 137° angle from both sides of southern face. The octagonal structure has an angle of 137° between two consecutive walls. Therefore we imagine that the ground plan of the 1st phase structure is octagonal shape. Maybe south-west face, western face, north-west face, north face and east face are similar length as like as south face of structure while south-eastern face and north-east face are of similar length. Or the south, north, west and east faces are similar in length and south-east face, south west face, north-east face and north-west faces are similar in length. The hypothesis could be confirmed until the entire area is excavated.

Location of construction wall face, alignment and distribution of bricks indicate that it belongs to the earlier phase construction. The second constructive phase of structure has started from regular face of the first constructive phase. There is no inter-locking between those structures which indicate different phases of construction.

The late constructive phase also extends 1.8 m in every face. It is decorated by horizontal and vertical projections which increased its beauty in this phase of structure. It has 4 vertical and 4 horizontal projections in every face of structure. The southwestern face has turned to 137° from the southern face of structure. In south-west face of structure 18-43 cm under current surface has been exposed. The southwest face is 4 m long. 85 cm from south end of south-western face structure projects outwards up to 14cm. There is another outward projection measuring 4-8 cm in a distance of 32-37 cm. After another distance of 166 cm, there is a projection measuring up to 6 cm. In a distance of 33 cm ahead, there lies a projection measuring 14-16 cm and the face runs up to another 22-28 cm. South face of structure is also decorated by projections as well as south-western face of structure. The length of south face is 3.5 m. The southern wall of the pillared-hall is 11.9 m long outside and 5.52 m long from inside. The maximum width of the preserved southern wall varies from 2.2 m to 2.6 m at the bottom. Southern wall has 5 vertical projections outside and only one projection inside. The 1st projection is located below the 90 cm from maximum height of preserved wall; 2nd projection is 67cm below the 1st projection; 3rd projection is located below the 18cm from 2nd projection; 4th projection is located under 10 cm below the 3rd projection; 5th projection is located 11 cm below the 4th projection. 46 cm has been exposed downward from the 5th projection. All the outside projections are 3-8 cm wide. The Inside projection located 58 cm below the maximum height of southern wall and another 28 cm has been exposed. The projection is 8 cm wide. Eastern wall's length is 10 m on the outside and 5.27 m on the inside of structure. The maximum width of eastern wall is 2.2 m on the top and 2.6 m at the bottom. The maximum height of preserved wall on the outside has been discovered under 40 cm from current surface. At north-east corner of the eastern wall, 6 projections on the outside and 1 projection at south-east corner have been exposed. 1st projection is located 66 cm below the maximum height of preserved wall.

2nd projection is located 53 cm below the 1st projection. 3rd projection is located 5 cm below the 2nd projection. 4th projection is located 29 cm below the 3rd projection. 5th projection is located 5 cm below the 4th projection. 6th projection is located 18 cm below the 5th projection. Moreover, another 46 cm has been exposed for last projection.

Four projections have been exposed on the eastern wall's inner face. 1st projection is located 23 cm below the maximum height of preserved wall. 2nd projection is located 23 below the 1st projection. 3rd projection is located 23cm below the 2nd projection. 4th projection is located 12cm below the 3rd projection. Moreover 46 cm has been exposed downward from 4th projection. Maybe this wall has been constructed and repaired several times. Outside projection indicates consecutive repairing and reconstruction.

At northern wall of pillared-hall 4.06 m from north-east corner towards the west has been exposed. The maximum width of northern wall is 2.2 m on the top and 2.6 m at the bottom. This wall has 1 projection on the outside and 3 projections on the inside. The maximum height of the outside face of the preserved wall is discovered 35 cm under the current surface. Only one projection is located 61cm below the maximum height of the outer face of preserved wall; another 74 cm has been exposed below the projection. But in inner face, 1st projection is located 46 cm below the maximum height of preserved northern wall. 2nd projection is located 48 cm below the 1st projection. 3rd projection is located 13cm below the 2nd projection and 14 cm is exposed below the 3rd projection.

Area of inside pillared-hall is 5.52 (East-West)×5.27 (North-South) m². Altar / pedestal is located on the western side of pillared-hall. The altar / pedestal is 5.27 m long in the direction of north to south and 2.89 m width from west to east. The brick platform is adjacent with western wall of pillared-hall. 2 vertical projections are also situated there. North and south touch with pillared-hall's wall but are not have inter-locking. Maybe it has extended in a later using period. Two separate structures in north-east corner and south-east corner of pillared-hall have been exposed, which also extend in later period. Area of these two structures is 2.2 m (E-W)×1.59 m (N-S). North-east structure is better than the south-east structure (Figure 3-22; Color Plate 3-67, 3-68, 3-69).

Octagonal Stupa 3

It is located in the southeastern corner of the excavation area, and exposed in the squares of UnitK7GridI9, I10, J9, and J10. At present, it is not completely excavated; most parts are still underground (Color Plate 3-70, 1).

Zigzag Boundary Wall 1

It is mainly distributed in the squares of UnitL7GridF10 G10, UnitL8GridG1, H1, H2, I1, I2, I3 ,I4, I5, J2, J3, J4, J5, J6 and UnitM8GridA3, A4, A5, A6, A7, A8, A9, B5, B6, B7, B8, B9, B10. In addition, a small part of a wall is found in unitM9GridC3, C4, C5, which possibly belongs to this zigzag wall. Some parts of the wall are seriously destroyed. The zigzag shape of the wall is not similar to other walls of the site.

It roughly runs from the southwest to the northeast, measuring 23.2 m long, 3.1 m wide and 1.9 m in preserved height. The exposed wall has three 90° turns on horizontal plan, and the widths of the projections are about 1.5 m inside and 2.15 m outside. Both sides of the wall show terraced vertical building technique, where the width of the wall is gradually narrower from bottom to top. The preserved inner wall has one terrace, whereas the outer wall has six terraces, and the width of each terrace is 5 – 10 cm. The lower part of the outer wall is less regular whereas the bricks in the upper part are uniform and smooth.

It is under Layer 2 and cuts Layer 4; House 1 and Road 1 are seen under this wall. According to the stratigraphic context, the zigzag wall belongs to the second period. It was probably built to serve as the boundary of the cruciform central temple (Figure 3-23; Color Plate 3-70: 2, 3).

Floor 1

The Floor 1, located on the east of cruciform central temple architecture and on the west of Octagonal Stupa 1 and zigzag wall, has been preserved a little in the northern and eastern area and extends into unexcavated southern area. The exposed part is mainly distributed in Unit L8 and Unit L9, and partially in Unit K8, involving a total of 95 Grids with an area of about 350 m^2. The northern boundary is in UnitL9GridB8, C8, D8, E8, the western boundary is in UnitL9GridB1 – B7, UnitL8GridB4, C5, B6 – B10, UnitK8GridI2, J3,the southern boundary is in UnitL8GridA1, B1, C1, and the east boundary is distributed to UnitL9GridE8, E7, E6, E5, E4, F3, F2, F1, UnitL8GridF10, F9, F8, G7, G6, F5, E4, D3, C2, C1. In addition, it can also be seen around the Octagonal Stupa 1 in UnitL9, L8, and near the zigzag boundary wall in the UnitL8GridJ9. On the north of the temple, there is also a red brick bust layer, with a few occasional flat bricks on its top. Although its structure has some difference with the Floor 1, the possibility that the floor extends to the northern end of Unit L10 (Color Plate 3-71) can not be excluded. When the southwest of the octagonal stupa was exacavated in 2013, it was proved to be the contemporary ground surface of the stupa. Because of the limited exposure, the distribution and the texture are still unclear. In order to fully understand it, a larger area was then excavated by the joint team in November and December, 2015. The deposit above the floor was removed and abandonde. Disturbed areas were not excavated. The concrete distribution of red bricks awaits further excavation.

The Floor 1 is distributed from north to south in a belt shape; the northern part is slightly straight while the southern part is arc-shaped towards the west. The longest dimension is 34.3 m across north and south, and widest 11.6 m form east to west. It is higher on the west and lower and flat on the east, gently sloping from west to east. The shallowest position is 2.45-2.85 m from the ground surface, and the deepest is 3.55 – 3.97 m. In general, the surface of the floor is uneven; the thickness is different from place to place.

The deposit is composed of the upper and lower parts, the former is the later disturbed accumulation, and the latter is the original accumulation of the road. Many sub-layers of various thicknesses are observed in the upper deposit, indicating that it is the remains of the destruction or abandonment of the buildings. The lower part is characterized by the fine red brick dusts, which is at the depth of 3.55 – 3.87 m from the ground floor, relatively continuously distributed in a large area. The function of this part as the pavement is clear. It is regular and horizontal in the northeast with a thickness of 5 cm, while it is loose and uneven in the south with a thickness of 5-12 cm. Under the brick dust layer, there is a layer of pure white powder sand, about 6 cm thick, distributed on almost all areas, but the question of whether they are formed by artificial filling or just natural accumulation is still unclear so far. A soil micromorpological analysis in the laboratory is needed to understand the nature and process of the deposit. In some squares, such as UnitL8GridD10, D9, there are also some complete bricks distributed in a strip shape, which may be the traces of the then untouched ground floor or courtyard structure (Color Plate 3-72).

The Floor 1 is mainly situated above Layer 4, and partially directly above Layer 5. There is no obvious gap between the outside wall of the Octagonal Stupa 1 and the Floor 1, indicating that they are possibly built at the same time. Floor 1 was constructed in the second period and functioned as the activity surface in the outdoor area, more precisely; it is likely to be the remnants of the circumambulatory passage or the corridor around the cruciform central stupa building.

According to our current understanding of the layout of the site, it is speculated that there may have been some of the corresponding brick structures, such as stairs and verandas, existing between the Floor 1 and the cruciform central stupa construction, constituting the passageway of the entire site from the low surrounding area to the top of the structures.

Floor 3

The floor ,which is mainly distributed in the squares of Unitl12GridF6 – J6, F7 – J7, F8 – J8, F9 – J9, F10 – J10, Unitl13GridG3 – J3, G4 – J4, has been exposed on the east side of Octagonal Stupa Complex 2 and both sides of the north gate. The floor demensions are 16.05 m from east to west, 12.4 m from north to south and 0.14 m thick. This floor is connected with north gate and is 30 cm east from the stupa complex. The floor of this area is almost a plane and suffers some kind of deterioration.

This floor is made of brick-dust, and possibly lime, but chemical test is needed to solve this issue. Some places also have a few scattered brickbats and potsherds. A 3 cm thick sand layer also exposed under the floor, which is probably for stability of the surface ground. Western part of the floor has some brickbats.

Another area is adjacent to the northern side of northern gate. It is almost 3 m from east to west and 1 m from north to south. The composite of this area is finer than southern side of the northern gate; some parts of the floor may be rammed. But the position of the northern side of the northern gate is 40 cm higher than that of the southern side.

This floor layer was exposed under Layer 3, and above the Layer 4. It was probably the contemporary living floor with the north gate and Octagonal Stupa 2 (Color Plate 3-73: 1, 2).

第四节 第三期遗迹
Section 4
The third period

第三期遗迹发现很少，在一些后期居民的取砖坑中，出土较为完整的陶器，推测与普通的②层有别，代表了某一时期的居民的生活行为。在收集这些陶器时，特以灰坑作为单位，以示区别，遗址中共发现5处（H1–H5），其中以H1最为典型。类似的取砖坑在遗址区数量众多，但大多都没有出土完整的陶器，因此，在发掘中都作为②层处理。

H1位于UnitI11GridJ1、J2和UnitJ11GridA1、A2内。开口于②层下，打破柱厅2柱基1。H1是后期人们取砖遗留下来的一个坑，平面呈圆形，剖面呈袋状，口径1.1、最大直径2.8、深度1.1米，填土浅灰褐色，可分多个小层，每层厚20—40厘米不等，填土中出土了多件罐、釜等陶器，出土的陶器与第一、二期有明显区别。推测H1是后期居民对于取砖坑的再次利用，作为贮藏或者丢弃垃圾使用，年代为本遗址的第三期。

H2位于柱厅4柱基3的顶部，陶器尚未整理。此外，未发现其他的活动遗迹（彩版3-73，3）。

Very few remains of the third period were found, but some complete potteries unearthed in the later pits indicate the difference from the ordinary cultural remains of Layer 2, representing a certain occupation period of the residents. 5 pits (H1-H5) were found in the site, of which H1 is the most typical one. The number of the similar pits is much bigger than this, most of them were included in the remains of Layer 2, because of the absence of complete wares.

H1, which is under the Layer 2 and cuts Pillar-Plinth 2 of Pillared-hall 1, is located in UnitI11GridJ1, J2 and UnitJ11GridA1, A2. It was dug by the later period villagers for the recovery of bricks and building materials. The ash pit is round in shape with maximum diameter of 2.8 m and 1.1 m in depth. The deposit inside the pit is light gray brown soil, with several sub-layers, each of 20-40 cm thick. A number of cooking pots and other pots were unearthed from the pit, showing a significant difference between the first and second periods. It is presumed that H1 was reused as storage or garbage.

H2 is located on the top of Pillar-plinth 3 of Pillared-hall 4, but the unearthed potteries have not yet been studied (Color Plate 3-73, 3).

彩版3-1
第一期遗迹全景
Color Plate 3-1
The panorama of the first period's cultural remains

1. 第一期遗迹全景

2. 2017年度发掘现场

彩版3-2
神殿1外墙
Color Plate 3-2
The outer wall of Temple 1

1. 西南—东北

2. 西北—东南

彩版3-3
神殿1全景
Color Plate 3-3
The panorama of Temple 1

1. 东—西

2. 南—北

彩版3-4
神殿1门厅
Color Plate 3-4
The entrance hall of Temple 1

1. 西北—东南

2. 西南—东北

3. 东北—西南

彩版3-5
神殿1相关遗迹
Color Plate 3-5
The related relics of Temple 1

1. 门厅墙基下人工填土

2. 东墙外地面及附属墙基

3. 内部墙面及基础火砖

彩版3-6
神殿1墙角瓮1、瓮2
Color Plate 3-6
The Urn 1 and Urn 2 at the corners of Temple 1

1. 瓮1

2. 瓮1下部陶器

3. 瓮1底部

4. 瓮2

彩版3-7
房屋6、房屋7和道路1
Color Plate 3-7
House 6, House 7 and Road 1

1. 房屋6局部

2. 房屋6局部

3. 房屋7（东—西）

4. 道路1（东南—西北）

彩版3-8
道路3北部
Color Plate 3-8
The north of Road 3

1. 南—北

2. 北—南

彩版3-9
道路3中南部
Color Plate 3-9
Southern and central part of Road 3

1. 东北—西南

2. 北—南

3. 局部特写

彩版3-10
浴室和排水沟
Color Plate 3-10
Bathroom and drainage

1. 浴室（西南—东北）

2. 排水沟（北—南）

彩版3-11
神殿2
Color Plate 3-11
Temple 2 (pyramid-shaped stupa)

1. 东墙（东南—西北）

2. 东墙（东北—西南）

3. 鸟瞰图

彩版3-12
神殿2东墙基
Color Plate 3-12
The eastern wall foundation of Temple 2 (pyramid-shaped stupa)

1. 东墙基（北—南）

2. 东墙基（南—北）

3. 东墙嵌入式结构（南—北）

彩版3-13

神殿2东墙外遗迹

Color Plate 3-131
The remains outside of the eastern wall of Temple 2 (pyramid-shaped stupa)

1. 东墙外废弃堆积（东北—西南）

2. 东墙外的墙基3和砖块堆积（东—西）

彩版3-14
神殿2东墙外陶器和河光石
Color Plate 3-14
The unearthed potteries and processed cobbles outside the eastern wall of Temple 2 (pyramid-shaped stupa)

1. 陶器

2. 陶器

3. 陶器

4. 河光石

彩版3-15
神殿2北墙

Color Plate 3-15
The northern wall of Temple 2 (pyramid-shaped stupa)

1. 北墙基内侧（南—北）

2. 第二期柱厅2北墙基打破神殿2北墙（南—北）

3. 第二期柱厅2北墙基打破神殿2北墙（东—西）

4. 北墙东段（北—南）

彩版3-16
隔墙
Color Plate 3-16
Partition wall

1. 隔墙南段

2. 隔墙南段（西南—东北）

3. 中段隔墙被八边形佛塔叠压（西北—东南）

彩版3-17
隔墙根下出土陶器
Color Plate 3-17
The potteries unearthed at the foot of partition wall

1. 第一期早段陶器

2. 第一期中段陶器

彩版3-18
隔墙根下出土陶器
Color Plate 3-18
The potteries unearthed at the foot of partition wall

1. 第一期早段陶器　　　　　　　　　　　2. 第一期早段陶器

3. 第一期早段陶器　　　　　　　　　　　4. 第一期中段陶器

5. 第一期中段陶器　　　　　　　　　　　6. 第一期中段陶器

彩版3-19
房屋1
Color Plate 3-19
House 1

1. 房屋1鸟瞰图

2. 东南—西北

3. 西南—东北

4. 柱洞（D9）

彩版3-20
房屋2
Color Plate 3-20
House 2

1. 房屋2平面

2. 南墙（西南—东北）

3. 南墙（东南—西北）

彩版3-21
房屋3、4
Color Plate 3-21
House 3, House 4

1. 房屋3墙基（西南—东北）

2. 房屋3墙基（东—西）

3. 房屋4（东南—西北）

4. 房屋4南墙（东南—西北）

彩版3-22
房屋5全景
Color Plate 3-22
The panorama of House 5

1. 房屋5全景

2. 房屋5全景（东北—西南）

彩版3-23
房屋5局部
Color Plate 3-23
Some parts of House 5

1. 发掘前地面

2. 台级

3. 砖辅道

4. 庭院砖辅地面

彩版3-24
墙1、2、3
Color Plate 3-24
Wall 1, Wall 2, and Wall 3

1. 墙1（南—北）

2. 墙2（东北—西南）

3. 墙2（北—南）

4. 墙3（东—西）

彩版3-25
路面4、道路4
Color Plate 3-25
Floor 4, Road 4

1. 路面4（西南—东北）

2. 道路4叠压道路3（北—南）

彩版3-26
十字形中心神殿全景
Color Plate 3-26
The panorama of the Cruciform Central Temple

彩版3-27
中心塔基地层和柱厅1发掘前地表
Color Plate 3-27
The stratigraphy of central temple foundation and the surface of Pillared-hall 1 before excavation

1. 中心塔基②层

2. 中心塔基②层

3. 柱厅1发掘前地表

彩版3-28
柱厅1全景
Color Plate 3-28
The panorama of Pillared-hall 1

彩版3-29
柱厅1全景
Color Plate 3-29
The panorama of Pillared-hall 1

1. 西—东

2. 东南—西北

彩版3-30
柱厅1东墙基
Color Plate 3-30
The eastern wall foundation of Pillared-hall 1

1. 西—东

2. 南—北

3. 东—西

4. 北—南

彩版3-31
柱厅1北墙基

Color Plate 3-31
The northern wall foundation of Pillared-hall 1

1. 西南—东北

2. 西—东

彩版3-32
柱厅1南墙基、西墙基
Color Plate 3-32
The southern and western wall foundations of Pillared-hall 1

1. 南墙基（西—东）

2. 南墙基（东—西）

3. 西墙基（南—北）

4. 西南墙角（南—北）

彩版3-33
柱厅1柱基1
Color Plate 3-33
The Pillar-plinth 1 of Pillared-hall 1

1. 南—北

2. 西—东

3. 西—东

4. 西北—东南

彩版3-34
柱厅1柱基2
Color Plate 3-34
The Pillar-plinth 2 of Pillared-hall 1

1. 北—南

2. 西北—东南

3. 西—东

4. 南—北

彩版3-35
柱厅1柱基3、4
Color Plate 3-35
The Pillar-plinth 3, 4 of Pillared-hall 1

1. 柱基3（南—北）

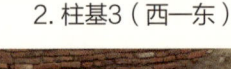

2. 柱基3（西—东）

3. 柱基4（东—西）

4. 柱基4（西—东）

彩版3-36
柱厅2全景
Color Plate 3-36
The panorama of Pillared-hall 2

彩版3-37

柱厅2全景（2014—2015年发掘后）

Color Plate 3-37

The panorama of Pillared-hall 2 (after excavation during 2014 – 2015)

1. 东北—西南　　　　　　　　　　　　2. 西—东

3. 北—南（墙基出露前）　　　　　　　4. 北—南

彩版3-38
柱厅2全景（2015—2016年发掘后）
Color Plate 3-38
The panorama of Pillared-hall 2 (after excavation during 2015 – 2016)

1. 东南—西北

2. 东北—西南

彩版3-39
柱厅2东墙基、南墙基
Color Plate 3-39
The eastern and southern wall foundations of Pillared-hall 2

1. 东墙基（北—南）

2. 南墙基（东—西）

彩版3-40
墙柱厅2西墙基
Color Plate 3-40
The western wall foundation of Pillared-hall 2

1. 西北—东南

2. 东北—西南

3. 墙基剖面（北—南）

4. 叠压神殿2北墙基（东北—西南）

彩版3-41
柱厅2北墙基
Color Plate 3-41
The northern wall foundation of Pillared-hall 2

1. 东段（东—西）

2. 中段（北—南）

3. 西段（北—南）

彩版3-42
柱厅2柱基1
Color Plate 3-42
The Pillar-plinth 1 of Pillared-hall 2

1. 西—东（1）

2. 西—东（2）

3. 东南—西北

4. 南—北

彩版3-43
柱厅2柱基2、3、4
Color Plate 3-43
The Pillar-plinth 2, 3 and 4 of Pillared-hall 2

1. 柱基2（南—北）　　　　　　　　　　　　　2. 柱基2（西—东）

3. 柱基3（东—西）　　　　　　　　　　　　　4. 柱基（东南—西北）

5. 柱基4（东南—西北）　　　　　　　　　　　6. 柱基4（南—北）

彩版3-44
柱厅3全景
Color Plate 3-44
The panorama of Pillared-hall 3

1. 南—北

彩版3-45
柱厅3墙基
Color Plate 3-45
The wall foundation of Pillared-hall 3

1. 东墙基（南—北）

2. 南墙基（西—东）

3. 西墙基（北—南）

4. 东、北墙基（东北—西南）

彩版3-46
柱厅3柱基
Color Plate 3-46
The Pillar-plinth of Pillared-hall 3

1. 柱基1、2（南—北）

2. 柱基2（南—北）

3. 柱基3（东南—西北）

4. 柱基4（西北—东南）

彩版3-47
柱厅4全景
Color Plate 3-47
The panorama of Pillared-hall 4

彩版3-48
柱厅4全景
Color Plate 3-48
The panorama of Pillared-hall 4

1. 东北—西南

2. 东—西

3. 西北—东南

4. 西—东

彩版3-49
柱厅4东墙基、南墙基
Color Plate 3-49
The eastern and southern wall foundations of Pillared-hall 4

1. 东墙基（东南—西北）

2. 南墙基（北—南）

3. 南墙基（南—北）

4. 南墙基（西—东）

彩版3-50
柱厅4西墙基、北墙基
Color Plate 3-50
The western and northern wall foundations of Pillared-hall 4

1. 西墙基（北—南）

2. 北墙基（东—西）

3. 北墙基（东南—西北）

4. 北墙基（西—东）

彩版3-51
柱厅4柱基1、2
Color Plate 3-51
The Pillar-plinth 1, 2 of Pillared-hall 4

1. 柱基1（北—南）

2. 柱基1（东北—西南）

3. 柱基2（北—南）

4. 柱基2（西北—东南）

彩版3-52
柱厅4柱基1、2
Color Plate 3-52
The Pillar-plinth 1, 2 of Pillared-hall 4

1. 柱基1、2（东北—西南）

2. 柱基1、2（西北—东南）

彩版3-53
柱厅4柱基3、4

Color Plate 3-53
The Pillar-plinth 3, 4 of Pillared-hall 4

1. 柱基（东—西）

2. 柱基3（西北—东南）

3. 柱基4（东北—西南）

4. 柱基4（西—东）

彩版3-54
连接墙基1
Color Plate 3-54
The Connective Wall Foundation 1

1. 东南—西北

2. 西北—东南

3. 西南—东北

4. 西北—东南

彩版3-55
连接墙基2
Color Plate 3-55
The Connective Wall Foundation 2

1. 北—南

2. 西—东

3. 东南—西北

4. 南—北

彩版3-56
连接墙基3、4
Color Plate 3-56
The Connective Wall Foundation 3 and 4

1. 连接墙基3（东—西）

2. 连接墙基3（南—北）

3. 连接墙基4（南—北）

4. 柱厅1西南角与连接墙基4（东—西）

彩版3-57
中心塔基和柱厅4全景
Color Plate 3-57
The panorama of central temple foundation and Pillared-hall 4

1. 中心塔基和柱厅4（2016年1月）

2. 中心塔基（2018年1月）

彩版3-58
中心塔基局部遗迹
Color Plate 3-58
The partial remains of central temple foundation

1. 塔基南端（西南—东北）

2. 塔基南端（东—西）

3. 塔基底部（西—东）

4. 墙基南端转折处（西北—东南）

彩版3-59
中心塔基东、北、西端
Color Plate 3-59
The east, north and west ends of central temple foundation

1. 东端（东—西）

2. 北端（西—东）

3. 西端（北—南）

彩版3-60
北门道全景
Color Plate 3-60
The panorama of north entrance

1. 北门道和八边形佛塔2

2. 北门道（东—西）

彩版3-61
北门道局部
Color Plate 3-61
Some local parts of north entrance

1. 门道墙体（西北—东南）

2. 西侧连接墙（东南—西北）

3. 门道残基（西—东）

彩版3-62

护墙基和巴哈布尔遗址复原图

Color Plate 3-62
The parapet wall and the imagination reconstruction of central temple at Paharpur monastery

1. 护墙基

2. 巴哈布尔复原图（1）

3. 巴哈布尔复原图（2）

彩版3-63
出土装饰砖
Color Plate 3-63
The unearthed decorative bricks

彩版3-64
八边形佛塔1全景
Color Plate 3-64
The panorama of Octagonal Stupa 1

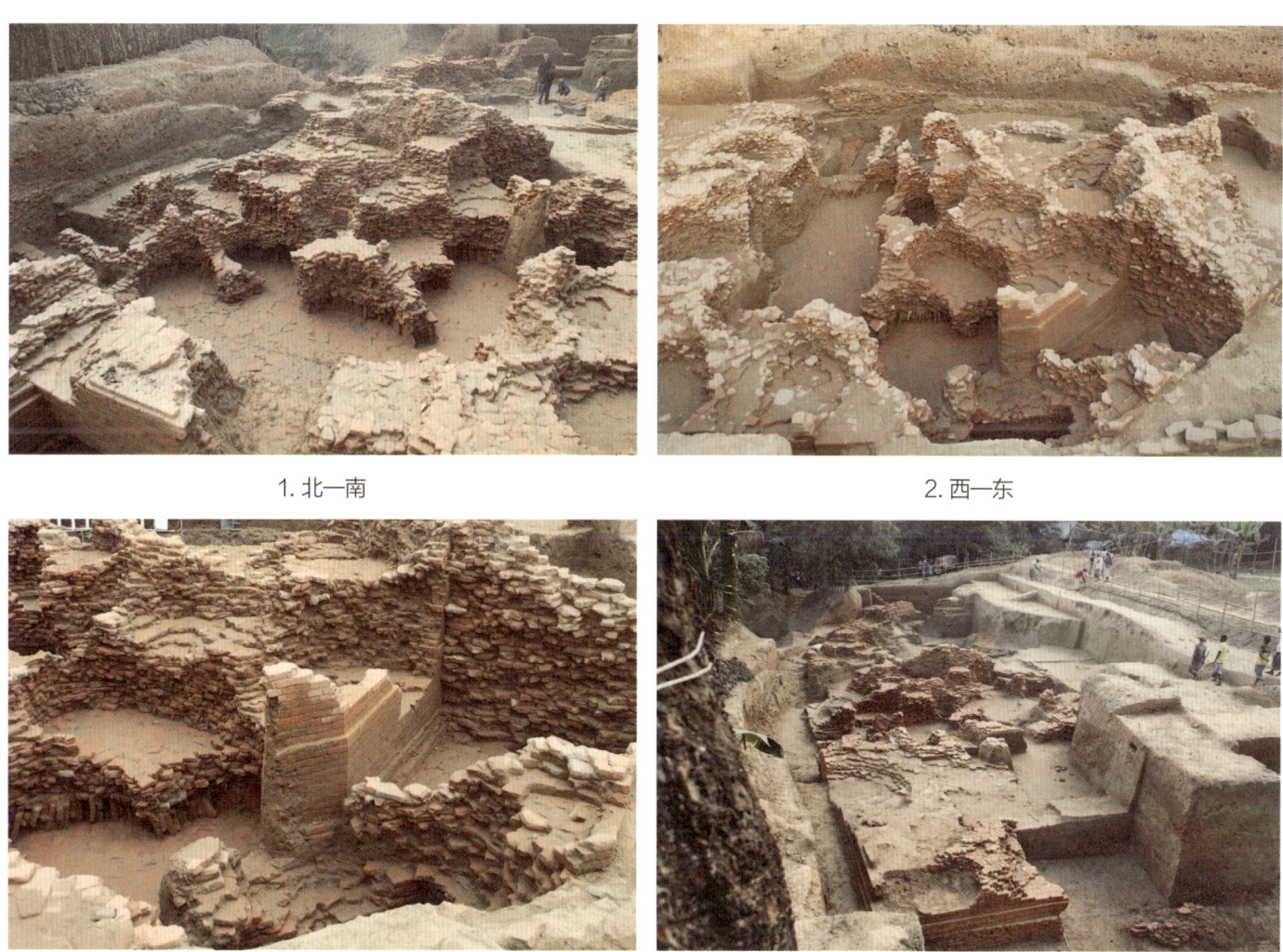

1. 北—南

2. 西—东

3. 西南—东北

4. 北—南

彩版3-65
八边形佛塔1内部
Color Plate 3-65
The interior of Octagon Stupa 1

1. 塔心室（1）

2. 塔心室（2）

3. 塔基底部结构

彩版3-66
八边形佛塔1局部
Color Plate 3-66
The exterior of Octagon Stupa 1

1. 前厅（西—东）

2. 塔基外墙（东南—西北）

3. 塔外地面

4. 塔基叠压第一期隔墙

彩版3-67
八边形佛塔2全景
Color Plate 3-67
The panorama of Octagonal Stupa 2

1. 发掘前（东南—西北）

2. 鸟瞰图

3. 南—北

4. 东—西

彩版3-68
八边形佛塔2塔身部分
Color Plate 3-68
The body of Octagonal Stupa 2

1. 内层佛塔

2. 外层佛塔

3. 两层佛塔

彩版3-69
八边形佛塔2前厅部分
Color Plate 3-69
The mandapa of Octagonal Stupa 2

1. 前厅东墙和南墙（东南—西北）

2. 前厅东墙（东南—西北）

3. 前厅内部砖结构（东北—西南）

4. 前厅内砖结构（北—南）

彩版3-70
八边形佛塔3、曲折形围墙1
Color Plate 3-70
The Octagonal Stupa 3, Zigzag Boundary Wall 1

1. 八边形佛塔3（东南—西北）

2. 曲折形围墙1（西南—东北）

3. 曲折形围墙1（北—南）

彩版3-71
路面1平面位置
Color Plate 3-71
The location plan of Floor 1

彩版3-72
路面1遗迹
Color Plate 3-72
Floor 1

1. 路面1表面（南—北）

2. 路面1表面（东南—西北）

3. 路面1表面局部砖块

4. 路面1叠压在第4层之上（东南—西北）

彩版3-73
路面3、H2
Color Plate 3-73
Floor 3, ash pit H2

1. 路面3（南—北）

2. 路面3（北—南）

3. H2（南—北）

Chapter

IV

第四章

Unearthed Artifacts

遗 物

纳提什瓦
Nateshwar

第一节
Section 1
Pottery
陶器

出土遗物以日用陶器的数量最大，本节将逐层对陶器标本进行介绍。首先，作以下相关说明：

1. 在发掘过程中，某些重要地层的上下部，或上下地层之间的标本，都加以了区分，整理时也未作合拼，因此，在标本中有“⑤层下部”、“⑥层表层”、“⑤—⑥层之间”这样的标志。其实，像“⑤层下部”、“⑤—⑥层之间”一般可以归入⑤层，“⑥层表层”可以归入⑥层，之所以没有合并，是想保存资料的原始性，以反映标本最真实的情况。

2. 2013 年发掘的 UnitL8、L9、L10 的部分区域，地层系统与 2014 年以后有较大调整，现根据当时的原始深度，将其换算成了统一地层，但可能存在一定的误差。此外，这部分器物的编号，为所选用标本的流水号。

3. 统计表中所用的数字，反映了遗物在量上的信息，但它们只代表已经整理的部分。由于出土遗物的数量很大，2015 年 6—7 月的整理，只选择了某些层位关系比较清楚、陶片收集比较准确的地层和遗迹单位（约占总量的一半），还有一部分未作整理。此外，2015 年 11 月—2016 年 1 月和 2017 年 11 月—2018 年 1 月发掘出土的陶器也尚未整理。所以，这些数字存在一定的局限性。

4. 行文中的标本号，都进行了简化处理，如“标本 UnitL10GridE5-F6 ④：11”，简化为“标本 L10E5-F6 ④：11”；“标本 UnitI10-I11 ④：12”，简化为“标本 I10-I11 ④：12”。

一、①层出土陶器

①层陶器实际上是遗址的扰乱地层，年代性质都比较杂乱。陶器基本为泥质夹细砂陶，以红陶为大多数，火候都较高，器类以罐、釜、壶、钵为常见，其中釜都为 B 型釜。以素面为主，纹饰有方格纹、凹弦纹、条状纹、叶脉纹等（表 2）。

标本介绍

UnitL10GridI5–J6，UnitJ11GridC1–D2 ① 层出土陶器：

标本 L10I5-J6 ①：3，壶，红陶，圆唇，卷沿外翻，束颈，弧肩，鼓腹，平底内凹，颈肩部饰多道弦纹。口径 10.5 厘米、腹径 13.2 厘米、高 14.2 厘米（图 4-1，1；彩版 4-1，1）。

标本 J11C1–D2 ①：1，钵，红陶，敛口，平底，肩饰多道弦纹。口径 6.4 厘米、高 3.1 厘米（图 4-1，2）。

标本 L10I5–J6 ①：2，器盖，红陶，圈足形纽，器盖呈覆斗状，沿面上饰一道凸棱。盖径 24 厘米、纽径 5.8 厘米、高 7.4 厘米（图 4-1，3；彩版 4-1，2）。

表 2　UnitI10、I11、J10、J11 ①层陶器统计表

纹饰＼陶色	红	黑	备注
素面	70	46	
方格	12	12	
凹弦	3	2	
条状	8		
叶脉	3		
器类（数量）	B 型釜 6 件，罐 21 件，壶 2 件，钵 1 件	罐 8 件，壶 2 件，器盖 1 件	

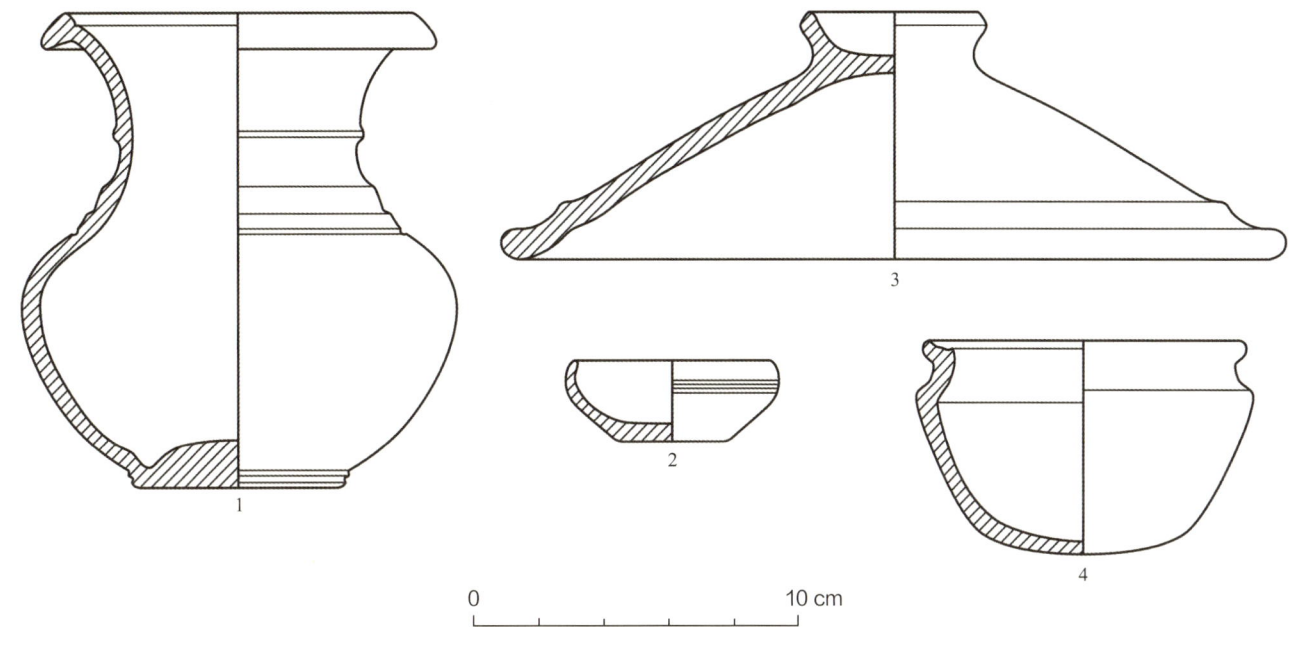

图 4-1　UnitL10GridI5-J6，UnitJ11GridC1-D2 ①层出土陶器
Fig. 4-1　The unearthed potteries of Layer 1 from UnitL10GridI5-J6, UnitJ11GridC1-D2

标本 L10I5-J6①：1，E 型罐，红陶，圆唇，直口，沿面内有一凹槽，束颈，折肩，圜底近平，素面，器底有烟炱痕迹。口径 10 厘米、腹径 10.4 厘米、高 6.4 厘米（图 4-1，4；彩版 4-1，3）。

二、②层出土陶器

②层是由取砖后的回填土形成的，因此，所包含的陶器中，既有晚期的，也混杂有早期的遗物，比较杂乱。皆为泥质夹细砂陶，红陶为绝大多数，新出现的一类陶器，陶色为较鲜的橙红色，火候普遍较高。器类有釜、罐、壶、钵等几类，釜、罐、壶的器体较大。素面为主，纹饰为方格纹、凹弦纹、条状纹、叶脉纹、星状纹等（表3）。

标本介绍

UnitL10GridE6 ②层出土陶器：

标本 L10E6②：29，C 型釜，盆形釜，红陶，颜色纯正，圆唇敞口，沿面内凹，束颈，弧腹斜收，腹部饰方格纹，圜底残，底部有黑色烟炱痕迹。口径 28 厘米、残高 12.8 厘米（图 4-2，1；彩版 4-1，4）。

标本 L10E6②：34，C 型釜，盆形釜，红陶，颜色纯正，圆唇敞口，沿面内凹，束颈，弧腹斜收，腹部饰方格纹，圜底。口径 28.4 厘米、残高 13 厘米（图 4-2，2；彩版 4-1，5）。

UnitI10GridI3，UnitL10，UnitJ11，UnitK9GridF10，UnitI11 ②层出土陶器：

标本 I10 I3②：6，C 型罐，红陶，敞口，圆唇，束颈，溜肩，鼓腹，圜底，肩部饰多道弦纹。口径 7.2 厘米、高 9.8 厘米（图 4-3，1；彩版 4-1，6）。

标本 L10②：7，C 型罐，红陶，敞口，圆唇，束颈，溜肩，鼓腹，圜底，肩部饰多道弦纹。口径 7.2 厘米、高 9 厘米（图 4-3，2；彩版 4-2，1）。

标本 J11②：3，缸，黑陶，敛口，圆唇，沿下残，沿下饰方格纹。口径 47.2 厘米、残高 6.4 厘米（图 4-3，3）。

标本 K9F10②：9，盂，红陶，圆唇，束颈，斜腹内收，圜底，素面。口径 17.8 厘米、高 8 厘米（图 4-3，4；彩版 4-2，2）。

标本 I11②：2，灯盏，红陶，尖圆唇，子母口，浅圜底，沿部有烧痕。口径 9.2 厘米、高 1.5 厘米（图 4-3，5；彩版 4-2，3）。

标本 J11②：4，器盖，红陶，圆形纽，盖身残，器壁较厚。纽径 4.8 厘米、残高 4.4 厘米（图 4-3，6）。

表 3　UnitI10、I11、J10、J11②层陶器统计表

纹饰 \ 陶色	红	黑	备注
素面	978	739	
方格	59	118	
凹弦	18	38	
条状	19		
叶脉	5		
星状	3	1	
器类（数量）	釜 27，罐 39，壶 12，钵 7，灯 2，器盖 3	罐 27，釜 6，壶 10，器盖 2	

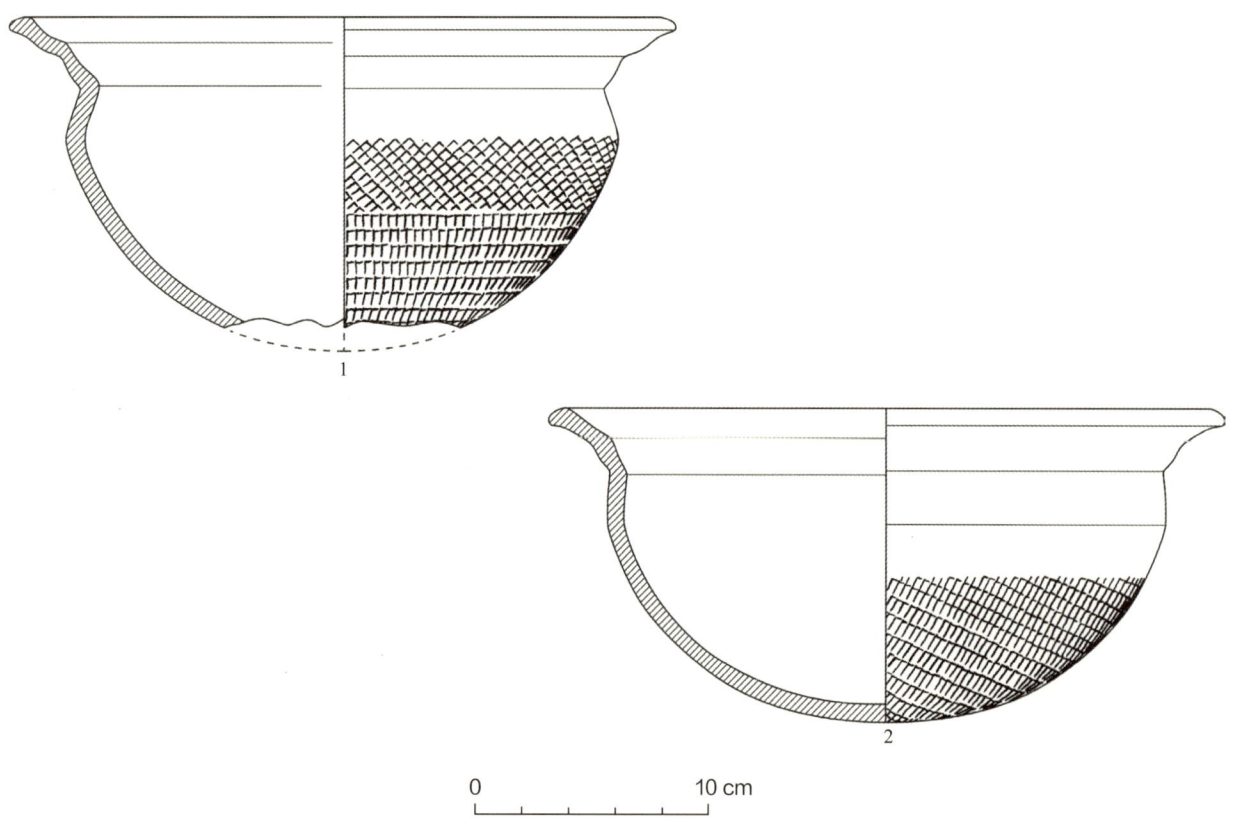

图 4-2　UnitL10GridE6②层出土陶器
Fig. 4-2　The unearthed potteries of Layer 2 from UnitL10GridE6

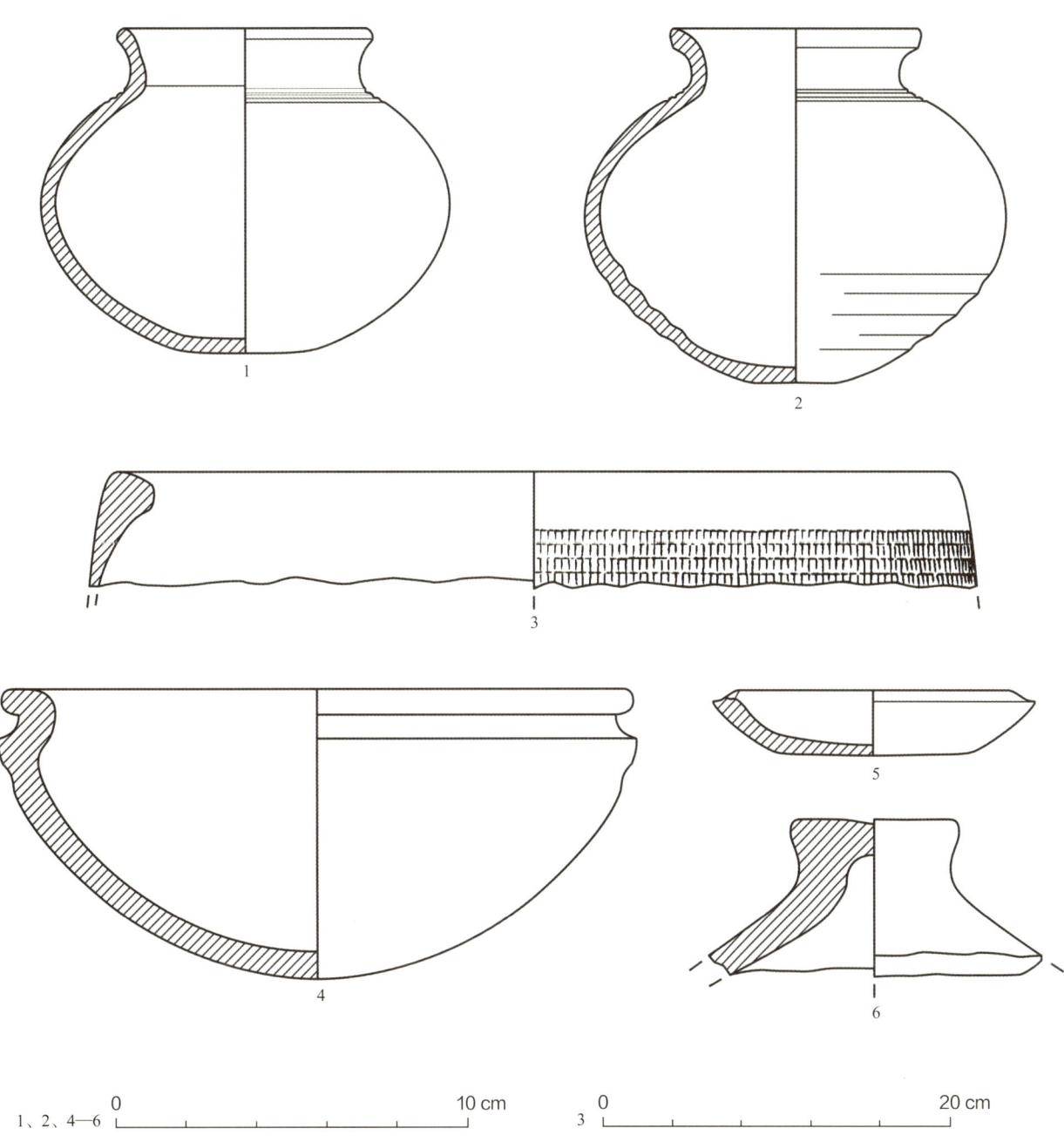

图 4-3 UnitI10GridI3，UnitL10，UnitJ11，UnitK9GridF10，UnitI11 ②层出土陶器

Fig. 4-3 The unearthed potteries of Layer 2 from UnitI10GridI3, UnitL10, UnitJ11, UnitK9GridF10 and UnitI11

三、灰坑 H1 出土陶器

H1 位于 UnitI11GridJ1、J2 和 UnitJ11GridA1、A2 内。开口于②层下，打破柱厅 2 柱基 1。H1 是后期人们取砖遗留下来的一个坑，填土中出土了多件陶器，出土的陶器为夹细砂陶，色彩鲜艳，薄胎，火候高，器形变大，与早期陶器有明显区别。器类以 C 型釜（盆形釜）、壶为主。器物颈部多素面，腹部有方格纹、弦纹、交叉拍印、条状印纹等。

标本介绍

标本 H1：1，C 型釜，盆形釜，红陶，圆唇敞口，沿下部略内凹，束颈，弧腹斜收，腹部饰方格纹，上部纹饰规整，下部交错拍印，器表有黑色烟炱痕迹。口径 36 厘米、残高 17.6 厘米（图 4-4，1；彩版 4-3，1）。

标本 H1：2，C 型釜，盆形釜，红陶，圆唇较厚，敞口，沿面内凹，束颈，弧腹斜收，腹部饰交错方格纹，腹部下有烟炱痕迹。口径 29.8 厘米、残高 10.8 厘米（图 4-4，2）。

标本 H1：5，C 型壶，红陶，色彩较纯，尖唇，敞口，口沿较厚，束颈，溜肩，圆腹，圜底，肩部有一道弦纹，腹上部饰拍印竖条纹，腹部下饰方格纹。口径 14.8 厘米、腹径 26.6 厘米、残高 27.4 厘米（图 4-5，1；彩版 4-3，2）。

标本 H1：3，A 型壶，红色较纯，器表施红衣，圆唇，口沿外翻内收，敞口，束颈，溜肩，肩部以下残。口径 17 厘米、残高 17.2 厘米（图 4-6，1）。

标本 H1：4，B 型壶，红陶，口沿外卷，敞口，束颈，溜肩，圆腹，腹部残，肩部饰弦纹，腹上部饰竖条纹，腹部下饰方格纹。口径 15 厘米、腹径 27 厘米、残高 23 厘米（图 4-6，2）。

四、④层出土陶器

④层是建造第二期寺院建筑而形成的填土，有一部分是利用原生的废弃物，所以年代上较为混杂。陶器皆为夹砂陶，泥质比重较大，红色陶比例大于黑色陶。器类以釜、罐、壶、钵为主，折腹、折肩类陶器转折风格逐渐从棱角分明趋向更加圆弧。C 型釜的数量有较大增加。以素面为主，纹饰主要为方格纹、凹弦纹、条状纹、交叉纹等（表 4）。

标本 L10E5-F6 ④：11，带柄杯，黑色，施黑衣，磨光精细，杯底中心有一实心凸起，四周饰有规整的同心圆圈纹，有学者认为，中央是山，四周为大海，其中有佛教世界模式的寓意（见后图 4-12，1）。这类精致的薄胎黑陶在遗址中有极少量发现，如标本 W1：17，C 型罐（见后图 4-28，3），也属此类，这种工艺特殊的罕见之物，似乎是外地传入品，值得注意。

标本介绍

UnitI10–I11 ④层出土陶器：

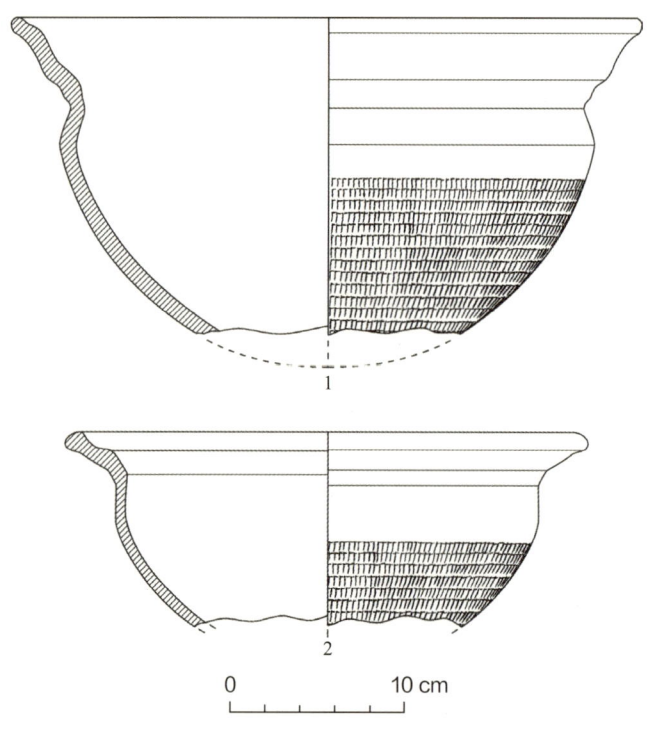

图 4-4　H1 出土陶器
Fig. 4-4　The unearthed potteries from H1

表4 UnitI10、I11、J10、J11 ④层陶器统计表

纹饰 \ 陶色	红	黑	备注
素面	1200	366	
方格	118	102	
凹弦	18	2	
交叉	3	2	
条状	17	4	
器类（数量）	Aa 型釜 9，Ab 型釜 8，C 型釜 18，A 型罐 14，B 型罐 16，C 型罐 17，D 型罐 8，A 型壶 12，C 型壶 2，钵 80，器盖 5，灯座 1，灯盏 3，缸 1	Aa 型釜 21，A 型罐 1，C 型罐 2，A 型壶 2，B 型壶 8，器盖 6，灯座 2，缸 1	

标本 I10–I11 ④：1，Aa 型釜，钵形，红陶，盘口，圆唇，束颈，圆肩，腹部残，颈部饰多道弦纹，肩部饰两道弦纹，腹部饰方格纹。口径 31.6 厘米、残高 7.6 厘米（图 4-7，1）。

标本 I10–I11 ④：3，Ab 型釜，红陶，敛口，宽沿，圆唇，溜肩，弧腹，腹部残，素面。口径 27.2 厘米、残高 6.6 厘米（图 4-7，2）。

标本 I10–I11 ④：4，Ab 型釜，红陶，敞口，圆唇，束颈，圆肩，腹部残，颈部饰多道弦纹，肩部饰一道凸棱，腹部饰刻划纹。口径 24 厘米、残高 4.8 厘米（图 4-7，3）。

标本 I10–I11 ④：6，C 型釜，盆形，红陶，侈口，圆唇，颈微束，圆肩，腹部残，素面。口径 25.6 厘米、残高 5.6 厘米（图 4-7，4）。

标本 I10–I11 ④：5，C 型釜，盆形，红陶，侈口，圆唇，束颈，圆肩，腹部残，腹部饰方格纹。口径 22.8 厘米、残高 6.2 厘米（图 4-7，5）。

标本 I10–I11 ④：2，Aa 型釜，红陶，盘口，圆唇，束颈，广肩，肩部残，沿内外饰多道弦纹。口径 19.2 厘米、残高 3 厘米（图 4-7，6）。

UnitI10–I11，UnitL10GridE6，UnitL10GridE5-F6 ④层出土陶器：

标本 L10E6 ④：4，Aa 型釜，黑陶，圆唇，沿面有一浅凹槽，束颈，圆鼓肩，浅腹内收，圜底，肩部饰两道弦纹，腹部饰方格纹。口径 15.6 厘米、残高 5.6 厘米（图 4-8，1；彩版 4-2，4）。

标本 L10E5–FE6 ④：26，Aa 型釜，灰黑陶，黑衣磨光，圆唇，盘口，束颈，圆肩，斜腹内收，圜底，口沿内饰两道弦纹，肩部饰一圈戳点纹，下有一道弦纹，腹部饰方格纹。口径 18.2 厘米、腹径 18.6 厘米、残高 5.3 厘米（图 4-8，2；彩版 4-2，5）。

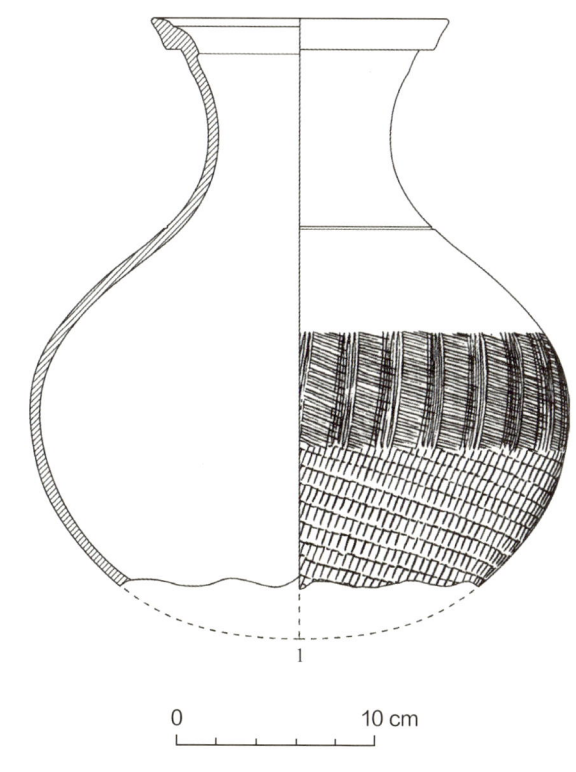

图 4-5 H1 出土陶器

Fig. 4-5 The unearthed potteries from H1

标本 I10–I11④：12，A 型壶，夹石英黑陶，喇叭口，圆唇，盘口，束颈，颈下残，沿内饰一道弦纹，沿下饰一道凸棱，颈部饰两道弦纹。口径 22 厘米、残高 5.4 厘米（图 4-8，3）。

标本 I10–I11④：13，A 型壶，红陶，敞口，圆唇，束颈，颈下残，沿下饰一道凸棱。口径 18.8 厘米、残高 5.8 厘米（图 4-8，4）。

标本 I10–I11④：14，缸，黑陶，喇叭口，圆唇，盘口，束颈，颈下残，沿内饰多道弦纹，沿下饰一道凸棱，沿上饰两道弦纹。口径 30 厘米、残高 5.4 厘米（图 4-8，5）。

标本 I10–I11④：15，缸，红陶，敛口，圆唇，沿下残，沿下饰一道弦纹。口径 26 厘米、残高 5.6 厘米（图 4-8，6）。

UnitI10GridI11，UnitJ10–I6，UnitK10GridI3④层出土陶器：

标本 I10–I11④：9，B 型罐，红陶，敛口，圆唇，束颈，广肩，肩下残，肩部饰多道弦纹。口径 11.4 厘米、残高 2.5 厘米（图 4-9，1）。

标本 I10–I11④：10，C 型罐，红陶，敞口，圆唇，束颈，广肩，肩下残，沿内饰多道弦纹，肩部饰两道弦纹和一周戳印纹。口径 17 厘米、残高 5 厘米（图 4-9，2）。

标本 I10–I11④：8，B 型罐，红陶，敛口，圆唇，束颈，斜肩，肩下残，素面。口径 20 厘米、残高 4.6 厘米（图 4-9，3）。

标本 I10–I11④：7，A 型罐，红陶，敞口，圆唇，束颈，斜肩，肩下残，沿内饰一道弦纹，肩部饰多道弦纹。口径 11.6 厘米、残高 4.6 厘米（图 4-9，4）。

标本 J10I6④：1，E 型罐，红陶，直口，窄沿，沿面有一浅凹槽，颈微束，弧腹，圜底内凹，素面，腹部见两孔，大孔直径 0.8 厘米，小孔直径 0.4 厘米，功能不详。口径 10.4 厘米、高 8 厘米（图 4-9，5；彩版 4-2，6）。

标本 K10I3④：8，小罐，黑陶，圆唇，侈口，束颈，肩部长弧，肩腹转折明显，平底，沿面内有凹弦纹，器体厚重。口径 5.6 厘米、腹径 8 厘米、底径 5 厘米、高 6 厘米（图 4-9，6；彩版 4-4，1）。

UnitK10–I4，UnitL10GridD6，UnitL10Grid E5–F6④层出土陶器：

标本 L10D6④：13，小壶，红陶，圆唇，喇叭口，唇中部有一凹槽，沿面平，束颈，广肩，斜腹内收，平底，沿面内有两道凹弦纹，肩部饰多道细弦纹。口径 8.2 厘米、底径 4.6 厘米、高 11 厘米（图 4-10，1；彩版 4-4，2）。

标本 L10E5–F6④：28，小壶，红陶，折肩，斜腹内收，平底，上部残，肩部饰四道弦纹。底径 5.2 厘米、腹径 12 厘米、残高 9 厘米（图 4-10，2；彩版 4-4，3）。

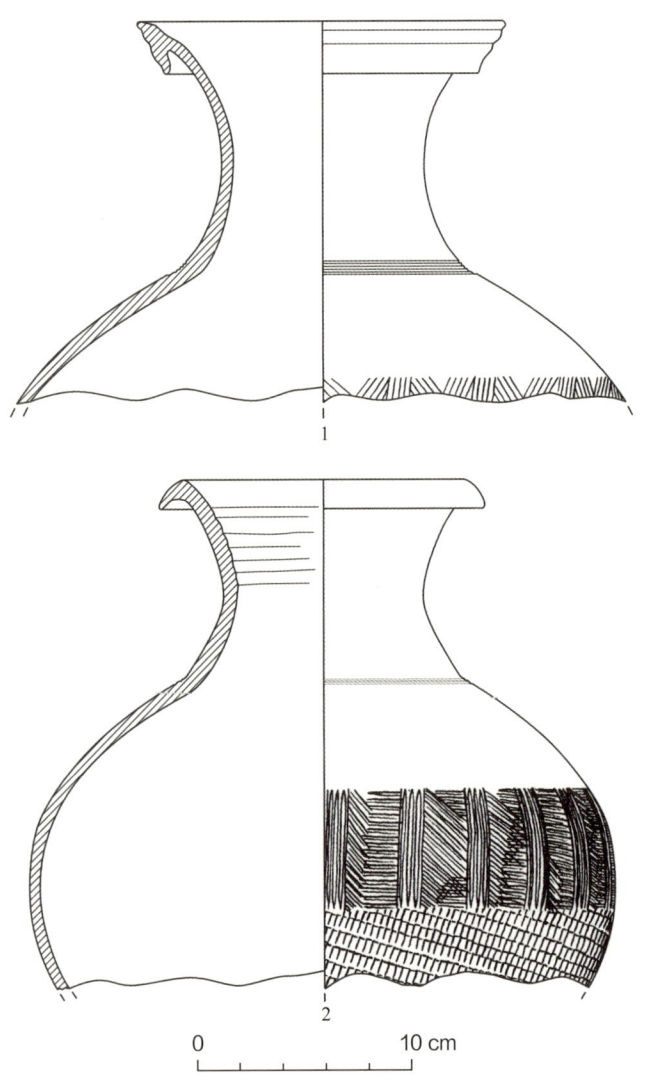

图 4-6　H1 出土陶器

Fig. 4-6　The unearthed potteries from H1

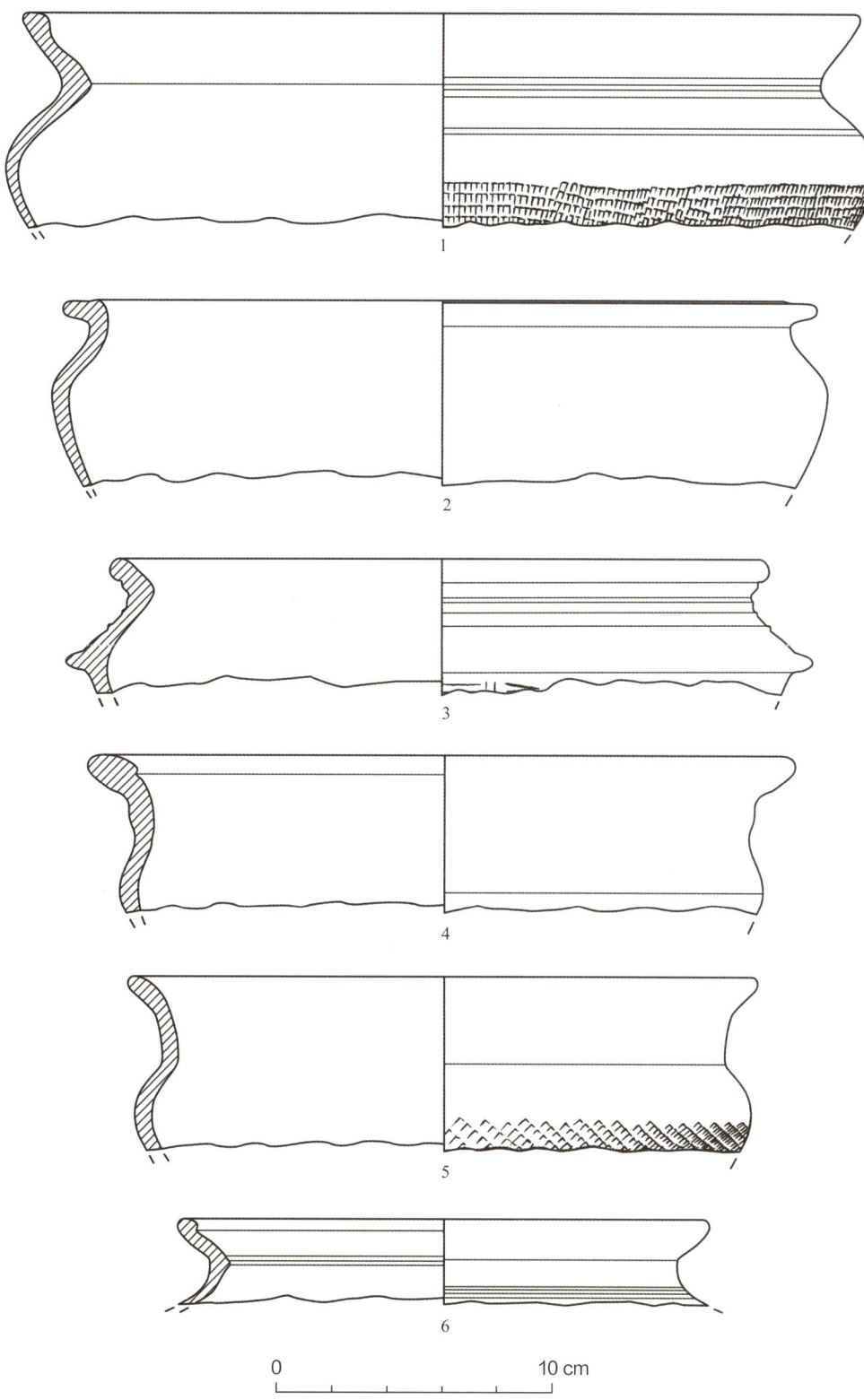

图 4-7　UnitI10-I11 ④层出土陶器

Fig. 4-7　The unearthed potteries of Layer 4 from UnitI10 – I11

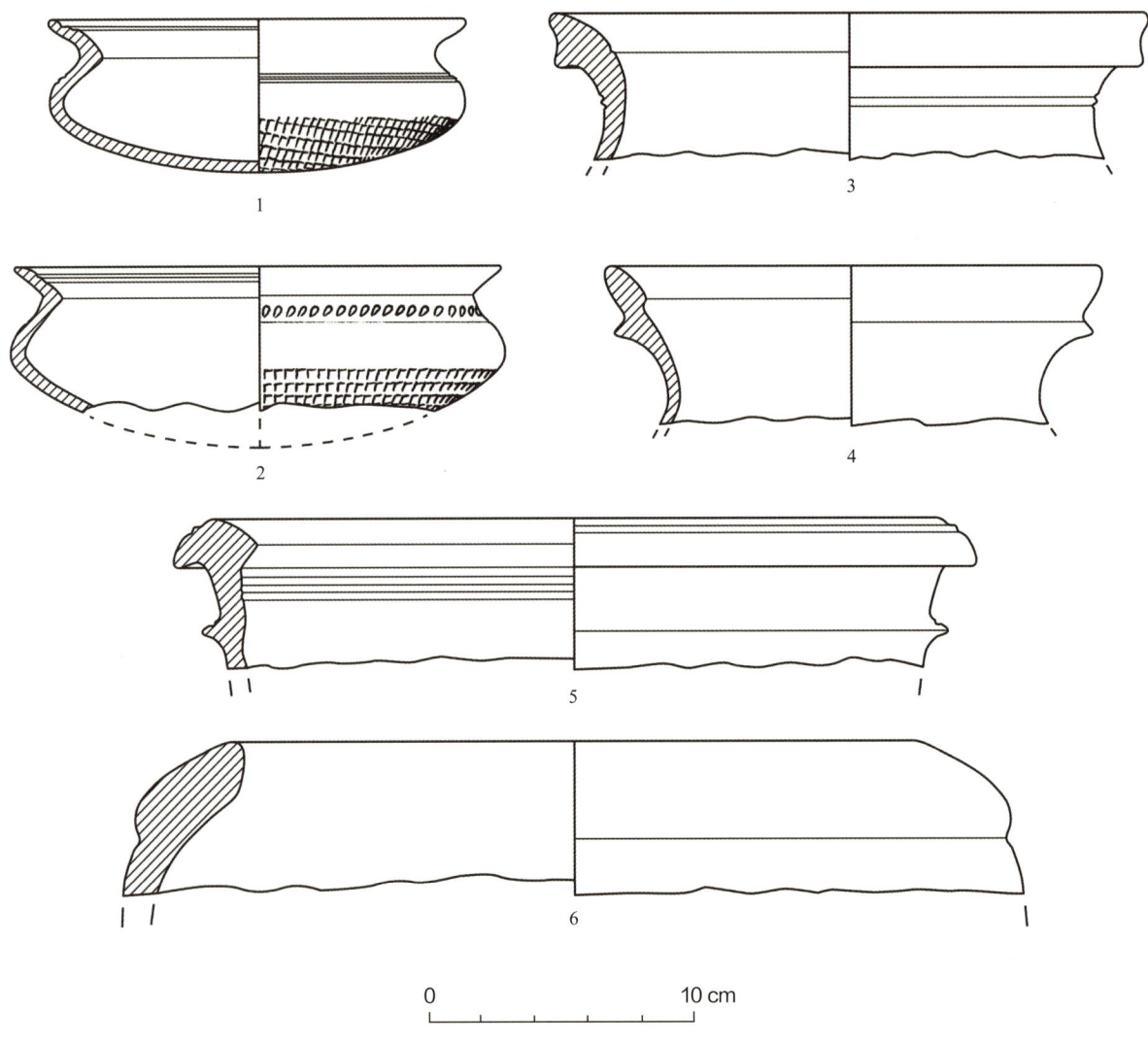

图 4-8　UnitI10-I11，UnitL10GridE6，UnitL10GridE5-F6 ④层出土陶器
Fig. 4-8　The unearthed potteries of Layer 4 from UnitI10-I11, UnitL10GridE6, UnitL10GridE5-F6

标本 L10E5-F6 ④：36，小壶，红陶，圆唇，侈口，沿面内凹，束颈，肩腹转折明显，斜腹内收，平底，肩部饰四道弦纹，腹部饰多道弦纹。口径 7.6 厘米、腹径 9.8 厘米、底径 4.2 厘米、高 9.7 厘米（图 4-10，3；彩版 4-4，4）。

标本 K10I4 ④：1，壶，红陶，外施红衣，沿残，束颈，颈肩部饰多道弦纹，腹部有凸棱，平底。腹径 10.5 厘米、底径 5.4 厘米、残高 9.4 厘米（图 4-10，4；彩版 4-4，5）。

标本 K10I4 ④：2，壶，红陶，上下均残，器身饰多道弦纹，腹部有凸棱。残高 7.8 厘米（图 4-10，5）。

UnitI10–I11，UnitL10GridE6 ④层出土陶器：

标本 L10 E6 ④：12，钵，红陶，敞口，圆唇，斜直腹，平底，器身内外饰多道弦纹。口径 17.8 厘米、底径 4.6 厘米、高 5.6 厘米（图 4-11，1；彩版 4-4，6）。

标本 I10–I11 ④：19，钵，红陶，敞口，圆唇，斜肩，平底，器身内外饰多道弦纹。口径 16.2 厘米、底径 5.2 厘米、高 4.6 厘米（图 4-11，2）。

标本 I10vI11④：20，钵，红陶，口沿残，斜肩，平底，器身内外饰多道弦纹。底径6.8厘米、残高3.8厘米（图4-11，3）。

标本 I10–I11④：21，钵，红陶，口沿残，斜肩，平底，器身内外饰多道弦纹。底径6.4厘米、残高3.6厘米（图4-11，4）。

标本 I10–I11④：22，钵，红陶，口沿残，斜肩，平底，器身内外饰多道弦纹。底径10厘米、残高3厘米（图4-11，5）。

UnitL10GridE5–F6，UnitI10–I11，UnitL10GridF6④层出土陶器：

标本 L10E5–F6④：11，带柄杯，黑色，施黑衣，磨光精细，上部残，杯壁处敞，底面平，中心有一实心凸起，四周饰有规整的同心圆圈纹，柄较细，柄中部有三个圆箍，由上至下逐渐加大加粗，杯底为实心平底。底径5.4厘米、残高6.9厘米（图4-12，1；彩版4-5，1、2）。

标本 I10–I11④：16，器盖，黑陶，圆形纽，器盖大部残，器壁较厚。纽径4.8厘米、残高4.6厘米（图4-12，2）。

标本 I10–I11④：17，器盖，黑陶，圆形纽，器盖大部残。纽径4厘米、残高3.8厘米（图4-12，3）。

标本 I10–I11④：18，器盖，黑陶，圆形纽，器盖大部残。纽径3.8厘米、残高3厘米（图4-12，4）。

标本 L10F6④：5，陶饼，红陶，圆形，较薄，剖面呈等腰梯形，底面有螺旋纹，直径4厘米、厚0.6厘米（图4-12，5；彩版4-5，3）。

UnitI10–I11，UnitL10GridA6、B6、C6、

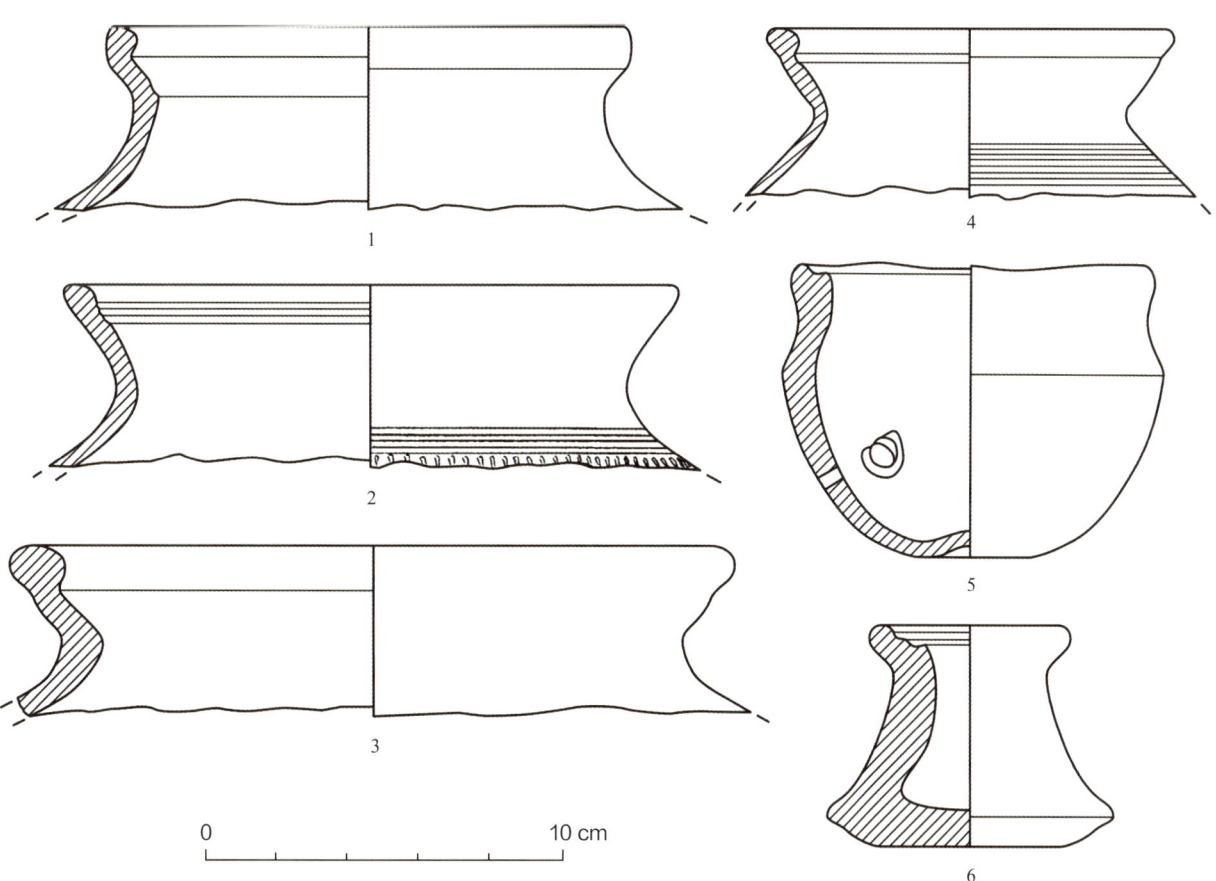

图4-9 UnitI10GridI11，UnitJ10-I6，UnitK10GridI3④层出土陶器
Fig. 4-9 The unearthed potteries of Layer 4 from UnitI10GridI11, UnitJ10-I6, UnitK10GridI3

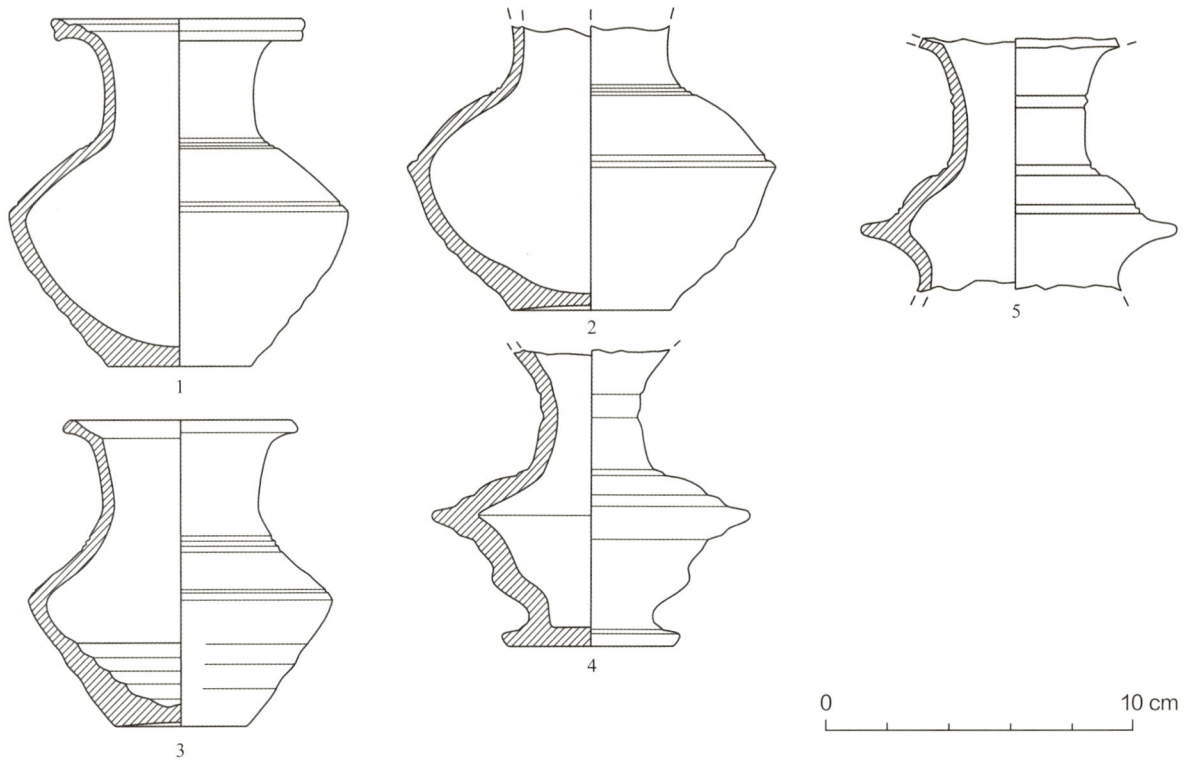

图 4-10　UnitK10-I4，UnitL10GridD6，UnitL10GridE5-F6 ④层出土陶器
Fig. 4-10　The unearthed potteries of Layer 4 from UnitK10-I4, UnitL10GridD6, UnitL10GridE5-F6

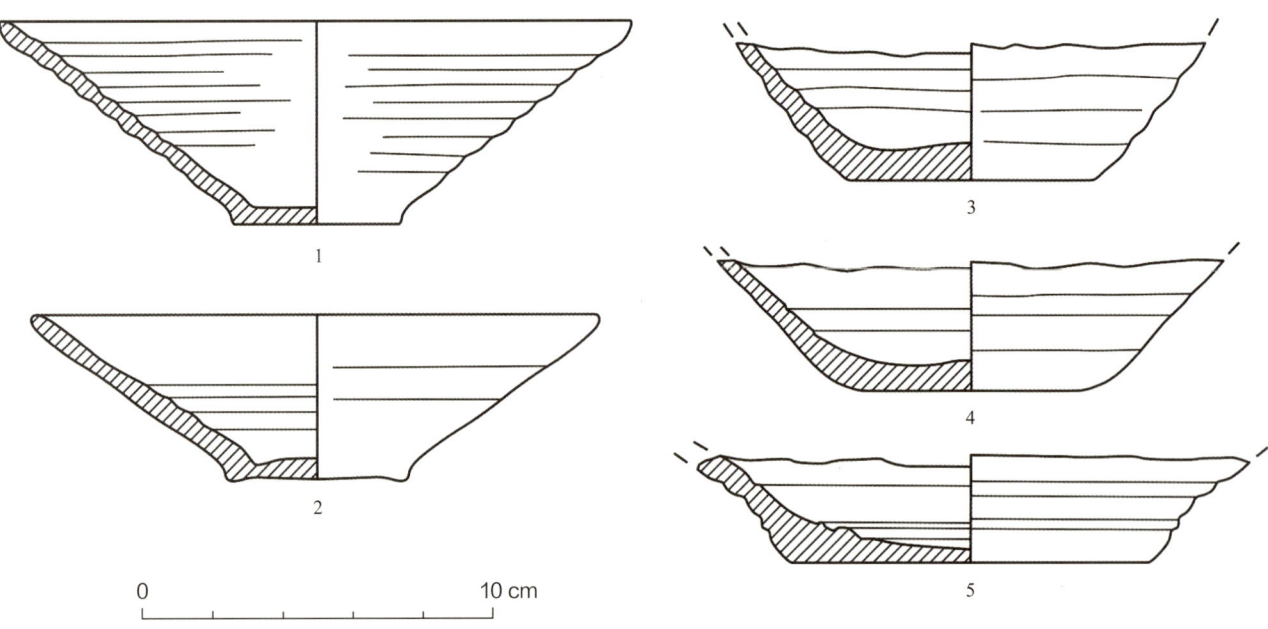

图 4-11　UnitI10-I11，UnitL10GridE6 ④层出土陶器
Fig. 4-11　The unearthed potteries of Layer 4 from UnitI10-I11, UnitL10GridE6

D6、E6，UnitL10GridE5、F6④层出土陶器：

标本L10dA6、B6、C6、D6、E6④：19，灯盏，红陶，尖唇，敛口，圜底，沿部有两处灯捻烧黑痕迹，其中一处在口沿凹陷的灯蕊处。口外径9.2厘米、高1.6厘米（图4-13，1；彩版4-5，4）。

标本I10-I11④：23，灯盏，红陶，圆唇，侈口，浅圜底，沿面有一处凹痕，沿下有一道凸棱。口径8厘米、高1.6厘米（图4-13，2）。

标本I10-I11④：24，灯盏，红陶，圆唇，侈口，斜腹，平底。口径8.4厘米、高1.7厘米（图4-13，3）。

标本I10-I11④：25，灯把，黑陶，上部残，呈圆柱状，中部有一道凸棱，下饰多道弦纹。底径5厘米、残高4.8厘米（图4-13，4）。

标本L10E5、F6④：23，灯，红陶，上部灯托部可见多处烧黑痕迹，灯托表面略内凹，中心有一凸点，灯柄上部有一圆形凸棱，下饰三组凹弦纹，柄底部外扩，圈足残。口径9.8厘米、残高23厘米（图4-13，5；彩版4-5，5）。

五、⑤层出土陶器

红陶以橙黄色居多，纯红或偏红者占少部分（不足10%），施红色陶衣者约30余件（片），

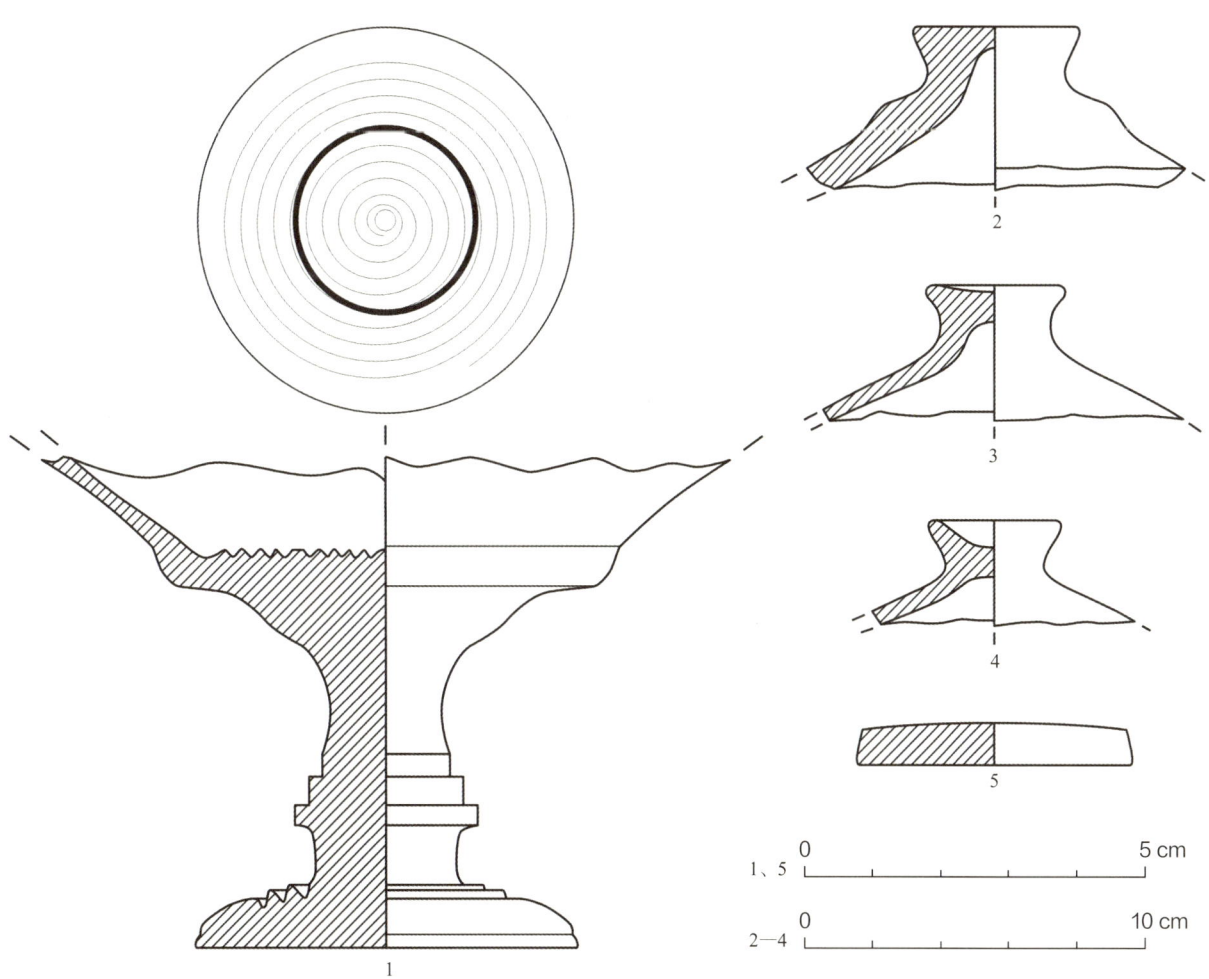

图4-12 UnitL10GridE5-F6，UnitI10-I11，UnitL10GridF6④层出土陶器
Fig. 4-12 The unearthed potteries of Layer 4 from UnitL10GridE5-F6, UnitI10-I11, UnitL10GridF6

个别罐、壶的外部和口沿施酱黄色陶衣。黑陶大部陶色为偏黑褐色，灰褐色者占近一半。主要器形为釜、罐、壶、钵类。素面为主，纹饰主要有方格纹、凹弦纹、戳刺纹、条状纹等（表5—7）。

标本介绍

UnitK10GridI2–I6、J2–J6 ⑤层出土陶器：

标本 K10I2–I6、J2–J6 ⑤：1，Aa 型釜，黑陶，盘口，圆唇，束颈，斜肩，底部残，肩部饰两道弦纹，腹部饰方格纹，有烟炱痕迹。口径 28.4 厘米、腹径 28 厘米、残高 6.4 厘米（图 4-14，1）。

标本 K10I2–I6、J2–J6 ⑤：2，B 型釜，黑陶，圆唇，侈口，沿内饰一道弦纹，下部残。口径 30.4 厘米、残高 3.6 厘米（图 4-14，2）。

标本 K10I2–I6、J2–J6 ⑤：9，灯座，残片，素面，直径 18.8 厘米、残高 4 厘米（图 4-14，3）。

标本 K10I2–I6、J2–J6 ⑤：8，灯，红陶，灯托圆形内凹，边缘有一道凸棱，灯柄呈圆柱状，上细下粗，饰三组弦纹。口径 7.2 厘米、残高 14 厘米（图 4-14，4；彩版 4-6，1）。

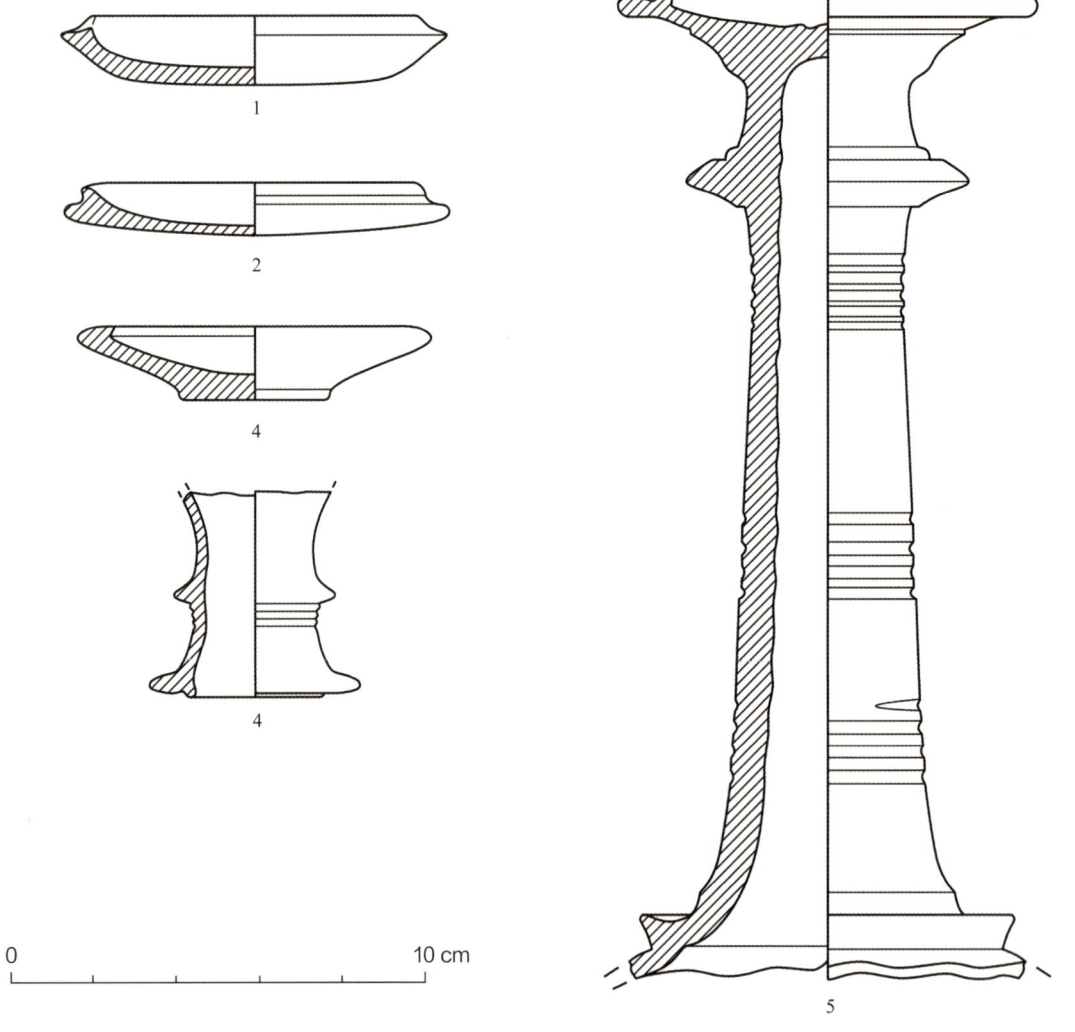

图 4-13　UnitI10-I11，UnitL10GridA6、B6、C6、D6、E6，UnitL10GridE5、F6 ④层出土陶器

Fig. 4-13　The unearthed potteries of Layer 4 from UnitI10-I11, UnitL10GridA6, B6, C6, D6, E6, UnitL10GridE5, F6

UnitK10GridI2–I6、J2–J6，UnitL10GridE5–F6⑤层出土陶器：

标本K10I2–I6、J2–J6⑤：3，A型罐，红陶，直口外侈，圆唇，束颈，广肩，腹部残，沿内饰两道弦纹，肩部饰多道弦纹，下饰戳印纹一周。口径15.6厘米、残高6.6厘米（图4-15，1）。

标本K10I2–I6、J2–J6⑤：4，B型罐，黄陶，盘口，圆唇，束颈，颈部下残，素面。口径14.8厘米、残高3.6厘米（图4-15，2）。

标本K10I2–I6、J2–J6⑤：5，A型壶，黑灰陶，圆唇，喇叭口，折沿，沿内有一道弦纹。口径18厘米、残高2.2厘米（图4-15，3）。

标本K10I2–I6、J2–J6⑤：6，C型壶，红陶，尖圆唇，喇叭口，沿内有多道弦纹，沿下有一道凸棱。口径14.8厘米、残高3厘米（图4-15，4）。

标本L10E5–F6⑤：14，小壶，红陶，上部残，溜肩，肩与腹转折明显，弧腹内收，平底，肩部有多道弦纹。腹径10.8厘米、底径5厘米、残高9.6厘米（图4-15，5；彩版4-6，2）。

标本K10I2–I6、J2–J6⑤：7，钵，红陶，口部残，斜直腹，平底，素面。底径6厘米、残高3厘米（图4-15，6）。

表5 UnitK10GridI2-I6、J2-J6⑤层陶器统计表

纹饰＼陶色	红	黑	备注
素面	535	189	
方格	80	73	
凹弦	29	51	
交叉	1		
条状	1		
太阳	1		
戳刺	1	8	
方点		1	
器类（数量）	Aa型釜3，Ab型釜3，A型壶1，C型壶3，A型罐3，B型罐4，钵9，灯盏2，灯柄1	Aa型釜31，Ab型釜1，A型壶4，A型罐1，B型罐3，器盖5	

表6 UnitL8GridG5-F5⑤层下部陶器统计表

纹饰＼陶色	红	黑	备注
素面	2705	539	
方格	271	608	
凹弦	55	272	
交叉	1		
条状	27	3	
太阳	21		
剔刺	6	3	
戳点	1	53	
器类（数量）	Aa型釜27，Ab型釜20，C型釜2，B型罐24，C型罐14，小罐7，B型壶10，C型壶1，钵140，灯盏9，灯座1，器盖1，不明器1	Aa型釜137，C型釜1，A型罐7，B型罐3，C型罐1，小罐7，A型壶1，B型壶3，C型壶5，钵7，器盖13，灯盏4，圆饼1	

UnitL8GridG5–F5 ⑤层下部出土陶器：

标本 L8G5–F5 ⑤下：1，Aa 型釜，黑陶，盘口，圆唇，束颈，圆肩，底部残，沿内饰一道弦纹，颈肩部饰戳印纹一周，下饰两道弦纹，腹部饰方格纹。口径 25.6 厘米、残高 9 厘米（图 4-16，1）。

标本 L8G5–F5 ⑤下：2，Ab 型釜，黑陶，盘口，圆唇，束颈，圆肩，底部残，肩部饰一道凸棱，腹部饰方格纹，有烟炱痕迹。口径 22 厘米、残高 8 厘米（图 4-16，2）。

标本 L8G5–F5 ⑤下：3，Aa 型釜，红陶，盘口，圆唇，束颈，圆肩，圜底，肩部饰一道弦纹，腹部饰方格纹，有烟炱痕迹。口径 24.4 厘米、腹径 24.8 厘米、高 9 厘米（图 4-16，3；彩版 4-6，3）。

表 7　UniL10GridA2-A3 ⑤—⑥层之间陶器统计表

纹饰 \ 陶色	红	黑	备注
素面	979	69	
方格	56	83	
凹弦	27	31	
条状	1	4	
剔刺纹	2		
戳点纹	1	7	
器类（数量）	Aa 型釜 4，Ab 型釜 1，C 型釜 1，B 型罐 4，C 型罐 3，B 型壶 10	Aa 型釜 18，A 型罐 6，C 型罐 1，A 型壶 3	

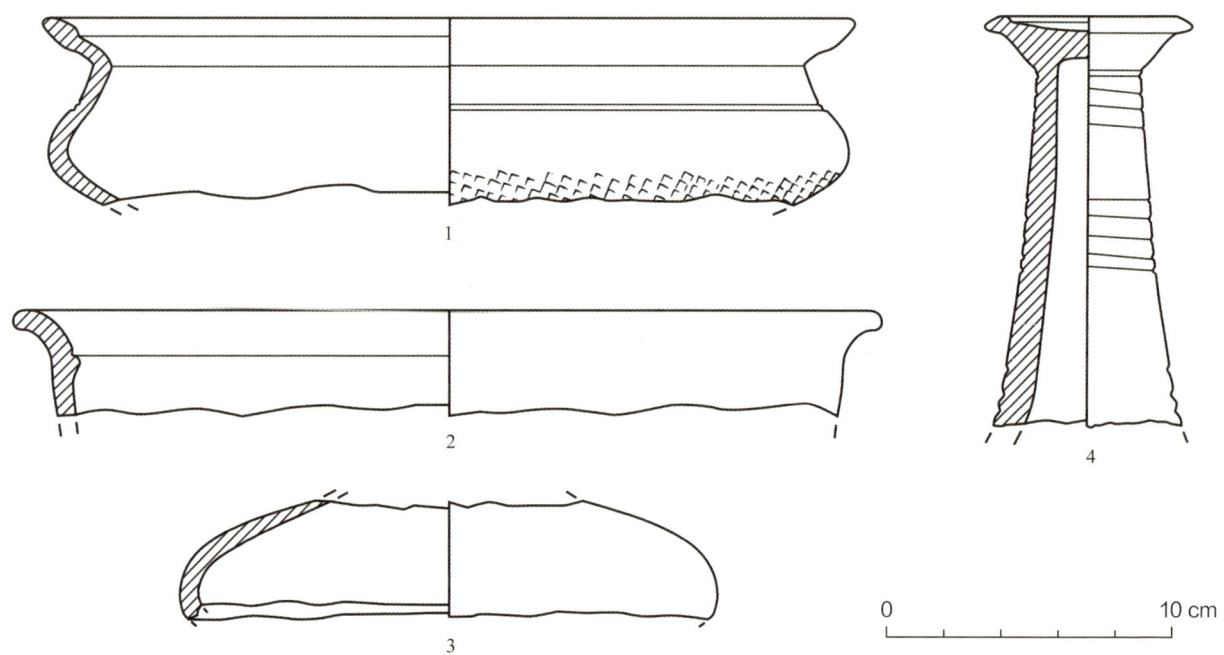

图 4-14　UnitK10GridI2-I6、J2-J6 ⑤层出土陶器

Fig. 4-14　The unearthed potteries of Layer 5 from UnitK10GridI2-I6, J2-J6

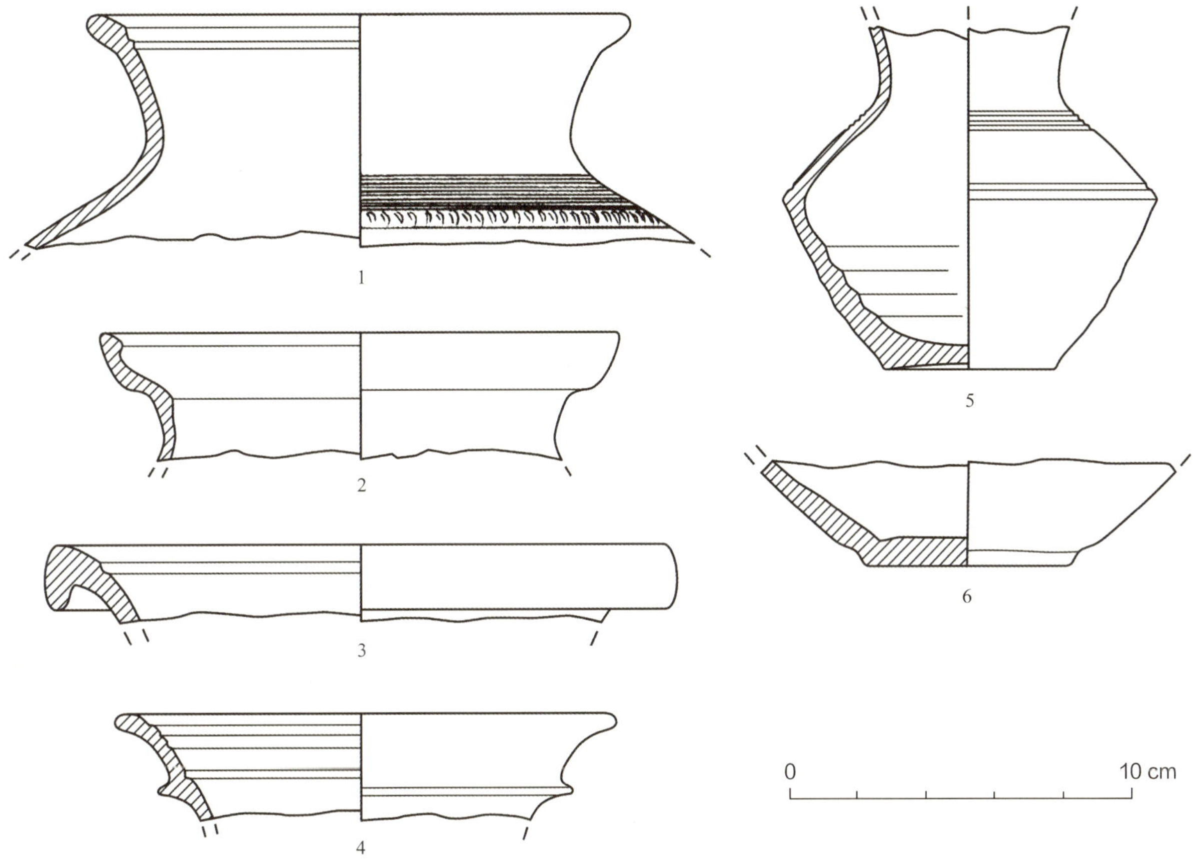

图 4-15　UnitK10GridI2-I6、J2-J6，UnitL10GridE5-F6 ⑤层出土陶器
Fig. 4-15　The unearthed potteries of Layer 5 from UnitK10GridI2-I6, J2-J6, UnitL10GridE5-F6

标本 L8G5–F5 ⑤下：4，Ab 型釜，红陶，盘口，圆唇，束颈，圆肩，圜底残，肩部饰两道弦纹，腹部饰方格纹。口径 18.2 厘米、残高 4.6 厘米（图 4-16，4）。

标本 L8G5–F5 ⑤下：5，Ab 型釜，红陶，盘口，圆唇，束颈，圆肩，圜底残，腹部饰方格纹，有烟炱痕迹。口径 18 厘米、残高 4.8 厘米（图 4-16，5）。

标本 L8G5–F5 ⑤下：6，B 型釜，红陶，上部残，长束颈，圆肩，肩腹转折明显，浅腹，圜底，圜底，颈部饰两道弦纹，肩部饰方格纹。底径 17.2 厘米、残高 13.4 厘米（图 4-16，6；彩版 4-6，4）。

UnitL8GridG5–F5 ⑤层下部出土陶器：

标本 L8G5–F5 ⑤下：7，A 型罐，红陶，敛口，圆唇，束颈，广肩，肩下残，肩部饰多道弦纹。口径 11.4 厘米、残高 2.5 厘米（图 4-17，1）。

标本 L8G5–F5 ⑤下：8，A 型罐，黑陶，直口，圆唇，束颈，肩下残，沿内饰多道弦纹。口径 17.8 厘米、残高 5 厘米（图 4-17，2）。

标本 L8G5–F5 ⑤下：9，B 型罐，红陶，敛口，圆唇，束颈，肩下残，素面。口径 14 厘米、残高 5 厘米（图 4-17，3）。

标本 L8G5–F5 ⑤下：10，B 型罐，红陶，圆唇，卷沿，束颈，长弧肩，肩下残，素面。口径 11.8 厘米、残高 6.4 厘米（图 4-17，4）。

标本 L8G5-F5⑤下：11，C 型罐，红陶，圆唇，折沿，束颈，斜肩，肩下残，素面。口径 12 厘米、残高 5.6 厘米（图 4-17，5）。

标本 L8G5-F5⑤下：12，C 型罐，红陶，圆唇，折沿，束颈，广肩，肩下残，素面。口径 12.4 厘米、残高 5.2 厘米（图 4-17，6）。

UnitL8GridG5-F5⑤层下部出土陶器：

标本 L8G5-F5⑤下：21，小罐，红陶，圆唇，侈口，溜肩，鼓腹，平底，素面。口径 4.3 厘米、腹径 6.2 厘米、高 4.5 厘米（图 4-18，1；彩版 4-6，5）。

标本 L8G5-F5⑤下：22，小罐，红陶，溜肩，鼓腹，平底，素面，肩饰四道弦纹。底径 4.6 厘米、残高 7 厘米（图 4-18，2）。

标本 L8G5-F5⑤下：23，小罐，红陶，直口，方唇，溜肩，肩下残，素面。口径 4 厘米、残高 2.8 厘米（图 4-18，3）。

标本 L8G5-F5⑤下：24，器盖，黑陶，圆形纽，器盖大部残。纽径 3.2 厘米、残高 3 厘米（图 4-18，4）。

标本 L8G5-F5⑤下：25，器盖，黑陶，纽残，器盖呈覆斗状，圆唇，素面。盖径 16.4 厘米、残高 4.4 厘米（图 4-18，5）。

标本 L8G5-F5⑤下：26，器盖，黑陶，纽残，

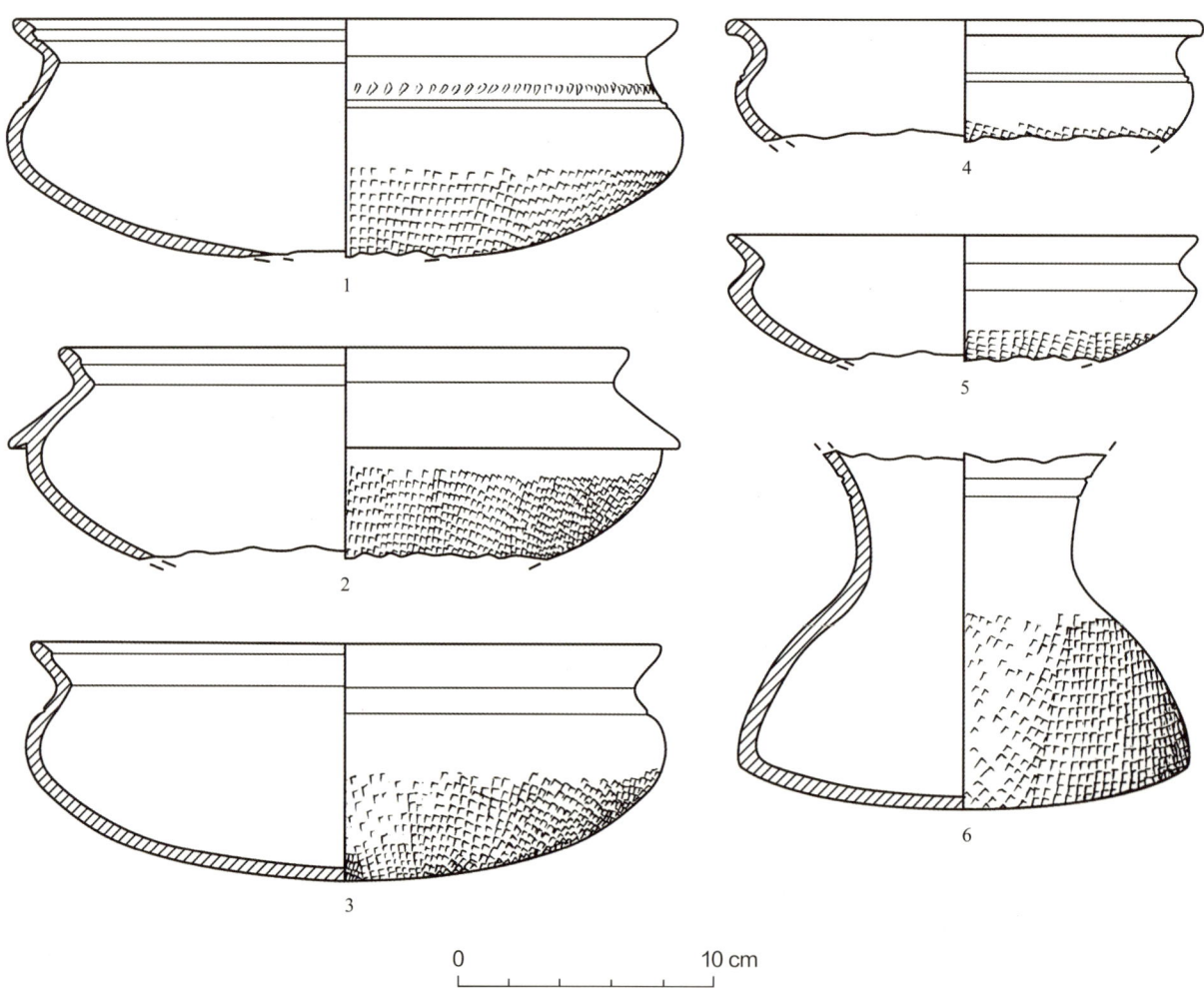

图 4-16　UnitL8GridG5-F5⑤层下部出土陶器

Fig. 4-16　The unearthed potteries of lower Layer 5 from UnitL8GridG5-F5

器盖呈覆斗状，圆唇，素面。盖径20厘米、残高4.6厘米（图4-18，6）。

UnitL8GridG5-F5 ⑤层下部出土陶器：

标本 L8G5-F5 ⑤下：13，A 型壶，红陶，圆唇，喇叭口，口沿外翻，沿内有一道弦纹。口径16.8厘米、残高4.8厘米（图4-19，1）。

标本 L8G5-F5 ⑤下：14，A 型壶，灰陶，圆唇，喇叭口，口沿下残，沿内有两道弦纹，沿下有一道凸棱。口径16.2厘米、残高2.8厘米（图4-19，2）。

标本 L8G5-F5 ⑤下：16，C 型壶，黑陶，圆唇，喇叭口，口沿下残，沿内有多道弦纹，沿下有一道凸棱。口径19.2厘米、残高3.8厘米（图4-19，3）。

标本 L8G5-F5 ⑤下：15，C 型壶，红陶，施红衣，圆唇，喇叭口，肩部下残，沿内有多道弦纹，沿下有一道凸棱，肩部有多道弦纹，其下饰一圈交错齿状纹。口径16厘米、残高11厘米（图4-19，4；彩版4-6，6）。

UnitL8GridG5-F5 ⑤层下部出土陶器：

标本 L8G5-F5 ⑤下：17，钵，红陶，敞口，圆唇，斜直腹，平底，器内外饰多道弦纹。口径19.6厘米、底径5.2厘米、高5.2厘米（图4-20，1；彩版4-7，1）。

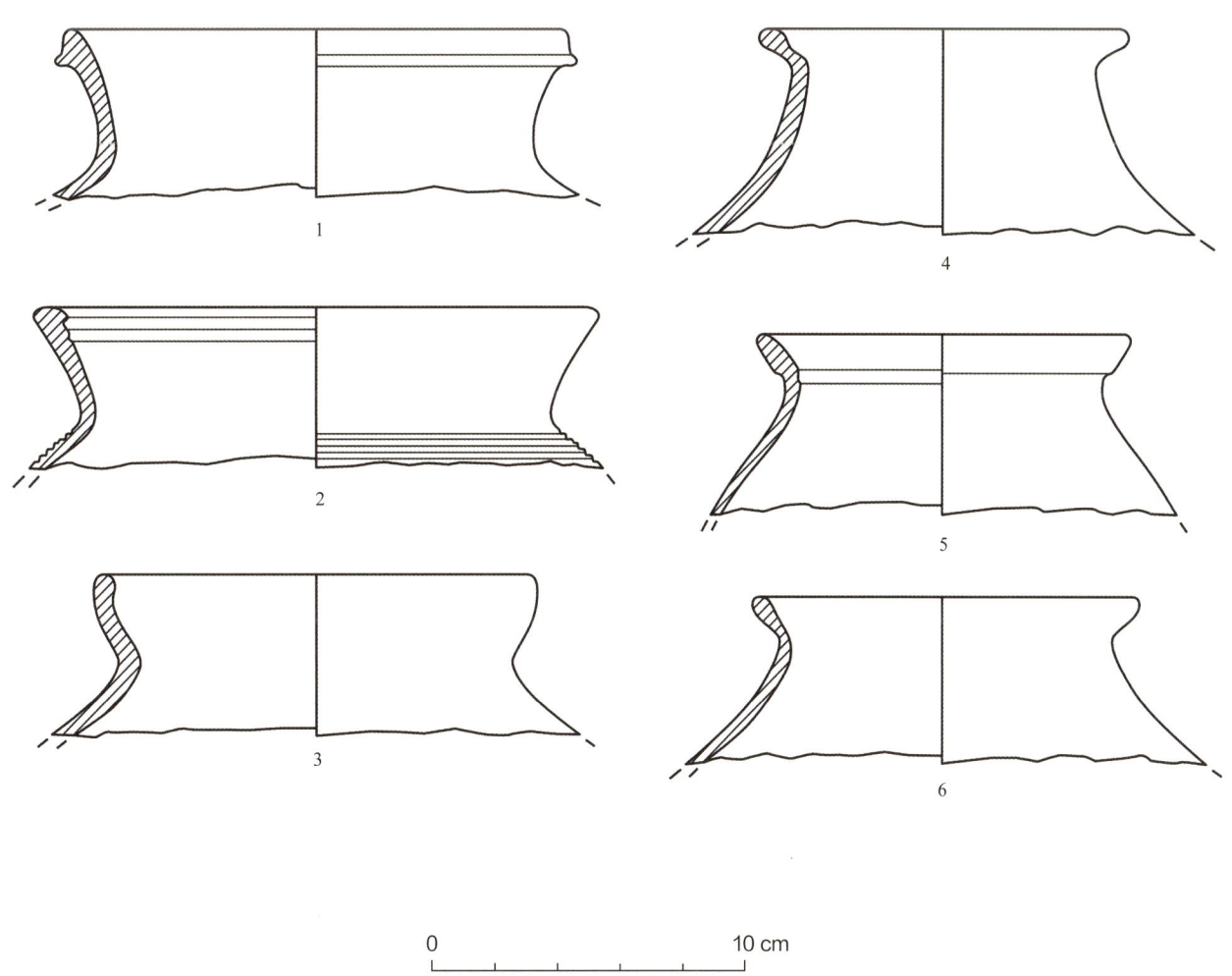

图4-17　UnitL8GridG5-F5 ⑤层下部出土陶器
Fig. 4-17　The unearthed potteries of lower Layer 5 from UnitL8GridG5-F5

标本 L8G5–F5 ⑤下：18，钵，红陶，敞口，圆唇，斜直腹，平底，器内外饰多道弦纹。口径 18 厘米、底径 4 厘米、高 4.8 厘米（图 4-20，2；彩版 4-7，2）。

标本 L8G5–F5 ⑤下：19，钵，红陶，敞口，圆唇，斜直腹，平底，器内外饰多道弦纹。口径 14.8 厘米、底径 5.6 厘米、高 4 厘米（图 4-20，3；彩版 4-7，3）。

标本 L8G5–F5 ⑤下：20，钵，红陶，敞口，圆唇，斜直腹，平底，器内外饰多道弦纹。口径 16.2 厘米、底径 5.6 厘米、高 4.2 厘米（图 4-20，4；彩版 4-7，4）。

UnitL8GridG5–F5 ⑤层下部出土陶器：

标本 L8G5–F5 ⑤下：27，灯盏，红陶，尖圆唇，敞口，折沿，浅直腹，平底。口径 9.2 厘米、底径 4 厘米、高 2.2 厘米（图 4-21，1）。

标本 L8G5–F5 ⑤下：28，灯盏，红陶，圆唇，直口，浅弧腹，圜底。口径 8.8 厘米、高 1.6 厘米（图 4-21，2）。

标本 L8G5–F5 ⑤下：29，灯盏，黑陶，圆唇，敛口，浅腹，平底。口径 8 厘米、底径 4.6 厘米、高 1.4 厘米（图 4-21，3）。

标本 L8G5–F5 ⑤下：30，灯柄，红陶，上下残，呈圆柱状，上细下粗，中空，灯柄饰弦纹。下部径 7.6 厘米、残高 6.4 厘米（图 4-21，4）。

标本 L8G5–F5 ⑤下：32，陶饼，灰黑陶，圆饼状，一边略凹，边缘可见打磨痕迹，两面均的刻划痕。直径 6.5 厘米、厚 1.2 厘米（图 4-21，

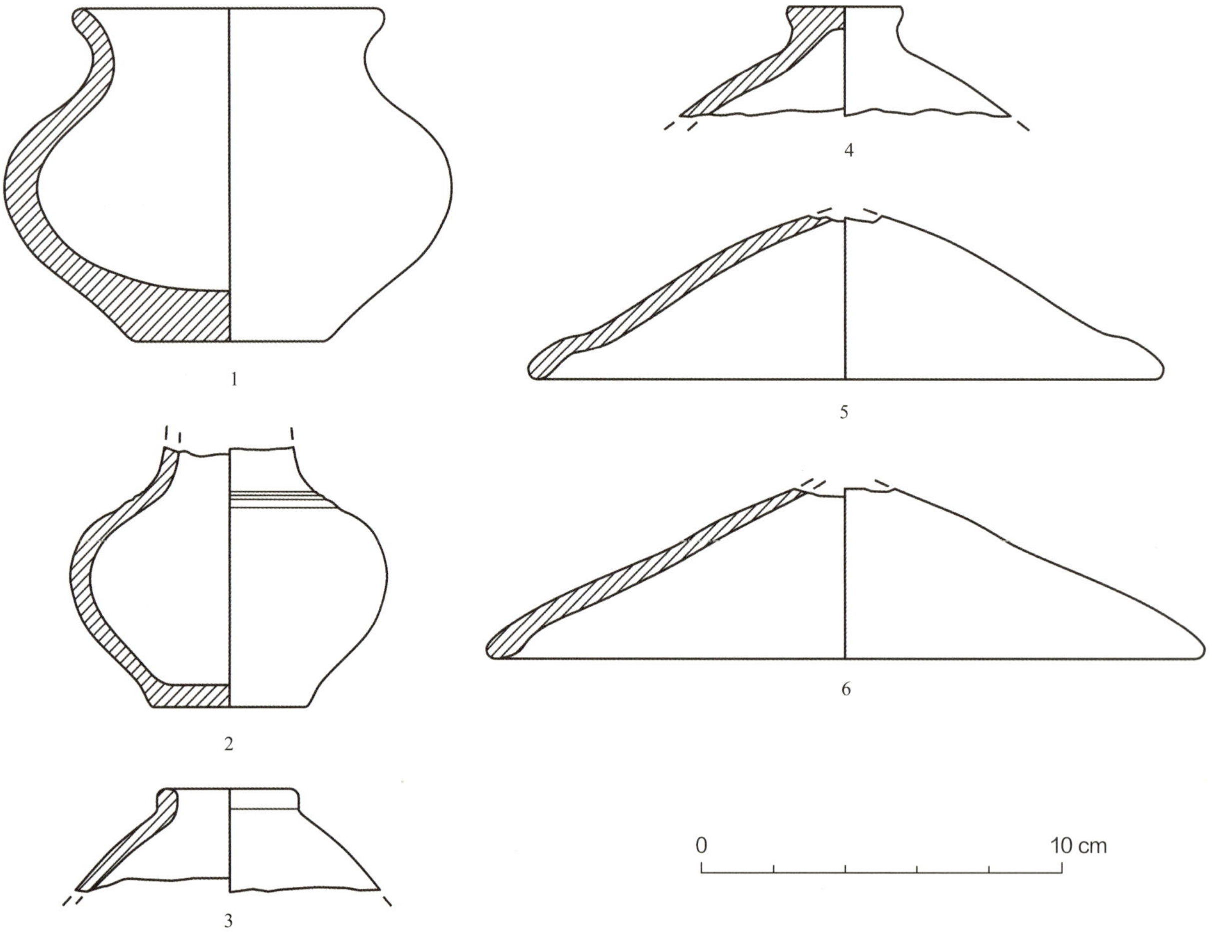

图 4–18 UnitL8GridG5–F5 ⑤层下部出土陶器

Fig. 4-18 The unearthed potteries of lower Layer 5 from UnitL8GridG5-F5

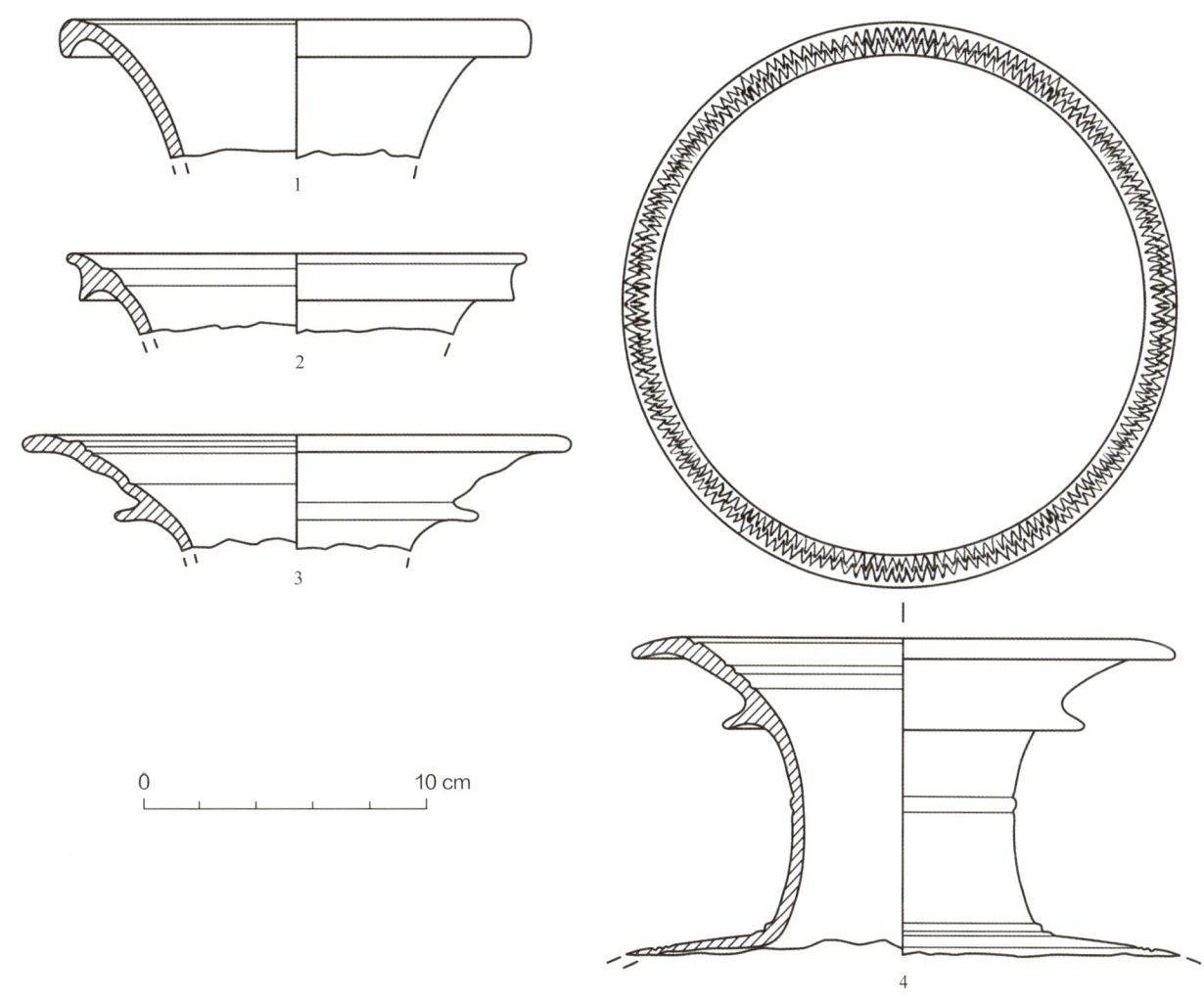

图 4-19 UnitL8GridG5-F5 ⑤层下部出土陶器
Fig. 4-19 The unearthed potteries of lower Layer 5 from UnitL8GridG5-F5

5；彩版 4-7，5）。

标本 L8G5–F5 ⑤下：31，灯座，红陶，残片，底边有一道凸棱。足径 22 厘米、残高 2 厘米（图 4-21，6）。

UnitL10GridA2–A3 ⑤—⑥层之间出土陶器：

标本 L10A2–A3 ⑤—⑥：1，Aa 型釜，黑陶，盘口，圆唇，束颈，圆肩，腹部残，肩部饰一道弦纹，一周戳印纹。口径 22.8 厘米、残高 4.2 厘米（图 4-22，1）。

标本 L10A2–A3 ⑤—⑥：3，A 型罐，红陶，喇叭口，圆唇，束颈，肩部下残，素面。口径 12.4 厘米、残高 3.4 厘米（图 4-22，2）。

标本 L10A2–A3 ⑤—⑥：4，B 型罐，红陶，敞口，圆唇，沿面有一道凹槽，束颈，斜肩，肩下残，肩部饰一道弦纹，下有戳印纹。口径 12 厘米、残高 4 厘米（图 4-22，3）。

标本 L10A2–A3 ⑤—⑥：5，小罐，红陶，侈口，圆唇，束颈，溜肩，小平底，肩部饰三道弦纹。口径 7.2 厘米、底径 2 厘米、高 10 厘米（图 4-22，4；彩版 4-7，6）。

243

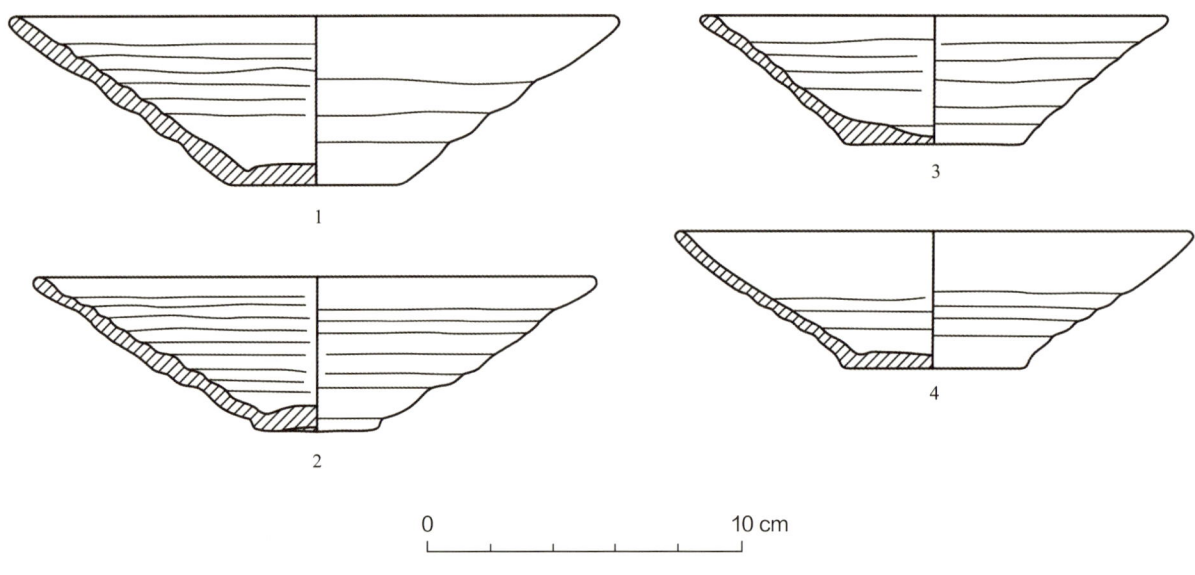

图 4-20　UnitL8GridG5-F5 ⑤层下部出土陶器
Fig. 4-20　The unearthed potteries of lower Layer 5 from UnitL8GridG5-F5

标本 L10A2–A3 ⑤—⑥：2，Ab 型釜，红陶，侈口，圆唇，束颈，圆肩，腹部残，素面。口径 16.8 厘米、高 4 厘米（图 4-22，5）。

标本 L10A2–A3 ⑤—⑥：6，A 型壶，黑陶，喇叭口，圆唇，口沿外翻，束颈，颈下残，沿内饰一道弦纹，沿下饰一道凸棱，颈部饰多道弦纹。口径 17.2 厘米、残高 8 厘米（图 4-22，6）。

标本 L10A2–A3 ⑤—⑥：7，B 型壶，红陶，盘口，圆唇，口沿下残，沿下饰一道凸棱。口径 17.6 厘米、残高 3 厘米（图 4-22，7）。

标本 L10A2–A3 ⑤—⑥：8，钵，红陶，敞口残，圆唇，斜直腹，平底。底径 5.6 厘米、残高 3.5 厘米（图 4-22，8）。

六、瓮 1、瓮 2 内出土陶器

神殿 1 前后有过两次修筑活动，在神殿 1 后期建筑的四角，可能各安放有圜底大瓮，地层上属于⑤层以下的遗迹。现发现的瓮 1 位于 UnitL10GridB4 内，瓮 2 位于 UnitL9GridB9 内，皆一半掩埋在地面以下。两瓮内各放置大量陶器。推测它们皆是在寺庙存在期间，放置在屋檐下，作为日常使用的。其中，瓮 1 保存完整，瓮内陶器均为夹细砂泥质陶，红陶（略带黄橙色）和黑褐色为多，少量为砖红色、灰褐色，多为素面，纹饰简单，有方格纹、弦纹、太阳纹，还有少量黑色彩绘。器类计有：Aa 釜 15 件、鼓腹罐 14 件、折肩罐 5 件、壶 3 件、钵 49 件、不明器若干件。瓮 2 未见口沿部分，瓮内器物全为夹细砂泥质陶，红陶（略带黄橙色）和黑褐色为主，少量为砖红色，多为素面，纹饰有方格纹、弦纹、太阳纹等。主要器类：Aa 釜 3 件、鼓腹罐 5 件、折肩罐 2 件、壶 3 件、钵 13 件、器盖 4 件、不明器 1 件。

瓮 1 标本介绍

标本 W1：19，瓮，位于 UnitL10GridB4 内。黑陶，表面施黑衣，敞口，沿部内敛，方唇，口沿内侧有一凹槽，束颈，颈部饰一道凸棱，溜肩，腹部呈长椭圆形，圜底，口部较厚，器身胎相对较薄，素面。口径（外）58 厘米、腹径 79 厘米、

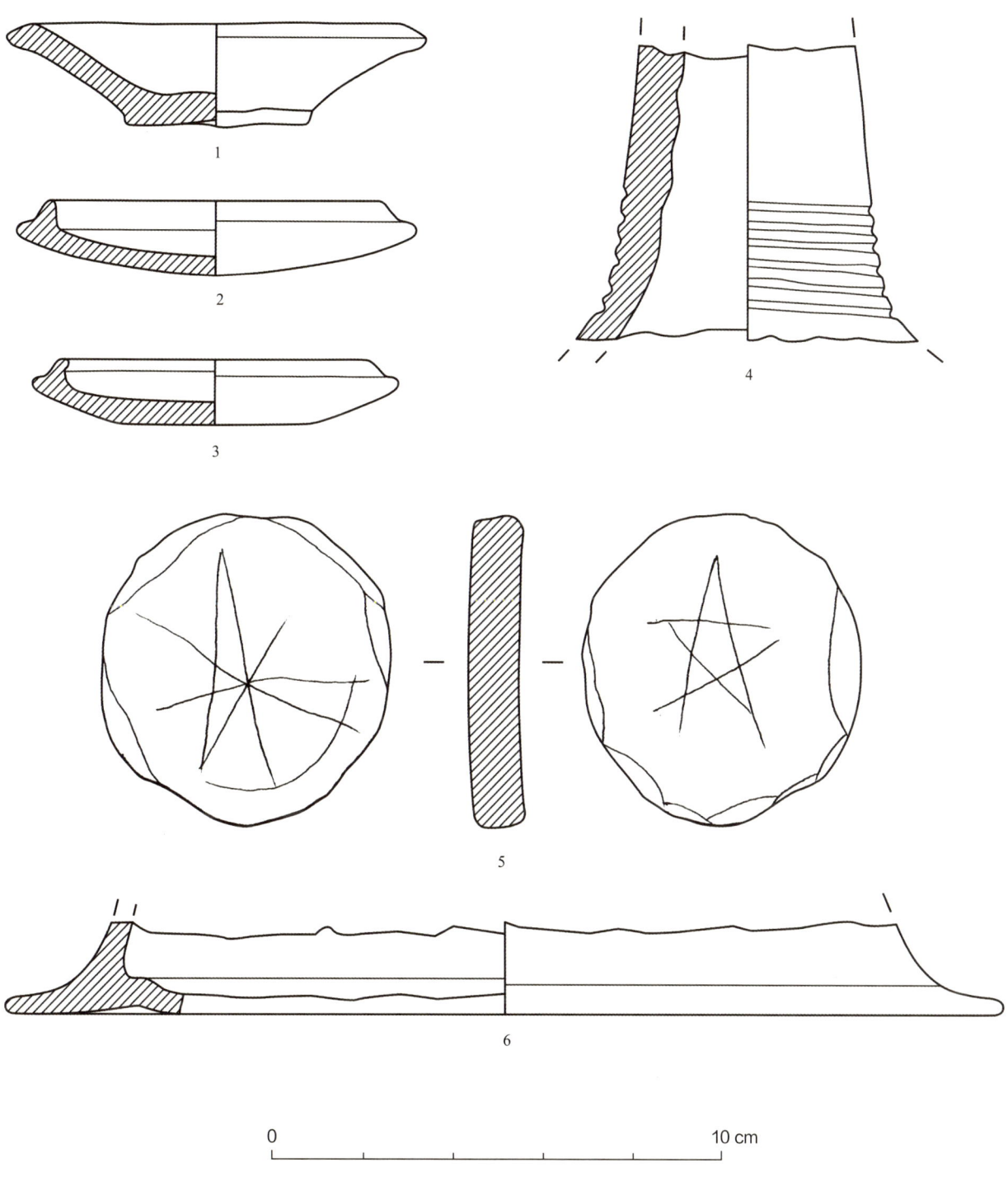

图 4-21　UnitL8GridG5-F5 ⑤层下部出土陶器

Fig. 4-21　The unearthed potteries of lower Layer 5 from UnitL8GridG5-F5

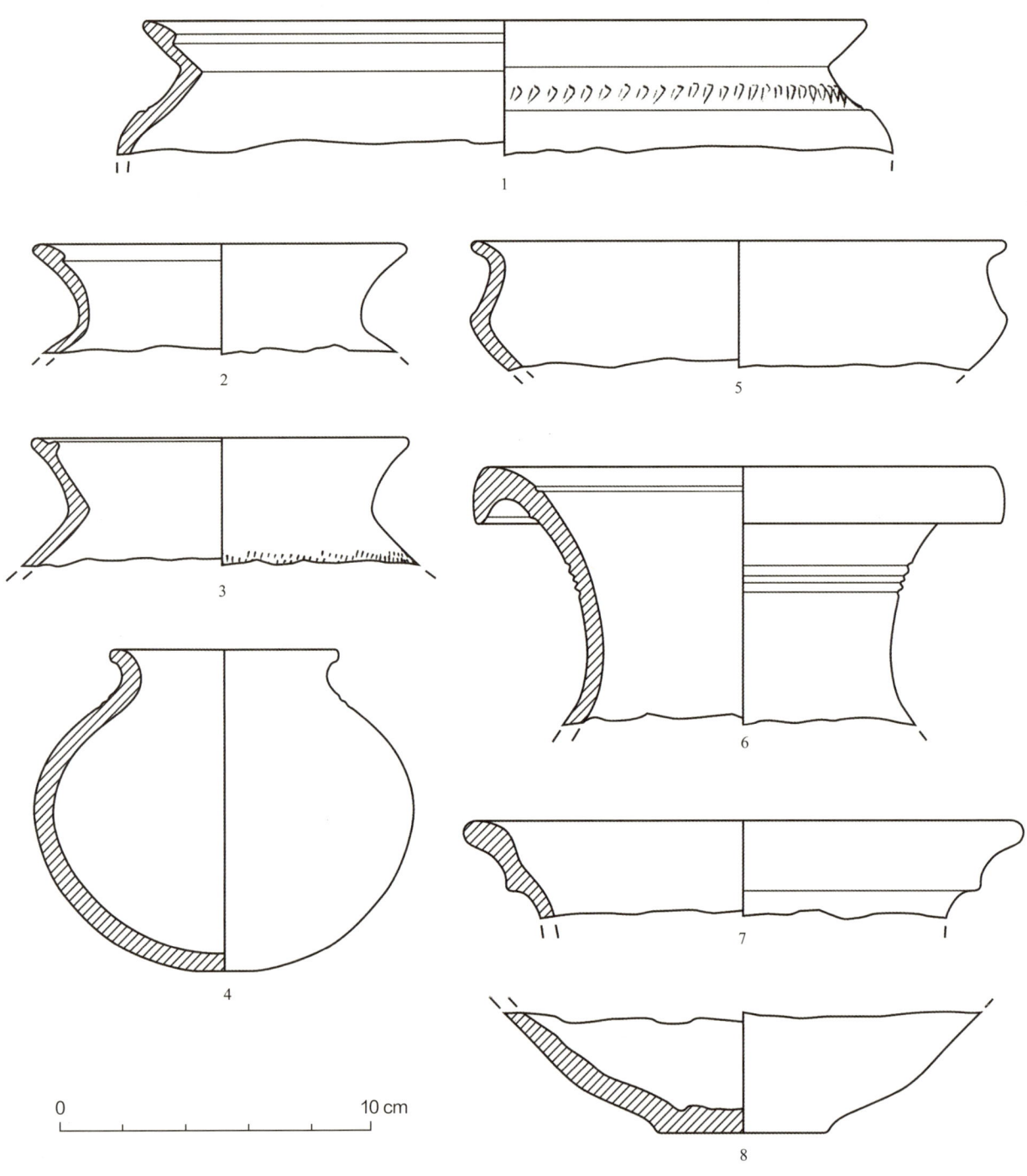

图 4-22　UnitL10GridA2-A3 ⑤—⑥层之间出土陶器

Fig. 4-22　The unearthed potteries between Layer 5 and layer 6 from UnitL10GridA2-A3

高 98 厘米（图 4-23；彩版 4-8，1）。

标本 W1：1，Aa 型釜，黑陶，表面有磨光痕迹，圆唇，折沿，沿面饰一凹弦纹，束颈，颈部有一圈交错斜曲折纹，圆肩，圜底残，腹部饰方格纹。口径 23 厘米、腹径 23.2 厘米、残高 8 厘米（图 4-24，1；彩版 4-8，2）。

标本 W1：2，Aa 型釜，红陶，圆唇，折沿，沿面饰一凹弦纹，束颈，折肩，圜底残，腹部饰方格纹，有烟炱痕迹。口径 24 厘米、腹径 25 厘米、残高 7.8 厘米（图 4-24，2）。

标本 W1：3，A 型罐，黑陶，表面有黑衣，侈口，圆唇，沿面外饰一道凸棱，束颈，微折肩，肩部饰多道弦纹，腹部饰方格纹，圜底。口径 19.6 厘米、腹径 35.8 厘米、残高 23 厘米（图 4-25，1；彩版 4-8，3）。

标本 W1：4，A 型罐，黑陶，表面有黑衣，侈口，圆唇，直领，微折肩，肩部饰多道弦纹和斜线彩绘，腹部饰方格纹，圜底。口径 19.6 厘米、腹径 35.8 厘米、残高 23 厘米（图 4-25，2；彩版 4-9，1）。

标本 W1：5，A 型罐，红陶，圆唇，口沿外翻，沿面内饰一道弦纹，直领，溜肩，肩部饰多道弦纹，圜底残，有烟炱痕迹。口径 14.6 厘米、腹径 20 厘米、残高 16.4 厘米（图 4-26，1；彩版 4-9，2）。

标本 W1：6，A 型罐，红陶，圆唇，沿面内饰一道凹弦纹，直领，溜肩，肩部饰多道弦纹，腹部饰方格纹，圜底，有烟炱痕迹。口径 13.4 厘米、腹径 21.2 厘米、残高 17 厘米（图 4-26，2；彩版 4-9，3）。

标本 W1：8，钵，红陶，圆唇，敞口，斜直腹，平底，内壁见多道弦纹。口径 23.4 厘米、高 6.8 厘米（图 4-27，1；彩版 4-10，1）。

标本 W1：9，钵，红陶，圆唇，敞口，斜直腹，平底，内壁见多道弦纹。口径 17.6 厘米、高 5.6 厘米（图 4-27，2；彩版 4-10，2）。

标本 W1：10，钵，红陶，圆唇，敞口，斜直腹，平底，内壁见多道弦纹。口径 18 厘米、高 5.8 厘米（图 4-27，3；彩版 4-10，3）。

标本 W1：11，钵，红陶，圆唇，敞口，斜直腹，平底，内壁见多道弦纹。口径 18 厘米、高 5.2 厘米（图 4-27，4；彩版 4-10，4）。

标本 W1：12，钵，红陶，圆唇，敞口，斜直腹，平底，内壁见多道弦纹。口径 16.8 厘米、高 5 厘米（图 4-27，5；彩版 4-10，5）。

标本 W1：13，钵，红陶，圆唇，敞口，斜直腹，平底，内壁见多道弦纹。口径 18.6 厘米、高 5.4 厘米（图 4-27，6）。

标本 W1：15，B 型釜，红陶，上部残，折腹，圜底，腹部饰方格纹，有烟炱痕迹。腹径 19 厘米、残高 7.2 厘米（图 4-28，1）。

标本 W1：14，C 型罐，红陶，有红衣，圆唇，敞口略外翻，束颈，溜肩，肩部饰多道弦纹，圜底。口径 8 厘米、腹径 12.4 厘米、高 10.1 厘米（图 4-28，2；彩版 4-10，6）。

标本 W1：17，罐，黑陶，外有红衣，上部残，圆腹，平底近圜，陶胎较薄，器内有多道弦纹。底径 4 厘米、残高 5.4 厘米（图 4-28，3）。

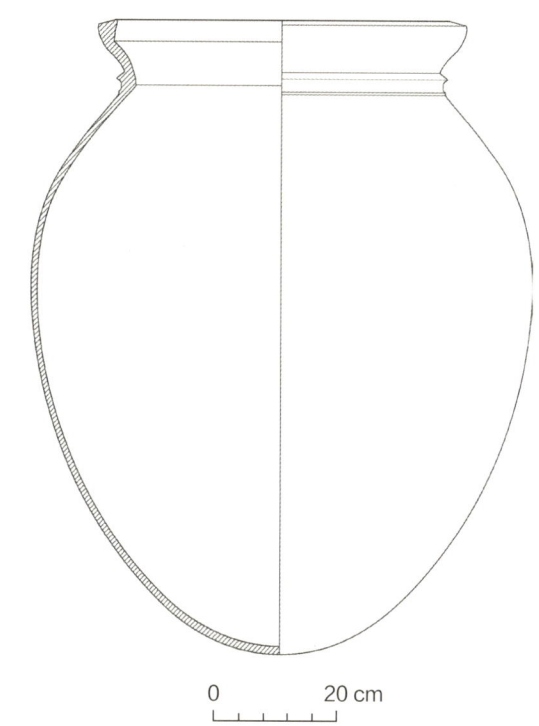

图 4-23　瓮（W1：19）
Fig. 4-23　The Urn (W1：19)

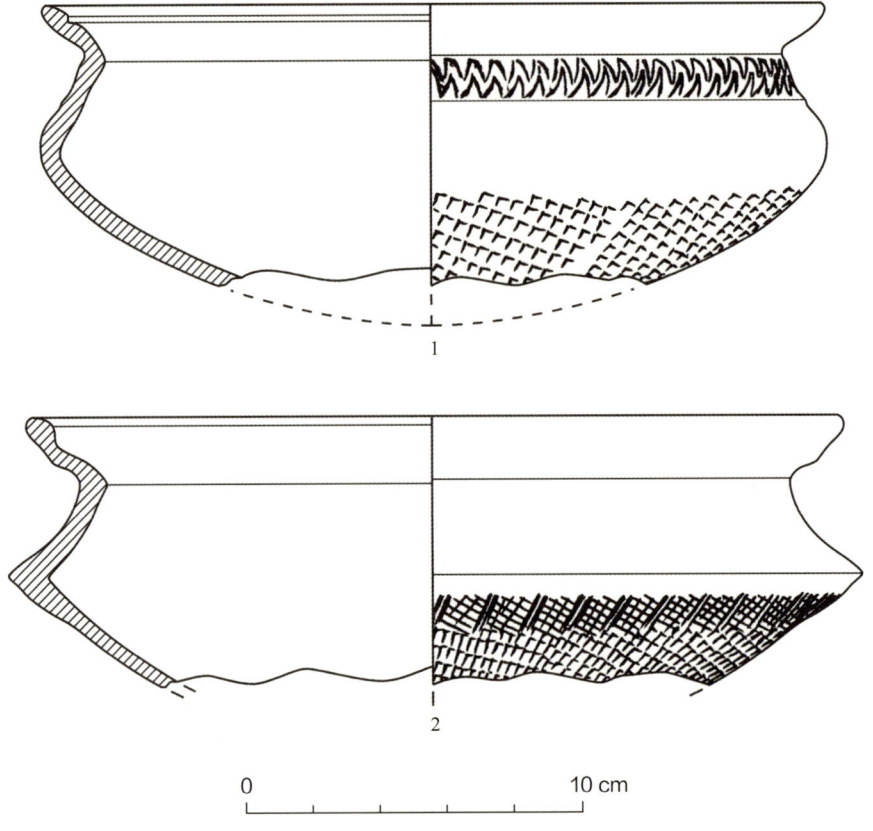

图 4-24　瓮 1 内出土陶器
Fig. 4-24　The unearthed potteries from Urn 1

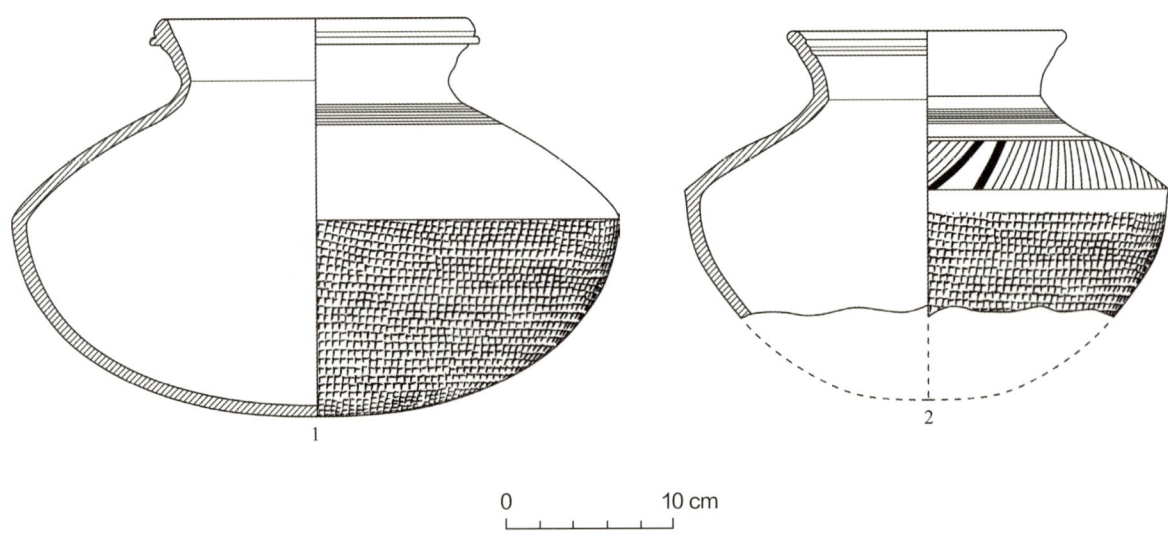

图 4-25　瓮 1 内出土陶器
Fig. 4-25　The unearthed potteries from Urn 1

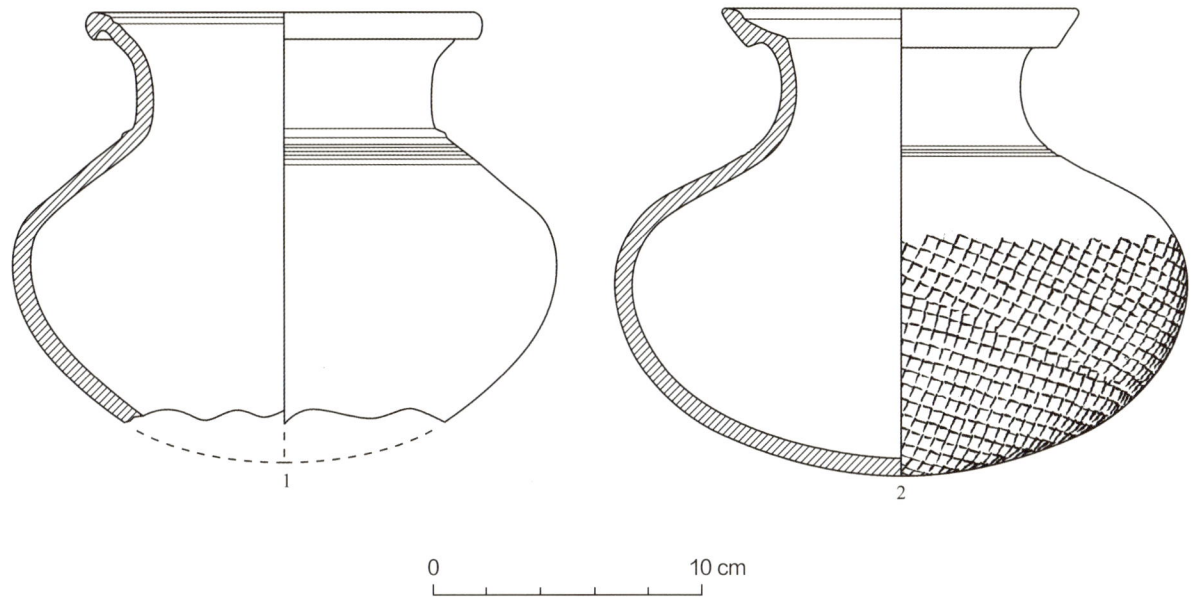

图 4-26　瓮 1 内出土陶器
Fig. 4-26　The unearthed potteries from Urn 1

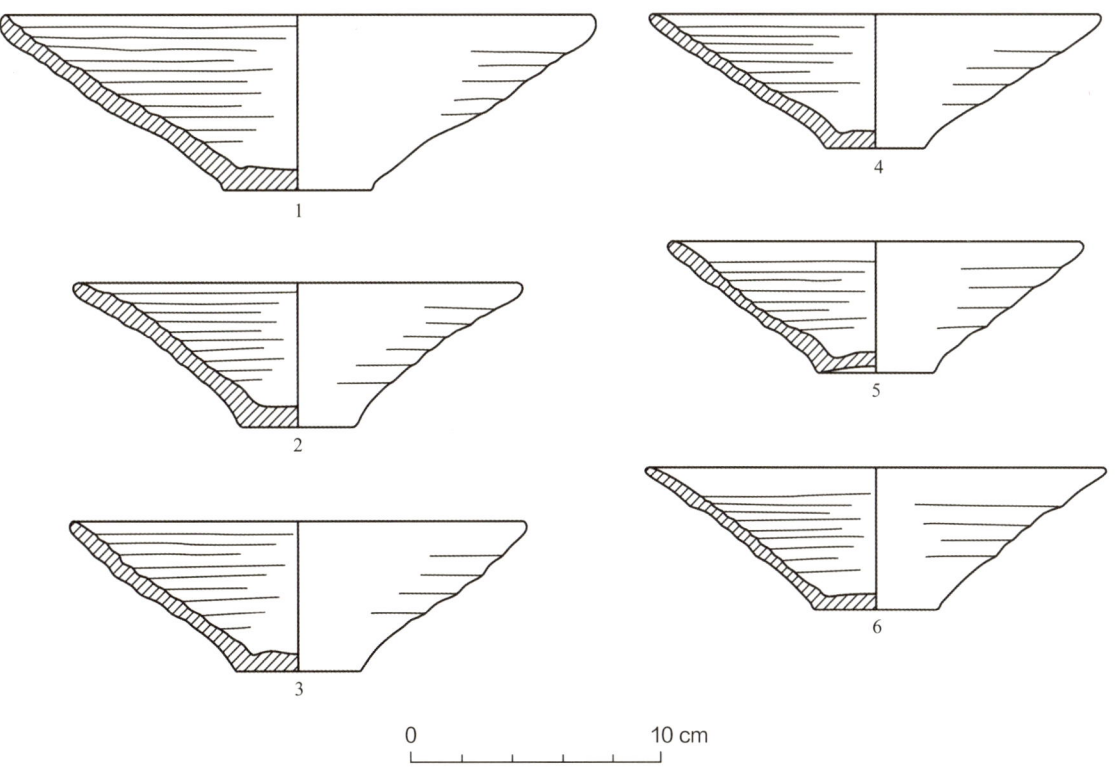

图 4-27　瓮 1 内出土陶器
Fig. 4-27　The unearthed potteries from Urn 1

标本 W1：18，罐，黑陶，上部残，圆腹，平底近圜，陶胎较薄，腹中有三道弦纹。底径 4.6 厘米、残高 6 厘米（图 4-28，4）。

标本 W1：7，C 型壶，红陶，尖圆唇，沿面近平，沿外有一圈凸棱，直领，折肩，肩部饰多道弦纹，圜底残。口径 14.4 厘米、腹径 20 厘米、残高 17.2 厘米（图 4-28，5；彩版 4-9，4）。

标本 W1：16，灯座，黑陶，上部残，柄部有一圆箍，底面饰一圈凸棱。底径 19 厘米、残高 10.2 厘米（图 4-28，6；彩版 4-11，1）。

标本 W1：20，器盖，黑陶，盖身向上，沿面有一凹槽，圆形纽，纽上饰几圈凸棱。盖径 11.6 厘米、高 2.4 厘米（图 4-28，7；彩版 4-11，2）。

瓮 2 内出土标本介绍

标本 W2：2，A 型壶，黑陶，圆唇，敞口，卷沿，束颈，溜肩，鼓腹，圜底，肩部饰多道弦纹、叶脉纹组合，肩下部饰斜线黑彩图案。口径 17 厘米、腹径 36 厘米、高 35.6 厘米（图 4-29；彩版 4-12，1）。

标本 W2：1，B 型罐，红陶，表面有红衣，圆唇，侈口，束颈，溜肩，鼓腹，圜底残，腹部饰方格纹。口径 14.7 厘米、腹径 24.6 厘米、残高 16.8 厘米（图 4-30；彩版 4-12，2）。

标本 W2：3，A 型壶，红陶，圆唇，敞口，卷沿外翻，束颈，溜肩，肩下残，肩部饰弦纹。口径 18.7 厘米、残高 9.6 厘米（图 4-31，1）。

标本 W2：4，A 型壶，红陶，圆唇，敞口外翻，束颈，溜肩，肩下残，颈部饰多道弦纹。口径 14.6 厘米、残高 9 厘米（图 4-31，2；彩版 4-11，3）。

标本 W2：4，小口壶，黑陶，唇部残，圆肩略扩，腹内收，下腹残，肩腹部饰多道弦纹。口径 3 厘米、腹径 12.8 厘米、残高 7.3 厘米（图 4-31，3）。

标本 W2：5，钵，红陶，敞口，圆唇，斜直腹，平底，器内外饰多道弦纹。口径 17 厘米、底径 4.4 厘米、高 5.6 厘米（图 4-31，4；彩版 4-11，4）。

标本 W2：6，钵，红陶，敞口，圆唇，斜直腹，平底，器内外饰多道弦纹。口径 16.8 厘米、底径 4.8 厘米、高 5 厘米（图 4-31，5）。

标本 W2：7，钵，红陶，敞口，圆唇，斜直腹，平底，器内外饰多道弦纹。口径 17 厘米、底径 4.6 厘米、高 4.6 厘米（图 4-31，6；彩版 4-11，5）。

标本 W2：8，器盖，黑陶，圆形纽，器盖呈覆斗状，内壁见多道弦纹。盖径 20 厘米、纽径 3.4 厘米、高 7 厘米（图 4-31，7；彩版 4-11，6）。

七、⑥层陶器

均为泥质夹细砂陶，以红陶为主，黑陶其次，红陶绝大部分为橙色陶，砖红色数量少，施红色陶衣 10 余件（片），黑陶以黑褐色为主，灰褐色次之。器类以釜、罐、壶、钵为主体。素面为主，纹饰主要有方格纹、凹弦纹、叶脉纹、条状纹、交叉纹等（表 8、9）。

标本介绍

UnitI11GridG2–G3 ⑥层表层出土陶器：

标本 I11G2–G3 ⑥表：1，钵，红陶，圆唇，敞口，斜直腹，平底，内壁见多道弦纹。口径 24.5 厘米、底径 6.6 厘米、高 7.2 厘米（图 4-32，1；彩版 4-13，1）。

标本 I11G2–G3 ⑥表：2，钵，红陶，圆唇，敞口，斜直腹，平底，内壁见多道弦纹。口径 22 厘米、底径 5.8 厘米、高 6.8 厘米（图 4-32，2；彩版 4-13，2）。

标本 I11G2–G3 ⑥表：3，钵，红陶，圆唇，敞口，斜直腹，平底，内壁见多道弦纹。口径 23.2 厘米、底径 5.6 厘米、高 6.6 厘米（图 4-32，3；彩版 4-13，3）。

标本 I11G2–G3 ⑥表：4，钵，红陶，圆唇，敞口，斜直腹，平底，内壁见多道弦纹。口径 23.2 厘米、底径 5.6 厘米、高 6.2 厘米（图 4-32，4；彩版 4-13，4）。

标本 I11G2–G3 ⑥表：5，钵，红陶，圆唇，敞口，斜直腹，平底，内壁见多道弦纹。口径 17 厘米、底径 4 厘米、高 5.4 厘米（图 4-32，5）。

图 4-28 瓮 1 内出土陶器
Fig. 4-28　The unearthed potteries from Urn 1

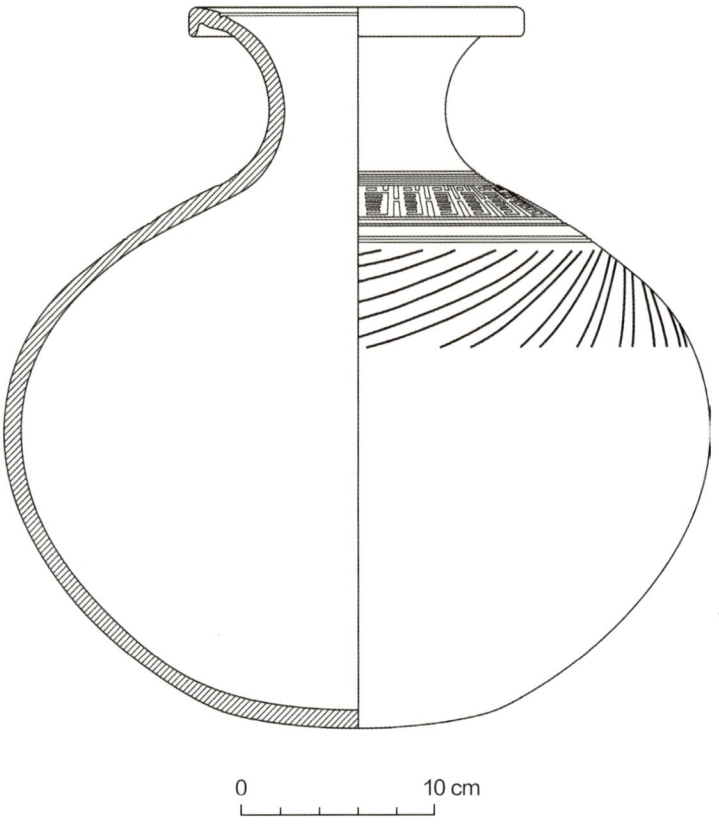

图 4-29 瓮 2 内出土 A 型壶
Fig. 4-29 The A-type jug unearthed from Urn 2

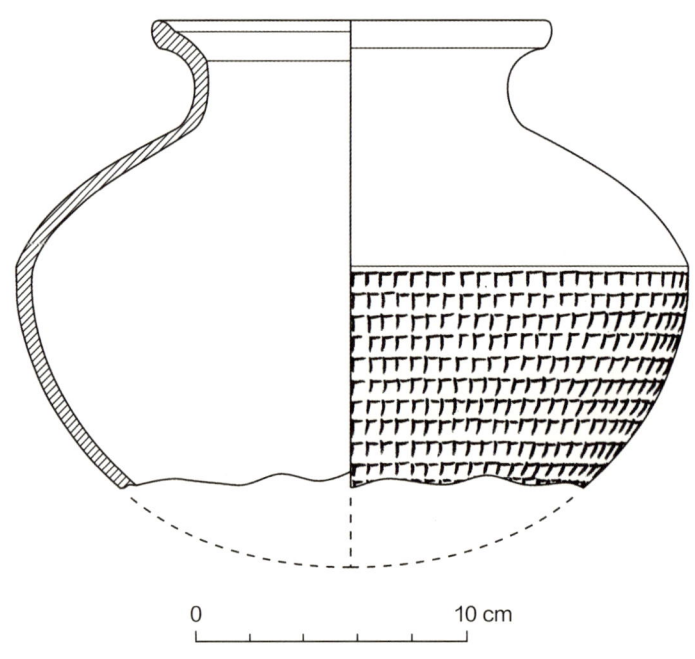

图 4-30 瓮 2 内出土 B 型罐
Fig. 4-30 The B-type pot unearthed from Urn 2

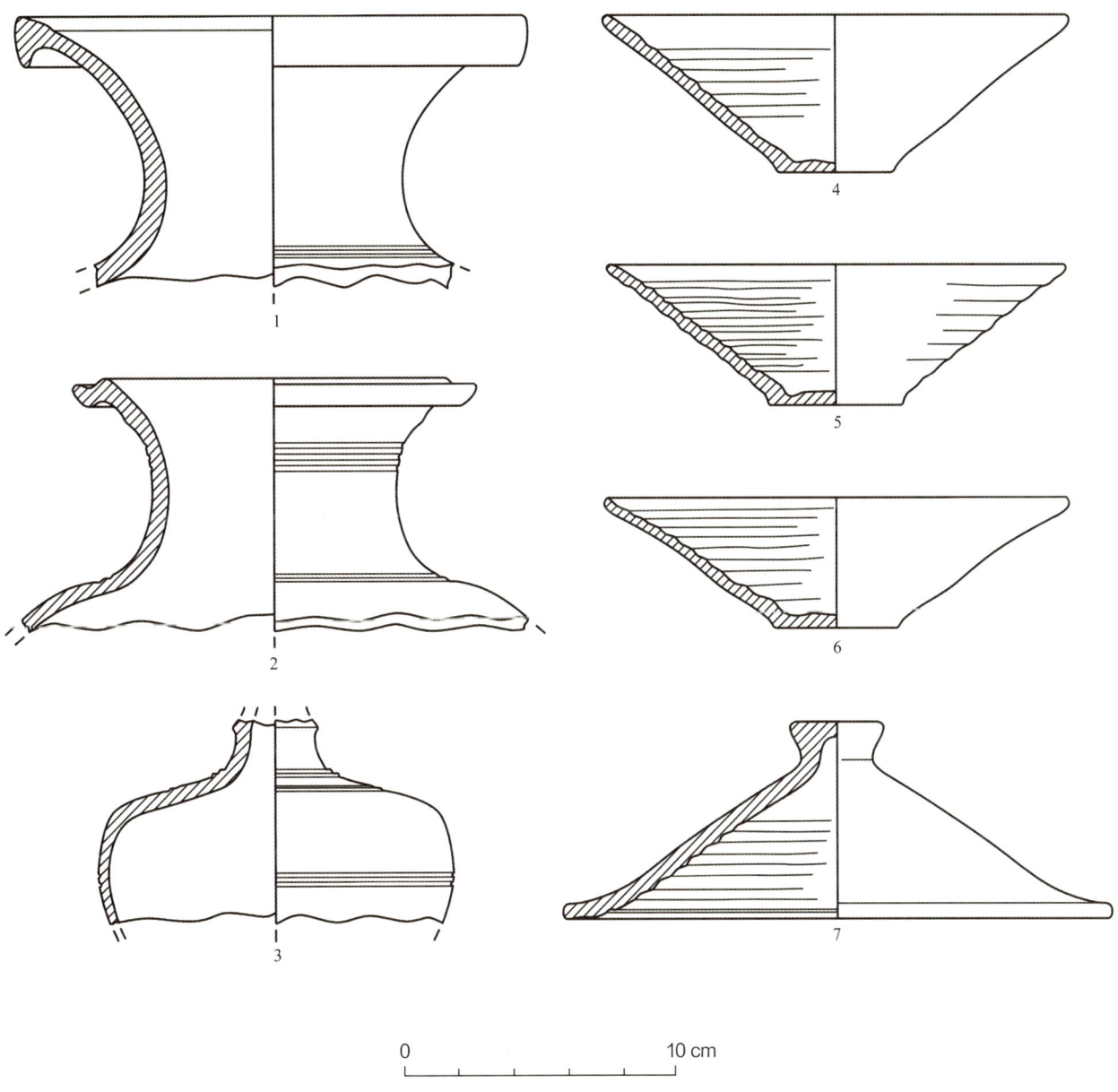

图 4-31　瓮 2 内出土陶器

Fig. 4-31　The unearthed potteries from Urn 2

253

标本 I11G2–G3 ⑥表：6，钵，红陶，圆唇，敞口，斜直腹，平底，内壁见多道弦纹。口径 14.4 厘米、底径 4.4 厘米、高 5.4 厘米（图 4-32，6）。

标本 I11G2–G3 ⑥表：7，钵，红陶，圆唇，敞口，斜直腹，平底，内壁见多道弦纹。口径 15.4 厘米、底径 4 厘米、高 4.8 厘米（图 4-32，7）。

标本 I11G2–G3 ⑥表：8，钵，红陶，圆唇，敞口，斜直腹，平底，内壁见多道弦纹。口径 15 厘米、底径 4.6 厘米、高 4.4 厘米（图 4-32，8）。

UnitI11GridG3，UnitI11GridG2–G3 ⑥层表层出土陶器：

标本 I11G3 ⑥表：10，Aa 型釜，红陶，施红衣，圆唇，束颈，折肩，弧腹内收，圜底，肩部饰一道凸棱，腹部施方格纹，有烟炱痕。口径 26.4 厘米、残高 11.2 厘米（图 4-33，1；彩版 4-13，5）。

标本 I11G2–G3 ⑥表：9，器盖，黑陶，圆形纽，器盖呈覆斗状，尖唇，器身内外饰多道弦纹。盖径 21.4 厘米、纽径 4 厘米、高 7 厘米（图 4-33，2；彩版 4-13，6）。

UnitI10GridG9–I11、G2、G3、G4、G5，UnitL10GridE5–F6,

UnitL8GridF5–G5 ⑥层出土陶器：

标本 I10G9–I11、G2、G3、G4、G5 ⑥：10，Aa 型釜，红陶，圆唇，束颈，圆肩，弧腹，圜底残，肩颈部饰多道弦纹，腹部饰方格纹。口径 26.4 厘米、腹径 29.8 厘米、残高 11.2 厘米（图 4-34，1）。

标本 L10E5–F6 ⑥：33，Ac 型釜，红陶，尖圆唇，口沿内有一凹槽，折肩，弧腹，圜底，

表 8　UnitI10GridG9，UnitI11GridG2、G3、G4、G5 ⑥层陶器统计表

纹饰 \ 陶色	红	黑	备注
素面	1310	410	
方格	137	207	
凹弦	43	56	
交叉	12	6	
条状	23	13	
叶脉	2	5	
器类（数量）	Aa 型釜 8，Ab 型釜 2，Ac 型釜 1，A 型罐 25，B 型罐 2，C 型罐 12，A 型壶 3，B 型壶 1，钵 74，灯座 3，器盖 2	Aa 型釜 102，Ab 型釜 1，A 型罐 3，C 型罐 3，A 型壶 2，B 型壶 4，钵 3，灯座 4，器盖 5	

表 9　UnitL10GridE5 - F6（神殿 1 北部探坑）⑥层陶器统计表

纹饰 \ 陶色	红	黑	备注
素面	1130	184	
方格	86	318	
凹弦	54	101	
条状	1		
叶脉	2		
太阳	1		
剔点纹		3	
戳点纹		12	
器类（数量）	Aa 型釜 15，B 型釜 1，Ac 型釜 4，A 型罐 3，B 型罐 2，A 型壶 4，钵 33	Aa 型釜 32，A 型罐 4，B 型罐 1，A 型壶 4，缸 1，器盖 4	

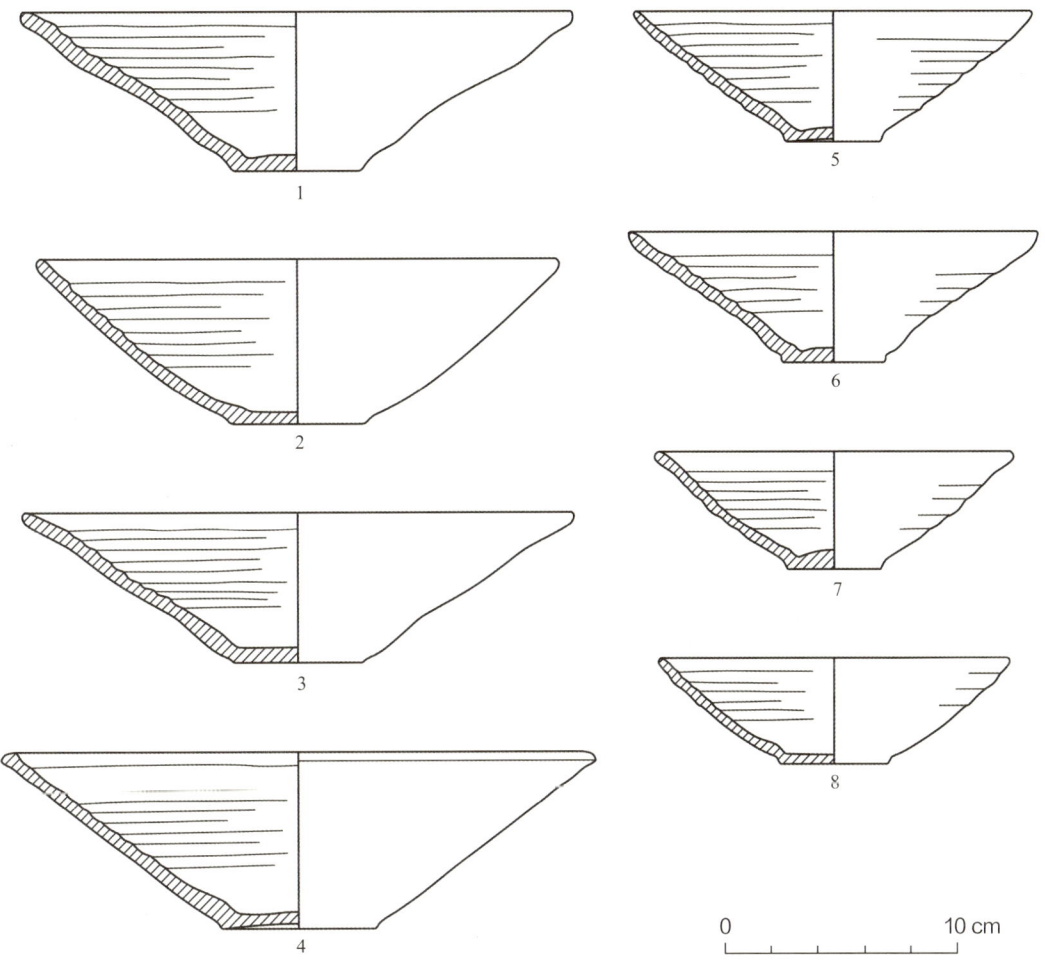

图 4-32 UnitI11GridG2-G3 ⑥层表层出土陶器
Fig. 4-32 The unearthed potteries of Layer 6 from UnitI11GridG2-G3

内壁有红色直线彩绘图案，腹部饰方格纹，有烟炱痕。口径 26.4 厘米、腹径 29.8 厘米、残高 11.2 厘米（图 4-34，2；彩版 4-14，1）。

标本 L8F5–G6⑥：25，B 型釜，红陶，圆唇，折肩，肩与腹转折明显，腹中鼓斜收，圜底，肩颈部饰多道弦纹，腹部饰方格纹，有烟炱痕。口径 12.6 厘米、腹径 18.8 厘米、残高 13.6 厘米（图 4-34，3；彩版 4-14，2）。

UnitI10GridG9–I11、G2、G3、G4、G5，UnitL8GridF5–G5 ⑥层出土陶器：

标本 I10G9–I11、G2、G3、G4、G5⑥：1，Aa 型釜，黑陶，圆唇，束颈，口沿内有一凸棱，折肩，弧腹，圜底较浅，肩腹转折处有一凸棱，肩部饰多道弦纹，肩下戳印纹一周，腹部饰方格纹。口径 19 厘米、高 7.4 厘米（图 4-35，1；彩版 4-14，3）。

标本 L8F5–G5⑥：35，Aa 型釜，黑陶，圆唇，圆肩，圜底，肩部饰两道弦纹，腹部饰方格纹，有烟炱痕。口径 19.6 厘米、高 7.4 厘米（图 4-35，2；彩版 4-15，1）。

标本 I10G9–I11、G2、G3、G4、G5⑥：4，B 型釜，红陶，圆唇，侈口，束颈，长弧形肩，弧腹，圜底较浅，肩腹转折处有一凸棱，肩部饰多

255

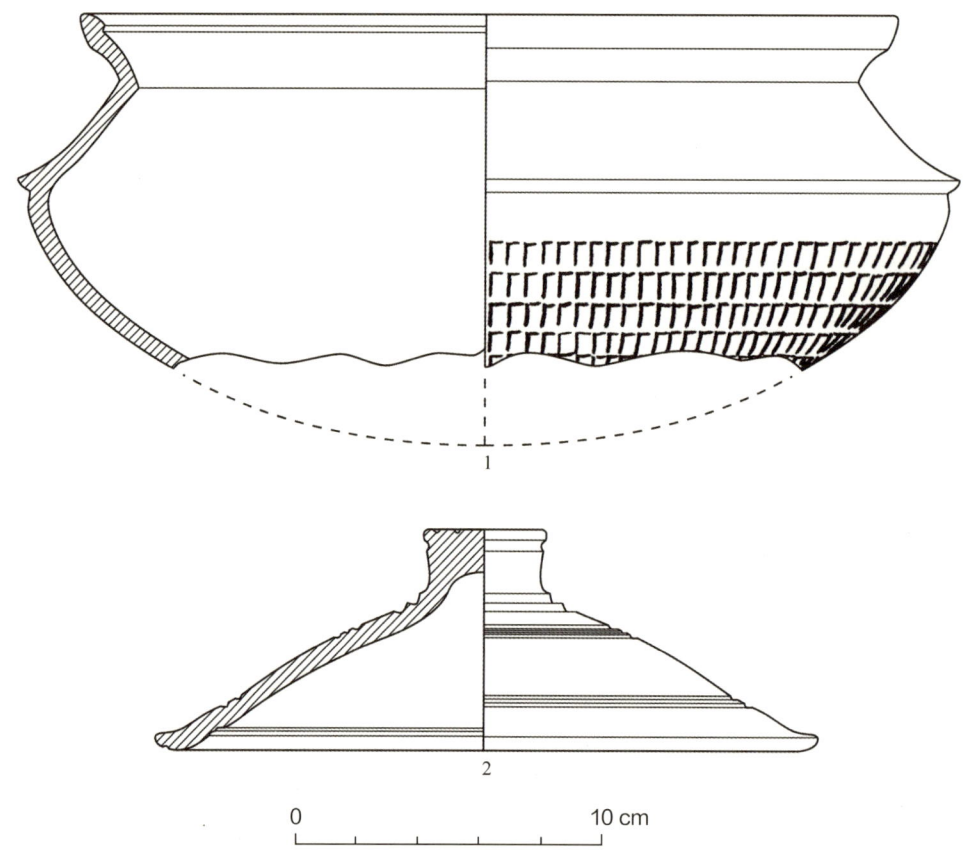

图 4-33 UnitI11GridG3，UnitI11GridG2-G3 ⑥层表层出土陶器

Fig. 4-33 The unearthed potteries of top Layer 6 from UnitI11GridG3, UnitI11GridG2-G3

道弦纹，腹部饰方格纹，有烟炱痕。口径 12.2 厘米、高 9.8 厘米（图 4-35，3；彩版 4-15，2）。

UnitL11GridE5–F6，UnitI10GridG9–I11、G2、G3、G4、G5 ⑥层出土陶器：

标本 L11E5–F6 ⑥：1，Aa 型釜，黑陶，圆唇，束颈，口沿内有一弦纹，溜肩，弧腹，圜底残，肩腹转折处有一凸棱，肩下戳印纹一周，腹部饰方格纹。口径 20 厘米、残高 6.4 厘米（图 4-36，1）。

标本 L11E5–F6 ⑥：2，Aa 型釜，黑陶，圆唇，束颈，口沿内有一弦纹，圆肩，斜腹，圜底残，肩部两道弦纹，腹部饰方格纹。口径 21.2 厘米、残高 5.8 厘米（图 4-36，2）。

标本 L11E5–F6 ⑥：3，Ac 型釜，红陶，圆唇，平折沿，束颈，口沿内有一弦纹，斜肩，肩部多道弦纹。口径 22 厘米、残高 2.2 厘米（图 4-36，3）。

标本 I10G9–I11、G2、G3、G4、G5 ⑥：2，Aa 型釜，黑陶，圆唇，束颈，口沿内有一弦纹，圆肩，斜腹，圜底残，肩部一道弦纹，腹部饰方格纹。口径 23.6 厘米、残高 6.2 厘米（图 4-36，4；彩版 4-15，3）。

标本 I10G9–I11、G2、G3、G4、G5 ⑥：3，Ac 型釜，红陶，圆唇，折沿，束颈，口沿内有一弦纹，肩部残。口径 24 厘米、残高 2 厘米（图 4-36，5）。

标本 I10G9–I11、G2、G3、G4、G5 ⑥：4，B 型釜，红陶，圆唇，折沿，束颈，斜肩，肩部饰一凸棱，肩下残。口径 24 厘米、残高 4.4 厘米（图 4-36，6）。

标本 I10G9–I11、G2、G3、G4、G5 ⑥：5，Aa 型釜，红陶，圆唇，束颈，圆肩，腹残。口径 18 厘米、残高 3.6 厘米（图 4-36，7）。

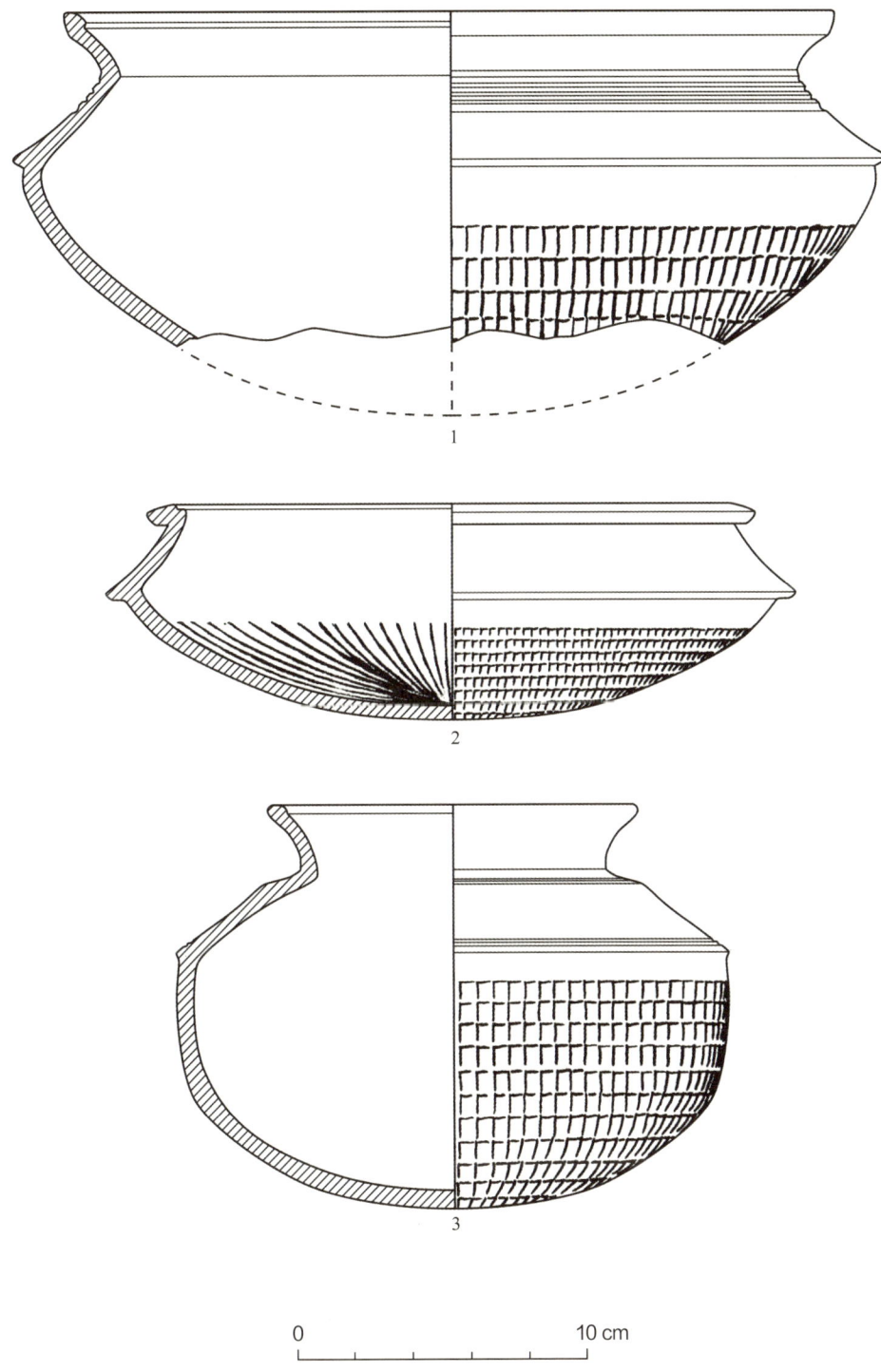

图 4-34　UnitI10GridG9-I11、G2、G3、G4、G5，UnitL10 GridE5-F6，UnitL8GridF5-G5 ⑥层出土陶器

Fig. 4-34　The unearthed potteries of Layer 6 from UnitI10GridG9-I11, G2, G3, G4, G5, UnitL10GridE5-F6, UnitL8GridF5-G5

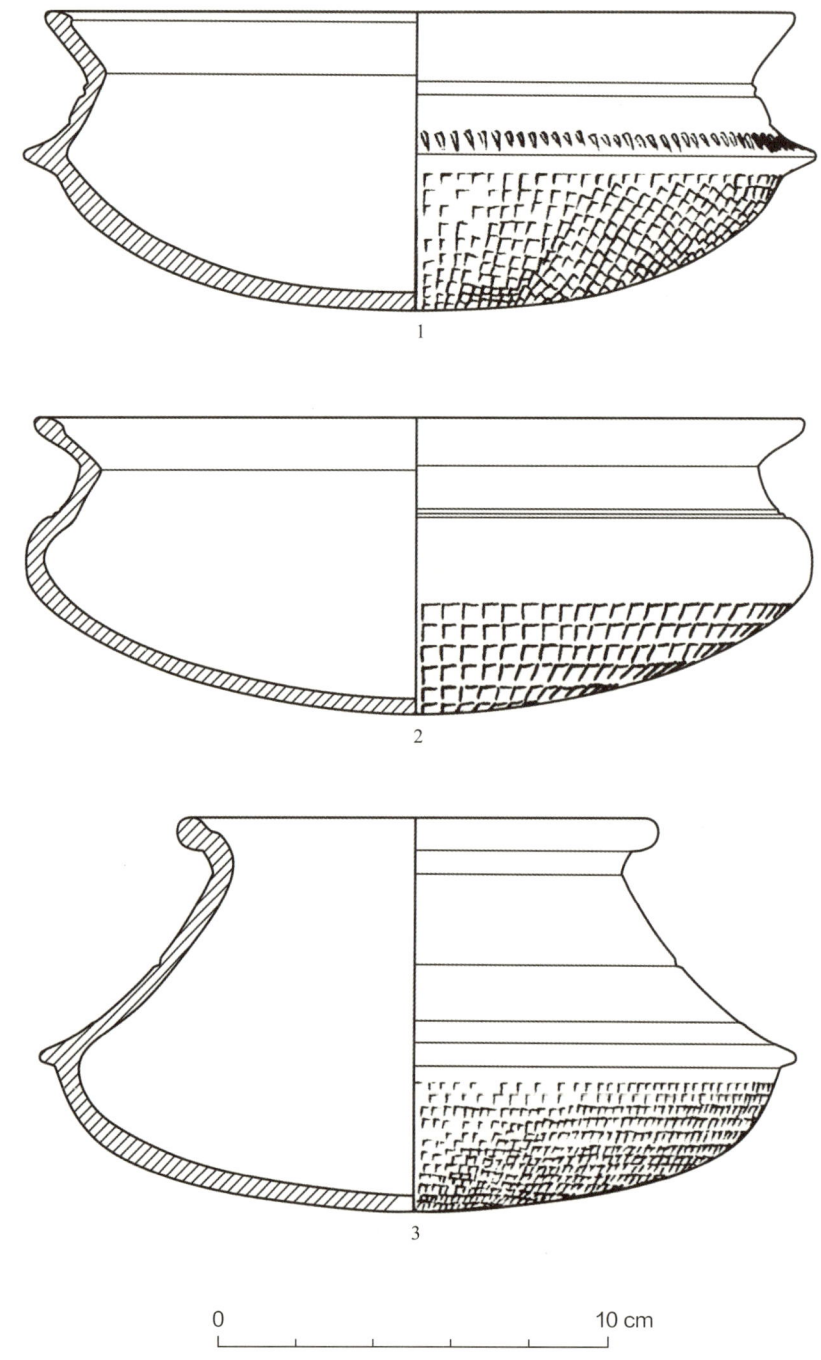

图 4-35　UnitI10GridG9-I11、G2、G3、G4、G5，UnitL8 GridF5-G5 ⑥层出土陶器

Fig. 4-35　The unearthed potteries of Layer 6 from UnitI10GridG9-I11, G2, G3, G4, G5, UnitL8GridF5-G5

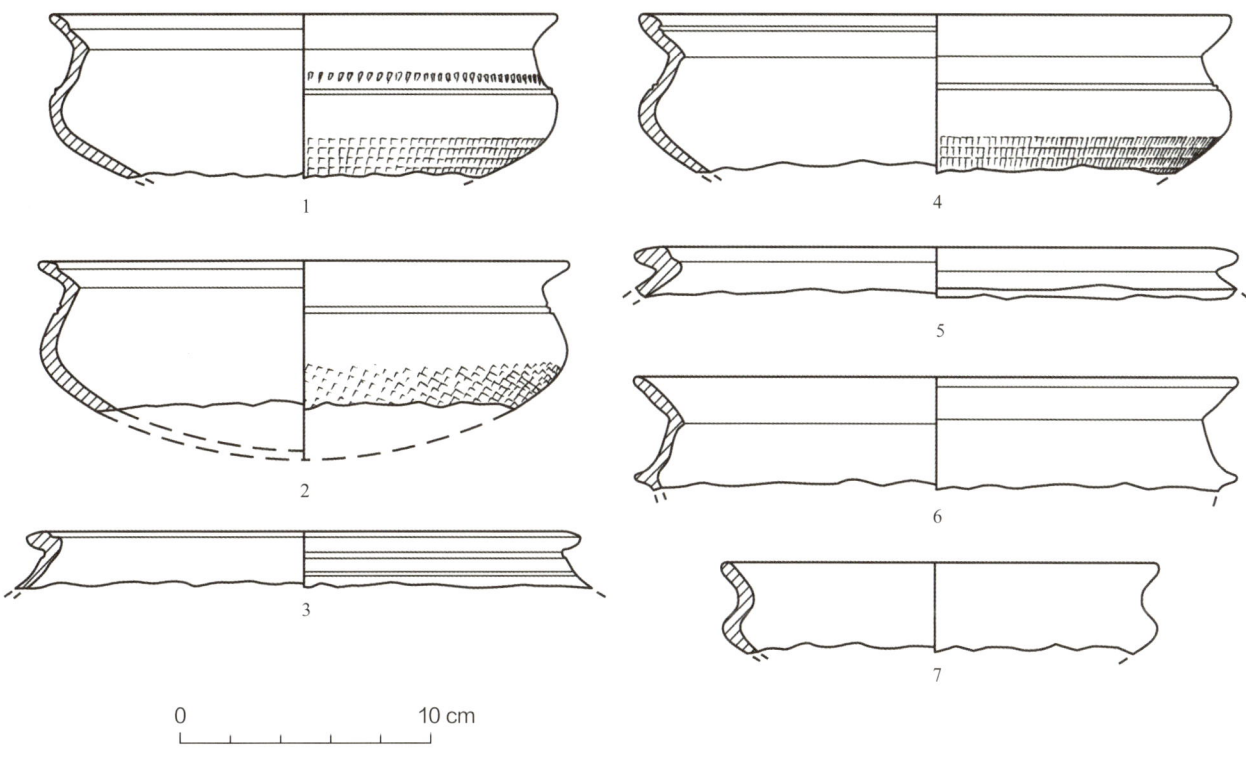

图 4-36　UnitL11GridE5-F6，UnitI10GridG9-I11、G2、G3、G4、G5 ⑥层出土陶器
Fig. 4-36　The unearthed potteries of Layer 6 from UnitL11GridE5-F6, UnitI10GridG9-I11, G2, G3, G4, G5

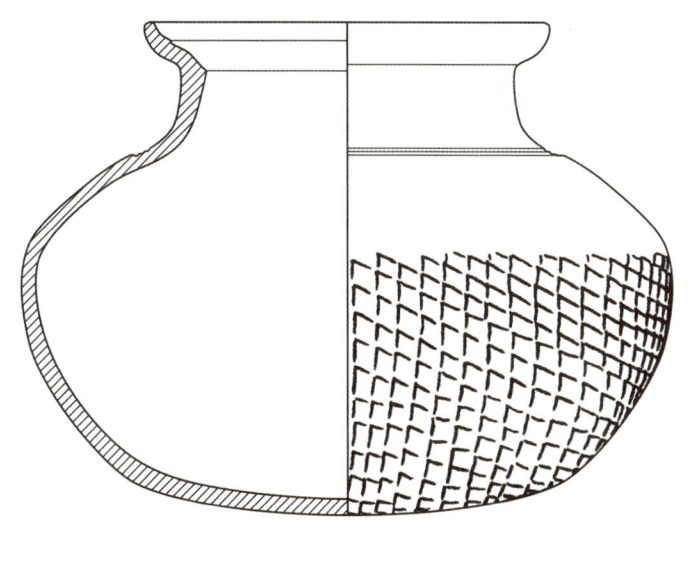

图 4-37　UnitL8GridF5-G5 ⑥层 B 型罐
Fig. 4-37　The B-type pot of Layer 6 from UnitL8GridF5-G5

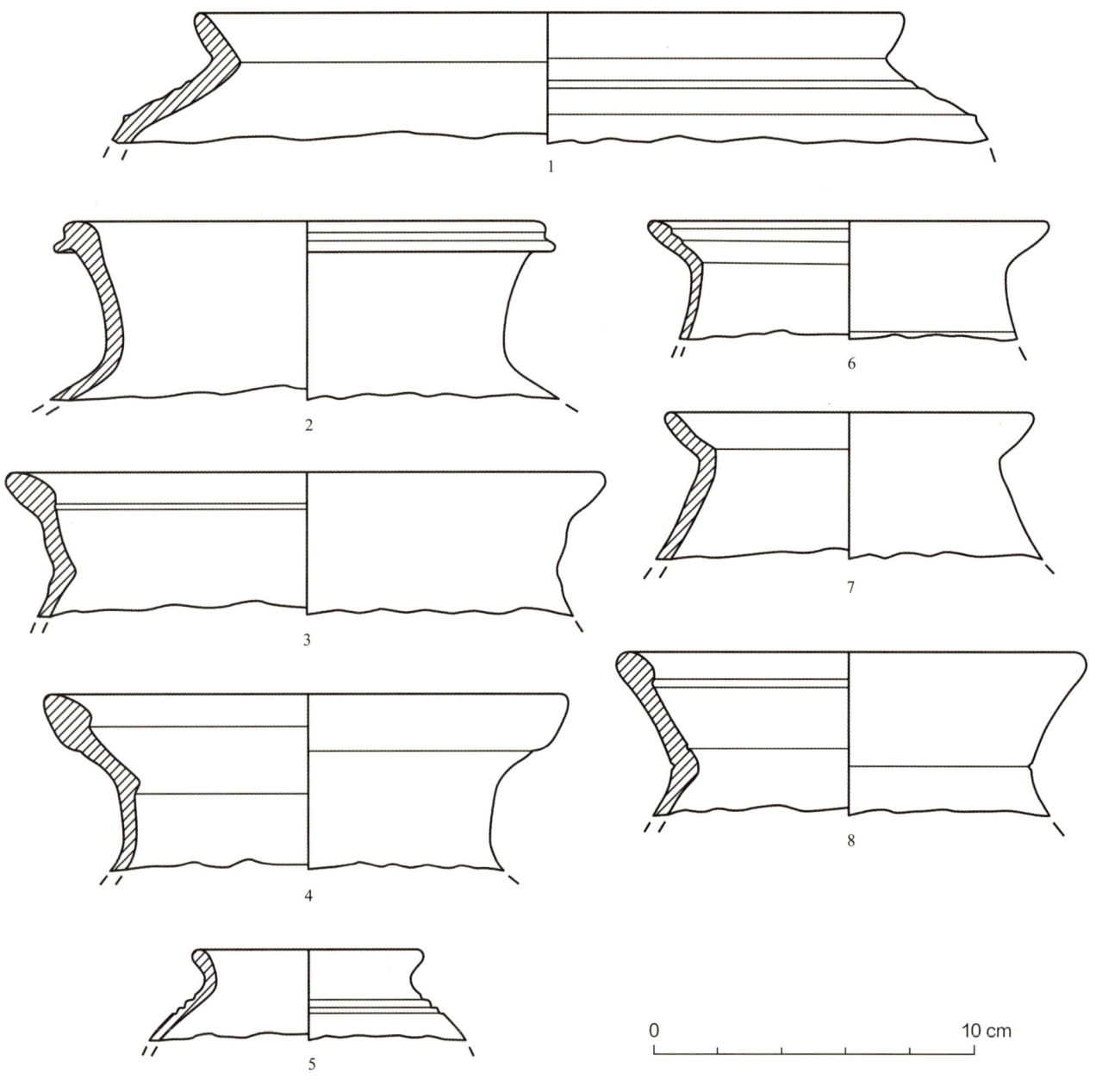

图 4-38 UnitL10GridE5-F6，Unitl10GridG9-I11、G2、G3、G4、G5 ⑥层出土陶器
Fig. 4-38 The unearthed potteries of Layer 6 from UnitL10GridE5-F6, Unitl10GridG9-I11, G2, G3, G4, G5

UnitL8GridF5–G5 ⑥层出土 B 型罐：

标本 L8F5–G5⑥：31，B 型罐，灰陶，外施红衣，圆唇，束颈，圆肩，弧腹，圜底，肩部饰三道弦纹，腹部饰方格纹，有烟炱痕。口径 12.6 厘米、腹径 20.2 厘米、高 15 厘米（图 4-37；彩版 4-15，4）。

UnitL10GridE5–F6，UnitI10GridG9–I11、G2、G3、G4、G5⑥层出土陶器：

标本 I10G9–I11、G2、G3、G4、G5⑥：9，C 型罐，红陶，折沿，圆唇，束颈，溜肩，肩下残，肩部有多道弦纹。口径 22 厘米、残高 4 厘米（图 4-38，1）。

标本 L10E5–F6⑥：5，A 型罐，黑陶，直口外敞，圆唇，束颈，颈下残，沿下饰一道凸棱。口径 15 厘米、残高 5.4 厘米（图 4-38，2）。

标本 I10G9–I11、G2、G3、G4、G5⑥：7，B 型罐，红陶，敞口微敛，圆唇，束颈，颈下残，沿内饰一道弦纹。口径 18.6 厘米、残高 4.4 厘米（图 4-38，3）。

标本 I10G9–I11、G2、G3、G4、G5⑥：8，B 型罐，黑陶，盘口，圆唇，束颈，颈下残，素面。口径 16.4 厘米、残高 5.4 厘米（图 4-38，4）。

标本 I10G9–I11、G2、G3、G4、G5⑥：10，小罐，红陶，侈口，圆唇，束颈，圆肩，肩下残，肩下饰多道弦纹。口径 6.4 厘米、残高 2.8 厘米（图 4-38，5）。

标本 L10E5–F6⑥：6，B 型罐，黑陶，敞口，圆唇，束颈，沿内饰多道弦纹，颈下残。口径 12.4 厘米、残高 3.6 厘米（图 4-38，6）。

标本 L10E5–F6⑥：7，C 型罐，红陶，敛口，圆唇，束颈，斜肩，肩下残，素面。口径 11.4 厘米、残高 4.4 厘米（图 4-38，7）。

标本 I10G9–I11、G2、G3、G4、G5⑥：6，A 型罐，红陶，盘口，圆唇，束颈，颈下残，沿内饰一道弦纹。口径 15.2 厘米、残高 5 厘米（图 4-38，8）。

UnitL8GridF5–G5，UnitL10GridE6⑥层出土陶器：

标本 L8F5–G5⑥：16，小壶，红陶，圆唇，喇叭口，沿面平，沿面有一道凹弦纹，颈较长，肩部饰多道弦纹，腹较鼓，平底，底面可见制作时留下的螺旋纹。口径 5 厘米、底径 3.4 厘米、高 8 厘米（图 4-39，1；彩版 4-16，1）。

标本 L8F5–G5⑥：17，小壶，红陶，圆唇，喇叭口，沿面平，沿面有一道凹弦纹，颈较长，肩部饰多道弦纹，腹较鼓，平底，底面可见制作时留下的螺旋纹。口径 4.8 厘米、底径 3.2 厘米、高 7.8 厘米（图 4-39，2；彩版 4-17，1）。

标本 L8F5–G5⑥：18，小壶，红陶，圆唇，喇叭口，沿面平，沿面有一道凹弦纹，颈较长，肩部饰多道弦纹，腹较鼓，平底，底面可见制作时留下的螺旋纹。口径 4.8 厘米、底径 3.4 厘米、高 8 厘米（图 4-39，3；彩版 4-17，2）。

标本 L10E6⑥：15，小壶，红陶，上部残，溜肩，肩腹转折处有一凸棱，腹斜收，底部外扩，平底，肩部饰多道细弦纹，腹部饰多道粗弦纹。底径 5.8 厘米、残高 7.2 厘米（图 4-39，4；彩版 4-17，3）。

标本 L8F5–G5⑥：27，小壶，红陶，上部残，折肩，肩腹转折处明显，腹斜收，平底，肩部腹部饰多道弦纹。底径 4.4 厘米、残高 7.5 厘米（图 4-39，5；彩版 4-17，4）。

UnitL10GridE5–F6，UnitI10GridG9–I11、G2、G3、G4、G5⑥层出土陶器：

标本 L10E5–F6⑥：9，A 型壶，红陶，圆唇，喇叭口，口沿外翻，口沿下残，沿内有多道弦纹。口径 15.2 厘米、残高 3.8 厘米（图 4-40，1）。

标本 L10E5–F6⑥：10，B 型壶，红陶，圆唇，喇叭口，口沿外翻，口沿下残，沿内有一道弦纹。口径 17 厘米、残高 3.6 厘米（图 4-40，2）。

标本 L10E5–F6⑥：11，C 型壶，灰陶，口沿残，喇叭口，颈下残，颈内有一道弦纹，沿下有一道凸棱。上径 12.4 厘米、残高 6.2 厘米（图 4-40，3）。

标本 L10E5–F6⑥：12，C 型壶，黑陶，圆唇，喇叭口，沿下残，沿内有多道弦纹，沿下有一道凸棱。口径 18 厘米、残高 3.8 厘米（图 4-40，4）。

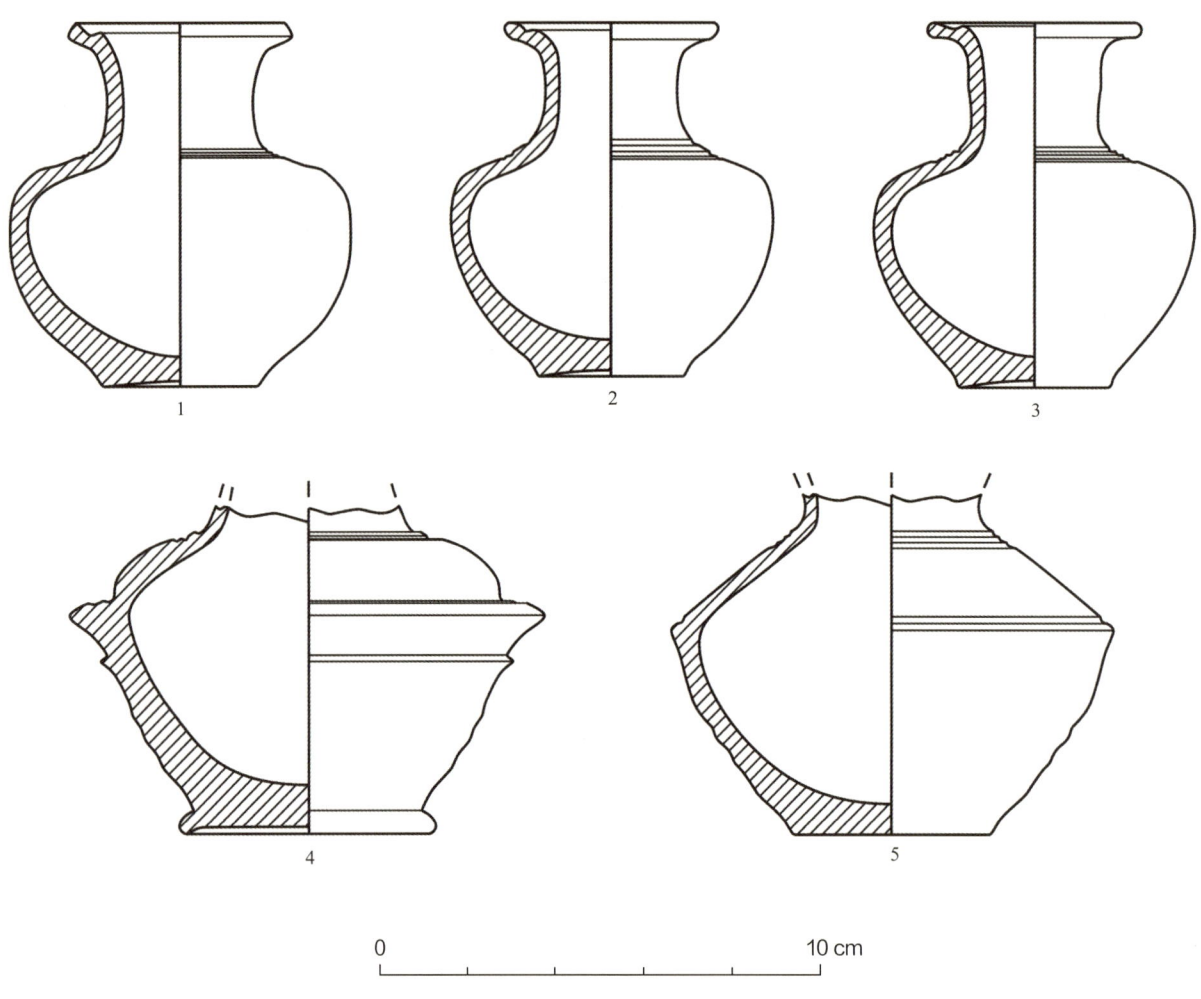

图 4-39　UnitL8GridF5-G5，UnitL10GridE6 ⑥层出土陶器
Fig. 4-39　The unearthed potteries of Layer 6 from UnitL8GridF5-G5, UnitL10GridE6

标本 I10G9–I11、G2、G3、G4、G5⑥：11，A 型壶，红陶，圆唇，喇叭口，口沿下残。口径 19 厘米、残高 6 厘米（图 4-40，5）。

标本 I10G9–I11、G2、G3、G4、G5⑥：12，B 型壶，黑陶，圆唇，喇叭口，口沿外翻，口沿下残，沿内有一道弦纹。口径 19 厘米、残高 3.8 厘米（图 4-40，6）。

标本 I10G9–I11、G2、G3、G4、G5⑥：13，C 型壶，红陶，圆唇，喇叭口，沿下残，沿内有一道凸棱。口径 19 厘米、残高 1.8 厘米（图 4-40，7）。

UnitL10GridE5–F6，UnitI10GridG9-I11、G2、G3、G4、G5，UnitL8GridF5-G5 ⑥层出土陶器：

标本 L10E5–F6⑥：14，钵，红陶，圆唇，敞口，斜直腹，平底，内壁见多道弦纹。口径 18.8 厘米、底径 5.6 厘米、高 4.6 厘米（图 4-41，1）。

标本 L10E5–F6⑥：15，钵，红陶，圆唇，敞口，斜直腹，平底，内壁见多道弦纹。口径 16.4 厘米、底径 4.2 厘米、高 5.4 厘米（图 4-41，2）。

标本 L10E5–F6⑥：3，钵，红陶，圆唇，敞口，斜直腹，平底，内壁见多道弦纹。口径 18.2 厘米、底径 4.8 厘米、高 5.2 厘米（图 4-41，3）。

标本 L8F5–G5⑥：10，钵，红陶，圆唇，敞

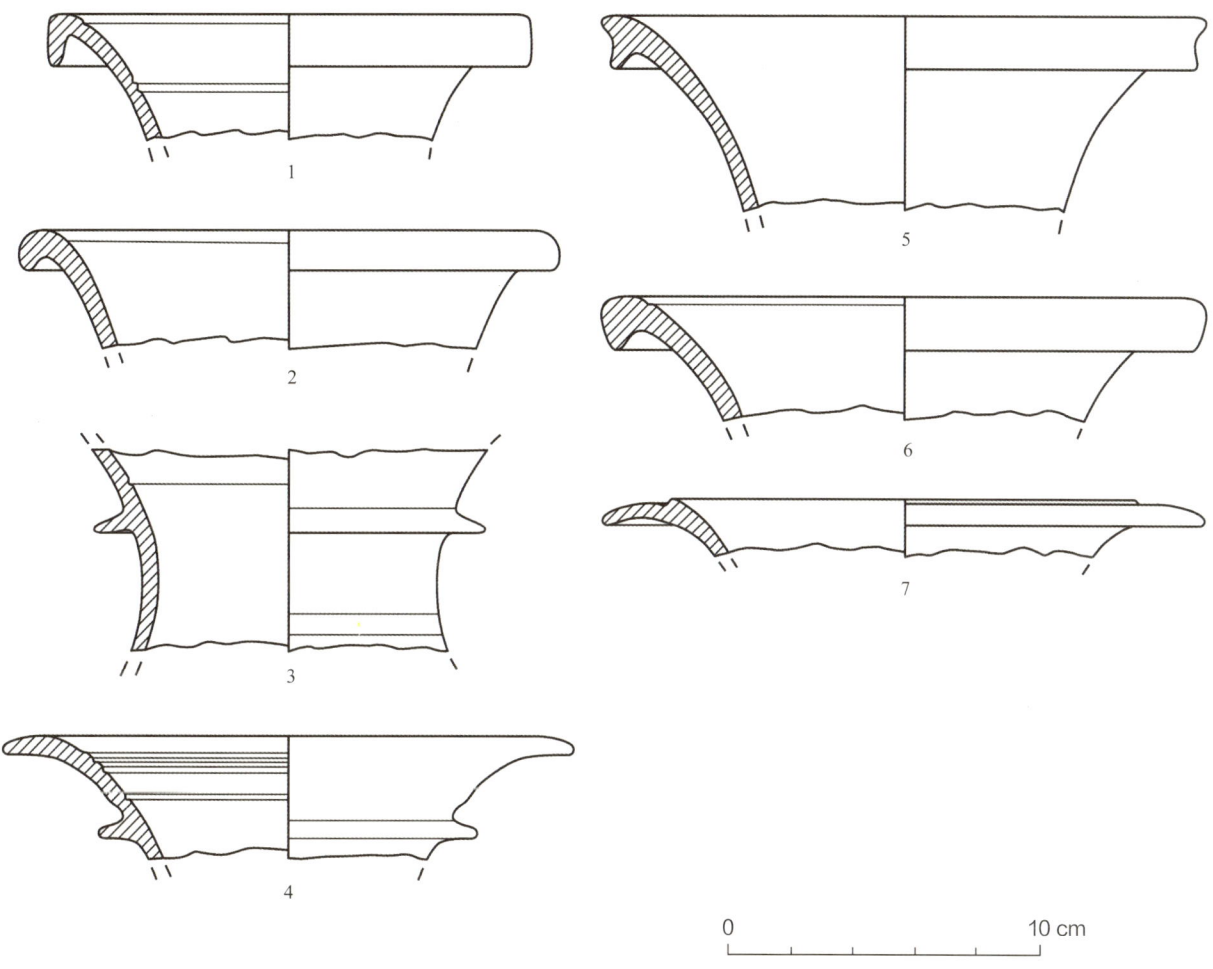

图 4-40　UnitL10GridE5-F6，UnitI10GridG9-I11、G2、G3、G4、G5⑥层出土陶器
Fig. 4-40　The unearthed potteries of Layer 6 from UnitL10GridE5-F6, UnitI10GridG9-I11, G2, G3, G4, G5

口，斜直腹，平底，内壁见多道弦纹，口沿部位有烧黑痕迹。口径16.4厘米、底径4.6厘米、高5厘米（图4-41，4）。

标本L10G5⑥：30，钵，红陶，圆唇，敞口，斜直腹，平底，内壁见多道弦纹。口径18.4厘米、底径4.4厘米、高5.6厘米（图4-41，5）。

标本L8G5⑥：32，钵，红陶，圆唇，敞口，斜直腹，平底，内壁见多道弦纹。口径17厘米、底径4.4厘米、高5厘米（图4-41，6）。

标本L8F5-G5⑥：37，钵，红陶，圆唇，敞口，斜直腹，平底，内壁见多道弦纹。口径17.6厘米、底径4.4厘米、高5.4厘米（图4-41，7）。

标本I10G9-I11、G2、G3、G4、G5⑥：21，钵，红陶，圆唇，敞口，斜直腹，平底，内壁见多道弦纹。口径16厘米、底径6厘米、高4.8厘米（图4-41，8）。

UnitL10GridE5-F6，UnitI10GridG9-I11、G2、G3、G4、G5⑥层出土陶器：

标本L10E5-F6⑥：8，缸，黑陶，残存口沿，沿下饰一道弦纹。口径49厘米、残高4厘米（图4-42，1）。

标本I10G9-I11、G2、G3、G4、G5⑥：14，器盖，红陶，圆形纽，盖身残。纽径4厘米、残高4厘米（图4-42，2）。

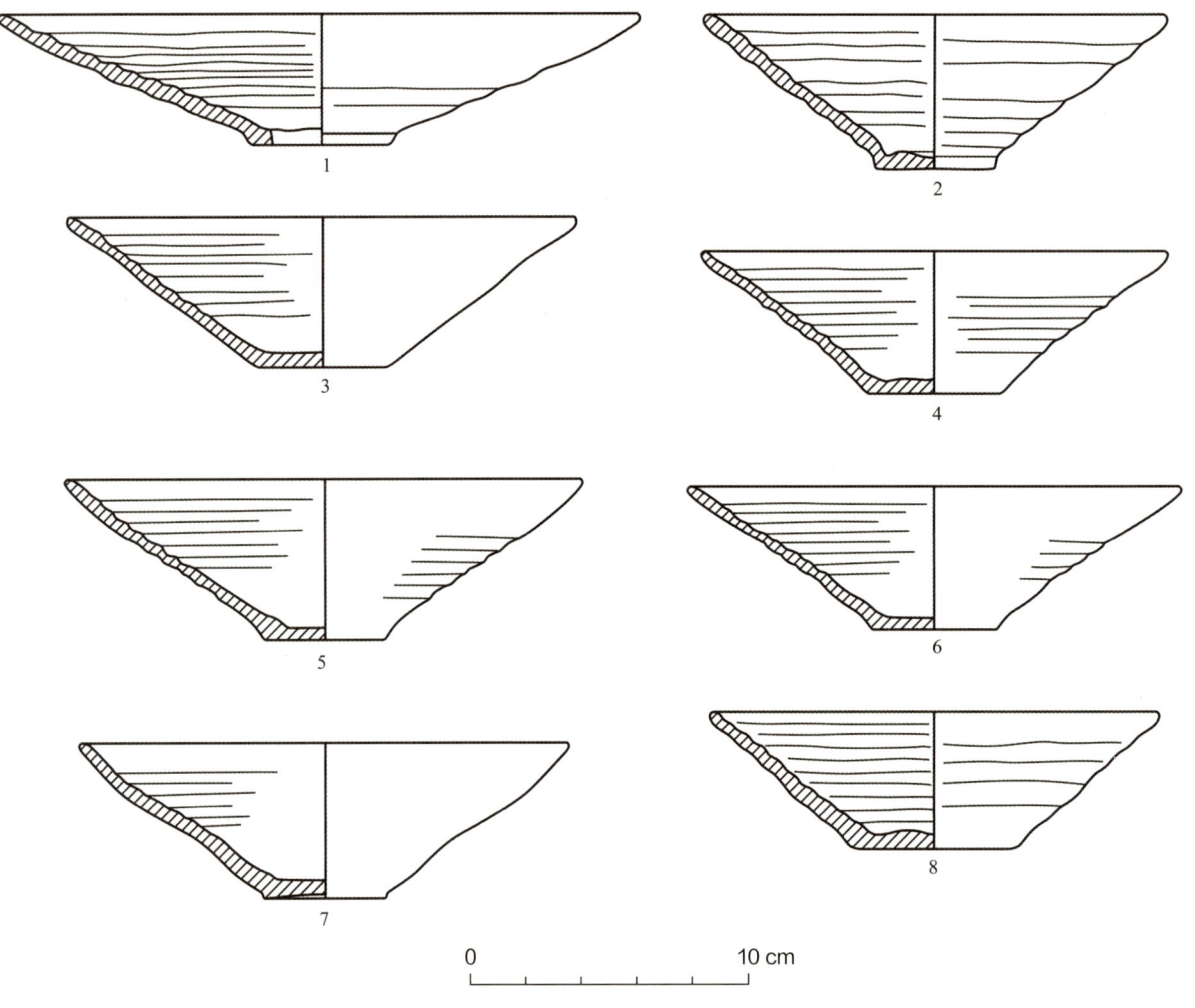

图 4-41 UnitL10GridE5-F6，UnitI10GridG9-I11、G2、G3、G4、G5，UnitL8GridF5-G5⑥层出土陶器

Fig. 4-41 The unearthed potteries of Layer 6 from UnitL10GridE5-F6, UnitI10GridG9-I11, G2, G3, G4, G5, UnitL8GridF5-G5

标本 I10G9–I11、G2、G3、G4、G5⑥：15，器盖，红陶，圆形纽，纽中间内凹，盖身残。纽径 3.2 厘米、残高 3.8 厘米（图 4-42，3）。

标本 I10G9–I11、G2、G3、G4、G5⑥：16，器盖，红陶，圆形纽，盖身残。纽径 4.4 厘米、残高 3.4 厘米（图 4-42，4）。

标本 L10E5–F6⑥：13，器盖，黑陶，纽残，器盖呈覆斗状。盖径 16.4 厘米、残高 3.6 厘米（图 4-42，5）。

标本 I10G9–I11、G2、G3、G4、G5⑥：22，钵，红陶，口部残，斜直腹，平底，内壁见多道弦纹。底径 5.6 厘米、残高 4.6 厘米（图 4-42，6）。

UnitL10GridE6，UnitL8GridF5–G5⑥层出土陶器：

标本 L10E6⑥：24，灯座，红陶，表面磨光，施红彩，上部残断，柄中部有两道凸弦纹，下部在两圈凸棱，其中饰以一周圆片状透雕，底座有一圈凸棱，圈足内有两道弦纹。底径 20.4 厘米、残高 15 厘米（图 4-43，1；彩版 4-16，2）。

标本 L8F5–G5⑥：20，灯座，灰黑陶，上

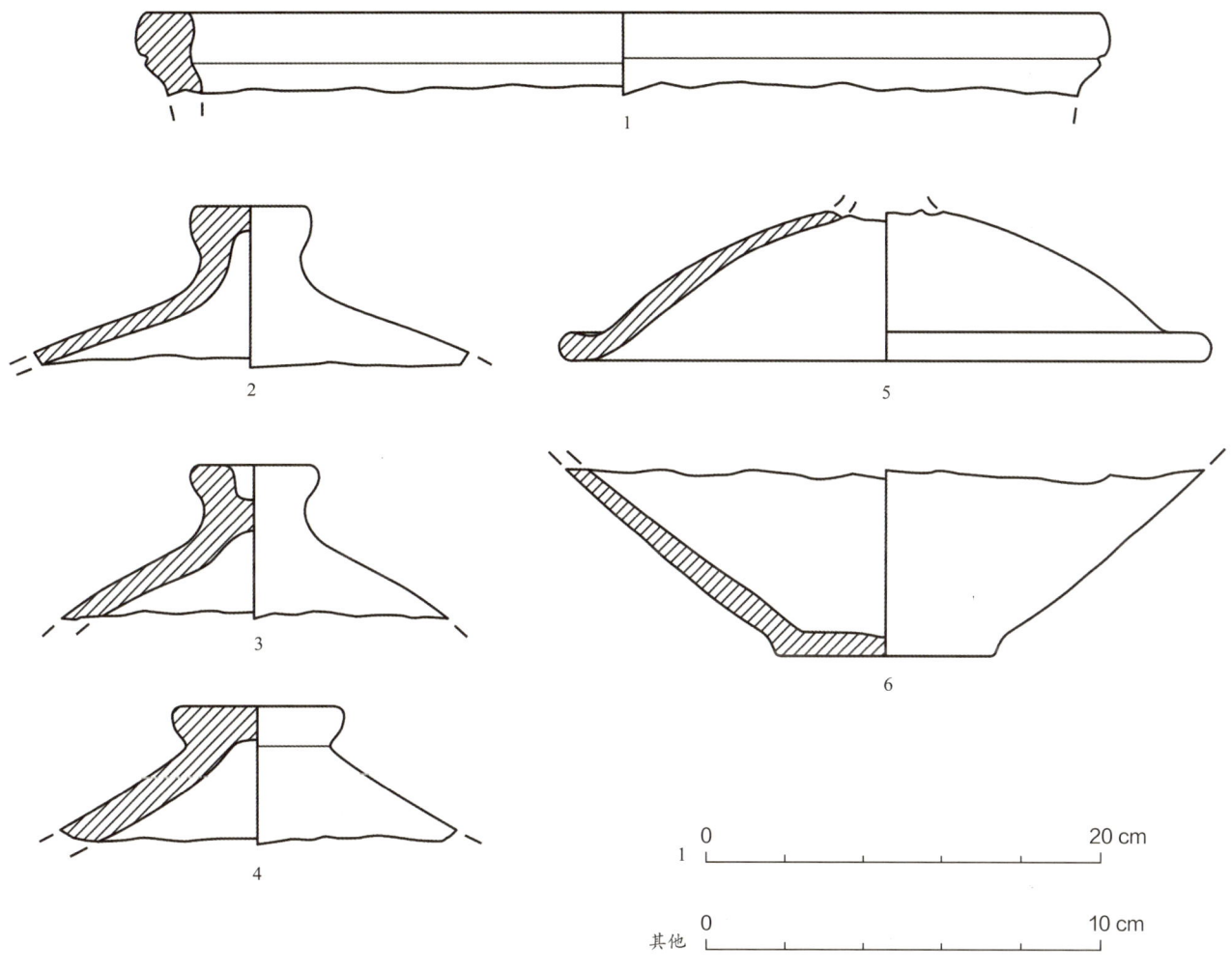

图 4-42 UnitL10GridE5-F6，UnitI10GridG9-I11、G2、G3、G4、G5⑥层出土陶器
Fig. 4-42 The unearthed potteries of Layer 6 from UnitL10GridE5-F6, UnitI10GridG9-I11, G2, G3, G4, G5

部残断，柄部有一道凸弦纹，底座有圈状凸棱，圈足内有多道弦纹。底径 15.8 厘米、残高 9.4 厘米（图 4-43，2；彩版 4-16，3）。

UnitI10GridG9-I11、G2、G3、G4、G5，UnitL10GridE5-F6，UnitL8GridF5-G5⑥层出土陶器：

标本 L10E5-F6⑥：8，灯座，红陶，底面饰两圈凸棱，器形不明。底径 29 厘米、残高 2.4 厘米（图 4-44，1）。

标本 L8F5-G5⑥：21，灯柄，红陶，磨光，施红彩，上下部残断，柄部有两组凹弦纹，长径 7.2 厘米、残高 21.9 厘米（图 4-44，2；彩版 4-17，5）。

标本 L8F5-G5⑥：22，灯柄，红陶，上下部残断，上部有圈状凸棱，柄部有两组凹弦纹，残高 15.8 厘米（图 4-44，3；彩版 4-17，6）。

标本 I10G9-I11、G2、G3、G4、G5⑥：17，灯盏，红陶，敛口，尖圆唇，斜腹，平底。口径 9.6 厘米、底径 4.8 厘米、高 2.2 厘米（图 4-44，4）。

265

标本 I10G9–I11、G2、G3、G4、G5⑥：18，灯柄，灰陶，上下部残断，上部有圈状凸棱，残高 4 厘米（图 4-44，5）。

标本 I10G9–I11、G2、G3、G4、G5⑥：19，灯柄，红陶，上下部残断，柄中部有道凸棱，圈足部有多道弦纹，残高 5 厘米（图 4-44，6）。

八、⑦层陶器

均为夹细砂泥质陶，以红陶为主，但黑陶所占比重也较大的，部分陶色较浅，近似于灰陶。器类以釜、罐、壶、钵为主，器形制作显得更为规范，其中 A 型釜及罐类的折肩、折腹风格较为流行。素面为主，纹饰主要有方格纹、凹弦纹、叶脉纹、条状纹、交叉纹、剔点纹、太阳纹等（表 10）。

标本介绍

UnitI10GridG9–I11、G2、G3、G4、G5，UnitI11GridG3 ⑦层出土陶器：

标本 I10G9–I11、G2、G3、G4、G5⑦：5，Aa 型釜，黑陶，圆唇，口沿内施多道弦纹，肩部饰一圈刻划纹，折肩处有道凸棱，腹部饰方格纹，圜底残。口径 23 厘米、残高 6.4 厘米（图 4-45，1）。

标本 I11G3⑦：34，Aa 型釜，红陶，施红衣，圆唇，盘口，束颈，圆肩，弧腹内收，圜底，肩部有两道弦纹，腹部饰方格纹，底部有烟炱痕迹。口径 21.2 厘米、腹径 21.4 厘米、高 8.2 厘米（图 4-45，2；彩版 4-18，1）。

标本 I11G3⑦：49，Aa 型釜，黑陶，施黑衣磨光，圆唇，盘口，束颈，折肩，弧腹内收，圜底残，折肩处有道凸棱，肩部有多道弦纹，腹部饰方格纹，底部有烟炱痕迹。口径 20.8 厘米、腹径 22.8 厘米、残高 7.9 厘米（图 4-45，3；彩版 4-18，2）。

UnitI10GridG9–I11、G2、G3、G4、G5⑦层出土陶器：

标本 I10G9–I11、G2、G3、G4、G5⑦：1，Aa 型釜，黑陶，圆唇，圆肩，斜腹，口沿内饰两道弦纹，肩部饰一道弦纹，腹部饰方格纹，圜底残。口径 20 厘米、残高 5.9 厘米（图 4-46，1）。

标本 I10G9vI11、G2、G3、G4、G5⑦：2，Aa 型釜，黑陶，圆唇，折肩，斜腹，口沿内饰一道弦纹，肩部饰多道弦纹，腹部饰方格纹，圜底残。口径 22 厘米、残高 5.4 厘米（图 4-46，2）。

标本 I10G9–I11、G2、G3、G4、G5⑦：3，Aa 型釜，黑陶，圆唇，溜肩，斜腹，肩部饰多道弦纹，腹部饰方格纹，圜底残。口径 23.6 厘米、残高 6 厘米（图 4-46，3）。

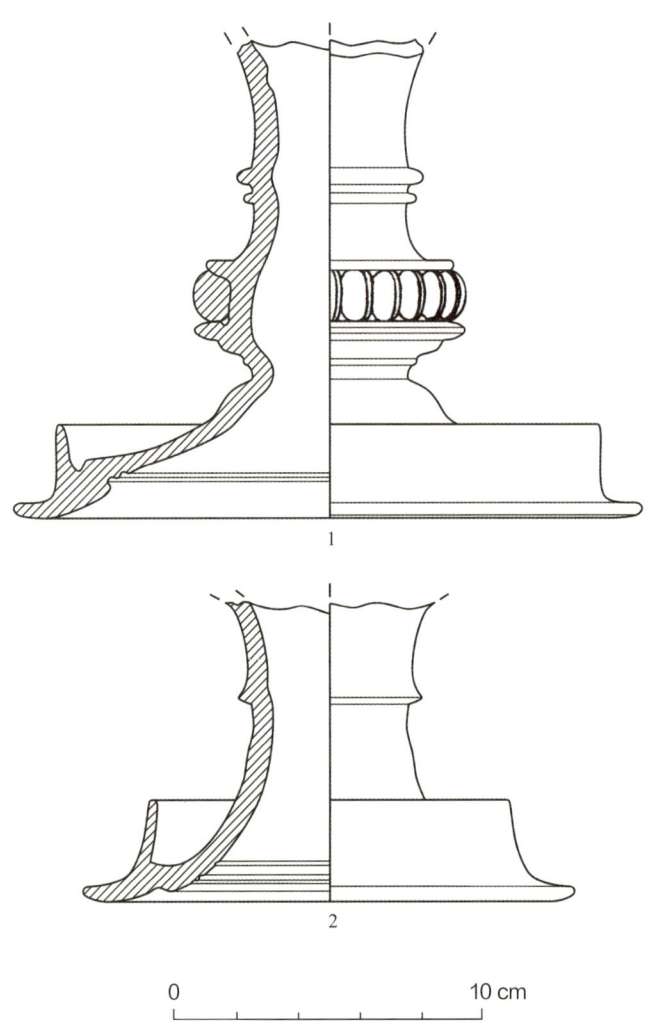

图 4-43　UnitL10GridE6，UnitL8GridF5-G5⑥层出土陶器
Fig. 4-43　The unearthed potteries of Layer 6 from UnitL10GridE6, UnitL8GridF5-G5

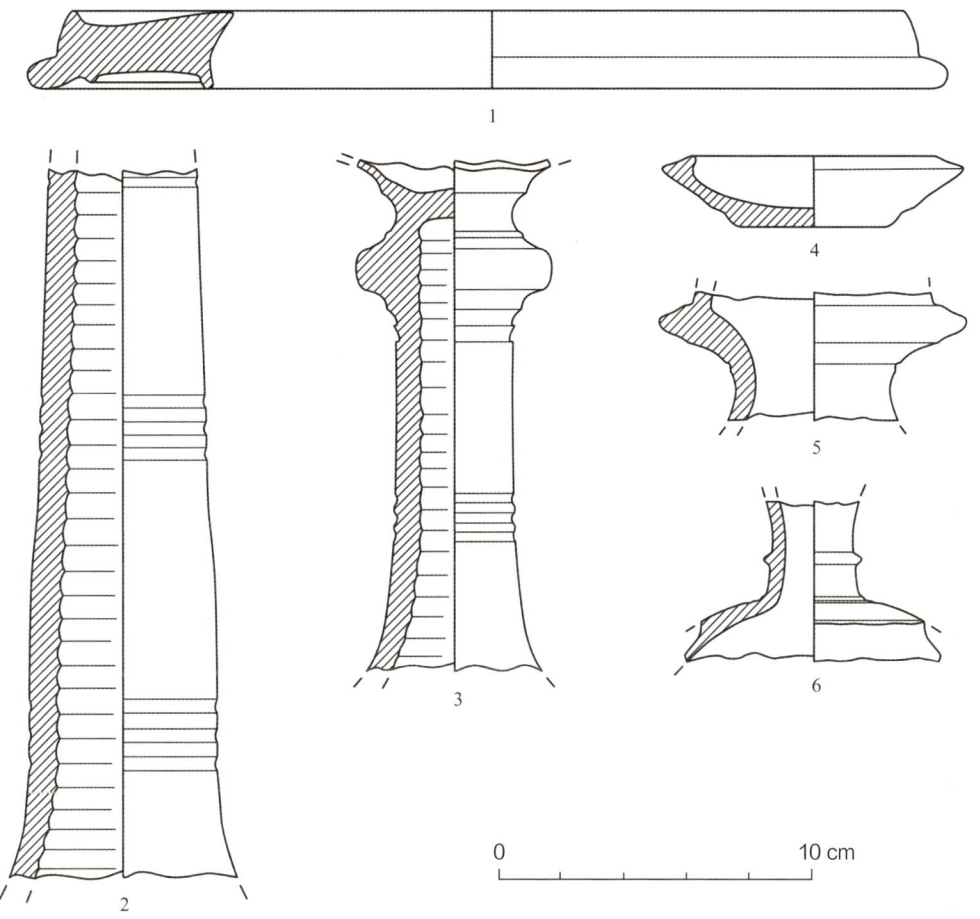

图 4-44　UnitI10GridG9-I11、G2、G3、G4、G5，UnitL10GridE5-F6，UnitL8GridF5-G5 ⑥层出土陶器
Fig. 4-44　The unearthed potteries of Layer 6 from UnitI10GridG9-I11, G2, G3, G4, G5, UnitL10GridE5-F6, UnitL8GridF5-G5

标本 I10G9-I11、G2、G3、G4、G5 ⑦：4，Aa 型釜，红陶，圆唇，敞口外翻，圆肩，斜腹，肩部饰两道弦纹，腹部饰方格纹，圜底残。口径 20 厘米、残高 4.7 厘米（图 4-46，4）。

UnitI10GridG9-I11、G2、G3、G4、G5 ⑦层出土陶器：

标本 I10G9-I11、G2、G3、G4、G5 ⑦：7，A 型罐，黑陶，直口外敞，圆唇，束颈，颈下残，沿下饰一道凸棱。口径 19.6 厘米、残高 4.5 厘米（图 4-47，1）。

标本 I10G9-I11、G2、G3、G4、G5 ⑦：8，A 型罐，红陶，敞口外侈，圆唇，束颈，颈下残，沿下饰一道凸棱。口径 15.4 厘米、残高 5 厘米（图 4-47，2）。

标本 I10G9-I11、G2、G3、G4、G5 ⑥：9，B 型罐，红陶，敞口微敛，圆唇，束颈，肩下残，肩部饰多道弦纹，沿下饰一道凸棱。口径 14.2 厘米、残高 4.8 厘米（图 4-47，3）。

标本 I10G9-I11、G2、G3、G4、G5 ⑥：10，B 型罐，灰陶，敞口，圆唇，束颈，广肩，肩下残，沿下饰一道凸棱。口径 17 厘米、残高 4.8 厘米（图 4-47，4）。

标本 I10G9-I11、G2、G3、G4、G5 ⑥：13，D 型罐，黑陶，侈口，圆唇，束颈，肩下残，肩部饰多道剔刺纹。口径 25.4 厘米、残高 6.8 厘米（图 4-47，5）。

表10　UnitI10GridG9，UnitI11GridG2、G3、G4、G5 ⑦层陶器统计表

陶色 纹饰	红	黑	备注
素面	4778	1860	
方格	1064	1772	
凹弦	585	384	
交叉	36	80	
条状	46	50	
叶脉	18	16	
太阳	9	1	
剔点	27		
器类（数量）	Aa型釜120，Ab型釜24，Ac型釜3，A型罐11，B型罐29，C型罐10，A型壶7，B型壶10，C型壶2，小壶1，钵119，灯座6，灯托18，器盖10	Aa型釜18，A型罐27，B型罐11，C型罐6，小罐2，A型壶6，B型壶1，C型壶1，带嘴壶1，钵4，缸2，灯座2，灯柄6，器盖6	

标本I10G9–I11、G2、G3、G4、G5 ⑥：14，罐，黑陶，侈口，圆唇，束颈，广肩，肩下残，肩饰一道凸棱。口径8.2厘米、残高3.4厘米（图4-47，6）。

UnitI10GridG9–I11、G2、G3、G4、G5 ⑦层出土陶器：

标本I10G9–I11、G2、G3、G4、G5 ⑦：6，Ac型釜，黑陶，敛口，尖圆唇，斜肩，肩下残，沿下饰一道凹弦纹。口径28.8厘米、残高3.2厘米（图4-48，1）。

标本I10G9–I11、G2、G3、G4、G5 ⑦：11，C型罐，黑陶，侈口，圆唇，束颈，颈下残，素面。口径34厘米、残高3.4厘米（图4-48，2）。

标本I10G9–I11、G2、G3、G4、G5 ⑦：12，D型罐，黑陶，敞口，圆唇，束颈，颈下残，沿内外饰多道弦纹。口径36厘米、残高5.2厘米（图4-48，3）。

标本I10G9–I11、G2、G3、G4、G5 ⑦：20，缸，黑陶，敞口微敛，沿外翻，束颈，颈下残，沿内饰一道弦纹，肩部有多道弦纹。口径60厘米、残高12厘米（图4-48，4）。

UnitI10GridG9–I11、G2、G3、G4、G5 ⑦层出土陶器：

标本I10G9–I11、G2、G3、G4、G5 ⑦：15，C型壶，红陶，喇叭口，圆唇，沿下残。口径23厘米、残高2.6厘米（图4-49，1）。

标本I10G9–I11、G2、G3、G4、G5 ⑦：16，C型壶，红陶，喇叭口，圆唇，折沿，沿下残。口径14.4厘米、残高2.6厘米（图4-49，2）。

标本I10G9–I11、G2、G3、G4、G5 ⑦：17，C型壶，灰陶，喇叭口，圆唇，沿外翻，沿下残。口径17厘米、残高3.2厘米（图4-49，3）。

标本I10G9–I11、G2、G3、G4、G5 ⑦：18，A型壶，红陶，敞口，圆唇，沿下饰一道凸棱，颈下残。口径19厘米、残高6.5厘米（图4-49，4）。

标本I10G9–I11、G2、G3、G4、G5 ⑦：35，A型壶，红陶，施红衣，敞口，方唇，沿外翻，沿内外饰多道弦纹，颈下残。口径18厘米、残高9厘米（图4-49，5）。

标本I10G9–I11、G2、G3、G4、G5 ⑦：19，带嘴壶，黑陶，直口外撇，肩部一侧有锥状壶嘴，弧腹，小平底，肩部腹部饰多道弦纹。口径7.2厘米、腹径11.2厘米、高9.2厘米（图4-49，6；彩版4-18，3）。

标本I10G9–I11、G2、G3、G4、G5 ⑦：36，小壶，红陶，圆唇，沿面较平，束颈，溜肩，肩腹部转折明显，小平底，肩部饰多道弦纹。口径7.8厘米、底径5厘米、高10.2厘米（图4-49，7；彩版4-18，4）。

UnitI10GridG9–I11、G2、G3、G4、G5 ⑦层出土陶器：

标本 I10G9–I11、G2、G3、G4、G5 ⑦：48，钵，红陶，圆唇，敞口，斜直腹，平底，内壁见多道弦纹。口径 18 厘米、底径 5.8 厘米、高 5.4 厘米（图 4-50，1；彩版 4-18，5）。

标本 I10G9–I11、G2、G3、G4、G5 ⑦：21，钵，红陶，圆唇，敞口，斜直腹，底残，内壁见多道弦纹。口径 16.4 厘米、残高 5.4 厘米（图 4-50，2）。

标本 I10G9–I11、G2、G3、G4、G5 ⑦：22，钵，红陶，圆唇，敞口，斜直腹，平底，内壁见多道弦纹。口径 19.8 厘米、高 5.8 厘米（图 4-50，3）。

标本 I10G9–I11、G2、G3、G4、G5 ⑦：23，钵，红陶，斜直腹，底残。底径 7.6 厘米、残高 2.8 厘米（图 4-50，4）。

UnitI10GridG9–I11、G2、G3、G4、G5 ⑦层出土陶器：

标本 I10G9–I11、G2、G3、G4、G5 ⑦：24，器盖，灰陶，圆形纽，盖身残，内壁见多道弦纹。纽径 4.2 厘米、残高 4.4 厘米（图 4-51，1）。

标本 I10G9–I11、G2、G3、G4、G5 ⑦：25，

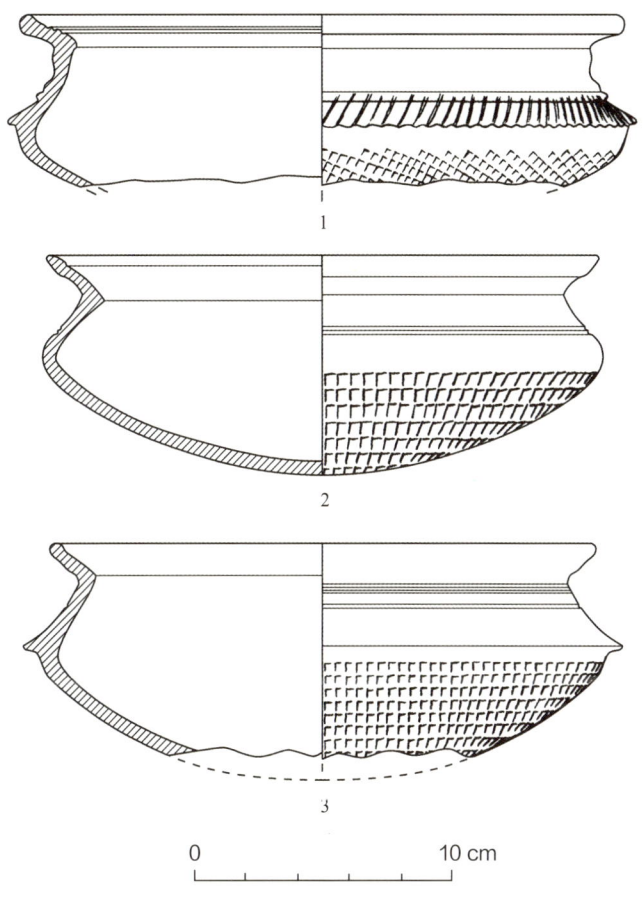

图 4-45　UnitI10GridG9-I11、G2、G3、G4、G5，UnitI11Grid G3 ⑦层出土陶器

Fig. 4-45　The unearthed potteries of Layer 7 from UnitI10GridG9-I11, G2, G3, G4, G5, UnitI11GridG3

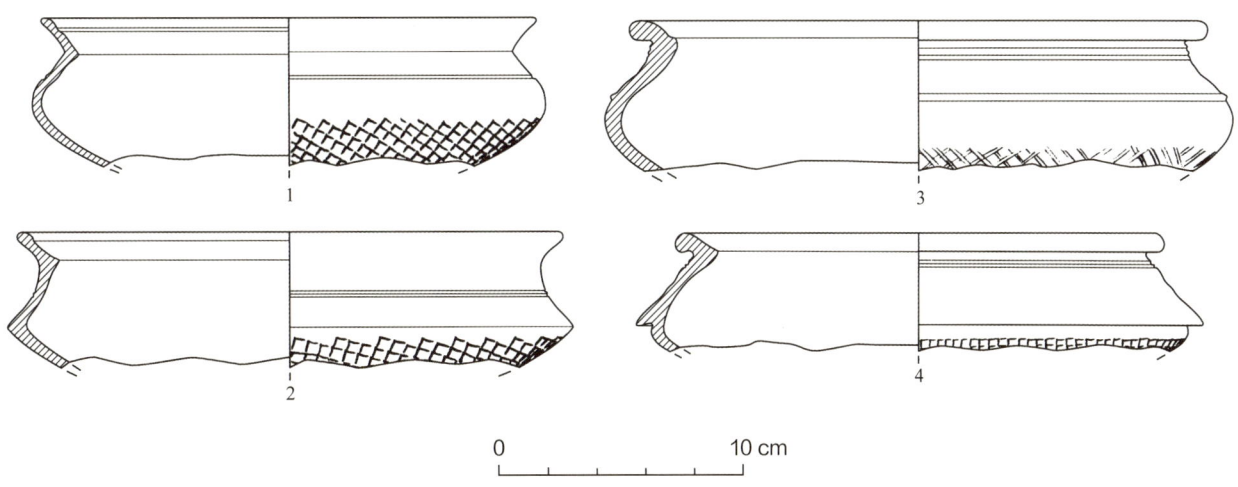

图 4-46　UnitI10GridG9-I11、G2、G3、G4、G5 ⑦层出土陶器

Fig. 4-46　The unearthed potteries of Layer 7 from UnitI10GridG9-I11, G2, G3, G4, G5

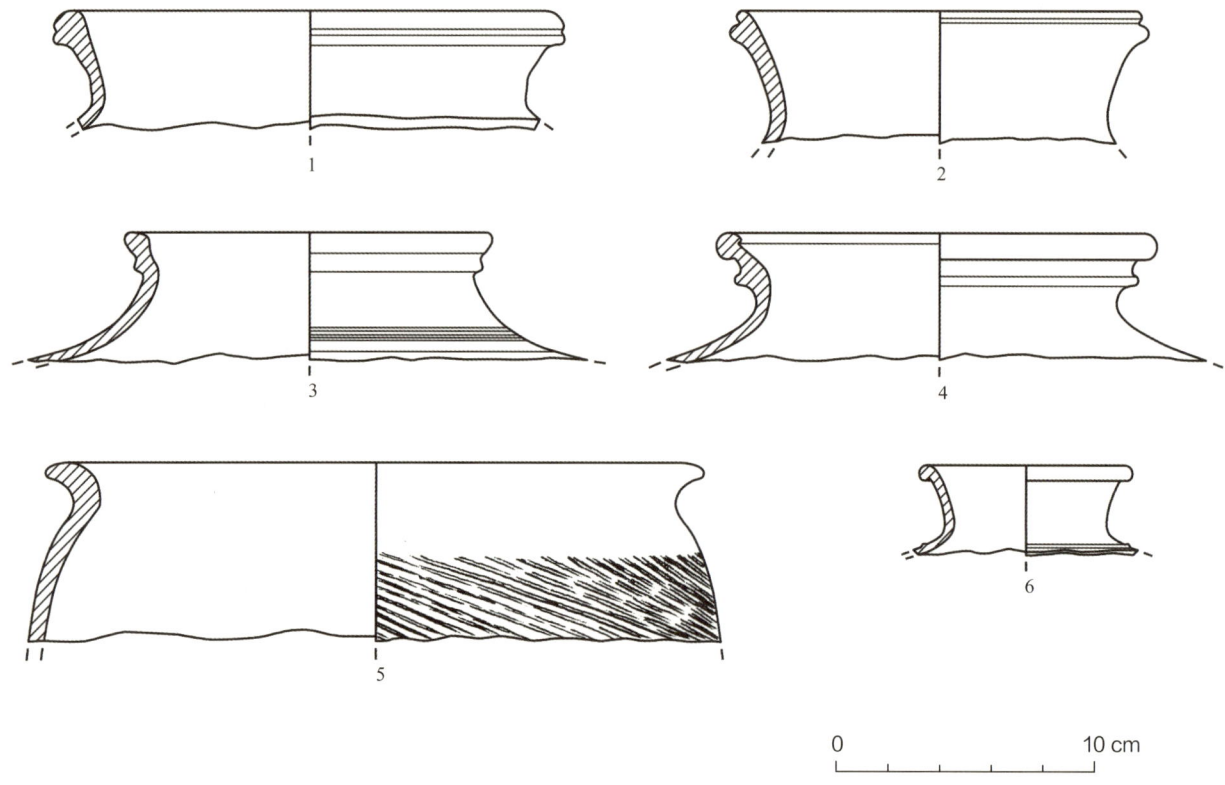

图 4-47 UnitI10GridG9–I11、G2、G3、G4、G5 ⑦层出土陶器
Fig. 4-47 The unearthed potteries of Layer 7 from UnitI10GridG9-I11, G2, G3, G4, G5

器盖，黄陶，圆形纽，器盖呈子母口。盖径 12 厘米、纽径 4.4 厘米、高 3.7 厘米（图 4-51，2；彩版 4-18，6）。

标本 I10G9–I11、G2、G3、G4、G5 ⑦：26，器盖，黑陶，圆形纽，顶部内凹，盖身残。纽径 3.2 厘米、残高 3.4 厘米（图 4-51，3）。

标本 I10G9–I11、G2、G3、G4、G5 ⑦：27，器盖，黑陶，球形纽，盖身残。残高 2 厘米（图 4-51，4）。

标本 I10G9–I11、G2、G3、G4、G5 ⑦：37，器盖，黑陶，圆形纽，顶部内凹，器盖呈覆斗状，内壁见多道斜线纹，接近沿部有一凹槽。盖径 19.2 厘米、纽径 3.4 厘米、高 5.6 厘米（图 4-51，5；彩版 4-19，1）。

UnitI10GridG9–I11、G2、G3、G4、G5 ⑦层出土陶器：

标本 I10G9–I11、G2、G3、G4、G5 ⑦：39，灯，红陶，灯盏敛口，尖圆唇，沿下饰一道凸棱，平底，口沿部有一处灯捻烧痕，柄部中空，下部残断，柄部有一组凹弦纹，制作精美。口径 7.6 厘米、残高 8.4 厘米（图 4-52，1；彩版 4-19，2）。

标本 I10G9–I11、G2、G3、G4、G5 ⑦：30，灯柄，红陶，柄部中空，上下部残断，残高 5 厘米（图 4-52，2）。

标本 I10G9–I11、G2、G3、G4、G5 ⑦：31，灯座，红陶，底面饰一圈凸棱，器形不明。底径 22 厘米、残高 2.8 厘米（图 4-52，3）。

标本 I10G9–I11、G2、G3、G4、G5 ⑦：40，灯盏，红陶，敛口，尖圆唇，子母口，浅平底，口沿部有一处灯捻烧痕。口径 8.3 厘米、高 1.4

厘米（图 4-52，4；彩版 4-19，3；彩版 4-20，1）。

标本 I10G9-I11、G2、G3、G4、G5⑦：41，灯盏，灰陶，敛口，尖圆唇，浅平底，口沿灯捻处有一按痕，外侧饰一圈花边形凸棱，口沿有一处烧痕。口径 8.5 厘米、高 1.6 厘米（图 4-52，5；彩版 4-19，4；彩版 4-20，2、3）。

标本 I10G9-I11、G2、G3、G4、G5⑦：28，灯盏，红陶，子母口，略残，平底。底径 6 厘米、残高 2.4 厘米（图 4-52，6）。

标本 I10G9-I11、G2、G3、G4、G5⑦：29，灯盏，灰陶，敛口，尖圆唇，子母口，浅圜底。口径 6.8 厘米、高 1.2 厘米（图 4-52，7）。

UnitI10GridG9-I11、G2、G3、G4、G5⑦层出土陶器：

标本 I10G9-I11、G2、G3、G4、G5⑦：38，器柄，红陶，末端壶嘴状，近端部饰一道凸棱，柄由上至下渐粗，实心，与器身交接处残。残长 13.8 厘米、末端直径 2 厘米（图 4-53，1；彩版 4-19，5）。

标本 I10G9-I11、G2、G3、G4、G5⑦：32，器柄，黑陶，末端壶嘴状，中间有孔，残，柄由上至下渐粗。残长 3.8 厘米（图 4-53，2）。

标本 I10G9-I11、G2、G3、G4、G5⑦：33，器柄，红陶，扁圆状，残。残长 4.5 厘米（图 4-53，3）。

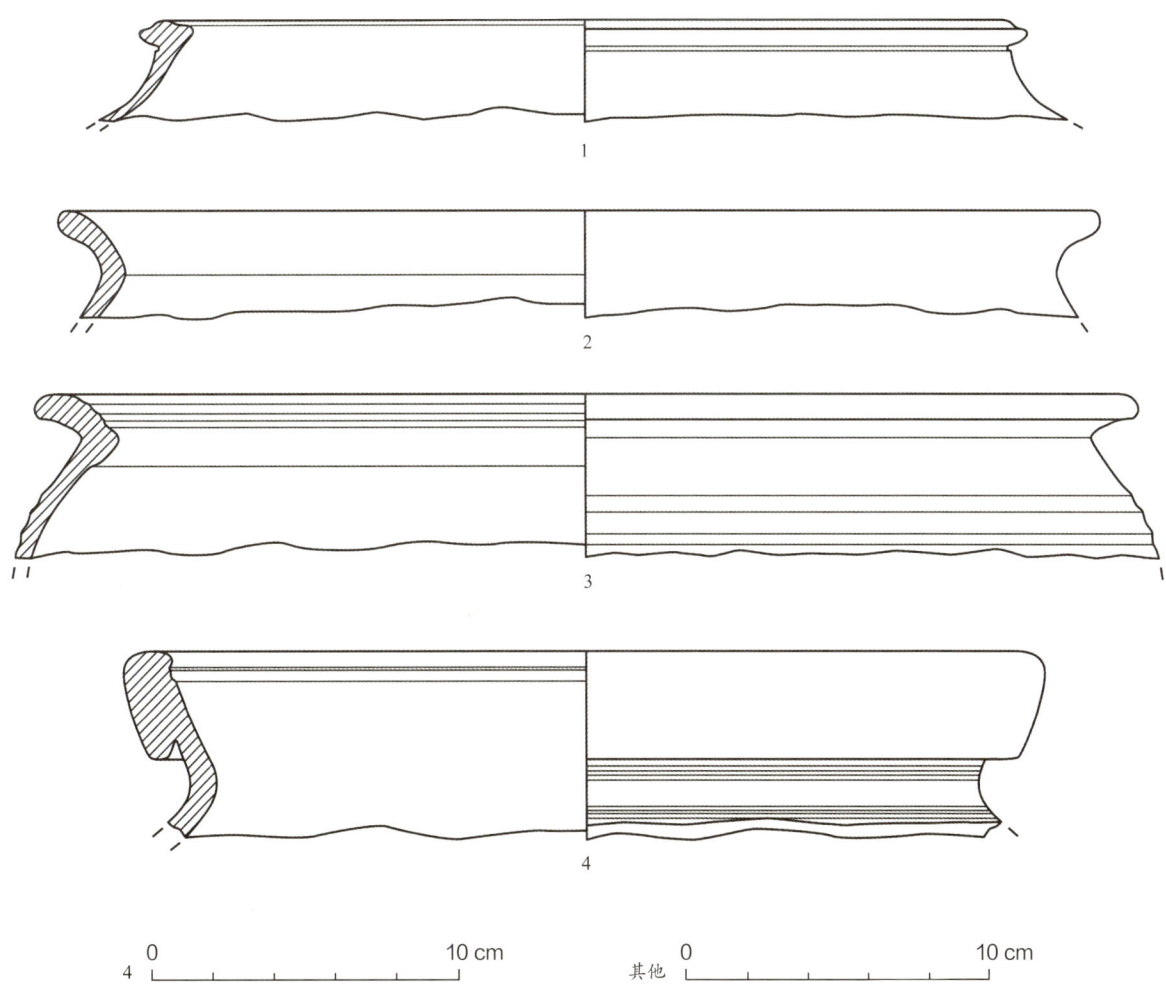

图 4-48　UnitI10GridG9-I11、G2、G3、G4、G5⑦层出土陶器
Fig. 4-48　The unearthed potteries of Layer 7 from UnitI10GridG9-I11, G2, G3, G4, G5

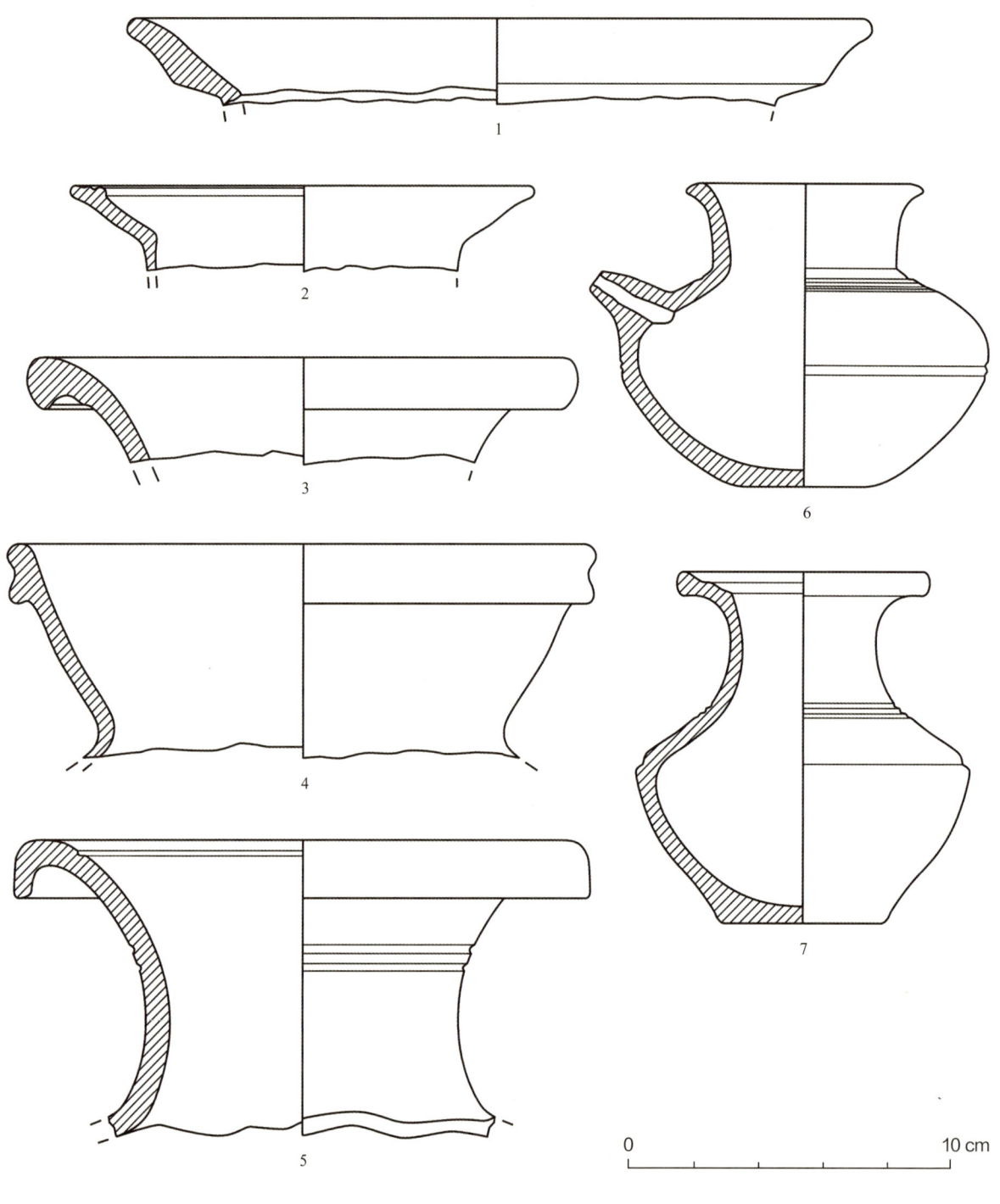

图 4-49　UnitI10GridG9-I11、G2、G3、G4、G5 ⑦层出土陶器

Fig. 4-49　The unearthed potteries of Layer 7 from UnitI10GridG9-I11, G2, G3, G4, G5

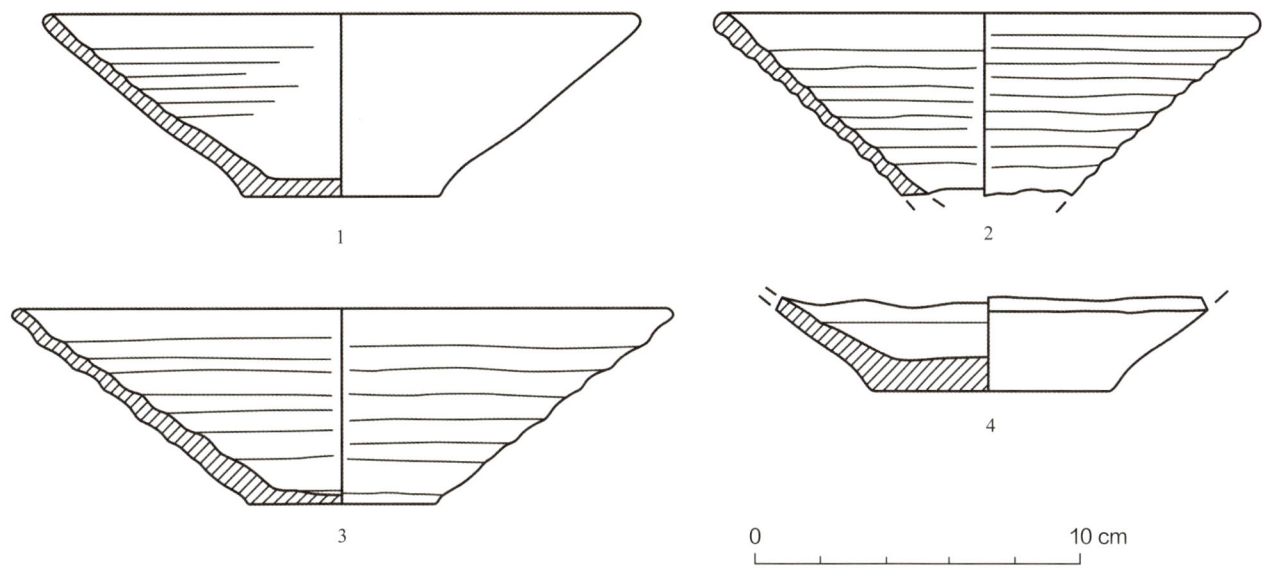

图 4-50　UnitI10GridG9-I11、G2、G3、G4、G5 ⑦层出土陶器
Fig. 4-50　The unearthed potteries of Layer 7 from UnitI10GridG9-I11, G2, G3, G4, G5

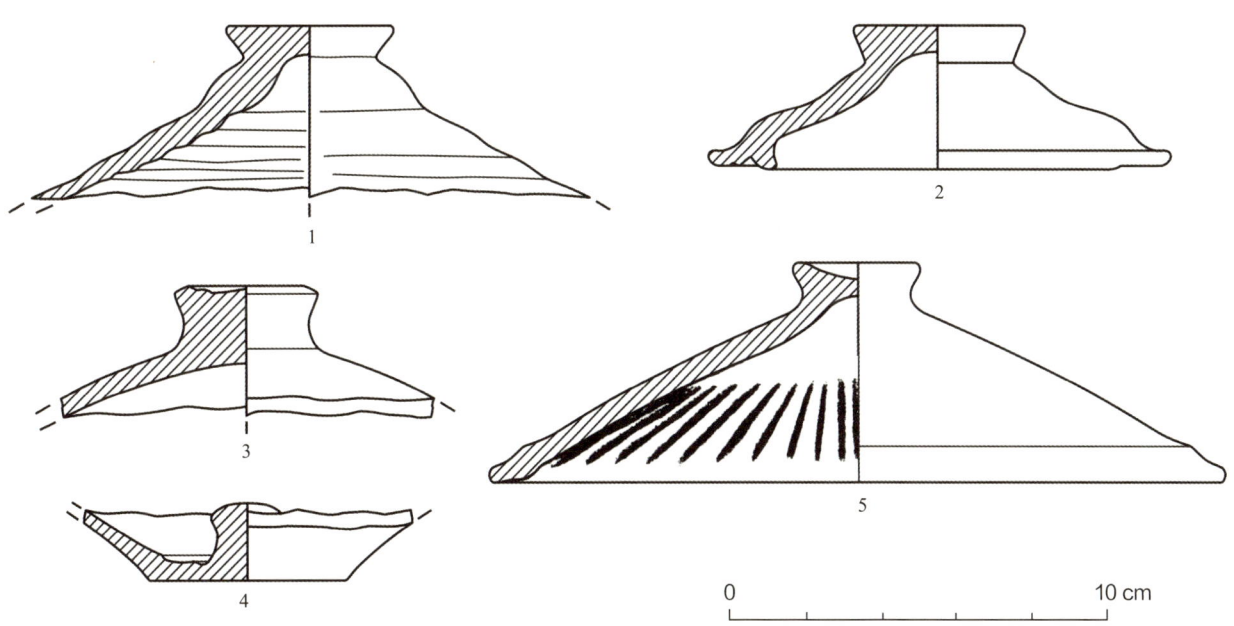

图 4-51　UnitI10GridG9-I11、G2、G3、G4、G5 ⑦层出土陶器
Fig. 4-51　The unearthed potteries of Layer 7 from UnitI10GridG9-I11, G2, G3, G4, G5

273

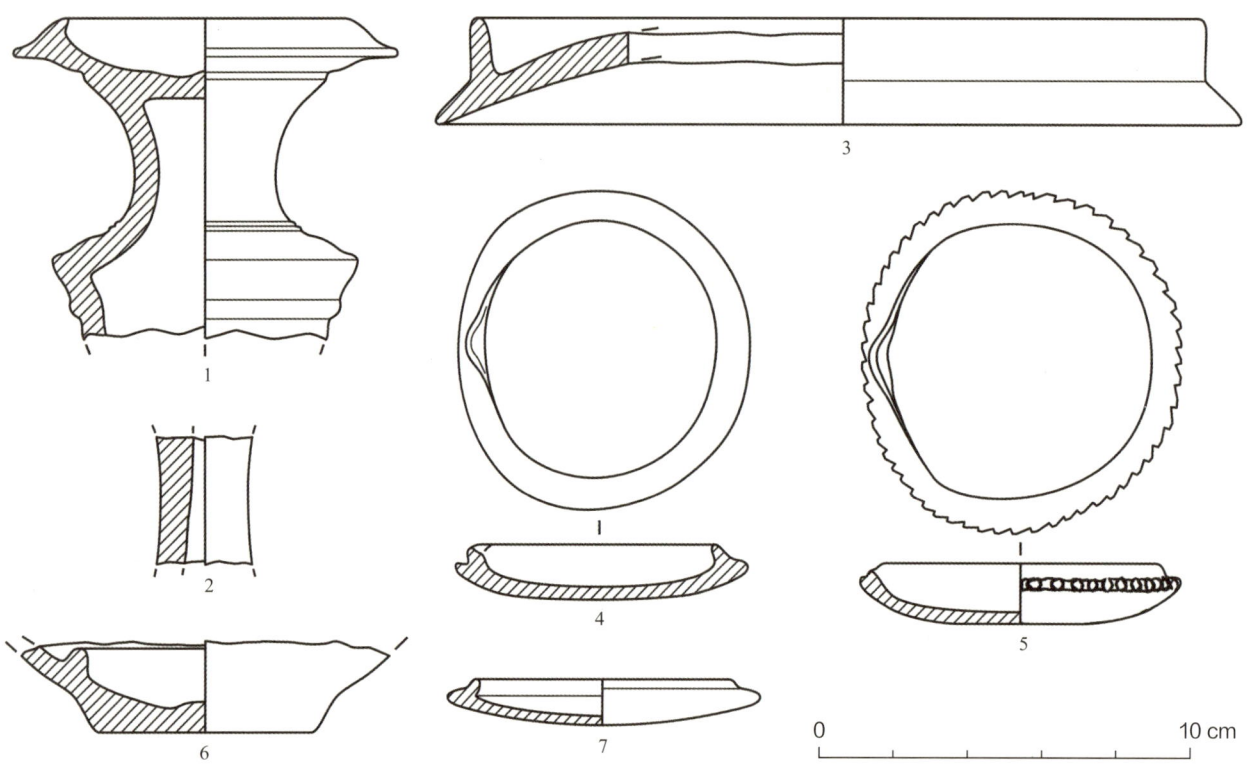

图 4-52　UnitI10GridG9-I11、G2、G3、G4、G5 ⑦层出土陶器

Fig. 4-52　The unearthed potteries of Layer 7 from UnitI10GridG9-I11, G2, G3, G4, G5

标本 I10G9-I11、G2、G3、G4、G5 ⑦:46，乳丁状纹饰，黑陶，陶器表面乳丁状纹。残长 5.3 厘米（图 4-53，4；彩版 4-20，4）。

标本 I10G9-I11、G2、G3、G4、G5 ⑦:47，太阳纹陶片，黑陶，陶器表面饰太阳纹和弦纹。残长 3.6 厘米（图 4-53，5）。

标本 I10G9-I11、G2、G3、G4、G5 ⑦:42，圆珠，黑陶，弧锥形，中部有穿孔，疑是佛珠，也可能是网坠。直径 1.9—2.3 厘米（图 4-53，6）。

标本 I10G9-I11、G2、G3、G4、G5 ⑦:43，圆珠，黑陶，弧锥形，中部有穿孔，疑是佛珠，也可能是网坠。直径 1.8—2.1 厘米（图 4-53，7）。

标本 I10G9-I11、G2、G3、G4、G5 ⑦:50，帽状器，黑陶，圆锥形，尖顶，中孔，用途不明。底径 3.6 厘米、高 4.2 厘米（图 4-53，8；彩版 4-19，6）。

九、讨论

1. 陶器均为夹细砂泥质陶，但夹砂的程度因器类不同而有所区别，总的说来，炊器釜的夹砂量大于罐钵类盛器。在陶色方面，主要分为红、黑两种，但颜色的深浅各不相同，显得斑驳混杂，在统计和描述中，简化为"红色"、"黑色"两种。

2. 各种纹饰分布于陶器相对固定的位置，如方格纹一般施于釜罐壶类器的下腹部和底部；凹弦纹多见于釜罐壶类器颈肩部和灯座上；叶脉状纹多与罐肩部的凹弦纹组合出现；太阳纹主要在罐壶的肩腹部；剔刺纹多在罐类器物上；拍印条

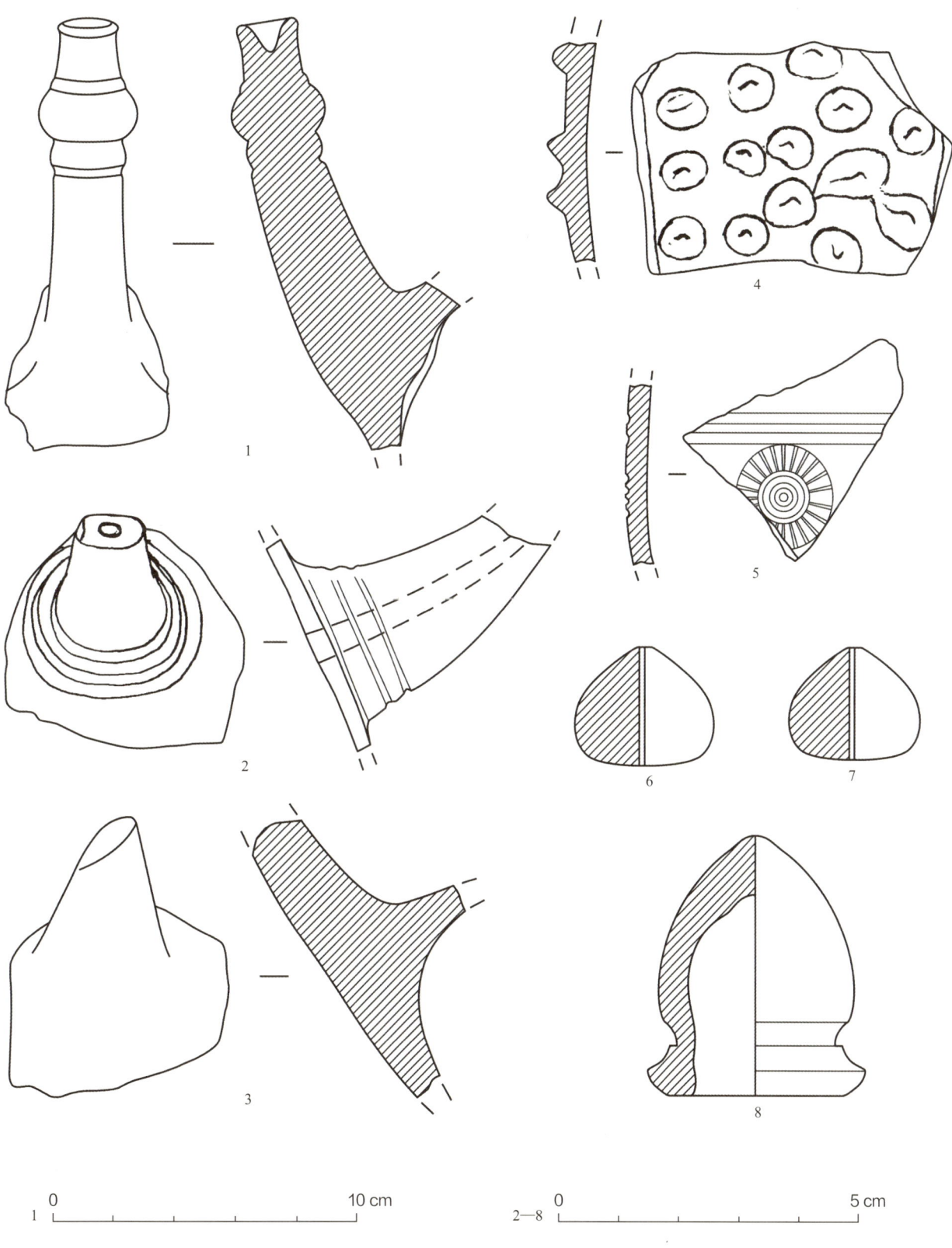

图 4-53 UnitI10GridG9-I11、G2、G3、G4、G5 ⑦层出土陶器

Fig. 4-53 The unearthed potteries of Layer 7 from UnitI10GridG9-I11, G2, G3, G4, G5

形纹多在壶类器物上；戳点纹与凹弦纹、方格纹共存于A型釜上（彩版4-21、4-22、4-23）。

3. 对出土数量较大的釜罐壶三类器物进行了分型。釜，根据器形的变化，分为三个型：A型，钵形釜；B型，罐形釜；C型，盆形釜。A型釜又根据口沿和唇部的特征，分abc三个亚型：Aa型，宽沿带棱；Ab型，平折沿，沿面略窄；Ac型，沿面更窄。罐，根据口沿的细微变化，分为五个型：A型，直口；B型，沿面内凹；C型，圆折沿；D型，侈口；E型，手制，直领。壶，根据口沿的变化，分为三型：A型，沿面外翻，方唇；B型，沿面略内凹，圆唇；C型，喇叭口。遗址中具有明确地层单位的陶器，主要集中在⑤、⑥、⑦层，由于时代接近，器形上的变化不大，难以作类型学上的排比，因此未分出式的变化。谨慎起见，本报告将出土陶器进行逐层的介绍，为进一步研究提供翔实的资料。

4. 第一期陶器，以⑤、⑥、⑦三层和瓮1、瓮2中出土的陶器为代表，在陶系、器形和纹饰上，没有太多区别，它们之间的共性是主要的，区别仅在某些细节处，如⑤层Ab型釜、B型釜、小罐的数量较多；⑦层陶器的红色较暗淡、斑驳，但这又可能与埋藏环境有关。这一时期的釜罐类陶器的折肩、折腹风格较为流行。瓮1、瓮2可代表这一时期的典型器物组合，两者出土的陶器区别不大，陶质陶色一致，只在罐、壶的口沿变化上有某些细微的区别。

第二期遗存遭到后期取砖破坏严重，至今还没有发现确切的使用时期的堆积，所以无法准确地指出第二期的典型陶器。代表第二期的陶器，可能出现在某些④层和②层的堆积中，通过整理，④层的陶器似乎可以分为两组，一组承袭早期的，另一组是新出现的因素，后者在②层中也有大量出现，以C型釜、E型罐、盂为代表，E型罐、盂为手制，显得粗糙。在陶色方面，黑色陶的比例有所减少，在器形方面，釜罐类陶器的折肩、折腹风格，逐渐从转角分明趋向更加圆弧。由于没有发现原生地层和器物组合，目前只能是比较浅表的认识。

第三期陶器以H1为代表，出土的陶器多为夹细砂陶，色彩鲜艳，薄胎，火候高，器形变大，与早期陶器有明显区别。器类以C型釜、壶为主，颈部素面，腹部有弦纹、方格纹、交叉拍印、条状印纹等，与早期区别较大，说明其年代跨度也较大，这批陶器的年代在13世纪寺庙废弃以后，具体年代，目前尚无 ^{14}C 测年数据。

5. 孟加拉国对于这个时期的陶器研究基本上还是一个空白，大型遗址的出土陶器，大多未曾进行系统的修复和整理工作，除了一般性的介绍，尚未进行系统的类型学研究。这次在纳提什瓦遗址所进行系统的陶器修复、整理和研究工作，对于建立这一时期的陶器类型学框架，无疑具有重要的意义。

The unearthed artifacts in the site are mainly daily-use potteries. Typical specimens found here are described in the following in accordance with the layers. Some necessary explanations are also given ahead for better understanding.

Firstly, some special finds from the crucial layers were collected and recorded. For example, apart from its three-dimensional coordinate, one specific given layer was divided into upper, lower or intermediate layers, so that the descriptions such as lower Layer 5, upper Layer 6, intermediate Layer 5 and Layer 6, can be found in the report. In order to keep and show the original information of the specimens, we continue to follow the original records during the studies of potteries. Therefore, such label of the layers on the specimens remains unchanged.

Secondly, some artifacts discovered in some units, such as L8, L9 and L10 in 2013; only the depths were recorded. When the study of these artifacts was conducted in 2015, we labeled them with layers under the gridding system according to their depth. For convenient purpose, the research serial numbers were used to refer to these mentioned selected objects.

Thirdly, the number of the artifacts, which were showed in the statistic tables, only represents the quantity of those already studied antiquities.

Actually, there were a large number of the artifacts unearthed in the site and so far only half of them were included into this interim report. The potteries discovered during the excavation of 2015 – 2016 will wait for future study. In this sense, limitation regarding the typological study is inevitable in our present work.

Lastly, the description on the layers of the specimens will be simplified in the following texts. For instance, the UnitL10GridE5-F6 : 11 is abbreviated to L10 E5-F6 ④ : 11.

I

The potteries unearthed from Layer 1

Layer 1 is actually a modern disturbed layer of the site, where the inclusions of different nature and age are mixed. Majority of the potteries from this are red in surface color, having silty sand fine temper and a high firing temperature. The repertory of types are commonly dominated by cooking pots, pots, jugs and bowls, among which all the cooking pots belong to type B. Most of the wares are plain, while those with the decorations including trellis pattern, concave string, strip design and leaf vein, etc. (Table 2).

Table 2 Statistic table of the potteries of Layer 1 in Unit I10, I11, J10 and J11

color decoration	red	black
plain	70	46
trellis pattern	12	12
concave string	3	2
strip design	8	—
leaf vein	3	—
types (quantity)	B-type cooking pot (6), pot (21), jug (2), bowl (1)	pot (8), jug (2), lid (1)

The potteries unearthed from Layer 2

Layer 2 was formed by backfill soils after removing the bricks from the earlier constructions. Therefore, the potteries in this layer were also mixed antiquities from late and early periods. All of them are produced with fine silty sand temper, and majority of the surface are red in color. One type which has orange-red surface color and higher firing temperature, newly appeared in this layer. The repertory of types includes cooking pots, pots, jugs, bowls etc. Among them, the body of the cooking pots, pots and jugs has a relative large size. The majority of the wares are plain, and others with decorations include trellis pattern, concave string, strip design, leaf vein and star design (Table 3).

The potteries unearthed from ash pit H1

Ash pit H1, which was under Layer 2, and destroyed the pillar-plinth 1 of Pillared-hall 2, was located in the squares of UnitI11GridJ1, J2 and UnitJ11GridA1, A2. It was the pit that was dug for the recovery of burnt bricks by later residents. Many potteries that are characterized by fine fabric, bright color, thin body and high firing temperature were found in this pit. The size of the potteries was larger than the earlier ones, displaying a significant difference. The dominating types were C-type cooking pots (basin-like cooking pot) and jugs. The wares were commonly plain on their necks, but the abodes were usually decorated with trellis pattern, concave string, cross patting design and strip pattern, etc.

The potteries unearthed from Layer 4

Layer 4 was mainly formed by the soils carried from outside the site for the basement of the second period's constructions. In addition, some previous structures were also demolished and leveled for this function. Therefore, the inclusions in this layer were also mixed with artifacts from different periods. All the unearthed potteries

Table 3 Statistic table of the potteries of Layer 2 in Unit I10, I11, J10 and J11

color decoration	red	black
plain	978	739
trellis pattern	59	118
concave string	18	38
strip design	19	—
leaf vein	5	—
Star design	3	1
types (quantity)	cooking pot (27), pot (39), jug (12), bowl (7), oil lamp (2), lid (3)	pot (27), cooking pot (6), jug (10), lid (2)

Table 4 Statistic table of the potteries of Layer 3 in Unit I10, I11, J10 and J11

decoration / color	red	black
plain	1200	366
trellis pattern	118	102
concave string	18	2
cross design	3	2
Star design	17	4
types (quantity)	Aa-type cooking pot (9), Ab-type cooking pot (8), C-type cooking pot (18), A-type pot (14), B-type pot (16), C-type pot (17), D-type pot (8), A-type jug (12), C-type jug (2), bowl (80), lamp stand (1), oil lamp (3), lid (5)	Aa-type cooking pot (21), A-type pot (1), C-type pot (2), A-type jug (2), B-type jug (8), lid (6), lamp stand (2), big jar (1)

are chiefly sandy fabric, and the proportion of the red potteries is larger than that of their black counterparts. The repertory of types was occupied by cooking pots, jugs, pots and bowls. In terms of the style of these potteries, the parts of their shoulder and belly are gradually becoming more circular. The number of C-type jugs has conspicuously increased. Majority of the wares are plain, and others with decorations include trellis pattern, concave string, strip design and cross design (Table 4).

The potteries unearthed from Layer 5

The red potteries are mostly orange in color, a small percentage (less than 10%) are pure red or reddish, only about 30 pieces were coated with red slip, and the yellow slip was individually coated on the surface of the rims of the pots and jugs. The black potteries are mainly in dark brown color, while gray brown color accounted for less than half of the amount. The main types consisted of cooking pots, pots, jugs, and bowls, which are mainly decorated with the trellis pattern, concave string, punched pattern, stripe design, etc (Table 5-7).

The potteries unearthed from Urn 1 and Urn 2

Current observation shows that the Temple 1 has two construction phases. Although only two urns, which are under the Layer 5, were discovered. So far, there are probably four big urns separately distributed in the four corners outside the Temple 1 during the second phase. The Urn 1 is located in UnitL10GridB4, and the Urn 2 is located in UnitL9GridB9. They were half buried in the ground when found, and lots of potteries were placed inside them. It is speculated that these urns were put under the eaves of the temple, functioning for daily-use during their existing time. The Urn 1 was preserved in a good condition, and the wares were all clay potteries with fine sand, and dominated by red (slightly yellow and orange) and dark brown color. Most of them are plain, except some decorated with trellis pattern, string pattern, sun design, and few with black painting. The types of the unearthed potteries include 15 pieces of Aa-type cooking pots, 14 pieces of pots with bulging belly, 5 pieces of pots with angular shoulder, 3 pieces of jugs, 49 pieces of bowls, and some

Table 5　Statistic table of the potteries of Layer 5 in UnitK10GridI2-I6 – J2-J6

color / decoration	red	black
plain	535	189
trellis pattern	80	73
concave string	29	51
cross design	1	–
strip design	1	–
sun design	1	–
incised design	1	8
square dot	–	1
types (quantity)	Aa-type cooking pot (3), Ab-type cooking pot (3), A-type jug (1), C-type jug (3), A-type pot (3), B-type pot (4), bowl (9), oil lamp (2), lamp handle (1)	Aa-type cooking pot (31), Ab-type cooking pot (1), A-type jug (4), A-type pot (1), B-type pot (3), lid (5)

Table 6　Statistic table of the potteries of lower Layer 5 in UnitL8GridG5-F5

color / decoration	red	black
plain	2705	539
trellis pattern	271	608
concave string	55	272
cross design	1	–
strip design	27	3
sun design	21	–
incised design	6	3
square dot	1	53
types (quantity)	Aa-type cooking pot (27), Ab-type cooking pot (20), C-type cooking pot (2), B-type pot (24), C-type jug (1), C-type pot (14), miniature jar (7), B-type jug (10), bowl (140), oil lamp (9), lamp stand (1), lid (1), unidentified ware (1)	Aa-type cooking pot (137), C-type cooking pot (1), A-type jug (1), B-type jug (3), C-type jug (5), B-type pot (3), C-type pot (1), miniature jar (7), bowl (7), lid (13), oil lamp (4), round disc (1)

Table 7 Statistic table of the potteries between Layer 5 and Layer 6 in UnitL10GridA2-A3

decoration \ color	red	black
plain	979	69
trellis pattern	56	83
concave string	27	31
strip design	1	4
incised design	2	—
square dot	1	7
types (quantity)	Aa-type cooking pot (4), Ab-type cooking pot (1), C-type cooking pot (1), B-type pot (4), C-type pot (3), B-type jug (10)	Aa-type cooking pot (18), Aa-type pot (6), C-type pot (1), Aa-type jug (3)

unidentified wares. The rim of the Urn 2 is missing, but the potteries found in it are also red (slightly yellow and orange) and dark brown wares. Most of them are plain, while some are decorated with trellis pattern, string pattern and sun design. The main types include 3 pieces of Aa-type cooking pots, 5 pieces of pots with bulging belly, 2 pieces of pots with angular shoulder, 3 pieces of jugs, 13 pieces of bowls, 4 pieces of lids and 1 unidentified ware.

The potteries unearthed from Layer 6

All the unearthed wares are clay potteries with fine sand inclusion, most of which are red and a few of them are black. The majority of the red potteries are in orange, less is in brick-red, and about 10 pieces are coated with the red slip. However, the black potteries are chiefly dark brown color, and followed by grayish brown. Like other layers, the cooking pots, pots, jugs and bowls are the main types; part of them are decorated with check pattern, concave string, leaf vein pattern, strip pattern, cross-pattern etc (Table 8 and 9).

The potteries unearthed from Layer 7

All the unearthed wares are clay potteries with fine sand inclusion, mainly red and second large number of potteries are black and gray. The dominating types include cooking pots, pots, jugs and bowls, which are more standardized than other unearthed wares. The A-type cooking pots and pots are characterized by the popular style of sharp turning shoulder and belly in this period. The majority of potteries are plain, but some are decorated with check pattern, concave string, leaf vein pattern, strip pattern, cross-pattern, dot pattern and sun design (Table 10).

Discussion

1. All the unearthed earthen wares are clay potteries with fine sand inclusion, but the quantities of sand content are various among different types. In general, the proportion of sand

inclusion in cooking vessels is larger than storage wares. In terms of color, there are also variations among them, for instance, some are much darker than that of others when they all can be attributed to a specific color. In the report, however, the pottery colors are simplified and classified as two main colors, red and black.

2. The comprehensive analysis of the decoration shows that some certain potteries are regularly decorated with one kind of pattern in the fixed position. There are many examples that can be given, such as the lower belly at the bottom of the cooking pot, pot and jug. The concave string decoration is more common on the shoulder or

Table 8　Statistic table of the potteries of Layer 6 in UnitI10GridG9，UnitI11GridG2、G3、G4、G5

color / decoration	red	black
plain	1310	410
trellis pattern	137	207
concave string	43	56
cross pattern	12	6
strip pattern	23	13
leaf vein	2	5
types (quantity)	Aa-type cooking pot (8), Ab-type cooking pot (2), Ac-type cooking pot (1), A-type pot (25), B-type pot (2), C-type pot (12), A-type jug (3), B-type jug (1), bowl (74), lamp stand (3), lid (2)	Aa-type cooking pot (102), Ab-type cooking pot (1), A-type pot (3), C-type pot (3), A-type pot (2), B-type pot (4), bowl (3), lamp stand (4), lid (5)

Table 9　Statistic table of the potteries of Layer 6 in UnitL10GridE5–F6

color / decoration	red	black
plain	1130	184
trellis pattern	86	318
concave string	54	101
strip pattern	1	—
leaf vein	2	—
sun design	1	—
square dot	—	3
incised design	—	12
types (quantity)	Aa-type cooking pot (15), B-type cooking pot (1), Ac-type cooking pot (4), A-type pot (3), B-type pot (2), A-type jug (4), bowl (33)	Aa-type cooking pot (32), A-type pot (4), B-type pot (1), A-type jug (4), big jar (1), lid (4)

Table 10 Statistic table of the potteries of Layer 7 in UnitI10GridG9, UnitI11GridG2、G3、G4、G5

color decoration	red	black
plain	4778	1860
trellis pattern	1064	1772
concave string	585	384
cross pattern	36	80
strip pattern	46	50
leaf vein	18	16
sun design	9	1
square dot	27	—
types (quantity)	Aa-type cooking pot (120), Ab-type cooking pot (24), Ac-type cooking pot (3), A-type pot (11), B-type pot (29), C-type pot (10), A-type jug (7), B-type jug (10), C-type jug (2), small vase (1), bowl (119), lamp stand (6), lamp support (18), lid (10)	Aa-type cooking pot (18), A-type pot (27), B-type pot (11), C-type pot (6), small jar (2), A-type jug (6), B-type jug (1), C-type jug (1), spouted jug (1), bowl (4), big jar (2), lamp stand (2), lamp handle (6), lid (6)

neck of a cooking pot, pot or jug. The leaf vein design together with concave string pattern always appears on the shoulder of the pot. The sun design mainly appears on the shoulder and belly of a pot or jug. The incised design and impressed strip decoration mostly appear in the pots and jugs respectively. The square dot, concave string pattern and trellis pattern coexist in the A-type cooking pot (Color Plate 4-21, 4-22, 4-23).

3. Among the unearthed objects, the cooking pots, pots and jugs, are the three dominating types. According to the changes in morphology, the cooking pots are divided into three types: type A is bowl-shaped, type B is pot-shaped and type C is basin-shaped. Among them, the A-type cooking pots are again divided into three sub-types due to the characteristics of their rims and lips: Aa-type, wide rim with ridge; Ab-type, flat and narrow edge; Ac-type, the narrowest rim. Judged from some subtle changes of the rims, the pots are also divided into five types: type A has straight mouth; type B has inner concave rim; type C has a round turning rim; type D has the spreading mouth; type E is handmade and has a straight collar. The jugs are divided into three types: type A has outward open rim and square lip; type B has slightly concave rim and round lip; type C has a trumpet-like mouth. It shows that most of the potteries with precise stratigraphic context are mainly collected from the Layers 5 – 7. However, because the ages of these layers are very close, there is no obvious big difference in their shapes. So far, we don't have enough interpretation on the evolution of the unearthed potteries of the first period. But this report will be beneficial for further research by presenting the artifacts according to layers.

4. The potteries of the first period, represented by those unearthed from Layers 5 – 7 and the Urn 1 and Urn 2, mainly share similarities with the exception of some minor differences in terms of

type, shape and decoration. The observed changes are reflected in some details. For example, the number of Ab-type and B-type cooking pots and the miniature jars is much larger in the Layer 5; the red potteries in Layer 7 seem a bit dull and mottled, of which the reason is unknown, but is probably related to the depositional environment. For cooking pots and pots, the style of the abrupt turning of the shoulder and belly is more popular during the first period. The Urn 1, Urn 2 and their contained wares represent the typical assemblage of artifacts in this period. However, little difference can be observed among them, except some minor differences occurred at the rim and lip of the potteries.

Due to the serious damage by later periods, the definite daily living deposit of the second period is unidentified so far; it is thus impossible to understand the typical assemblage of this period. The potteries, which can represent the second period, are probably unearthed from Layer 4 and Layer 2. After systematical study, the potteries from Layer 4 are divided into two groups: one is inherited from the earlier stage; the other newly appears. The latter is also found in the Layer 2, which can be represented by C-type cooking pot, E-type pot. For the color of the potteries, the proportion of black is reduced, while in terms of the shape, the belly and shoulder is gradually becoming circular. Because of the above-mentioned reasons, the current conclusion is still a superficial understanding.

The potteries of the third period are represented by the ash pit H1. A large number of clay potteries with bright color, thin body and high temperature are unearthed. They are bigger in size, and significantly different from the earlier potteries. The types are dominated by C-type cooking pots and jugs. These potteries probably last for a long time, but the accurate date cannot be obtained since ^{14}C sample is not available.

5. The research on the potteries in this period is rare in Bangladesh. Most of the unearthed potteries in previous excavated sites are not systematically restored and studied. Except some simple introductions, the formal typological research is seldom conducted. The restoration, classification and analysis of the potteries at Nateshwar site are undoubtedly of great significance in establishing the chronological framework of the pottery during this period.

彩版 4-1
①、②层陶器
Color Plate 4-1
The potteries of Layer 1 and Layer 2

1. 标本L10I5-J6①：3，壶
specimen L10I5-J6 ① : 3, jug

2. 标本L10I5-J6①：2，器盖
specimen L10I5-J6 ① : 2, lid

3. 标本L10I5-J6①：1，E型罐
specimen L10I5-J6 ① : 1, E-type pot

4. 标本L10E6②：29，C型釜
specimen L10E6 ② : 29, C-type cooking pot

5. 标本L10E6②：34，C型釜
specimen L10E6 ② : 34, C-type cooking pot

6. 标本l10I3②：6，C型罐
specimen l10I3 ② : 6, C-type pot

彩版4-2
②、④层陶器

Color Plate 4-2
The potteries of Layer 2 and Layer 4

1. 标本L10②：7，C型罐

specimen L10 ② ： 7, C-type pot

2. 标本K9F10②：9，盂

specimen K9 F10 ② ： 9, pot

3. 标本I11②：2，灯盏

specimen I11 ② ： 2, oil lamp

4. 标本L10E6④：4，Aa型釜

specimen L10 E6 ④ ： 4, Aa-type cooking pot

5. 标本L10E5-FE6④：26，Aa型釜

specimen L10E5-FE6 ④ ： 26, Aa-type cooking pot

6. 标本J10I6④：1，E型罐

specimens J10 I6 ④ ： 1, E-type pot

彩版4-3
H1陶器
Color Plate 4-3
The potteries from H1

1. 标本H1：1，C型釜
specimen H1 ： 1, C-type cooking pot

2. 标本H1：5，C型壶
specimen H1 ： 5, C-type jug

彩版4-4

④层陶器

Color Plate 4-4
The potteries of Layer 4

1. 标本K10 I3④：8，小罐

specimen K10 I3 ④ ：8, miniature pot

2. 标本L10 D6④：13，小壶

specimen L10 D6 ④ ：13, miniature jug

3. 标本L10 E5-F6④：28，小壶

specimen L10 E5-F6 ④ ：28, miniature jug

4. 标本L10 E5-F6④：36，小壶

specimen L10 E5 F6 ④ ：36, miniature jug

5. 标本K10I4④：1，壶

Specimen K10I4 ④ ：1, jug

6. 标本L10 E6④：12，钵

specimen L10 E6 ④ ：12, bowl

彩版4-5
④层陶器
Color Plate 4-5
The potteries of Layer 4

1、2. 标本L10 E5-F6④：11，带柄杯
specimen L10 E5-F6 ④ ： 11, knobbed ware

3. 标本L10 F6④：5，陶饼
specimen L10 F6 ④ ： 5, pottery disc

4. 标本L10dA6、B6、C6、D6、E6④：19，灯盏
specimen L10dA6, B6, C6, D6, E6 ④ ： 19, oil lamp

5. 标本L10E5、F6④：23，灯，红陶
specimen L10E5, F6 ： 23, lamp-on-stand (red pottery)

彩版4-6

⑤层陶器

Color Plate 4-6

The potteries of Layer 5

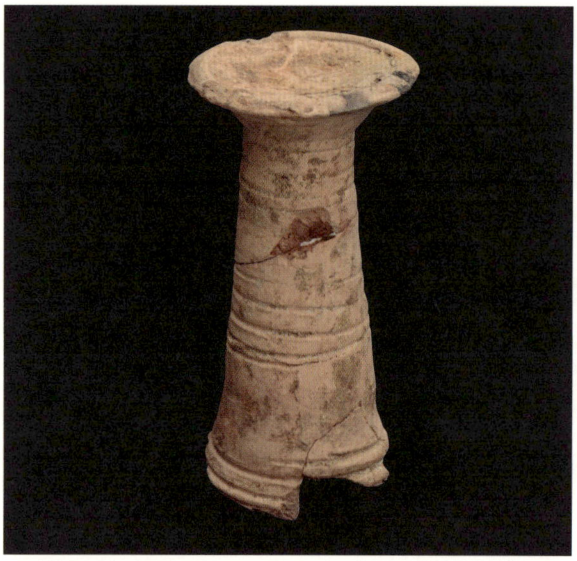

1. 标本K10I2-I6、J2-J6⑤：8，灯

specimen K10I2-I6, J2-J6 ⑤ ： 8, lamp-on-stand

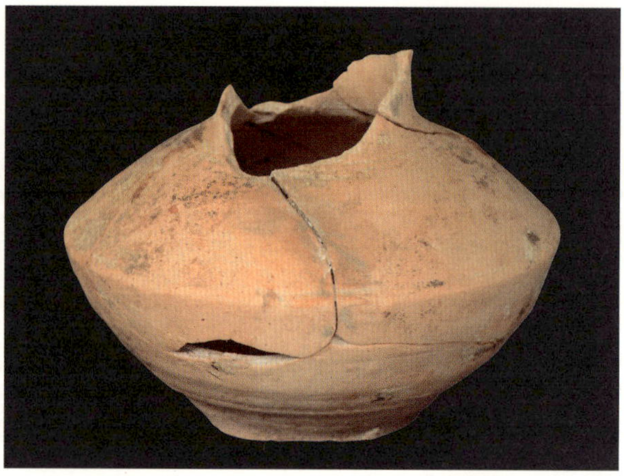

2.标本L10E5-F6⑤：14，小壶

specimen L10E5-F6 ⑤ ： 14, miniature jug

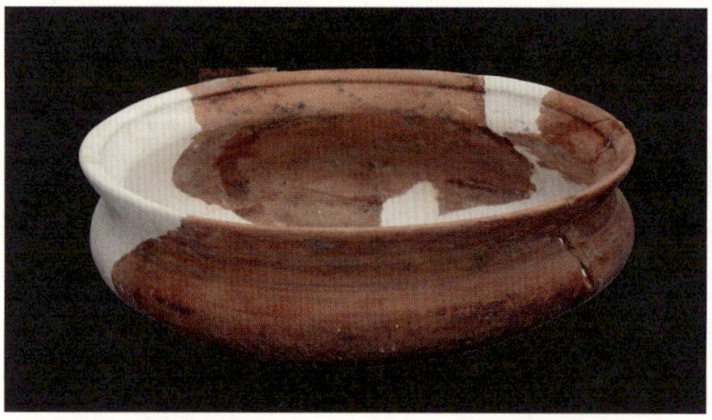

3. 标本L8G5-F5⑤下：3，Aa型釜

specimen L8G5-F5 ⑤ ： 3, Aa-type cooking pot

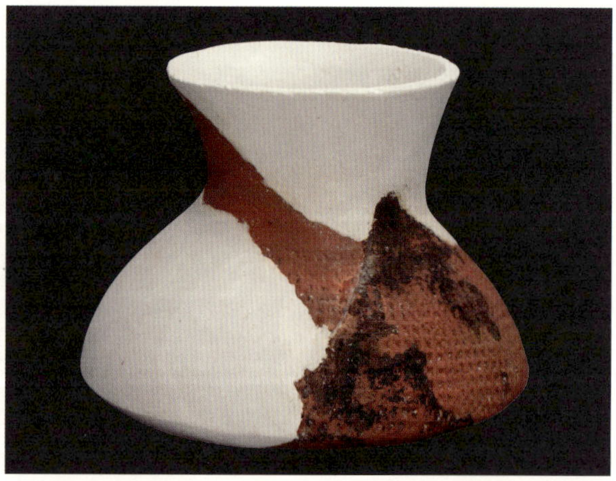

4. 标本L8G5-F5⑤下：6，B型釜

specimen L8G5-F5 ⑤ ： 3, B-type cooking pot

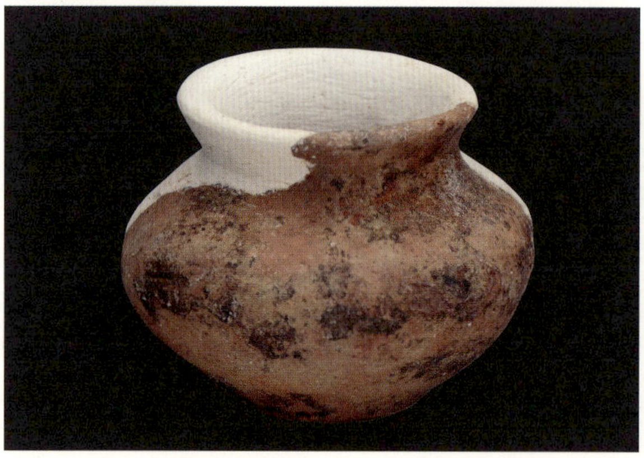

5. 标本L8G5-F5⑤下：21，小罐

specimen L8G5-F5 ⑤ ： 21, miniature pot

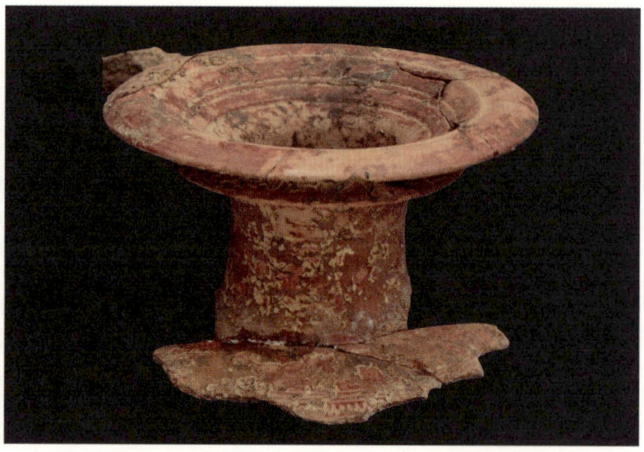

6. 标本L8G5-F5⑤下：15，C型壶

specimen L8G5-F5 ⑤ ： 15, C-type jug

彩版4-7
⑤层陶器
Color Plate 4-7
The potteries of Layer 5

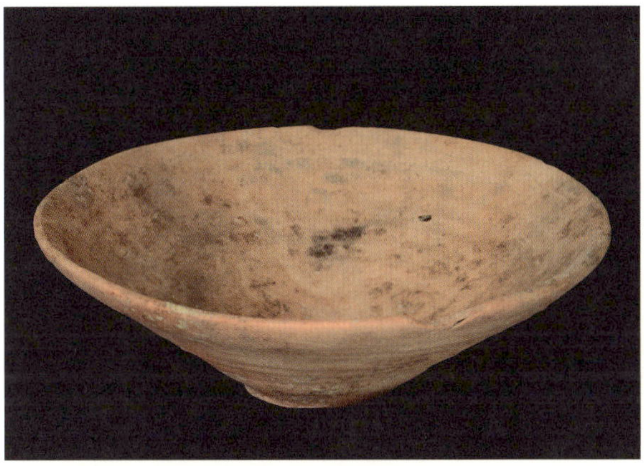

1. 标本L8G5-F5⑤下：17，钵
specimen L8G5-F5 ⑤ ： 17, bowl

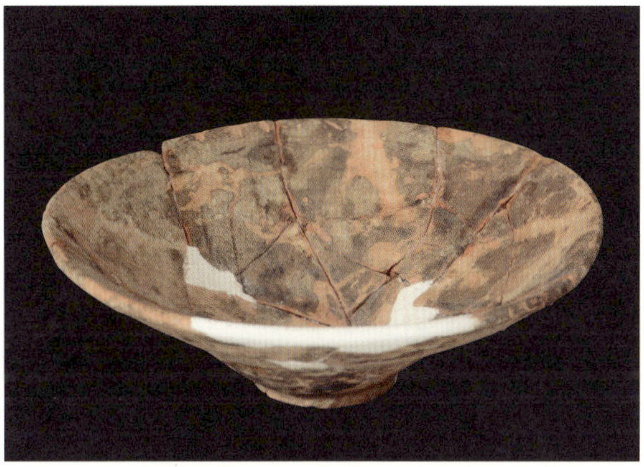

2. 标本L8G5-F5⑤下：18，钵
specimen L8G5-F5 ⑤ ： 18, bowl

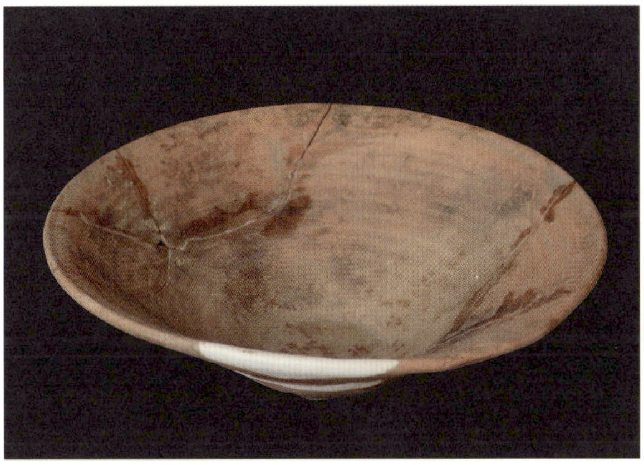

3. 标本L8G5-F5⑤下：19，钵
specimen L8G5-F5 ⑤ ： 19, bowl

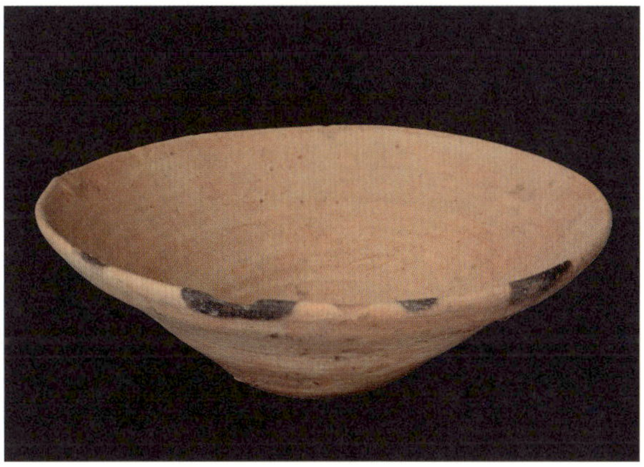

4. 标本L8G5-F5⑤下：20，钵
specimen L8G5-F5 ⑤ ： 20, bowl

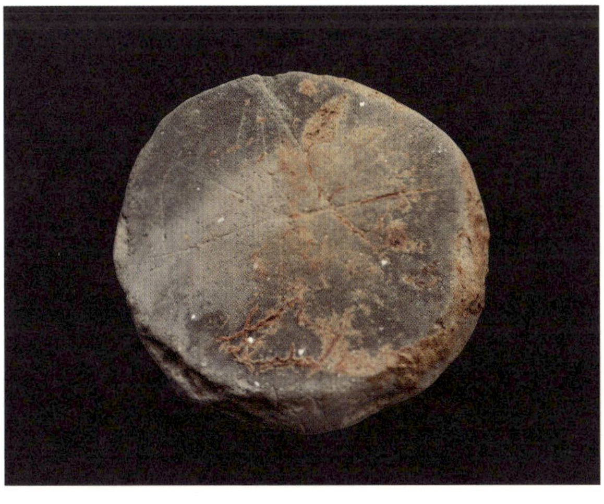

5. 标本L8G5-F5⑤下：32，陶饼
Specimen L8G5-F5 ⑤ ： 32, pottery disc

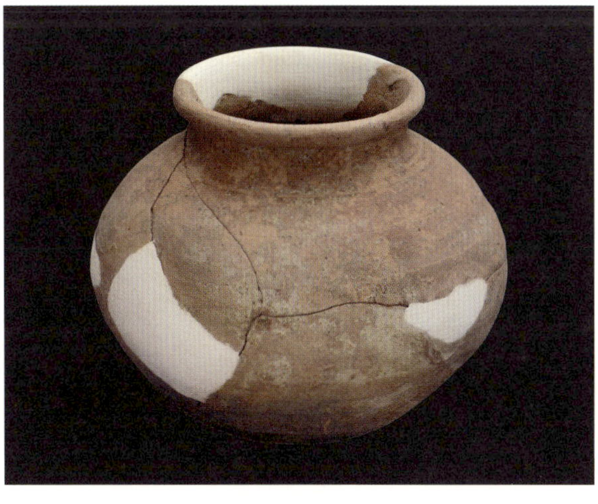

6. 标本L10A2-A3⑤—⑥：5，小罐
specimen L10A2-A3 ⑤ – ⑥ ： 5, miniature pot

彩版4-8
瓮1陶器
Color Plate 4-8
The potteries from Urn 1

1. 标本W1∶19，瓮
Specimen W1 ： 19, urn / storage jar

2. 标本W1∶1，Aa型釜
Specimen W1 ： 1, Aa-Type cooking pot

3. 标本W1∶3，A型罐
Specimen W1 ： 3, A-Type pot

彩版 4-9
瓮1陶器
Color Plate 4-9
The potteries from Urn 1

1. 标本 W1：4，A型罐
specimen W1 : 4, A-type pot

2. 标本 W1：5，A型罐
specimen W1 : 5, A-type pot

3. 标本 W1：6，A型罐
specimen W1 : 6, A-type pot

4. 标本 W1：7，C型壶
specimen W1 : 7, C-type jug

彩版4-10
瓮1陶器
Color Plate 4-10
The potteries of Urn 1

1. 标本W1：8，钵
Specimen W1 ： 8, bowl

2. 标本W1：9，钵
Specimen W1 ： 9, bowl

3. 标本W1：10，钵
Specimen W1 ： 10, bowl

4. 标本W1：11，钵
Specimen W1 ： 11, bowl

5. 标本W1：12，钵
Specimen W1 ： 12, bowl

6. 标本W1：14，C型罐
Specimen W1 ： 14, C-type pot

彩版4-11
瓮1、瓮2陶器

Color Plate 4-11
The potteries of Urn 1 and Urn 2

1. 标本W1：16，灯座

Specimen W1 ： 16, lamp holder

2. 标本W1：20，器盖

Specimen W1 ： 20, lid

3. 标本W2：4，A型壶

Specimen W2 ： 4, A-Type pot

4. 标本W2：5，钵

Specimen W2 ： 5, bowl

5. 标本W2：7，钵

Specimen W2 ： 7, bowl

6. 标本W2：8，器盖

Specimen W2 ： 8, lid

彩版4-12
瓮2陶器
Color Plate 4-12
The potteries from Urn 2

1. 标本W2：2，A型壶
specimen W2 ∶ 2, A-type jug

2. 标本W2：1，B型罐
specimen W2 ∶ 1, B-type pot

彩版4-13
⑥层表面陶器

Color Plate 4-13
The potteries on the surface of Layer 6

1. 标本I11G2-G3⑥表：1，钵
specimen I11G2-G3 ⑥ ：1, bowl

2. 标本I11G2-G3⑥表：2，钵
specimen I11G2-G3 ⑥ ：2, bowl

3. 标本I11G2-G3⑥表：3，钵
specimen I11G2-G3 ⑥ ：3, bowl

4. 标本I11G2-G3⑥表：4，钵
specimen I11G2-G3 ⑥ ：4, bowl

5. 标本I11G3⑥表：10，Aa型釜
Specimen I11G3 ⑥ ：10, Aa-type cooking pot

6. 标本I11 G2-G3⑥表：9，器盖
specimen I11 G2-G3 ⑥ ：9, lid

彩版4-14
⑥层陶器
Color Plate 4-14
The potteries of Layer 6

1. 标本L10E5-F6⑥:33,Ac型釜
specimen L10E5-F6 ⑥ : 33, Ac-type cooking pot

2. 标本L8F5-G6⑥:25,B型釜
specimen L8F5-G6 ⑥ : 25, B-type cooking pot

3. 标本l10G9-I11、G2、G3、G4、G5⑥:1,Aa型釜
specimen l10G9-I11, G2, G3, G4, G5 ⑥ : 1, Aa-type cooking pot

彩版 4-15
⑥层陶器
Color Plate 4-15
The potteries of Layer 6

1. 标本L8F5-G5⑥：35，Aa型釜
specimen L8F5-G5⑥ ：35, Aa-type cooking pot

3. 标本I10G9-I11、G2、G3、G4、G5⑥：2，Aa型釜
specimen I10G9-I11, G2, G3, G4, G5⑥ ：2, Aa-type cooking pot

2. 标本I10G9-I11、G2、G3、G4、G5⑥：4，B型釜
specimen I10G9-I11, G2, G3, G4, G5⑥ ：4, B-type cooking pot

4. 标本L8F5-G5⑥：31，B型罐
specimen L8F5-G5⑥ ：31, B-type pot

彩版4-16
⑥层陶器
Color Plate 4-16
The potteries of Layer 6

1. 标本L8F5-G5⑥：16，小壶
specimen L8F5-G5⑥ ：16, small jug

2. 标本L10E6⑥：24，灯座
specimens L10E6⑥ ：24, lamp holder

3. 标本L8F5-G5⑥：20，灯座
specimens L8F5-G5⑥ ：20, lamp holder

彩版4-17
⑥层陶器

Color Plate 4-17
The potteries of Layer 6

1. 标本L8F5-G5⑥：17，小壶
specimen L8F5-G5 ⑥ ：17, jug

2. 标本L8F5-G5⑥：18，小壶
specimen L8F5-G5 ⑥ ：18, jug

3. 标本L10E6⑥：15，小壶
specimen L10E6 ⑥ ：15, jug

4. 标本L8F5-G5⑥：27，小壶
specimen L8F5-G5 ⑥ ：27, jug

5. 标本L8F5-G5⑥：21，灯柄
specimen L8F5-G5 ⑥ ：21, lamp handle

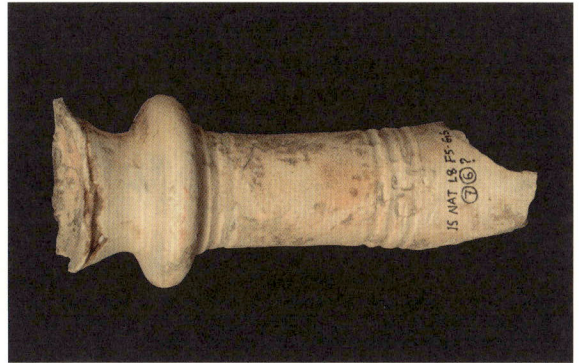

6. 标本L8F5-G5⑥：22，灯柄
specimen L8F5-G5 ⑥ ：22, lamp handle

彩版4-18
⑦层陶器

Color Plate 4-18
The potteries of Layer 7

1. 标本I11G3⑦：34，Aa型釜
specimen I11G3 ⑦ ： 34, Aa-type cooking pot

2. 标本I11G3⑦：49，Aa型釜
specimen I11G3 ⑦ ： 49, Aa-type cooking pot

3. 标本I10G9-I11、G2、G3、G4、G5⑦：19，带嘴壶
specimen I10G9-I11, G2, G3, G4, G5 ⑦ ： 19, jug with snout

4. 标本I10G9-I11、G2、G3、G4、G5⑦：36，小壶
specimen I10G9-I11 G2, G3, G4, G5 ⑦ ： 36, jug

5. 标本I10G9-I11、G2、G3、G4、G5⑦：48，钵
specimen I10G9-I11, G2, G3, G4, G5 ⑦ ： 48, bowl

6. 标本I10G9-I11、G2、G3、G4、G5⑦：25，器盖
specimen I10G9-I11, G2, G3, G4, G5⑦ ： 25, lid

彩版4-19
⑦层陶器
Color Plate 4-19
The potteries of Layer 7

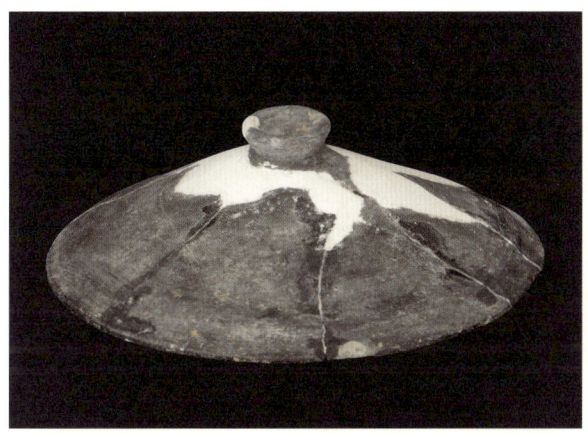

1. 标本I10G9-I11、G2、G3、G4、G5⑦：37，器盖
specimen I10G9-I11, G2, G3, G4, G5⑦ : 37, lid

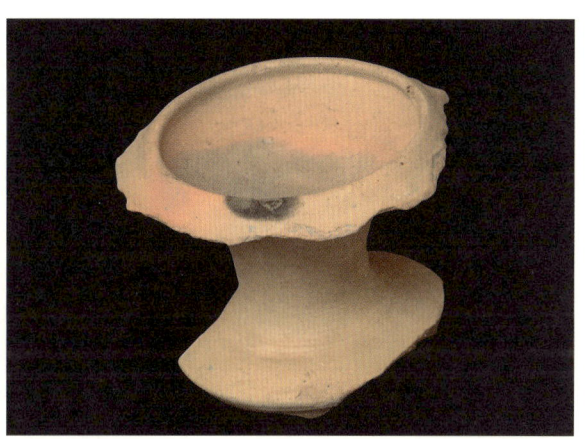

2. 标本I10G9-I11、G2、G3、G4、G5⑦：39，灯
specimen I10G9-I11, G2, G3, G4, G5⑦: 40, lamp

3. 标本I10G9-I11、G2、G3、G4、G5⑦：40，灯盏
specimen I10G9-I11, G2, G3, G4, G5⑦ : 40, lamp

4. 标本I10G9-I11、G2、G3、G4、G5⑦：41，灯盏
specimen I10G9-I11, G2, G3, G4, G5⑦ : 41, lamp

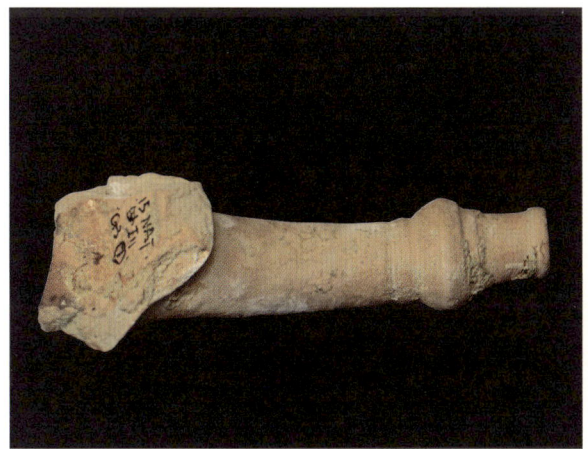

5. 标本I10G9-I11、G2、G3、G4、G5⑦：38，器柄
specimen I10G9-I11, G2, G3, G4, G5⑦ : 38, handle

6. 标本I10G9-I11、G2、G3、G4、G5⑦：50，帽状器
specimen I10G9-I11, G2, G3, G4, G5⑦ : 50, cap

彩版4-20
⑦层陶器
Color Plate 4-20
The potteries of Layer 7

1. ⑦层灯盏
the Layer 7 lamp

2. ⑦层灯盏
the Layer 7 lamp

3. 标本I10G9-I11、G2、G3、G4、G5⑦：41，灯盏
specimen I10G9-I11, G2, G3, G4, G5⑦：41, lamp

4. 标本I10G9-I11、G2、G3、G4、G5⑦：46，乳丁状纹饰
specimen I10G9-I11, G2, G3, G4, G5⑦：46, nail grain pattern

彩版4-21
陶片纹饰
Color Plate 4-21
Pottery decoration

1. ①层
Layer 1

2. ②层
Layer 2

3. ③层
Layer 3

4. ④层
Layer 4

彩版4-22 陶片纹饰
Color Plate 4-22
Pottery decoration

1. ⑤层下部
Lower Layer 5

2. ⑤层下部
Lower Layer 5

3. ⑥层
Layer 6

4. ⑥层
Layer 6

彩版4-23
陶片纹饰
Color Plate 4-23
Pottery decoration

1. ⑦层
Layer 7

2. ⑦层
Layer 7

3. ⑦层
Layer 7

4. ⑦层
Layer 7

第二节
Section 2
Other Unearthed Objects
其他出土遗物

出土遗物除日用陶器外，还有少量的瓷片、金箔残片、铁钉、玻璃制品、建筑石材和石雕造像的残片、陶塑等。尽管在发掘出土的精美文物有限，但却提供了埋藏种类的信息。特别值得注意的是，长期以来，在毗诃罗普尔遗址所在的蒙希甘杰地区，经常出土砖雕、石雕、陶器、木船、铜币、铭刻文字等珍贵文物，成为国内外许多博物馆的收藏品。在达卡国家博物馆的展品中，蒙希甘杰出土的石雕几乎占据所展出石雕的一半，还有建筑构件上的木雕像，如女神（Sundari）、文殊菩萨（Lokanatha）等，都从一个侧面反映了遗址在存活时期的盛况（彩版4-24）。

一、瓷片

1. 青瓷，碗足，出土地点 UnitL8GridG2，⑤层（彩版4-25，1、2）。

林梅村先生鉴定意见："胎质发灰黄色，不够质密，釉层薄，不坚实，烧制温度较低，应该是罐之类的广东青瓷片，年代似在宋末元初（12—13世纪）。"

2. 青瓷，出土地点 UnitL8GridA8，在L3表面的⑤层（彩版4-25，3，中）。

林先生鉴定意见："刻花青瓷片，釉层较薄，有划花。看不见胎质细节，疑似南宋越窑类型产品，可能为福建窑口产品。"

3. 白瓷，出土地点 UnitJ9GridI9，②层（彩版4-25，3，左）。

林先生鉴定意见："白瓷片，胎质较为质密，釉色不够白，看似宋末元初（12—13世纪）德化白瓷片，但是标本太小，难以准确判断。"

4. 青花瓷，出土地点 UnitL9GridJ6，②层（彩版4-25，3，右）。

林先生鉴定意见："青花瓷片，尽管看不到胎质细节，钴料发色不似元代或明代早期蓝中闪黑的颜色，尤其是画法与元青花有所不同，估计是清代早中期的产品。"

5. 白瓷，出土地点 UnitL9GridD4，⑤层（彩版4-25，4）。

⑤层瓷片鉴定的年代与地层年代不合，不排除局部地层扰乱的可能，有待进一步分析。

二、金箔残片

UnitI9GridB9，距地表深度5.4米，位于④层。极薄，不足1毫米，残高2.9厘米，造像作跏趺坐，脚心朝上，作说法印，上身突出双乳，双耳长，尖顶帽冠，下为莲花座，造像的神格不明（彩版4-26，1）。

三、铁钉

标本I10G3⑦：44，尖锥状，扁圆形帽，有锈迹。盖径3.5厘米、钉身长4.9厘米（图4-54，1）。

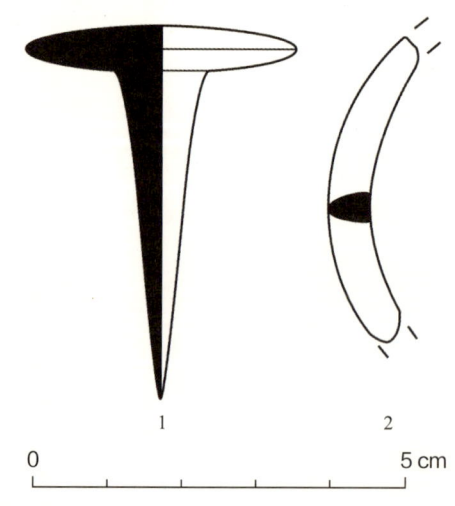

图 4-54　铁钉
Fig. 4-54　Iron nail

四、玻璃环

标本 UnitI10GridG3 ⑦：45，深绿色，截面呈弧三角形。残长 4 厘米（图 4-54，2；彩版 4-26，2）。

五、骨锥

残长 7 厘米（彩版 4-26，3）。

六、念珠

陶质，中空，长 2.6 厘米、外径 2.2 厘米、孔径 0.8 厘米（彩版 4-26，4）

七、建筑石材

柱厅 4 西墙的②层中发现，长方体，一面的中间有一棱，形成上下台面，两侧中部有一人工凿成的浅漕，可能属于建筑中的石材，被取砖者遗弃的（彩版 4-26，5）。此外，彩版 4-26，6 石基座采集自纳提什瓦遗址，彩版 4-26，7 采集自拉库罗普尔（Raghurampur）遗址。

八、石雕残片

UnitJ9GridC9，距地表深度 0.23 米，②层。黑色石雕的残片，造像臂部，带有臂钏的花纹（彩版 4-26，8）。

九、陶塑（Tettacotta）

这个平坦的冲积地区缺乏石料，将黏土变成丰富的陶塑，是一门古老的手工艺，孟加拉 7 世纪以后的寺庙遗址中，广泛发现陶塑作为寺庙墙面的装饰。彩版 4-27、4-28 是 2010—2013 年在拉库罗普尔（Raghurampur）和纳提什瓦（Nateshwar）遗址出土的部分陶塑。

其中彩版 4-27：1. 头像；2. 头像；3. 人像；4. 妇女人像；5. 佛陀（?）；6. 四臂观音；彩版 4-28：1. 神像；2. 象头神；3. 夜叉；4. 象头神擦擦，高 9.5 厘米、宽 5.8 厘米、厚 1—2.6 厘米，纳提什瓦遗址 UnitK8GridC7 ④层出土。

十、达卡国家博物馆展出的蒙希甘杰石雕像

在达卡国家博物馆展出的石雕像中，有一批出自蒙希甘杰地区，皆为黑石雕，年代为 9—12 世纪，与毗诃罗普尔遗址作为都城的时期吻合。大部分石雕像是印度教造像，占三分之二以上，印度教主神毗湿奴及其化身又占其半数以上，这与孟加拉地区盛行毗湿奴教的历史相吻合，其他有湿婆、林伽、太阳神、雪山女神帕尔瓦蒂及化身旃蒙陀女神、高利女神等。当时印度教庙宇遍布各地，各自安置有神像，印度教徒不出家，全民皆是。这也与《阿底峡尊者传》所说"尔时邦伽罗境内，外道与内道辩诤，内不抵外，是故内教道场，多失于外道"情况相吻合。佛教造像不足三分之一，主要神祇有禅那佛中的不动佛、阿弥陀佛以及观音、叶衣观音、佛母、度母、绿度母等，基本反映了佛教金刚乘阶段的神格特征。

1. 不动佛，梵文 Dhyani Buddha Akshobhya，11 世纪（彩版 4-29，1）。

2. 阿弥陀佛，梵文 Dhyani Buddha Amitava，11 世纪（彩版 4-29，2）。

3. 观音菩萨，梵文 Bodisattva Lokanath，10 世纪（彩版 4-29，3）。

4. 大随求佛母，梵文 Mahapratisara，10 世纪（彩版 4-29，4）。

5. 叶衣观音，梵文 Parnasavari，10 世纪（彩版 4-30，1）。

6. 绿度母，梵文 Shyama Tara，10 世纪（彩版 4-30，2）。

7. 度母，梵文 Astamahabhaya Tara，10 世纪（彩版 4-30，3）。

8. 度母，梵文 Vrikutitara，11 世纪（彩版 4-30，4）。

9. 毗湿奴，梵文 Vishnu，12 世纪。

印度教有三大神，分别是创造之神梵天，维系之神毗湿奴和毁灭之神湿婆。梵天、湿婆、毗湿奴"三神一体"，体现创造宇宙过程中的三种力量。毗湿奴的形象为全身蓝色，一面四臂二目，右手持轮和莲花，左手持海螺和大棒。头戴皇冠，身上戴有各种金银珠宝，他的坐骑为金翅大鹏鸟嘎茹达（Garuda)，毗湿奴在佛教中被译为遍入天，意思是以化身遍入世间救度众生（彩版 4-31，1）。

10. 毗湿奴，梵文 Vishnu，11 世纪（彩版 4-31，2）。

11. 毗湿奴，梵文 Vishnu，10 世纪（彩版 4-31，3）。

12. 那茹阿星哈毗湿奴，梵文 Vishnu: Narasimha Avataya，11 世纪。毗湿奴化身为人狮那茹阿星哈，作为人类强大的保护者，在尼泊尔和印度有很多这类神像（彩版 4-31，4）。

13. 雄猪毗湿奴，梵文 Vishnu: Baraha Avataya，12 世纪。毗湿奴神显现为了一头顶天立地的巨型雄猪，用它的两颗长牙将地球从宇宙的汪洋之中托了起来，让它重新归位（彩版 4-31，5）。

14. 毗湿奴，梵文 Vishnu: Matsya Avataya，9 世纪。经典上记载，毗湿奴现为一条鱼，在海洋里救回了吠陀圣典（彩版 4-31，6）。

15. 毗湿奴，梵文 Visvarupa Vishnu，12 世纪（彩版 4-32，1）。

16. 那罗延天毗湿奴，梵文 Narayana Vishnu，12 世纪。那罗延天为毗湿奴的化身，代表最原初之神（彩版 4-32，2）。

17. 瓦玛那毗湿奴，梵文 Vamana Vishnu，10 世纪。瓦玛那为毗湿奴神的第五个化身，一个美丽可爱的侏儒形象（彩版 4-32，3）。

18. 父神湿婆和母神乌玛（帕蒂），梵文 Umamahesvara，12 世纪（彩版 4-32，4）。

19. 湿婆林伽，梵文 Sivalinga，9 世纪。湿婆最显著的象征物是林伽，即男性生殖器，林伽与女阴交合，代表创造和再生的力量，是生命之源，在神庙中心放置林伽（彩版 4-32，5）。

20. 湿婆化身（？），梵文 Aghora，11 世纪（彩版 4-32，6）。

21. 太阳神，梵文 Surya，11 世纪。太阳神苏利耶是源于古代婆罗门教的古老神祇，左右手各拿一枝莲花，乘四马大车。"孟加拉"一词源于太阳神的南方语词"邦加"，古代陶片上广泛的有太阳纹，代表太阳崇拜（彩版 4-33，1）。

22. 太阳神，梵文 Surya，11 世纪（彩版 4-33，2）。

23. 印度教神祇，梵文 Kalayana Sundara，11 世纪（彩版 4-33，3）。

24. 湿婆林伽（？），梵文 Mahamaya，12 世纪（彩版 4-33，4）。

25. 卡莉女神，梵文 Gauri，10 世纪。卡莉女神是杜尔嘎女神（Durga）的化身，在世界被恶魔统治之时化现为愤怒形象。在藏传佛教中，玛哈卡莉作为玛哈嘎拉的明妃，是藏传佛教最重要的出世间解脱护法之一（彩版 4-34，1）。

26. 坎迪女神，梵文 Chandi，10 世纪。坎迪女神即湿婆大神的妻子帕尔瓦蒂（Parvati）的化身（彩版 4-34，2）。

27. 旃蒙陀女神，梵文 Chamunda，11 世纪。旃蒙陀女神为雪山女神帕尔瓦蒂（Parvati）之化身（彩版 4-34，3）。

28. 拉克什米女神（？），梵文 Gajalaksmi，10 世纪。拉克什米女神（Lakshmi）毗湿奴的妻子，也被称为月亮之妹。当拉克什米女神从海洋中诞生之时，诸天都被她的美貌所震惊，她嫁给了毗湿奴神，象征财富、美丽和繁荣（彩版 4-34，4）。

There was a small amount of porcelains, gold foil fragments, iron nails, glass products, architectural stones, stone sculpture fragments and terracotta objects unearthed in the site, besides common daily-use potteries. Despite the limited number of the fine objects, it provides important information on the various local lifestyles. It is noteworthy that for a long time the significant cultural relics such as Buddhist stone sculptures, wooden boats, pillars and inscriptions were found in Munshiganj district, where Vikrampura ancient city was located. They now belong to the collections of many museums both at home and abroad. In the exhibits of National Museum in Dhaka, the stone statues unearthed in Munshiganj almost occupy half of the exhibited stone sculptures. In addition, there are some other wooden sculptures such as the Sursundari and Lokanatha. They all reflect the prosperity of the Buddhism during the functioning existence time of the site (Color Plate 4-24).

Porcelain fragments

1. Celadon, bowl foot, UnitL8GridG2, Layer 5 (Color Plate 4-25: 1, 2).
The identification by Prof. Lin Meicun from Peking University in China: "the porcelain body is grayish yellow in color, not enough hard and dense enaugh, and the glaze is thin and not solid, reflecting low firing temperature. It possibly originated from the celadon wares in Guangdong Province, China, around in 12th – 13th century". This speculation doesn't match with the ^{14}C dates of Layer 5, possibly because of uncorrectedly identified context of this porcelain.

2. Celadon, UnitL8GridA8, Layer 5 ,on the surface of Road 3 (Color Plate 4-25: 3, middle)
Prof. Lin's identification: "incised celadon, thin glaze, and the details of its body are unclear to see. It is speculated to originate from the products of Yue porcelain kiln in Southern Song dynasty, possibly belonging to the kiln products in Fujian ".

3. White porcelain, UnitJ9GridI9, Layer 2 (Color Plate 4-25: 3, left).
Prof. Lin's identification: "white porcelain fragment, hard and dense body, the glaze is not white enough, seemingly the Dehua kiln during the late Song Dynasty and early Yuan dynasty (1271 – 1368 AD). Due to the small size of the specimen, it is difficult to give final conclusion".

4. Blue and white porcelain, UnitL9GridJ6, Layer 2 (Color Plate 4-25: 3, right).
Prof. Lin's identification: "the fragment of blue and white porcelain, although the details of its body are unknown , the color of the cobalt material is not like black-blue color in the Yuan Dynasty (1271 – 1368 AD) or the early Ming Dynasty (1368 – 1644 AD), especially the painting is different with blue and white ceramics of Yuan dynasty. Therefore, it is estimated that it belongs to the product of early and mid-Qing dynasty".

5. White porcelain, uncovered in UnitL9GridD4, Layer 5 (Color Plate 4-13, 4)
The archaeological datings of porcelains discovered at Nateshwar indicate that these were produced before the Yuan and Ming dynasty.

Sculpture and Icon

Many sculptures and icons have been reported as chance finds and a few have been found in excavation. The inventory of sculptures and icons are under progress. However, a special icon is described below:

Gautama Sakyamuni (Gold foil fragment)
The specimen is located in Layer 4 in UnitI9GridB9, at the depth of 5.4 m. from the surface-ground. It is very thin, less than 1 mm thick, and the remaining length is 2.9 cm. The figure has two prominent breasts and two long ears. The two-armed deity is seated in *Vajrasana on a podmasana* (double petaled lotus) and exhibited *dharmachakra mudra* in hands. He is wearing a three-pointed crown on his head. The gold miniature image has been identified as *Gautama Sakyamuni* (*Manusi Buddha*) (Color Plate 4-26, 1).

Iron nails

The specimen I10G3⑦ : 44 is pointed-shape with flat round cap, already rusted. The body length is 4.9 cm, and the diameter of the cap is 3.5 cm (Figure 4-54, 1).

Glass ring fragment

The specimen UnitI10GridG3⑦ : 45 is dark green color, arc triangular-shaped cross section. The remaining length is 4 cm (Figure 4-54, 2; Color Plate 4-26, 2).

Bone Awl

7 cm in remnant length (Color Plate 4-26, 3).

Prayer Bead

Pottery, hollow, 2.6 cm long, 2.2 cm outside diameter and 0.8 cm bore diameter (Color Plate 4-26, 4).

Stone Architectural parts

One was uncovered in the Layer 2 of the west wall of Pillared-hall 4. It is rectangular in shape, which a ridge is in the middle of one side, forming two table-boards. Other two side flanks each has an artificial chisel shallow groove in the middle. It could be used for architecture construction, such as the pillar pedestal and the threshold (Color Plate 4-26, 3). Some other large stone parts were ever collected in this area, such as the stone pedestal collected from Nateshwar (Color Plate 4-26, 4) and Raghurampur (Color Plate 4-26, 5).

Carved stone fragment

The specimen UnitJ9GridC9 is from Layer 2 at the depth of 0.23 m below surface-ground. It is the fragment of black basalt carved statue. An armlet pattern can be seen on the arm of the figure (Color Plate 4-26, 6).

Terracotta sculptures

This area is a low-lying alluvial plain so that it is lack of stone materials. Using clay to produce terracotta objects is an ancient handicraft. Terracotta plaques were widely used for the decoration of the construction walls. In the Buddhist monasteries in Bangladesh after seventh century. The followings terracotta sculptures were unearthed in the excavations of Raghurampur and Nateshwar from 2010 to 2013 (Color Plate 4-27).

Munshiganj district, which are contemporary with the age of Vikrampura ancient city, i.e 9 – 12 century AD. Most of the statues belong to Hinduism, accounting for more than two-thirds, of which the Hindu god Vishnu and its incarnation account for more than half of the number. It is coincided with the history that Vishnu was prevalent in ancient Bengal. Others such as Sun god, Chamunda godness, and Gauri godness were also existent. Many Hindu temples were distributed here at that time, each of which has a statue. The Buddhist statues were less than one-third, and the main gods include Zen Acala Buddha, Amitabha and, Tara, etc., which basically reflects the characteristics of Vajrayana Buddhism (Color Plate 4-29 – 4-34).

Stone carved statues from Munshiganj distirct exhibited in National Museum

In the exhibition of National Museum in Dhaka city, there are some black basalt sculptures from

彩版4-24
毗诃罗普尔地区出土文物
Color Plate 4-24
The artifacts unearthed in Vikrampura area

1. 青铜造像
Bronze sculptures

2. 碑铭
Stone inscription (Bhoja Varman Deva C.1137-1145)

3. 木雕
Sursundari

4. 木雕
Lokanatha

5. 木柱
Wooden pillar

6. 木船
Wooden boat

彩版4-25
出土瓷片
Color Plate 4-25
The unearthed porcelain fragments

1

2

3

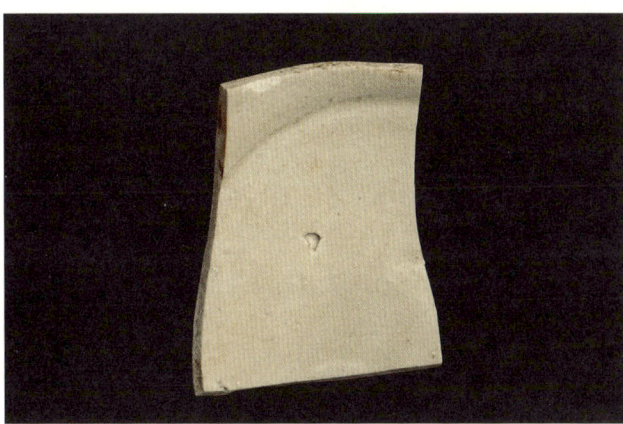

4

彩版4-26
出土文物
Color Plate 4-26
The unearthed artifacts

1. 金箔残片（UnitI9GridB9④层）
Gautama Sakymuni (Manusi Buddha) (UnitI9GridB9 Layer 4)

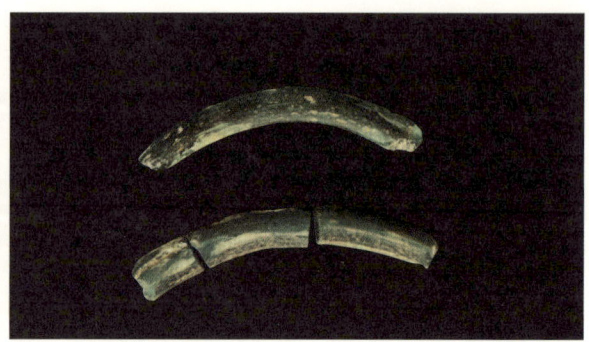

2. 玻璃环（标本UnitI10GridG3⑦：45）
glass ring (specimen UnitI10GridG3⑦：45)

3. 骨锥
bone awl

4. 念珠
perfored stone bead

5. 建筑石材（柱厅4西墙的②层）
architectural stone (from Western wall of Pillared-hall 4, Layer 2)

6. 石基座，采集自纳提什瓦遗址
Stone pedestal, collected from Raghurampur site

7. 石基座，采集自拉库罗普尔遗址
Stone pedestal, collected from Raghurampur site

8 石雕残片（UnitJ9GridC9②层）
stone sculptural fragment (Layer 2 UnitJ9GridC9)

彩版 4-27
毗诃罗普尔地区出土砖雕
Color Plate 4-27
The brick scuptures unearthed in Vikrampura area

1. 头像
Head

2. 头像
Head

3. 人像
Figure

4. 妇女人像
Female figure

5. 佛陀
Buddha

6. 四臂观音
Four-armed Avalokitesvara

彩版4-28
毗诃罗普尔地区出土砖雕
Color Plate 4-28
The brick scuptures unearthed in Vikrampura area

1. 神像
Atisha / king (?)

2. 象头神
Ganash

3. 夜叉
Yaksha

4. 象头神
Ganash

彩版4-29
毗诃罗普尔地区出土石雕造像
Color Plate 4-29
The stone statues unearthed in Vikrampura area

1. 不动佛，梵文Dhyani Buddha Akshobhya，11世纪
Dhyany Buddha Akshobhya, 11th century

2. 阿弥陀佛，梵文Dhyani Buddha Amitava，11世纪
Dhyany Buddha Amitabha, 11th century

3. 观音菩萨，梵文Bodisattva Lokanath，10世纪
Khasarpana-Lokesvara, 10th century

4. 大随求佛母，梵文Mahapratisara，10世纪
Moharotisara, 10th AD

彩版 4-30
毗诃罗普尔地区出土石雕造像
Color Plate 4-30
The stone statues unearthed in Vikrampura area

1. 叶衣观音，梵文 Parnasavari，10世纪
Parnasavari Buddhist Godness of desease and epidemic, 10th century

2. 绿度母，梵文 Shyama Tara，10世纪
Shyama Tara (Green Tara), 10th century

3. 度母，梵文 Astamahabhaya Tara，10世纪
Shyama Tara, 10th century

4. 度母，梵文 Vrikuti Tara，11世纪
Brikuti Tara, 10th century

彩版4-31
毗诃罗普尔地区出土石雕造像
Color Plate 4-31
The stone statues unearthed in Vikrampura area

1. 毗湿奴，梵文Vishnu，12世纪
Vishnu, Sanskrit Vishnu, 12th century

2. 毗湿奴，梵文Vishnu，11世纪
Vishnu, Sanskrit Vishnu, 11th century

3. 毗湿奴，梵文Vishnu，10世纪
Vishnu, Sanskrit Vishnu, 10th century

4. 那茹阿星哈毗湿奴，梵文Vishnu: Narasimha Avataya，11世纪
Narasiimha, Incarnation Vishnu, 11th century

5. 雄猪毗湿奴，梵文Vishnu: Baraha Avataya，12世纪
Varaha Avatara, Incarnation of Vishnu, 12th century

6. 毗湿奴，梵文Vishnu: Matsya Avataya，9世纪
Matsya Avatara, Incarnation of Vishnu, 9th century

彩版4-32
毗诃罗普尔地区出土石雕造像
Color Plate 4-32
The stone statues unearthed in Vikrampura area

1. 毗湿奴，梵文Visvarupa Vishnu，12世纪

Visvarupa Vishnu, 12th century

2. 那罗延天毗湿奴，梵文Narayana Vishnu，12世纪

Vishnu, 12th century

3. 瓦玛那毗湿奴，梵文Vamana Vishnu，10世纪

Vamana Avatara, Incarnation of Vishnu, 10th century

4. 父神湿婆和母神乌玛（帕蒂），梵文Uma Mahesvara，12世纪

Uma-Mahesvara, 12th century

5. 湿婆林伽，梵文Sivalinga，9世纪

Gauripotta and Linga, 9th century

6. 湿婆化身，梵文Aghora，11世纪

Aghora, a manifestation of Siva, 11th century

彩版4-33
毗诃罗普尔地区出土石雕造像
Color Plate 4-33
The stone statues unearthed in Vikrampura area

1. 太阳神，梵文Surya，11世纪
Sun god, Surya, 11th century

2. 太阳神，梵文Surya，11世纪
Sun god, Surya, 11th century

3. 印度教神祇，梵文Kalayana Sundara，11世纪
Kalayana Sundara, 11th century

4. 湿婆林伽，梵文Mahamaya，12世纪
Mahamaya, 12th century

彩版4-34
毗诃罗普尔地区出土石雕造像
Color Plate 4-34
The stone statues unearthed in Vikrampura area

1. 卡莉女神，梵文Gauri，10世纪
Gauri Godness, Gauri, 10th century

2. 坎迪女神，梵文Chandi，10世纪
Chandi Godness, Chandi, 10th century

3. 旃蒙陀女神，梵文Chamunda，11世纪
Chamunda, 11th century

4. 拉克什米女神，梵文Gajalaksmi，10世纪
Gajalaksmi, 10th century

Chapter

V

第五章

Conclusion

结语

纳提什瓦
Nateshwar

第一节

Section 1

The Chronological Periods and the Rise and Decline of the Site

纳提什瓦遗址的年代分期和遗址兴废过程的历时性描述

根据上述 ^{14}C 数据，结合遗址的地层关系，建筑遗迹和地层间的叠压打破关系，并依据孟加拉这一时期的历史背景，我们得出纳提什瓦遗址地层和遗迹单位的年代分期（图 5-1；表 11）。

第一期：第一次佛教寺院时期

推测年代：780—950 年。所包含的地层为⑤、⑥、⑦层。这一期的遗迹可以分出早中晚 3 个不同的时间段。

根据孟加拉国相关史料，这个时期应为德瓦王朝（750—800 年）时期至旃陀罗王朝（900—1050 年）的前期。德瓦王朝的势力范围主要在三摩达吒疆域，统治中心应当在库米拉地区，国都位于德瓦帕瓦吒（Devaparvata），即现今的拉尔迈—迈纳马蒂（Laimai-mainamati）区域。德瓦王朝时期佛教兴盛，迈纳马蒂是当时的佛教中心。其中，800—900 年间的历史记载比较少，人们对这段历史的认识也很模糊，因此，这一时期遗址中所获取的信息，对于建立孟加拉国的历史编年，具有重要的意义。

第一期早段的寺院修建于德瓦王朝时期，大约发生在 780 年左右，有学者认为，在莫卧尔王朝以前，现今蒙希甘杰所在的毗诃罗普尔（Vikrampura）地区，可能是恒河和贾木纳河（在印度称布拉马普特拉河，在中国称雅鲁藏布江）的交汇之地。最初，在水网之地开始修建寺院，这一时期的地面高出四周的地平面 1 米左右，考虑到该地区长期洪水的作用，地面在逐年增高，因此，在当时的景观中，遗址所在的地势还是相对较高的。这一时期的排水设施、道路几乎直接叠压在原始的泥沙堆积之上。

第一期早段对应的地层暂定为第⑦层，发现的遗迹包括：神殿 1 前期遗迹，道路 1、2、3、5，

表 11　纳提什瓦遗址地层和遗迹单位的分期表

期	段	地层	^{14}C 年代	遗迹
一期	早段	⑦层（暂定）	780AD—950AD	神殿 1 前期遗迹，房屋 6、房屋 7、道路 1、2、3、5，浴室和排水沟等
	中段	⑥层		神殿 1 后期遗迹，神殿 2，道路 3（延用早段），隔墙，房屋 1、2、3、4、5，墙 1、2、3，路面 2、4 等
	晚段	⑤层		道路 4
二期		④层	950AD—1223AD	十字形神殿建筑，八边形佛塔 1、2、3、曲折形围墙 1、路面 1、3 等
三期		①②③层	1223AD 至近现代	H1—H5

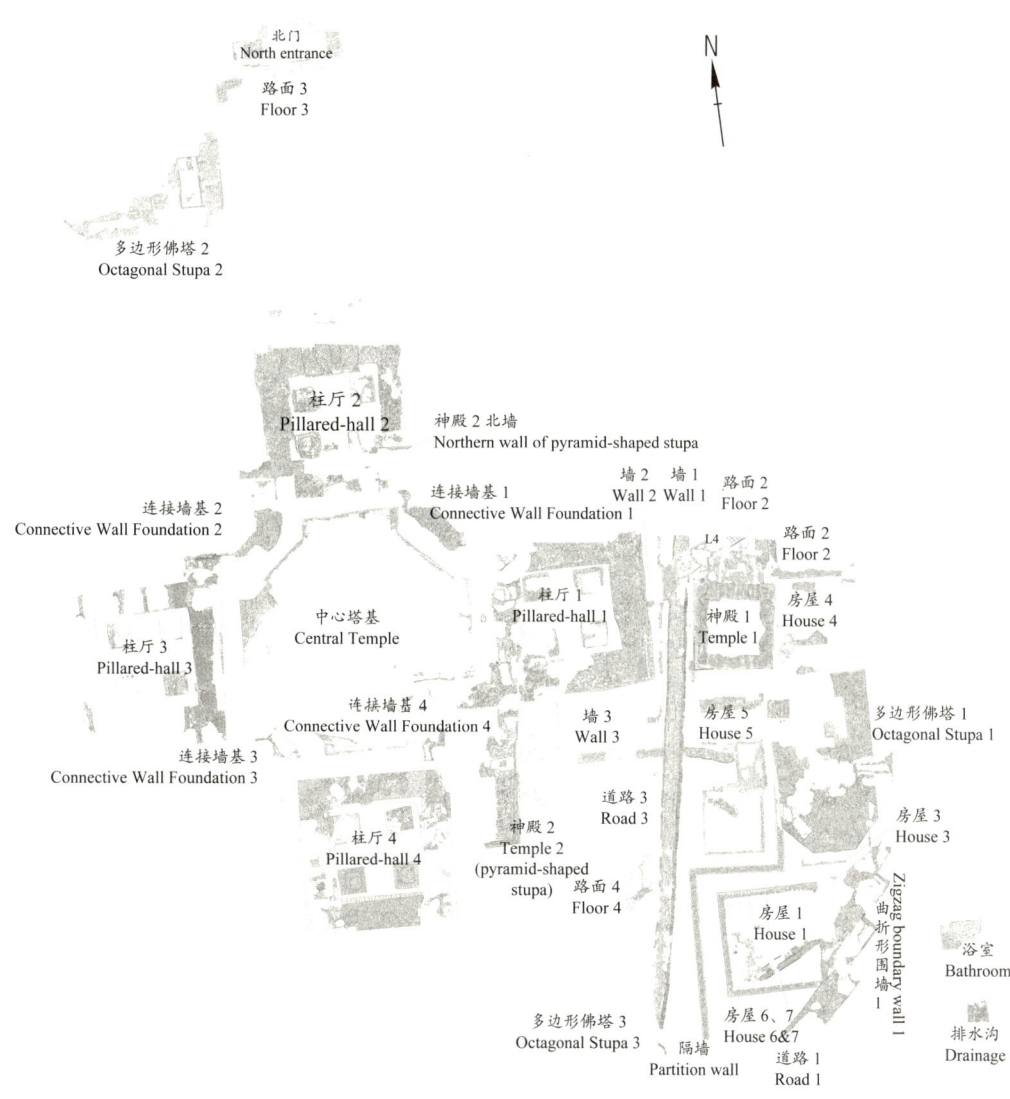

图 5-1 纳提什瓦遗址遗迹总平面图

Fig. 5-1　The master plan of cultural remains at Nateshwar excavation site

浴室和排水沟等。其中神殿1应是早期宗教建筑的核心，主要体现在该建筑的体量和建筑的精美结构上。目前揭露的第一期建筑位于遗址的中部和东部，但在第二期十字形中心神殿遗存的底部，也发现过零星的一期遗迹，如第二期的柱厅1、柱厅2都有利用早期建筑废墟的情况，柱厅1西墙基有一段建立在早期建筑之上，该早期墙体被推倒后，做了④层的垫基层；柱厅2的南墙北侧的墙基下也有早期墙体。这两个早期建筑的体量都较大。

在UnitL10GridB5的探坑中发现纯黄土，位于神庙1的墙基之下，可断定为当时建筑的填土。⑦层是目前我们所确认的最早一期人类活动堆积。它应是早期建筑的填土层。此外，⑥、⑦层颜色为什么呈现灰青色，是本身土质的问题，还是长期在低水位中浸泡有关？为了保存第二期十字形中心神殿建筑，中心区域未进一步下挖。这一时段的建筑多使用小而较薄的红砖，砖砌比较规整。⑦层出土的红陶较暗淡、斑驳，器型较为简单，釜罐类陶器的折肩、折腹风格较为流行，陶器中敞口钵数量较多，陶器较薄，火候较低，但器形规整。

第一期中段对应的地层为⑥层，发现的遗迹包括：神殿1后期遗迹，神殿2，道路3（延用早段），隔墙，房屋1、2、3、4、5，墙1、2、3，路面2、4等。

中段最大的变化是新修了神殿2这座庞大的建筑，并利用早段的建筑空地，新建了隔墙及多处僧院建筑，象征着寺庙本身的继承和发展。另一方面对原有建筑进行改造利用，如对神殿1的后期改造，路3是毗邻神殿1的道路，此时也有相应的改变。总体来看，这一时段砖的尺寸更大更厚，建筑体量也变大，但建筑的规整程度比第一期早段有所下降。这一时期遗址延续至旃陀罗王朝前期，毁灭的原因，也许是人为的原因，也许是火灾、水灾等自然的原因。这一时期在UnitI11GridG2–G3⑥层表面，在一个很小的区域内出土了二十余件可修复的完整陶器，在神殿1两个拐角处发掘了两个大瓮，大瓮中贮藏有各种陶器，反映当时人们使用生活器皿的情况。出土的陶器在种类上增加了各种圜底卷沿罐，底部多有烟熏痕迹。

第一期晚段对应的地层为⑤层，这一时段的遗迹为道路4。发掘显示，中段建筑废弃后的一段时间内，有人在此废墟上平整、重修，并继续使用，如路4打破路3，压在神殿的出口，与后期神殿1的废弃是相应的。神殿2墙根下分布着密集的陶器和炭末，也是晚段留下的遗存，晚段没有发现大体量的建筑，可能此时已转变为普遍的小聚落。⑤层陶器和⑥、⑦层陶器之间的共性是主要的，在陶系、器形和纹饰上，没有太多区别，区别仅在某些细节处，如⑤层Ab型釜、B型釜、小罐的数量较多。

第二期：第二次佛教寺院时期

推测年代：950—1223年。所包含的地层为④层。根据孟加拉相关史料，这个时期为旃陀罗王朝（900—1050年）后期、跋摩王朝（1080—1150年）时期和犀那王朝（1100—1223年）时期。这三个王朝，都曾建都城于毗诃罗普尔。

旃陀罗王朝是一个非常强大的时期，是孟加拉东部和南部长久繁荣的黄金时代，完全能够与孟加拉西部和北部的波罗王朝相抗衡。据有关资料，至迟在第三个君主时，已经在毗诃罗普尔建都了。第四任君主Srichandra时期（929—979年），王朝的势力范围已包括了整个文伽（Vanga）、三摩达吒（Samatata）、锡尔赫特（Srihatta）和诃利科罗（Harikela），迈门辛（Mymensingh）县的部分地区也应在其控制中，其都城即是位于蒙希甘杰地区的毗诃罗普尔。

跋摩王朝的早期统治者可能来自于印度奥里萨邦地区，在11世纪后半期兴起于文伽地区，其后势力也扩至西北的高达地区，王朝的都城亦位于毗诃罗普尔，前后历经5任君主。

犀那（Sena）王朝在12世纪后半期由毗阇

耶犀那（Vijayasena）在西孟加拉邦地区的Radha兴起，它起初是波罗王朝在这一地区的封地，在波罗王朝的最后一位国君时，毗阇耶犀那打败孟加拉东南部的跋摩王朝，巩固了自己的政治基础，然后推翻了孟加拉西、北部的波罗王朝，从而建立起了一个广阔的帝国，最盛时领土范围向北扩至印度的北比哈尔（North Bihar），整个西孟加拉邦和文伽地区。1204—1223年，犀那王朝由于受到西北方的穆斯林突袭和侵入，将都城迁至毗诃罗普尔地区，其后的二任君主继续在孟加拉东部和南部实施统治。

第二期寺院的兴建年代，大抵在旃陀罗王朝第四任君主索凯觉罗（Srichandra）（929—979年）时期。大规模的营造活动大致发生在950年左右，人们在前一次建筑废墟的基础上，就地填充各种混杂着泥土和红砖碎块作为垫基物，还有意搬入附近河流纯净的灰黄色泥沙，完全覆盖了早期的废弃建筑，厚度达3米以上的堆积大幅度抬升了地面。新营建的建筑再在此基础上挖基槽，用红砖砌筑墙体的基部，推测当时的地面应与现在地面接近，但由于后期人类的活动，已经难以分辨。目前看到的遗迹，都是地面以下的地基部分，从其深度和体量，可以想见当年建筑的辉煌。

这个时期最主要的遗迹即为十字形中心神殿建筑，此外，还有八边形佛塔1、2、3，曲折形围墙1，路面1、3等附属建筑。

从目前发掘情况看，第二期的遗存由于后期破坏严重，未能具体分段。其中，八边形佛塔存在着前后不同阶段的扩建行为；第二期的寺院的中心区应与第一期寺院重合，但具体的四至目前还不能确定。这一时期寺院的年代下限没有 ^{14}C 数据，但根据历史背景推测，它应毁于1223年穆斯林的侵入，作为佛教寺庙遗址，至此走完了它的全部历程。

第二期遗存遭到后期取砖的严重破坏，至今还没有发现确切的使用时期的堆积，所以无法准确地指出第二期的典型陶器。②层和④层堆积中的陶器，与第一期陶器相比，釜罐类陶器的折肩、折腹风格，逐渐从转角分明趋向更加圆弧。此后，还出现了某些新的因素，以C型釜、E型罐、盂为代表，但这些只是推测性的意见。

毗诃罗普尔（Vikrampura）是孟加拉历史上一个神秘的名字，长期以来，这里经常出土石雕、砖雕、陶器、木船、铜币、铭刻文字等珍贵文物，成为国内外许多博物馆的收藏品。当地村民在开挖池塘和房屋地基时，也经常发现有古代的砖墙和遗物。毗诃罗普尔遗址目前包括东、西两个遗址，分别为拉库罗普尔（Raghurampur）和纳提什瓦（Nateshwar），两者相距约2千米。从发掘的遗迹显示，拉库罗普尔遗址为周匝绕置小居室（僧房）的僧院（vihara），这是东印度常见的僧院格局，其建筑规模非常庞大。这种建筑在孟加拉国的博格拉、库米拉等地多有发现。这一时期，纳提什瓦遗址的主要发现为十字形中心神殿建筑及相关的附属设施。这种十字形中心神殿建筑的宗教本质，为金刚乘中的曼陀罗，这是金刚乘对于世界结构的想像，具体化为寺院建筑的形式。据 ^{14}C 年代数据，这两处遗址属于同一时期。这个规模庞大、具有不同功能的大型佛教遗址，正好与文献中的都城相匹配。通过与巴哈布尔（Pahapur）的苏摩普里寺（Somapuri）遗址中心柱厅的比较，纳提什瓦这座十字形中心神殿的柱厅规模要大于苏摩普里寺。因此，它是孟加拉国目前所见到的规模最大的单体建筑。毫无疑问，作为南亚次大陆最后一个佛教中心的珍贵遗产，这个遗址将永载世界考古学的史册。

第三期：佛教寺院废弃以后

1204年，巴克蒂亚克洛杰（Ikhtiaruddin Mohammad Bakhtiar Khalji）打败了犀那王朝，于1205年在高达（Gauda）建立了穆斯林政权，1223年，穆斯林占领毗诃罗普尔地区，犀那（Sena）王朝从此结束，毗诃罗普尔佛教遗址大体也在此时终结。

穆斯林入侵者通过剑与火结束了佛教在印度丰富多彩的文明，在此过程中，佛教徒纷纷亡命于尼泊尔、西藏、克什米尔山区，还有一些则逃往缅甸和柬埔寨，在孟加拉地区，大部分居民皈依了伊斯兰教，有些加入了印度教，但佛教的残余仍不绝于缕。据文献记载，西藏的译师法主曾于1234年左右游历比哈尔与孟加拉，在那里聆听到一名班智达的说法，他即罗睺罗师利跋陀罗（Rahulacribhadta）。

第三期是指佛教寺院废弃以后形成的堆积，这一时期所包含的地层为①②③层，年代为1223年至近现代。自从佛教寺院废弃后，作为宗教中心的性质已经消失，但仍有小股人群在此旧废墟上生活，以H1至H5为其标志。这一时期使用的陶器为颜色纯正的红色陶器，器形变大，陶器的火候更高、更规整，器类以C型釜、壶为主，与早期陶器有明显区别，说明其年代跨度也较大，目前尚未有 ^{14}C 测年数据。

从目前发掘情况看，这一期还可以分出若干时间段，有多次人类活动所留下的的遗存。此外，至少经历两次由晚期生活于此的伊斯兰教或印度教教徒非常严重的取砖行为，对遗址造成了严重的破坏。目前所见的建筑遗存皆为砖墙的基础部分，建筑的墙体部分已不可考。据调查，近代有许多印度教徒生活在这个村子里，后来大多迁往印度，又有新的穆斯林居民移居此地，直到现在，村子里仍有少数印度教徒生活，而数百年连续生活于此的佛教僧侣，仅留下了高出周围地面数米的废墟堆积，即现今展现在我们眼前的丘状土台。

According to radiocarbon data and the stratigraphy of the site, combined with the historical background in ancient Bangladesh, the chronological periodization of the cultural layers and cultural features at Nateshwar site can-be concluded as follows (Fig.5-1,Table 11).

(a) First Period: Early Buddhist Monastery

The age of this period, which includes Layer 5, Layer 6 and Layer 7, is presumed to be 780 – 950 AD and can be divided into three stages.

The relevant historical documents of Bangladesh show that this period corresponded to the Deva dynasty (750 – 800 AD) and early Chandra dynasty (900 – 1050 AD). The ruling territory of the Deva dynasty was mainly in Samatata janapada, with the capital of Devaparvata, located in present Lalmai-Mainamati area of Comilla district. Buddhism was flouring in the Deva dynasty, and Lalmai-Mainamati was the then Buddhist center. However, historical records between 800 AD and 900 AD are relatively scarce and so understanding of the history of this period is still very vague. Therefore, the data obtained from this site is significant for the further establishment of the chronological framework of ancient Bangladesh history.

The construction of the early stage of the first period happened around 780 AD. According to the opinion of some scholars, the present Munshiganj district, where the Nateshwar site was located, was the intersection of the Ganges River (Padma in Bangldesh) and the old Brahmaputra River (the Yarlung Tsangpo in China) before the Mughal dynasty. Initially, the settlement started on the lowland area, the then living floor being about one meter higher than the surrounding ground level. If we consider the effect of the long-term fluvial in this region, the terrain of the site should be a relative highland at that time. The earliest drainage system and the roads almost directly overlie on the top of the natural soil.

Layer 7 is currently recognized to have been built in the early stage of the first period, and the exposed features include early phase of Temple 1, Road 1, Road 2, Road 3, Road 5, House 6, House 7, bathroom and drainage. The Temple 1 was possibly the center of the Buddhist structures in this stage, reflected from the delicate decoration and overall layout of the site. So far, the exposed

Table 11   The periodization of layers and cultural remains at Nateshwar site

Period	Stage	Layer	^{14}C date	Cultural Remains
First	Early	Layer 7 (presumed)	780 – 950AD	Early phase of Temple 1, Road 1, Road 2, Road 3, Road 5, House 6, House 7, bathroom and drainage
	Middle	Layer 6		Late phase of Temple 1, Temple 2 pyramid-shaped stupa, Road 3, partition wall, House 1, House 2, House 3, House 4, House 5, Wall 1, Wall2, Wall3, Floor2, Floor 4
	Late	Layer 5		Road 4
Second		Layer 4	950 – 1223AD	Cruciform Central Temple, Octagonal Stupa 1, Octagonal Stupa 2, Octagonal Stupa 3, North Entrance, Zigzag Boundary Wall, Floor 1, Floor 3
Third		Layer 1 – 3	12th century – Now	H1 – H5

architectures of the first period were mainly located in the middle and eastern excavation area, but some other structures were also overlaid by the cultural remains of the second period. In order to protect the cruciform central temple in the center of the second period, many other constructions under it were not excavated. Based on the excavation, so far, the size of the bricks used in this stage was thin and small, and most architectures were regularly and finely built. The red potteries unearthed in Layer 7 can be characterized by a dull and mottled color, thin body, low firing temperature and regular shape. The type of pottery is simple, dominated by bowls. The middle stage of the first period corresponds to Layer 6. Many cultural remains were uncovered in this layer, including the late phase of Temple 1 (including the two urns in the corners), a colossal pyramid-shaped stupa, Road 3, partition wall, House 1, House 2, House 3, House 4, House 5, Wall 1, Wall2, Wall3, Floor2 and Floor 4. The main change of this stage is the newly built architecture of the colossal stupa; new structures were built in the unoccupied space, such as partition wall and some houses for monks, indicating the inheritance and development of the Buddhist monastery. Meanwhile, some previous structures were also slightly changed or rebuilt. For example, the temple was rebuilt by making use of partial foundation of the early phase, and the Road 3 was also correspondingly maintained.

Overall, the size of the used bricks became a little bit bigger and thicker; the scale of the buildings was also increased. It lasted a long time until the early Chandra dynasty, but the reason of destruction is unknown, perhaps it was because of the fire, floods or other natural causes. On the surface of Layer 6 in the UnitI11GridG2 – G3, more than 20 pieces of complete or semi-complete potteries were unearthed in a small area. Two large urns, containing various earthen wares, were also separately discovered in the two corners of Temple 1, which contains much information about the daily life of the people at that time. The number of the pots with round bottom and coiling rim increased, and smoked traces can be observed at the bottoms of most of them.

The late stage of the first period correspondingly belongs to Layer 5. After the abandonment of the architecture of the middle stage, a small group of people still occupied some limited areas of the site. The definite cultural feature of this stage is only the Road 4.

The potteries unearthed from Layer 5, Layer 6 and Layer 7 possess the main features, and there are only minor differences among them in aspects of type, shape and decoration. For instance, the number of Ab-type cooking pot, and miniature pot was much larger in Layer 5 than that in other two layers.

(b) Second Period: Late Buddhist Monastery

The second period of Buddhist settlement, which is equivalent to Layer 4, was around 950 – 1223 AD, when late Chandra, Varman dynasty (1080 – 1150AD) and Sena dynasty (1095 – 1223 AD) successively ruled this region. Their capitals were all located in Vikrampura according to several copper plate inscriptions.

Chandra dynasty, which was fully able to compete with the northern contemporary Pala dynasty, was very powerful. Their rule is considered as a golden age in south-east Bengal. According to relevant historical records, at least from the third king, the capital of the dynasty was established in Vikrampura. At about the 9th century AD, the main territory of the Harikela janapada covered Sylhet mountain tract, extending from the original Chittagong area. In the period of the fourth king Srichandra (929 – 979 AD), the territory was expanded to Vanga, Samatata, Srihatta, Harikela and parts of Mymensingh area.

The early rulers of the Varman dynasty (1080 – 1150 AD) might come from the Orissa region of India. In the second half of the 11th century, the Varman dynasty arose in the Vanga and later expanded to the Gauda region on the northwest. The dynasty, which successively experienced five monarchs, also positioned its capital in Vikrampura. Vijaysena founded the Sena dynasty (1095 – 1223 AD) in Gauna. Vijaysena's father Hemantasena was ruling chief of Pala king. The Sena dynasty had consolidated its political foundation and established a broad Empire. The largest territory was extended to North Bihar of India, the entire West Bengal and the Vanga region. Vikrampura was Lakmansena's capital.

However, the second period of Buddhist settlement was built possibly during the rule of Srichandra (929 – 979 AD) who was the fourth king of Chandra dynasty. Large scale construction activties took place at the site at around 950 AD. After locally filling various mixed sediments of soil and brickbats on the top of the debris of the first period, the grey-yellow clayey sand was then intentionally carried from nearby places to cover the early abandoned buildings; the ground surface level was substantially raised about 3 m. It is clear that the new builders in the second period firstly dug the trenches in the man-made soil platform to create an architectural foundation, and then built the structures with burnt bricks. However, the original floor in this period was difficult to identify because of then recent human activities; the exposed remains were almost the foundation parts under the present ground surface. Nevertheless, we can reasonably imagine the glory of the architectures at that time by observing the depth and volume of the preserved foundations. The main remains in this period include a cruciform central temple, composed of four pillared-halls, three octagonal stupas, the north entrance, a huge zigzag boundary wall, Floor 1 and Floor 3. It is difficult to identify different stages due to serious destruction. However, the octagonal stupas were expanded and rebuilt several times, and the scale of construction also developed, but the specific distribution area cannot be determined. There is no suitable ^{14}C data concerning the abandonment age of the monastery. According to cultural layers, it was destroyed approximately during 12th century.

Due to the activities of later brick hunters, the distinct living deposits of the second period are unidentified so far, and it is thus impossible to learn about the typical assemblage. Compared with Layer 1, the cooking pots and pots unearthed from Layer 2 and Layer 4 display the circular characteristics on their belly and shoulder. Some other new elements also appeared, representing by C-type cooking pot and E-type pot. However, the current understanding is not the final conclusion.

Vikrampura is a mysterious name in the history of Bangladesh. For a long time, the precious cultural relics such as Buddhist stone sculptures, terracotta objects, potteries, wooden boat and inscriptions were frequently found here, becoming part of the collections of many museums in and outside of Bangladesh. Ancient brick walls and objects were also uncovered when local villagers dug the ponds or built foundation of their houses. Presently, Vikrampura ancient city includes two sites, Raghurampur and Nateshwar, which are about 2 kilometers apart in distance. The exposed features in Raghurampur show that it is a part of Buddhist vihara with cells placed all around. This is a common vihara pattern of eastern India, and also found in Bogura and Comilla. The main features of this period are the cruciform central temple and related affiliated facilities. The spiritual feature of this kind cruciform construction is the *Mandala*, which represents the vision of Vajrayana Buddhism to the cosmology, but virtually embodied by the Buddhist monastery. According to the ^{14}C dates, the two sites are almost contemporary. It is worthwhile to mention that this large scale Buddhist site with different functional components corroborates the existence of the capital city mentioned in the inscription data. The size of the four pillared-halls (mandapas) and the cruciform central temple together in Nateshwar are larger than that of Paharpur central temple. There is no doubt that this site will be written into the history of world archaeology as the last precious Buddhist heritage in South Asia.

(c) Third Period:
After the Abandonment of the Monastery

Ikhtiaruddin Mohammad Bakhtiar Khalji defeated Sena king Laksmansena in 1204 AD at Gauda but Lakmansena and his successors continued to rule in Vikrampura till 1223 AD.

The Buddhist left Vikrampura but the remains of Buddhism are endless. According to the literature, a Tibetan translator traveled around Bihar and Bengal in 1234, where he listened to a teacher's sermon, who was named Rahulacribhadta.

The third period refers to the deposit of the Layers 1 – 3 after the abandonment of the Buddhist monastery. Since the Buddhist monastery was abandoned and stopped functioning as a religious center, there were still small groups of people living in this place, which is indicated by some ash pits (H1 – H5). Potteries used in this period were characterized by pure red color, larger size, higher firing temperature and finer shape. Among them the C-type cooking pots and jugs were dominant, displaying significant differences from earlier potteries. But ^{14}C data are not available in this period.

This period can also be divided into several sub-phases, reflecting many phases of human activities. In addition, bricks were severely extracted by local residents at least two times, causing serious destruction. The exposed structural remains are almost just the foundation of the architectures; the upper parts of the brick walls were missing. As investigation shows, many Hindus lived in the village in recent times before they moved to India, and later Muslims occupied this place. Until now, a few Hindus still live in the village. However, the Buddhist monks, who lived here for hundreds of years, only left the mound-like cultural debris a few meters below the ground floor.

第二节　纳提什瓦遗址的核心价值

Section 2　The Main Value of the Nateshwar Site

1. 纳提什瓦遗址的早期遗存，是一组塔院（stupa court）和僧院（vihara）的综合体，遗址规模、整体布局及单体建筑的特点，在孟加拉国都是前所未有。晚期遗存是以一座十字形中心神殿为主体的金刚乘建筑。这两个时期的遗存反映了佛教建筑的重要变迁，遗存的完整性和叠压关系的清晰性，提供了南亚次大陆佛教考古的重要标尺。遗址中出土了大量的陶器，具有明确的地层关系，初步建立了陶器年代学序列，填补了孟加拉国这一研究领域的空白。

2. 毗诃罗普尔是孟加拉国旃陀罗（Chandra）、跋摩（Varman）和犀那（Sena）王朝的都城，规模庞大的佛教遗址也印证了文献的记载，孟加拉国 800—900 年间的历史记载比较少，考古发掘所获取的信息，丰富了孟加拉国这一时期的历史叙述。

3. 毗诃罗普尔在藏文典籍中也是一个神圣的名字，阿底峡是孟加拉人民的优秀儿子，也是中国人民心中尊贵的圣者，毗诃罗普尔佛教遗址因此被赋予了佛教文明传播和中孟友谊的伟大象征。

根据上述三条理由，毗诃罗普尔遗址已具备了申报世界文化遗产的条件。同时，遗址的规模和体量符合建设考古遗址公园的条件，新的展示理念和和科技保护手段，将为孟加拉国的文化遗产事业探索出广阔的空间。

1. The first period of cultural remains at Nateshwar site was a stupa complex; the scale of the site, the overall layout and the characteristic of the single structure are unique in Bangladesh. The second period cultural remains were representative of Vajrayana architecture, focusing on the cruciform central temple. The remains of these two periods reflect the important changes in Buddhist architecture. The integrity of preserved remains and the clarity of the stratigraphic context provide important reference for Buddhist archaeology in South Asia. The large number of potteries unearthed in the site, with a clear stratigraphic relationship, preliminary established the chronological sequence of the ceramics, filling the research gap in this area of Bangladesh.

2. Vikrampura was the capital of the successive dynasties of Chandra, Varman and Sena in ancient Bangladesh. The large Buddhist site also confirms the records of the historical literature. In Bangladesh, the history between 800 AD and 900 AD is especially ambiguous, so the information obtained from archaeological excavation at two sites of Vikrampura will definitely enrich the understanding of the ancient history in Bangladesh.

3. Vikrampura is also a sacred name in the Tibetan scriptures. Atisha Dipankara Srijnana is not only the excellent son of the people of Bangladesh, but also a noble sage in the hearts of Chinese people. The Vikrampura Buddhist site was thus the great symbol of the diffusion of Buddhist civilization and the friendship between China and Bangladesh.

Due to the above three reasons, the site has already qualified to be declared as a world heritage. Meanwhile, it also meets the prerequisites for the construction of an archaeological site park in terms of size and volume. Adopting scientific concepts and methods of conservation and display, we will explore the great potentials for cultural heritage management in Bangladesh.

第三节
Section 3
The Further Excavation and Conservation at Nateshwar Site

纳提什瓦遗址
进一步发掘、保护的设想

一、考古勘探与发掘

1. 纳提什瓦遗址的第一期，已经发掘出神殿1、神殿2、道路3及多个僧院建筑，出土陶器也比较丰富，但对于这一时期寺院的边界和整体格局，还是不太清楚，有待勘探和进一步发掘。

2. 纳提什瓦遗址的十字形中心神殿建筑，与巴哈布尔的苏摩普里寺一样，是一个带有围墙的建筑群。苏摩普里寺中心遗址四周，有多达177间的僧舍以及上百座佛塔和其他生活设施。纳提什瓦周边也应有相应的附属设施。目前，纳提什瓦遗址所在的中心区域比周边高出1.5米左右，但建筑的具体四至有待进一步的勘测和确认。目前发现的北门道遗迹和曲折形围墙1为线索，可以进一步寻找四周围墙位置，以及相应的东、南、西寺门的位置。台地边缘发现的一些大型石料，也是重要的线索。此外，在柱厅1的东北部和南墙基南侧、柱厅3的西北部、柱厅4的西南部，都发现有打破④层的砖结构，与柱厅的墙基相连接，可能是四个柱厅之间的附属建筑，也有待进一步的清理。

3. 从宏观上说，一是有必要采用普查与重点详查的办法，厘清纳提什瓦与拉库罗普尔两个遗址的范围，两者之间的自然边界。二是开始启动城市考古的项目，确认毗诃罗普尔古城的分布情况。它们可能是以纳提什瓦与拉库罗普尔为中心的周围数十里作为内城，有护城河，如同玄奘所看到的印度古城的普遍情形，城墙周长以20—30里为多。另一种可能，如在莫诃斯坦，都城与寺庙保持一定的距离，如现在的蒙希甘杰县城，是否有当时世俗都城存在。这些都要参照莫诃斯坦和库米拉的德瓦帕瓦吒（Devaparvata）城址考古的实践，来制定相应的勘探方案。此外，作为政治、经济、文化中心的都城，一般都有复杂的水道系统，承担交通和贸易的功能，这需要根据地形图，考察其历史上的痕迹。当地原住民非常熟悉附近文物出土情况，可以通过他们的口述，给考古调查提供重要的线索。同时，可运用电子地表雷达探测系统（GPRS）等科技手段，进行准确而有效的勘探工作。

4. 在发掘过程中，进行一些微观上的研究，采集更多的动、植物标本，以了解环境和生计方面的信息；通过土壤微结构分析，了解堆积形成原因、过程等方面信息，开展包括人类行为方式在内的多学科研究。

二、遗址保护和展示

经过多年的大规模的考古发掘，纳提什瓦遗址的整体面貌已经基本明朗，接下来的任务是对遗址的保护和展示，考古发掘工作将配合保护和展示的需要而进行。

1. 遗址本体的临时性保护措施

鉴于发掘出土的遗址本体，已经出现不同程度的开裂、垮坍现象，遗址保护已经刻不容缓。目前已经对遗址采取了一些临时性保护措施。这些措施包括：将耸立在地面上的墙体、柱基，用牢固的木柱和竹席捆扎加固，以避免垮坍；大量使用沙袋作为护墙，放置在墙体旁和容易损毁的遗迹的凹陷处；在遗迹上覆盖塑料薄膜，再在其上用土回填；在遗址周围疏通排水沟渠，以避免长时间的积水对遗址的入侵；另外，在遗迹遗物特别重要的区域，有限度地采取一些抢险加固措施，实施局部保护。

2. 制定保护规划，实施遗址本体保护工程。

纳提什瓦遗址的保护模式，将尽可能地展示遗址的真实本体，不采取回填后在其上仿建的模式。在保护过程中，将遵循对遗址本体的最低干预原则，尽量实施预防性保护措施，同时确保工程材料的可逆性，保证遗址的原状不受损害。当然，如何解决南亚地区多雨和存在地下水位高诸多技术问题，将是对保护工作的主要挑战。

3. 建设考古遗址公园

纳提什瓦遗址遗迹体量极为壮观，具有很高的观赏价值，具备了建设考古遗址公园的良好条件。作为附属的遗址博物馆，陈列内容除介绍遗址本体外，还可包括：中国历史文化、中孟交往史、阿底峡和藏传佛教文化等，使它成为传播中国文化和中孟友谊的一个窗口。它们将与拉库罗普尔遗址、中国援建的阿底峡纪念堂结合在一起，构成一道风格独特的人文景观，成为当地民众的休闲场所和外国游客的观光目的地，这将是中孟友谊的又一里程碑。

Archaeological exploration and excavation

1. Some important cultural features of the first period such as Temple 1, pyramid-shaped stupa, Road 3, bathroom and drainage had already been uncovered at Nateshwar site, and a large number of potteries were also unearthed, but the layout and stratigraphy of the monastery are still unclear.

2. Almost similar to the Somapura monastery in Paharpur, the cruciform central temple of the second period at Nateshwar site is probably an architectural complex with boundary wall. There are 177 cells and many stupas and other facilities surrounding the main temple in Somapura monastery. It can be speculated that similar ancillary structures will also be found at Nateshwar and Raghurampur. From the indication of the exposed zigzag boundary wall and north entrance, we can continue to explore the extension scope of the boundary wall and the corresponding east, south, west and north gates' position in each side. Besides, some of the large stone pedestals on the edge of the mound are also an important clue. Moreover, on the northeast and south of the Pillared-hall 1, the northwest of the Pillared-hall 3 and the southwest of the Pillared-hall 4, the brick structures were found to connect with the foundation of the walls. However, further work is needed to clarify whether they are affiliated facilities.

3. From a macropoint of view, it is necessary to clarify the scope of the two sites of Nateshwar and Raghurampur as well as each of their natural boundaries by the methods of full-scale and a key area exploration. In addition, it is time the archaeological project to start to confirm the location and functional distribution of the ancient city of Vikrampura. According to previous researches, there are two possibilities for the layout of ancient Vikrampura city: one is just as Hiuen Tsang saw in this place——a moat surrounding the inner city-wall, which is about 20 li (10 kilometers) long (Xuanzang, 2014). The other possibility is that it is like Mahasthangrh and Wari-Bateshuar, most of monasteries and settlements are situated outside the fortified wall, with a certain distance between them (Rahman 2000; Rahman and Pathan 2012). For the next step survey of Vikrampura city site, a detailed plan should be formulated, based on the previous relevant practice of archaeological exploration and excavation. The city served as a generally political, economic, and cultural center, and should have a complex waterway system for traffic and trade functions. Topographic maps can provide us some clues on this. The application of the Ground Penetrating Radar System (GPRS) also can make exploration work more accurate and effective.

4. In the following excavation process, scientific archaeological techniques and methods should be applied to carry out more microscopic research. For instance, more faunal and botanic samples will be collected and analyzed to understand the environment and subsistence. The study of soil micromorphology will allow a better understanding of the formation process and the cause of the sediment. Other multidisciplinary research will also be included to make people know more about the human behaviors on the site.

The conservation and display of the site

After continuous large-scale archaeological work for several years, conservation and display work are becoming the next main tasks while some archaeological excavations will also be carried out in cooperation with the need of protection and dispaly.

1. The temporary conservation measures of the site. The uncovered brick structures have been already endangered by various damages such as cracking and collapse, so it is urgent to take some temporary measures to protect them before final proper conservation. At present, some measures have been implemented by Bangladesh-China joint team during and after every season's excavation. For instance, wooden pillars and bamboo mats are used to protect the brick walls above the ground floor from collapsing again. Many sandbags are put outside the structures. At hollow places, to protect wall, plastic films are used to cover the top of all exposed features and then these places are backfilled with soil, and drainage ditches are dug around the site to dredge raining water.

2. Formulating the protection plan to implement the conservation project on the site

In terms of final conservation, the Nateshwar site will be kept and displayed as much as possible when the project is carried out, instead of rebuilding other new structures as what is typically done in Bangladesh. The principle of the minimum intervention and preventive protection measures on the site will be strictly followed during the process while ensuring the reversibility of engineering materials. Of course, since most of the architectural remains are situated lower than current ground floor, it will be a big challenge to solve the problems of excessive raining water and groundwater in this low-lying area.

3. The construction of archaeological site park

It is no doubt that Nateshwar Buddhist settlement meets the essential requirements for constructing an archaeological site park, with a spectacular volume of brick structures and a high ornamental value. As for the site museum, the exhibition can also include: Chinese history and culture, communication history between Bangladesh and China, Atisha Dipankar and Tibetan Buddhism. This will create a new window of knowledge about Chinese culture and China-Bangladesh friendship. Together with the cultural remains uncovered in Raghurampur site and the Chinese-built Atisha's Memorial Hall, this unique cultural landscape will attract more and more people both from domestic and overseas areas.

References:

Barua, Dipak Kumar. *Viharas in Ancient India (A survey of Buddhist Monasteries)*, Indian Publications, Calcutta, 1969, p177.

Bhattasali, Nalini Kanta. *Iconography of Buddhist and Brahmanical Sculptures in the Dacca Museum*, Dacca Museum, Dacca, 1929, pVI.

Charkrabarti, Dilip K. *Ancient Bangladesh*, UPL, Dhaka, 1992.

Dikshit, Rao Bahadur K. N. *Excavation at Paharpur, Bengal. Memoirs of the ASI*, no. 55. DG, ASI, New Delhi, 1938.

Ghosh, Ambikacaran, 1275 BS. Vikrampurer Itihas Pracin O Adhunik Vivaran, Dhaka.

Gupta, Jagendranath, 1316 BS. Vikrampurer Itihas, Kolkata.

Islam, Shariful. *New Light on the History of the South-East Bengal*, ASB, Dhaka, 2014, pp.85-105.

Rahman, Sufi Mostafizur and Bulbul Ahmed, 'Janapada Punch-marked Coins from Wari-Bateshwar, Narsingdi, Bangladesh', in K. Krishna Naik and E. Siva Nagi Reddy edited. *Cultural Contour of History and Archaeology*, vol. IV, B. R. Publishing Corporation, Delhi, 2015, pp. 1-9.

Rahman, Shah Sufi Mostafizur. *Archaeological Investigation in Bogra District*. ICSBA, Dhaka, 2000.

Rahman, Sufi Mostafizur and Muhammad Habibullah Pathan. *Wari-Bateshwar: Shekarer Sandhane*, Prothoma Prokasan, Dhaka, 2012.

Ven Fazun (translator). *The Biography of Venerable Atisha*, (in Chinese), Chengdu Press and Publication Bureau, vol. 1, 1995.

Xuanzang, (translated by Dong Zhiqiao). *Journey to the West in Tang Dynasty*, Zhonghua Book Company, 2014.

Zong Kaba. *The Great Treatise on the Path to Enlightenment*. (in Tibetan language). Qinghai People's Press, 1985, p4.

Appendix

附 录

纳提什瓦
Nateshwar

附录一

REPORT OF RADIOCARBON DATING ANALYSES

Dr. Haibin Gu
Report Date: 3/24/2015

Hunan Archaeological
3/10/2015

Material Received:

Sample Data	Measured Radiocarbon Age	d13C	Conventional Radiocarbon Age(*)
Beta - 406425	890 +/- 30 BP	-11.2 o/oo	1120 +/- 30

BP SAMPLE : 1, I11G3(4)
ANALYSIS : AMS-Standard delivery
MATERIAL/PRETREATMENT : (charred material): acid/alkali/acid
2 SIGMA CALIBRATION :   Cal AD 780 to 785 (Cal BP 1170 to 1165) and Cal AD 880 to 990 (Cal BP 1070 to 960)

Beta - 406426	1090 +/- 30 BP	-26.0 o/oo	1070 +/- 30

BP SAMPLE : 2, I11G3(4)
ANALYSIS : AMS-Standard delivery
MATERIAL/PRETREATMENT : (charred material): acid/alkali/acid
2 SIGMA CALIBRATION :   Cal AD 895 to 925 (Cal BP 1055 to 1025) and Cal AD 940 to 1020 (Cal BP 1010 to 930)

Beta - 406427	840 +/- 30 BP	-10.4 o/oo	1080 +/- 30

BP SAMPLE : 3, I11G2-G3(4)
ANALYSIS : AMS-Standard delivery
MATERIAL/PRETREATMENT : (charred material): acid/alkali/acid
2 SIGMA CALIBRATION :   Cal AD 895 to 1020 (Cal BP 1055 to 930)

Beta - 406428	1210 +/- 30 BP	-27.3 o/oo	1170 +/- 30

BP SAMPLE : 4, I11G2-G3(7)
ANALYSIS : AMS-Standard delivery
MATERIAL/PRETREATMENT : (charred material): acid/alkali/acid
2 SIGMA CALIBRATION :   Cal AD 770 to 905 (Cal BP 1180 to 1045) and Cal AD 920 to 965 (Cal BP 1030 to 985)

Sample Data	Measured Radiocarbon Age	d13C	Conventional Radiocarbon Age(*)
Beta - 406429 BP SAMPLE : 5, J11G-A4(5) ANALYSIS : AMS-Standard delivery MATERIAL/PRETREATMENT : (charred material): acid/alkali/acid 2 SIGMA CALIBRATION : Cal AD 775 to 790 (Cal BP 1175 to 1160) and Cal AD 800 to 980 (Cal BP 1150 to 970)	1160 +/- 30 BP	-26.5 o/oo	1140 +/- 30
Beta - 406430 BP SAMPLE : 6, J11G-A4(7)? ANALYSIS : AMS-Standard delivery MATERIAL/PRETREATMENT : (charred material): acid/alkali/acid 2 SIGMA CALIBRATION : Cal AD 885 to 995 (Cal BP 1065 to 955)	1140 +/- 30 BP	-26.7 o/oo	1110 +/- 30
Beta - 406431 BP SAMPLE : 7, I11G2-G3(8) ANALYSIS : AMS-Standard delivery MATERIAL/PRETREATMENT : (charred material): acid/alkali/acid 2 SIGMA CALIBRATION : Cal AD 895 to 925 (Cal BP 1055 to 1025) and Cal AD 940 to 1020 (Cal BP 1010 to 930)	1050 +/- 30 BP	-23.8 o/oo	1070 +/- 30
Beta - 406433 BP SAMPLE : 9, I11G2-G3(8) ANALYSIS : AMS-Standard delivery MATERIAL/PRETREATMENT : (charred material): acid/alkali/acid 2 SIGMA CALIBRATION : Cal AD 770 to 905 (Cal BP 1180 to 1045) and Cal AD 920 to 965 (Cal BP 1030 to 985)	1150 +/- 30 BP	-23.6 o/oo	1170 +/- 30

Sample Data	Measured Radiocarbon Age	d13C	Conventional Radiocarbon Age(*)
Beta - 406434 BP SAMPLE : 10, I10G9(8) ANALYSIS : AMS-Standard delivery MATERIAL/PRETREATMENT : (charred material): acid/alkali/acid 2 SIGMA CALIBRATION : Cal AD 775 to 975 (Cal BP 1175 to 975)	1170 +/- 30 BP	-26.0 o/oo	1150 +/- 30
Beta - 406436 BP SAMPLE : 12, J11G-D3(5) ANALYSIS : AMS-Standard delivery MATERIAL/PRETREATMENT : (charred material): acid/alkali/acid 2 SIGMA CALIBRATION : Cal AD 885 to 995 (Cal BP 1065 to 955)	1100 +/- 30 BP	-24.2 o/oo	1110 +/- 30

Beta - 406437   1000 +/- 30 BP   -25.7 o/oo   990 +/- 30
BP SAMPLE : 13, K10I4(5)
ANALYSIS : AMS-Standard delivery
MATERIAL/PRETREATMENT : (charred material): acid/alkali/acid
2 SIGMA CALIBRATION : Cal AD 995 to 1050 (Cal BP 955 to 900) and Cal AD 1085 to 1125 (Cal BP 865 to 825) and Cal AD 1140 to 1150 (Cal BP 810 to 800)

Beta - 406438   1160 +/- 30 BP   -27.6 o/oo   1120 +/- 30
BP SAMPLE : 14, K9J9(5)
ANALYSIS : AMS-Standard delivery
MATERIAL/PRETREATMENT : (charred material): acid/alkali/acid
2 SIGMA CALIBRATION : Cal AD 780 to 785 (Cal BP 1170 to 1165) and Cal AD 880 to 990 (Cal BP 1070 to 960)

Sample Data	Measured Radiocarbon Age	d13C	Conventional Radiocarbon Age(*)

Beta - 406439   1050 +/- 30 BP   -25.9 o/oo   1040 +/- 30
BP SAMPLE : 15, K10J3(5)
ANALYSIS : AMS-Standard delivery
MATERIAL/PRETREATMENT : (charred material): acid/alkali/acid
2 SIGMA CALIBRATION :   Cal AD 970 to 1025 (Cal BP 980 to 925)

Beta - 406441   920 +/- 30 BP   -11.1 o/oo   1150 +/- 30
BP SAMPLE : 17, K10I1J2(5)
ANALYSIS : AMS-Standard delivery
MATERIAL/PRETREATMENT : (charred material): acid/alkali/acid
2 SIGMA CALIBRATION :   Cal AD 775 to 975 (Cal BP 1175 to 975)

Beta - 406442   1010 +/- 30 BP   -25.8 o/oo   1000 +/- 30
BP SAMPLE : 18, K10I3(5)
ANALYSIS : AMS-Standard delivery
MATERIAL/PRETREATMENT : (charred material): acid/alkali/acid
2 SIGMA CALIBRATION : Cal AD 990 to 1045 (Cal BP 960 to 905) and Cal AD 1095 to 1120 (Cal BP 855 to 830) and Cal AD 1140 to 1145 (Cal BP 810 to 805)

Beta - 406443   1230 +/- 30 BP   -29.7 o/oo   1150 +/- 30
BP SAMPLE : 19, K10E3(4)
ANALYSIS : AMS-Standard delivery
MATERIAL/PRETREATMENT : (charred material): acid/alkali/acid
2 SIGMA CALIBRATION : Cal AD 775 to 975 (Cal BP 1175 to 975)

Sample Data	Measured Radiocarbon Age	d13C	Conventional Radiocarbon Age(*)
Beta - 406444	1100 +/- 30 BP	-27.7 o/oo	1060 +/- 30

BP SAMPLE : 20, K9J9(4)
ANALYSIS : AMS-Standard delivery
MATERIAL/PRETREATMENT : (charred material): acid/alkali/acid
2 SIGMA CALIBRATION :   Cal AD 900 to 925 (Cal BP 1050 to 1025) and Cal AD 945 to 1020 (Cal BP 1005 to 930)

Sample Data	Measured Radiocarbon Age	d13C	Conventional Radiocarbon Age(*)
Beta - 406445	1120 +/- 30 BP	-26.7 o/oo	1090 +/- 30

BP SAMPLE : 21, L10E5F6(4)
ANALYSIS : AMS-Standard delivery
MATERIAL/PRETREATMENT : (charred material): acid/alkali/acid
2 SIGMA CALIBRATION :   Cal AD 890 to 1015 (Cal BP 1060 to 935)

Sample Data	Measured Radiocarbon Age	d13C	Conventional Radiocarbon Age(*)
Beta - 406446	1140 +/- 30 BP	-28.4 o/oo	1080 +/- 30

BP SAMPLE : 22, L10G-B5
ANALYSIS : AMS-Standard delivery
MATERIAL/PRETREATMENT : (charred material): acid/alkali/acid
2 SIGMA CALIBRATION :   Cal AD 895 to 1020 (Cal BP 1055 to 930)

Sample Data	Measured Radiocarbon Age	d13C	Conventional Radiocarbon Age(*)
Beta - 406447	1180 +/- 30 BP	-28.2 o/oo	1130 +/- 30

BP SAMPLE : 23, L10G-B5
ANALYSIS : AMS-Standard delivery
MATERIAL/PRETREATMENT : (charred material): acid/alkali/acid
2 SIGMA CALIBRATION :   Cal AD 780 to 790 (Cal BP 1170 to 1160) and Cal AD 870 to 985 (Cal BP 1080 to 965)

Sample Data	Measured Radiocarbon Age	d13C	Conventional Radiocarbon Age(*)
Beta - 406448	1160 +/- 30 BP	-24.7 o/oo	1160 +/- 30

BP SAMPLE : 24, L10G-B5
ANALYSIS : AMS-Standard delivery
MATERIAL/PRETREATMENT : (charred material): acid/alkali/acid
2 SIGMA CALIBRATION :   Cal AD 775 to 970 (Cal BP 1175 to 980)

Sample Data	Measured Radiocarbon Age	d13C	Conventional Radiocarbon Age(*)
Beta - 406449	1180 +/- 30 BP	-25.2 o/oo	1180 +/- 30

BP SAMPLE : 25, L10G-B5
ANALYSIS : AMS-Standard delivery
MATERIAL/PRETREATMENT : (charred material): acid/alkali/acid
2 SIGMA CALIBRATION :   Cal AD 770 to 900 (Cal BP 1180 to 1050) and Cal AD 925 to 945 (Cal BP 1025 to 1005)

Beta - 406450　　　　　　　　　　1190 +/- 30 BP　　　　　　　　-26.3 o/oo　　　　　　　　1170 +/- 30
BP SAMPLE : 26, L10B4
ANALYSIS : AMS-Standard delivery
MATERIAL/PRETREATMENT : (charred material): acid/alkali/acid
2 SIGMA CALIBRATION : Cal AD 770 to 905 (Cal BP 1180 to 1045) and Cal AD 920 to 965 (Cal BP 1030 to 985)

Beta - 406451　　　　　　　　　　1100 +/- 30 BP　　　　　　　　-25.6 o/oo　　　　　　　　1090 +/- 30
BP SAMPLE : 27, L10B4
ANALYSIS : AMS-Standard delivery
MATERIAL/PRETREATMENT : (charred material): acid/alkali/acid
2 SIGMA CALIBRATION : Cal AD 890 to 1015 (Cal BP 1060 to 935)

Sample Data	Measured Radiocarbon Age	d13C	Conventional Radiocarbon Age(*)

Beta - 406452　　　　　　　　　　1030 +/- 30 BP　　　　　　　　-26.8 o/oo　　　　　　　　1000 +/- 30
BP SAMPLE : 28, L8G3H4(5)
ANALYSIS : AMS-Standard delivery
MATERIAL/PRETREATMENT : (charred material): acid/alkali/acid
2 SIGMA CALIBRATION :　Cal AD 990 to 1045 (Cal BP 960 to 905) and Cal AD 1095 to 1120 (Cal BP 855 to 830) and Cal
　　　　　　　　　　　　　AD 1140 to 1145 (Cal BP 810 to 805)

Beta - 406453　　　　　　　　　　1050 +/- 30 BP　　　　　　　　-24.5 o/oo　　　　　　　　1060 +/- 30
BP SAMPLE : 29, L8G3H4(5)
ANALYSIS : AMS-Standard delivery
MATERIAL/PRETREATMENT : (charred material): acid/alkali/acid
2 SIGMA CALIBRATION :　 Cal AD 900 to 925 (Cal BP 1050 to 1025) and Cal AD 945 to 1020 (Cal BP 1005 to 930)

Dates are reported as RCYBP (radiocarbon years before present, "present" = AD 1950). By international convention, the modern reference standard was 95% the 14C activity of the National Institute of Standards and Technology (NIST) Oxalic Acid (SRM 4990C) and calculated using the Libby 14C half-life (5568 years). Quoted errors represent 1 relative standard deviation statistics (68% probability) counting errors based on the combined measurements of the sample, background, and modern reference standards. Measured 13C/12C ratios (delta 13C) were calculated relative to the PDB-1 standard.

The Conventional Radiocarbon Age represents the Measured Radiocarbon Age corrected for isotopic fractionation, calculated using the delta 13C. On rare occasion where the Conventional Radiocarbon Age was calculated using an assumed delta 13C, the ratio and the Conventional Radiocarbon Age will be followed by "*". The Conventional Radiocarbon Age is not calendar calibrated. When available, the Calendar Calibrated result is calculated from the Conventional Radiocarbon Age and is listed as the "Two Sigma Calibrated Result" for each sample.

附录二

孟加拉国纳提什瓦遗址出土动物遗存

湖南省文物考古研究所　莫林恒

一、遗址出土动物种属

孟加拉国纳提什瓦 (Nateshwar) 遗址 2014 年 12 月至 2018 年 1 月考古发掘出土的动物骨骼共计 938 件。通过对骨骼鉴定研究，可将这批材料分为两种情况。一部分是可以鉴定到种属 (NISP) 的动物骨骼，共 432 件，占总数的 46%；另一部分是由于太过破碎等原因无法进行种属鉴定的，共 506 件，占总数 54%。目前鉴定到种属的动物包括水牛、黄牛、猪、山羊、马、狗、小麂、水鹿、鸡、鼠、鱼、陆龟、蟹守螺、玉螺等，包括 5 纲、8 目、11 科、15 种属。具体种属如下：

软体动物门 Mollusca	腹足纲 Gastropoda	中腹足目 Mesogastropoda	蟹守螺科 Cerithiidae	蟹守螺属 *Telesecopium*	
			玉螺科 Naticidae	玉螺属 *Natica*	
脊索动物门 Chordata	硬骨鱼纲 Osteichthyes				
	爬行纲 Reptilia	龟鳖目 Testudinata	陆龟科 Testudinidae	陆龟属 *Testudo*	陆龟 *Testudo* sp.
	鸟纲 Aves	鸡形目 Galliformes	雉科 Phasianidae	原鸡属 *Gallus*	家鸡 *Gallus gallus domesticus* Brisson
	哺乳纲 Mammalia	啮齿目 Rodentia	鼠科 Muridae	家鼠属 *Rattus*	
		食肉目 Carnivora	犬科 Canidae	犬属 *Canis*	狗 *Canis familiaris* Linnaeus
		长鼻目 Proboscidea	象科 Eelphantidea	亚洲象属 *Elephas*	亚洲象 *Elephas maximus* Linnaeus
		奇蹄目 Perissodactyla	马科 Equidae	马属 *Equus*	马 *Equus caballus* sp.
		偶蹄目 Artiodactyla	猪科 Suidae	猪属 *Sus*	家猪 *Sus scrofa domesticus* Linnaeus
			鹿科 Cervidae	麂属 *Muntiacus*	小麂 *Muntiacus reevesi* Ogilby
				鹿属 *Cervus*	水鹿 *Cervus unicolor* (Kerr)
			牛科 Bovidae	牛属 *Bos*	黄牛（未定种）*Bos* sp.
				水牛属 *Bubalus*	水牛（未定种）*Bubalus* sp.
				山羊属 *Capra*	山羊（未定种）*Capra* sp.

二、各种动物骨骼出土概况及典型标本描述

以下对各种动物骨骼的出土情况进行一种概述，介绍各种动物骨骼出土数量、保存状况，挑选典型骨骼标本举例。

（一）蟹守螺 Telesecopium

共22件，保存蟹守螺的壳体部分，每件壳体都有不同程度的残损。

1. 螺壳

（1）标本：UnitK9GridI2②：1（图版一、1）。

（2）测量数据：上下长28.9 mm、左右长16.3 mm。

（3）描述：壳体呈竖三角形，底部残损。

（二）玉螺 Natica

共35件，保存玉螺的壳体，大部分骨骼残损，少量保存完整。

1. 螺壳

（1）标本：UnitK9GridA1②：1（图版一、2）。

（2）测量数据：最大长55.1 mm、螺口口径37.9 mm。

（3）描述：壳体保存完整。

（三）鱼 Osteichthyes

共30件，以小型鱼类骨骼为主，骨骼多已破碎，可辨识的骨骼部位有鳃盖骨、脊椎骨及其它头部骨骼。

1. 主鳃盖骨

（1）标本：UnitG10GridD8⑥：1（图版一、4）。

（2）测量数据：上下长19.9 mm、前后长14.1 mm、厚1.1 mm。

（3）描述：左侧主鳃盖骨，保存完整。

（四）陆龟 Testudo sp.

共49件，以陆龟的腹甲、背甲为主，骨骼都较为破碎。

1. 腹甲

（1）标本：UnitJ13GridA5②：1（图版一、6）。

（2）测量数据：前后长68.4 mm、左右长73.1mm、厚8.6 mm。

（3）描述：左前侧底板，左侧、后侧为骨缝结合部位。

（五）鸡 Gallus gallus domesticus Brisson

共1件，为胫骨部位。

1. 胫骨

（1）标本：UnitI10GridG9⑦：1（图版一、4）。

（2）测量数据：长度58.4 mm、宽度13.3 mm。

（3）描述：左侧胫骨，近端未愈合，远端残缺。骨骼外侧面有两处刮削痕迹。

（六）家鼠 Rattus

共1件，为门齿骨骼部位。

1. 门齿

（1）标本：F6：2（图版一、5）。

（2）测量数据：上下长21.7 mm、前后长2.0 mm、左右长1.6 mm。

（3）描述：为左侧下门齿，门齿保存基本完整，根部略残。

（七）狗 Canis familiaris Linnaeus

共2件，为1件残损牙齿和1件肱骨骨骼。

1. 肱骨

（1）标本：UnitJ13GridA5②：1（图版二、1）。

（2）测量数据：长度67.8 mm、宽度24.82 mm。

（3）描述：右侧肱骨，保存骨骼中远部。

（八）亚洲象 Elephas maximus Linnaeus

共1件，为1残缺臼齿。

图版一

1. 蟹守螺 2. 玉螺 3. 鸡胫骨 4. 鱼鳃盖骨 5. 家鼠门齿 6. 陆龟腹甲

1. 臼齿

（1）标本：UnitK8GridH8⑤：1（图版二、2）。

（2）测量数据：上下长44.5 mm、左右长59.1 mm、前后长25.3mm。

（3）描述：残存两排臼齿齿板，齿面磨蚀较重。

（九）马 Equus caballus sp.

共出土2件骨骼，分别为臼齿和第1指（趾）骨。

1. 臼齿

（1）标本：UnitI11GridG3③：1（图版二、6）。

（2）测量数据：齿长72.4 mm、齿面长28.1 mm；齿齿面宽18.2mm。

（3）描述：为一左侧单颗臼齿，保存基本完整。

2. 第1指（趾）骨

（1）标本：UnitL7GridG10⑦：1（图版二、5）。

（2）测量数据：最大长（GL）76.5 mm、近端宽51.1 mm、远端宽（Bd）37.6mm。

（3）描述：骨骼保存完整。

（十）猪
Sus scrofa domesticus Linnaeus

共22件，包括牙齿5件，肱骨2件，股骨1件，胫骨14件，。

1. 臼齿

（1）标本：UnitL10GridL1④：1（图版二、3）。

（2）测量数据：前后长23.4mm、左右长16.6 mm、上下长15.6 mm。

（3）描述：为一单颗臼齿，臼齿后部残缺，齿面基本未磨蚀。

2. 肱骨

（1）标本：UnitK9GridI4⑤：1（图版二、4）。

（2）测量数据：长度120.1mm、远端宽（Bd）29.8 mm。

（3）描述：保存肱骨中远部，近端断裂处可见砍断痕迹。

（十一）小麂
Muntiacus reevesi Ogilby

共10件，为一个单位内集中出土，骨骼部位包括牙齿、桡骨、掌骨、跖骨、中央跗骨、距骨、第1指（趾）骨、第2指（趾）骨。

1. 桡骨

（1）标本：UnitK9GridG2⑤：5（图版三、1）。

（2）测量数据：残长30.3mm、远端宽（Bd）28.7mm。

（3）描述：右侧桡骨，保存骨骼远端部分。骨骼局部可见浅红褐色烤痕。

2. 炮骨

（1）标本：UnitK9GridG2⑤：3（图版三、2）。

（2）测量数据：残长60.4 mm、近端宽（Bp）18.5 mm。

（3）描述：右侧炮骨，残存骨骼远端部分。远端关节面有红褐色烤痕。

3. 掌骨

（1）标本：UnitK9GridG2⑤：9（图版三、3）。

（2）测量数据：残长34.1mm、近端宽（Bp）21.9mm。

（3）描述：右侧掌骨，保存骨骼近端部分。近端关节面有烤痕。

4. 跖骨

（1）标本：UnitK9GridG2⑤：1（图版三、6）。

（2）测量数据：残长60.4 mm、近端宽（Bp）18.5 mm。

（3）描述：右侧跖骨，保存骨骼近中部分。近端关节面有烤痕。

5. 中央跗骨

（1）标本：UnitK9GridG2⑤：10（图版三、4）。

（2）测量数据：前后长19.5 mm、最大宽（GB）21.3 mm。

（3）描述：右侧中央跗骨，骨骼保存完整。骨骼局部有红褐色烤痕。

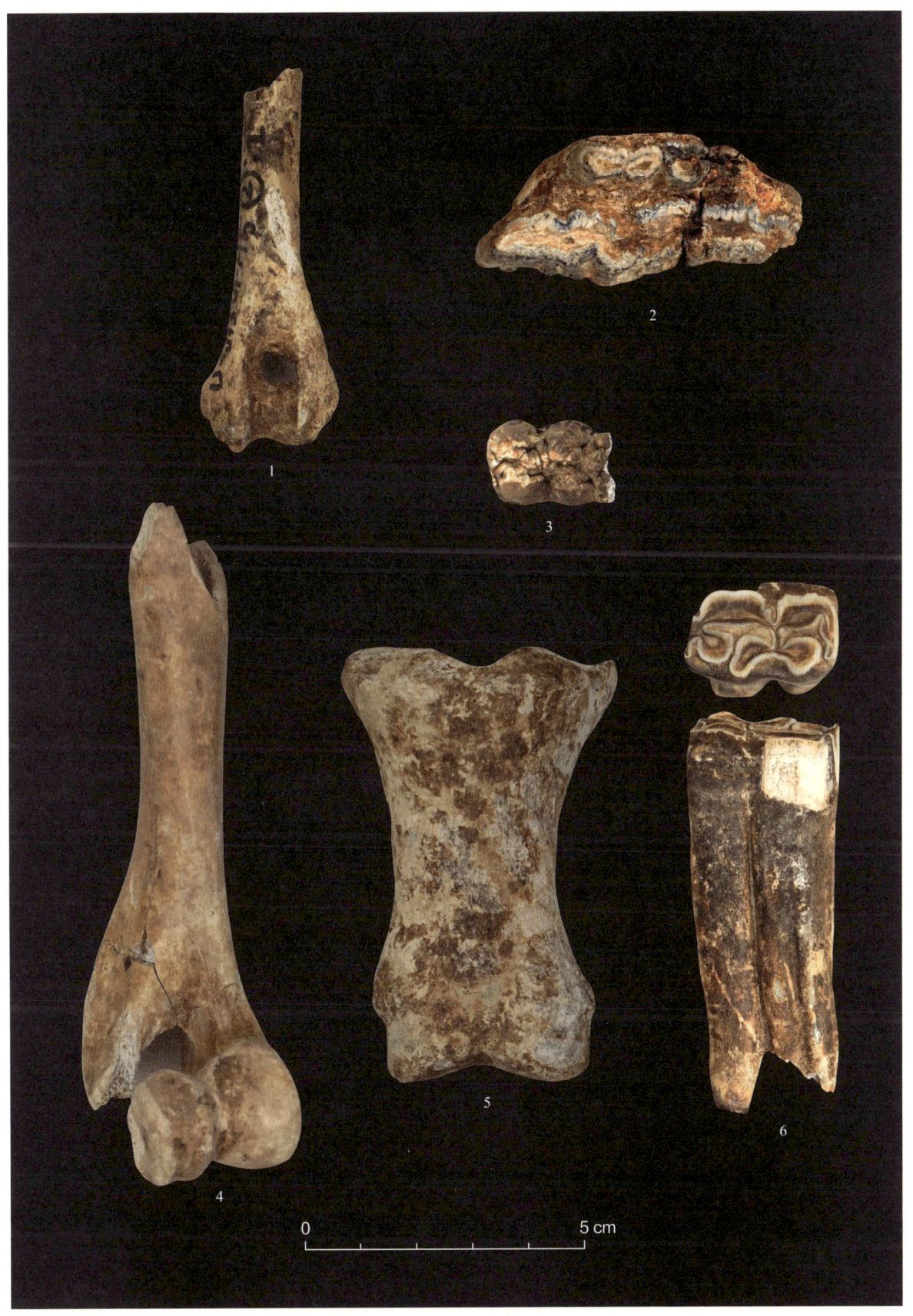

图版二
1. 狗肱骨　2. 亚州象臼齿　3. 猪臼齿　4. 猪肱骨　5. 马第1指（趾）骨　6. 马臼齿

6. 距骨

（1）标本：UnitK9GridG2⑤：7（图版三、6）。

（2）测量数据：外部最大长（GLl）23.6 mm、最大宽（GB）21.3mm。

（3）描述：右侧距骨，骨骼保存完整。骨骼局部有红褐色烤痕。

7. 第1指（趾）骨

（1）标本：UnitK9GridG2⑤：2（图版三、5）。

（2）测量数据：最大长（GL）29.6 mm、近端宽（Bp）11.7 mm。

（3）描述：骨骼保存完整。骨骼局部有红褐色烤痕。

8. 第2指（趾）骨

（1）标本：UnitK9GridG2⑤：12（图版三、8）。

（2）测量数据：最大长（GL）17.9 mm、近端宽（Bp）9.9 mm。

（3）描述：骨骼保存完整。骨骼局部有红褐色烤痕。

（十二）水鹿 Cervus unicolor (Kerr)

共1件，为水鹿跖骨。

1. 跖骨

（1）标本：UnitI12GridI5④：1（图版四、3）。

（2）测量数据：长度98.3 mm、近端宽（Bp）35.9mm。

（3）描述：右侧跖骨，保存骨骼近中部分，远端关节头砍断。

（十三）黄牛 Bos sp.

牛骨骼出土较多，共242件。骨骼出土状况都较为破碎。受水平能力及条件限制，在牛骨骼中鉴定出3件为黄牛，分别是黄牛的下颌骨、肱骨、跖骨。

1. 下颌骨

（1）标本：UnitJ10GridD10②：1（图版四、1）。

（2）测量数据：前后长77.0 mm、上下长44.5 mm、左右长22.9 mm。

（3）描述：右侧下颌骨，保存下颌骨中部一段，附有M1、M2、P4三颗牙齿。

2. 肱骨

（1）标本：UnitL9GridA9③：1（图版四、2）。

（2）测量数据：长度126.3 mm、远端宽（Bd）59.6 mm。

（3）描述：左侧肱骨，保存骨骼远端，骨骼表面可见砍痕、切痕。

3. 跖骨

（1）标本：UnitK9GridG9⑤：1（图版四、4）。

（2）测量数据：长度182.2 mm、近端宽（Bp）37.4 mm。

（3）描述：右侧跖骨，保存骨骼近中部分，远端关节头砍断。

（十四）水牛 Bubalus sp.

牛骨骼出土较多，其中在UnitL9GridF6第⑤层集中出土了一批牛骨骼，鉴定判断这批骨骼属于同一水牛个体，骨骼部位包括下颌骨、肱骨、桡骨、尺骨、颈椎、腰椎、肋骨、掌骨、跖骨、膝盖骨、距骨、中央跗骨、第1指（趾）骨、第2指（趾）骨等。

1. 下颌骨

（1）标本：UnitL9GridF6⑤：18（图版五、1）。

（2）测量数据：前后长136.2 mm、上下长81.2 mm、左右长22.9 mm。M1齿面长29.9 mm、齿面宽17.2 mm；M2齿面长30.4 mm、齿面宽17.7 mm；M3齿面长45.1 mm、齿面宽16.9 mm。

（3）描述：左侧下颌骨，包含有M1、M2、M3三颗牙齿。

2. 颈椎

（1）标本：UnitL9GridF6⑤：8（图版五、2）。

（2）测量数据：前关节突到后关节突长（GLPa）90.5mm、前关节突最大宽（BPacr）81.5 mm、后关节突最大宽（BPacd）95.1mm。

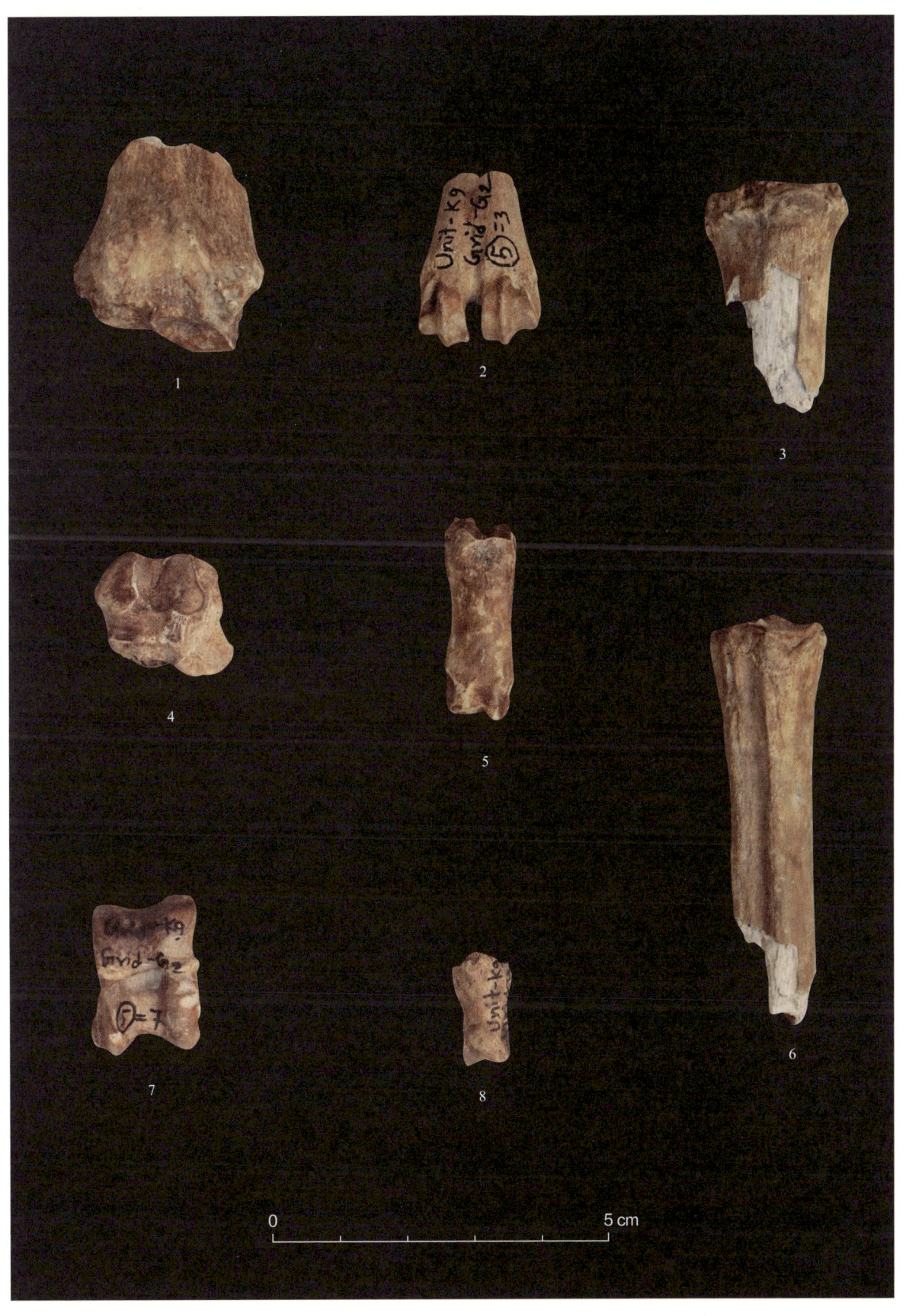

图版三
1. 小麂桡骨　2. 小麂炮骨　3. 小麂掌骨　4. 小麂中央跗骨　5. 小麂第1指（趾）骨　6. 小麂跖骨
7. 小麂距骨　8. 小麂第2指（趾）骨

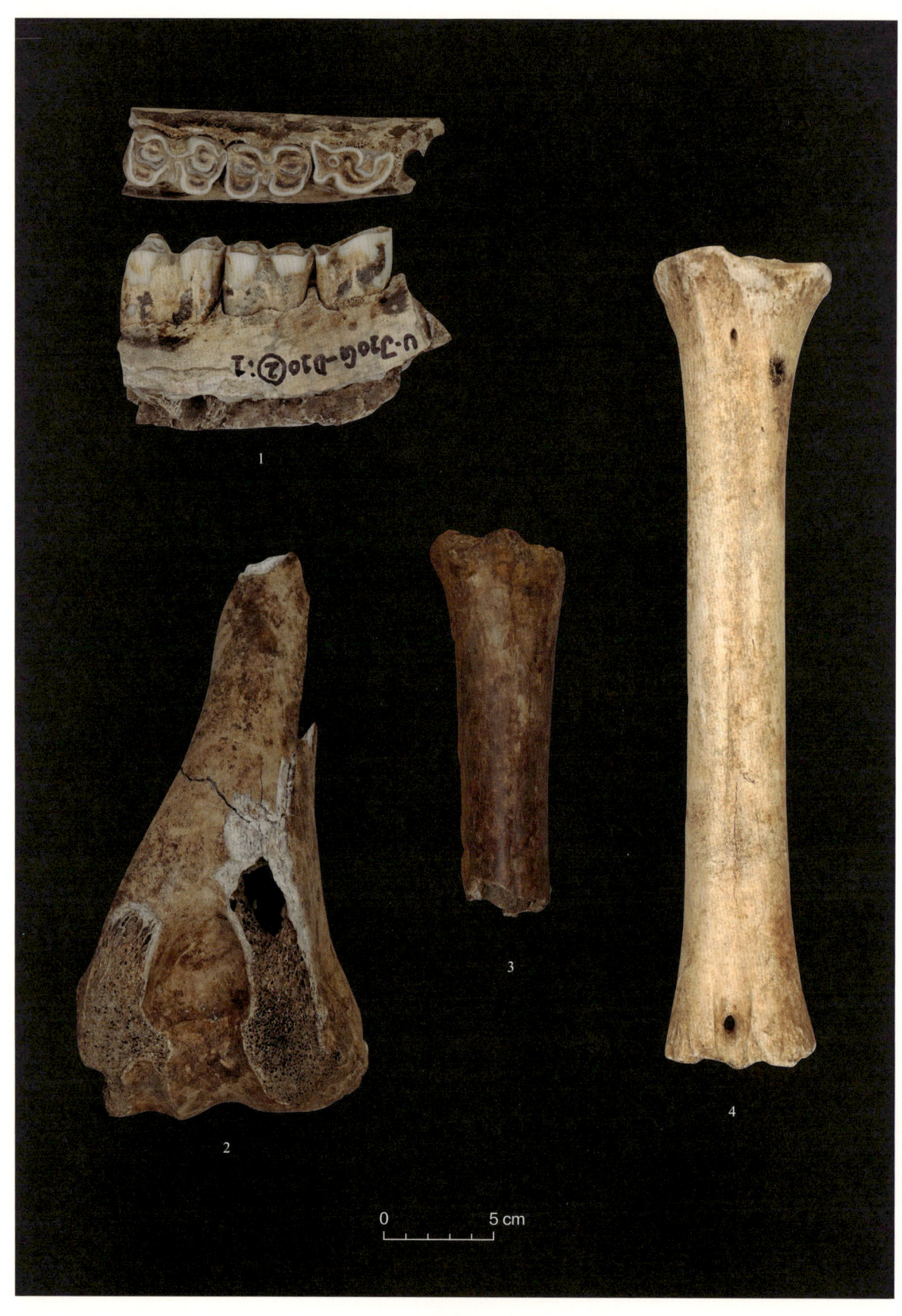

图版四
1. 黄牛下颌骨 2. 黄牛肱骨 3. 水鹿跖骨 4. 黄牛跖骨

（3）描述：骨骼保存基本完整，横突、棘突略残。

3. 肱骨

（1）标本：UnitL9GridF6⑤：7（图版五、3）。

（2）测量数据：残长201.1mm、远端前后长98.5 mm。

（3）描述：左侧肱骨，骨骼保存远端部分。远端关节有一道切割痕迹长16.1mm、宽1mm。

4. 桡骨

（1）标本：UnitL9GridF6⑤：2（图版五、4）。

（2）测量数据：残长167.6 mm、近端宽（Bp）102.8 mm。

（3）描述：右侧桡骨，保存骨骼近端部分，骨骼断裂处可见砸痕。

5. 中央跗骨

（1）标本：UnitL9GridF6⑤：11（图版六、1）。

（2）测量数据：前后长68.4mm、最大宽（GB）79.1 mm。

（3）描述：左侧中央跗骨，骨骼保存完整。外侧面有两道切痕。

6. 距骨

（1）标本：UnitL9GridF6⑤：5（图版六、3）。

（2）测量数据：外半部最大长（GLl）89.9mm、内半部最大厚（Dm）37.2 mm。

（3）描述：左侧距骨，骨骼保存基本完整，内半部略残。

8. 第1指（趾）骨

（1）标本：UnitL10GridA2②：1（图版六、2）。

（2）测量数据：最大长（GL）79.5mm、近端宽（Bp）42.9 mm。

（3）描述：骨骼保存完整。

9. 第2指（趾）骨

（1）标本：UnitL9GridF6⑤：11（图版六、5）。

（2）测量数据：最大长（GL）58.2mm、近端最大宽（Bp）41.8 mm。

（3）描述：骨骼保存完整，外侧面有一道切痕。

10. 蹄骨

（1）标本：UnitL9GridF6⑤：3（图版六、4）。

（2）测量数据：蹄底残长89.5 mm、蹄底中部宽（MBS）37.2 mm。

（3）描述：左侧蹄骨，骨骼保存基本完整，远端略残。

（十五）山羊 *Capra* sp.

共出土7件，骨骼部位包括下颌骨、牙齿、桡骨与脊椎骨。

1. 下颌骨

（1）标本：UnitK9GridI2⑤：1（图版六、6）。

（2）测量数据：长度56.1 mm、高度36.5 mm；M3齿前后长21.5mm、齿面宽6.9mm；M2齿前后长12.6mm、齿面宽6.5mm。

（3）描述：左侧下颌骨，保存M2、M3两颗臼齿。

2. 桡骨

（1）标本：UnitK9GridI4②：1（图版六、7）。

（2）测量数据：长度76.9 mm、近端宽（Bp）25.1 mm。

（3）描述：左侧桡骨，桡骨与尺骨结合在一起，远端缺损。

三、相关问题探讨

纳提什瓦遗址出土的动物骨骼都较为破碎，根据观察，部分骨骼存在对动物的肢解、加工利用痕迹，如砍、砸、切、刮、烤等，并有部分加工成骨器，分析这些动物骨骼主要是古代人类消费的食物残骸。遗址共出土938件动物骨骼，其中432件为可鉴定标本，从各种动物骨骼出土的数量来看，家养动物共计274件，可鉴定标本数的63.89%，可见是以家养动物为主要的消费对象。这其中牛总数为242件，占家养动物的88.32%，其次是猪22件、山羊7件，可见这几种动物是主要的消费对象。其它的家养动物只有少量出土，其中马2件、狗2件、鸡1件，推测鸡的骨骼出

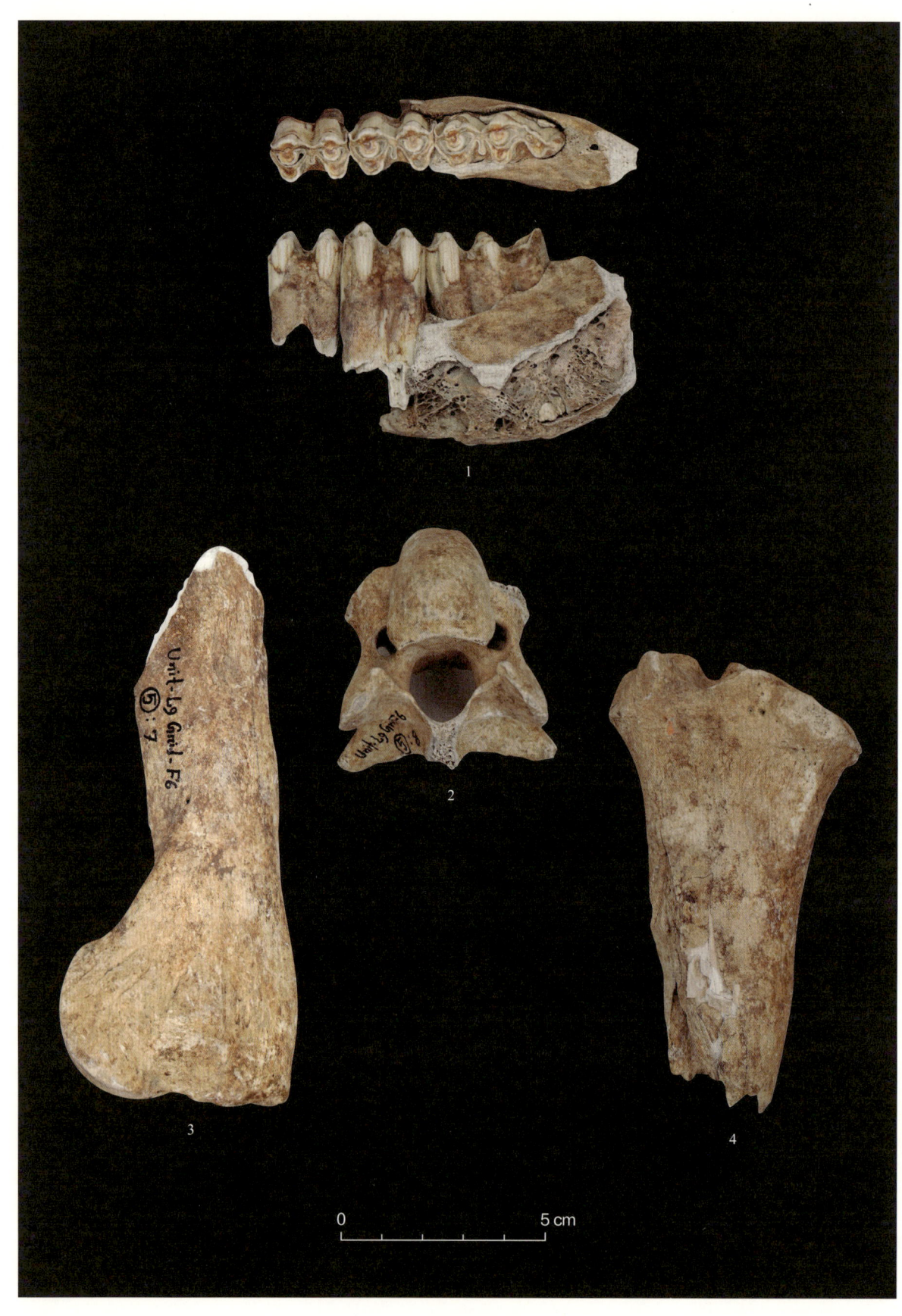

图版五
1. 水牛下颌骨 2. 水牛颈椎 3. 水牛肱骨 4. 水牛桡骨

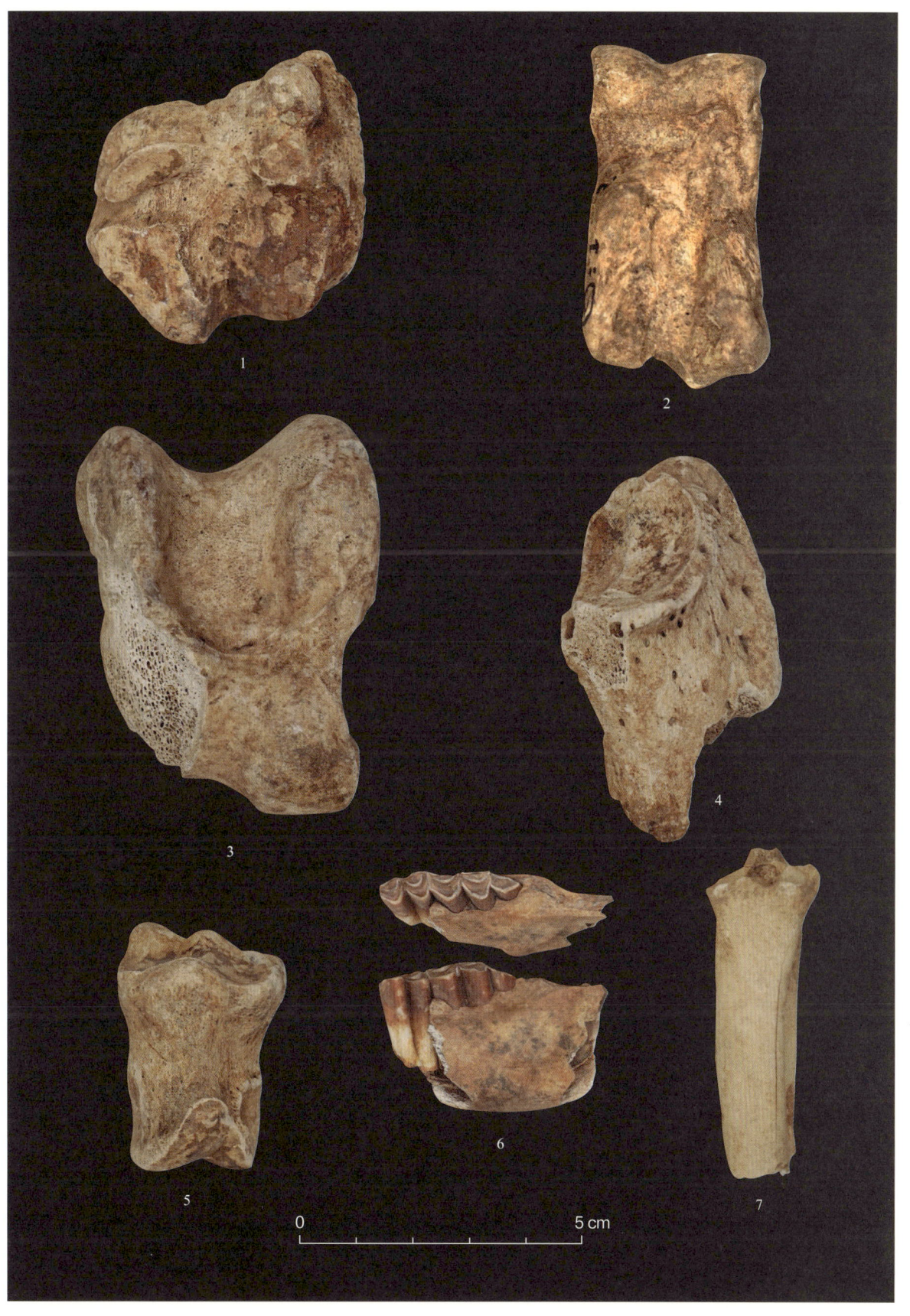

图版六
1. 水牛中央跗骨 2. 水牛第1指（趾）骨 3. 水牛距骨 4. 水牛蹄骨
5. 水牛第2指（趾）骨 6. 山羊下颌骨 7. 山羊桡骨

土较少或许与这种小动物的骨骼在遗址中不易保存收集有关。野生动物中，鱼类30件，陆龟49件，蟹守螺22件，玉螺35件，小鹿10件，水鹿1件，亚洲象1件。从数量上看以鱼类、蟹守螺、玉螺、陆龟代表的水生动物数量较多，另外小鹿和水鹿代表的鹿科动物也存在一定比例。

动物骨骼在各个地层都有出土。经统计第①层出土3件，第②层出土497件，第③层出土7件，第④层出土204件，第⑤层出土190件，第⑥层出土14件，第⑦层出土12件，F6出土11件。第①层出土动物骨骼代表近现代人类生活消费，在此不予探讨。属于古代遗存的动物骨骼共计935件，分为早晚两期，第一期的年代在公元780至950年，第二期的年代在公元950至1223年。以第⑤层、第⑥层、第⑦层以及F6代表的第一期遗存共出土227件，占古代动物遗存的24.28%；以第②层、第③层、第④层代表的第二期遗存共出土708件，占古代动物遗存总数的75.72%；因此从数量上分析，第二期人类消费动物资源的数量大于第一期，但这在一定程度上受发掘深度影响，即发掘区内第一期的第⑤层、第⑥层、第⑦层有相当部分未做发掘。F6出土有小鱼骨骼和家鼠骨骼，结合房址的结构和所处的位置，推测这与F6房址属于食堂性质有关。

纳提什瓦遗址是毗诃罗普尔古城一处重要的佛教寺院遗址，遗址中出土的动物骨骼丰富了对该遗址的研究内容，也为研究孟加拉国古代社会生活和自然环境提供了一批宝贵的材料。

附记：湖南省文物考古研究所袁家荣先生和中国社会科学院考古研究所吕鹏博士在动物鉴定上提供了宝贵的指导意见，在此深表谢意！

附录三

孟加拉国纳提什瓦遗址炭化米分析

湖南省文物考古研究所　顾海滨

2017年在孟加拉国纳什提瓦遗址考古发掘中，在房址F6中出土3粒炭化米，编号分别为F6-1、F6v2、F6-3（图1），其检测结果如下。

3粒炭化米粒长分别为4.67mm、4.5mm、4.29mm，粒宽为2.23 mm、2.33 mm、2.15 mm，粒厚为1.89mm、2.1mm、2.21mm，胚长1.48mm、1.39 mm、1.32 mm，胚宽1.25mm、1.21mm、1.25mm，长宽比分别为2.09、1.93、2.0，详见表1。

从粒长的数据来看，出土的炭化水稻个体比较小，与我国的小粒稻数值较为接近。在我国一般将粒长小于4.5mm的水稻称为小粒稻，由于米粒小，目前已经很少栽培了。

从长宽比数据看，其数值介于1.93—2.09之间，与现代的粳稻数据更为接近。一般情况下，籼稻的长宽比介于2.1—3，粳稻长宽比介于1.8—2.5。孟加拉地处亚热带季风气候区，目前种植的水稻主要以籼稻为主（图2），是什么原因导致遗址出土的水稻粒形数据更加接近粳稻，是当时气候的原因？还是农作物交流的结果？还需进一步做更多的工作。

将表1中3个炭化米的粒长、粒宽、粒厚、胚长、胚宽5个参数数据带入野生稻和栽培稻判别公式中，分别计算野生稻（Y野）和栽培稻（Y栽）的得分值，当Y栽值大于Y野值时，我们认为其为栽培稻，反之则为野生稻。经计算3粒炭化米的Y栽值均大于Y野值，因此出土的水稻均为栽培稻。Y栽与Y野得分值见表2。

综上所述，我们认为纳什提瓦遗址出土的3粒炭化米，为栽培稻，其粒形长宽比数据更加接近粳稻。

表1　炭化水稻数据（单位：mm）

样品编号	粒长（L1）	粒宽（S1）	粒厚（H）	胚长（L2）	胚宽（S2）	长宽比
F6-1	4.67	2.23	1.89	1.48	1.25	2.09
F6-2	4.5	2.33	2.1	1.39	1.21	1.93
F6-3	4.29	2.15	2.21	1.32	1.25	2

表2　野生稻和栽培稻得分

样品编号	Y野	Y栽	Y栽-Y野
F6-1	107.90	108.34	0.44
F6-2	105.89	106.15	0.26
F6-3	97.07	97.45	0.38

野生稻和栽培稻判别公式：

$Y野 = -144.775 + 26.282*L1 + 23.353*S1 + 12.641*H + 18.836*L2 + 20.871*S2$

$Y栽 = -174.142 + 24.323*L1 + 24.559*S1 + 16.525*H + 31.057*L2 + 29.542*S2$

图1 纳什提瓦遗址出土炭化米

图2 现代籼稻
（产自孟加拉，摄于2017年）

专文

Special Article

8—12世纪
东印度佛教建筑、造像
对于西藏的传播

柴焕波

纳提什瓦
Nateshwar

提要

2014年以来,湖南省文物考古研究所和孟加拉国欧提亚·欧耐斯恩(Oitihya Onneswan)考古研究中心联合发掘了阿底峡尊者的故乡毗诃罗普尔(Vikrampura)古城的纳提什瓦(Nateshwar)遗址。在编写《纳提什瓦》发掘报告的过程中,笔者考察了孟加拉国各地的佛教遗存,研读原始发掘报告[1],通过对同类遗址的解读,以理解纳提什瓦遗址的内涵(图1),进而将遗存放在8—12世纪宏观的时空框架内,梳理其历史变迁的脉络以及对于藏传佛教的深刻影响。

上篇论述"建筑",分"以佛塔为中心的塔院式寺院""以佛殿为中心的僧院式寺庙""以神殿为中心的寺庙"三个层次,论述了印度寺院建筑的发展和演变,尤其对十字形中心神殿建筑的起源、结构、传播及宗教象征进行了详细的叙述。下篇论述"造像",在"造像的分类及其风格特征"部分,对孟加拉国和西藏的青铜铸像、泥灰塑像、木雕、石雕、赤陶砖雕、擦擦进行了一般性的综述。在"造像的题材其及教义背景"部分,分"大乘佛教和持明密教造像""金刚乘造像体系""无上瑜伽密教造像的源头与流衍""印度教神像体系和佛教护法神"四个层次,对庞杂的造像神格进行了系统的梳理,由此构成了孟加拉国和西藏8—12世纪宗教遗存的宏观框架。本文以孟加拉国和西藏的材料为主体,同时兼及印度的相关的研究实例,附有各种照片、线图资料200余幅,可作为本报告的背景研究资料。

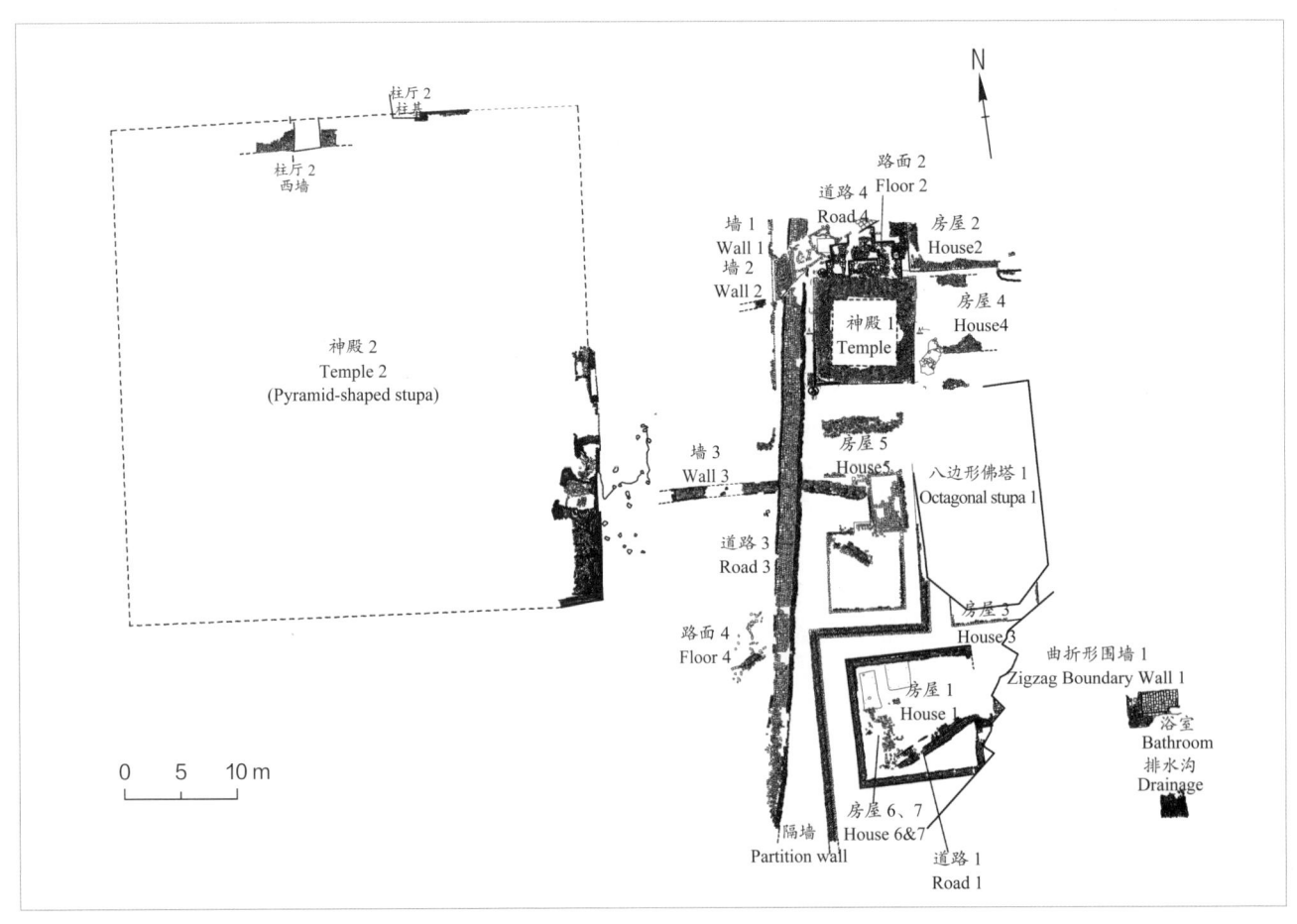

图1　纳提什瓦遗址第一期总平面图

Abstract

Since 2014, Nateshwar Buddhist ancient city site, where is the hometown of Atisha Dipanka, has beer excavated by the joint team of the Agrashar Vikrampur Foundation of Bangladesh and Hunan Provincial Institute of Cultural Relics of China. During writing the Nateshwar site excavation report, the author investigated the Buddhist sites in Bangladesh, and studied the original excavation reports[1]. By comparing with the similar Buddhist sites, this paper aims to better understand the cultural connotation of the Nateshwar site (Fig 1-1), and analyze the changes of religious remains and the relationships of Buddhism between East India and Tibet from the macroscopic space-time context of the 8th-12th centuries.

The first part is about the "architectures", which is divided into three aspects: "the court centered by stupa", "the vihara centered by Buddhist temple" and "the shrine-centered monastery". It discusses the development of the architecture of Indian monasteries, especially presents the origin, structure, diffusion and religious symbol of the cruciform central temple. The second part is about the "statues". The "classification and style of the statues" part generally reviews the bronze sculptures, earthen statues, wood carvings, stone sculptures, terracotta objects and tsha-tsha discovered both in Bangladesh and Tibet. "The theme of the statues and the background of the doctrines" part systematically studies the diachronic changes of the complex statues. Through into four sections of "the statues of Mahayana Buddhism and Vidyahara-holder Esoteric Buddhism", "the Vajrayana statue system", "the origin and distribution of Supreme Yoga Esotericism statues" and "Hindu statues system and the Dharma protecting deities of Buddhism", it forms the macroscopic framework of religious remains in Bangladesh and Tibet between the 8th and the 12th centuries. Based on the materials of Bangladesh and Tibet, this article covers some related research examples in India, with more than 200 photos and line drawings, which also can be seen as the research background of this report.

上篇

建筑

一、以佛塔为中心的塔院式寺院

在印度佛像兴起以前，佛塔作为佛陀涅槃的象征，在佛教徒心目中享有崇高的地位。礼塔即礼佛，具有获得无上福报的功德。慧琳《一切经音义》卷六八："塔，具云窣堵波，谓置佛舍利处也，寺名依梵本中呼为鞞诃罗，此云游，谓众生共游止之所也。"（《大正藏》卷五四）道宣《四分律删繁补阙行事钞》卷下《主客相待篇》曰："客僧受房已，问主人已，应先礼佛塔。"（《大正藏》卷四〇）可见，佛塔为伽蓝之中心，僧房为寺院之必置。

桑奇（Sanchi）大塔位于印度中央邦首府博帕尔附近的桑奇，中心为半球形的覆钵，始建于孔雀王朝阿育王时代。公元前1世纪晚期至1世纪初叶，又在大塔围栏四方陆续修建了四座砂石的塔门。

《法显传》记载的所有佛迹或佛教史上发生过重大事件的地方，都起塔纪念，成为礼祈之所，其中大部分是阿育王塔。《大唐西域记》卷四："《印度记》曰：窣堵波中有多舍利，或有斋日，时放光明。"在那烂陀寺，教徒反复念诵佛名、坐禅和赞咏是日常的修持。义净在《南海寄归内法传》卷四描绘到："即如西方制底（支提）畔睇，及常途礼敬，每于晡后，或黄昏时，大众出门，绕塔三匝，香花具设，并悉蹲踞。令其能者作哀雅声，明彻雄朗，讃大师德。或十颂，或二十颂。"法尊法师《阿底峡尊者传》记载："时种敦为首，藏地诸善知识，请问绕佛之教授。尊者曰：诸有为善根，更无余大于旋绕者。并广说印度有绕大城得成就，绕寺院得成就，绕观音圣殿得成就等历史，广说旋绕之教授。"

印度夏季炎热，石窟具有良好的避暑效果，印度的佛教石窟主要集中在西印度马哈拉施特拉邦境内，年代在公元前150—625年期间，数量多、延续时间长，为世界石窟建筑的摇篮。这一时期的石窟可分为僧伽起居的僧坊窟和用于宗教礼拜的塔庙窟两类，其中塔庙窟平面呈狭长的马蹄形，里端中部置一覆钵塔，环塔布置廊柱，可供信徒绕塔礼拜（图2）。塔庙窟的产生，显然为了向佛教徒提供不受天气干扰而进行朝拜活动的场所。

礼塔的传统在印度许多地区一直流传，三摩达吒是东印度最重要的古国之一，都城德瓦帕瓦吒（Devaparvata）位于孟加拉国库米拉（Comilla）县，玄奘《大唐西域记》卷十载："国大都城方圆二十余里""伽蓝三十余所，僧徒二千余人，并皆遵习上座部学。天祠百所，异道杂居。""去城不远有窣堵坡，无忧王之所建也，昔者如来为诸天人于此七日说深妙法。旁有四佛座及经行遗迹之所，去此不远伽蓝中有青玉佛像，其高八尺，

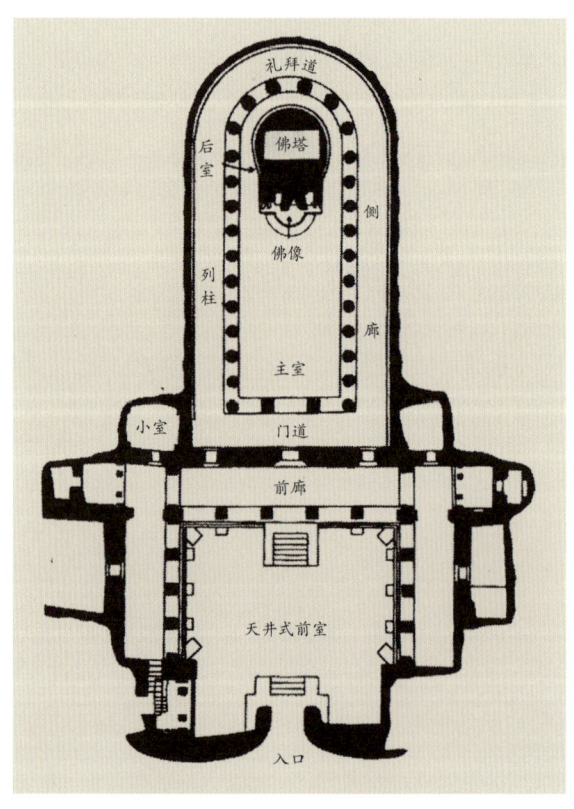

图2 埃洛拉第10窟平面图，475—625年
李崇峰：《佛教考古——从印度到中国》，上海古籍出版社，2014年，第26页。

相好圆备，灵应时效。"目前考古揭露的遗址中，7世纪的库提拉神庙（Kutila Mura）可能是上座部佛教的遗迹，三个佛塔代表佛法僧，一侧有对应的小室，中央塔肚四面有四个小龛，应是放置四方佛或者放置油灯的（图3）。

纳提什瓦遗址发现的三座八边形佛塔，年代在10—12世纪，形态大致相似，其中八边形佛塔1，南北残长11米，东西宽10.7米，残高2米，中心部位有存放圣物的塔心室，未见塔基的佛龛遗迹，佛塔北部连着附属房间，应与冥想证入三摩地有关。整体布局与库提拉神庙（Kutila Mura）有相似之处（图4、图5）。

从理论上，佛塔有八种类型，西藏常见的有天降塔、噶当塔和多门塔。图6是古格王朝时期托林寺的天降塔，年代约在11—13世纪；图7是西藏康马县雪囊寺后弘早期的佛塔，方形基座，逐次内收四层，属噶当式佛塔，年代不晚于14世纪。西藏隆子县日当镇发现的"果拉康"遗址，是由中心佛塔和环塔的殿室、围廊组成完整的塔庙建筑，遗址残长20、宽17.8米，很可能是西藏前弘期到后弘期早期一种业已失传的建筑模式（图8）[2]。

毗诃罗（Vihara）指早期的佛教寺院，在开阔的庭院周围建密匝匝的僧舍，这些敞开的小室有走廊相通，为僧人度雨季而建。毗诃罗也往往开凿于峭壁上，印度西部的僧坊窟可以阿旃陀第12窟为例，中央为方形大厅，大厅的左右后三面凿出供僧侣栖息之小禅室，年代在公元前2—公元1世纪，外观极为简单。这种形态，也是地面上最早毗诃罗的翻版（图9）。

犍陀罗早期地面上的寺院，具有大厅和带游廊的小室、餐厅、厨房、浴室、围廊俱全，经常有一条建筑轴心线，有的在中心修建佛塔或者组成封闭的神殿，被虔诚的居住者所供奉。呾叉始罗国（今巴基斯坦拉瓦尔品第附近）焦莲僧院遗址是由僧院（vihara）和塔院（stupa court）组成的一座寺庙。主塔和周围的奉献塔为神圣的礼拜所在，而在僧院内，以僧舍为主体，

图3　Kutila Mura模型，迈纳马蒂（Mainamati）博物馆 笔者拍摄

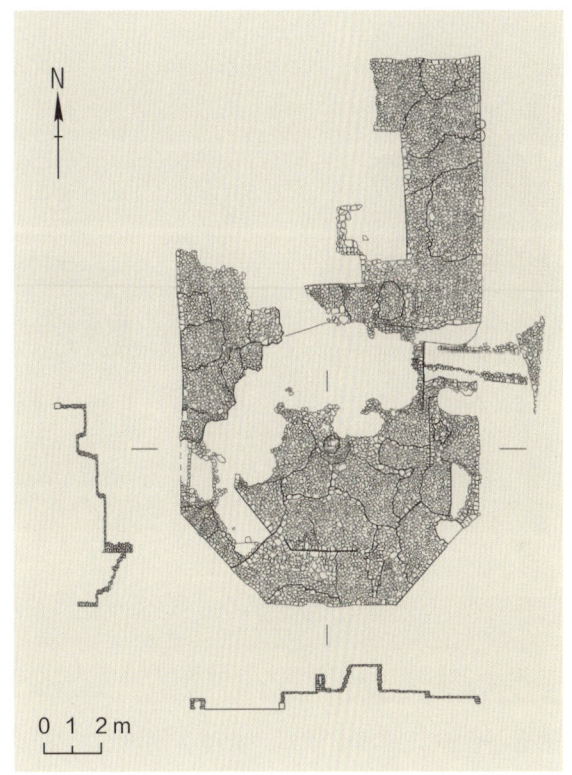

图4　八边形佛塔1平面图，10—12世纪，毗诃罗普尔（Vikrampura）古城纳提什瓦（Nateshwar）遗址

图5　八边形佛塔1遗迹，10—12世纪，毗诃罗普尔（Vikrampura）古城纳提什瓦（Nateshwar）遗址

图6 古格王朝托林寺天降塔，约11—13世纪 笔者拍摄

图7 康马县雪囊寺后弘早期佛塔
宿白：《藏传佛教寺院考古》，文物出版社，1996年，图版54。

图8 果拉康遗址，后弘期早期，西藏隆子县日当镇

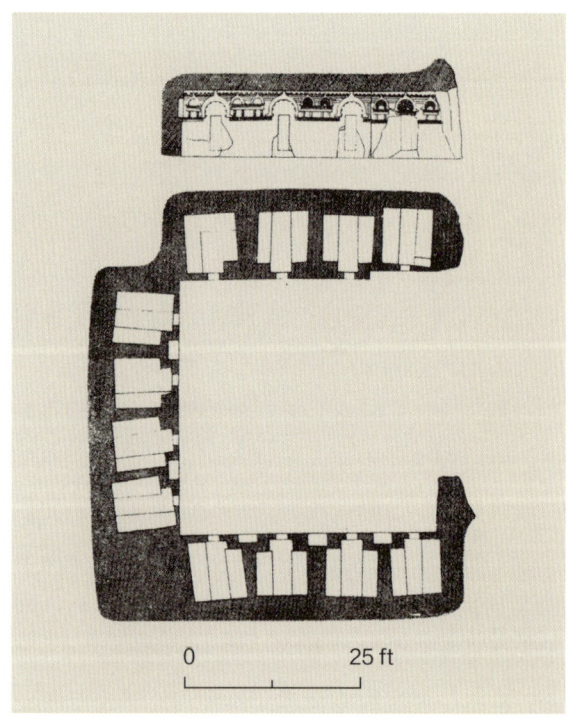

图9 阿旃陀第12窟平剖面图
李崇峰：《佛教考古——从印度到中国》，上海古籍出版社，2014，第79页。

有放置神像的佛龛（chapel）、布萨处、贮藏室、厨房、食堂、厕所、楼梯、水池、阴沟、灯龛、经行石路等日用设施。一般认为，这些寺院可能始建于1世纪，4世纪后趋于衰落，5世纪时废止[3]。

犍陀罗地区位于中印交通的必经之地，唐代以前，汉地的朝圣僧人，都是沿着中亚丝路商道，先抵印度河流域，后赴恒河流域，4世纪和5世纪，在匈奴人的冲击下，犍陀罗地区的圣地受到重创，另一方面也促使佛教向北传播，进入中亚和汉地。犍陀罗早期寺庙建筑的样式，还见于1979—1981年发掘的洛阳北魏永宁寺遗址和2009—2010年发掘的山西大同云冈石窟窟顶北魏寺院遗址，后者中间是塔基，四面有廊房，显然亦属这类寺院的模式[4]。

4—5世纪，东部孟加拉砖结构寺院发展，这种寺院形式也成为主流，并一直流传后世。纳提什瓦第一期遗址有一组庞大的塔院（stupa court）和僧院（vihara）的综合体，其中塔院区位于寺院的中部，包括四座神殿、带有居住和储藏功能的公共房子、主干道和位于神殿周围的广场；僧院区位于寺院的边缘，包括若干座僧舍和经多次修缮的食堂建筑、浴室和排水沟。一道曲折形隔墙将塔院（神圣空间）与僧院（生活空间）分割开来。目前所揭露的寺院遗迹只是遗迹的一部分，年代约在8—10世纪（图10）。

图10 纳提什瓦第一期寺院遗迹航拍照，约8—10世纪

二、以佛殿为中心的僧院式寺庙

早期佛教没有圣像，因为佛陀反对偶像崇拜，佛像是在大乘时代才出现的。在鹿野苑（Sarnath），佛塔圆穹的八个方向设有神龛，其中放置佛像。最早的佛殿供奉佛陀与菩萨像，常见的有僧房式佛殿和中心殿式佛堂两种。

1. 僧房式佛殿

僧房式佛殿的平面布局，是在方形院落的四壁内侧，规整地建造成列的僧房，其中正方向的一间或三间，作为供佛的佛殿。

阿旃陀第1号窟是5—6世纪开凿的，该窟平面由前廊、中央柱式大厅、大厅周匝小室和正壁所开凿的佛殿组成。这种石窟被称为"佛殿僧坊混成式窟"[5]，窟内雕造华丽，空间复杂，壁画精美，其中佛殿成为僧人、信众观想、礼忏、供养之处，最初的佛塔在这里已经转变为佛像（图11）。

印度巴特那县的那烂陀（Nalanda）寺可能初建于5世纪，历代皆有营建。5世纪初，法显到达王舍城附近，并未提到那烂陀。7世纪玄奘朝圣时，寺院已经极为宏丽。义净在那烂陀寺居住了整整10年，他在《大唐西域求法高僧传》中，专辟一节，对其进行了详尽的描述："其城形略方如城""如观一寺，余七同然。背上平直，通人还往。凡观寺者，须面西看之，欲使西出其门，方得真势"，这是从寺院的整体格局而说的；"其僧房也，面有九焉"，这是指每边各有九间僧舍；"于寺东面取房，或一或三，用安尊像，或可即于此面前出多少，别起台观，

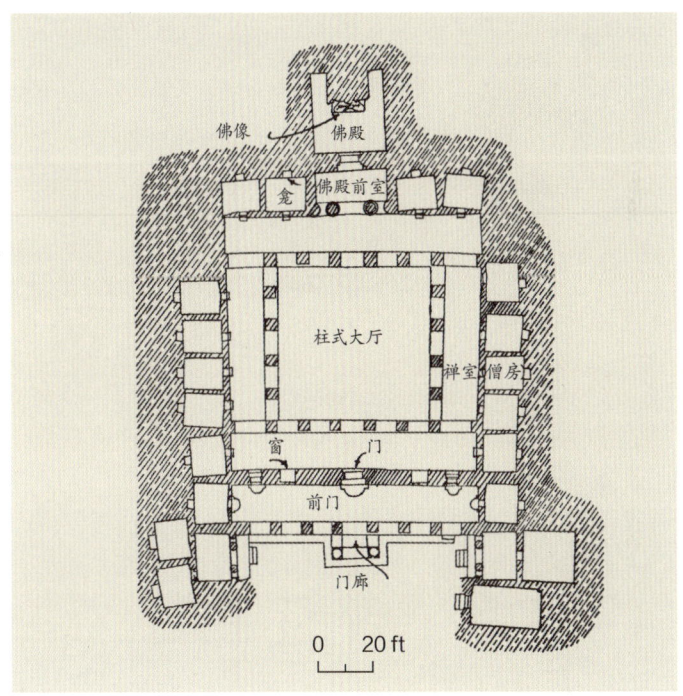

图11 阿旃陀第1号窟平面图
李崇峰：《佛教考古——从印度到中国》，上海古籍出版社，2014年，第84页。

为佛殿矣"，这是指东墙中间的一间或三间，略作增建，用作佛殿使用。这些描述与考古发掘的遗址极为吻合（图12）。

7世纪松赞干布时期修建的拉萨大昭寺是用来供奉佛像的方形伽蓝，其最大的特点是主厅四周绕置小凹室（僧房）、并树立有华丽雕饰的廊柱（图13），宿白先生最早指出，这种格局可以追溯到僧房式佛殿的印度原型。据《五部遗教》，大昭寺范本源自"毗讫罗摩尸罗寺"，《贤者喜

宴》中称"天竺嘎摩罗寺",说的都是超戒寺（Vikramasila）。此外,大昭寺并不是孤立的寺庙,它的四周原有吐蕃时期庞大的寺庙建筑群。据《西藏王臣记》记载,吐蕃赞普赤热巴巾（815—838年）的大臣在大昭寺四周修建了六座佛殿,东南有噶如和墨如,南有噶瓦和噶瓦卫,北有产康和产康它玛。现存的惜德林、墨如宁巴等建筑,寺院中心是佛殿和经堂,庭院的四周,是僧房和日用功能的房间,都是比较纯粹的印度风格,它们与大昭寺结合在一起,构成一个庞大的寺庙群体。

古格古城Ⅳ F48-60建筑群,年代为10—11世纪,密匝匝的僧舍围绕着中心佛殿,也是印度

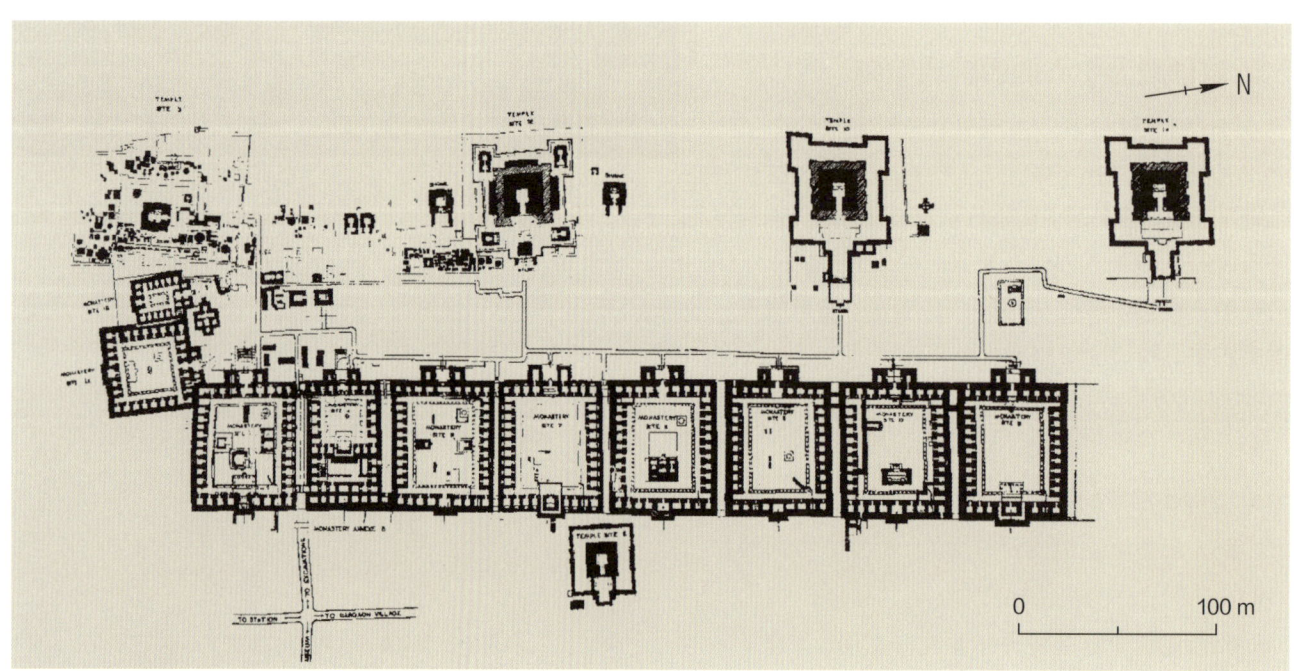

图12 那烂陀寺遗址平面图
李崇峰：《佛教考古——从印度到中国》,上海古籍出版社,2014年,第565页。

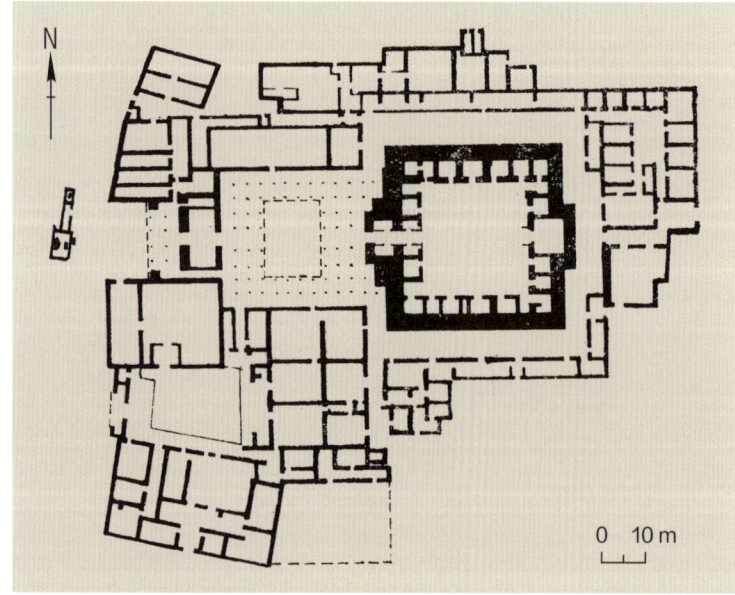

图13 拉萨大昭寺平面图
西藏自治区文物管理委员会编：《拉萨文物志》,内部资料,1985年。

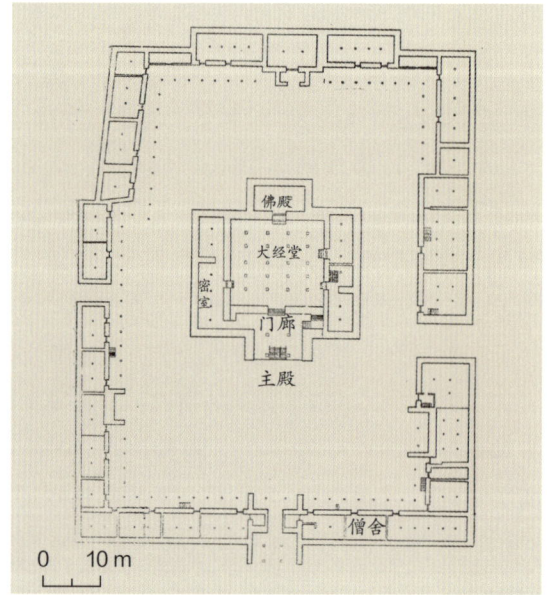

图14 扎囊县葱推措巴寺平面图
西藏自治区文物管理委员会编：《扎囊县文物志》,内部资料,1986年。

僧房模式的延续。

喀旦班钦·释迦室利（1127—1225）是印度那烂陀寺的最后一任寺主，1204年，年近80岁高龄的大师被迎请到西藏传教弘法，并创建了扎囊县葱堆措巴寺，该寺的平面结构也明显带有印度的僧房风格（图14）。

2. 中心殿式佛堂

随着崇拜佛像渐成风气，佛教建筑也在发生相应的变化，佛殿作为一般性礼拜、供养佛像的场所，逐渐成为寺院建筑的主体。以佛殿为中心，产生了围绕佛殿的内部转经道，最初绕塔礼拜演变为绕殿礼拜。

塔波寺（Tabo）位于印度喜马偕尔邦的斯比蒂（Spiti）地区，996年由仁青桑布所创建，46年后，绛曲沃重新修葺，1076年，在此寺举行了佛教大法会。寺院主体是一个向东的佛堂，由门厅、经堂和带内部转经道的佛殿组成（图15）[6]。

中心殿式佛堂建筑在新疆地区也有广泛的分布，年代在4—8世纪[7]。这种建筑也成为西藏和汉地最为普遍的寺庙模式。7世纪中期由文成公主所建的拉萨小昭寺，座西朝东，也是由门厅、前庭、经堂和带礼拜道的中心佛殿组成（图16）。西藏吉隆县的帕巴寺、强准祖拉康也是建于前弘期的千年古寺，都是带有中心佛殿和内部转经廊的建筑，由于地处中尼边境，建筑样式带有更多南亚地区的风格（图17）。山南市桑耶寺的乌孜大殿及强巴林、札觉加嘎林、康松桑松林以及日喀则那塘寺觉冈大殿（13世纪）、白居寺措庆大殿（15世纪）等，都是中心殿式佛堂。

中心殿式佛堂门向大多朝东，西藏的桑耶、托林、萨迦、夏鲁等寺，以及孟加拉国7世纪许多佛殿，皆门向朝东。有学者认为，如果将庙门打开，从远山上射来的第一抹朝阳将照到朝向东方的墙上、门窗上，"看起来早期寺庙确实在寺庙选址与太阳方位有着一定的联系"[8]。其实，在佛经中，佛陀在菩提树下冥想时，是朝东而坐的，后来演变成东方不动佛的神格。

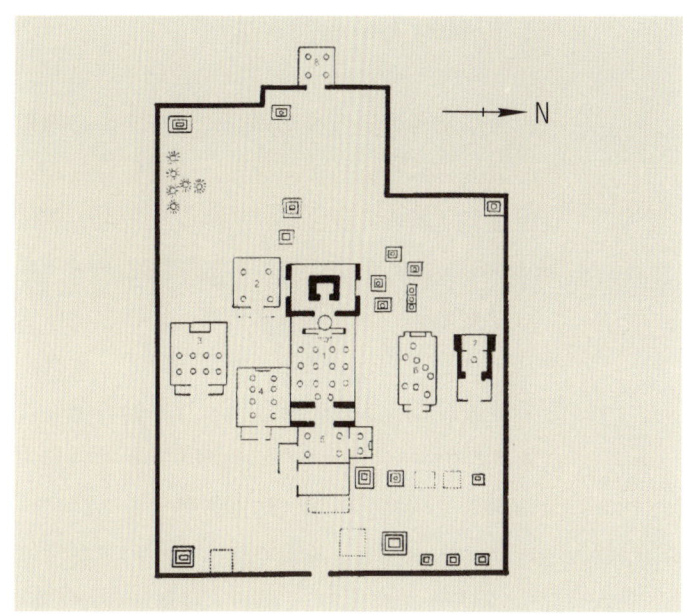

图15　塔波寺平面图

[意]杜齐著，魏正中、萨尔吉主编，李翎等译：《梵天佛地》第3卷，上海古籍出版社，2010年。

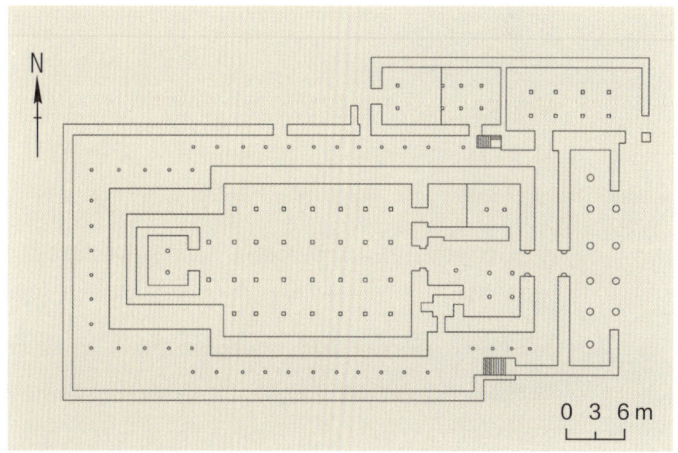

图16　拉萨小昭寺平面图

西藏自治区文物管理委员会编：《拉萨文物志》，内部资料，1985年。

图17　强准祖拉康　笔者拍摄

三、以神殿为中心的寺庙

佛塔和神殿是两种不同的建筑,佛塔是佛涅槃的象征,本身就是崇拜对象,神殿是安放神灵肖像神龛之所、礼拜之地。从佛塔到神殿,意味着从封闭的建筑变成了内部开放的空间。

早期婆罗门教并没有永久性的宗教设施,杀牲祭祀往往在树木、坟冢、巨石间举行。4世纪笈多王朝时期,婆罗门教复兴,并开始为神灵建造永久性的神庙。8世纪的商羯罗(788—820年)大师创立了吠檀多哲学,印度教进入黄金时代。印度教神庙由门廊(导引空间)、柱厅(礼拜空间)、前厅(过渡空间)、圣室(神灵空间)组成。圣室具有印度教曼陀罗平面结构,与佛教一样,也有顺时针绕神的礼拜道。圣室封闭黑暗,意为胎室,隐喻着宇宙生命的胚胎,其中供奉着毗湿奴神像或湿婆象征物林伽,象征创造的无尽活力,圣室上方是高耸的塔状屋顶,象征神灵居住的宇宙之山。每个神庙都是世界的轴心,天地冥界的交汇点,这是"梵我同一"哲学的图像化体现。圣室前面的柱厅,是神灵世界与世俗世界的过渡,也是信徒的膜拜之地,也有上升的屋顶。整座神庙的台基、柱子、墙壁、天花板、屋顶,到处布满雕刻,强烈的视觉效果,代表了印度教积极向上的入世态度,与追求宁静肃穆佛教体系明显不同[9]。

印度教神庙也是社会活动的中心,法显《佛国记》记载于阗国、摩揭陀国婆罗门徒请佛像到城中,作倡伎乐,华香供养,道俗皆集,长者居士,进行食物、医药布施。玄奘《大唐西域记》卷五中提到一曲长城附近印度教神庙:"有大自在天祠,并莹青石,俱穷雕刻,规模度量,同佛精舍,各有千户充其洒扫,鼓乐弦歌不舍昼夜。"

位于孟加拉国库米拉县的恰帕伽神庙(Charpatra Mura)遗址,长46.7、宽16.8米,由柱式大厅与小室构成,年代为10世纪,是孟加拉东部最早的印度教神庙遗址[10]。

在法显和玄奘的记录中,孟加拉地区还是耆那教(Jainism)昌盛之地,文献中称尼乾外道、裸形外道、外道,耆那教是起源于公元前6世纪的古老宗教之一,主张通过苦修来达到精神上的永久解脱,主要活动地区在印度的东北部。8—12世纪,耆那教受到部分统治者的重视而得到发展。耆那教神殿结构与印度教神庙接近。孟加拉国巴哈布尔最初就是一座耆那教的寺庙,据当地出土碑文记载,5世纪末,当地有一个婆罗门,在此购置土地建立神庙,由一名耆那教教师掌管。

从笈多晚期开始,佛教建筑受到同时期印度教、耆那教神庙建筑的影响,寺院中出现了佛塔式神殿以及后来的十字形中心神殿建筑。

1. 佛塔式神殿

印度早期流行的佛塔为覆钵式塔,2—4世纪,印度比哈尔邦菩提伽耶(Bodhgaya)出现了一座金刚座式的正觉大塔,巨大的须弥台成为了塔的主体,而象征性保留的覆钵和塔刹,反而成了顶部的点缀(图18)。菩提伽耶是佛陀成道之地,这座大塔即是7世纪玄奘见到过的佛教精舍:塔高一百六七十尺,下边的基座每面宽二十多步,用青砖垒起,每层龛中有金像,墙壁上雕刻着花纹和天仙像,顶部安放金光闪闪的铜质宝瓶;东面连接着楼阁,三重洞门相连,外门左右神龛中分别是观音、弥勒像,用白银铸成,高十多尺;在此精舍的旧地,阿育王曾建有小精舍,后来有婆罗门将其扩建;精舍内的佛像,结跏趺坐,右脚叠在上面,左手提起,右手下垂指地,面朝东而坐,俨然如在世一般(《大唐西域记》卷八)。

细细分析这座建筑,它的性质已经变成了高耸的佛塔式神殿,附有柱厅、门廊,门向朝东,中心佛殿和寺门顶部皆具五塔,即中间大塔和四隅各一小塔,这些显然是印度教建筑的因素,但佛像配置完全符合大乘佛教的模式。菩提伽耶在西藏称为"金刚座"(Vajrasana),西藏那塘寺藏有由21座石雕和木雕组成的菩提伽耶模型,其中有一件镌刻有"大明永乐年施"的题记(图19、20)。

图 18　印度菩提伽耶正觉大塔

图 19　菩提伽耶的模型
宿白：《藏传佛教寺院考古》，文物出版社，1996 年，图版 58。

图 20　印度神庙石雕像，藏于江孜县热隆寺，后弘期初期 笔者拍摄

玄奘还到过曲女城附近的一处佛寺，亦属这类佛塔式神殿（《大唐西域记》卷五）："伽蓝东南不远，有大精舍，石基砖室，高二百余尺。中作如来立像，高三十余尺，铸以鍮石，饰诸妙宝。精舍四周石壁之上，雕画如来修菩萨行所经事迹，备尽镌镂。"

那烂陀寺遗址平面图中（见图 12），与僧院建筑相对应的，有大小十余处佛塔式神殿，义净在《大唐西域求法高僧传》中亦提到："于寺西面，大院之外，方列窣堵波，及诸制底（支提），数乃盈百。圣迹相连，不可称说。"[11] 从图上看，神殿门皆朝东，每座僧房式佛殿与某座佛塔式神殿似乎有对应关系。在神殿内部，义净没有文字说明，但从平面图上看，应该也是放置佛像的。

毗诃罗普尔古城纳提什瓦遗址发现的神殿 1 位于遗址的东北部，南北长 9.4、东西宽 9.1、残高 2.6 米，方向 5°。东南西三面外壁，由几排弧状砖叠涩而成，外凸内收，并用装饰砖砌成精致的花卉图案，外观为典型的佛塔，但其内部却是一个方形的室内空间，内围东西长 5.8、南北宽 5.6 米。发掘清理了佛殿北部的门道遗迹，门道的东、西两侧墙壁以连续三次直角转折与神殿北墙相接，两侧砖面上发现三个圆形柱洞，可以推想门道内部空间是沿神殿中轴线的柱廊式门厅结构。在神殿和门厅上方，原来应有高耸的塔状屋顶。建筑的四角可能安放有罨底大瓮，所保存的两处皆一半掩埋在地面以下，瓮内放置了数十件陶器，计有釜、鼓腹罐、折肩罐、壶、钵、器盖等，推测它们应是神殿存在期间放置在廊檐下，作为日常使用的。神殿 1 的建筑年代约在 8—

10世纪，为孟加拉国此前佛教遗址中所未见，所以，孟加拉国学者称之为"佛塔和寺庙的联合体"[12]，其实，它就是一座开放式的佛塔式神殿（图21、22）。

孟加拉国现存7世纪的佛教遗址中，还有一类封闭型的佛塔式神殿，这类神殿的塔基是封闭的，内部只有安放舍利的塔心室，但在佛塔的东边，设有佛龛，主像多为跏趺座的不动佛，前面或连接一个方形殿堂，为礼拜或禅定之所。它们一般都位于寺院的中心，周围有敞开的小室或围墙。孟加拉国库米拉县之西的拉尔迈—迈纳马蒂（Laimai-mainamati）区域，是古代三摩达吒国的都城德瓦帕瓦吒（Devaparvata）所在地，其中鲁帕班神庙（Rupban Mura）第一期建筑，年代约6世纪或7世纪初，是边长为20米的正方形建筑，即是这类封闭型的佛塔式神殿，四方形塔基支撑着高耸的塔顶，东面佛龛中放置佛像，三个小室连着三条通道，保留着早期一佛两菩萨的配置（图23）[13]。

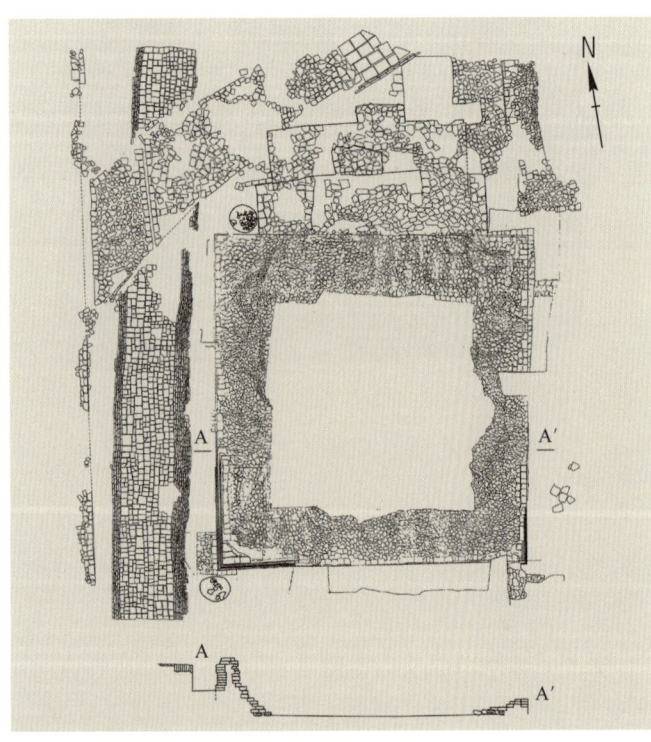

图21　毗诃罗普尔古城纳提什瓦遗址佛塔式神殿1平面图

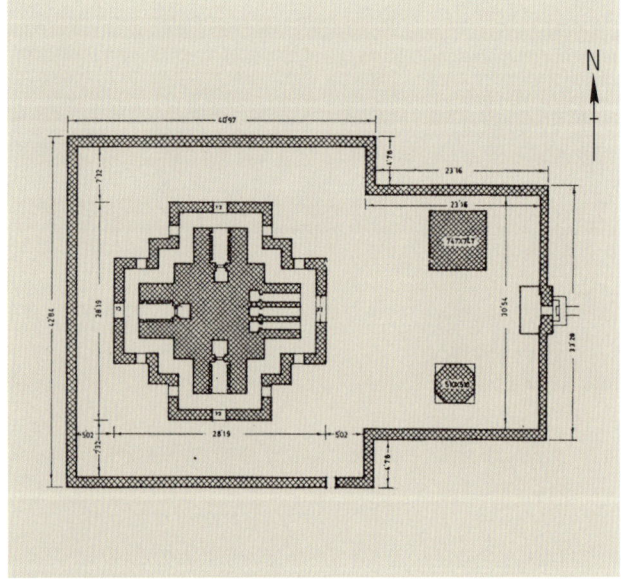

图23　Rupban Mura 平面图

Dr. Md. Shafiqul Alam edited: *Proceedings for Paharpur World Heritage Site and its Environment (Bangladesh)*, International Seminar on Elaboration of an Archaeological Research Strategy for Paharpur World Heritage Site and its Environment 20-25 March 2004, Dhaka, P62.

图22　毗诃罗普尔古城纳提什瓦遗址佛塔式神殿1外墙　笔者拍摄

图24　Itakhola Mura 佛龛甬道，为大众祈祷、供养的礼拜道，两侧砖墙上镶嵌着安置造像或灯台的小龛　笔者拍摄

爱塔克霍拉神庙（Itakhola Mura）是德瓦帕瓦吒一座由五个时期遗迹叠压而成的遗址，前三个时期的遗迹都在地下，笔者查阅了7世纪时期的建筑平面图，发现其为封闭型佛塔式神殿，寺门朝东，有三条甬道，中间是不动佛的泥塑像（图24）[14]。

毗诃罗普尔古城纳提什瓦遗址发现的神殿2建筑，年代约9—10世纪，属于德瓦王朝统治下的流行格局。神殿2基座墙体可分为上下两部分，下部墙体与墙基相连，垂直平砌，高0.8米，墙体宽度为1.7米；上部墙体用斜侧砖砌成，墙体向中心转折上升，墙体的宽度约为4.3米。外侧从底部开始就呈现出光洁的墙面，而内侧尚未见到任何整齐的墙面，尽管神殿2墙基与建筑内部的结构关系尚不清楚，但从现有的剖面分析，神殿的外墙内侧存在一层厚实的纯净填土，很可能是支撑整个塔顶的基础。更重要的是，外墙的趋势是向中部转折、斜向上升的，坡度为53度。尽管顶部的建筑结构不清，但从残砖中，多见斜侧砖，由此推测，神殿2应是实心的、带有厚墙的高耸建筑，或者说，是一种封闭型的佛塔式神殿。塔心部位可能存在一个面积不大的方形空间，作为神殿的神圣中心，建筑内部还会有支撑塔顶的复杂的建筑结构。

神殿2东边基座墙体中部，墙面上砌成几道具有装饰意味的凹凸棱角，墙体的外侧，还有一道长8.4米的嵌入式结构，推测应是一个佛龛的所在，其毗邻的墙根下，有一片密集的砖块，范围正好与佛龛相始终，东边广场上有两条的孤立的砖墙（墙2、墙3），向西垂直对着东边基座墙体，从两者位置和形态上分析，应是佛龛两侧的礼拜墙。如果这种分析成立，神殿2正是这类封闭型的佛塔式神殿建筑，为开放式的佛塔式神殿向十字形中心神殿发展的过渡形态（图25）。

迈纳马蒂的萨尔班寺（Salban Vihara）出土一座约7世纪的青铜佛塔像，带有覆斗状的塔基和圆柱形塔肚，塔基四面带有佛龛，大体可以反映纳提什瓦神殿2的形貌（图26）。

图25 毗诃罗普尔古城纳提什瓦遗址神殿2鸟瞰图，约9—10世纪

图26 迈纳马蒂萨尔班寺（Salban Vihara）出土青铜佛塔，约7世纪

Dr. Md. Shafiqul Alam edited: *Proceedings for Paharpur World Heritage Site and its Environment (Bangladesh)*, International Seminar on Elaboration of an Archaeological Research Strategy for Paharpur World Heritage Site and its Environment 20-25 March 2004, Dhaka, P64.

2. 十字形中心神殿

在法显、玄奘、义净的记录中，中天竺摩揭陀国是大乘佛教的核心地区，有以"大乘教为主"的明确记载，印度其他地区佛教，或以小乘为主，或大小并存，还有印度教等宗教。玄奘记载7世纪中期的那烂陀寺，"其有不谈三藏玄旨者，则形影自愧矣"（《大唐西域记》卷九）。到义净时，"所云大乘无过二种，一则中观，二乃瑜伽"（《南海寄归内法传》卷一），这是7世纪末的情形。

大乘佛教开始是以改革的面目出现的，不论在思想上还是在修行实践上，都倡导大众化，因而得到了很大的发展。但后来逐渐丧失了积极进取的精神，走向繁琐的经院哲学。密教正是在大乘佛教颓废衰败之际应运而生，它倡导佛教回到众生之中，采取入世的修行方法。

7世纪中叶，印度密教先后兴起两大新派别，中印一带的真言乘和南印一带的金刚乘，前者代表经典是《大日经》，后者是《金刚顶经》。《大日经》的基本原理体现在"住心"二字上，通过缘虑一处、心一境性而调伏散乱的心识，在观想中注重本尊与自身的无差别合一。《金刚顶经》则是一部注重密教实践的经典，它通过一整套特定的仪轨，手结印契、口念真言、心想本尊，成就身、口、意三密而达到"即身成佛"。佛教的修行方式已经变化，义理只是基础，但实修的价值更大，占主导地位的不再是单纯的对于经文的智解，而是证解和瑜伽。随着密教的传播，大乘的中观派、唯识派开始融合，形成了中观瑜伽行派，作为支撑密教怛特罗的宇宙论、本体论的基础，修行者通过微观与宏观的融合，将大乘义理与密教修持融为一体，生机勃勃的新教法具有摧枯拉朽的力量，使衰微的佛教再度昌盛。

《金刚顶经》借金刚阿阇黎之口，明确说过，凡是未见过、入过曼陀罗的人，念诵真言咒语是不能成就的。曼陀罗（梵文 Mandala）一词中，Manda 是本体、本质、根本，la 是包含，曼陀罗具"含藏宇宙本体"之意，也是摆脱任何干扰的、封闭的地盘。人们从曼陀罗中找到了自己的位置和归属，感受到宇宙与人之间的对应性，这是古老亚洲的一种宇宙模式。

在曼陀罗思想的支配下，佛教建筑结构和佛像的配置也进入了新的阶段。建筑中心是一个佛塔，基座上有四面佛龛，空间上的"五部佛"与印度数论的五大（水、地、火、风、空）概念相对应。本尊毗卢遮那佛居于中心，相当于空，象征物是轮；阿閦佛相当于风，位于东方，象征物是金刚杵；宝生佛相当于火，位于南方，象征物是宝珠；阿弥陀佛相当于水，位于西方，象征物是莲花；不空成就佛相当于地，位于北方，象征物是交杵金刚。佛龛正对着一个柱厅（Antechamber），再连接着一个入口（Mandapa）和一个露台（Terrace）。印度神庙式建筑变成了完全敞开的、带五佛的十字形神殿，这与传统大乘寺院建筑明显不同，是金刚乘的全新的创造，也可以称为"金刚乘建筑"。约从9世纪开始，以怛特罗为基础的宗教修习占据了绝对的优势，在波罗王朝统治区内，一批按其教法和仪轨而建的密教中心诞生了。除了大乘中心的那烂陀（Nalanda）寺本身也成为密教中心外，还建造了三处重要的密教中心，它们是第一代瞿波罗王（Gopala）于那烂陀寺附近建立的欧丹多富梨寺（Odantapuri），第二代达磨波罗（Dharmapala）于恒河沿岸建立的毗诃摩尸罗寺（Vikramacila，即超戒寺），第三代提婆波罗（Devapala）在孟加拉北部的巴哈布尔（Paharpur）建立的苏摩普里寺（Somapuri）。

欧丹多富梨寺已经湮没无闻。超戒寺位于恒河右岸山坡岩石上，遗址于1960—1961年在印度比哈尔邦帕格尔布尔地区安拉查克村被发掘出来。中央是神殿，周围有密宗殿53座，一般佛殿54座。由于国王支持，逐渐取代了笈多王朝时代的那烂陀寺，成为印度的佛教中心。阿底峡1034—1038年间在此寺任住持，西藏后弘期的译师大多在此修学。1203年，超戒寺毁于穆斯林的入侵。超戒寺遗址残存可见，近处是带塔心室的大菩提塔和周围密集的小塔，学界通称为供奉塔或还愿塔（Votive Stupa）。毗邻是由僧舍环绕的寺院，中心是一座十字形中心神殿。图35是中心神殿照片，中央是有四方佛龛的塔基，佛龛前有带四个柱子的柱厅，有镶嵌着砖雕的露台墙基，这与巴哈布尔的中心神殿非常相似。

在毗诃罗普尔古城发现之前，孟加拉国最重要的佛教遗址共有三处：拉杰沙希县的巴哈布尔（Pahadpur，详见后文）、博格拉的摩诃斯坦（Mahasthan）和库米拉的拉尔迈-迈纳马蒂（Laimai-Mainamati）。

摩诃斯坦城址的历史可以追溯到公元前2世纪，是《大唐西域记》中"奔那伐弹那国"（Pundravarddhana）的都城所在地，它的周围分布有众多的佛教寺院遗址，是一个以都城为中心的宗教圣地（图27）。

库米拉的拉尔迈-迈纳马蒂是《大唐西域记》中"三摩呾吒"国都德瓦帕瓦吒所在地。从6世纪起，这里开始出现佛寺，德瓦（Devas）王朝（750—800年）时期佛教兴盛，迈纳马蒂成为一个佛教中心，阿难陀寺（Ananda Vihara）和萨尔班寺（Salban Vihara）均以国王的名字命名。有学者认为，十字形中心神殿建筑发轫于7—8世纪 Khadgas、德瓦王朝统治时代，在此发现的众多中等规模的寺庙遗址，佛塔式神殿的四面设立神龛，既不同于那烂陀寺大乘佛塔建筑，也不同于巴哈布尔的十字形神殿，而显示出过渡时期的特征。8世纪末或9世纪初，十字形神殿开始流行于印度的比哈尔和孟加拉其他地区。旃陀罗王朝（900—1050年）是一个非常强大的王朝，是孟加拉东部和南部一个长久繁荣的黄金时代，完全能够与孟加拉西部和北部的波罗王朝相抗衡，大约在此时，为了领土的扩张，旃陀罗王朝将都城从德瓦帕瓦吒迁至毗诃罗普尔。但直到13世纪，拉尔迈-迈纳马蒂仍是著名的密教中心。

毗诃罗普尔古城是2010年由孟加拉国考古学家发现的，现已发掘的包括东、西两个遗址，分别为拉库罗普尔（Raghurampur）和纳提什瓦（Nateshwar）。从2014年—2017年，中国湖南省文物考古研究所和孟加拉国欧提亚·欧耐斯恩（Oitihya Onneswan）考古研究中心组成联合考古队，先后三次对纳提什瓦（Nateshwar）遗址进行了大规模的考古发掘，发掘面积已达五千多平方米，通过地层学和一系列测年数

图27　摩诃斯坦古城墙　笔者拍摄

据，认为纳提什瓦遗址的佛教寺院遗址可分为两个不同时期。第一期年代约在780—950年，为德瓦王朝（750—800年），沿续至旃陀罗王朝（900—1050年）的前期。第二期年代约在950—1223年，这段时期为旃陀罗王朝后期、跋摩王朝（1080—1150年）和犀那王朝（1100—1223年）时期。纳提什瓦遗址的早期遗存，是一组僧院和佛塔式神殿的综合体，这是印度大乘寺院的普遍模式；晚期遗存是一座十字形中心神殿的庞大建筑群，是印度金刚乘建筑的成熟模式，应是旃陀罗王朝将都城从德瓦帕瓦吒迁至毗诃罗普尔后所修建的，为南亚次大陆最后一个佛教中心。

纳提什瓦遗址十字形神殿的中心是八边形佛塔，佛塔整体是实心的，中心应有狭小的塔心室。从《大日经》发展出来的胎藏界曼陀罗正是由八叶莲花组成中台，毗卢遮那住于花台正中，象征法身智慧，四叶四佛象征四智，四隅四菩萨象征四行。中台、八叶、三重，是胎藏界曼陀罗的基本形式。僧众从中领悟到曼陀罗所体现的意义，渐次证入三摩地中。塔基四周相关建筑都围绕着这个中心对称布局，八边形塔基与四个方向的柱厅之间，有一条环形道，应是围绕佛塔的行经道，每个柱厅与中央佛塔之间，都会设立一门，通过这个门，既可进入行经道，也可以通往其他三处柱厅，所有建筑之间的关系圆融有序（图28—30）。

尽管纳提什瓦遗址考古发掘取得了很大的成果，但由于长期对于墙砖的肆意盗掘，考古发掘

图 28　毗诃罗普尔古城拉库罗普尔 Raghurampur 遗址

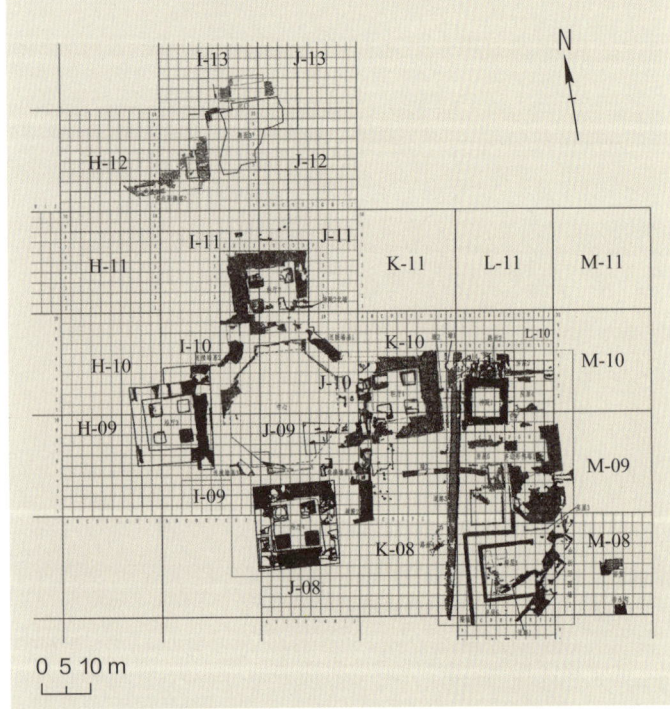

图 29　毗诃罗普尔古城纳提什瓦（Nateshwar）遗址平面图

图 30　毗诃罗普尔古城纳提什瓦（Nateshwar）遗址航拍图

所揭露的，仅仅是建筑的基础部分，地面以上的遗迹基本殆尽，原来的造像散布在世界各大博物馆，在遗址中仅见残片，遗址所提供的信息显得残破而有限。相比之下，巴哈布尔遗址的保存情况要好得多，与那烂陀或库米拉等历史累积起来的布局不同，巴哈布尔遗址是单一设计的结果，虽有修复、附加、改动，但没有影响最初的设计思想，体现了十字形中心神殿的特征[15]。

巴哈布尔遗址位于孟加拉国西北部拉杰沙希县恼冈（Naogaon）地区的巴哈布尔村，西距 Jaypurhat 火车站约 5 千米。1807—1812 年，东印度公司的布查纳·哈密顿（Buchanan Hamilton）发现并报道了该遗址，他从缅甸和尼泊尔寺院的比较中，判定其为佛教寺院，将砖雕上女神判定为印度教女神卡莉（Kali），并推测年代属于波罗时代。1922 至 1923 年，古印度历史和文化教授 D. R. Bhandarkar 主持了遗址的首次发掘。随后，发掘工作由印度考古局接管，一直持续到 1934 年以后。通过发掘，遗址被确认为波罗时代著名的苏摩普里寺（Somapuri）遗址，为世界上第二大单体佛教僧院，由波罗王朝第三任国王提婆波罗于 8 世纪末与 9 世纪初敕建，13 世纪初毁于穆斯林的侵入（图 31、32）。

现在的巴哈布尔遗址是经保护修缮过的，从 20 世纪 80 年代的航拍照片上，可以分辨出石柱础、石条的位置与现在是一致的，并不是修缮时从别处搬过去的。建筑整体与原始发掘线图大体一致。

巴哈布尔遗址主体建筑是十字形中心神殿，中心为高大的佛塔，现存一个"井"字形凹形的方形砖结构，作为巨大塔顶的支撑，方形结构除了狭窄的塔心室，整体上是实心的，不是空心的殿堂，上下没有任何入口。塔心室象征着宇宙之心，可能是放置大日如来或者后来是持金刚造像。库米拉的 Bhoja Viharap 神庙，也有相似的结构，其殿堂中心也是一个方形砖体，作为屋顶的支撑，而不是柱子，其建筑年代为 9—10 世纪，这种结构与纳提什瓦八边形佛塔有一定的区别（图 33、34）。

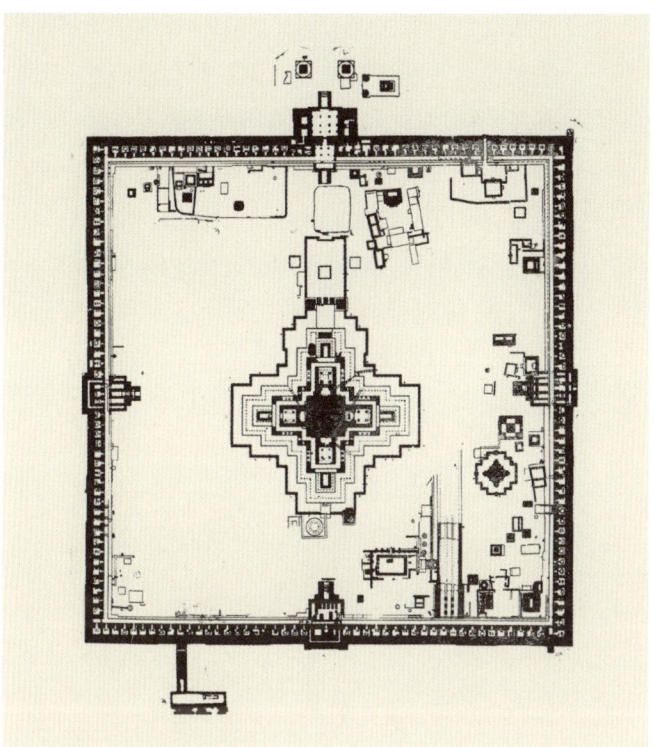

图 31 巴哈布尔遗址平面图
Dr. Md. Shafiqul Alam edited: *Proceedings for Paharpur World Heritage Site and its Environment (Bangladesh)*, International Seminar on Elaboration of an Archaeological Research Strategy for Paharpur World Heritage Site and its Environment 20-25 March 2004, Dhaka, P72.

图 32 巴哈布尔遗址复原图
Dr. Md. Shafiqul Alam edited: *Proceedings for Paharpur World Heritage Site and its Environment (Bangladesh)*, International Seminar on Elaboration of an Archaeological Research Strategy for Paharpur World Heritage Site and its Environment 20-25 March 2004, Dhaka, P77.

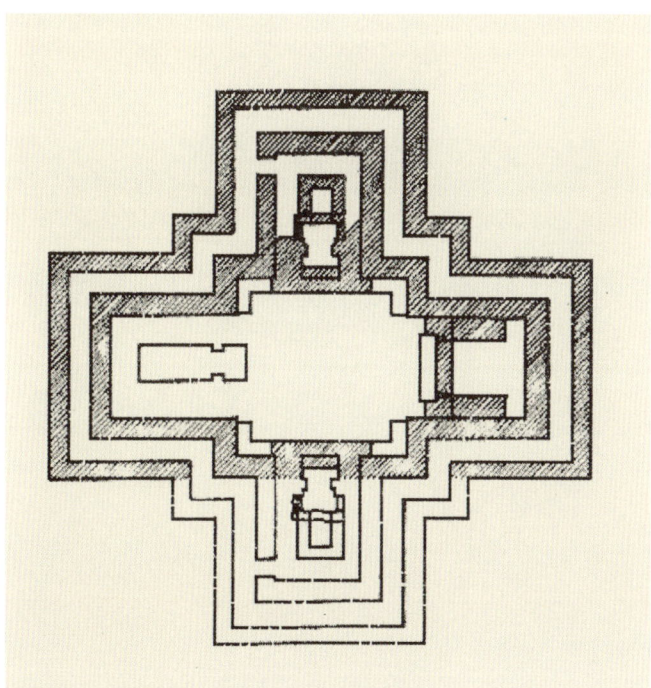

图 33 库米拉 Bhoja Viharap 神庙平面图
Dr. Md. Shafiqul Alam edited: *Proceedings for Paharpur World Heritage Site and its Environment (Bangladesh)*, International Seminar on Elaboration of an Archaeological Research Strategy for Paharpur World Heritage Site and its Environment 20-25 March 2004, Dhaka, P61.

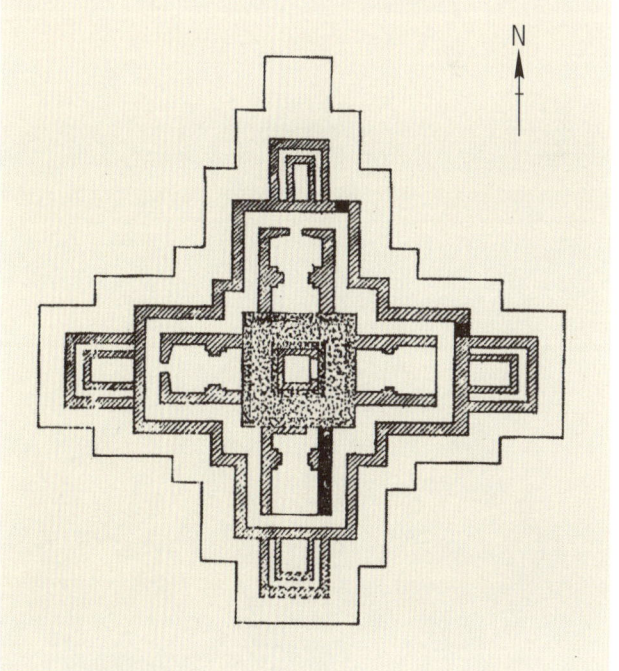

图 34 巴哈布尔中心神殿平面图
Dr. Md. Shafiqul Alam edited: *Proceedings for Paharpur World Heritage Site and its Environment (Bangladesh)*, International Seminar on Elaboration of an Archaeological Research Strategy for Paharpur World Heritage Site and its Environment 20-25 March 2004, Dhaka, P61.

金刚乘的五禅那佛，每个都是大日如来的不同形貌，面向四个方向。从巴哈布尔遗址看，四方墙面上嵌有品字形的三个小壁龛，可能是放置神像或油灯的小龛，并没有正中的大龛，四个方向的禅那佛可能是靠墙安置在佛殿内的。以佛塔南面的佛殿为例，东西长6.1米，南北宽3.55米，即为安置佛像的佛殿，前面有门道通向带四个柱础石的柱厅，四个柱础石上原来应有石柱，承担屋顶的重量。柱厅除用于僧徒礼拜外，也可能用于集会、讲解教义、诵经和举行各种仪轨。佛殿之间没有相互连通的转经道，但有沿塔基上升的梯子。柱厅之外，便是四个方向的入口和三级露台，露台上有连续的廊柱，墙面上装饰着丰富的砖雕，风格一致的砖雕也说明建筑时间的同一性，通过南北台级，通向开阔的庭院（图35）。

图36是推测的缅甸式尖状塔顶，有16个转角楼、塔楼或螺塔。图37是根据印度神庙所作的推测图。

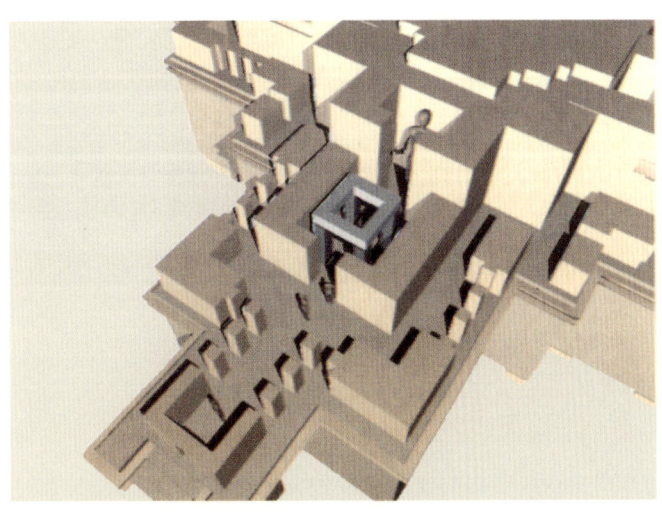

图35 巴哈布尔从入口到柱厅到实心塔的复原图
Dr. Md. Shafiqul Alam edited: *Proceedings for Paharpur World Heritage Site and its Environment (Bangladesh)*, International Seminar on Elaboration of an Archaeological Research Strategy for Paharpur World Heritage Site and its Environment 20-25 March 2004, Dhaka, P79.

图36 巴哈布尔中心建筑顶部复原图
Dr. Md. Shafiqul Alam edited: *Proceedings for Paharpur World Heritage Site and its Environment (Bangladesh)*, International Seminar on Elaboration of an Archaeological Research Strategy for Paharpur World Heritage Site and its Environment 20-25 March 2004, Dhaka, P77.

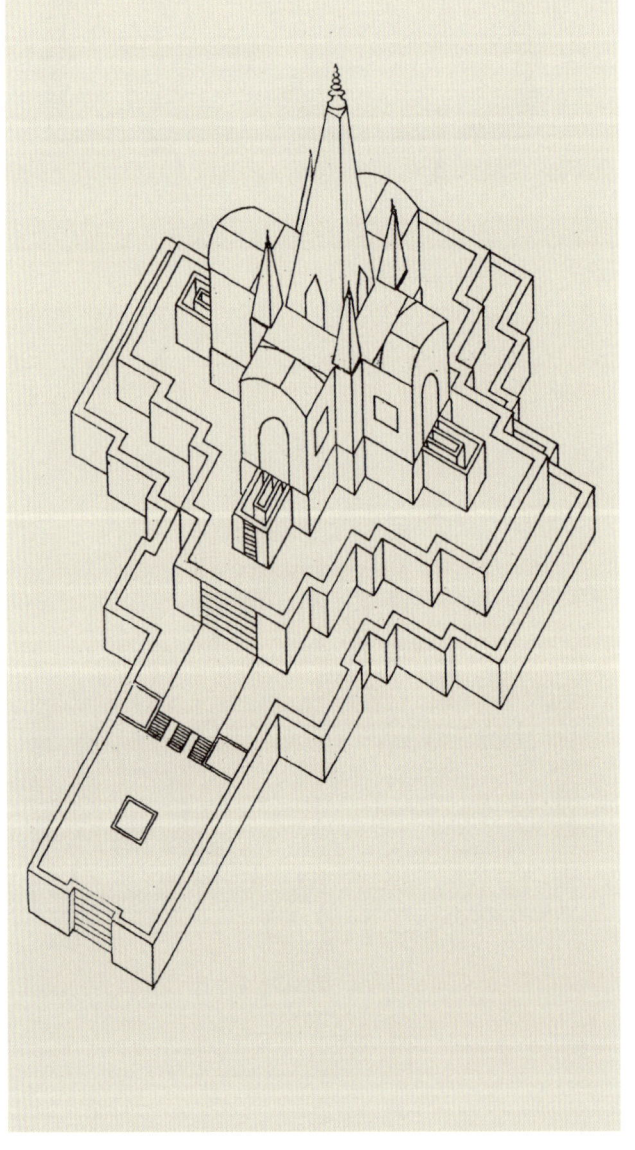

图37 巴哈布尔中心建筑顶部复原图
Dr. Md. Shafiqul Alam edited: *Proceedings for Paharpur World Heritage Site and its Environment (Bangladesh)*, International Seminar on Elaboration of an Archaeological Research Strategy for Paharpur World Heritage Site and its Environment 20-25 March 2004, Dhaka, P85.

中心神殿的外围，围绕着 177 间小居室，小居室前面是一条带柱子的游廊，四门有高大的门楼。小居室最初是僧人的生活用房，墙壁上有安置神像的壁龛，室内放置日常用物，至少有 92 间后期小居室安置了神像基座，可能意味着修行方式的变化。据发掘报告，37 号小居室内发现的 9—10 世纪佛陀等身像，是一个低眉沉思的合金像，残高 1.27 米；159 号小居室前的庭院发现一个象头神青铜像；170 号小居室前的庭院发现一尊耆那教神像；175 号小居室的廊道上发现 Prabhavali 神像。义净在《南海寄归内法传》卷三曾描绘："又复僧房之内，有安尊像，或于窗上，或故作龛。食坐之时，像前以布幔遮障，朝朝洗沐，每荐香花。午午虔恭，随餐奉献。"

大约在 10 世纪末到 11 世纪初，开阔的庭院中修建了许多建筑，围墙之外修建了 Satyapir Bhita 度母庙和密宗的奉献塔。

建筑材料以不同尺寸的砖为主，少量石材用作门窗的过梁、门槛、门柱、柱础、柱子、神像基座等，石块之间用铁条链结（图 38—40）。位于恼冈的 Dhamoirhat 的 Jagaddala 寺院遗址修建于 11—12 世纪，距离巴哈布尔约 30 千米，遗址中发现了大量精美的建筑石材，其中排水口有漂亮的石雕龙嘴（图 41、42），反映了这一时期建

图 38　巴哈布尔遗址柱厅内的石柱础、石门槛　笔者拍摄

图 39　门框雕刻，Bangarh, West Dinajpur，10—11 世纪，达卡国家博物馆　笔者拍摄

图 40　门框雕刻，Bangarh, West Dinajpur，10—11 世纪，达卡国家博物馆　笔者拍摄

图41　Jagaddala 寺院遗址中的石材　笔者拍摄

图42　Jagaddala 寺院遗址排水口。又称娑竭罗龙嘴，为梵文音译，娑竭罗龙为降雨的龙神，古来祈雨皆以之为本尊。《海龙王经》《佛为海龙王说法印经》《佛为娑伽罗龙王所说大乘经》诸经，皆为佛对此龙王所说之法。水沟中流动水让人联想到龙王的咆哮声　笔者拍摄

筑石雕的水平。

波罗王朝被认为是孟加拉历史上的黄金时代，孟加拉民族的荣耀和对外影响在这一时期达到了前所未有的程度，十字形中心神殿也传播到周边的许多地区。加德满都博达佛塔相传为11世纪重修，佛塔修在三层宽阶之上，外形为曼陀罗，中心为塔顶的伞盖，四周有108个供奉阿弥陀佛的佛龛。在东南亚，柬埔寨的吴哥窟、爪哇的婆罗浮屠（Borobudhur）佛塔也是这种十字形风格。

考古学家在印度克什米尔一带的考古调查中注意到，大约在7—8世纪前后，克什米尔、旦叉始罗等地区也开始流行十字形的佛塔，犍陀罗贾吉克德里大塔就是其中一例，中亚阿基那寺，也是呈十字形的大塔位于塔院的中心，四周建以方形围廊[16]。印度河流域乌仗那是杂密的中心，金刚乘中心在印度中东部，这种建筑风格应该从东部传来的。

桑耶寺是西藏历史上的第一座寺院，创建于赤松德赞时期（755—797年）。史载，出生于孟加拉萨霍尔（Zahor）地方的佛学大师寂护在青朴住了四个月，向赞普宣讲了"十善"、"十八界"、"十二因缘"，又设计了桑耶寺。桑耶寺的整体结构与同时期的印度寺院非常相近，与后来的西藏寺庙迥然有别。据布顿《佛教史大宝藏论》，莲花生在此按照欧丹多富梨寺（Odantapuri）模式，设计了整体图样。桑耶寺建筑分布上体现了佛教"大千世界"的思想，这是佛教对世界结构的想像，其目的是要用新世界来摧毁被佛教视为受邪恶力量支配的地方信仰。乌策大殿四面每一边的中部四门凸出，形成曼陀罗形状，即《巴协》所谓的"吉祥毗卢遮那救渡恶趣曼陀罗"（图43、44）。但细细分析桑耶寺乌孜大殿的平面结构，它还不是典型的十字形中心神殿建筑，在乌策大殿中，佛堂仍是仪轨的中心，其中还有三条绕殿礼拜的内部转经道。准确地说，乌孜大殿并不是典型的曼陀罗建筑，至多算是大乘佛教传统建筑和曼陀罗新思维融合的产物。过了近两个世纪，益西沃于985—990前后创建了古格的托林寺，据文献记载，托林寺的朗巴朗则拉康也是仿照欧丹多富梨（Otantapuri）寺而建造的，与桑耶寺相比，它才是西藏典型十字形中心神殿建筑的代表。在此后一百多年中，托林寺一直是西藏西部地区最为重要的佛教中心（图45、46）。

扎塘寺始建于1081年，创建人是扎囊十二贤人中的扎巴恩协（1012—1090年），扎塘寺的布局也是按曼陀罗结构建造的，围墙原有内、中、外三重围墙，内、中围墙呈多角形，大部分被毁，现仅存主殿和部分残缺围墙。

江孜白居塔建于1427—1436年间，建筑的结构和雕塑、壁画中五部佛的配置，完全是按曼

陀罗结构安排的。白居寺措庆大殿建于1418年，内部是中心殿式佛堂，外部四面突出，即《汉藏史集》所记之"十二道大棱"，形成复式十字形结构，是融合了大乘佛教礼佛和密宗曼陀罗两种意念的创造，体现了藏传佛教显密并重的宗教特点（图47—49）。

四、继承和流变：西藏寺院建筑风格的变迁

西藏寺庙建筑源于印度的蓝本，建筑的样式，既带着宗教精神的深刻印记，也与当地的气候、建材和建筑传统有关。东印度多为砖砌建筑、砖石建筑，顶部是高耸的塔尖，西藏则是土石、土木建筑，顶部多为平顶。

西藏早期寺院多建于谷底的平地上，僧舍是庭院四周一系列凹室，这种布局可以追溯到印度犍陀罗的许多早期佛寺。多数情况下，这些凹室简化为一圈夯土围墙，保证佛殿的隐蔽与静谧。除了桑耶寺、托林寺等皇家寺院直接摹仿东印度寺院外，西藏众多的中小型寺庙，大多以一座单一的建筑为中心，作为僧人诵经、集会和信众供奉之地。僧人修行还选择在附近僻静的洞窟中，与寺庙有一定距离，以方便过无扰的禅修生活。

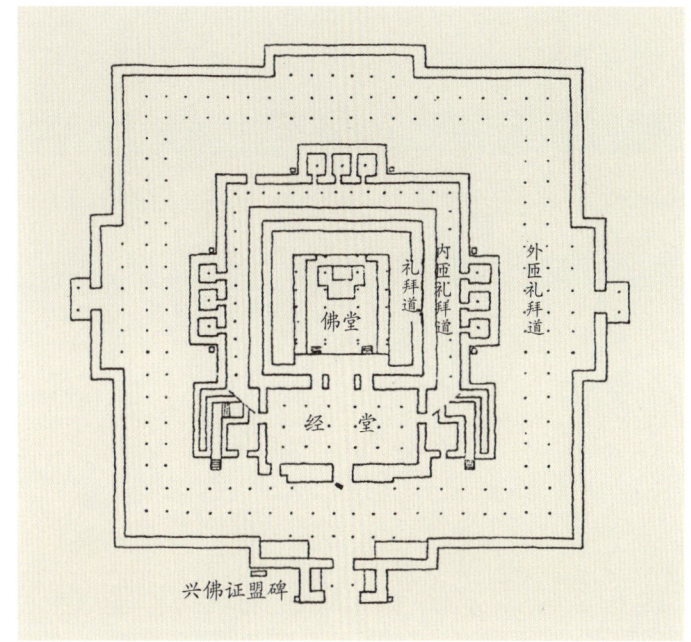

图43　桑耶寺乌策大殿平面图
宿白：《藏传佛教寺院考古》，文物出版社，1996年。

图44　桑耶寺乌策大殿　贾英杰拍摄

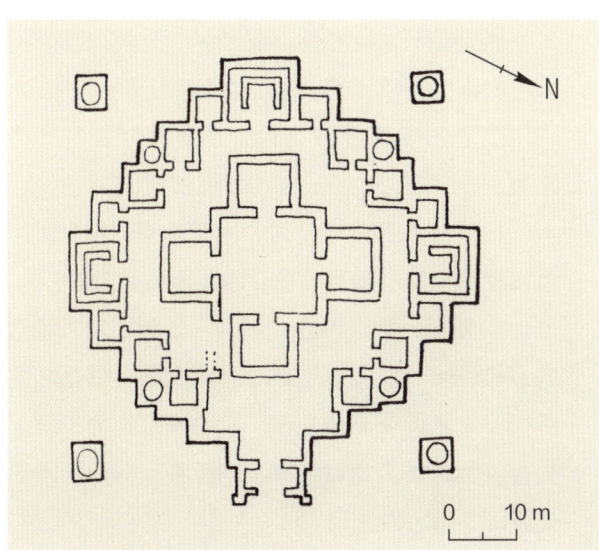

图45　托林寺朗巴朗则拉康平面图
宿白：《藏传佛教寺院考古》，文物出版社，1996年。

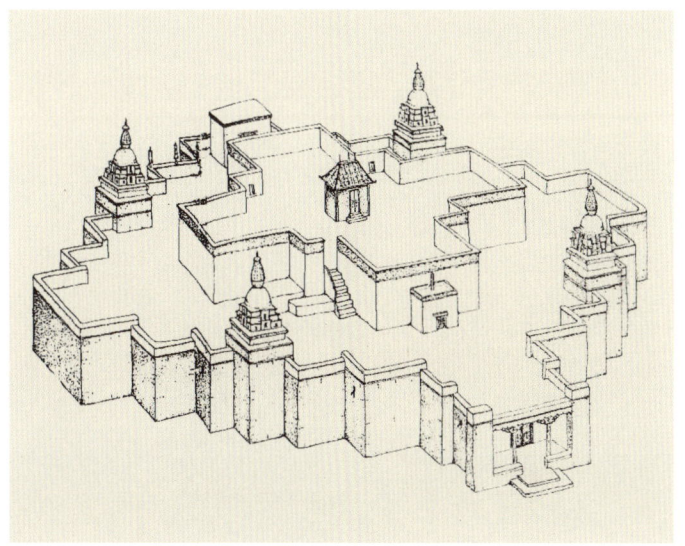

图46　托林寺朗巴朗则拉康复原图　托林寺提供

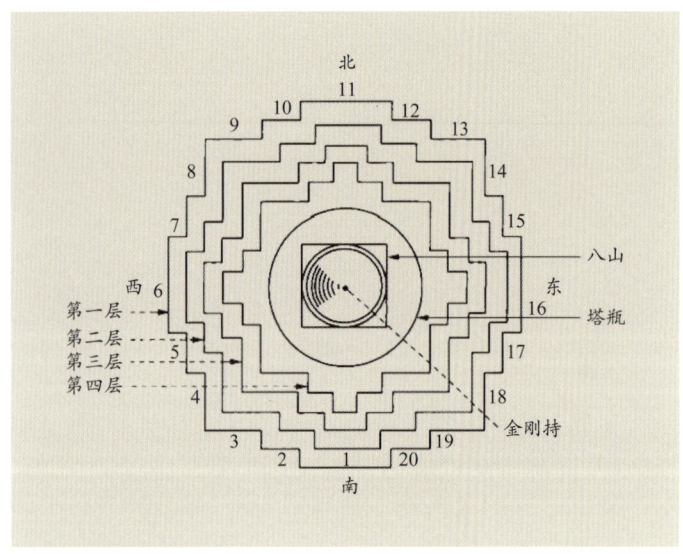

图47 白居塔平面图
〔意〕杜齐著，魏正中、萨尔吉主编，李翎等译：《梵天佛地》第4卷第1册，上海古籍出版社，2010年。

图48 白居塔 笔者拍摄

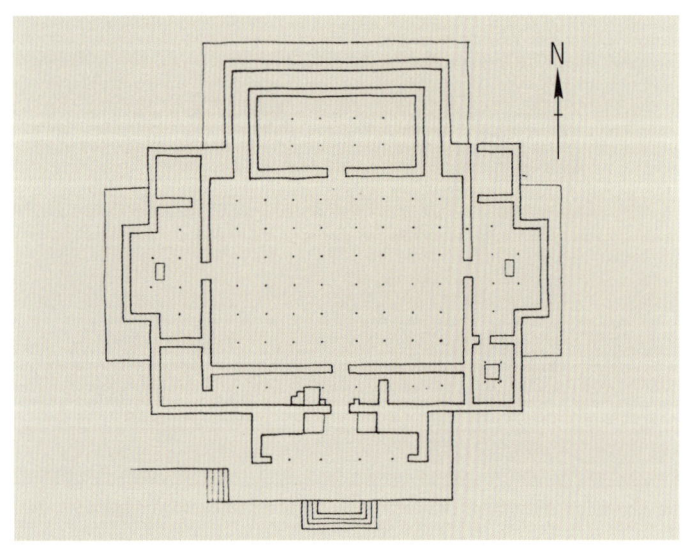

图49 白居寺措庆大殿平面图
宿白：《藏传佛教寺院考古》，文物出版社，1996年。

僧人在石窟中禅修结束后，通常回到附近地面上的寺庙。在西藏西部地区，河谷地带两岸崖壁上的石窟多与河谷中的佛塔、崖顶的寺院组合出现，时代从11世纪到15世纪。

前弘期和后弘期初期，西藏各教派与波罗王朝佛教中心的交流是畅通的。1204年超戒寺被烧毁，印藏之间的交流因此中断，标志着佛教在印度的毁灭，这也标志着一个新阶段的到来。此时正值西藏大寺院的兴建时代，由于僧团的扩充，寺院成为护法施主捐建的中心，高僧的驻锡吸引了无数的信众。新建的寺院在印度建筑模式的基础上，加快了与西藏本土的融合。1264年，元世祖忽必烈命八思巴领总制院事，"掌释教僧徒及吐蕃之境而隶治之"，寺庙作为地方的文化和精神中心，王朝的赏赐和村庄的贡奉，使得寺庙的财富猛增，从而使之成为易受袭击的目标，1274年竣工的萨迦南寺，在寺庙的外围修筑了坚固的方形城堡。此外，随着元代汉藏交流的频繁，建筑中出现了许多汉地因素，如广泛采用汉式建筑的木结构和"金饰起脊屋顶"，萨迦寺、夏鲁寺都是明显的例子。

西藏寺院的一般格局中，中心殿式佛堂成了寺院建筑的中心，大经堂的四周或建筑的各层，发展出护法殿、密宗殿、祖师灵塔殿等附属殿堂，将多种修行仪轨功能合而为一[17]，一般是如下结构。

转经廊：主殿外有一条土路，环墙设有经筒，香客们围绕主殿转经，边走边拨动经筒。

庭院：寺门前的空地，也是进行节日庆典之地。

门厅：外部世俗空间和内部神圣领域之间的过渡地带，门厅两边一般有四大护法天王像。

大经堂：僧人讲经、诵经、集会之地。经堂有多排柱子，使大厅变得尽可能宽敞。靠近经堂后端设立佛像或高僧法座。以中央甬道为中轴设数排座位，僧人相对而坐，四面和天井的壁画烘托着浓厚的宗教氛围。

佛殿：经堂后面是佛殿的入口，佛殿一般呈四方形，是供奉神像的神圣之地，这是从印度原型中承袭而来的古老形制。在佛殿之外，有一条围绕佛殿的内部转经廊，作为僧众的礼拜道。

护法殿：一般位于经堂的侧殿，有黑色背景的线描壁画和本地的各种护法神造像，僧人在此诵经和举行消灾、祝祷、祛禳、仪轨。

密宗殿：用于密宗灌顶、修炼等秘密用途，单层建筑一般在佛殿附近的侧殿，多层建筑多置于高层隐秘之所。密宗殿堂内安置相应的造像或壁画，作为观想和灌顶仪轨的辅助工具。

总的来说，寺庙的功能不外于僧侣的修行、观想和对信众的教化，白居寺措庆大殿、夏鲁寺、贡嘎曲德寺、打隆下寺等都是这类寺庙风格的典范。

1409年拉萨大昭寺举办的祈愿大法会，标志着格鲁派的兴盛，宗喀巴以继承阿底峡传统为号召，使大批噶当派寺庙改宗格鲁派，四大黄教寺院的兴建，使格鲁派的影响遍及全藏。格鲁派将早期诸译师传入的传规按次第修习，教义上显密兼备，也影响着建筑及造像、壁画的配置。可能是为了缓解寺庙礼拜者的剧增的压力，从16世纪起，废除环绕佛殿的内礼拜道，这并非忽视礼拜佛像、佛塔的仪轨，而是将礼拜道的位置从殿内移向殿外，出现了围绕主殿、寺庙甚至城市的多层外礼拜道。这样一来，原来经堂之后设佛堂之制也随之改变，变为并列的三佛堂，供奉之像、塔皆列于经堂后壁之前，16世纪以来的拉萨三大寺各札仓皆流行此制[18]。此外，有的寺庙将旧经堂分割，或在两侧加以扩建，形成左右配殿；有的甚至不设佛殿，仅设经堂；僧舍或其他设施与佛堂混杂在一起，曼陀罗格局已经不再明显；建筑的方位、对称性等特征往往出于实用，不再由象征意义决定；晚期寺院多建于在山坡上，采用城堡式形制以利于防御；拉萨三大寺和日喀则扎什伦布寺，建筑层叠如城镇、街衢，宗教与生活融为一体，政教合一比佛陀的象征更加重要，建筑模式也与印度最初的范本越走越远。

下篇
造像

一、造像的分类及其风格特征

（1）孟加拉国

孟加拉国的佛教造像包括青铜铸像、泥灰塑像、木雕、石雕和赤陶砖雕，其中青铜铸像、泥灰塑像、石雕多是圣像，蕴含着深刻的宗教含义，与建筑结合在一起，承担着宗教崇拜的功能。东印度的孟加拉、比哈尔和奥里萨等地，既是密宗中心，也是造像的制作中心，这些地区留下了严格按照仪轨制作的、美学上臻于完美的众多造像，被称为"波罗式样"。赤陶砖雕多作为建筑的装饰，主要为传说故事和反映现实生活的题材。

孟加拉国出土的金铜像不多，大部分是些小尊造像，可能与当地缺乏矿产资源有关。像莫河斯坦附近的Balaidhap出土的6世纪鎏金文殊铜像；巴哈布尔第37号小居室内发现的9—10世纪的佛陀等身合金像；库米拉县迈纳马蒂（Mainamati）区域 Bhoja Vihara 发现的巨大的持金刚青铜像（见后图132），其精美的造型和铸造工艺，都令人震惊，使人们对于波罗—旃陀罗（Chandra）铸像艺术有了全新的认识。

泥灰塑像保存下来的很少，典型的样本是库米拉县迈纳马蒂区域的爱塔克霍拉神庙（Itakhola Mura）出土的不动佛泥塑像，年代在7世纪（图50）。

图50　不动佛泥塑像，7世纪，Itakhola Mura　笔者拍摄

木雕造像在孟加拉国各地佛教遗址中均有出土，达卡国家博物馆展出的蒙希甘杰（Munshiganj）县出土的木雕，属于古代毗诃罗普尔古城寺院建筑构件及门柱门楣的装饰，有文殊菩萨、世间怙主（Lokanatha）、女神（Sundari，图51）等，年代为11世纪，反映了当时佛教建筑的盛况。

石雕艺术发源于印度河、恒河流域，在印度古老的农耕文明中，达罗毗荼人对于药叉（Yaksa）与那迦蛇王（龙王）的崇拜根深蒂固，中印度秣菟罗地区农田或堤坝上频繁出现那迦雕刻，具有人的身体和头部上方展开的多个蛇头帽冠。在家宅内，都有一尊巨大的药叉立像，作为保护之神。它们出现在雅利安人以前，成为婆罗门教和佛教造像的最初模型。

巴尔胡特—菩提伽耶—山奇的三处栏杆石雕，可看作是从公元前150到公元50年这两个世纪中佛教艺术逐渐演进的三大里程碑。

笈多（Gupta）王朝（320—500年）是大乘佛教的极盛时期，与前古典时期朴素、粗犷、对生活充满乐趣的神像不同，笈多艺术呈现出一种充满风韵的优美外观，一种超越世俗的表情和姿态，是理想主义与高度和谐感的结合。它采取了大自然中活的曲线，亚热带阳光下纤丽、细腻的人体，扭突斜耸的三道弯风格，象征着青春和人

图51　女神木雕，11世纪，Munshiganj，达卡国家博物馆藏　笔者拍摄

体之美，代替了慈悲出世的表情。这是清新的自然主义和虔敬的神秘主义的和谐融合，是5世纪无著、世亲光辉流畅大乘玄学的外在表现，并在以后的几个世纪中得到传承。

笈多王朝之后，印度再度分裂，印度教盛行，佛教的香火只限于西北的克什米尔和东印度波罗王朝治下的比哈尔和孟加拉地区。波罗造像继承了笈多的美学传统，接受了秣菟罗样式的启发，日渐成熟，人体结构简约，线条优美，姿态自然典雅，华丽的璎珞和头冠刻划精细。

在孟加拉国一些博物馆中，7世纪以前的石雕造像以佛陀、菩萨以及持明密教中的度母像为主。7世纪以后，随着金刚乘的发展，出现了数量可观的五智禅那佛和密教菩萨。大约9世纪以后，黑石雕数量庞大，石材来自孟加拉与比哈尔之间的Rajmahal山区。10世纪密教进入无上瑜伽阶段，为了体现密宗修行的奥义及降魔的职能，造像多具有狰狞的外貌：三只眼睛象征看穿世界的智慧，五颗头颅的头冠，意指"五智"，还有多臂多头的守护神，或拥抱着明妃，或双脚踏着教义的敌人，繁杂的装饰以及对于尖、拱、火焰的嗜用，都是从人的心识中产生出来的象征。孟加拉8—12世纪的佛教和印度教造像，成为笈多艺术和尼泊尔艺术之间的桥梁，西藏造像艺术更是直接由此衍化而来[19]。

砖雕是石雕的姊妹艺术，在5000年前的印度河流域已经流行。孟加拉地区石材少，建筑多用砖材，砖雕因此特别发达，至迟到7世纪，以砖雕装饰墙体已成风尚。8—12世纪的波罗时代，砖雕大多用于装饰佛塔和神庙的墙基。艺术家从大自然和笈多时代传统中撷取题材，有的故事出自佛教《本生经》（Jataka），如释迦太子执刀割下头发，大象、猴子向佛陀奉献蜂蜜等；有的来自《罗摩衍那》《摩诃婆罗多》和《五卷书》（Panchatantra，用梵文写成的古印度故事集）中的知名故事；也有6世纪古希腊寓言作家伊索的寓言；都是当时民间喜闻乐见的故事。按印度轮回观念，动物与人是同宗兄弟，许多神祇都与动物有关。植物花草则象征生命、活力和丰收。这些观念超越了教派，代表了多彩的心灵，是印度民族共同的传统。艺术家在对于人物、动植物的自然主义描摹中，冲破了宗教规范的昏昧神秘，自由地表达了对于神祇、大自然和日常生活的感情，以及一切生物都应和平相处的佛教哲理[20]（图52—55）。

图52 镶嵌砖雕的墙基，7—9世纪，Salban Vihara 迈纳马蒂博物馆资料

图53 砖雕（牛），7—9世纪，Mainamati出土，迈纳马蒂博物馆 笔者拍摄

图54 砖雕（罗摩故事），博格拉（Bogra）地区Palashbari出土，6—7世纪，达卡国家博物馆收藏 笔者拍摄

图55 巴哈布尔遗址墙基砖雕 笔者拍摄

图56 象头神（Ganash）擦擦，约8—10世纪纳提什瓦遗址出土

古代印度有佛塔内存放去世高僧遗骨、硬币、念珠等圣物的风俗，将高僧的骨灰与土掺和在一起，制成佛塔或刻有法轮、经咒的小泥塑，称为"擦擦"（Seals），它起源于古代及中世纪印度中部和北部方言中的一个词汇[21]。擦擦上压印的塔，可能与迦毗罗卫（Kapilavastu）、菩提伽耶（Bodhgaya）、波罗奈斯（Benares）、拘尸那揭罗（Kusinagara）等八大佛教胜地有关，代表了释迦牟尼游化宣教的八大履所[22]，擦擦可能是印度佛教圣地的纪念品[23]。

玄奘《大唐西域记》卷九曾描写道："印度之法，香末为泥，做小窣堵波，高五六寸，书写经文，以置其中，谓之法舍利也。数渐盈积，建大窣堵波，总聚于内，常修供养。"

孟加拉国的巴哈布尔、库米拉等地的佛教遗址中，皆有许多擦擦及压印擦擦的模具出土。擦擦的制法是揉好泥团后，直接用模具压印成形，因此，多有翻起的边缘，题材主要为佛塔、法轮、佛像以及梵文经咒[24]。但在西印度斯瓦特这样庞大的佛教圣地发掘中，却没有发现擦擦，所以它可能是东印度的习俗。擦擦从东印度传入西藏，擦擦中的图像也成为西藏造像艺术的灵感来源。

图56为毗诃罗普尔古城纳提什瓦遗址出土的象头神（Ganash）擦擦，高9.5、宽5.8、厚1—2.6厘米，带有印度教神祇的帽冠，肥胖的肚子，长长的象鼻已残损，顶部有水果图案，左侧执武器（Mace）。象头神是湿婆大神和帕尔瓦蒂女神的长子，佛教中被称为大圣欢喜天，藏密中称为象鼻财神或象头财神。孟加拉国早期擦擦多为圆饼状，带着翻起的边缘，这类尖顶的陶制擦擦可能仿自当时放置在神龛中的石雕造像，过去少有发现，西藏流行的擦擦皆为尖顶，可能源出东印度。

（2）西藏地区

1. 金铜造像

松赞干布（617—650年）时期，尼泊尔尺尊公主将当时流行的不动佛、救度母、十一面观音像带入吐蕃。大唐文成公主将释迦牟尼像带入吐蕃。同时也带来了各自的佛典和工匠，这是西藏佛教造像的起点。

7—12世纪，印度有两个造像中心，西北部的迦湿弥罗汲取了斯瓦特地区的犍陀罗传统，并受到希腊造像的影响，十分注意肌肉的轮廓和身体上每一个细节的精确性，风格雄浑硬朗，衣饰带有粗大的摺痕，没有太多的饰物，从10—14世纪初，一直影响着西藏西部地区；另一个造像中心是印度东北部及孟加拉地区，它直接影响尼泊尔和卫藏地区，尤其在10—12世纪，那烂陀寺和超戒寺汇集了来自印度各地和西藏、尼泊尔、汉地、东南亚的求法僧侣，许多小型造像作为吉祥物装在他们的行囊中，成为各地图像的源泉。

1204年，超戒寺被穆斯林摧毁后，许多僧侣、工匠避走尼泊尔或穿越喜玛拉雅山来到西藏，并长期留居下来。

尼泊尔造像继承了笈多后期的古典风格和波罗造像传统，带有柔软的三道弯风格，在几个世纪中没有太多的变化。此外，由于受曼陀罗图像影响，东印度佛像台座喜用多角多折的样式。由于东印度造像往往嵌在佛塔或佛龛中，所以造像的背光出现了佛塔或佛龛的形态。尼泊尔也是后期密教的中心，后宏期许多西藏译师都在尼泊尔求学，学习"大威德"等密宗教法。加德满都金铜造像作为持续的影响源，深刻地影响了西藏造像的风格。

西藏许多后弘期大寺庙，都保存大量的金铜造像，如扎什伦布寺藏有来自东北印度、斯瓦特、克什米尔、尼泊尔和西藏本地的大量金铜像；萨迦寺保存了大量波罗王朝风格的造像；布达拉宫、大昭寺也有大量来自不同地区的造像。

15世纪前，噶当派佛像主要在洛扎、涅（隆子）、劳若、雅隆等地铸造。西藏早期的本土作品稍显僵硬，背部制作粗糙，头部镶嵌绿松石。15—18世纪，拉萨、扎什伦布、孜东是卫藏地区三大铸造中心，其中不乏闪耀着天才智慧的杰作，是艺术家禅修时所获灵感的结晶。来乌群巴是15世纪拉萨地区的一个著名工匠，有不少作品传世，他的作品身体比例匀称，卵形脸庞很美，脚趾和手指准确，可跟汉地造像相混淆。扎雅活佛指出，来乌群巴的四臂观音像，面相秀美，眉宇间传达出一种忧郁感，表现了观音悲悯众生的情怀[25]。此外，明清宫廷有制造作坊，雇请了尼泊尔、西藏地区工匠。大明永乐年间（1403—1424年）青铜造像常见尊格包括：佛陀、度母、文殊、观音、大威德、大黑天等。特点是面相扁平，圆形或方形的脸，东亚人的眼睛。正面和背面一样，都精细雕琢，题记镌刻在莲花座前方的中间部位，双层莲座，底部的花瓣比上部花瓣大约长出一半，上下有密密的珍珠，花瓣都是双层的，里层花瓣的瓣尖略尖一些，微微凸起[26]。16、17世纪以后，商业生产和粗制滥造剧增，造像带上了世俗的情调，并进入了僵化状态，典雅的造像传统走到了尽头。

2. 泥塑

西藏前弘期就有塑像的传统，据《巴协》记载，桑耶寺曾挑出最俊美的男子枯达擦做观音像，照最美丽的女子觉若妃子布琼、拉布门、桑达勒的模样，塑造了天女、观音、度母。

8世纪前期，一批于阗僧人因国内排佛事件而逃到吐蕃，当时赤德祖赞收留了他们，在今山南乃东县建吉如拉康作为他们的修行之地。吉如拉康的释迦牟尼塑像是于阗僧人按西域风格制作的。艾旺寺位于日喀则市康马县萨马达乡萨鲁村冲巴涌曲河岸，距康马县城15千米，可能创建于11世纪初，塑像也为典型的中亚—于阗风格（图57）[27]。

印度喜马偕尔邦斯比蒂地区的塔波寺，其杜康大殿后殿正中为无量光佛塑像，两侧为菩萨等身塑像，躯体呈沙漏计时器状，菩萨肚脐蜗牛状卷曲不在正中位置，从而产生一种动感。这是11世纪克什米尔风格的杰作。

西藏塑像主要受东印度和尼泊尔的影响，只是在摹仿过程中，南亚的柔美、野性的繁荣有所抑制，逐渐趋于严谨。白居寺措庆大殿中心佛殿的大菩提佛和十六菩萨塑像，承袭了东印度摩揭陀金刚座大佛像的崇高和庄严，精神集中，目光表

图57　艾旺寺雕塑，11世纪初　何强拍摄

情都是创造性的，是西藏塑像的杰作（图58）。措庆大殿西净土殿供养天女塑像，涡蔓状圆圈内是一个个独立的神祇，沿五佛周围展开，肢体曼妙舒展，是尼泊尔风格的典型作品（图59）。

3. 木雕

大昭寺一、二层的木质门楣、廊柱上满施雕饰，题材有佛传故事、飞天、动物、花草、人头卧狮等（图60）。这种传统源自古印度，那烂陀寺的枋橡也周雕人头卧狮，如义净所说，"上作人头""雕刻奇形，妙尽工饰"[28]。

科加寺门楣上有108组木雕，也是比较纯粹的印度风格，其中佛传故事27组，《罗摩衍那》（Ramayana）故事27组，那迦（Naga）和迦如达

图58　白居寺措庆大殿大菩提佛塑像　笔者拍摄

图60　大昭寺吐蕃时期木雕

国家文物局主编：《中国文物地图集·西藏自治区分册》，文物出版社，2010年。

图59　白居寺措庆大殿西净土殿供养天女塑像　笔者拍摄

图61　科加寺木雕门框，10世纪末　笔者拍摄

图62　佛传故事经版，约15—16世纪，康马县南尼寺　笔者拍摄

（Garuda）54组，年代为10世纪末（图61）。

古格遗址红殿的两扇木门的表面，刻有梵文"六字真言"；门楣上方正中，刻有金刚手，两侧各有一人结跏趺坐于莲台上，身旁各有飞天，应是说法图；两侧外框刻有人物、动物图案，可能是佛本生故事一类的题材；中楣刻有对称的连续忍冬卷草浮雕。年代不详。

这种门楣、廊柱上的木雕后来不再流行，西藏木雕工艺以别的形式继承下来，如印制唐卡、坛城、风马、祈幡的木刻版及经版雕刻等，成为西藏独特的艺术形式（图62）。

4. 石刻

"在通往圣地的路上，在浅滩或其他地势险峻的地方，在悬浮桥附近或有塌方的地方，常常可以看到在天然崖面上的岩雕。其中最古老的是佛陀，后期还有具有护法神力的其他神灵。特别常见的是观世音和救度母……岩雕同时也为朝圣者标明了行进的路线"[29]。

《西藏王臣记》记载，松赞干布来到红山上，亲眼看见自显的六字真言和对面药王山上的观音救度母、马头金刚等神像，立即请来尼泊尔工匠依照自显的形貌雕刻神像。又云，帕邦喀三怙主殿内的四臂观音、文殊、金刚手等摩崖造像，亦是松赞干布请尼泊尔工匠雕刻的。

前佛教时代，为了排斥凶恶的神灵，西藏有立石或堆石的习俗。到佛教时代，石头上镌刻了造像和经文，因为经文的内容多为六字真言（唵、嘛、呢、叭、咪、吽），故俗称"玛尼石刻"。在西藏高原，无论城镇、乡村、寺庙或山口，随处可见用石块垒成的玛尼堆，上面插些木棒，用绳子牵向一棵树或山崖，绳上挂满了经幡，它是目不识丁信徒们的经书，风吹经幡是信徒向上苍的诵经之声，这是让来访者印象深刻的高原景观。玛尼石刻除了佛教题材外，还有许多日常生活的内容，是一个民族包罗万象的心灵记录，它所流露出来的对于日常生活的真挚感受和技法上摆脱陈腐程式的自由，散发出一股清新的气息。

六字真言，即观音六字大明神咒，这是真言乘的标志，在7世纪左右获得巨大的发展。西藏铺天盖地的经幡、六字真言石刻、连绵不绝的吟诵声，就象空气一样，充塞在街头巷尾、山野和圣地之间。大众部信徒声称，佛陀以一个音节阐述了其全部教法，这也是莲花生的法宝，从那时起，西藏就弥漫在这个声音之中，并塑造了西藏宗教的独特品格（图63）。

图63　六字真言石刻，扎囊县青朴修行地　笔者拍摄

5. 擦擦

西藏最早的"擦擦"大约出现于11世纪，在古格故城和皮央—东嘎遗址中均有出土。相传阿底峡在为寺院或佛像开光时，多布施"擦擦"，或放入佛塔中作为胎藏。杜齐在西北印度和西藏西部的采集品中，早期的擦擦与东印度风格接近。图64—67采自杜齐《梵天佛地》第1卷，其中图64是原书中第5件，发现于底克塞（Tikse），三座天降塔，周围是藏文转写的缘起法颂："诸法从缘起，如来说是因，彼法因缘尽，是大沙门说。"这是佛塔开光仪式时所要诵念的偈颂，由于这个偈颂总摄整个教法，因此塔内装藏的擦擦

图64　擦擦，发现于底克塞（Tikse）
［意］杜齐著，魏正中、萨尔吉主编，李翎等译：《梵天佛地》，上海古籍出版社，2010年。

图65　擦擦，发现于雪韶（Shushot）
［意］杜齐著，魏正中、萨尔吉主编，李翎等译：《梵天佛地》，上海古籍出版社，2010年。

图66　擦擦，发现于斯多克（Stok）
［意］杜齐著，魏正中、萨尔吉主编，李翎等译：《梵天佛地》，上海古籍出版社，2010年。

图67　擦擦，发现于嘉地（Gya）
［意］杜齐著，魏正中、萨尔吉主编，李翎等译：《梵天佛地》，上海古籍出版社，2010年。

多压印有这个偈颂。结尾是陀罗尼明咒。图65是原书中第7件,发现于雪韶(Shushot),带有飞幡、伞盖、日轮、新月的天降塔,铭文是10世纪的北印度字体书写的缘起法颂。图66是原书中第63件,发现于斯多克(Stok),释迦牟尼成道像,两侧是菩萨或天人,顶部有三座天降塔,铭文是9—10世纪的北印度字体书写的缘起法颂。与发现于菩提伽耶(Bodhgaya)并在印度各地流通的擦擦极为相似。图67是原书中第71件,发现于嘉地(Gya),世间怙主(Lokanatha)于莲花上呈轮王坐,施与愿印,右侧有一小塔,塔旁有铃,这个样式完全是依照《成就法鬘》中第十八成就法而来。周围是藏文转写的缘起法颂,塔下部是六字真言[30]。

西藏最早的擦擦来自印度,不久就开始了本土的模制。梵文逐渐消失,代之以藏文六字真言,或者无任何铭文。开始时制作粗劣,随后,图像变得复杂、精致起来,翻起的泥边逐渐消失,浅浮雕向圆雕方向发展。擦擦的题材与寺庙的年代、教派和教义旨趣相关,每个时代都有不同的特征。

二、造像的题材其及教义背景

小乘佛教是一种哲理性的宗教,不仅否定神灵的存在,也否定佛的神性。佛陀反对偶像崇拜,在佛像产生之前,人们用佛塔、法轮或佛足印来代表佛陀(图68)。大乘佛教使佛带上了神性,成为存在于三界的神灵化身。密宗造像是礼祈、观想的重要辅助,从大瑜伽以五佛为中心,到无上瑜伽以持金刚为中心,都有相关的仪轨论书和相伴的天众,体现着教义的精髓,它们都是根据有情的根器业行的不同化现。在佛教的不同阶段,佛教神祇总会按照其象征意义而一次次重新诠释,只有放在相应宗教仪轨中,造像才能得到真正的理解。同时,寺庙中的造像又是杂糅的,每一个时期所流行的造像,总是包含着前一个阶段的造像,甚至包括人类由始以来的各种鬼怪神灵,它们并存交叠,由此构成了佛教造像的存在体系。

图68　佛足印,年代不详,斯瓦特地区出土
栗田功:《大美之佛像——犍陀罗艺术》,文物出版社,2017年

(1)大乘佛教和持明密教造像

用人的形象来表现佛陀,可能是从中印度的马土腊开始的。从此,印度艺术中最优秀的精心之作,都是要以佛的形象来表现印度的精神理想,这是印度造型艺术中最伟大的创造。早期佛像几乎是男性药叉神的翻版,马土腊艺术崇尚肉感的美学原则,构成一种朦胧、含蓄而又神秘的美感,同时通过恬静的面部神情,流露出领悟了"四圣谛""八正见"之后内心彻悟的微笑和对尘世的悲悯[31]。

早期的佛陀造像相当单一,立像和坐像占据了绝大部分。这里,佛陀是作为一个人的形象,尽管超凡脱俗,但仍是人(图69)。

佛陀跏趺坐像,右手垂直指地,称为"降魔指地印"或"触地印",表明释迦在成佛前,经过无数磨难,降服了破坏修法的恶魔,终于得道,大地之神可以作证。此外,常见的有禅定印、说法印等。造像融合了帝王和禅定者的姿态,目光趋向内心,精神集中超越,忍受一切,固守自我的道路,这是解脱者的写照,也是印度笈多造像的基本特征(图70—72)[32][33]。

早期佛像风格朴素,无装饰物,到后期,装

图69 立佛,2世纪后半叶—3世纪初,犍陀罗风格
栗田功:《大美之佛像——犍陀罗艺术》,文物出版社,2017年。

图70 佛陀坐像,3世纪末—4世纪初,巴焦尔地区
栗田功:《大美之佛像——犍陀罗艺术》,文物出版社,2017年。

图71 佛陀坐像,1世纪,北方邦马土腊,马土腊考古博物馆藏
[德]吴黎熙:《佛像解说》,社会科学文献出版社,2010年。

图72 佛陀坐像,5世纪,萨尔纳特,萨尔纳特博物馆收藏
[德]吴黎熙:《佛像解说》,社会科学文献出版社,2010年。

饰变得繁缛，佩璎珞环钏或戴宝冠，形象往往与当代国王相同。造像本身也从大乘教义中派生出各种象征意义，造像的神格往往难以分辨，从成佛的时间顺序上，有三世佛（燃灯佛、释迦佛、弥勒佛）；从佛所处的空间位置上，有三方佛（药师佛、释迦佛、阿弥陀佛）。这些造像并不是世间生命的真实存在，而是从禅定的意念中产生出来的，是通往涅槃道路上形象化的辅助工具。

图73—79为孟加拉国各地的石雕佛陀像。图80释迦牟尼铜造像，造像略前倾，低眉凝思，身体呈三道弯形，一手作与愿印。螺状发型，通肩袍，褶痕疏朗，呈圆而隆起圆绳状，这是笈多时代马土腊地区佛像的特征，应为6—7世纪的东印度作品，现藏于西藏索县军巴区甲青乡穷果寺。图81释迦牟尼铜造像，头部为螺状发型，身着薄袈裟，一手作说法印。面部表情端庄，宽肩细腰，气宇轩昂，肌肉圆润起伏，但不呈现块状，头光与背光以火焰作装饰，脚下无莲座，直接站立于简单的垫片上，可能为7—9世纪东印度造像，现藏于西藏江孜白居寺。图82石刻圆雕立像，高28厘米，体身呈三道弯式，装饰简朴，腹部肌肉呈块状，头戴三叶宝冠，这种头冠流行于8世纪北印度的喜马查和尼泊尔，这尊造像出自西藏阿里古格遗址，是后弘期早期受克什米尔风格影响的西藏作品。图83弥勒佛铜造像，高74厘米，造像身佩璎珞、珠饰、臂钏、环铛，一手执净瓶，一手可能执有花枝，身体线条柔和平滑，表情含蓄，具有波罗艺术的优雅气质，可能出自尼泊尔，年代约15世纪，现藏于西藏比如县热丹寺。图84佛陀石雕坐像，风格雄浑，具有波罗艺术的风格特点，为吐蕃时期桑耶寺石刻。图85佛陀石雕坐像，高32厘米，佛作跏趺坐，作禅定印，薄衣贴体，有褶痕，背光及莲座下法座为东印度波罗风格，约9—11世纪，现藏于西藏贡嘎县德勤穷国寺。图86佛陀石雕坐像，高34厘米，佛作跏趺坐，体态饱满，神情端庄，神龛状背光，图案细腻，并刻有梵文，为典型的东印度波罗风格，约为9—11世纪，现藏于西藏贡嘎县德勤穷国寺。

菩萨，即菩提萨埵，他们已经与佛平等，因出于慈悲，不想失去与世间的联系，甘愿推迟获得佛果和最后涅槃而在人间弘扬佛法，直至众生都获得觉悟并从生死轮回中解脱出来。常见的大乘菩萨有弥勒（Maitreya）、文殊师利（Manjucri）、观世音（Avlokitecvara）、普贤（Samantabhadra）、金刚手（Vajrapani）等。

观音是与"化身"概念连在一起的，是佛教中最受人崇拜的菩萨，是大乘精神的标志性神祇。早在1、2世纪，观音信仰已在印度建立，贵霜时期就有手持莲花的观音像（又称莲花手菩萨），阿旃陀石窟有5世纪观音壁画像，随侍阿弥陀佛是观音图像的一大特征。藏传佛教对观音的崇拜也非常虔诚，观音的化身特别多，信徒们念诵的六字真言意为"皈依莲花上的宝珠"，就是赞颂观音的（图87—89）。

文殊，即文殊师利，传说是释迦牟尼的左胁侍，专司"智慧"，印度教徒称为"毗湿奴"，曾挥利剑斩出河道，标识为顶结五髻，手持宝剑，肩部有经书或卷轴，坐莲花宝座，骑狮子，为最常见的形象，是智慧、辩才、威猛的象征（图90—94）。

大乘晚期，出现了一些事部密教的神祇。密教的原始成分源于婆罗门教，杂密称为事部，包括明咒（吠陀经之咒术）、瑜伽（婆罗门教禅定）、护摩（婆罗门教火供，以物投火，藉火神阿耆尼之力而达于梵），以此来调伏鬼神、息灾避祸、增益致福。陀罗尼密教于2世纪在印度、西域一带形成，包含在方广般若法门之中，3世纪初传入中国。事部密宗中，观音、金刚手、不动明王、救度母是最标志性的神祇。持明密教属于事部密教的最高阶段，西印度龙树弟子难陀，在4世纪前后，撮集《持明咒藏》，在持诵陀罗尼经时，手持印契，起强化、提示、顺序作用，后被赋予神力，用于召请众神。莲花生在吐蕃传播的，正是这一时期在北印乌仗那一带流传的陀罗尼和持明密教。

图 73 佛陀，12 世纪，Dinajpur 出土，拉杰沙希 Varendra 研究博物馆藏　笔者拍摄

图 74 佛陀，5 世纪，Rajshahi 出土，拉杰沙希 Varendra 研究博物馆藏　笔者拍摄

图 75 立佛，7 世纪，Bogra 出土，莫河斯坦遗址博物馆藏　笔者拍摄

图 76 立佛，9 世纪，Bogra 出土，莫河斯坦遗址博物馆藏　笔者拍摄

图 77 坐佛，9—10 世纪，Khulna 出土，库尔纳博物馆藏　笔者拍摄

图 78 阿弥陀佛，8 世纪，Pahadpur 出土，达卡国家博物馆藏　笔者拍摄

图 79 禅定佛，8 世纪，出土地点不清，达卡国家博物馆藏　笔者拍摄

图 80 释迦牟尼铜造像，6—7 世纪，西藏索县军巴区甲青乡穷果寺　笔者拍摄

图 81 释迦牟尼铜造像，7—9 世纪，西藏江孜白居寺　笔者拍摄

图 82 佛陀石雕立像，后弘期初期，西藏阿里古格遗址　笔者拍摄

图 83 弥勒佛铜造像，约 15 世纪，西藏比如县热丹寺　笔者拍摄

图 84 佛陀石雕坐像，吐蕃时期，西藏桑耶寺　笔者拍摄

图 85 佛陀石雕坐像，9—11 世纪，西藏贡嘎县德勤穷国寺　笔者拍摄

图 86 佛陀石雕坐像，9—11 世纪，西藏贡嘎县德勤穷国寺　笔者拍摄

图 87 观音，10 世纪，Munshiganj 出土，达卡国家博物馆藏　笔者拍摄

图 88 观音，3 世纪，印度那烂陀寺遗址出土，拉杰沙希 Varendra 研究博物馆藏　笔者拍摄

图 89 观音，10 世纪，Shibpur, Rajshahi 出土，达卡国家博物馆藏　笔者拍摄

图 90　文殊师利，10 世纪，Hatpukuria, Noakhali 出土，达卡国家博物馆藏　笔者拍摄

图 91　文殊师利，11 世纪，Jalakundi, Narayanganj 出土，达卡国家博物馆藏　笔者拍摄

图 92　义殊师利，11 凵纪，Niamatpur, Naogaon 出土，达卡国家博物馆藏　笔者拍摄

图 93　文殊师利，10 世纪，Talanda, Rajshahi 出土，拉杰沙希 Varendra 研究博物馆藏　笔者拍摄

图 94　文殊像，约 15—16 世纪，西藏巴青县普那寺　笔者拍摄

在持明密教中，观音、度母最为流行，观音表现为多面多臂及忿怒相，常见的有四臂、十一面、千手千眼、马头、罥索、叶衣、如意轮、千转等。除此之外，佛母、摩利支天、诃利帝、天女（Apsaras）、夜叉、乾达婆（Gandharva）也是持明密教常见的天神，承担着护法的功能。

常见的四臂观音分为寂静相和忿怒相两种。寂静相表情平静，造型优美，一头四臂，主臂两手作合掌印，另外两手分别持念珠和莲花，结跏趺坐在莲花座上（图95）。8世纪末藏文《佛说大乘庄严宝王经》记载，要获得六字真言大明咒的法力，必须进入四臂观音坛场。八臂观音像中间两手作合十形，其他各手或作说法印或作与愿印（图96）。十一面观音像出现于5世纪末，十一面分为五层，顶上又有一阿弥陀佛像（称为顶严），按照《造像量度经》说法，罗刹鬼有十个脑袋，非常狂妄自大，观音为了降伏他，变成十一个头，将他降伏了（图97）。图98这尊十一面观音像，高33厘米，约10—11世纪，是一尊工艺精美之作，莲枝下的女使与花枝融为一体，这种风格也见于11世纪的东印度造像。叶衣观音，梵名Parnasavari，为披叶衣的意思，全身裹于莲叶中，是观音三十三变化身之一，在胎藏曼陀罗中位列观音院，密号异行金刚。依据《叶衣观自在菩萨经》所述，叶衣观音在极乐世界的法会中，应金刚手菩萨的请求而宣说此经。经中说，此陀罗尼不但能除诸有情之疫疾饥馑、劫贼刀兵、水旱不调、宿曜失序等一切灾祸，并有增长福德、国界丰盛、人民安乐等殊胜功德（图99、100）。这尊叶衣观音像上带有五佛，显然是进入瑜伽密教时代的印记。

按西藏密教的说法，依大随求佛母的仪轨修行，火不能烧，水不能淹，不为风吹，不被地陷，不遭意外兵祸殃害，不生病痛，远离魔障，寿命延长，智慧增长，大随求佛母最殊胜的功德是摄众生心，令其悦服（图101、102）。

摩利支天（Marichi），护法二十诸天之一，意为"阳焰"或"威光"，实际上是古印度的光明女神。相传她是帝释天的部属，当她随从日宫天子出巡时，她在前头飞走如箭。她最大神通是能隐身，故无人能害，无人能缚，因此为武士所特别信奉。摩利支天有二臂像、六臂像以及八臂像等多种（图103—105）。在中国道教中，被称为"斗姆元君"（北斗妈妈）。

诃利帝（Hariti），又称鬼子母神，护法二十诸天之一，原为婆罗门恶神，专吃小孩，后受佛陀教化，弃恶从善，成为小孩的保护神（图106）。密宗有为祈祷妇女顺利生产而修的"诃利帝母法"，在中国俗称"送子观音"。

度母，又称多罗菩萨，一位平民化的女神，源自印度教爱欲之神洛乞史茗（梵文Lakshmi），她是与7世纪的金刚乘同时出现的，在早期大乘经文中找不到她。据《度母本源记》，观音以法眼观照六道众生，见众生无量，沉浮其间，度之不尽，不觉流下两滴泪水，泪水落入大海中，海面随即浮现两朵莲花，度母由莲花中化生而出，对观音发愿道："汝心勿忧闷，我为汝伴助，作度脱无量众生之事业。"《大日经疏》记载度母仪轨"其像合掌，掌中持青莲，如微笑形。"度母像多为半佛座，或一脚踩在从莲座衍生出来的莲朵上，一手作说法印，一手作与愿印，这也是《造像量度经》中度母的标准姿态（图107—114）。

藏传佛教以度母为观音的化身，与观音并存，是广受崇拜的神祇。度母按颜色区分为二十一相，以白度母与绿度母最为常见。藏民认为白度母是尺尊公主的化身，绿度母是文成公主的化身。度母也是阿底峡推崇的神祇之一，"尊者凡有所疑，则设供于度母像前，祈祷所怀""至藏之后……圣观自在及度母，随念即现"（法尊法师《阿底峡尊者传》）。

图115度母像，高30厘米，面庞饱满，神态雅娴，有位置偏高的双乳，呈三道弯的笈多式体态和火焰纹头光，应为8—11世纪东印度的作品，原藏定结县萨尔乡穷古寺。图116度母像，高42厘米，姿态安详，神情优雅，约13—15世纪，可能出自西藏工匠之手，现藏西藏白朗县旺旦乡

图 95 四臂观音，7 世纪，迈纳马蒂博物馆藏　笔者拍摄

图 97　十一面观音像，约 14—15 世纪，西藏措美县雪拉乡曲林寺　笔者拍摄

图 96　八臂观音像，10 世纪，Kashipur，Dinajpur 出土，拉杰沙希 Varendra 研究博物馆藏　笔者拍摄

图 98　十一面观音像，约 10—11 世纪，西藏比如县比如寺　笔者拍摄

图99 观音，11世纪，Vill-Narayanpur 出土，达卡国家博物馆藏　笔者拍摄

图100 叶衣观音，10世纪，Vajrayogini, Munshiganj 出土，达卡国家博物馆藏　笔者拍摄

图101 大随求佛母，10世纪，Munshiganj 出土，达卡国家博物馆藏　笔者拍摄

图102 大随求佛母，10世纪，Dinajpur 出土，达卡国家博物馆藏　笔者拍摄

图103 摩利支天，10世纪，Panditsar, Faridpur 出土，达卡国家博物馆藏　笔者拍摄

图104 摩利支天，11世纪，Rajshahi 出土，拉杰沙希 Varendra 研究博物馆藏　笔者拍摄

图105 摩利支天，Kachua Bagerhat 出土，库尔纳博物馆藏　笔者拍摄

图106 诃利帝，青铜，12世纪，Dinajpur 出土，达卡国家博物馆藏　笔者拍摄

图107 绿度母，10世纪，Sukhayaspur, Munshiganj 出土，达卡国家博物馆藏　笔者拍摄

图108 Astamahabhaya 度母，10世纪，Sompara, Munshiganj 出土，达卡国家博物馆藏　笔者拍摄

图109 Vrikuti 度母，11世纪，Bhabanipur, Munshiganj 出土，达卡国家博物馆藏　笔者拍摄

图110 度母，11世纪，Jagaddal Vihara 出土，巴哈布尔遗址博物馆藏　笔者拍摄

图111　度母，9世纪，Comilla 出土，达卡国家博物馆藏　笔者拍摄

图112　度母，11世纪，Bogra 出土，拉杰沙希 Varendra 研究博物馆藏　笔者拍摄

图113　度母，12世纪，Naogaon 出土，拉杰沙希 Varendra 研究博物馆藏　笔者拍摄

图114　度母，5—6世纪，Joypurhat 出土，莫诃斯坦遗址博物馆藏　笔者拍摄

图115　度母，8—11世纪，征集自定结县萨尔乡穷古寺，现藏西藏文管会　笔者拍摄

图116　度母，约13—15世纪，白朗县旺旦乡穷果寺　笔者拍摄

图117　乾达婆砖雕，10—11世纪，Vasu-Bihar出土，莫河斯坦遗址博物馆藏　笔者拍摄

图118　乾达婆，玛尼石刻，约12—13世纪，白朗县曲奴乡桑林寺　笔者拍摄

穷果寺。

乾达婆（Gandharva），乐神名，俗称"飞天"，其职是奉侍佛陀，因其能歌善舞，并能散发香气，又称伎乐神、香音神等。身形介于人和动物之间、飞翔于空中，她们是古代部落崇拜的遗产（图117、118）。

（2）金刚乘造像体系

7世纪中叶以后，中印一带的真言乘和南印一带的金刚乘先后兴起，前者代表经典是《大日经》，后者是《金刚顶经》，早期事部密教被赋予了深奥的哲理。金刚乘是一种可以实行的真实的宗教生活，修行以瑜伽观想为主，瑜伽（Yoga），词根为"给牛上轭"，引申为"连接、接合"，密宗经典取名怛特罗（Tantra），意为纺织的纬线，西藏译名为"本续"或"续"。静修者在坛场中，将自己升华为神祇，体验、证实"果"的乐趣，僧侣从繁琐教义的宣传者变成了人和菩萨间的媒介，具有了术士和神巫的性质。

大乘佛教向怛特罗转变过程中，创造了十字形中心神殿建筑，作为新教义的直观象征，造像也根据仪轨的要求，发生了同步的变化。金刚界圣众分五部，佛部、金刚部、宝部、莲花部、羯磨部。佛部以毗卢遮那佛（大日，汉译普明）为部主，大日如来最初是从波斯太阳神中派生出来的。以五部佛、四波罗蜜、十六大菩萨、内外八供养、四摄菩萨等三十七尊为主，构成金刚界的造像体系。五部佛或称五禅那（Dhyani）佛，是金刚乘体系中最基本的造像。修行者在入定之前和仪式之后，都要对造像进行礼拜。召神是静修过程中的重要环节，召到的神祇置于曼陀罗各自的空间中。静修时，要对特定神祇的形貌进行观想，这些镶嵌在佛龛内的造像，代表内证真实的可视象征。密教修行以念诵、观想种子真言的形、音、义为主，神咒中的音节，充满了召神之力，在六字真言中，毗卢遮那佛通过第一个音节"唵"而显现，之后的"吽"，产生阿閦佛。五佛中的每尊佛皆具有独特的颜色、特有的坐骑、一个种子音节、一个对应的修法女伴，他们不仅仅主持着空间的一个方向，代表自然界"体性广大"的五大之一，也主持一种生理感觉和一种感官（根）、一种典型的人欲。

孟加拉国库米拉县之西的拉尔迈-迈纳马蒂区域，是古代三摩达吒国的都城德瓦帕瓦吒所在地，所发现的佛教遗址大抵处于持明密教与金刚乘密教阶段。其中的鲁帕班神庙（Rupban Mura）遗址第三期（8世纪）才产生出十字形的结构，南西北三面是都有放置神像的神龛，东边有三个神龛，可能是突出不动佛的殊胜地位，在遗址中出土了阿弥陀佛像；7世纪的爱塔克霍拉神庙（Itakhola Mura）遗址中，发现了两个不动佛、三个阿弥陀佛青铜像[34]。

巴哈布尔遗址也处于金刚乘阶段，建筑年代约8—9世纪，固定在露台墙体上约2000件装饰砖雕，年代可能在此后的200年内，题材以反映自然界和日常生活为主，印度教内容占总数的7.37%，佛教神像占总数的3.81%，其中以佛、菩萨为主，有一尊带有金刚乘意义的不动佛，以菩提树为背景，施触地印，镶嵌在东墙的中心位置（图119），这显然是按照曼陀罗的要求而安排的，是绕行者礼拜的对象[35]。这个发现，使得纷繁庞杂的砖雕因此变得有序，折射出金刚乘精神理念的存在。

以毗卢遮那佛为中心的五部佛，在11世纪印度西部也非常普遍，从塔波、阿济、芒域等地寺庙以及西藏古格都可以得到印证。塔波寺位于印度喜马偕尔邦的斯比蒂，仁青桑布建于996年，其杜康大殿有一个光线昏暗、两侧有几尊粗糙塑像的门廊，杜康殿内有精美的壁画和塑像，32尊塑像环绕着立体的金刚界坛城和雄伟的四头大日如来塑像，这正是纯正的佛教金刚乘遗存（图120）[36]。

据多罗那他《印度佛教史》记载，《大日经注释》的作者佛密（Buddha Guhya）生活于8世纪的达摩波罗王朝时期，为密教大师觉智足早年的上首弟子，精通事、行、瑜伽三部密法，曾在波罗奈斯（Varanasi，今恒河左岸之瓦腊纳西）修行文殊法，获得神通。他与法兄佛寂（Buddha Santi）同往南印普陀洛迦山亲谒观世音菩萨，得到指授而获成就。后来又到冈底斯山（Kailasa）修行，亲见金刚界大曼陀罗。吐蕃赞普赤松德赞曾派遣使者前去迎请，因年老未能应聘入藏，但将事、行、瑜伽三部密法传授于使者，并让使者将《金刚界修法入瑜伽》《大日经注释》《后静虑广释》等典籍带回藏地。藏文大藏经有佛密《大日经集义》一卷、《说曼陀罗法经》《秘经义入门》等密教著作。

桑耶寺中心大殿的造像系统，从底层到三层，是按大乘和金刚乘的次第设计的。据《巴协》记载，底层是佛陀和八大菩萨；中层主像是大日如来佛，以横三世佛与纵三世佛构成曼陀罗结构；上层"主像是大日如来和普见四面一性佛"[37]。现在桑耶寺三层的主像仍是大日如来像。这个神像系统与曼陀罗建筑结合在一起，与东印度佛教金刚乘发展阶段是同步的。可见，从一开始，寂护大师就将东印度同时期最系统、最纯正的佛教体系移植到了西藏，这也是8世纪宁玛派主供大日如来四面像的原因（图121—123）。

据多罗那他《后藏志》记载："坐落在泽乃萨寺的西经堂系赤热巴坚创建的，现今称为嘉丕，殿内主尊是四尊背靠背的大日如来和八大随佛子。一般而言，金刚界坛城的主尊是大日如来，另有三十七尊神佛，此系《性空胜会根本续》四品中第一品规定的。"[38]西藏这类四面的大日如来像年代很早，所以成为后弘期伏藏师寻宝的目标。《后藏志》接着记载，从前伏藏师谷如·益喜琼扎装扮成泽乃萨寺庙祝的侍从，当了两年仆役后，从大日如来像胸部的背面请出婆罗门的木乃伊。另一个伏藏师的弟子从圣像内请出莲花生大师灌顶用的水晶宝瓶，宝瓶内装满书写有甚深九法类的黄纸。约12世纪，后藏桀·白杂玛瓦在曼隆寺建幻化殿，主要佛像也是大日如来。

白居寺措庆大殿经堂西侧的金刚界殿，供奉有大日如来曼陀罗塑像，正中为四面二臂之大日

图119　不动佛砖雕，巴哈布尔遗址
Rao Bahadur K.N. Dikshit, M.A., F. R. A. S. B.: *Excavations at Paharpur, Bengal*, Deli: Manager of Publications, 1938.

图120　塔波寺的大日如来像
〔意〕杜齐著，魏正中 萨尔吉主编，李翎等译：《梵天佛地》第3卷，上海古籍出版社，2010年。

如来，周围为其他四佛，诸佛均伴有相应的菩萨，四壁供养天造像凸塑于墙上三叶拱中，沿五佛周围展开，有简洁的涡蔓纹饰，精致洗炼，优雅庄严，塑像之间有作棋格状排列之供养天壁画，为尼泊尔风格，共同构成一组立体的曼陀罗。经典源自《金刚顶经》第一品的金刚界曼陀罗，目的在于去除障碍解脱的根本烦恼之一贪欲，这是卫藏地区15世纪中叶流行的样式，在夏鲁寺、古格遗址中皆有发现。

8世纪以来，孟加拉国出现大量表现手结触地印的阿閦佛（即不动佛）石雕造像，这一手印与释迦牟尼降魔成道有关，相关经典如《阿閦佛国经》。不动佛在西藏也有普遍的信仰，造像极多。此外，阿弥陀佛信仰在东印度和西藏也较为普遍（图124—130）。

1937年，杜齐在考察后藏康马县萨马达寺时，发现一座制作美轮美奂的佛塔，表面用浮雕的技法，表现了金刚界曼陀罗三十七尊神及其部众，杜齐推测，这是一件由尼泊尔传入藏地的晚期波罗时代的孟加拉作品（图131—132）。

东印度造像常见背光是佛龛和佛塔，12世纪以后的西藏唐卡和壁画中，这类背光装饰变得华丽复杂：底部由两头狮子支撑佛龛；两侧有神兽，均面向外侧；佛龛肩部有一横木，两端有摩羯鱼，

图 121　大日如来金铜像，11 世纪，尼泊尔　熊文彬、叶灵毅主编：《东去西来——11—14 世纪藏传佛教金铜佛像精品展》文物出版社，2016 年。

图 122　大日如来四面相泥塑，年代不详，西藏贡嘎县达波扎仓　笔者拍摄

图 123　大日如来四面相，年代不详，拉萨药王山摩崖石刻　笔者拍摄

图 124　阿弥陀佛，11 世纪，Mahakali, Munshiganj 出土，达卡国家博物馆藏　笔者拍摄

图 125　阿弥陀佛，9—10 世纪，Bhojavihara, Comilla 出土，库尔纳博物馆藏　笔者拍摄

图 126　不动佛，11 世纪，Vikrampura, Munshiganj 出土，达卡国家博物馆藏　笔者拍摄

图127 不动佛，约15世纪，西藏贡嘎县贡嘎曲德寺　笔者拍摄

图128 不动佛，约12—15世纪，西藏聂荣县大众乡朗色寺　笔者拍摄

图129 不动佛，10世纪，Ujani, Gopalganj出土，达卡国家博物馆藏　笔者拍摄

图130 弥勒佛，12世纪，Dinajpur出土，达卡国家博物馆藏　笔者拍摄

图131 奉献塔，10世纪，Bangarh, West Dinajpur出土，达卡国家博物馆藏　笔者拍摄

图132 奉献塔，6世纪，Dhaka出土，达卡国家博物馆藏　笔者拍摄

图133　白居寺5层（覆钵体）门外侧及上方的六拿具门饰　笔者拍摄

鱼身上或骑有童子；佛龛顶部有金翅大鹏鸟，口中衔着摩羯鱼尾的蛇身部分，有时两旁有飞天形象，这就是《造像量度经》中所谓的"六挈（拿）具"。无畏的狮子象征大日如来，十力的大象象征不动佛，四神足的马象征宝生佛，十自在的孔雀象征无量光佛，一切无著力的金翅鸟象征不空成就佛。此题材用于陪衬装饰主神，意谓主神力大无穷，法力无边，也用于建筑门楣等处（图133）。

（3）无上瑜伽密教造像的源头与流衍

9世纪以后，金刚乘出现分化，《金刚顶经》十八会中的一些瑜伽不断扩编改造，形成新的流派，如理趣瑜伽流衍为大乐派，秘密集会瑜伽流衍为密集派，统称为大瑜伽（即纯密），盛行于以超戒寺为中心的波罗时代。10世纪以后，在大乐瑜伽以及无二瑜伽基础上，吸收了印度教毗湿奴俱生派的影响，主张性力解脱，其派系进一步流衍为胜乐、喜金刚、四座、幻化等流派，统称无上瑜伽。

无上瑜伽修行分为生起次第和圆满次第，修生起次第是观想本尊形象，在曼陀罗前成年累月的修，本尊会出现在梦境中，如同真实一般，自己的身、口、意也会修成与本尊一样。修圆满次第，观想中出现了脉、轮、风等概念，控制体内风（脉息）的流动。所谓大秘密，就是观想本尊与明妃相抱，金刚住于莲花中，"乐空双运"，目的是通过观想两性和合，使气脉流通，脐火炽燃，明点充足，获得大乐、空的体验，此境界即是"菩提"（觉），这是常人通过修炼可以达到的境界。

印度河文明最早流行的宗教，主要是对地母神、动植物（特别是牛）、性器官和祖灵的崇拜。原始居民将耕耘活动与人类生殖行为联系起来，女性是田亩，男性生殖器为锄头，精液为种子，为祈祷丰产而建立祭祀仪式，这就是性力派修法的古老渊源。乌仗那是许多瑜伽母怛特罗的编纂之地，是无上瑜伽的发源地之一，主要流行地则在中印度和孟加拉、阿萨姆一带，因此，瑜伽母密典大多以中世纪俗语和早期孟加拉语写成。11—12世纪，波罗王朝的新密（即俱生乘、时轮乘）流行，13世纪初，佛教在伊斯兰教武力摧毁下趋于消亡。

宋初，法天（中印人，980年来华）、天息灾（中印人，980年来华）、施护（北印人，与天息灾同时来华）在中国传播的密教，主要是波罗王朝时期流行于孟加拉、奥利萨地区的无上瑜伽一系，即左道密。推行对于女神（明妃）的崇拜，以及灌顶、双修、轮座，由于与中国封建伦理不合，只局限于部分上层之间[39]。

无上瑜伽的最高神祇是金刚萨埵，它是大日如来的"正法轮身"，或"真实身"。金刚界三十七智身，其中诸菩萨之首大普贤即是金刚萨埵，普贤菩萨从毗卢遮那双手接受金刚杵，并得到灌顶而称为金刚手，或持金刚。金刚萨埵、法身普贤和持金刚都是异名而同体，金刚萨埵也有双身的，拥抱着明妃。密宗认为，这是释迦佛说密法时所呈现的形象，是释迦佛的秘密化身，所以又叫秘密主，它是佛陀本性的化身，是智慧与空性结合中的神秘统一，其标志是执金刚杵、宝玲两件法器。

图134为巨大的金刚萨埵青铜像，出土于孟加拉国库米拉县Bhoja Vihara遗址的中心神殿北部，造像结跏趺坐，一手持金刚杵，一手持金刚铃，

作冥想状,年代为9—10世纪。

无上瑜伽部主要本尊有密集、大威德、喜金刚、胜乐、时轮等,它们是菩萨的"正法轮身"或"真实身",是持金刚的各种化身。本尊的活力以女性的形体来表现,都有各自的明妃。它们受邀居于修习者心中,既是智慧、慈悲、空的人格化,又是一种真实的实体、一种保护神或爱神。它们又泛称为"黑茹伽",意为邪恶势力的破坏者,兼具本尊神和护法神的性质。"黑表离因等,茹字离集合,迦表无所住。""因等谓离自生他生共生及无因生。集合谓虽住坏(成住坏空)之聚。无所住谓双运大印。其教授谓随力随能心住光明而修。"(宗喀巴《密宗道次第广论》卷二一)无上瑜伽是在印度文明与伊斯兰入侵者的对抗中产生的,既然这个世界是由心识产生,因此,战场不是在现实的世界中,而是在人的内心展开,不是外障,更多是内障,不是致力于打造现实的兵器,而是在心理中锻造更加锋利的武器。显宗讲"欲火入心,犹如鬼著",密宗将欲作为桥梁,认为"斯乃非欲之欲,以欲止欲,如以屑出屑,将声止声"(《金光明文句二》)。狂笑的狰狞的面容,脚踏因挤压而扭曲变形的人身,正是湿婆宇宙之舞的翻版。通过般若与方便的结合,心灵在危脆无常世界前合一,受灌顶者体证到无法言诠的解脱喜乐,体现着印度的最高智慧。而多头、多臂、多足,动物肢体与人体结合在一起,都是密法借以表达的内境、心相、意乐和深刻的生命悲剧感,这些人类心识的分析大师认为:天魔鬼怪非为外境及出世间真实,而是散乱心识的无常变相,内识中支离破碎的影事幻象,源自心识深处的贪欲烦恼习气。上师为了调伏它们,在仪式中以禅修瑜伽之火将其烧灭。在那个国破家亡、生灵涂炭的年代,这是一种抗争,一种救赎,只是现在,我们已经失去了这个语境。

孟加拉国巴哈布尔的苏摩普梨(Somapuri)寺,不仅经历了最初的纯密阶段,还经历了无上瑜伽的阶段。在巴哈布尔遗址的发掘中,发现了一些残碎的石雕像,其中一尊为喜金刚(Hevajra-Sakti)造像,6面,每个面上有3只眼睛,16臂,各执充填不明物的颅骨碗,中间一臂拥抱性力女神沙克蒂(Shakti),后者代表性力、生命力。石雕像年代约在11世纪后期(图135)[40]。距此约30千米的Jagaddala寺院遗址中,也发现了一件同样性质的喜金刚造像,年代在10—11世纪。

据藏文史料,黑行者,孟加拉人,八十四大成就者之一,得到胜乐本尊法真传后,在苏摩普梨寺等地传法,教化了许多僧人,在与一位女咒

图134 金刚萨埵青铜像,9—10世纪,Bhoja Vihara出土,迈纳马蒂博物馆藏 笔者拍摄

图135 喜金刚(Hevajra),11世纪后期,巴哈布尔遗址出土
Rao Bahadur K.N. Dikshit, M.A., F. R. A. S. B.: Excavations at Paharpur, Bengal, Deli: Manager of Publications, 1938.

师比赛法力时,染病身亡。他的著作涉及密集、大威德、胜乐,他所传"胜乐四灌顶"在西藏影响很大。胜乐教法传承中,还有一大批学者,如底洛巴、那若巴等。9—12世纪,许多西藏僧人也参观过苏摩普梨寺,阿底峡曾在此住寺多年,于1034年向那措译师传授《中观心论注思择焰》。

毗哇巴(寂护之师)是南印度的一位王子,悄悄离开王宫直接来到密教较盛行的苏摩普梨寺,研修佛教义理和密法,通过长期修炼,直接领受了金刚持开示给无我母的密法,首次提出了"道果"法,创立了一套自己的实践方法[41]。毗哇巴也是八十四大成就者之一,被认为是萨迦派密法的祖师,持金刚、无我母、毗哇巴三尊一铺的形象几乎出现在萨迦派的所有寺院中,标示着教法的心髓、开示和世间化现,而喜金刚正是萨迦道果法最主要的本尊。

孟加拉国密宗造像以早期杂密和中期纯密时期的造像为主,无上瑜伽的双身像极为稀少,原因是无上瑜伽是金刚乘的最后形态,流行的时间较短。苏摩普梨寺和Jagaddala寺出土的这两件喜金刚造像,是孟加拉无上瑜伽的重要资料,也为西藏无上瑜伽造像找到了真正的源头。

图136胜乐金刚金铜像,藏于加尔各答印度博物馆,出自波罗王朝的比哈尔地区,年代约11世纪。图137黑茹伽雕像,迈纳马蒂博物馆收藏,年代约11世纪。相传净劫开始时,众生相互袭杀,将尸体送往八方,形成八大寒林,尔时,金刚手所化的大自在天以神通到达须弥山和赡部洲,化现二十四个地方,调伏教化他们的本尊是嘿茹迦胜乐金刚[42]。图138是江孜白居寺所藏的金属坛城,年代不清。

西藏密宗与东印度密宗基本上是平行发展的,前弘期西藏所传译的密教称为旧密,后弘期所传译的称为新密,正好代表东印度密教的两个

图136 胜乐金刚金铜像,约11世纪,比哈尔地区出土,加尔各答印度博物馆藏

谢继胜:《西夏藏传绘画—黑水城出土西夏唐卡研究》,河北教育出版社,2002年。

图137 黑茹伽,11世纪,迈纳马蒂博物馆藏 笔者拍摄

图138 金属坛城,年代不详,西藏江孜白居寺 笔者拍摄

时期。10世纪中叶后,新密开始大量传入西藏,仁青桑波、卓弥、玛尔巴、郭库巴等译师译出了密集、胜乐、喜金刚、大威德、时轮等教法,并相与传习。宁玛派以大瑜伽密集教法的大圆满法为主;噶举派以无上瑜伽胜乐教法的大手印为主;萨迦派以喜金刚的道果法为主;夏鲁派、觉囊派以时轮教法为主;格鲁派兼修密集、时轮、大威德、胜乐、喜金刚等,但以诵习陀罗尼以及持明类教法为主[43]。

尽管无上瑜伽密法很早就有所翻译,但在相当长一段时间内,并没有被王室宗教体系吸收与消化。后弘期上路弘法主要是持明密教和大瑜伽密教两种;下路弘法主要是戒律一类大乘显教。在西藏早期寺庙遗存中,不见无上瑜伽密宗的图像。14世纪以后,布顿在编排经论、定型《甘》《丹》的同时,力图拟定一种仪式轨则,超越各种异见,建立正统清净传承,在此理论氛围中,无上瑜伽密教的传承脉络得以梳理。布顿《佛教史大宝藏论》成书于1322年[44],书中罗列了当时译成藏文的密宗经典约400种,从经典名称中可见所涉及的密宗神名,其中大瑜伽续部包括毗卢遮那、密集金刚、大威德金刚、能怖金刚、金刚手、呼金刚、空行母、胜乐金刚、度母、瑜伽母、金刚亥母和各种世间怙主。这是布顿对于印度密宗遗产的总结,源于密宗文献中的尊格系统变得更加确定,从而形成一个整然有序的诸神世界,夏鲁寺、白居寺的造像体系就是藏传佛教本土化梳理的典范。白居塔十万佛塔营造的灵感来自布顿,造像和壁画交叠着大乘以来的全部精髓,持金刚放置在十万佛塔的顶端,象征着无上瑜伽密宗的全部传承已经完成,从此,无上瑜伽密教图像在西藏呈现出泛滥之势,并达到顶峰。

图139普贤像、图140持金刚,皆出自洛扎县拉隆寺。图141普巴金刚为噶玛黑茹伽(金刚萨埵的忿怒相)之化身,又称橛金刚,是宁玛派和萨迦派的本尊。

密集金刚,藏名"桑堆",呈坐式,下有莲花座。其像三面六臂,主臂两手持金刚杵,拥抱的

图139 普贤像,约18世纪,西藏拉隆寺喜珠拉康　笔者拍摄

图140 持金刚,约15世纪,洛扎县拉隆寺藏　笔者拍摄

明妃也是六臂，尊像据说是从阿閦佛变化而来的，格鲁派非常重视修习密集金刚法（图142）。

大威德金刚，藏名"吉杰多吉"，因其"有伏恶之势，谓之大威，有护善之功，谓之大德"。形象为九面三十六臂十六足，正面为牛头，坐骑大白牛，缺乏通常的明妃。此像为无量寿佛的忿怒身，以威猛力摧灭调伏教法及其修法中的一切违缘障碍，以智慧力摧破烦恼业障，使众生从无明中解脱出来。大自在天与其妃乌摩在其脚下，影射佛教与印度教的敌意。据《吉祥大金刚怖畏生起次第安立·显耀顶饰》："文殊为对治三十三天化现出三十四臂，为对治地下阿修罗骑众化现出水牛面，为对治地上八病及八邪魔化现出十六足，为对治大自在天示现直立之男根，而后宣说金刚怖畏十万怛特罗。"首次广弘大威德怛特罗的是嬉金刚（Lalitavajra），他是底洛巴的弟子，约生活在10世纪前后。大威德金刚也是格鲁派主修的本尊神（图143）。

喜金刚，藏名"杰巴多吉"，又称饮血金刚，也称欢喜金刚，八面十六臂，主臂拥抱着明妃，每只手里都托着一个白色的骷髅碗，内盛神物，身上悬挂着有五十个骷髅的项链，象征着梵文的五十个字母，足踏两仰卧人，表示降伏邪恶与无明（图144）。

胜乐金刚，藏名"德巧"，其像四面脸，有十二臂，主臂分别持金刚杵和金刚铃，拥抱明妃，右腿踏一伏首趴身恐怖男者，左脚踏一仰面躺身女者，背后是火焰光背，下有莲花座。噶举派多修此本尊（图145）。

时轮金刚，藏名"堆柯"，为双尊像，有单头或五头的，双臂或多臂，也有三十二臂的，持斧、棒、轮、月刀、戟、短剑、弓箭、骷髅鼓、海螺、莲花、钩、索、骷髅碗等，寓福德、智慧、钩召、吉祥、摧破等义，脚下踩着许多挣扎的生灵，表降伏意，下有莲花座，后有火焰光背。时轮密法认为，众生都在过去、现在、未来"三时"的迷界之中，故时轮以示三时。时轮密法关注宇宙、历法与人的关系，将占星术和天文学转换成咒术之力和救度之道，又称天文学部（图146）。

金刚亥母，藏名"多吉帕母"，噶举派密宗本尊，为胜乐金刚明妃，饰骷髅念珠和璎珞，手执颅器和金刚钺，头的右侧现一猪头（图147）。

空行佛母也是藏传密宗常见的护法神，形象为一裸身女像，一手上举，一手朝下，执法器，身佩骷髅缀成的璎珞，一腿直，一腿曲，脚踏生灵（图148）。

后弘期藏传佛教的一个重要特征，是唯敬上师，以代敬事三宝。西藏所迎请的印度法本，只是无解的字句，需要上师探寻密意、现证境界，否则就无法理解，也无法灌顶。上师是经典与修习者之间的媒介，如果没有上师，经文仅仅是一具僵尸，世界上没有任何力量能使它还阳。上师本人犹如明灯，使清净正法得以薪火相传。噶举派僧人在做祈祷时，多念"上师、本尊、护法神"，而不提释迦牟尼。《大日经》也说："供养佛者，当供养此善男子善女人，若乐欲见佛，即当观彼。"那若巴也说："上师未曾出现时，连佛名字也未闻，所有千劫诸佛陀，皆依上师而出现。"[45]

西藏活佛、上师像流行于13世纪以后，在曼陀罗中，上师像几乎从未缺席，同样，对他们的迎请也是仪式之必须。同时，他们往往也是政治舞台上的人物，交织着政治的、民族的、宗教的诸多情结，成为西藏造像的一大特征（图149—153）。

（4）印度教神像体系和佛教护法神

在孟加拉国乡村，经常可以看到孤耸的印度教神庙，因为相信宇宙的主宰，都有向天空发展的尖顶，与早期佛教强调轮回的覆钵形佛塔迥然不同。印度教是入世的宗教，主张世俗生活与宗教生活密不可分，教徒都居住在村庄中，神庙中只有人数不多的祭司和神职人员，没有佛教那样庞大的僧团。印度教神庙在乡村城镇无处不在，在社会生活中扮演着多种角色，不像出世的佛教，往往远离喧嚣和繁杂的城市，有意与世俗分离。在法显和玄奘的记述中，通篇都有天神祠的记载，

图 141 普巴金刚石雕像，12—13 世纪
熊文彬、叶灵毅主编：《东去西来——11—14 世纪藏传佛教金铜佛像精品展》，文物出版社，2016 年。

图 142 密集金刚，约 15—16 世纪，西藏比如县白嘎乡盆嘎日寺　笔者拍摄

图 143 大威德金刚，15—18 世纪，西藏索县穷果寺
笔者拍摄

图 144 喜金刚，约 15—18 世纪，西藏洛扎县拉隆寺
笔者拍摄

图145　胜乐金刚，14世纪，私人收藏
熊文彬、叶灵毅主编：《东去西来——11—14世纪藏传佛教金铜佛像精品展》，文物出版社，2016年。

图146　时轮金刚，约15—18世纪，西藏巴青县巴冲寺
笔者拍摄

图147　金刚亥母，约15—16世纪，西藏比如县热丹寺
笔者拍摄

图148　空行佛母，约17世纪，西藏班戈县雪如乡萨木寺
笔者拍摄

图149 莲花生石刻，吐蕃时期，桑耶寺 笔者拍摄

图150 阿底峡"酷肖我"塑像，年代不清，西藏聂塘卓玛拉康 笔者拍摄

图151 阿底峡像，约15世纪，西藏青铜像，现存达卡法王寺 笔者拍摄

图152 绛曲坚赞像，16世纪，私人收藏
黄春和：《西藏丹萨替寺历史研究》，文物出版社，2016年。

图153 宗喀巴像，18世纪，私人收藏
黄春和：《西藏丹萨替寺历史研究》，文物出版社，2016年。

图154 蒙希甘杰 Kalir Atpara 湿婆神庙，近代 笔者拍摄

图155 印度教祭祀活动，Kalir Atpara 湿婆神庙 笔者拍摄

一般情况下，天祠的数量总是远远高于佛寺。据法尊法师《阿底峡尊者传》："尔时邦伽罗（即孟加拉）境内，外道与内道辩诤，内不抵外，是故内教道场，多失于外道。"这是10世纪初孟加拉印度教盛行的情况。在孟加拉国的各地博物馆中，大部分造像都是印度教的，来自各地的印度教神庙中，年代一般在9—12世纪，石材、雕刻风格与同时期的佛教造像相似。

2015年12月，笔者在纳提什瓦遗址附近的 Kalir Atpara 湿婆神庙遇到一次印度教徒的祭祀活动，这是一座颓败的近代神庙，神殿墙面上带尖顶状的神龛，正是安置石雕神像之所（图154、155）。

古代印度有许多分裂的小王国，有各自古老的地方神，印度教据此建立起自己庞杂的神祇体系[46]。

1. 梵天

印度教有三大主神，分别是创造之神梵天，维系之神毗湿奴和毁灭之神湿婆。梵天、湿婆、毗湿奴"三神一体"，体现创造宇宙过程中的三种力量。

梵天，梵文 Brahama，有清净之意。梵天常见的形象为四面四臂，四只手分别持莲花、念珠、水罐和吠陀圣典，盘坐于莲花之上。他的坐骑为白天鹅。在佛教里他被吸收成为一名伟大的护教者（图156、157）。

2. 妙音天女

梵天的妻子是著名的妙音天女萨茹阿斯瓦蒂，梵语 Saraswati，是印度教中司学问、智慧、艺术、音乐之神，在印度最古老的经典《梨俱吠陀》中就有了对她的记载。佛教经典旧译为娑罗室伐底，为佛教二十天之辩才天。藏密的形象一般作两臂持琴像（图158）。

3. 湿婆

梵文 Shiva，意为吉祥，是毁灭、再生之神。湿婆神的形象是三只眼，头上有恒河女神，因为恒河从天上降落人间之时，先从他的头上流下，以减轻压力。他的居所是神圣的冈底斯山。更多的时候，他安住于甚深的禅定之中，观察宇宙实相（图159）。

湿婆又被称为玛哈嘎拉（Mahakala），超越时间的伟大之神，藏传佛教也将玛哈嘎拉作为出世间的护法供奉，《大智度论》卷二载其形（图160）。湿婆还被称为摩醯首罗，梵文 Maheswara，意为大自在天，被佛教列为护法神。父神湿婆和母神乌玛（帕蒂）造像在孟加拉常见（图161—164）。图165造像现藏洛扎县拉隆寺，这尊造像具有波罗造像的特点，约8—11世纪，可能出自东印度或尼泊尔。

湿婆神根据不同的形象和传说，有许多不同的名字。其中一个是那塔茹阿吉，梵文 Nataraj，

图156 梵天，10世纪，Kalihar, Rajshahi 出土，达卡国家博物馆藏 笔者拍摄

图157 梵天，10世纪，Bogra 出土，莫河斯坦遗址博物馆藏 笔者拍摄

图158 妙音天女，12世纪，Vikrampura, Munshiganj 出土，臭河斯坦遗址博物馆藏 笔者拍摄

图159 湿婆，10世纪，Comilla 出土，拉杰沙希 Varendra 研究博物馆藏 笔者拍摄

图160 玛哈嘎拉，14世纪，西藏金铜像
熊文彬、叶灵毅主编：《东去西来——11—14世纪藏传佛教金铜佛像精品展》，文物出版社，2016年。

图161 父神湿婆和母神乌玛（帕蒂），10世纪，Comilla 出土，达卡国家博物馆藏 笔者拍摄

图162 父神湿婆和母神乌玛（帕蒂），12世纪，Naogaon 出土，拉杰沙希 Varendra 研究博物馆藏 笔者拍摄

图163 父神湿婆和母神乌玛（帕蒂），9世纪，Bogra 出土，莫河斯坦遗址博物馆藏 笔者拍摄

图164 父神湿婆和母神乌玛（帕蒂），12世纪，Naogaon 出土，巴哈布尔遗址博物馆藏 笔者拍摄

图165 湿婆及其明妃乌玛，约8—11世纪，西藏洛扎县拉隆寺 笔者拍摄

图166 湿婆舞蹈像，10世纪，Comilla 出土，达卡国家博物馆藏 笔者拍摄

图167 湿婆舞蹈像，12世纪，Naogaon 出土，拉杰沙希 Varendra 研究博物馆藏 笔者拍摄

图168 湿婆舞蹈像，13世纪，南印度出土，拉杰沙希 Varendra 研究博物馆藏 笔者拍摄

图169 青颈湿婆像，11世纪，Kashipur, Barisal 出土，达卡国家博物馆藏 笔者拍摄

意为舞蹈之王。多臂两足，踩踏在阿修罗的身上跳着著名的坦塔瓦舞。阿含说，"世界、诞生的维护、它的灭亡、灵魂的蒙昧和解放是他的舞蹈的五幕"；周围火环代表所有幻想的宇宙、苦难和痛苦；乱蓬蓬发间的新月代表夜间神的爱；通过月亮的圆缺，湿婆创造了不同季节；一条蛇盘绕在他的手臂和脖子，蛇自然蜕皮象征着灵魂从一个生命到另一个轮回；一只脚踏着无知的侏儒。整个造像隐含着对于宇宙的深刻理解（图166—168）。湿婆还有一个名字叫那丽堪塔，梵文 Nilakantha，意为青颈。传说劫初之时，天人和阿修罗为挣夺不死甘露而搅拌牛奶之洋，在牛奶之洋中搅出了一瓶毒药威胁到了众生的安全，于是湿婆大神将其喝下，存在脖子处，脖子因此变为青色（图169）。这个传说影响了后期的佛教密宗，由此创造了青颈观世音菩萨。湿婆最显著的象征物是林伽（梵文 Linga），指男性生殖器，林伽

图170 湿婆林伽，9世纪，Sompara, Munshiganj 出土，达卡国家博物馆藏 笔者拍摄

与女阴交合，代表创造和再生的力量，在印度教神庙中心往往会放置湿婆林伽（图170）。

4. 杜尔嘎女神

杜尔嘎（Durga）女神是湿婆大神的妻子，杜尔嘎女神非常漂亮，通常被视为宇宙的能量，因此也被称为萨克提（Sakti，性力）女神。她也代表了幻化宇宙的力量，所以也被称为摩耶（Maya，幻觉能量）（图171、172）。后来，萨克提女神转世为喜马拉雅山的女儿帕尔瓦蒂。帕尔瓦蒂女神显现为八臂愤怒的形象，将化身为水牛的恶魔玛黑萨（Mahisa）杀死，将宇宙从罪恶之中拯救了出来，因此她被奉为战争女神、胜利女神（图173、174）。帕尔瓦蒂女神因为千年的苦行将甚深禅定中的湿婆大神唤醒，重新结为夫妻，生下了象头神迦尼什和六面童子战神塞犍陀（图175、176）。象头神是湿婆大神和帕尔瓦蒂女神的长子，他有许多名字，如迦尼什（Ganash）、嘎纳帕提（Ganapat）、毗那夜迦（Vinayaka）等，能除一切障碍，成就一切利益，在佛教中被称为大圣欢喜天，藏密中称为象鼻财神或象头财神，胖胖的身体和象头是他的标志（图177—179）。六面童子战神塞犍陀（Skanda），即为佛教二十天之韦驮天。

卡莉（Kumari）女神是杜尔嘎女神的化身，在世界被恶魔统治之时，女神为了利益世间而化现出来的愤怒形象（图180、181）。在藏传佛教中，卡莉作为玛哈嘎拉的明妃，占有重要的地位，是藏传佛教最重要的出世间解脱护法之一，保留了三目、深蓝色皮肤、人头项链、人头耳环、头戴新月、全身赤裸唯着皮裙的特征，骑着骡子在血海之上。

5. 毗湿奴

梵文 Vishnu，维系之神。维湿奴的形象为全身蓝色，一面四臂，右手持轮和莲花，左手持海螺和大棒，头戴皇冠，身佩各种金银珠宝、花环作为装饰（图182—185）。他的坐骑为大鹏金翅

图171 性力女神，12—13世纪，私人收藏，库尔纳博物馆藏 笔者拍摄

图172 杜尔嘎女神，10世纪，Rajshahi 出土，达卡国家博物馆藏 笔者拍摄

图173 帕尔瓦蒂女神，12世纪，Rajshahi 出土，拉杰沙希 Varendra 研究博物馆藏　笔者拍摄

图174 帕尔瓦蒂女神，10世纪，Munshiganj 出土，达卡国家博物馆藏　笔者拍摄

图175 杜尔嘎女神和儿子，两侧分别是象头神迦尼什和六面童子战神塞犍陀，Palashbari, Bogra 出土，达卡国家博物馆藏　笔者拍摄

图176 母亲与孩子，6世纪，Bogra 出土，达卡国家博物馆藏　笔者拍摄

图177 象头神，前弘期，拉萨市郊　笔者拍摄

图178 象头神，11世纪，Dhanuka, Faridpur 出土，达卡国家博物馆藏　笔者拍摄

图179 象头神，10—11世纪，Bogra 出土，莫河斯坦遗址博物馆藏　笔者拍摄

图180 卡莉女神，年代不详，Tarash, Sirajganj 出土，莫河斯坦遗址博物馆藏　笔者拍摄

图181 卡莉女神，12世纪，莫河斯坦遗址博物馆藏　笔者拍摄

图 182 毗湿奴，10 世纪，巴哈布尔遗址博物馆藏 笔者拍摄

图 183 毗湿奴，7—8 世纪，Naogaon 出土，巴哈布尔遗址博物馆藏 笔者拍摄

图 184 毗湿奴，12 世纪，Naogaon 出土，达卡国家博物馆藏 笔者拍摄

图 185 毗湿奴，10—11 世纪，Naogaon 出土，达卡国家博物馆藏 笔者拍摄

鸟嘎茹达（Garuda）。波罗王朝时期，毗湿奴崇拜在孟加拉发展到顶峰，怪异的半神半兽造像象征着旺盛的生命力、积极向上的入世态度。在佛教中，毗湿奴被意译为遍入天，意思是以化身遍入世间救度众生。经典上记载他有无数的化身，最重要的化身有十种。第一次劫初，他显现为一条鱼，在海洋里救回了吠陀圣典（图186）。第二次，在阿修罗和天人争夺不死甘露时，他化身龟支撑起须弥山，以便天人作为搅拌时的支点。第三次，化现为雄猪瓦茹阿哈（梵文Varaha）（图187、188），雄猪化身找到了恶魔黑冉亚克沙，和他开始了激烈的战斗，最后将他杀死。然后用它的两颗长牙将地球从宇宙的汪洋之中托了起来，让它重新归位。第四次，化现为人狮尼星哈（Nrsimha），将君主帕拉德从恶魔父亲那里救出。作为强大的保护者，在印度和尼泊尔有很多自然显现的尼星哈的神像（图189—191）。第五次，当暴君巴利征服地球时，他化现为可爱的侏儒婆罗门瓦玛那（Vamana）（图192），向大君乞求三步土地，他走了第一步，身体就无限地变大，第二步就将整个宇宙覆盖，脚趾将宇宙的外壳捅破了，恒河之水从宇宙外流向了天堂，然后流到了人间，洁净了整个地球，第三步跨穿宇宙，要回了地球。第六次，当世上充满了邪恶的统治者时，他化现为持斧罗摩（Rama）将邪恶的君主和战士毁灭了二十一次。第七次，恶魔罗婆那统治世界时，他化现为最理想的君主罗摩，将恶魔杀死，罗摩的故事被记载在史诗《罗摩衍那》中，是印度广受崇拜的神（图193、194）。第八次，他化现为牧牛童奎师那，梵文Krishna，意思是皮肤黑色的人，或最有吸引力的人，因此被译为"黑天"，形象是全身蓝黑色，手持笛子，头上有着孔雀羽作为装饰（图195—197）。奎师那的故事非常多，世界最长的史诗《摩诃婆罗多》上有着详细的记载。第九次，当人们滥用吠陀圣典杀生祭祀时，他化现为反对吠陀圣典的佛陀释迦牟尼，重宣非暴力的哲学。第十次，在四十二万七千年后，铁器时代的末期，恶魔充满世间之时，他会化现为骑着白马的考克伊，毁灭世界，将虔诚的人带回他的国土。毗湿奴也被称为那罗延天，为梵文Narayana，有多重意思，一为躺在水上的人，一为人之本初之意，代表他是最原初之神（图198）。

6. 洛乞史茗女神

梵文Lakshmi，毗湿奴的妻子，也被称为月亮之妹。当洛乞史茗女神从海洋中诞生之时，诸天都被她的美貌所震惊，但她还是嫁给了英俊的毗湿奴神。她是财富、美丽和繁荣的象征。当毗湿奴神躺在神蛇之床时，她总是温柔地为他按摩着莲花足（图199）。当毗湿奴作为各种化身显现人间时，她随着化现在人间。当毗湿奴化现为罗摩时，她化现为美丽的悉塔。当毗湿奴化为奎师那时，她化现为牧女茹阿达茹阿妮和皇后茹珂蜜妮。在印度教徒心中，她是温柔的众生之母（图200—202）。毗湿奴胸前有着美丽的"卐"符号，就是洛乞史茗女神的象征，因此被称为吉祥喜旋。洛乞史茗女神也受到了大乘佛教的供奉，《佛说大吉祥天女十二名号经》说，佛陀宣讲了大吉祥天女的十二个名号，如能受持读诵修习供养，能除一切贫穷业障，获丰饶财宝。藏语称为班达拉姆，即吉祥天母，是藏密中十分重要的护法神。

7. 太阳神

太阳神（Surya）源于古代婆罗门教的古老神祇（图203—206）。作为佛教护法神，又称日宫天子，为观音菩萨之变化身，住在太阳内的宫殿里。日宫天子的形象，为肉红色脸膛，左右手各拿一枝莲花，乘四马大车；也有的手捧日轮，骑三至八匹马，在水陆道场所用的水陆画中，日宫天子为头戴冕旒，双手捧圭的帝王形象。

8. 因陀罗

梵文Indra，为天堂众生之主和雷电之神，是《吠陀》中很早就出现的神祇，司职雷电与战斗，坐骑是六牙大白象（图207），为佛教二十天之

图 186 毗湿奴化现为一条鱼，9 世纪，Vajrayogini，Munshiganj 出土，达卡国家博物馆藏　笔者拍摄

图 187 瓦茹阿哈，12 世纪，Vajrayogini，Munshiganj 出土，达卡国家博物馆藏　笔者拍摄

图 188 瓦茹阿哈，10 世纪，Silinpur，Bogra 出土，拉杰沙希 Varendra 研究博物馆藏　笔者拍摄

图 189 人狮尼星哈，10 世纪，Bogra 出土，巴哈布尔遗址博物馆藏　笔者拍摄

图190 人狮尼星哈，11世纪，Vikrampura, Munshiganj出土，达卡国家博物馆藏 笔者拍摄

图191 狮面护法，约15世纪，西藏洛扎县拉隆寺 笔者拍摄

图192 瓦玛那，10世纪，Munshiganj出土，达卡国家博物馆藏 笔者拍摄

图193 罗摩故事，6—7世纪，Palashbari, Bogra出土，达卡国家博物馆藏 笔者拍摄

图194 罗摩故事，6—7世纪，Palashbari, Bogra出土，达卡国家博物馆藏 笔者拍摄

图195 奎师那，6世纪，Paharpur出土，巴哈布尔遗址博物馆藏 笔者拍摄

图196 奎师那，11世纪，Dhaka出土，达卡国家博物馆藏 笔者拍摄

图197 奎师那，5—6世纪，巴哈布尔遗址博物馆藏 笔者拍摄

图198 那罗延天，12世纪，Munshiganj出土，达卡国家博物馆藏 笔者拍摄

图199　毗湿奴和洛乞史茗Lakshmi女神，12世纪，Naogaon出土，拉杰沙希Varendra研究博物馆藏
笔者拍摄

图200　洛乞史茗，10世纪，巴哈布尔遗址博物馆藏
笔者拍摄

图201　洛乞史茗，10—11世纪，Bogra出土，莫河斯坦遗址博物馆藏　笔者拍摄

图202　洛乞史茗，9—10世纪，Pabna出土，莫河斯坦遗址博物馆藏　笔者拍摄

图203　太阳神，9—10世纪，Naogaon出土，巴哈布尔遗址博物馆藏　笔者拍摄

图204　太阳神，11世纪，Comilla出土，达卡国家博物馆藏　笔者拍摄

图205　太阳神，12世纪，Chapai Nababganj出土，拉杰沙希Varendra研究博物馆藏　笔者拍摄

图 206 太阳神，6 世纪，Bogra 出土，莫河斯坦遗址博物馆藏　笔者拍摄

图 207 因陀罗，5—6 世纪，巴哈布尔博物馆藏　笔者拍摄

帝释天。因陀罗的武器是雷电，梵文 Vajra，在中文被译为金刚杵。有些金刚橛和金刚杵的上端有护法神的愤怒相或金翅鸟等图像，而手柄另一侧连接三刃刀的地方，可以清楚地看到鼻子两侧的两颗犬齿和中间的其他牙齿，在刃身部有缠在一起的蛇（图 208）。手柄与刀刃之间的象唇装饰，石泰安先生指出它是摩竭罗嘴，即通常所说的龙嘴，三角形的剑上面有龙头，笔者引藏族喇嘛的话："不仅仅从水龙头中伸出三棱剑，而且还有火光、火焰、烟雾和伴有千声雷的暴风雨，龙的鼻孔也放出烟和龙卷风，龙卷风笼罩了黑暗的三界并把它要驯服的人带到了神的面前。"在佛经中，金刚橛被视为"烧毁三毒之劫的火"，一部本教经文也介绍过"极端残忍的摩竭罗嘴"和"三棱剑、妖魔的舌头"[47]。

9. 阎罗王

阎罗王（Yamaraja）是印度教的正义、法制和死亡之神，他掌管着亡灵的世界，根据人们生前的业报对众生进行审判。他的一只手拿着钩索，可以将死去的罪人勾招到他那里，另一只手拿着大头棒，代表了惩罚，他的坐骑是一头水牛，有时候他自己也化现为水牛的形象。阎罗王的许多故事被记载在吠陀圣典和《摩诃婆罗多》里。在佛教、道教之中都有他的身影，道教之中甚至扩大为十位阎罗王，称为十殿阎罗。藏传佛教密教的大威德明王，是由阎罗王和难近母（杜尔伽）演化的，藏文称"党金却甲"，为格鲁派的主要出世间护法。

图208 金刚杵，年代不详，拉萨八廓街市场 笔者拍摄

图209 夜叉，公元前2世纪，Patharghata，Joypurhat出土，达卡国家博物馆藏 笔者拍摄

10. 夜叉

夜叉（Yaksa）在古印度神话中是半神，据《毗湿奴往世书》所述，夜叉与罗刹同时由梵天脚掌生出，但双方通常相互敌对，女性夜叉被描绘为带有丰满乳房与臀部的美丽女子（图209）。

11. 金翅大鹏鸟

金翅大鹏鸟嘎茹达（Garuda），是印度和西藏本教神话中的鸟中之王（图210）。印度是一个多毒蛇的热带国家，嘎茹达是蛇的天敌，人们经常念颂金翅鸟的咒语来防范毒蛇的袭击。传说中它是人头鸟身的神鸟，有时被绘成鸟头人身，它是毗湿奴神的坐骑，它的故事在《摩诃婆罗多》和《往世书》中都有提到。据说莲花生未曾调伏龙（蛇）的心，导致藏地龙病不断，因此传下了许多金翅鸟的修法。

12. Kirtimukha（兽面）

Kirtimukha（兽面）为一个吞噬一切的形象，常用于装饰神庙或神像的顶部，具有守卫的意义（图211）。

密宗教义不是从大乘佛教内部生长的，而是来自于外部印度教的影响，8—12世纪波罗王朝时期，性力派极为流行，崇拜湿婆之妻难近母、毗湿奴之妻吉祥天女、梵天之妻辩才天女、黑天之妻罗陀等，供奉酒、肉、鱼、谷物，采用秘密仪式，瑜珈、巫咒甚至轮座（男女杂交），这成了佛教新的源泉，印度教的造像体系也被佛教密宗所吸收，成为密宗最基本的神祇。

图210 金翅大鹏鸟，11世纪，Chakhar，Barisai 出土，达卡国家博物馆藏　笔者拍摄

图211 怪物 Kirtimukha，11世纪，库尔纳博物馆藏　笔者拍摄

图212 巴哈布尔石雕出土时情景

Rao Bahadur K. N. Dikshit, M. A.，F. R. A. S. B.：*Excavation at Paharpur, Bengal*, Delhi: Manager of Publications, 1938.

在巴哈布尔的苏摩普梨寺遗址中，63件石雕固定在中心神庙的墙基部位，除了一个是佛教菩萨（观音）像，其余皆是印度教神祇。从原始资料分析，石雕像置于砖雕的下方，位于墙基的中部、转角和排水孔上方，是曼陀罗建筑的有机组成部分（图212）。石雕像的题材以黑天传说和各种湿婆神像为主，包括《罗摩衍那》《摩诃婆罗多》中的故事。现在，雕像已被取走，分置于多处博物馆中，在巴哈布尔遗址博物馆中陈列着其中的三件石雕：一件因陀罗（Indra）砂石雕，年代为5—6世纪（见图207）；二件奎师那砂石雕，年代为6世纪（见图195、197）。镶嵌这些石雕的地方现在已经被土填平，但这个位置显然不是信众礼拜的位置，它们只是作为护法神而固定在那里的。有学者认为，这些石雕是从早期神庙中取下来再镶嵌在墙基上的，所以石雕的年代较早[48]。尽管如此，这并不影响它们在佛教寺庙中作为护法神的宗教功能。西藏丹萨替寺京俄舍利灵塔，塔身上有数百尊装饰造像，最低层也是护法层。佛教二十诸天以及藏传密教的许多本尊、护法，几乎与印度教的主要神祇重叠，反过来说，印度教神祇成了密宗造像体系的重要来源。

注释

[1] AKM Zakariah: *The Archaeology Heritage of Bangladesh*, Asiatic Society of Bangladesh, 2011.

[2] 柴焕波、强巴次仁：《西藏隆子县发现早期塔庙建筑及其壁画》，《中国文物报》2017 年 10 月 20 日。

[3] [5] 李崇峰：《佛教考古——从印度到中国》，上海古籍出版社，2014 年。

[4] 云冈石窟研究院等：《云冈石窟窟顶西区北魏寺院遗址》，《考古学报》2016 年第 4 期。

[6] [36]〔意〕杜齐著，魏正中、萨尔吉主编，李翎等译：《梵天佛地》第 3 卷，上海古籍出版社，2010 年。

[7] 李文瑛：《新疆地区中心殿式佛堂试析》，《中国文物报》1996 年 6 月 4 日。

[8] [17] 儒弥·考斯勒《西喜玛拉雅的佛教建筑》，《西藏研究》1992 年第 1 期。

[9] 沈亚军：《印度教神庙研究》，南京工业大学硕士学位论文，2013 年。

[10] [13] [14] [34] A.B.M.Husain: *Mainamati-Devaparvata*, Asiatic Society Of Bangladesh, 1997.

[11] [28] 义净著，王维邦校：《大唐西域求法高僧传校注》，中华书局，1988 年。

[12][24] Bulbul Ahmed edited: *Buddhist Heritage Sites of Bangladesh*, Nymphea Publication, 2015.

[15] [35] Rao Bahadur K.N. Dikshit, M.A., F. R. A. S. B.: *Excavations at Paharpur, Bengal*, Deli: Manager of Publications, 1938. Dr. Md. Shafiqul Alam edited edited: *Proceedings for Paharpur World Heritage Site and its Environment (Bangladesh)*, nternational Seminar on Elaboration of an Archaeological Research Strategy for Paharpur World Heritage Site and its Environment 20-25 March 2004, Dhaka.

[16] 霍巍：《古格与冈底斯山一带佛寺遗迹的类型及初步分析》，《中国藏学》1997 年第 1 期。

[18] 宿白：《藏传佛教寺院考古》，文物出版社，1996 年。

[19] [31]〔印〕R. C. 马宗达著，张澍霖等译：《高级印度史》，商务印书馆，1986 年。〔法〕雷奈·格鲁塞著，常任侠、袁音译：《印度的文明》商务印书馆，1967 年。

[20] [40] Rao Bahadur K. N. Dikshit，M. A., F. R. A. S. B.: *Excavation at Paharpur, Bengal*, Delhi: Manager of Publications, 1938.

[21] [29]〔意〕杜齐著，向红笳译：《西藏考古》，西藏人民出版社，1987 年。

[22] [30]〔意〕杜齐著，魏正中、萨尔吉主编，李翎等译：《梵天佛地》第 1 卷，上海古籍出版社，2010 年。

[23] 李翎：《佛教与图像论稿》，文物出版社，2011 年。

[25] 扎雅·诺丹西绕著，谢继胜译：《西藏宗教艺术》，西藏人民出版社，1989 年。

[26]〔法〕海瑟·噶尔美著，熊文彬译：《早期汉藏艺术》，中国藏学出版社，1994 年。

[27] 张亚莎：《11 世纪西藏的佛教艺术》，中国藏学出版社，2008 年。

[32]〔德〕吴黎熙：《佛像解说》，社会科学文献出版社，2010 年。

[33] 相关神祇参考 http://www.ebaifo.com/fojiao-226359.html

[37] 拔塞囊：《巴协》（增补本）译注，四川民族出版社，1990 年。

[38] 觉囊达热那特著，余万治译：《后藏志》西藏人民出版社，1994 年。

[39] [43] 吕建福：《中国密教史》（修订版），中国社会科学出版社，2011 年。

[41] [42] 索南才让（许得存）：《西藏密教史》，中国社会科学出版社，1998 年。

[44] 布顿：《佛教史大宝藏论》，民族出版社，1986 年。

[45] 查同结布著，张天锁等译：《玛尔巴译师传》，西藏人民出版社，1989 年。

[46] 参考《印度教诸神简介》，http://www.360.doc.com

[47]〔法〕石泰安著，岳岩译：《摩竭罗嘴——某些法器的一种特点》，《国外藏学研究译文集》第 6 辑，西藏人民出版社。

[48] Dr. Md. Shafiqul Alam: *Paharpur and Bagerhot: Two World Cultural Heritage Sites of Bangladesh*, 2004.

鸣 谢
Acknowledgement

中国国家文物局

中国湖南省人民政府

中国湖南省文物局

中国驻孟加拉国大使馆

孟加拉国文化部

孟加拉国考古局

贾汉吉纳格尔大学考古系

库米拉大学考古系

蒙希甘杰青年培训中心

蒙希甘杰县政府

Naresh Chandra Das 先生

For providing funds:

Ministry of Cultural Affairs, People's Republic of Bangladesh

For various cooperation:

Department of Archaeology, Ministry of Cultural Affairs

Department of Archaeology, Jahangirnagar University

Department of Archaeology, Comilla University

Munshiganj Youth Training centre

Munshiganj District Administration

Naresh Chandra Das

National Cultural Heritage Administration, People's Republic of China

People's Government of Hunan Province, People's Republic of China

Hunan Provincial Cultural Relics Bureau, People's Republic of China

Embassy of People's Republic of China, Dhaka